W9-AJS-151

econoguide
'97-'98

Golf Resorts and Courses USA

Corey Sandler

CB
CONTEMPORARY BOOKS

Library of Congress Cataloging-in-Publication Data

Sandler, Corey, 1950–
    Econoguide '97–'98, golf resorts and courses USA / Corey
Sandler.
      p.   cm.
    ISBN 0-8092-3090-9
    1. Golf resorts—United States—Directories.   2. Golf courses—
United States—Directories.   3. Deals—United States—Directories.
I. Title.
GV981.S27   1997
796.352'06—dc20   96-44809
                                                CIP

To Willie and Tessa, my favorite links.

This book is not authorized or endorsed by any attraction or business described in its pages. All attractions, product names, or other works mentioned in this book are trademarks or registered trademarks of their respective owners or developers and are used in this book strictly for editorial purposes and to the benefit of the trademark owner; no commercial claim to their use is made by the author or the publisher.

Cover photo: Fifth Hole of the Bay Course, Kapalua, Maui. Photo by John Severson.
Cover design by Kim Bartko

Econoguide is a registered trademark of Word Association, Inc.

Contents

Acknowledgments **vii**

1 Introduction to the 1997–98 Edition 1
About This Book   1
Think About the Game   2
About the Course Ratings   3
Buying Golf Equipment   4
   Used Equipment, Recycled Balls, and X-Outs   5
The Best Days to Go Golfing   6
Special Golf Services   6
   Tee-Time Services   6
   Discount Cards   7
   Discount Coupons   7

2 How to Save Money on Air Travel and Golf Packages 9
Alice in Airlineland   9
   Air Wars   11
   Convention Fares   12
   A Loophole Closes a Bit   13
   Standing Up for Standing By   14
Your Consumer Rights   14
   Overbooking   15
   How to Get Bumped   16
How to Book a Package or Charter Flight   17
About Travel Agencies   18
Golf Packages   18
Drive, He Said?   20
   Renting a Car   20
   Saving Money at the Rental Counter   21

3 Hotels   23

A Place to Lay Your Head   23
   Negotiating for a Room   25
   Dialing for Dollars   26
   Protecting Yourself Against an Unfulfilled Reservation   27
Discount Hotel Deals   28
Discount Hotel Companies   28
A Selection of Some of America's Best Golf Resorts   29

4 Golf Travelers' Most Frequently Asked Questions   31

Golf Equipment   31
   Clubs   31
   Balls   35
Hitting the Ball with the Club   36
Handicap, Course, and Slope Ratings   37
The Toughest Courses in America   39

5 Econoguide Golf State-by-State   41

The East   41
   Connecticut   41
   Delaware   45
   Maine   46
   Maryland   48
   Massachusetts   51
   New Hampshire   56
   New Jersey   59
   New York   63
   Pennsylvania   74
   Rhode Island   84
   Vermont   85
   Virginia   88
   Washington, D.C.   94
The Central States   95
   Illinois   95
   Indiana   104
   Iowa   110
   Kansas   113
   Kentucky   115
   Michigan   118
   Minnesota   125
   Missouri   131
   Nebraska   134
   North Dakota   136
   Ohio   138
   South Dakota   148

West Virginia   150
Wisconsin   152
The South   158
Alabama   159
Arkansas   162
Florida   164
Georgia   186
Louisiana   194
Mississippi   195
North Carolina   197
Oklahoma   208
South Carolina   212
Tennessee   222
Texas   226
The West, Alaska, and Hawaii   235
Alaska   235
Arizona   236
California   244
Colorado   262
Hawaii   269
Idaho   276
Montana   278
Nevada   280
New Mexico   283
Oregon   286
Utah   290
Washington   293
Wyoming   298

Discount Coupons   301

Quick-Find Index to Golf Courses   325

Acknowledgments

Dozens of hardworking and creative people helped move my words from the keyboard to the pages of this book.

Among the many to thank are editor Linda Gray and publisher Christine Albritton of Contemporary Books for working with me as we expand the Econoguide series. Thanks to Dan Bial for his capable agentry. Thanks to Eugene Brissie, our original champion, and to Bill Gladstone of Waterside Productions.

Julia Anderson of Contemporary Books gave the text a professional polish, and Kathy Willhoite managed the editorial and production processes with professionalism and good humor.

Thanks to the capable production staff at Contemporary Books, including: Kim Bartko, Monica Baziuk, Dana Draxten, Gigi Grajdura, Pamela Juárez, Todd Petersen, Audrey Sails, and Terry Stone.

Thanks to the golf courses, resorts, hotels, equipment makers, mail-order companies, and attractions that offered discount coupons to our readers. Special thanks go to Andrew Paul and Janice Keefe, who worked long and hard in the Word Association offices to collect and process the discount coupons. Thanks also to Dan Keefe, the official Econoguide golf pro.

And finally, thanks to you for buying this book. We all hope you find it of value; we'd appreciate it if you would let us know how we can improve the book in future editions. (Please enclose a self-addressed stamped envelope if you'd like a reply; no phone calls.)

We're also available over the Internet. To send us electronic mail, use the following address: econoguide@pobox.com *or* sandler@pobox.com

You can also consult our Web page at:

http://www.pobox.com/~econoguide *or*

http://www.netcom.com/~econo-gd/travel.html

(Don't forget that little squiggly character called a tilde in the Web address. You'll find it on your computer keyboard.)

Corey Sandler
Econoguide Travel Books
P.O. Box 2779
Nantucket, MA 02584

Chapter 1
Introduction to the 1997–98 Edition

At its most basic, golf is a very simple and inexpensive game. Hammer a peg into the ground, place a ball on top of the peg, swing a stick at the ball, and aim at a hole in the ground at the other end of the field.

That was about all that was required back when the game was new. Today, though, from the tee to the ball to the club to the golfer to the spectacular golf resort, the price of entry and the complexity of the sport have soared about as high as a well-struck drive from an elevated tee. There are an estimated 25 million American golfers among us now, up about 43 percent from a decade ago, according to the United States Golf Association (USGA).

You can pay $150 for a round of golf at a fancy resort, with $50 gloves holding a $500 custom-fitted titanium wood, and wear a monogrammed $300 golfing ensemble that makes you look just like the Shark or the Golden Bear or whoever is the pro star of the moment.

Or you can pay $25 for 18 holes at a well-maintained municipal course, wear a pair of slacks from the closet and a tee shirt from Kmart and swing at the ball with an off-the-shelf club purchased from a discount store.

Either way, you're swinging a stick at a ball on a peg. The ball costs a buck or two, no matter how expensive the rest of your golfing setup.

About This Book

Let's get something straight right up front: The purpose of the books in the Econoguide series* is not to help you be unreasonably cheap. This is not a guide to windswept and dusty $5 courses with make-it-yourself clubs and

---

*Titles in the series by author Corey Sandler include *Econoguide '97—Walt Disney World, Universal Studios Florida, Epcot, and Other Major Central Florida Attractions*; *Econoguide '97—Las Vegas, Reno, Laughlin, Lake Tahoe*; *Econoguide '97—Disneyland, Universal Studios Hollywood, and Other Major Southern California Attractions*; *Econoguide '97—Washington, D.C., Williamsburg, Busch Gardens, Richmond, and Other Area Attractions*; and *Econoguide '97–'98: Ski and Snowboard America*. All are published by Contemporary Books and are available at your local bookstore. You can find details about the books on the World Wide Web, at http://www.netcom.com/~econo-gd/travel.html

second-hand balls. Instead, our goal is to help you get the most for your money and make the best use of your time.

We've collected information on the best courses at any price, along with details of how to get the most for your money—no matter how much you spend—on equipment, and advice on how to travel in economic style from coast to coast.

And we offer a selection of money-saving coupons. There is no connection between the information in this book and the coupons we publish, except that everything between the covers is intended to save you money.

Pardon us for saying so, but we think the cost-effectiveness of this book will speak for itself. You should easily be able to save several times the price of the book.

Think About the Game

Before you pick up the telephone to make reservations for the golfing vacation of your dreams, we suggest you stop and think about your personal definition of that dream. Ask yourself the following questions, and remember that there are no right or wrong answers. The only penalty comes from not asking them at all.

1. *What kind of a golf course and resort do you want to visit?* Do you want to go to an easy course where you can boost your ego by shooting the lowest score of your golfing career? Or would you rather visit one of America's most difficult courses, where your score will climb into the stratosphere but, oh, what stories you'll be able to tell back at the 19th hole of your local muni?

2. *Is price an object?* The courses in this book, all of them selected as above average, range from as low as $10 per round to $150 and even more. It's all golf, and there are some classic challenges and gorgeous locations at the less-expensive courses; it's up to you to decide whether a brand name is worth the extra fare.

3. *Do you want a luxurious resort setting, or is a clean Motel Cheapo acceptable?* There are many advantages to staying at a world-class resort, especially if you are in mixed company (golfers and nongolfers) or if you plan to stay in one area for an extended period of time and want to make use of other amenities. And, as we will point out in Chapter 3 on hotels, a luxury resort is not always that much more expensive than a strip motel if you plan to play golf at the resort's course. You'll have to do the math yourself, based on your own preferences and plans.

4. *Do you need to travel at the height of high season?* The warm spring of Florida and much of the South is a huge lure to frostbitten northerners, and the rewards are real. But sometimes it seems as if the entire state of New Hampshire is in line in front of you . . . and airline, auto rental, hotel, and greens fees are at their highest levels.

5. *Are you willing to spend a little bit of time to save a lot of money?* If so, read on; you'll find all of the information you need to make the most of your money and time on a golfing vacation.

About the Course Ratings

In Chapter 5 on courses, you'll find information on more than 2,500 public, resort, and semiprivate courses around the nation. In order to make the cut, the course had to be above average to exceptional, and open to visitors.

We based our ratings on published reviews and reports by players. The chart awards from one to four golf balls, as follows:

☺	Worth a Visit
☺☺	Above Average
☺☺☺	Exceptional
☺☺☺☺	Very Best

We show you the best courses open to the public, and the best deals—a combination of highest quality and most reasonable rates. Look for these icons:

BEST	Econoguide's Best American Courses
DEAL	Econoguide's Best Golfing Deals
STATE	Econoguide's Best Courses in the State

There are nearly 350 Econoguide Best and State courses in the book. The Econoguide Deal icon is awarded to any course that is listed as Exceptional or Very Best and is priced at bargain or budget levels of less than $40 for a round of golf. There are more than 700 Econoguide Deals spread across the 50 states.

The *Econoguide* includes only those golf courses or resorts that are open to the public. That doesn't mean, alas, that you will be able to walk up to the pro shop at 9 A.M. and claim an immediate starting time. In fact, in the height of the season, some of the most popular public courses are booked up for weeks in advance. Call ahead of time—at the same time you make your travel plans—to arrange a reservation, and try to avoid those days sure to be busy, including most holidays and Saturdays.

We also include listings for semiprivate (or semipublic, if you prefer) courses. These are mostly membership clubs that offer a limited number of slots to visitors; availability may be limited to specific days or times, or you may be able to obtain a reservation for any slot not already spoken for by a member.

Finally, there are the resort courses that usually give priority to guests at the resort itself or a limited number of nearby hotels. Most resort courses will permit visitors at a premium rate.

The codes in the listings are:

P	Public Course
R	Resort Course
SP	Semiprivate Course

You'll also find listings on regularly offered discounts. Low season at golf courses varies depending on the weather and regional practice. In the Northeast, Midwest, and mountainous regions, low season often means early spring when the snows have melted and again in the late fall as the air turns cold and storm clouds gather. In the hotter climes of the South and the desert West, the low season may be declared during the heart of the summer in July and

August when only mad dogs, Englishmen, and the most dedicated of golfers brave the midday sun.

Discounts in the listings include:

W	Weekdays
L	Low Season
R	Resort Guests
T	Twilight
S	Seniors
J	Juniors

The greens fees for courses listed in the *Econoguide* are indicated by symbols representing ranges from bargain to very expensive and beyond to exclusive.

The rates indicate a typical discount rate and standard full rate. Rates are subject to change, and though base rates are almost always adjusted upward, be sure to ask about discount rates when you call for a reservation.

Here are the price ranges for the listings in this book:

$	Bargain	Less than $20
$$	Budget	About $20 to $39
$$$	Moderate	About $40 to $59
$$$$	Expensive	About $60 to $79
$$$$$	Very Expensive	About $80 to $100
$$$$$$	Exclusive	More than $100

You will see price icons for greens on every course, and another price icon if there is an additional charge for rental of a cart. If this information was unavailable to us, we've indicated that you should "Inquire" at the course for rental rates.

Then we have the essential statistics for the courses. We begin by organizing courses by region within each state. In larger states, regions can cover several hundred square miles; consult a map or make a phone call to be sure your golfing goal is a reasonable drive (by car) from where you live or where you're staying. Confirm directions to the course when you call to make a reservation.

Other information in the listings includes the number of holes (we list only courses with 18 or more holes). Next is the par. For 18-hole courses we tell you the pars from the back and front tees; for 27-hole courses the par is indicated from the back tees only. Yardage is listed from the front and back tees for 18-hole courses and the back tees only for 27-hole challenges.

The rating tells you the USGA course rating from the back and front tees for 18-hole courses and the back tees for 27-hole courses. The same pattern is used to report the USGA slope rating.

Finally, you'll learn the course's official season and its published high season. You'll want to call to check on a course's schedule before you go, however.

Buying Golf Equipment

Titleist golf balls are the same whether you buy them at full list price from the pro shop just before tee time or by mail at deep discount. So, too, are golf accessories, clothing, and even clubs.

In general, you'll find the highest prices on golf equipment at pro shops or at full-service retail shops.

The best deals on equipment are often available through a mail-order operation or at a discount store, including golf-only shops as well as sporting goods superstores.

You will have to decide, though, whether the service you receive from a competent golf retailer—including repair of grips and other minor repairs—might make it worthwhile to buy your clubs locally.

Be sure to compare guarantees and service promises from anyone who tries to sell you equipment. There are some instances where mail-order sources offer both the best price and the best support after the sale; other times you may find that mail-order operations want to take your order only and have little in the way of advice to offer.

I am a big fan of mail-order purchases in certain situations. Over the years I have purchased tens of thousands of dollars' worth of items over the phone, from sporting equipment to video cameras to personal computers to a car. Before I read out the digits on my credit card, though, I ask a ton of questions about the product and its current availability, billing and shipping policies, product return and warranty procedures, and anything else I can think of. My theory is this: if they won't respond to my questions before they have my money, what would make me think they would respond after they've deposited my money in their bank account?

Always use a credit card when you purchase by mail order; doing so gives you some legal rights to recover money in the event of nonperformance by the seller, and some contractual rights to get your credit card company's assistance if you have a problem.

You'll find a selection of coupons from some direct marketers of golfing equipment in this book; you'll find other listings for mail-order companies in golf magazines, in newspapers, and on the Internet.

Outlet stores offer another important way to shop for equipment and clothing. Some outlet stores are operated by manufacturers and others by discounters. As with any other purchase, compare prices with full retail price and spend your money wisely.

Used Equipment, Recycled Balls, and X-Outs

One good way to save money on practice equipment or to outfit a beginner is to buy used equipment. You may find clubs at a tag sale or listed in the classified ads. Check with local pro shops and retail stores to see if they have used demo or rental sets available for sale.

In recent years we have also seen the growth of used sporting goods stores that specialize in buying and reselling last year's clubs, outgrown boots and skis, and all of that other stuff that clutters our basements.

And did you ever wonder just how many perfectly good balls sit at the bottom of the pond at your favorite course? Well, there may be thousands . . .

or they may have been recently harvested by one of many companies that clean them up and resell them at a deep discount.

Another way to save money is to purchase X-out balls, which are new balls marked with an *X* or other symbol through the brand name to indicate a defect. In theory, an X-out ball is sold at a discount because of cosmetic flaws—misprints, off colors, or mottled covers. That means you should be able to use the ball in your game and pocket the price difference. Unfortunately, there may be other problems that are not so benign: imperfect covers, improper weight, or off-center construction.

You should have no problem using X-out balls on the driving range or even in an informal round. You may not want to use an X-out on your one and only game at a spectacular resort, or in a competition.

The Best Days to Go Golfing

Some of the best days to play golf are during the off-season (which varies from place to place) or when others have other things to do, including Easter Sunday, Christmas Day (if the course is open), New Year's Day, Mother's Day, and any day when there is an important sporting event going on. You might try hitting the links on the afternoon of Super Bowl Sunday, for example.

Although the Fourth of July may be a glorious day on Cape Cod, in the Colorado Rockies, or in Saratoga Springs, it may be an unbearably hot day in Palm Springs, West Palm Beach, or Houston. Likewise, a warm and sunny March or October day in Orlando may be a miserably wet and cold day in Minnesota.

Therein lies one money-saving strategy for the exceptionally hardy golfer: courses in sun spots including Florida, the deep South, and southern California often offer significant discounts in the heart of the summer, and courses in colder climes will have value pricing in the spring and fall (and sometimes snowless winter) while full rates are charged in the fair days of summer.

Special Golf Services

The world of golf seems to exist in a perpetual state of imbalance: there are either too many golfers seeking too few tee times, or too many golf courses and not enough golfers.

The first situation can ruin your golfing vacation or clean out your wallet; the second situation can work to your benefit. But sometimes the place where you want to play turns out to be the spot where it is the most difficult to obtain a reservation.

Tee-Time Services

One way to obtain a tee time at the most popular courses is to use a reservation service. These companies usually arrange for blocks of time at courses in their area and offer them to their clients. At some of the nation's most popular courses, using a service may be the only way to obtain a tee time.

Some services make their money by charging a commission to the golf courses; others will charge you a fee by adding a premium to the regular greens fee.

In some situations, you may even be able to obtain a discounted greens fee through one of these services, especially during off-season periods. The service may have some reservations it needs to unload at the last minute, or a golf course may cut its rates for clients of the service to fill up a slow day. Don't hesitate to ask for a discount—asking costs nothing, and you just may be rewarded for your effort.

Discount Cards

There are a number of national and regional discount programs that offer reduced greens fees, two-for-the-price-of-one deals, and other special programs for golfers. In general, you will find that the programs offer discounts during low-season periods and at courses that are less popular than those on everyone's leader board of the best of the best. But that doesn't mean there aren't great deals available, or that you won't find the perfect course at a discounted price.

There are three types of discount programs we have seen:

1. *Nonprofit organizations.* The American Lung Association and other groups have offered discount golf programs at the local, regional, or national level.
2. *Golf and travel clubs.* A number of commercial organizations, including travel packagers, golf magazines, and others, sell discount golf cards.
3. *Groups of golf courses.* Corporate families of courses, including those at the Walt Disney World in Florida and the Robert Trent Jones Golf Trail in Alabama, regularly offer multiday or annual discount passes. Elsewhere you will find discount golf cards offered by associations of golf courses within a particular area.

Pay attention to small print on any discount card offer; not all discounts or special offers are as great a deal as they appear. Look for the following:

1. *Exclusion periods.* Are the discounts valid only at twilight on rainy Thursdays in February, or can you use the card at any time?
2. *Limitations.* Can you only use the card once at each course that participates? Must each golfer in your party have his or her own card?
3. *Hidden charges.* Some discount cards promise free or half-price greens fees, but include in the small print a requirement that you rent a golf cart at the full rate.

As with any other purchase, compare prices with and without the discount cards. Some of the programs are great deals, while others are a triple bogey on a par 3.

Discount Coupons

Be sure to check the discount coupons at the back of this book. The companies represented there promise money-saving offers for Econoguide readers. The presence of a coupon in this section is not in any way related to the author's opinions published in this book.

Chapter 2
How to Save Money on Air Travel and Golf Packages

I'm flying south to a slice of golf heaven in North Carolina. My ticket cost $309 for a round-trip. The businessman across the aisle will suffer through the same mystery meal, watch the same crummy movie, and arrive at Pinehurst's Southern Pines Airport at the same millisecond I do. The only difference will be the fact that he paid $804 for his ticket.

Somewhere else on this plane there is probably a couple who were bumped off a previous flight because of overbooking. They are no doubt happily discussing where to use the two free round-trip tickets they received in compensation.

Up front in first class, where the food is ever so slightly better and you arrive a millisecond earlier, a family of four is traveling on free tickets earned through Mom's frequent flier plan.

Me, I've got that cut-rate ticket and I'm due for a 5 percent rebate on airfare, hotel, and car rental, all arranged through my travel agent.

And on my trip back home, I will get on the flight I really wanted to take instead of the less-convenient reservation I was forced to sign up for when I bought that cut-rate ticket. How will I do this? Read on.

Alice in Airlineland

In today's strange world of air travel, there is a lot of room for the dollarwise and clever traveler to wiggle. You can pay an inflated full price, you can take advantage of the lowest fares, or you can play the ultimate game and parlay tickets into free travel. In this chapter, we'll show you how to do each.

There are three golden rules: When it comes to saving hundreds of dollars on travel, be flexible, be flexible, and be flexible. Here's how to translate that flexibility into extra dollars in your pocket:

Checking in again. Having a boarding pass issued by a travel agent is not the same as checking in at the airport. You'll still need to show your ticket at the counter so that the agent knows you're there.

• Be flexible about when you choose to travel. Go during the off-season or low-season when airfares, hotel rooms, and other attractions are offered at substantial discounts. Try to avoid school vacations, including the prime summer travel months of July and August, unless you enjoy a lot of company. However, if you can stand the heat, the summer is a great time to go to the hot spots of Florida, Texas, and southern California to play in the semicool early mornings or late afternoons of the off-season.

• Be flexible about the day of the week you travel. In many cases you can save hundreds of dollars by bumping your departure date one or two days in either direction. Ask your travel agent or airline ticket agent for current fare rules and restrictions.

The days of lightest air travel are generally midweek, Saturday afternoon, and Sunday morning. The busiest days are Sunday evening, Monday morning, and Friday afternoon and evening.

In general, you will receive the lowest possible fare if you include a Saturday in your trip, buying what is called an excursion fare. Airlines use this as a way to exclude business travelers from the cheapest fares, assuming that businesspeople will want to be home by Friday night.

• Be flexible about the hour of your departure. There is generally lower demand—and therefore lower prices—for flights that leave in the middle of the day or very late at night. The highest rates are usually assigned to breakfast-time (7 A.M.–11 A.M.) and cocktail-hour (4 P.M.–7 P.M.) departures.

• Be flexible on the route you will take, and be willing to put up with a change of plane or stopover. Once again, you are putting the law of supply and demand in your favor. For example, a direct flight from Boston to Orlando for a family of four may cost hundreds more than a flight from Boston that includes a change of planes in Atlanta (a Delta hub) before proceeding on to Florida.

• Consider flying on one of the newer, deep-discount airlines, but don't let economy cloud your judgment. Some carriers are simply better run than others. In the aftermath of the 1996 ValuJet plane crash and other incidents, the FAA promised to step up its oversight of maintenance and operations of off-brand carriers. Read the newspapers, check with a trusted travel agent, and use common sense. As far as we're concerned, the best thing about the cheapo airlines is the pressure they put on the established carriers to lower prices or even to match fares on certain flights. Look for the cheapest fare you can find and then call your favorite big airline and see if it will sell you a ticket at the same price—it just might work.

• Don't overlook the possibility of flying out of a different airport either. For example, metropolitan New Yorkers can find domestic flights from La Guardia, Newark, or White Plains as an alternative to Kennedy Airport. Suburbanites of Boston might want to consider flights from Worcester or Providence as possibly cheaper alternatives to Logan Airport. Chicago has O'Hare and Midway. From the Los Angeles area there are airports at Los Angeles, Orange County, Burbank, and San Diego.

• Plan way ahead of time and purchase the most deeply discounted advance tickets, which usually are noncancelable. Most carriers limit the number of discount tickets on any particular flight. Although there may be plenty of seats left on the day you want to travel, they may be offered at higher rates.

• In a significant change over the past few years, most airlines have modified nonrefundable fares to be noncancelable. What this means is that if your plans change or you are forced to cancel your trip, your tickets retain their value and can be applied against another trip, usually for a fee of about $35 or $50 per ticket.

• If you're feeling adventurous, you can take a big chance and wait for the last possible moment, keeping in contact with charter tour operators and accepting a bargain price on a leftover seat and hotel reservation. You may also find that some airlines will reduce the prices on leftover seats within a few weeks of your departure date; don't be afraid to check with the airline regularly, or ask your travel agent to do it for you. In fact, some travel agencies have automated computer programs that keep a constant electronic eagle eye on available seats and fares.

• Take advantage of special discount programs like senior citizens' clubs, military discounts, or offerings from other organizations to which you may belong. If you are in the over-60 category, you may not even have to belong to a group like AARP; simply ask the airline ticket agent if there is a discount available. You may have to prove your age when you pick up your ticket or boarding pass.

Air Wars

Airlines are forever gnashing their teeth and weeping about huge losses due to cutthroat competition. And then they regularly turn around and drop their prices radically with major sales.

We won't waste time worrying about the bottom line of the airlines; it's our own wallets we want to keep full. Therefore, the savvy traveler keeps an eye out for airline fare wars all the time. Read the ads in daily newspapers and keep an ear open to news broadcasts that often cover the outbreak of price wars. If you have a good relationship with a travel agent, you can ask to be notified of any good fare deals.

The most common times for airfare wars are in the weeks leading up to the travel industry's off-season. Look for sales in late summer for flights in the period between Labor Day and Thanksgiving and again in the fall to cover the slow winter season with the exception of Christmas, New Year's, and Presidents' Day holiday periods.

There are three important strategies to employ here:

1. Hold off on vacation travel plans for as long as you can. Hopefully you'll snare a discount fare. Don't wait too long, though—the deepest standard discounts are for tickets purchased at least 21 days before the date of travel. And remember that the chances for a fare sale for Memorial Day weekend or Thanksgiving are very slim, and in fact tickets may be hard to obtain at any price.
2. Consider grabbing a discount-fare ticket even if your travel dates are not

firm. In most cases (be sure to check with the airline) you will be able to adjust dates for a small penalty; the final price of the ticket should still be less than a regular fare.

3. Ask for a refund on previously purchased tickets if fares go down for the period of your travel. The airline may refund the difference, or you may be able to reticket your itinerary at the new fare, paying a $35 to $50 penalty for cashing in the old tickets. Be persistent—if the difference in fare is significant, it may be worthwhile to make a visit to the airport to meet with a supervisor at the ticket counter.

Another money-saving strategy involves the use of discount coupons distributed directly by the airlines, or through third parties such as supermarkets, catalog companies, and direct marketers. A typical coupon offers $50 or $100 off full fares or certain types of discount fares. It has been our experience that these coupons are often less valuable than they seem—while they are certainly better than paying full fare, they often result in a price that is higher than other readily available discounts. Read the fine print carefully and be sure to ask ticket agents if the price they quote you with the coupon is higher than another fare you qualify for.

Convention Fares

If you are traveling to a convention that happens to take place near the golf course of your dreams, you may be able to get in on a discount negotiated by the group with a particular airline. In fact, you may not need any affiliation at all with a convention group in order to take advantage of the special rates offered. All the airline will ask is the name or number of the discount

Torrey Pines Golf Course, San Diego, California
James Blank photo courtesy of the San Diego Convention & Visitors Bureau.

plan for the convention; the ticket agent is almost certainly not going to ask to see your union card or funny hat.

Check with conventions and visitors bureaus at your destination to see if any large groups are traveling when you plan to fly. Is this sneaky and underhanded? Yes. But we think it is also sneaky and underhanded for an airline to charge hundreds of dollars more for the seats to the left and right of the one we're sitting in. Here are a few more tips:

• Consider doing business with discounters, known in the industry as consolidators or, less flatteringly, as bucket shops. These companies buy the airlines' slow-to-sell tickets in volume and resell them to consumers at rock-bottom prices. Look for their ads in the classified listings of many Sunday newspaper travel sections. Be sure to study and understand the restrictions; if they fit your needs and wants, this is a good way to fly.

> **Finding a bucket shop.** Look for ads for ticket brokers and bucket shops in places like the classified ads in *USA Today*, the "Mart" section of the *Wall Street Journal*, or in specialty magazines like *Frequent Flyer*.

• A bit more in the shadows are ticket brokers who specialize in the resale of frequent flier coupons and other free or almost-free tickets. Although most airlines attempt to prohibit the resale or transfer of free tickets from the original ticket holder to a second or third party, the fact is that very rarely are they successful in preventing such reuse. Are you willing to take a small financial risk with the chances of saving hundreds or even thousands of dollars on a long trip? If you aren't interested in any risk, make sure that the tickets you receive are listed in your name.

We're not going to make a recommendation about using such brokers, but we will note that many fliers use them with success. If you join them, be sure to read and understand the terms of your contract with the broker, and pay for your ticket with a credit card, if possible. (Using a credit card gives you some leverage through the issuer of the card.)

A Loophole Closes a Bit

The biggest change to hit the airline industry in recent years had nothing to do with fancy new jetliners, improved service, or (heaven forbid) a decent meal at 30,000 feet. Instead it was the near-universal end to transferable tickets.

It used to be that for any domestic airline flight, all you needed to get on board the plane was your ticket. Just like showing your ticket at the theater, all that mattered was that you had an admission pass.

Travelers were often able to resell or give away unneeded nested ticket pairs, sell off promotional free tickets, or sell tickets issued under a frequent flier program.

But in the fall of 1995, the federal government called a security alert at the nation's airports because of perceived threats from the Middle East and elsewhere. As part of a package that included elimination of some parking spaces directly in front of terminals, increased scrutiny of carry-on and checked baggage, and other measures, airline check-in agents began asking for a photo ID for each ticket holder and comparing that name against the ticket.

Although the security alert was reduced later in the year (subject to future reinstatement), most airlines have continued to ask for identification. Why? Industry observers noted that airlines took to this practice with particular relish, and news reports said that some of the major carriers found they were earning a significant increase in profits by blocking the use of tickets issued under another name.

Standing Up for Standing By

One of the little-known secrets of air travel on most airlines and most types of tickets is the fact that travelers with valid tickets are allowed to stand by for flights other than the ones for which they have reservations; if there are empty seats on the flight, standby ticket holders are permitted to board.

Some airlines are very liberal in their acceptance of standbys within a few days of the reserved flight, while others will charge a small fee (usually $35 to $50) for changes in itinerary. And some airline personnel are stricter about the regulation than others.

Here's what I do know: if I cannot get the exact flight I want for a trip, I make the closest acceptable reservations available after that flight and then show up early at the airport and head for the check-in counter for the flight I really want to take. Unless you are seeking to travel during an impossibly overbooked holiday period or arrive on a bad weather day when flights have been canceled, your chances of successfully standing by for a flight are usually pretty good.

One trick is to call the airline the day before the flight and check on the availability of seats for the flight you want to try for. Some reservation clerks are very forthcoming with information; many times I have been told something like, "There are 70 seats open on that flight."

Be careful with standby maneuvers if your itinerary requires a change of plane en route; you'll need to check the availability of seats on all of the legs of your journey.

And a final note: be especially careful about standing by for the very last flight of the night. If you somehow are unable to get on that flight, you're stuck for the night.

Double indemnity. Your home owner's or renter's insurance policy may include coverage for theft of your possessions while you travel, making it unnecessary to purchase a special policy. Check with your insurance agent.

My personal strategy usually involves making a reservation for that last flight and standing by for one or more earlier flights on the same day.

Your Consumer Rights

The era of airline deregulation has been a mixed blessing for the industry and the consumer. After a period of wild competition based mostly on price, we now are left with fewer but larger airlines and a dizzying array of confusing rules.

The U.S. Department of Transportation and

its Federal Aviation Administration (FAA) still regulate safety issues. Almost everything else is between you and the airline.

Policies on fares, cancellations, reconfirmation, check-in requirements, and compensation for lost or damaged baggage or for delays all vary by airline. Your rights are limited and defined by the terms of the contract you make with an airline when you buy your ticket. You may find the contract included with the ticket you purchase, or the airlines may "incorporate terms by reference" to a separate document which you will have to request to see.

Whether you are buying your ticket through a travel agent or dealing directly with the airline, here are some important questions to ask:

• Is the price guaranteed, or can it change from the time of the reservation until you actually purchase the ticket?

• Can the price change between the time you buy the ticket and the date of departure?

• Is there a penalty for cancellation of the ticket?

• Can the reservation be changed without penalty, or for a reasonable fee? Be sure you understand the sort of service you are buying.

• Is this a nonstop flight, a direct flight (an itinerary where your plane will make one or more stops en route to its destination), or a flight that requires you to change planes one or more times?

• What seat has been issued? Do you really want the center seat in a three-seat row, between two strangers?

You might also want to ask your travel agent:

• Is there anything I should know about the financial health of the airline offering me this ticket?

• Are you aware of any significant threats of work stoppages or legal actions that could ruin my trip?

Overbooking

Overbooking is a polite industry term for the legal business practice of selling more than an airline can deliver. It all stems, alas, from the rudeness of many travelers who neglect to cancel flight reservations that will not be used. Airlines study the patterns on various flights and city pairs and apply a formula that allows them to sell more tickets than there are seats on the plane in the expectation that a certain percentage of ticket holders will not show up at the airport.

But what happens if all passengers holding a reservation do show up? Obviously, the result will be more passengers than seats, and some will have to be left behind.

The involuntary bump list will begin with the names of passengers who are late to check in. Airlines must ask for volunteers before bumping any passengers who have followed the rules on check-in.

Now, assuming that no one is willing to give up his or her seat just for the fun of it, the airline will offer some sort of compensation—either a free ticket or cash, or both. It is up to the passenger and the airline to negotiate an acceptable deal.

Second chance. Tour cancellations are rare. Most tour operators, if forced to cancel, will offer another package or other incentives as a goodwill gesture. If a charter flight or charter tour is canceled, the tour operator must refund your money within 14 days.

Lug-it-yourself. If you are using a scheduled airline to connect with a charter flight or vice versa, your baggage will not be transferred automatically. You must make the transfer yourself.

Charter and tour flights operate independently of other flights. If you are on a trip that combines scheduled and non-scheduled flights, or two unrelated charter flights, you may end up losing your money and flight because of delays.

It may make sense to avoid such combinations for that reason, or to leave extra hours or even days between connections. Some tour operators offer travel-delay insurance that pays for accommodations or alternative travel arrangements necessitated by certain types of delays.

The U.S. Department of Transportation's consumer protection regulations set some minimum levels of compensation for passengers who are bumped from a flight due to overbooking.

If a passenger is bumped involuntarily, the airline must provide a ticket on its next available flight. Unfortunately, there is no guarantee that there will be a seat on that plane, or that it will arrive at your destination at a convenient time.

If a passenger is bumped involuntarily and is booked on a flight that arrives within one hour of the original arrival time, no compensation need be paid. If the airline gets the bumpee to his or her destination more than one hour but less than two hours after the scheduled arrival, the traveler is entitled to receive an amount equal to the one-way fare of the oversold flight, up to $200. If the delay is more than two hours, the bumpee will receive an amount equal to twice the one-way fare of the original flight, up to $400.

It is not considered bumping if a flight is canceled because of weather, equipment problems, or the lack of a flight crew. You are also not eligible for compensation if the airline substitutes a smaller aircraft for operational or safety reasons, or if the flight involves an aircraft with 60 seats or less.

How to Get Bumped

Why in the world would you want to be bumped? Well, perhaps you'd like to look at missing your plane as an opportunity to earn a little money for your time instead of an annoyance. Is a two-hour delay worth $100 an hour to you? For the inconvenience of waiting a few hours on the way home a family of four might receive a voucher for $800—that could pay for a week's hotel plus a heck of a meal at the airport.

If you're not in a tremendous rush to get to Florida—or to get back home—you might want to volunteer to be bumped. We wouldn't recommend doing this on the busiest travel days of the year, or if you are booked on the last flight of the day, unless you are also looking forward to a free night in an airport motel.

How to Book a Package or Charter Flight

If possible, use a travel agent—preferably one you know and trust from prior experience. In general, the tour operator pays the travel agent's commission. Some tour packages, however, are available only from the operator who organized the tour; in certain cases, you may be able to negotiate a better price by dealing directly with the operator, although you are giving up one layer of protection for your rights.

Pay for your ticket with a credit card; this is a cardinal rule for almost any situation in which you are prepaying for a service or product.

Realize that charter airlines don't have large fleets of planes available to substitute in the event of a mechanical problem or an extensive weather delay. They may or may not be able to arrange for a substitute plane from another carrier.

If you are still willing to try a charter after all of these warnings, check the bottom line once more before you sign the contract. First of all, is the air travel significantly less expensive than the lowest nonrefundable fare from a scheduled carrier? (Remember that you are, in effect, buying a nonrefundable fare with most charter flight contracts.)

Have you included taxes, service charges, baggage transfer fees, or other charges the tour operator may put into the contract?

Are the savings significantly more than the 10 percent the charter operator may boost the price without your permission? Do any savings come at a cost of time? Put a monetary value on your time.

Finally, don't buy a complete package until you have compared it with the à la carte cost of such a trip. Call the hotels offered by the tour operator, or similar ones in the same area, and ask them a simple question: "What is your best price for a room?" Be sure to mention any discount programs that are applicable, including AAA or other organizations. Do the same for car rental agencies, and remember to place a call to

Traveling with golf clubs. Many major airlines make special accommodations for golf bags. They may offer a free cardboard box to surround your case, or a heavy plastic bag to encase your clubs; some even sell special travel bags made of canvas or nylon that cover your equipment. Call your airline in advance to find out what it may have available; confirm that bags are offered at the airport where you will start your trip. Finally, add at least 30 minutes to your preflight check-in time to take care of packing business.

You can protect your own equipment. You might consider purchasing a hard travel case to cover your clubs. Consider wrapping your clubs in padding— bubble plastic or foam rubber will do, but so will your underwear, socks, and sweaters.

Finally, consult with your home insurance agent to see what coverage you already have on your belongings while you travel. If you make several vacation trips each year, it may be worthwhile to purchase a relatively inexpensive rider to your home owner's or renter's policy to cover your equipment beyond the basic liability of airlines.

Don't hesitate to drop a card. Keep in touch with your travel agent or tour operator. In many cases he or she can anticipate major changes before departure time and let you know how the changes will affect your plans. And many operators will try hard to keep you from demanding a refund if you find a major change unacceptable. They may offer a discount or an upgrade on a substitute trip or adjust the price of the changed tour.

Disneyland and any other attractions you plan to visit to get current prices.

And, of course, don't overlook the discount coupons for hotels, motels, restaurants, and attractions that are included in this book—that's why we put them there.

About Travel Agencies

Here's my advice about travel agents, in a nutshell: get a really good one, or go it alone.

A good travel agent is someone who remembers who he or she works for: you.

Of course there is a built-in conflict of interest here, since the agent is in most cases paid by someone else. Agents receive a commission on airline tickets, hotel reservations, car rentals, and many other services they sell you. The more they sell (or the higher the price), the more they earn.

I would recommend you start the planning for any trip by calling the airlines and a few hotels and finding the best package you can put together for yourself. Then call your travel agent and ask him or her to do better.

If your agent contributes knowledge or experience, comes up with dollar-saving alternatives to your own package, or offers some other kind of convenience, then go ahead and book through the agency. If, as I often find, you know a lot more about your destination and are willing to spend a lot more time to save money than the agent will, do it yourself.

There is one special type of travel agency worth considering. A number of large agencies offer their customers rebates of part of their commissions. Some of these companies cater only to frequent fliers who will bring in a lot of business; other rebate agencies offer only limited services to clients.

I use an agency that sends me a check after each trip equal to 5 percent of all reservations booked through them. I have never set foot in their offices, and I conduct all of my business over the phone; tickets arrive by mail or by overnight courier when necessary.

You can find discount travel agencies through many major credit card companies (Citibank and American Express among them) or through associations and clubs. Some warehouse shopping clubs have rebate travel agencies.

And if you establish a regular relationship with your local travel agency and bring them enough business to make them glad to see you walk through their door, don't be afraid to ask them for a discount equal to a few percentage points.

Golf Packages

Some of the best deals for golfers can be found by booking a package golf tour from a resort, or from a specialized travel agency or tour packager.

The packages often bring together discounted airfare, cheap car rentals, off-rate hotel rooms, and free or deeply discounted greens fees. That's the good news.

The potential bad news is that you have to pay attention to the details of the package to make certain it is a better deal than an à la carte vacation you assemble for yourself or an equivalent level of convenience and luxury.

Here is an example of a package to Hilton Head Island offered by one major packager:

• Round-trip air transportation to Hilton Head or Savannah from major East Coast and Midwest locations

• Accommodations for three nights

• Rental car with unlimited mileage

• Four daily greens fees with guaranteed advance tee times

Low-season rates (summer in Hilton Head) are as low as $499 per person at a motel and up to $629 at a resort at one of the name golf courses. High-season rates (spring in Hilton Head) range from about $559 to $699 per person.

This particular package has a relatively small amount of fine print, although some of the elements are important: the participating golf resorts all require rental of a golf cart at an additional fee of $15 to $19 per person; some of the tonier golf resorts may add an unspecified surcharge, and rental car taxes, fees, and insurance.

Some other notes include penalties of up to $150 if reservations have to be changed after documents have been issued, and a cancellation policy that includes the following:

• Up to 45 days before departure, $25 per person cancellation fee

• Within 45 to 15 days before departure, $100 per person cancellation fee, plus any applicable air-, hotel-, car-, or golf-related penalties (with the penalties not specified in the brochure)

• Within 15 days and up to 72 hours before departure, $150 per person cancellation fee, plus any applicable air-, hotel-, car-, or golf-related penalties

• Within 72 hours of departure, forfeiture of the full advance payment

Does this mean that golf packages are not a good deal? Absolutely not. It just means that you have to study the fine print very carefully. The more oner-

Kids in midair. If you are flying with children, discuss with your airline or travel agent any special needs you might have. These might include a request for a bulkhead seat to give children a little extra room for fidgeting (although you will lose the storage space underneath the seat in front of you) or special meals (most airlines offer a child's meal of a hot dog or hamburger upon request, which may be more appealing to a youngster than standard airline cuisine).

Be sure to pack a special utility bag for young children and carry it on board the plane. Extra diapers in the baggage compartment won't help you at all in an emergency at 25,000 feet. Include formula, food, and snacks as well as a few toys and books to occupy young ones.

Changes in altitude at takeoff and landing may cause some children discomfort in their ears. Try to teach them to clear their ears with an exaggerated yawn. Bubble gum or candy, or a bottle for babies, can help too.

ous the cancellation fees, the more valuable a cancellation insurance policy becomes.

And finally, don't be afraid to attempt to negotiate with a tour packager for a better deal or better conditions. Some companies may have contractual obligations with airlines, hotels, and courses; they may be willing to cut their rates close to departure dates.

Drive, He Said?

Everyone's conception of the perfect vacation is different, but for me, I draw a distinction between getting there and being there. I want the getting there part to be as quick and simple as possible, and the being there part to be as long as I can manage and afford. Therefore, I fly to just about any destination that is more than a few hundred miles from my home. The cost of driving, hotels, meals en route, and general physical and mental wear and tear rarely equals a deeply discounted excursion fare.

If you do drive, though, you can save a few dollars by using the services of AAA or another major automobile club. Before you head out, spend a bit of time and money to make certain your vehicle is in traveling shape: a tune-up and fully inflated, fully inspected tires will certainly save gas, money, and headaches.

If you plan to travel by bus or train, be aware that the national carriers generally have the same sort of peak and off-peak pricing as the airlines. The cheapest time to buy tickets is when the fewest people want them.

Renting a Car

Extra miles. Don't let it force you to pay too much for a rental car, but all things being equal, use a rental agency that awards frequent flier mileage in a program you use.

Renting a car can be a liberating experience, freeing you from the hassles of finding a taxi, allowing you to explore the area at will, permitting you to rent a less-expensive hotel room a bit of a drive away from the golf resort, and giving you the freedom to drive to that exciting restaurant—the one with better food and better prices than those offered by room service.

Renting a car can also be an anchor around your neck. You'll need to find a place to park, a set of maps of the area, and the location of gas stations. Finally, you'll need to leave time on getaway day to fill up the tank and drop off the car.

I recommend you sit down with a piece of paper and a pencil and calculate the value of a rental car. Expect to pay somewhere between $30 and $50 per day for a small car—plus tax, gas, and parking. Compare the bottom line with the cost of taxis, shuttle services (does your hotel offer a free service?), and even with the cost of hiring a car and driver for a few hours.

I generally find that renting a car is more expensive than using a taxi or car service for most travel in and near major cities and resorts, but I prefer to pay the extra money for the freedom to explore at will. Renting a car is usually a cost-effective decision when you have a long distance to travel between airport and resort, or from hotel to golf course.

Saving Money at the Rental Counter

Car rental companies will try—with varying levels of pressure—to convince you to purchase special insurance coverage. They'll tell you it's "only" $7 or $9 per day. What a deal! That works out to about $2,500 or $3,330 per year for a set of rental wheels. Of course the coverage is intended primarily to protect the rental company, not you.

Before you travel check with your insurance agent to determine how well your personal automobile policy will cover a rental car and its contents. We strongly recommend you use a credit card that offers rental car insurance; such insurance usually covers the deductible below your personal policy. The extra auto insurance by itself is usually worth an upgrade to a gold card or other extra-service credit card.

The only sticky area comes for those visitors with a driver's license but no car, and therefore no insurance. Again, consult your credit card company and your insurance agent to see what kind of coverage you have, or what kind you need.

Your travel agent may be of assistance in finding the best rates; you can make a few phone calls by yourself too. Rental rates generally follow the same structure. We have obtained rates as low as $59 a week for a tiny subcompact (a convertible, no less) in low season.

Although it is theoretically possible to rent a car without a credit card, you will find it to be a rather inconvenient process. If the rental agency cannot hold your credit card account hostage, it will most often require a large cash deposit—perhaps as much as several thousand dollars—before it will give you the keys.

Be aware that the least-expensive car rental agencies usually do not have their stations at the airport itself. You will have to wait for a shuttle bus to take you from the terminal to the rental lot, and you must return the car to that same outlying area at the end of your trip. This may add about 20 to 30 minutes to your arrival and departure schedule.

Pay attention, too, when the rental agent explains the gas policy. The most common plan

The best policy. Consider buying trip-cancellation insurance from a travel agency, tour operator, or insurance company (ask your insurance agent for advice). The policies are intended to reimburse you for any lost deposits or prepayments if you must cancel a trip because you or certain specified members of your family become ill. Read the policy carefully to understand the circumstances under which the company will pay.

Take care not to purchase more coverage than you need; if your tour package costs $5,000 but you would lose only $1,000 in a cancellation, then the amount of the insurance payoff required is just $1,000. Some policies will cover you for health and accident benefits while on vacation, excluding any preexisting conditions.

And be sure you understand your contract with your airline. You may be able to reschedule a flight or even receive a refund after payment of a service charge. Some airlines will give full refunds or free rescheduling if you can prove a medical reason for the change.

If your trip is based on refundable tickets and

cancelable hotel reservations you don't need trip-cancellation insurance at all—the policy won't pay you anything at all if you can get your money back without it.

says that you must return the car with a full tank; if the agency must refill the tank, you will be billed a service charge plus what is usually a very high per-gallon rate.

Other optional plans include one where the rental agency sells you a full tank when you first drive away and takes no note of how much gas remains when you return the car. Unless you somehow manage to return the car with the engine running on fumes, you are in effect making a gift to the agency with every gallon you bring back.

We prefer the first option, which requires making it a point to refill the tank on the way to the airport on getaway day.

Chapter 3
Hotels

A Place to Lay Your Head

Let us start out by saying that some travelers—let's call them type A people—consider a hotel to be a place to catch a minimal amount of shut-eye and store their stuff between expeditions. They want their hotel clean, convenient . . . and cheap. They don't care whether the television has rabbit ears or 32 cable channels, whether there is a health club, or whether the view out the window is an asphalt parking lot. Amenities don't mean very much to the type A who arrives at 11 P.M. and departs each morning at 7 A.M. for the links.

For others—type B folk—the place they stay is one of the main aspects of the vacation. They demand large rooms with three telephones, two television sets with satellite channels, in-room saunas, on-call massage therapists, spectacular restaurants and room service, extravagant furnishings, and million-dollar views of the beach, the golf course, or the mountain peaks.

There is nothing wrong with either preference, unless you are a type A person forced to pay for a view you never see and a swimming pool you never visit, or a type B person unhappily stuck in an economy motel without HBO and room service.

So, the first decision you should make in planning a vacation is to decide what level of luxury you are willing to pay for. But before you make a reservation, you should also perform a cost/benefit analysis for the trip you have in mind.

Here's a hypothetical comparison of five hotel options for a golfing vacation, using typical prices from in and around a four-star golf resort in Arizona.

Example 1

Economy Motel: Public Golf, Economy Dining
Basic room (per person, double-occupancy)	$30
Breakfast and dinner at economy restaurants	$20

| Greens fee at public golf course | $30 |
| Car rental (per person, for two golfers) | $30 |

Total: $110 per person per night

Example 2

Economy Motel: Resort Golf, Economy Dining

Basic room (per person, double-occupancy)	$30
Breakfast and dinner at economy restaurants	$20
Greens fee at resort golf course	$100
Car rental (per person, for two golfers)	$30

Total: $180 per person per night

Example 3

Luxury Golf Resort: Resort Golf, Economy Dining

Luxury room (per person, double-occupancy)	$75
Breakfast and dinner at economy restaurants	$20
Discounted resort greens fee for guests	$75
Car rental (per person, for two golfers)	$30

Total: $200 per person per night

Example 4

Luxury Golf Resort: Resort Golf, Fine Dining

Luxury room (per person, double-occupancy)	$75
Breakfast and dinner at resort restaurants	$50
Discounted resort greens fee for guests	$75
Car rental (not needed)	0

Total: $200 per person per night

Example 5

Luxury Golf Resort: Resort Golf Package

Luxury room (per person, double-occupancy)	$200
Breakfast and dinner on modified American plan	$60
Unlimited resort greens fee (included)	0
Car rental (not needed)	0

Total: $260 per person per night

What can be learned from this one comparison?

The least-expensive option is to stay at an economy motel, eat at economy restaurants, and visit a reasonably priced public course. You knew that, right?

But things become more complicated when your goal is to play at one of America's premier resorts. The best deal might be found at a luxury resort that offers discounts on golf rounds or even a golf resort that offers a package, including golf and other amenities, such as lessons, practice time, and more.

A few more notes: car rental is included in Examples 1, 2, and 3 since travelers will need to get to the courses and to restaurants. We have removed the cost of a car rental from Examples 4 and 5 since golfers should be able to make use of the resort's facilities to get to the course and restaurants; most luxury resorts offer courtesy transportation to nearby airports for guests.

In our experience, we have found that modified American plan packages (breakfast and dinner included in room rates) are often priced above the value we would place on those meals, but that's a purely subjective judgment.

Other elements that you should consider are health clubs, pools, tennis courts, jogging tracks, and other amenities. You may also want to consider attractions for nongolfers in your party (be sure to seek credit for any golf greens fees that will not be used). Families who travel together might want to consider the appeal of courses located within or near major attractions. Mom or dad can go golfing for the day while the kids and the nongolfing spouse can visit such places as Walt Disney World, Williamsburg, Disneyland, and Las Vegas.

Negotiating for a Room

Notice the title of this section; it's not called "Buying a Room." The fact of the matter is that hotel rooms, like almost everything else, are subject to negotiation and change.

Here is how to pay the highest possible price for a hotel room: walk up to the front desk without a reservation and say, "I'd like a room." Unless the "No Vacancy" sign is lit, you may be charged the rack rate, which is the published maximum nightly charge. You not only want to avoid paying the rack rate, you want to pay the lowest possible price.

Before you head for your vacation, spend an hour on the phone and call half a dozen hotels that seem to be in the price range you're comfortable with. (We recommend membership in AAA; you can use their annual tour books as starting points for your research.)

Start by asking for the room rate. Then ask the reservation clerk for the hotel's best rate. Does that sound like an unnecessary second request? Trust us, it's not. We can't begin to count the number of times the rates have dropped substantially when we asked a second time.

True story: I once called the reservation desk of a major hotel chain and asked for the rates for a night at a Chicago location. "That will be $149 per night," I was told. "Ouch," I said. "Oh, would you like to spend less?" the reservation clerk answered. I admitted that I would, and she punched a few keys on her keyboard. "They have a special promotion going on. How about $109 per night?" she asked.

Not bad for a city hotel, I reasoned, but still I hadn't asked the big question. "What is your best rate?" I asked. "Oh, our best rate? That would be $79," said the agent.

Here's my card. Membership in AAA brings some important benefits for the traveler, although you may not be able to apply the club's usual 10 percent discount on top of whatever hotel rate you negotiate. (It doesn't hurt to ask, though.) Be sure to request a tour book and maps from AAA, even if you plan to fly; AAA maps are much better than those given by car rental agencies.

If you are age 50 or older, consider membership in AARP (American Association of Retired Persons) for discounts on hotel, car rental, and travel packages. A number of hotels have their own senior discount programs as well.

Weekly, not weakly.
Are you planning to stay
for a full week? Ask for
the weekly rate. If the
reservation clerk says
there is no such rate, ask
to speak to the manager;
he or she may be willing
to shave a few dollars per
day off the rate for a
long-term stay.

"OK, I'll take it," I told the clerk. "I'm a AAA member, by the way." Another pause. "That's fine, Mr. Sandler. The nightly room rate will be $71.10. Have a nice day."

When you feel you've negotiated the best deal you can over the phone, make a reservation at the hotel of your choice. Be sure to go over the dates and prices one more time, and obtain the name of the person you spoke with and a confirmation number if available.

But wait. When you show up at your hotel on the first night, stop and look at the marquee outside and see if the hotel is advertising a discount rate. Most of the hotels in the Walt Disney World area adjust their prices based on attendance levels at the park. It is not uncommon to see prices change by $10 or more over the course of a day.

Here's where you need to be bold. Walk up to the desk as if you do not have a reservation, and ask the clerk: "What is your best room rate for tonight?" If the rate you are quoted is less than the rate in your reservation, you are now properly armed to ask for a reduction in your room rate.

Similarly, if the room rate advertised out front on the marquee drops during your stay, don't be shy about asking that your charges be reduced. Just be sure to ask for the reduction before you spend another night at the old rate, and obtain the name of the clerk who promises a change. If the hotel tries a lame excuse like "That's only for new check-ins," you can offer to check out and then check back in again. That will usually work; you can always check out and go to the hotel across the road that will usually match the rates of its competitor.

And here is the way to make the most informed choice, but try it in the low season only. Arrive at your destination without a reservation, and then cruise one of the motel strips. Check the outdoor marquees for discount prices. I make notes. Find a phone booth and make a few phone calls to the ones you found attractive. Once again be sure to ask for the best price. The later in the day you search for a room, the more likely you are to find a hotel ready to make a deal.

Dialing for Dollars

By now we hope you realize that you must be aggressive in your negotiations with a reservation clerk. Sometimes you will also need to be very persistent.

A few years back, a major travel magazine conducted a survey of hotel rates and found wide discrepancies between the prices quoted by central toll-free services, reservations clerks at a particular hotel, and travel agents. The survey was indecisive; no one source consistently yielded the lowest prices.

The magazine's recommendation was to use the services of a travel agent you trust, and request that the agent verify the lowest rate with a direct call. The agent can check the computer first and then compare that rate against the hotel's offer.

Protecting Yourself Against an Unfulfilled Reservation

A reservation guarantees you a place to stay, right? Well . . . *usually*.

At busy times of the year, hotels hope to operate at or near capacity. And like airlines and car rental companies, a hotel may even take more reservations than it has rooms, figuring that a certain percentage of people will cancel at the last minute or fail to show up. Nevertheless, it is still possible that you can show up at the front desk with your reservation in hand and find out that there is no room at the inn.

First of all, let's understand one of the deep, dark little secrets of hotels: in most cases it is almost impossible for a hotel to oust a guest who stays beyond his or her reserved length of stay. The manager can object, the chambermaids can refuse to deliver fresh towels, and room service can take forever to deliver dinner (well, they do that anyway, but you get the idea). Hotels may have to resort to a court order to remove someone who refuses to go peacefully. (We're not going to suggest this as a strategy, but it is true that some brazen travelers will accept a one-night-only reservation on the day before a sold-out convention and then stay as long as they want.)

How can you protect yourself from losing a room? Guarantee your room for late arrival using a major credit card; by itself this gives you a bought-and-paid-for contract for a room that should be honored, and some credit card companies go even further to add guarantees of their own in such a case. If you have any doubts about availability of rooms, call the hotel directly to make a reservation instead of using an 800 number; this is generally a good practice anyhow, since you may sometimes find better prices by calling directly.

If you are a member of a hotel frequent-guest program, use the priority reservation services of the program. (The same applies for car rental services—if you are in a club, use the special number you receive to increase your clout.)

The policies at various hotels differ, but you should be able to make some demands if your reservation is not honored. Start by asking for a suite or a business-class room (at the same rate you were quoted for your original reservation). If that doesn't work, insist that the hotel find you another room of equal or better quality nearby. The hotel should provide transportation to the other hotel if you need it, and if it's a good operation it may offer to give you one or more nights free. Keep notes of the names of the front-desk person-

Wrong numbers. Be sure you understand a hotel's telephone billing policy. Some establishments allow free local calls, while others charge as much as 75 cents for such calls. (We're especially unhappy with service charges for 800 numbers.) Be sure to examine your bill carefully at checkout and make sure it is correct. We strongly suggest you obtain a telephone credit card and use it when you travel.

Clearing the air. If you don't indulge, ask for a nonsmoking room at check-in. With luck, the air will be somewhat cleaner and furniture coverings and drapes somewhat fresher.

nel and manager and don't be shy about writing to the customer service department of any national chain involved—it may earn you a free room in the future.

Discount Hotel Deals

It's pretty clear that we shudder at the thought of paying full price for travel and hotel arrangements. Here are a few steps every travel shopper should follow:

• Join an association that offers discounts at participating hotel chains and individual locations. These include the AAA and CAA automobile clubs, AARP (American Association of Retired Persons), and professional groups.

• Use credit cards that offer special discounts to their members; American Express and Discover cards are among the many companies that regularly offer special deals.

• Check into wholesale buying clubs such as Price Club, Costco, BJ's, and others that may offer special deals to members.

• If you are a frequent traveler, consider joining a membership club associated with major hotel chains. Some of these clubs offer discounts off nightly rates, or they may reward you with free nights after a certain number of paid visits.

Discount Hotel Companies

One other avenue to explore is hotel booking services and hotel consolidators. These companies may have made special arrangements with individual hotels to allow them to offer discounted rates at off-peak times of the year, or they may have actually committed to purchase and resell blocks of rooms around the country.

As with any other special offer, be sure to compare the rates offered you with other deals. I suggest you begin by finding the lowest possible rate by yourself. Then call a discount company to see if it has a better deal to offer.

The timing of your reservation entails a metaphorical roll of the dice. You may find that last-minute availability is limited to the most expensive properties. Or you may find a discount company with some rooms it needs to unload or lose money on.

One of these companies is the Hotel Reservations Network, which claims savings of up to 65 percent at hotels in cities including Anaheim, Boston, Chicago, Los Angeles, Miami, New Orleans, New York, Orlando, San Diego, and San Francisco.

Here are some discount hotel companies:

Hotel Reservations Network
(800) 964-6835
http://www.hoteldiscount.com

TravelNow
(800) 568-1972
http://www.TravelNow.com

Capitol Reservations
(800) 847-4832
http://hotelsdc.com/reserv.html

A Selection of Some of America's Best Golf Resorts

Condé Nast Traveler conducted a poll of thousands of its readers in 1996 to determine their favorite golf resort. Bear in mind that this is a rather elite group and their tastes (and pocketbooks) may run to more luxury than the average golfer's. Consider this a cost-is-no-object ranking. Note that 6 of the top 10 (see page 30) are located in the Hawaiian Islands.

Safety first. The small safes available in some hotels can be valuable to the traveler; be sure to inquire whether there is a service charge for their use. We've been in hotels that apply the charge whether we used the safe or not; look over your bill at checkout and object to any charges that are not proper. In any case, we'd suggest that any objects that are so valuable that you feel it necessary to lock them up should probably be left at home.

The top-ranked was the Lodge at Koele, on the Hawaiian island of Lanai. Readers lauded the gorgeous fairways that include waterfalls and views of nearby Molokai and Maui. They also paid tribute to the formal setting of the lodge on the course itself. Prices at the Lodge range from about $300 to $500 per night, and greens fees are about $100.

Second place among American resorts went to The Greenbrier in White Sulphur Springs, West Virginia, which won kudos for the attentiveness of the staff and the challenge of the courses, especially the Championship Course. Rooms at the large hotel, including breakfast and dinner, range from about $400 to $550 per night.

Northstar-at-Tahoe's high altitude, 18-hole resort golf course features a wide-open front nine and a technical, tree-lined back nine.
David Madison photo courtesy of Northstar-at-Tahoe.

◌◌◌◌ **Top 25 Resorts** ◌◌◌◌

1. Lodge at Koele, Lanai, Hawaii
2. The Greenbrier, White Sulphur Springs, West Virginia
3. American Club, Kohler, Wisconsin
4. Mauna Lani Bay Hotel & Bungalows, Hawaii, Hawaii
5. Mauna Kea Beach Hotel, Hawaii, Hawaii
6. The Cloister, Sea Island, Georgia
7. Manele Bay Hotel, Lanai, Hawaii
8. The Homestead, Hot Springs, Virginia
9. Aston Wailea Resort, Maui, Hawaii
10. Princeville Resort, Kauai, Hawaii
11. Hyatt Regency Kauai, Kauai, Hawaii
12. Ritz-Carlton Kapalua, Maui, Hawaii
13. Marriott at Sawgrass, Ponte Vedra Beach, Florida
14. Williamsburg Inn, Williamsburg, Virginia
15. Barton Creek Resort, Austin, Texas
16. Litchfield Beach & Golf Resort, Pawleys Island, South Carolina
17. Hyatt Regency Grand Cypress Resort, Orlando, Florida
18. Scottsdale Princess, Scottsdale, Arizona
19. Kapalua Bay Hotel and Villas, Maui, Hawaii (This complex shares courses with the Ritz-Carlton Kapalua.)
20. Innisbrook Hilton Resort, Tarpon Springs, Florida
21. Sunriver Lodge and Resort, Sunriver, Oregon
22. Loews Ventana Canyon Resort, Tucson, Arizona
23. Ojai Valley Inn, Ojai, California
24. La Quinta Hotel Golf and Tennis Resort, La Quinta, California
25. Kiawah Island Inn and Villas, Kiawah Island, South Carolina

Source: *Condé Nast Traveler*, June 1996.

Chapter 4
Golf Travelers' Most Frequently Asked Questions

One of the most welcome additions to our publishing lexicon comes from the world of the Internet, where common-interest groups on almost any conceivable topic introduce themselves with lists of frequently asked questions, known in the computer world as FAQs.

We're committed to the world of paper and ink; books travel so much better than PCs (no batteries or extension cords), and dropping a book into the bathtub is much less of a catastrophe than drowning a laptop computer. However, we're not above borrowing a good idea when we see one. So, here are the golfing FAQs, just the FAQs.

Golf Equipment

Even a great golfer needs the right equipment. What constitutes the right equipment? Read on.

Clubs

1. *What is a* wood, *and why are some of them made of materials that never grew in a forest?* The classic definition of a wood is a club for use when distance down the fairway or a carry across a body of water is more important than accuracy. Originally such clubs were made of solid wood, but there are now woods made of laminated timber, metal, and advanced man-made substances such as graphite.

Wooden woods usually are made of persimmon for solid heads that are turned using a master model or on an automated lathe; laminated heads are made of thin veneers of wood that are pressure-formed and turned on a lathe. There is little difference in performance or feel between the two types of wooden woods, although a laminated club may be sturdier than a solid one.

Metal woods generally are made of cast metal including stainless steel, aluminum, and more exotic materials such as titanium. The club heads are usually hollow when first cast; they are then precisely balanced—or sometimes purposely made off-balance to achieve a certain effect—when they are filled with polyurethane or other compounds.

Because the metal in the metal woods is usually cast pretty thin, it is sometimes subject to being crushed or dented. One way to get around this is to make the metal wood slightly smaller but with thicker walls, a so-called mid-size head; another solution involves the use of plastic, graphite, or harder metal face inserts in the sweet spot of metal woods.

Graphite, which has increasingly become the material of choice for club shafts, is also used for molding woods. Graphite woods usually are about the same weight as wood or metal woods, but because the material is about 40 percent lighter than steel the resulting club is much larger. As such, it gives the golfer a larger sweet spot, which may be a comfort for some players, and is a bit more forgiving for slightly off-center hits.

By the way, some especially strong and accurate swingers on the pro tour will use a 1- or 2-iron off the tee on some holes.

2. *What is meant by the "loft" of a club?* Loft is a measurement of the angle of the club face compared with a flat surface beneath it. A club with 0 degrees of loft is perpendicular to the ground; a 1-wood usually has between 8 and 12 degrees of loft.

3. *What is an* iron, *and are any of them made from that basic element?* Irons, used when accuracy is more important than distance, originally were made of iron. Today few are. More common are stainless steel irons. Some are made of aluminum, and the newest thing is the forged titanium iron, that promises accuracy and more distance than iron irons. Irons are either cast or forged.

A cast club is created by pouring molten metal into a mold that includes markings and design elements. A form of cast club is the cavity back iron, which distributes the weight of the head around its perimeter and yields a large sweet spot that is more forgiving of off-center shots.

A forged club is made by hammering and otherwise shaping a superheated chunk of metal; the completed piece must then go through a finishing process including milling and grinding. A form of forged iron is a muscleback, or blade, design that is formed in such a way as to distribute the weight of the iron across all of the head, producing a small sweet spot in its center. This makes a properly hit shot fly straight and long, but penalizes any off-center hit. However, some golfers believe that a muscleback iron delivers a truer feel.

4. *What do the numbers on clubs mean?* The numbers evolved over time as more weapons were added to the golfer's arsenal, but they generally refer to the relative loft of a club—the lower the number, the lower the loft and the "longer" the club. A low-loft long club is supposed to deliver the greatest distance at the cost of accuracy; a higher number means higher loft—meaning shorter distance and better accuracy.

5. *Is there a standard "set" of clubs?* A golfer is supposed to have no more than 14 clubs in a set—you can have less but not more. The makeup of your optimal set should vary according to your strength and abilities as well as the particular challenges you expect to see on the course you are playing.

A typical set might include:

> Woods: 1, 3, and 5
> Irons: 3, 4, 5, 6, 7, 8, 9, and a pitching wedge
> Putter

Some players will sacrifice a 5-iron or a 6-iron for a sand wedge, especially when playing on beachlike courses.

6. *What kind of shaft should stand between the grip and the club?* If you think about its function, you'll realize that the shaft is actually the most complex part of a golf club. It has to be strong yet light, able to transfer the power of your swing to the club and ball yet able to flex properly, and it must be the proper length for varying skill levels and sizes of golfers. Designers talk about weight, stiffness, torque, and flex points.

Shafts were originally made of wood, but these are mostly relegated to the antique shelves these days. More common now are steel, graphite, or titanium. Stainless steel or carbon steel shafts are drawn to the proper length, thickness, and wall design, and then hardened and chrome plated. The flex of the shaft typically is adjusted by making it thinner at the grip (more likely to flex) and thicker at the club. Steel shafts have the advantage of carrying an identical or similar feel from one club in a set to another, and they are generally the least expensive and most durable.

Graphite shafts generally are made by wrapping graphite tape around a form, which is later cut and polished. Graphite shafts are noticeably lighter than steel, and able to dampen the vibration transmitted up the shaft by contact with the ball or ground. Graphite shafts, though, can vary in feel from one club in a set to another; they are also more expensive than steel. Even more expensive are graphite shafts with filament winding, which is supposed to combine the light weight and feel of graphite with the consistency of steel.

Most expensive are titanium shafts, which are light and strong; some players find them too stiff.

7. *How do I judge the stiffness of a shaft?* As with any other piece of equipment, whatever works best for you is the right thing. Experts say that the faster your swing speed the stiffer the shaft you should use (this is to prevent the club head from lagging behind the shaft as it meets the ball). Conversely, slower swingers can benefit from the extra kick a flexible shaft will deliver.

Shafts are often rated by manufacturers as R (regular), S (stiff), and X (extra stiff). There are also A (men's flexible) and L (ladies' flexible) classes.

A more technical way to rate a shaft is to list its frequency, a measure of the number of vibration cycles per minute for the shaft. The stiffer the shaft, the faster its vibration rate; an extra-stiff shaft vibrates at about 270 cycles.

Let's talk about *torque.* Let's do the twist, which is what a shaft's torque is all about. In general, the stiffer the shaft the less torque the club will have. Steel shafts typically have a torque rating of about 2.5 degrees, a relatively slight potential twisting action. Graphite shafts are twistier, usually ranging from about 3.5 to 5.5 degrees of torque. Some exotic graphite shafts extend beyond this range in either direction.

8. *What's the purpose of flex points?* The flex point, also called the kick point or the bend point, is the place where a shaft will bend. A high flex point will result in a low trajectory. A low flex point will tend to make the ball fly higher; the shaft will feel as if it whips the club into the ball.

9. *How do I get a grip for myself?* Even the seemingly minor issue of how to hold onto your club can become as complicated as any other part of golf-

ing equipment. Golf grips are typically made of rubber, leather, or cord. They are available in standard, oversized, and undersized versions.

The original design for grips used cowhide or calfskin leather. These are soft and comfortable with a bit of tackiness that helps you hold onto the club. Leather grips are a bit more expensive than man-made materials and may require professional installation and repair.

Rubber grips are usually a composition material made up of rubber and granulated cork. The advantage of rubber includes its lower price, ease of installation, and the ability to mold into the grip markers for hand placement and other special comfort and playability features.

Cord grips add fabric or man-made filament to a rubber grip to create a nonslip surface, especially valuable in wet, hot, or humid weather. A variation is a half-cord grip that puts smooth rubber at thumb level and corded rubber where the fingers wrap around.

Grip sizes can be adjusted with padding or tape on the shaft beneath the grip. Alternatively you can order your grips in special sizes.

Oversized grips can be more comfortable for certain players, especially those with arthritis or other problems, as well as players who simply have extra-large paws. The overlarge grip may reduce hand movement, increasing a tendency to slice.

An undersized grip is geared toward women and others with smaller hands. The hand is more likely to move, increasing a tendency to hook.

10. *How do I select the best clubs for me?* The best suggestion is to combine some informed advice with some real-world testing. In other words, ask a golf pro, golf equipment salesperson, or good golfer you know and trust about the latest and greatest equipment as well as the oldest and most-proven.

The next step is to try out the clubs. Beg or borrow—don't steal—a set from the golf shop, the pro shop at a golf club, or a friend. You might be able to rent a set from a golf club too. Play a round or two with the clubs.

It would be wonderful if you suddenly found that the new clubs shaved a dozen strokes off your typical game. In fact, you may find that the new clubs feel so very different from your current set that your score goes up. What you are looking for are cures for known problems, an improved feel, and an overall better match between the equipment and your abilities.

11. *Should I purchase a custom-fitted or custom-built set of clubs?* In the best of all possible worlds, a custom-fitted or custom-built set of clubs would be standard. That's because no two golfers are the same height, and no two golfers have identical strength, ability, or preferences.

Off-the-shelf sets are assembled based on a club manufacturer's definition of an average golfer; you will find sets of clubs best suited for rank amateurs, competent longtime players, and pro-level players. Although prices will fit within a wide range, off-the-shelf sets are relatively less expensive than custom sets.

A custom-built set is one that is manufactured specifically for a single golfer. It may include nonstandard shaft lengths, customized weighting, special grips, and other accommodations. Parts for the clubs can be made by a club maker or can be ordered from a name-brand manufacturer and assembled to meet your needs. No matter how you cut it, buying custom-built clubs is the most expensive way to go.

In between is a custom-fit set. This is a set that is made up of ready-made components selected to match your particular needs. For example, you can order nonstandard lengths from most major name-brand club makers. Or you can mix and match club lengths and weights within a set.

Whether you end up buying your clubs from the pro shop or from a retail or mail-order operation, a visit to your local pro—especially one who is familiar with your game—can help you save money and time.

12. *Can I build my own clubs?* Yes. A number of club makers sell components—club heads, shafts, and grips—that you can assemble by yourself. You'll find listings in some of the golf magazines. You may be able to save some money this way, but you'll need to do your own research for advice on customization.

Balls

1. *My local pro shop has golf balls for sale with prices from about a buck to $5 each. Will an expensive ball make me a star on the PGA Tour?* No, but it might help the owner of your pro shop make a boat payment.

Let's start with the numbers: some golfers are willing to spend thousands of dollars on a set of clubs, hundreds on clothing, hundreds on greens fees . . . but everyone ends up swinging at a ball that sells for just a few dollars.

Approximately 2.3 million balls are sold worldwide every day—about 832 million a year. Two-thirds of the ball sales are made in the American market. The average retail price of a ball is about $2.50, but some are sold for about half that and others for twice the price. Insiders say that balls—no matter what the selling price—cost less than 50 cents to manufacture.

Ball makers have tried mightily over the past decade to make the simple golf ball more complicated and expensive. In 1985 only 147 ball designs were officially accepted for play in tournaments. In 1995, that number had reached more than 1,500. (In 1996, leading golfer Greg Norman took himself out of a tournament when he apparently used a ball that was mislabeled.)

Consider this: In 1968, the average length of a drive on the pro tour was 258 yards; in 1995 it was 263 yards. That's about a 2 percent increase, which most observers credit to the improved physical condition of today's players, not to improved equipment.

2. *What kind of balls are legal for play?* There are two basic designs: three-piece, used by nearly every professional golfer, and two-piece, used by nearly everyone else.

The three-piece ball has a solid or liquefied center that is wound with rubber threads and then covered with a synthetic balata outer surface. Balata is a latexlike dried juice of trees in the sapodilla family. Today, real balata is hard to find; instead there are synthetic substitutes that have the same properties.

A balata ball is more expensive, has a short life span, cuts easily, and goes out of round after just a few solid hits. But it supposedly has a superior feel and offers more control to those golfers able to apply hooks, slices, and spins at will to fade or draw a shot or apply backspin.

Two-piece balls have a solid plastic center and a plastic cover, usually based on Surlyn (courtesy of a DuPont factory instead of a noble tree). Less expensive and less likely to cut or nick, a Surlyn ball goes farther than a three-piece ball, but it is harder to control.

3. *Can a manufacturer stuff the ball with feathers or flubber?* Yes, more or less. The official specifications say that a golf ball cannot weigh more than 1.62 ounces and cannot be smaller than 1.68 inches in diameter. The balls also must pass a test with a golf swing machine: they can't have an initial velocity off the club face of more than 250 feet per second, and can't travel more than 280 yards when hit by the machine.

So, a basketball-sized ball filled with feathers just might qualify.

4. *What about those cute dimples?* First of all, they're not just cute; they are essential to the flight of the ball. The purpose of the dimples is to make the ball aerodynamically appropriate, pulling air over the top and creating pressure underneath, which makes the ball fly somewhat like an airplane wing. The number of dimples has varied from a few hundred to nearly a thousand. The common range for officially accepted balls is from 318 to 552.

5. *What about the compression rating for golf balls?* You think you're under pressure when you step up to the tee? Inside your golf ball, the core is under extreme pressure; typical golf balls are given compression ratings between 80 and 100, with 90 a common choice. There is no proven correlation between compression and the distance or accuracy of a shot, although some golfers claim to be able to feel a difference between high- and low-rated balls.

6. *Which type of ball should I use?* The one you can drive the farthest, approach the green with the most accuracy with, and putt with deadeye aim. Some players can discern no difference between the most expensive balls on the market and the scuffs they find on the driving range; others are more particular about the golf ball they choose than anything else in their lives.

Hitting the Ball with the Club

1. *Why do my drives not fly straight to where I aim them?* If we were able to solve that problem with just a few words here, we could become instant millionaires—so rich we could afford to hire someone else to play golf for us.

Aside from missing the ball—which none of us has ever done, right?—the most common problems are hooks and slices, pushes and pulls, and fades or draws. These are not always problems, though, since a capable golfer can purposely change his or her swing to direct the ball for a tricky shot.

2. *What is a hook and how is it different from a slice?* A slice happens when the ball is given a sidespin that makes it curve in flight from left to right, generally costing you a bit of distance as well as putting you in danger of landing in the rough.

A hook is the opposite of a slice.

A slice happens when the club face strikes the ball open several degrees relative to the club path. A hook is caused by striking the ball with the club face a bit closed on contact.

Other causes of slices are an outside-to-in swing plane, an incomplete hand release, or a collapsed left wrist. You might also slice if you place the ball too far back in your stance.

A hook can come about from an inside-to-out swing plane, an early hand release, or a bowed left wrist. Placing the ball too far forward in your stance also contributes to your chances of shooting a hook.

The best way to fix a hook or a slice is to seek professional help. A competent instructor or pro should be able to diagnose the source of your problem.

Better players can purposely add a slice to bend a drive around a dogleg to the right, or a hook to go the other direction.

3. *What is a push and how is it different from a pull?* A push is a ball that has very little sidespin and a straight flight path but ends up to the right of the target.

A pull is the opposite of a push, with a straight shot ending up to the left of the target.

4. *What is a fade and how is it different from a draw?* A fade is a straight shot with just a bit of sidespin that gives it left-to-right travel at the end of its flight. Because the forward energy of the ball is greater than the slight sidespin, the fade of the ball doesn't take effect until it slows down near the end of its flight. A fade is accomplished by a straight swing aimed at the target with the club face open just a few degrees at impact.

A draw is the opposite of a fade, with a small amount of right-to-left travel at the end of its flight. A draw is accomplished by a straight swing aimed at the target with the club face closed just a few degrees at impact.

Handicap, Course, and Slope Ratings

1. *What is a USGA handicap index?* A handicap is one way to equalize the level of skill among a party of golfers, across a large tournament of contestants, or between you and Greg Norman, Corey Pavin, and whoever is the PGA star of the day.

In formal terms, a handicap is an estimation of a player's expected performance on a standardized course (more about that later). A handicap of 0 means a player can be expected to shoot par on an ordinary course. A handicap of 18 means the player can be expected to average a stroke over par on an ordinary course.

In practical terms, a player subtracts his or her handicap from actual strokes at the end of a round for a net score.

The next step is to find a way to compare performance on one course with another; we'll get to slope and course ratings in a moment.

2. *How do I obtain an official USGA handicap index?* The only way to receive a rating is to be assigned one by a golf club that subscribes to the USGA system. The handicap is based on the average of your 10 best scores among the last 20 rounds you have played.

You don't necessarily have to become a member of an exclusive and expensive golf club for the purpose, though; there are golf clubs at many public courses that charge only modest fees and often afford you special privileges, including reduced greens fees and preferred tee times. Clubs don't even necessarily have to be associated with a golf course, but can run traveling competitions and events at a number of locations.

There is also another way to obtain a close equivalent to a USGA handicap. The quick reference allowance (QRA) can be used by a tournament committee for ranking players. The QRA takes the three best scores made in the last year on a regulation course with a par of 68 or higher. Also included are any scores made in a tournament over the past two years. The QRA is calculated as the second-best score, minus 70 for men or minus 73 for women.

3. *What do the USGA course and slope ratings mean?* The United States Golf Association (USGA) attempts to create a way to compare one golfer with another, and one golf course with another.

Courses are rated based on criteria set up by the USGA; the ratings are supposed to be performed by authorized golf associations rather than the particular club itself.

A yardage rating classifies the difficulty of play based only on yardage; as such it does not take into account obstacles and terrain and other natural and unnatural elements of the design that can make a 4,500-foot killer and a 7,500-foot cream puff. The rating is expressed as the score a scratch player would be expected to make when playing a course of average difficulty.

A scratch player is defined by the USGA as an amateur player who plays to

Sea Trail Golf Links, Sunset Beach, North Carolina
Courtesy of the North Carolina Division of Travel and Tourism.

the standard of the stroke-play qualifiers competing in the U.S. Amateur Championship. A male scratch golfer can hit tee shots an average of 250 yards and can reach a 470-yard hole in two shots. This generally equates to a player with a 0 handicap up to about a 2 handicap. A female scratch golfer is an amateur player who plays to the standard of the match-play qualifiers in the U.S. Women's Amateur Championship and can hit tee shots an average of 210 yards and can reach a 400-yard hole in two shots.

Another important rating, though not often published, is the bogey rating. First of all, a bogey golfer is a player who is about a stroke above par, specifically one who has a USGA handicap index between 17.5 and 22.4 for men and between 21.5 and 26.4 for women; a male bogey golfer can be expected to hit tee shots an average of 200 yards and reach a 370-yard hole in two shots, while a female bogey golfer can hit tee shots of 150 yards and reach a 280-yard hole in two shots.

A bogey rating is an evaluation of the difficulty of a course for a bogey golfer under normal course and weather conditions and includes yardage and obstacles to the extent that they affect scoring. It is calculated as the average of the better half of a bogey golfer's scores under normal playing conditions.

We'll come to the importance of the bogey rating in a moment.

A USGA course rating is a classification of the playing difficulty of a course under normal course and weather conditions, specifically taking into account yardage and other obstacles that affect the scoring ability of a scratch player. The course rating is expressed in strokes.

Note that a yardage rating and USGA course rating are not the same as par, and not directly related to that measure.

The slope rating classifies the relative difficulty of a course for players with handicaps above scratch. The lowest slope rating is 55 and the highest is 155, and the average slope rating for men and women is 113.

In case you were wondering, here's how a slope rating is calculated: the difference between the bogey rating and the course rating is multiplied by 5.381 for men and 4.24 for women.

Courses make available a conversion chart that relates the slope rating to the USGA handicap of individual players. Ratings are also listed for each of the various sets of tees at a course. The golfer checks the chart at the course to see where his or her handicap index falls on the chart; at a difficult course, your handicap will be adjusted upward, and at an easier-than-average course it will be adjusted downward.

The course ratings also take into account play from the back and front tees, again with the aim of equalizing play among golfers of different skill levels.

The Toughest Courses in America

Based on the slope rating, which are the most difficult courses in America? The top end of the rating chart is set at 155, and at least two courses come very close to the ceiling with ratings from championship tees. Page 40 lists the top 40 18-hole courses.

1. **Marriott's Bay Point Resort.** Lagoon Legend Course,
   Panama City Beach, Florida   152
2. **PGA West.** TPC Stadium Course, La Quinta, California   151
3. **Blackwolf Run Golf Club.** River Course, Kohler, Wisconsin   151
4. **Thunder Hill Golf Club.** South Madison, Ohio   151
5. **Industry Hills Sheraton Resort.** Eisenhower Course,
   City of Industry, California   149
6. **Redhawk Golf Club.** Temecula, California   149
7. **Kiawah Island Resort.** Ocean Course, Kiawah Island,
   South Carolina   149
8. **Grand Traverse Resort.** Bear Course, Acme, Michigan   149
9. **Thoroughbred Golf Club.** Rothbury, Michigan   147
10. **Treetops Sylvan Resort.** Jones Masterpiece Course, Gaylord,
    Michigan   146
11. **Breckenridge Golf Club.** Breckenridge, Colorado   146
12. **Troon North Golf Club.** Scottsdale, Arizona   146
13. **Ventana Canyon Golf and Racquet Club.** Mountain Course,
    Tucson, Arizona   146
14. **Desert Falls Country Club.** Palm Desert, California   145
15. **Pinehurst Resort.** No. 7, Pinehurst, North Carolina   145
16. **The Club at Cordillera.** Edwards, Colorado   145
17. **Wilderness Valley Golf Club.** Black Forest Course, Gaylord,
    Michigan   145
18. **Quicksilver Golf Club.** Midway, Pennsylvania   145
19. **North Port National Golf Club.** Lake Ozark, Missouri   145
20. **Shattuck Golf Course.** Jaffrey, New Hampshire   145
21. **Stoney Creek Golf Club.** East Stoney Creek, North Carolina   144
22. **Sentryworld Golf Course.** Stevens Point, Wisconsin   144
23. **Industry Hills Sheraton Resort.** Zaharias Course,
    City of Industry, California   144
24. **Tamarron Resort.** Cliffs Course, Durango, Colorado   144
25. **Carlton Oaks Country Club.** Santee, California   144
26. **The Prince Golf Club.** Princeville, Kauai, Hawaii   144
27. **Elk Ridge Golf Club.** Atlanta, Michigan   144
28. **Tapawingo National Golf Club.** St. Louis, Missouri   144
29. **Hulman Links Golf Course.** Terre Haute, Indiana   144
30. **Fox Creek Golf Club.** Edwardsville, Illinois   144
31. **Blackwolf Run Golf Club.** Meadow Valleys Course, Kohler,
    Wisconsin   143
32. **Marriott's Tan-Tar.** Oaks Course, Osage Beach, Missouri   143
33. **The Golf Courses at Kenton County.** Independence, Kentucky   143
34. **Bald Head Island Club.** Bald Head Island, North Carolina   143
35. **Bluffs on Thompson Creek Golf Club.** St. Francisville, Louisiana   143
36. **Spyglass Hill Golf Course.** Pebble Beach, California   143
37. **Poppy Hills Golf Course.** Pebble Beach, California   143
38. **La Purisma Golf Course.** Lompoc, California   143
39. **Makalei Hawaii Country Club.** Kailua-Kona, Hawaii   143
40. **Talamore Resort.** Southern Pines, North Carolina   142

Chapter 5
Econoguide Golf State-by-State

The East

Connecticut

Delaware

Maine

Maryland

Massachusetts

New Hampshire

New Jersey

New York

Pennsylvania

Rhode Island

Vermont

Virginia

Washington, D.C.

Connecticut

Golf in Connecticut can be very green and very busy in the spring and summer.

The **Richter Park Golf Club** in Danbury, a bit more than an hour from New York City, is a not-so-hidden jewel where it can be quite difficult to obtain a tee time if you are not a local resident; still, it's worth a try.

Sterling Farms Golf Club in Stamford is another surprisingly lush municipal course, again with restrictions on out-of-towners.

Also worth a visit is the **Crestbrook Park Golf Course** in Watertown, just north of Waterbury.

In the Hartford area is the **Tallwood Country Club** in Hebron, a green and watery course.

Some Connecticut courses manage to stay open year-round, with deep discounts in the winter. In the snowbelts of the state, courses may close in the heart of the winter.

Look for highest prices in the heart of the summer, with the best deals in the coolest months.

Econoguide Leader Board: Best Public Course in Connecticut

◎◎◎◎   Richter Park Golf Club

Econoguide Leader Board: Best Deals in Connecticut

$$/☺☺☺	Blackledge Country Club (Anderson, Gilead, Links)
$$/☺☺☺	Cedar Knob Golf Club
$$/☺☺☺	Crestbrook Park Golf Course
$$/☺☺☺	Lyman Orchards Golf Club (Robert Trent Jones Course)
$$/☺☺☺	Pequabuck Golf Club
$$/☺☺☺	Pine Valley Country Club
$$/☺☺☺	Portland Golf Course
$$/☺☺☺	Ridgefield Golf Course
$$/☺☺☺	Rockledge Country Club
$$/☺☺☺	Shennecossett Municipal Golf Course
$$/☺☺☺	Simsbury Farms Golf Club
$$/☺☺☺	H. Smith Richardson Golf Course
$$/☺☺☺	Stanley Golf Club (Blue, Red, White)
$$/☺☺☺	Sterling Farms Golf Club
$$/☺☺☺	Tallwood Country Club
$$/☺☺☺	Timberlin Golf Club
$$/☺☺☺	Tunxis Plantation Country Club (Red, Green)

Key to Symbols

Rating: 1 to 4 Golf Balls

☺	Worth a Visit
☺☺	Above Average
☺☺☺	Exceptional
☺☺☺☺	Very Best

Price Ranges

$	<$20	Bargain
$$	$20–$39	Budget
$$$	$40–$59	Moderate
$$$$	$60–$79	Expensive
$$$$$	$80–$100	Very Expensive
$$$$$$	>$100	Exclusive

Course Type

P	Public
R	Resort
SP	Semiprivate

Discounts

W	=	Weekdays
L	=	Low Season
R	=	Resort Guests
T	=	Twilight
S	=	Seniors
J	=	Juniors

BEST	Econoguide Best American Courses
DEAL	Econoguide Best Golfing Deals
STATE	Econoguide Best in State

Connecticut Golf Guide

Stamford

P	**Sterling Farms Golf Club**	Greens: $–$$	W L T S J
☺☺☺	Newfield Ave., Stamford. (203) 329-7888	Carts: $	
DEAL	18 holes. Par 72/73. Yards: 6,410/5,600	Rating: 71.7/72.6	
	Year-round. High: July–Aug.	Slope: 127/121	

Bridgeport Area

P	**Candlewood Valley Country Club**	Greens: $$	W T S
☺☺	Danbury Rd., New Milford. (203) 354-9359	Carts: $	
	18 holes. Par 72/72. Yards: 6,295/5,403	Rating: 70.3/70.9	
	Mar.–Dec. High: May–Sept.	Slope: 120/126	

P	**H. Smith Richardson Golf Course**	Greens: $$	
☺☺☺	Morehouse Hwy., Fairfield. (203) 255-6094	Carts: $	
DEAL	18 holes. Par 72/72. Yards: 6,676/5,764	Rating: 71.0/72.8	
	Apr.–Feb. High: May–Oct.	Slope: 127/129	

P	**Tashua Knolls Golf Course**	Greens: $$	S J
☺☺	Tashua Knolls Lane, Trumbull. (203) 261-5989	Carts: $$	
	18 holes. Par 72/72. Yards: 6,502/5,454	Rating: 71.5/72.0	
	Mar.–Dec. High: May–Sept.	Slope: 125/118	

P	**Whitney Farms Golf Course**	Greens: $$$	W
☺☺	Shelton Rd., Monroe. (203) 268-0707	Carts: Incl.	
	18 holes. Par 72/73. Yards: 6,628/5,832	Rating: 72.4/72.9	
	Mar.–Dec. High: June–Aug.	Slope: 130/124	

New Haven Area

P	**Grassy Hill Country Club**	Greens: $$	W S
☺☺	Clark Lane, Orange. (203) 795-1422	Carts: $	
	18 holes. Par 70/71. Yards: 6,118/5,209	Rating: 70.5/71.1	
	Apr.–Nov. High: Apr.–Oct.	Slope: 122/118	

P	**Orange Hills Country Club**	Greens: $$	
☺☺	Racebrook Rd., Orange. (203) 795-4161	Carts: $$	
	18 holes. Par 71/74. Yards: 6,389/5,729	Rating: 71.2/71.5	
	Mar.–Nov. High: May–Oct.	Slope: 114/120	

New London/Norwich Area

P	**Elmridge Golf Course**	Greens: $$	L T
	Elmridge Rd., Pawcatuck. (203) 599-2248	Carts: $	
☺☺	*Red/Blue/White*	Rating: 121/NA	
	27 holes. Par 71/72/71. Yards: 6,402/6,639/6,449	Slope: 72.3/NA	
	Mar.–Dec. High: May–Sept.		

P	**Norwich Golf Course**	Greens: $$	
☺☺	New London Turnpike, Norwich. (203) 889-6973	Carts: $	
	18 holes. Par 71/71. Yards: 6,183/5,104	Rating: 69.6/70.2	
	Apr.–Dec. High: May–Aug.	Slope: 123/118	

P	**Shennecossett Municipal Golf Course**	Greens: $$	
☺☺☺	Plant St., Groton. (203) 445-0262	Carts: $	
DEAL	18 holes. Par 72/76. Yards: 6,491/5,796	Rating: 71.1/73.2	
	Year-round. High: July–Aug.	Slope: 122/121	

Waterbury/Watertown/Bristol Area

P	**Crestbrook Park Golf Course**	Greens: $–$$	W S J
☺☺☺	Northfield Rd., Watertown. (203) 945-5249	Carts: $$	
DEAL	18 holes. Par 71/75. Yards: 6,376/5,718	Rating: 73.2/73.8	
	Apr.–Dec. High: June–Aug.	Slope: 132/128	

SP	**Pequabuck Golf Club**	Greens: $$	
☺☺☺	School St., Pequabuck. (203) 583-7307	Carts: $	
DEAL	18 holes. Par 69/72. Yards: 6,015/5,388	Rating: 69.1/71.0	
	Apr.–Dec. High: May–Sept.	Slope: 122/117	

Connecticut Golf Guide

Danbury Area

P	**Richter Park Golf Club**	Greens:	$$–$$$ T S J
☺☺☺☺	Aunt Hack Rd., Danbury. (203) 792-2552	Carts:	$
BEST	18 holes. Par 72/72. Yards: 6,740/5,627	Rating:	73.0/72.8
	Apr.–Nov. High: June–Aug.	Slope:	130/122

P	**Ridgefield Golf Course**	Greens:	$–$$ T S J
☺☺☺	Ridgebury Rd., Ridgefield. (203) 748-7008	Carts:	$$
DEAL	18 holes. Par 70/71. Yards: 6,380/5,295	Rating:	70.0/70.7
	Apr.–Dec. High: June–Aug.	Slope:	122/120

Hartford Area

P	**Bel Compo Golf Club**	Greens:	$$
☺☺	Nod Rd., Avon. (203) 678-1679	Carts:	$$
	18 holes. Par 72/72. Yards: 7,028/5,452	Rating:	73.4/71.6
	Apr.–Nov. High: May–Sept.	Slope:	131/112

P	**Blackledge Country Club**	Greens:	$$ W L T S J
	West St., Hebron. (203) 228-0250	Carts:	$
☺☺☺	*Anderson/Gilead/Links*	Rating:	72.3/NA/NA
DEAL	27 holes. Par 72/72/72. Yards: 6,853/6,823/6,880	Slope:	123/NA/NA
	Mar.–Dec. High: June–Aug.		

P	**Cedar Knob Golf Club**	Greens:	$ W L S J
☺☺☺	Billings Rd., Somers. (203) 749-3550	Carts:	$
DEAL	18 holes. Par 72/74. Yards: 6,734/5,784	Rating:	72.3/73.8
	Year-round. High: Apr.–Sept.	Slope:	119/126

P	**Hunter Golf Club**	Greens:	$–$$ W S J
☺☺	Westfield Rd., Meriden. (203) 634-3366	Carts:	$$
	18 holes. Par 71/72. Yards: 6,700/5,764	Rating:	71.9/72.7
	Mar.–Dec. High: June–Aug.	Slope:	124/131

SP	**Lyman Orchards Golf Club**	Greens:	$$ W T S J
	Rt. 157, Middlefield. (203) 349-8055	Carts:	Incl.
☺☺	*Gary Player Course*	Rating:	73.0/67.8
	18 holes. Par 71/71. Yards: 6,660/4,667	Slope:	135/116
	Mar.–Nov. High: May–Oct.		

☺☺☺	*Robert Trent Jones Course*	Greens:	$$
DEAL	18 holes. Par 72/72. Yards: 7,011/5,812	Carts:	$
		Rating:	73.5/73.5
		Slope:	129/122

P	**Millbrook Golf Course**	Greens:	$$
☺☺	Pigeon Hill Rd., Windsor. (203) 688-2575	Carts:	$
	18 holes. Par 71/73. Yards: 6,258/5,715	Rating:	71.0/71.0
	Apr.–Nov. High: May–Oct.	Slope:	125/124

P	**Pine Valley Country Club**	Greens:	$$
☺☺☺	Welch Rd., Southington. (203) 628-0879	Carts:	$
DEAL	18 holes. Par 71/73. Yards: 6,325/5,443	Rating:	70.6/72.0
	Mar.–Dec. High: June–Aug.	Slope:	122/122

SP	**Portland Golf Course**	Greens:	$$ W S J
☺☺☺	Bartlett St., Portland. (203) 342-6107	Carts:	$
DEAL	18 holes. Par 71/71. Yards: 6,213/5,039	Rating:	70.8/68.6
	Mar.–Dec. High: May–Oct.	Slope:	124/118

P	**Rockledge Country Club**	Greens:	$–$$ S
☺☺☺	S. Main St., W. Hartford. (203) 521-3156	Carts:	$
DEAL	18 holes. Par 72/74. Yards: 6,307/5,608	Rating:	71.3/71.5
	Apr.–Dec. High: June–July	Slope:	121/118

P	**Simsbury Farms Golf Club**	Greens:	$$
☺☺☺	Old Farms Rd., West Simsbury. (203) 658-6246	Carts:	$$

Connecticut Golf Guide

Hartford Area

DEAL	18 holes. Par 72/72. Yards: 6,421/5,439	Rating:	71.1/70.1	
	Apr.–Nov. High: May–Sept.	Slope:	124/117	
P	**Stanley Golf Club**	Greens:	$$	W
	Hartford Rd., New Britain. (203) 827-8144	Carts:	$$	
☺☺☺	*Blue/Red/White*	Rating:	70.5/72.0	
DEAL	27 holes. Par 72/71. Yards: 6,453/6,311/6,138	Slope:	120/122	
	Apr.–Dec. High: June–Sept.			
P	**Tallwood Country Club**	Greens:	$–$$	L T S J
☺☺☺	North St., Rte. 85. Hebron. (203) 646-3437	Carts:	$	
DEAL	18 holes. Par 72/72. Yards: 6,366/5,430	Rating:	70.2/70.8	
	Mar.–Dec. High: May–Sept.	Slope:	119/114	
P	**Timberlin Golf Club**	Greens:	$–$$	S J
☺☺☺	Ken Bates Dr., Kensington. (203) 828-3228	Carts:	$	
DEAL	18 holes. Par 72/72. Yards: 6,733/5,477	Rating:	71.9/70.5	
	Apr.–Nov. High: June–Sept.	Slope:	127/109	
P	**Tunxis Plantation Country Club**	Greens:	$$	S J
	Town Farm Rd., Farmington. (203) 677-1367	Carts:	$$	
☺☺☺	*Red/Green Course*	Rating:	71.5/71.5	
DEAL	18 holes. Par 72/72. Yards: 6,647/5,378	Slope:	125/116	
	Apr.–Nov. High: May–Aug.			
☺☺	*White Course*	Rating:	72.2/71.5	
	18 holes. Par 72/72. Yards: 6,638/5,744	Slope:	129/125	

Delaware

The brief list of courses in this small state is led by the **Three Little Bakers Country Club** in Wilmington, formerly a private course in the hills with some very difficult challenges, especially on the back nine. Even with a monopoly at the high end of the market in the state, it is offered at bargain rates.

Delaware's generally moderate climate allows most courses to remain open year-round. Look for deepest discounts in fall through winter, with peak rates in effect from about May to September.

Econoguide Leader Board: Best Public Course in Delaware

☺☺☺   Three Little Bakers Country Club

Econoguide Leader Board: Best Deal in Delaware

$$/☺☺☺   Three Little Bakers Country Club

Delaware Golf Guide

P	**Del Castle Golf Course**	Greens:	$	W L T S J
☺	McKennans Church Rd., Wilmington. (302) 995-1990	Carts:	$	
	18 holes. Par 72/72. Yards: 6,628/5,396	Rating:	70.4/70.9	
	Year-round. High: Apr.–Nov.	Slope:	116/116	
P	**Ed "Porky" Oliver Golf Course**	Greens:	$–$$	W L T S J
☺	N. DuPont Rd., Wilmington. (302) 571-9041	Carts:	Inquire	
	18 holes. Par 69/71. Yards: 6,115/5,692	Rating:	69.8/71.8	
	Year-round. High: May–Sept.	Slope:	118/121	
P	**Ron Jaworski's Garrisons Lake Golf Club**	Greens:	$–$$	L T S
☺☺	Smyrna. (302) 653-6349	Carts:	$	

	18 holes. Par 72/72. Yards: 7,028/5,460	Rating:	73.1/71.6	
	Year-round. High: June–Aug.	Slope:	127/126	
SP	**Three Little Bakers Country Club**	Greens:	$$	W L T S J
⊙⊙⊙	Foxcroft Dr., Wilmington. (302) 737-1877	Carts:	$	
DEAL	18 holes. Par 71/72. Yards: 6,609/5,209	Rating:	71.8/70.3	
STATE	Year-round. High: Apr.–Oct.	Slope:	129/117	

Maine

The king of the hill among public and resort courses in Maine is **Sugarloaf**, near the ski area of the same name in Carrabassett Valley. It's a spectacular and challenging mountain course carved out of the woods; each hole is isolated as a form of golfer's green tunnel vision, limiting your attention to one hole at a time.

In Rockport you'll find the **Samoset Resort**, a gorgeous ocean course along the rocky coast of Penobscot Bay. The course has its very own lighthouse and Atlantic views from 13 holes.

Near the middle of the state is **Waterville**, a superb semiprivate challenge that also captures a spot on the Econoguide Deals list.

The snow can pile up pretty high in the Maine winter, and it's followed by the spring mud season. Most courses in Maine are open from about April through November, with peak rates and best conditions available in the short but sweet summer months of June through early September.

Econoguide Leader Board: Best Public Courses in Maine

⊙⊙⊙   Samoset Resort Golf Club
⊙⊙⊙⊙   Sugarloaf Golf Club
⊙⊙⊙⊙   Waterville Country Club

Econoguide Leader Board: Best Deals in Maine

$$/⊙⊙⊙   Aroostock Valley Country Club
$$/⊙⊙⊙   Biddleford Saco Golf Club
$$/⊙⊙⊙   Kebo Valley Golf Course
$$/⊙⊙⊙   Sable Oaks Golf Club
$$/⊙⊙⊙   Val Halla Golf Course
$$/⊙⊙⊙⊙   Waterville Country Club

Northern Maine

SP	**Aroostock Valley Country Club**	Greens:	$$	L
⊙⊙⊙	Russell Rd., Fort Fairfield. (207) 476-8083	Carts:	$	
DEAL	18 holes. Par 72/72. Yards: 6,304/5,393	Rating:	71.5/71.5	
	May–Oct. High: July–Aug.	Slope:	117/108	
SP	**Mingo Springs Golf Course**	Greens:	$$	
⊙	Proctor Rd. and Rte. 4, Rangeley. (207) 864-5021	Carts:	Inquire	
	18 holes. Par 70/70. Yards: 5,923/5,334	Rating:	66.3/67.4	
	May–Oct. High: July–Sept.	Slope:	109/110	
R	**Sugarloaf Golf Club**	Greens:	$$$	L R T J
⊙⊙⊙⊙	RR 1, Carrabassett Valley. (207) 237-2000	Carts:	$	
BEST	18 holes. Par 72/72. Yards: 6,451/5,376	Rating:	70.8/73.7	
	May–Oct. High: Aug.–Sept.	Slope:	137/136	

Maine Golf Guide

Northern Maine

R	**Va Jo Wa Golf Course**	Greens:	$$	R T
☺☺	Walker Rd., Island Falls. (207) 463-2128	Carts:	Inquire	
	18 holes. Par 72/72. Yards: 6,223/5,065	Rating:	70.4/69.6	
	May–Oct. High: July–Sept.	Slope:	121/115	

Bangor Area

P	**Bangor Municipal Golf Course**	Greens:	$	W T
☺☺	Webster Ave., Bangor. (207) 941-0232	Carts:	Inquire	
	18 holes. Par 71/71. Yards: 6,345/5,173	Rating:	67.9/69.1	
	Apr.–Nov. High: June–Aug.	Slope:	112/111	

P	**Kebo Valley Golf Course**	Greens:	$$	L
☺☺☺	Eagle Lake Rd., Bar Harbor. (207) 288-3000	Carts:	$	
DEAL	18 holes. Par 70/72. Yards: 6,112/5,440	Rating:	69.0/68.0	
	Apr.–Nov. High: July–Aug.	Slope:	129/125	

SP	**Penobscot Valley Country Club**	Greens:	$$$	
☺☺☺	Main St., Orono. (207) 866-2423	Carts:	$$	
	18 holes. Par 72/74. Yards: 6,450/5,856	Rating:	70.3/73.2	
	Apr.–Oct. High: June–Aug.	Slope:	123/126	

Augusta Area

SP	**Rockland Golf Club**	Greens:	$$	T
☺☺	Old County Rd., Rockland. (207) 594-9322	Carts:	$	
	18 holes. Par 70/73. Yards: 6,121/5,583	Rating:	68.6/71.8	
	Apr.–Oct. High: June–Sept.	Slope:	114/119	

SP	**Waterville Country Club**	Greens:	$$	
☺☺☺☺	Oakland. (207) 465-9861	Carts:	$$	
DEAL	18 holes. Par 70/73. Yards: 6,412/5,466	Rating:	69.6/71.4	
STATE	Apr.–Nov. High: May–Sept.	Slope:	124/121	

Portland Area

R	**Bethel Inn and Country Club**	Greens:	$$	W L R T
☺☺	Broad St., Bethel. (207) 824-6276, (800) 564-0125	Carts:	$$	
	18 holes. Par 72/72. Yards: 6,663/5,280	Rating:	72.3/71.4	
	May–Oct. High: July–Aug.	Slope:	133/129	

SP	**Biddleford Saco Golf Club**	Greens:	$$	T
☺☺☺	Old Orchard Rd., Saco. (207) 282-5883	Carts:	$$	
DEAL	18 holes. Par 71/72. Yards: 6,192/5,053	Rating:	69.6/69.2	
	Apr.–Nov. High: June–Aug.	Slope:	123/110	

SP	**Cape Arundel Golf Club**	Greens:	$$	
☺☺	Old River Rd., Kennebunkport. (207) 967-3494	Carts:	$$	
	18 holes. Par 69/70. Yards: 5,869/5,134	Rating:	67.0/68.6	
	Apr.–Oct. High: July–Sept.	Slope:	117/106	

P	**Dutch Elm Golf Club**	Greens:	$$	W L R T S
☺☺	Brimstone Rd., Arundel. (207) 282-9850	Carts:	Inquire	
	18 holes. Par 72/73. Yards: 6,230/5,384	Rating:	68.8/70.1	
	Apr.–Nov. High: July–Aug.	Slope:	119/115	

R	**Poland Spring Country Club**	Greens:	$	R
☺☺	Rte. 26, Poland Spring. (207) 998-6002	Carts:	$	
	18 holes. Par 71/74. Yards: 6,450/5,856	Rating:	68.2/71.6	
	Apr.–Oct. High: June–Aug.	Slope:	119/117	

P	**Riverside Municipal Golf Course**	Greens:	$	S J
☺☺	Riverside St., Portland. (207) 797-3524	Carts:	$	
	18 holes. Par 72/72. Yards: 6,450/5,640	Rating:	69.5/70.7	
	Apr.–Nov. High: July–Aug.	Slope:	115/112	

P	**Sable Oaks Golf Club**	Greens:	$$	T
☺☺☺	S. Portland. (207) 775-6257	Carts:	$$	
DEAL	18 holes. Par 70/72. Yards: 6,359/4,786	Rating:	71.8/NA	
	Apr.–Dec. High: Apr.–Sept.	Slope:	138/121	

Portland Area

P	**Val Halla Golf Course**	Greens:	$–$$	W S J
☺☺☺	Val Halla Rd., Cumberland. (207) 829-2225	Carts:	Inquire	
DEAL	18 holes. Par 72/72. Yards: 6,574/5,437	Rating:	71.0/70.4	
	Apr.–Oct. High: June–Sept.	Slope:	126/116	

P	**Willowdale Golf Club**	Greens:	$	T
☺☺	Willowdale Rd., Scarborough. (207) 883-9351	Carts:	$	
	18 holes. Par 70/70. Yards: 5,980/5,344	Rating:	68.7/73.7	
	Apr.–Oct. High: July–Aug.	Slope:	110/112	

Central Coast

R	**Samoset Resort Golf Club**	Greens:	$$–$$$$	L R
☺☺☺	Warrenton St., Rockport. (207) 594-1431	Carts:	$	
BEST	18 holes. Par 70/71. Yards: 6,417/5,360	Rating:	69.3/69.1	
	Apr.–Nov. High: June–Sept.	Slope:	125/117	

Maryland

Hog Neck on the DelMarVa Peninsula is a spectacular, demanding challenge with sand and water on the front nine, and long, narrow fairways on the way home. And you'll save a bit of green, since it is listed on the Econoguide Deals list.

Queenstown Harbor, southeast of Baltimore, offers beautiful river settings.

Most courses in Maryland manage to stay open year-round. Expect the best conditions and peak prices from about April through October.

Econoguide Leader Board: Best Public Courses in Maryland

☺☺☺☺ Hog Neck Golf Course
☺☺☺☺ Queenstown Harbor Golf Links (River)

Econoguide Leader Board: Best Deals in Maryland

$$/☺☺☺	Black Rock Golf Course
$/☺☺☺	Breton Bay Golf and Country Club
$$/☺☺☺	Eagle's Landing Golf Club
$$/☺☺☺	Enterprise Golf Course
$$/☺☺☺	Harbourtowne Golf Resort & Country Club
$$/☺☺☺☺	Hog Neck Golf Course
$/☺☺☺	Mount Pleasant Golf Club
$/☺☺☺	Pine Ridge Golf Course
$$/☺☺☺	Redgate Municipal Golf Course
$$/☺☺☺	River Run Golf Club
$$/☺☺☺	Wakefield Valley Golf & Conference Center

Western Maryland

R	**The Golf Club at Wisp**	Greens:	$$$	T S J
☺☺☺	Marsh Hill Rd., McHenry. (301) 387-4911	Carts:	Incl.	
	18 holes. Par 72/72. Yards: 7,122/5,542	Rating:	73.0/72.0	
	Apr.–Oct. High: July–Sept.	Slope:	137/128	

Hagerstown Area

P	**Black Rock Golf Course**	Greens:	$–$$	T S J
☺☺☺	Mt. Aetna Rd., Hagerstown. (301) 791-3040	Carts:	$	

Maryland Golf Guide

Hagerstown Area

DEAL	18 holes. Par 72/74. Yards: 6,646/5,179	Rating:	70.7/64.7
	Year-round. High: May–Sept.	Slope:	124/112

Baltimore Area

SP ☺☺	**Bay Hills Golf Club**	Greens:	$$	T
	Bay Hills Dr., Arnold. (410) 974-0669	Carts:	Incl.	
	18 holes. Par 70/70. Yards: 6,423/5,029	Rating:	70.8/69.2	
	Year-round. High: Apr.–Oct.	Slope:	118/121	

SP ☺☺	**Beaver Creek Country Club**	Greens:	$–$$	W L R T
	Mapleville Rd., Hagerstown. (301) 733-5152	Carts:	$	
	18 holes. Par 72/73. Yards: 6,878/5,636	Rating:	71.6/71.4	
	Year-round. High: May–Oct.	Slope:	120/124	

P ☺☺	**Clustered Spires Golf Course**	Greens:	$–$$	W T S J
	Gas House Pike, Frederick. (301) 694-6249	Carts:	$	
	18 holes. Par 72/72. Yards: 6,769/5,230	Rating:	70.5/70.0	
	Year-round. High: Apr.–Oct.	Slope:	115/124	

P ☺☺	**Diamond Ridge Golf Course**	Greens:	$	T S J
	Ridge Rd., Woodlawn. (410) 944-6607	Carts:	$	
	18 holes. Par 70/72. Yards: 6,550/5,833	Rating:	71.0/73.2	
	Year-round. High: Apr.–Oct.	Slope:	120/123	

P ☺☺☺☺ BEST DEAL	**Hog Neck Golf Course**	Greens:	$$	T J
	Old Cordova Rd., Easton. (410) 822-6079	Carts:	$	
	18 holes. Par 72/72. Yards: 7,000/5,500	Rating:	73.8/71.1	
	Feb.–Dec. High: Apr.–Oct.	Slope:	125/118	

P ☺☺☺ DEAL	**Mount Pleasant Golf Club**	Greens:	$	W T S J
	Hillen Rd., Baltimore. (410) 254-5100	Carts:	$	
	18 holes. Par 71/73. Yards: 6,7575/5,489	Rating:	72.0/71.0	
	Year-round. High: June–Aug.	Slope:	121/120	

P ☺☺☺ DEAL	**Pine Ridge Golf Course**	Greens:	$	W T S J
	Dulaney Valley Rd., Lutherville. (410) 252-1408	Carts:	Inquire	
	18 holes. Par 72/72. Yards: 6,820/5,732	Rating:	72.0/72.0	
	Year-round. High: Mar.–Oct.	Slope:	122/120	

P	**Queenstown Harbor Golf Links**	Greens:	$$$	W T
	Queenstown. (410) 827-6611	Carts:	Incl.	
☺☺☺	*Lakes Course*	Rating:	71.0/66.6	
	18 holes. Par 71/71. Yards: 6,537/4,576	Slope:	124/111	
	Year-round. High: Apr.–Oct.			

☺☺☺☺ STATE	*River Course*	Rating:	74.2/69.0
	18 holes. Par 72/72. Yards: 7,110/5,026	Slope:	138/123

P ☺☺	**Rocky Point Golf Club**	Greens:	$	W T S J
	Back River Neck Rd., Essex. (410) 391-2906	Carts:	$	
	18 holes. Par 72/74. Yards: 6,785/5,510	Rating:	72.3/73.1	
	Year-round. High: Apr.–Sept.	Slope:	122/121	

R	**Turf Valley Hotel and Country Club**	Greens:	$$–$$$	W L R T
	Turf Valley Rd., Ellicott City. (410) 465-1504	Carts:	Incl.	
☺☺	*North Course*	Rating:	69.5/71.8	
	18 holes. Par 71/71. Yards: 6,633/5,600	Slope:	117/124	
	Year-round. High: Apr.–Oct.			

☺☺	*East Course*	Rating:	72.0/71.6
	18 holes. Par 71/71. Yards: 6,592/5,564	Slope:	128/131

☺☺	*South Course*	Rating:	69.2/72.8
	18 holes. Par 70/72. Yards: 6,323/5,572	Slope:	113/126

Maryland Golf Guide

Baltimore Area

SP	**Wakefield Valley Golf & Conference Center**	Greens:	$$	L T S J
☺☺☺	Fenby Farm Rd., Westminster. (410) 876-6662	Carts:	Incl.
DEAL	27 holes. Par 72/72/72. Yards: 6,933/7,038/6,823	Rating:	74.4/74.1/73.6
	Mar.–Dec. High: June–Sept.	Slope:	139/138/139

Washington, D.C., Area

SP	**Breton Bay Golf and Country Club**	Greens:	$	J
☺☺☺	Rte. 3, Leonardtown. (301) 475-2300	Carts:	$$
DEAL	18 holes. Par 72/73. Yards: 6,933/5,457	Rating:	73.0/70.0
	Mar.–Dec. High: May–Aug.	Slope:	126/117

P	**Enterprise Golf Course**	Greens:	$–$$	W L T S J
☺☺☺	Enterprise Rd., Mitchellville. (301) 249-2040	Carts:	$$
DEAL	18 holes. Par 72/72. Yards: 6,586/5,157	Rating:	71.7/69.6
	Year-round. High: Mar.–Oct.	Slope:	128/114

P	**Glenn Dale Country Club**	Greens:	$$	L T S J
☺☺	Old Prospect Hill Rd., Glenn Dale. (301) 464-0904	Carts:	$$
	18 holes. Par 70/70. Yards: 6,282/4,809	Rating:	70.0/67.2
	Year-round. High: Apr.–Oct.	Slope:	115/107

R	**Harbourtowne Golf Resort & Country Club**	Greens:	$$	L R
☺☺☺	Rte. 33, St. Michaels. (410) 745-5183, (800) 446-9066	Carts:	$
DEAL	18 holes. Par 70/71. Yards: 6,320/5,036	Rating:	69.5/68.5
	Year-round. High: Apr.–Oct.	Slope:	120/113

P	**Needwood Golf Course**	Greens:	$–$$	S J
☺☺	Needwood Rd., Derwood. (301) 948-1075	Carts:	$$
	18 holes. Par 70/72. Yards: 6,254/5,112	Rating:	69.1/69.2
	Year-round. High: May–Sept.	Slope:	113/105

P	**Northwest Park Golf Course**	Greens:	$	T S J
☺☺	Layhill Rd., Wheaton. (301) 598-6100	Carts:	$
	18 holes. Par 72/74. Yards: 7,185/6,325	Rating:	74.0/74.5
	Year-round. High: June–Aug.	Slope:	122/126

P	**Poolesville Golf Course**	Greens:	$–$$	S J
☺☺	W. Willard Rd., Poolesville. (301) 428-8143	Carts:	Inquire
	18 holes. Par 71/73. Yards: 6,757/5,599	Rating:	72.3/71.4
	Year-round. High: June	Slope:	123/118

P	**Redgate Municipal Golf Course**	Greens:	$–$$	S J
☺☺☺	Avery Rd., Rockville. (301) 309-3055	Carts:	$
DEAL	18 holes. Par 71/71. Yards: 6,432/5,271	Rating:	71.7/70.2
	Year-round. High: Apr.–Nov.	Slope:	131/121

P	**River Run Golf Club**	Greens:	$–$$	W L R T
☺☺☺	Beauchamp Rd., Berlin. (410) 641-7200	Carts:	$
DEAL	18 holes. Par 71/71. Yards: 6,705/5,002	Rating:	70.4/73.1
	Year-round. High: Apr.–Oct.	Slope:	128/117

SP	**Swan Point Golf Club**	Greens:	$$–$$$$	W L T S J
☺☺☺☺	Swan Point Blvd., Issue. (301) 259-0047	Carts:	Incl.
	18 holes. Par 72/72. Yards: 6,761/5,009	Rating:	72.5/69.3
	Mar.–Dec. High: June–Sept.	Slope:	126/116

P	**Trotters Glen Golf Course**	Greens:	$–$$	W L
☺☺	Batchellors Forest Rd., Olney. (301) 570-4951	Carts:	$$
	18 holes. Par 72/72. Yards: 6,220/4,983	Rating:	69.3/68.2
	Year-round. High: June–Aug.	Slope:	113/111

P	**Twin Shields Golf Club**	Greens:	$$	W L
☺☺	Roarty Rd., Dunkirk. (410) 257-7800	Carts:	$$
	18 holes. Par 70/70. Yards: 6,321/5,305	Rating:	68.2/67.0
	Year-round. High: Apr.–Oct.	Slope:	118/113

Maryland Golf Guide

Washington, D.C., Area

SP ◐◐	**University of Maryland Golf Course** University Blvd., College Park. (301) 403-4299 18 holes. Par 71/72. Yards: 6,654/5,563 Year-round. High: Apr.–Oct.	Greens: Carts: Rating: Slope:	$$ $ 71.7/71.1 120/117	W L T S J
P ◐◐	**Wicomico Shores Municipal Golf Course** Rte. 234, Chaptico. (301) 934-8191 18 holes. Par 72/72. Yards: 6,482/5,460 Year-round. High: May–Sept.	Greens: Carts: Rating: Slope:	$ $ 70.7/68.3 120/120	W T S J

DelMarVa Peninsula

R ◐◐	**The Bay Club** Libertytown Rd., Berlin. (800) 229-2582 18 holes. Par 72/72. Yards: 6,958/5,609 Year-round. High: Apr.–Oct.	Greens: Carts: Rating: Slope:	$$–$$$ Incl. 73.1/71.3 126/118	W L R T
SP ◐◐◐	**The Beach Club Golf Links** Deer Park Rd., Berlin. (410) 641-4653 18 holes. Par 72/72. Yards: 7,020/5,167 Year-round. High: Apr.–Oct.	Greens: Carts: Rating: Slope:	$$–$$$ Incl. 73.0/69.0 128/117	L T
SP ◐◐	**Cambridge Country Club** Horns Point Rd., Cambridge. (410) 228-4808 18 holes. Par 72/73. Yards: 6,387/5,416 Year-round. High: May–Oct.	Greens: Carts: Rating: Slope:	$$ Inquire 69.3/71.0 113/118	R
P ◐◐◐ DEAL	**Eagle's Landing Golf Club** Eagle's Nest Rd., Berlin. (410) 213-7277 18 holes. Par 72/72. Yards: 7,003/4,896 Year-round. High: Apr.–Oct.	Greens: Carts: Rating: Slope:	$–$$ $ 74.3/69.3 126/115	W L T
SP ◐◐	**Nassawango Country Club** Nassawango Rd., Snow Hill. (410) 632-3144 18 holes. Par 72/73. Yards: 6,644/5,760 Year-round. High: May–Oct.	Greens: Carts: Rating: Slope:	$$ $ 70.2/72.1 125/125	L
SP ◐◐	**Nutters Crossing Golf Club** S. Hampton Bridge Rd., Salisbury. (410) 860-4653 18 holes. Par 70/70. Yards: 6,033/4,800 Year-round. High: Apr.–Oct.	Greens: Carts: Rating: Slope:	$$ Incl. 67.1/66.5 115/110	T
R ◐◐	**Ocean City Golf and Yacht Club** Berlin. (410) 641-1779 *Bayside Course* 18 holes. Par 72/72. Yards: 6,526/5,396 Year-round. High: Apr.–Oct.	Greens: Carts: Rating: Slope:	$–$$ $ 71.7/71.3 121/119	W L
◐◐	*Seaside Course* 18 holes. Par 73/75. Yards: 6,520/5,456	Rating: Slope:	70.9/73.1 115/119	

Massachusetts

The Bay State's golfing shrine is located among the shrub pines, sand dunes, fog, and wind of Cape Cod; three of the state's best public and resort courses are located there. The championship Blue Course along the ocean at **New Seabury** includes No. 3, which is surrounded by water on three sides. The **Captains**, in Brewster, winds its way through a thick scrub pine forest. It's also on our Econoguide Deals list. The gorgeous **Farm Neck** hugs the shore of Martha's Vineyard.

In the hills around the Connecticut River above Springfield is the well-regarded **Crumpin-Fox Club**, named after a long-defunct soda company that occupied the site. It offers breathtaking views from some of its elevated tees. And all the way west in the Green Mountains along the New York border is the **Taconic Golf Club**.

Some golf courses in Massachusetts, including many on Cape Cod and along the southern coast, endeavor to stay open year-round, although snow closures do occur. Massachusetts's snowbelt includes Worcester and the Berkshire Mountains in the western portion of the state. For the rest of the state, a realistic season is from April through early December. The high season at most courses runs from about May through September.

Econoguide Leader Board: Best Public Courses in Massachusetts

☉☉☉	Captains Golf Course
☉☉☉☉	Crumpin-Fox Club
☉☉☉☉	Farm Neck Golf Club
☉☉☉☉	New Seabury Country Club (Blue)
☉☉☉☉	Taconic Golf Club

Econoguide Leader Board: Best Deals in Massachusetts

$$/☉☉☉	Atlantic Country Club
$$/☉☉☉	Bayberry Hills Golf Course
$$/☉☉☉	Cape Cod Country Club
$$/☉☉☉	Captains Golf Course
$$/☉☉☉	Cranberry Valley Golf Course
$$/☉☉☉	Dennis Highlands Golf Course
$$/☉☉☉	Dennis Pines Golf Course
$$/☉☉☉	Gardner Municipal Golf Course
$$/☉☉☉	George Wright Golf Course
$$/☉☉☉	Maplegate Country Club
$$/☉☉☉	Oak Ridge Golf Club
$$/☉☉☉	Olde Barnstable Fairgrounds Golf Course
$$/☉☉☉	Stow Acres Country Club (North, South)
$$/☉☉☉	Trull Brook Golf Course
$$/☉☉☉	Wachusett Country Club
$$/☉☉☉	Waubeeka Golf Links

Massachusetts Golf Guide

Western Massachusetts

SP ☉☉☉☉ STATE	**Taconic Golf Club** Meacham St., Williamstown. (413) 458-3997 18 holes. Par 71/NA. Yards: 6,614/NA Apr.–Nov.	Greens: $$$$$ Carts: Incl. Rating: 70.5/NA Slope: 127/111
SP ☉☉☉	**Wahconah Country Club** Orchard Rd., Dalton. (413) 684-1333 18 holes. Par 71/73. Yards: 6,541/5,597 Apr.–Nov.	Greens: $$$ Carts: $$ Rating: 71.4/71.2 Slope: 122/113
P ☉☉☉ DEAL	**Waubeeka Golf Links** New Ashford Rd., S. Williamstown. (413) 458-8355 18 holes. Par 72/72. Yards: 6,296/5,086 Apr.–Nov. High: July–Aug.	Greens: $–$$ L J Carts: Inquire Rating: 70.9/71.2 Slope: 127/111

Massachusetts Golf Guide

Springfield Area

P	**Crumpin-Fox Club**	Greens:	$$$	R J
○○○○	Parmenter Rd., Bernardston. (413) 648-9101	Carts:	$	
STATE	18 holes. Par 72/72. Yards: 7,007/5,432	Rating:	73.8/71.5	
	Apr.–Nov. High: June–Oct.	Slope:	141/131	

SP	**Hickory Ridge Country Club**	Greens:	$$–$$$	W J
○○○	W. Pomeroy Lane, Amherst. (413) 253-9320	Carts:	$$	
	18 holes. Par 72/72. Yards: 6,794/5,340	Rating:	72.5/70.3	
	Apr.–Nov. High: May–Sept.	Slope:	129/114	

P	**Oak Ridge Golf Club**	Greens:	$–$$	W L T J
○○○	S. Westfield St., Feeding Hills. (413) 789-7307	Carts:	$	
DEAL	18 holes. Par 70/70. Yards: 6,819/5,307	Rating:	71.2/70.0	
	Mar.–Dec. High: June–Sept.	Slope:	124/NA	

P	**Westover Golf Course**	Greens:	$	L J
○○	South St., Granby. (413) 547-8610	Carts:	$	
	18 holes. Par 72/72. Yards: 7,025/5,980	Rating:	73.9/72.0	
	Apr.–Dec. High: June–Sept.	Slope:	131/118	

Worcester Area

SP	**Blissful Meadows Golf Club**	Greens:	$–$$	L T S
○○	Chockalog Rd., Uxbridge. (508) 278-6133	Carts:	$	
	18 holes. Par 72/72. Yards: 6,656/5,072	Rating:	NA	
	Apr.–Nov. High: May–Oct.	Slope:	120	

P	**Gardner Municipal Golf Course**	Greens:	$–$$	W T
○○○	Eaton Dr., Gardner. (508) 632-9703	Carts:	$	
DEAL	18 holes. Par 71/75. Yards: 6,106/5,653	Rating:	68.9/72.2	
	Apr.–first snow. High: June–Sept.	Slope:	124/123	

SP	**Wachusett Country Club**	Greens:	$$	W L T
○○○	Prospect St., West Boylston. (508) 835-4453	Carts:	$	
DEAL	18 holes. Par 72/NA. Yards: 6,608/6,216	Rating:	71.7/NA	
	Apr.–Nov. High: May–Oct.	Slope:	124/NA	

SP	**Westminster Country Club**	Greens:	$$	T
○○	Ellis Rd., Westminster. (508) 874-5938	Carts:	$$	
	18 holes. Par 71/71. Yards: 6,491/5,453	Rating:	70.9/70.0	
	Apr.–Nov. High: May–Sept.	Slope:	133/115	

Boston Area

P	**Atlantic Country Club**	Greens:	$$	W T
○○○	Little Sandy Pond Rd., Plymouth. (508) 888-6644	Carts:	$	
DEAL	18 holes. Par 72/72. Yards: 6,728/4,918	Rating:	71.5/67.4	
	Mar.–Dec. High: June–Aug.	Slope:	130/113	

P	**Bradford Country Club**	Greens:	$–$$	L
○○	Chadwick Rd., Bradford. (508) 372-8587	Carts:	$	
	18 holes. Par 70/70. Yards: 6,511/4,939	Rating:	72.8/67.8	
	Apr.–Dec. High: May–Sept.	Slope:	141/129	

P	**Colonial Country Club**	Greens:	$$$$	L T S J
○○	Audobon Rd., Wakefield. (617) 245-9300	Carts:	Incl.	
	18 holes. Par 70/72. Yards: 6,565/5280	Rating:	72.8/69.5	
	Apr.–Dec. High: May–Sept.	Slope:	130/109	

P	**George Wright Golf Course**	Greens:	$–$$	S J
○○○	West St., Hyde Park. (617) 364-8997	Carts:	$$	
DEAL	18 holes. Par 70/70. Yards: 6,400/5,500	Rating:	69.5/70.3	
	Year-round. High: June–Aug.	Slope:	126/115	

P	**Lakeville Country Club**	Greens:	$$	
○○	Clear Pond Rd., Lakeville. (508) 947-6630	Carts:	$$	
	18 holes. Par 72/72. Yards: 6,274/5,297	Rating:	70.1/68.5	
	Year-round. High: May–Sept.	Slope:	123/118	

Massachusetts Golf Guide

Boston Area

P ☺☺☺ DEAL	**Maplegate Country Club** Maple St., Bellingham. (508) 966-4040 18 holes. Par 72/72. Yards: 6,815/4,852 Apr.–Dec. High: May–Sept.	Greens: Carts: Rating: Slope:	$–$$ $$$ 74.2/70.2 133/124	W L T J
P ☺☺☺	**New England Country Club** Paine St., Bellingham. (508) 883-2300 18 holes. Par 71/71. Yards: 6,378/4,908 Apr.–Nov. High: June–Sept.	Greens: Carts: Rating: Slope:	$$–$$$ Incl. 71.1/68.7 129/121	W L T
P ☺☺	**Sagamore Springs Golf Club** Main St., Lynnfield. (617) 334-6969 18 holes. Par 70/70. Yards: 5,936/4,784 Mar.–Dec. High: June–Sept.	Greens: Carts: Rating: Slope:	$$ $ 68.6/66.5 119/112	L S
P ☺☺☺	**Shaker Hills Golf Club** Shaker Rd., Harvard. (508) 772-2227 18 holes. Par 71/71. Yards: 6,850/5,001 Apr.–Nov. High: June–Sept.	Greens: Carts: Rating: Slope:	$$$ Incl. 72.3/67.9 135/116	T
P ☺☺☺ DEAL	**Stow Acres Country Club** Randall Rd., Stow. (508) 568-1100 *North Course* 18 holes. Par 72/72. Yards: 6,950/6,011 Mar.–Dec. High: Apr.–Nov.	Greens: Carts: Rating: Slope:	$$ $$ 72.8/70.6 130/120	W L T S J
☺☺☺ DEAL	*South Course* 18 holes. Par 72/72. Yards: 6,520/5,642	Rating: Slope:	71.8/69.7 120/116	
R ☺☺☺	**Tara Ferncroft Country Club** Ferncroft Rd., Danver. (508) 777-5614 18 holes. Par 72/73. Yards: 6,601/5,543 Apr.–Dec. High: May–Oct.	Greens: Carts: Rating: Slope:	$$$$ Incl. 73.2/71.4 131/118	
P ☺☺☺ DEAL	**Trull Brook Golf Course** River Rd., Tewksbury. (508) 851-6731 18 holes. Par 72/72. Yards: 6,350/5,385 Mar.–Nov. High: June–Aug.	Greens: Carts: Rating: Slope:	$$ $ 68.4/70.2 118/118	L T

Cape Cod/Martha's Vineyard

SP ☺☺☺	**Ballymeade Country Club** Falmouth Woods Rd., N. Falmouth. (508) 540-4005 18 holes. Par 72/70. Yards: 6,928/4,722 Year-round. High: June–Aug.	Greens: Carts: Rating: Slope:	$$$–$$$$ Incl. 72.3/66.3 137/112	W L T S
P ☺☺	**Bass River Golf Course** Highbank Rd., South Yarmouth. (508) 398-9079 18 holes. Par 72/72. Yards: 6,129/5,343 Year-round. High: May–Sept.	Greens: Carts: Rating: Slope:	$–$$ $$ 79.3/69.3 122/111	L T
SP ☺☺☺ DEAL	**Bayberry Hills Golf Course** W. Yarmouth Rd., W. Yarmouth. (508) 394-5597 18 holes. Par 72/72. Yards: 7,172/5,275 Apr.–Dec. High: May–Oct.	Greens: Carts: Rating: Slope:	$$ $$ 73.5/69.2 132/111	L T
P ☺☺☺ DEAL	**Cape Cod Country Club** Theater Rd., Hatchville. (508) 563-9842 18 holes. Par 71/72. Yards: 6,404/5,348 Year-round. High: Mar.–Oct.	Greens: Carts: Rating: Slope:	$$ $$ 71.0/70.6 122/119	W L T J
P ☺☺☺ BEST DEAL	**Captains Golf Course** Freeman's Way, Brewster. (508) 896-5100 18 holes. Par 72/72. Yards: 6,794/5,388 Mar.–Dec. High: May–Oct.	Greens: Carts: Rating: Slope:	$$ Inquire 72.7/70.5 130/117	L T

Massachusetts Golf Guide

Cape Cod/Martha's Vineyard

P	**Cranberry Valley Golf Course**	Greens:	$$	W L T
☺☺☺	Oak St., Harwich. (508) 430-7560	Carts:	$$	
DEAL	18 holes. Par 72/72. Yards: 6,745/5,518	Rating:	71.9/71.3	
	Year-round. High: Mar.–Nov.	Slope:	129/115	

P	**Dennis Highlands Golf Course**	Greens:	$$	L T
☺☺☺	Old Bass River Rd., Dennis. (508) 385-8698	Carts:	$$	
DEAL	18 holes. Par 71/71. Yards: 6,464/4,927	Rating:	70.4/67.4	
	Year-round. High: Apr.–Nov.	Slope:	118/112	

P	**Dennis Pines Golf Course**	Greens:	$$	L T
☺☺☺	E. Dennis. (508) 385-8698	Carts:	$$	
DEAL	18 holes. Par 72/73. Yards: 7,029/5,798	Rating:	71.9/73.2	
	Year-round. High: Apr.–Nov.	Slope:	127/128	

SP	**Farm Neck Golf Club**	Greens:	$$–$$$$	L
☺☺☺☺	Farm Neck Way, Oak Bluffs. (508) 693-3057	Carts:	$$	
STATE	18 holes. Par 72/72. Yards: 6,709/5,022	Rating:	71.8/68.9	
	Apr.–Dec. High: July–Aug.	Slope:	130/109	

P	**Highland Golf Links**	Greens:	$$	L
☺☺	Highland Light Rd., N. Truro. (508) 487-9201	Carts:	$$	
	18 holes. Par 70/74. Yards: 5,299/4,782	Rating:	65.0/67.4	
	Apr.–Nov. High: June–Sept.	Slope:	103/107	

SP	**Hyannis Golf Club at Iyanough Hills**	Greens:	$$	W L T S
☺☺	Rte. 132, Hyannis. (508) 362-2606	Carts:	$	
	18 holes. Par 71/72. Yards: 6,514/5,149	Rating:	70.2/69.0	
	Year-round. High: June–Sept.	Slope:	121/125	

R	**New Seabury Country Club**	Greens:	$$–$$$$	L T
	New Seabury. (508) 477-9110	Carts:	$	
☺☺☺☺	*Blue Course*	Rating:	75.3/73.8	
BEST	18 holes. Par 72/72. Yards: 7,200/5,764	Slope:	130/128	
	Year-round. High: July–Aug.			

☺☺☺	*Green Course*	Rating:	67.0/66.3	
	18 holes. Par 70/68. Yards: 5,939/5,105	Slope:	117/110	

R	**Ocean Edge Golf Club**	Greens:	$$–$$$	W L R J
☺☺☺	Villages Dr., Brewster. (508) 896-5911	Carts:	$	
	18 holes. Par 72/72. Yards: 6,665/5,098	Rating:	71.9/73.2	
	Mar.–Dec. High: June–Sept.	Slope:	129/129	

P	**Olde Barnstable Fairgrounds Golf Course**	Greens:	$$	W T
☺☺☺	Rte. 149, Marstons Mills. (508) 420-1141	Carts:	$$	
DEAL	18 holes. Par 71/71. Yards: 6,503/5,162	Rating:	70.7/69.2	
	Year-round. High: Apr.–Nov.	Slope:	123/118	

SP	**Quashnet Valley Country Club**	Greens:	$–$$	L T
☺☺	Old Barnstable Rd., Mashpee. (508) 477-4412	Carts:	$	
	18 holes. Par 72/72. Yards: 6,602/5,094	Rating:	71.7/70.3	
	Year-round. High: Apr.–Oct.	Slope:	132/119	

SP	**Round Hill Country Club**	Greens:	$$$	L T J
☺☺	Round Hill Rd., E. Sandwich. (508) 888-3384	Carts:	Incl.	
	18 holes. Par 71/70. Yards: 6,300/4,800	Rating:	71.4/68.1	
	Year-round. High: May–Oct.	Slope:	124/115	

Fall River Area

P	**Swansea Country Club**	Greens:	$$	L T
☺☺	Market St., Swansea. (508) 379-9886	Carts:	Inquire	
	18 holes. Par 72/72. Yards: 6,809/5,103	Rating:	72.6/69.3	
	Year-round. High: May–Sept.	Slope:	129/111	

New Hampshire

The Granite State has a nice selection of fine public and resort golf courses. At the front of the pack is the very difficult **Shattuck Golf Course** in Jaffrey, east of Keene.

In the picturesque White Mountains you'll find the **North Conway Country Club**, shoehorned in among the hills. By the sea, near Portsmouth, you'll find the windswept **Portsmouth Country Club**.

The Manchester and Concord area, big cities by New Hampshire standards, offers two first-class courses: the **Country Club of New Hampshire**, in a thickly wooded wilderness setting in North Sutton at the base of Mount Kearsarge, and the **Eastman Golf Links**, a hilly challenge in Grantham.

Sky Meadow is a low mountain course in Nashua, just 30 miles north of Boston, with spectacular views in all directions. Another handsome setting is the rolling **Bretwood Golf Course** in Keene.

Five of New Hampshire's best coexist on the Econoguide Deals list: Bretwood, Country Club of New Hampshire, Eastman Golf Links, North Conway Country Club, and Shattuck Golf Course.

The New England winters limit golf course schedules in New Hampshire to April through November. Peak season rates are in effect from about May through late September.

Econoguide Leader Board: Best Public Courses in New Hampshire

⊙⊙⊙⊙	Bretwood Golf Course
⊙⊙⊙	Country Club of New Hampshire
⊙⊙⊙	Eastman Golf Links
⊙⊙⊙	North Conway Country Club
⊙⊙⊙⊙	Portsmouth Country Club
⊙⊙⊙⊙	Shattuck Golf Course
⊙⊙⊙⊙	Sky Meadow Country Club

Econoguide Leader Board: Best Deals in New Hampshire

$$/⊙⊙⊙⊙	Bretwood Golf Course
$$/⊙⊙⊙	Campbell's Scottish Highlands Golf Course
$$/⊙⊙⊙	Country Club of New Hampshire
$$/⊙⊙⊙	Eastman Golf Links
$$/⊙⊙⊙	Hanover Country Club
$$/⊙⊙⊙	John H. Cain Golf Club
$$/⊙⊙⊙	North Conway Country Club
$$/⊙⊙⊙	Overlook Country Club
$$/⊙⊙⊙	Passaconaway Country Club
$$/⊙⊙⊙⊙	Shattuck Golf Course

New Hampshire Golf Guide

Northern New Hampshire

R	**The Balsams Grand Resort**	Greens:	$$$	R
	Rte. 26, Dixville Notch. (603) 255-4961	Carts:	$	
⊙⊙⊙	*Panorama Golf Club*	Rating:	73.9/69.6	

New Hampshire Golf Guide

Northern New Hampshire

	18 holes. Par 72/72. Yards: 6,804/5,069	Slope:	136/124
	May–Oct. High: July–Aug.		

R	**Mount Washington Golf Course**	Greens:	$$	R
☺	Rte. 302, Bretton Woods. (603) 278-1000	Carts:	$$	
	18 holes. Par 71/71. Yards: 6,638/5,336	Rating:	70.1/70.1	
	May–Oct. High: July–Sept.	Slope:	123/118	

SP	**North Conway Country Club**	Greens:	$$	L T S J
☺☺☺	Norcross Circle, N. Conway. (603) 356-9391	Carts:	$$	
DEAL	18 holes. Par 71/71. Yards: 6,659/5,530	Rating:	71.9/71.4	
STATE	May–Oct. High: June–Oct.	Slope:	126/120	

P	**White Mountain Country Club**	Greens:	$–$$	W L T
☺☺	Ashland Rd., Ashland. (603) 536-2227	Carts:	$	
	18 holes. Par 71/73. Yards: 6,408/5,410	Rating:	70.4/70.2	
	Apr.–Nov. High: May–Sept.	Slope:	125/118	

Lebanon Area

P	**Hanover Country Club**	Greens:	$$	T
☺☺☺	Rope Ferry Rd., Hanover. (603) 646-2000	Carts:	$	
DEAL	18 holes. Par 69/73. Yards: 5,876/5,648	Rating:	68.7/72.7	
	Apr.–Nov. High: June–Sept.	Slope:	118/127	

Portsmouth Area

P	**Pease Golf Course**	Greens:	$$
☺☺	Portsmouth. (603) 433-1331	Carts:	$$
	18 holes. Par 70/70. Yards: 6,228/5,291	Rating:	70.8/69.9
	Apr.–Nov. High: June–Aug.	Slope:	128/120

SP	**Portsmouth Country Club**	Greens:	$$$	T
☺☺☺☺	Greenland. (603) 436-9719	Carts:	$$	
STATE	18 holes. Par 72/78. Yards: 7,050/6,202	Rating:	74.1/77.1	
	Apr.–Nov. High: June–Sept.	Slope:	127/135	

SP	**Rochester Country Club**	Greens:	$$–$$$
☺☺	Church St., Gonic. (603) 332-9892	Carts:	Incl.
	18 holes. Par 72/73. Yards: 6,596/5,414	Rating:	72.7/70.4
	Apr.–Nov. High: June–Aug.	Slope:	125/123

SP	**Wentworth-by-the-Sea Country Club**	Greens:	$$$–$$$$	W L
☺☺☺	Wentworth Rd., Portsmouth. (603) 433-5010	Carts:	$	
	18 holes. Par 70/70. Yards: 6,162/5,097	Rating:	67.8/70.5	
	Apr.–Nov. High: May–Sept.	Slope:	123/119	

Keene Area

P	**Bretwood Golf Course**	Greens:	$$	T
☺☺☺☺	East Surry Rd., Keene. (603) 352-7626	Carts:	$	
DEAL	18 holes. Par 72/72. Yards: 6,974/5,140	Rating:	73.9/70.1	
STATE	Apr.–Nov. High: June–Oct.	Slope:	134/120	

SP	**Keene Country Club**	Greens:	$$$
☺☺☺	West Hill Rd., Keene. (603) 352-9722	Carts:	$$
	18 holes. Par 72/75. Yards: 6,200/5,900	Rating:	69.0/72.2
	Apr.–Nov. High: May–Sept.	Slope:	121/130

P	**Shattuck Golf Course**	Greens:	$$	W L T
☺☺☺☺	Dublin Rd., Jaffrey. (603) 532-4300	Carts:	$	
DEAL	18 holes. Par 71/71. Yards: 6,701/4,632	Rating:	74.1/73.1	
STATE	May–Oct. High: June–Sept.	Slope:	145/139	

Manchester/Concord Area

P	**Beaver Meadow Golf Club**	Greens:	$–$$	W L T S J
☺☺	Beaver Meadow Dr., Concord. (603) 228-8954	Carts:	Inquire	
	18 holes. Par 72/72. Yards: 6,356/5,519	Rating:	70.0/71.8	
	Apr.–Nov. High: May–Sept.	Slope:	121/123	

New Hampshire Golf Guide

Manchester/Concord Area

P ⊙⊙	**Candia Woods Golf Links** South Rd., Candia. (603) 483-2307 18 holes. Par 71/73. Yards: 6,558/5,582 Mar.–Dec. High: June	Greens: Carts: Rating: Slope:	$$ $ 70.9/72.2 121/130	W L T J	

P ⊙⊙⊙ DEAL STATE	**Country Club of New Hampshire** Kearsarge Valley Rd., N. Sutton. (603) 927-4246 18 holes. Par 72/72. Yards: 6,727/5,446 Apr.–Nov. High: July–Sept.	Greens: $$ Carts: $ Rating: 71.6/71.7 Slope: 125/127	W T

P ⊙⊙⊙ DEAL STATE	**Eastman Golf Links** Grantham. (603) 863-4500 18 holes. Par 71/73. Yards: 6,731/5,369 May–Nov. High: July–Sept.	Greens: $$ Carts: $ Rating: 73.5/71.9 Slope: 137/128	

P ⊙	**Green Meadow Golf Club** Steele Rd., Hudson. (603) 889-1555 *North Course* 18 holes. Par 72/72. Yards: 6,495/5,102 Mar.–Dec. High: Apr.–Aug.	Greens: $$ Carts: Inquire Rating: 67.6/68.3 Slope: 109/113	W L T S J

P ⊙⊙	**Jack O'Lantern Resort** Rte. 3, Woodstock. (603) 745-3636 18 holes. Par 70/70. Yards: 5,829/4,725 May–Oct.	Greens: $$ Carts: $ Rating: 67.5/67.5 Slope: 113/113	W R T

SP ⊙⊙⊙ DEAL	**John H. Cain Golf Club** Unity Rd., Newport. (603) 863-7787 18 holes. Par 71/71. Yards: 6,415/4,738 Apr.–Nov. High: July–Sept.	Greens: $$ Carts: $ Rating: 71.4/63.8 Slope: 133/112	W L T S J

SP ⊙⊙⊙	**Laconia Country Club** Elm St., Laconia. (603) 524-1273 18 holes. Par 72/72. Yards: 6,483/5,552 Apr.–Nov. High: June–Sept.	Greens: $$$$ Carts: Incl. Rating: 71.7/72.1 Slope: 128/125	L R J

P ⊙⊙⊙ DEAL	**Overlook Country Club** Overlook Dr., Hollis. (603) 465-2909 18 holes. Par 71/72. Yards: 6,290/5,230 Apr.–Dec. High: June–Aug.	Greens: $$ Carts: $$ Rating: 69.7/70.4 Slope: 130/126	W T

P ⊙⊙⊙ DEAL	**Passaconaway Country Club** Midway Ave., Litchfield. (603) 424-4653 18 holes. Par 71/72. Yards: 6,855/5,369 Apr.–Dec. High: May–Sept.	Greens: $$ Carts: Inquire Rating: 72.2/70.3 Slope: 126/118	W L T S J

P ⊙⊙	**Waukewan Golf Club** Meredith. (603) 279-6661 18 holes. Par 71/73. Yards: 5,735/5,010 May–Oct. High: June–Sept.	Greens: $$ Carts: $$ Rating: 67.1/68.7 Slope: 120/112	L

P ⊙⊙	**Windham Golf and Country Club** Londonderry Rd., Windham. (603) 434-2093 18 holes. Par 72/72. Yards: 6,442/5,127 Year-round. High: May–Oct.	Greens: $$ Carts: $ Rating: 71.3/69.0 Slope: 136/132	

Nashua Area

P ⊙⊙	**Amherst Country Club** Ponemah Rd., Amherst. (603) 673-9908 18 holes. Par 72/74. Yards: 6,520/5,532 Mar.–Dec. High: May–Oct.	Greens: $$ Carts: $ Rating: 71.0/74.2 Slope: 123/129	W S

P ⊙⊙⊙	**Campbell's Scottish Highlands Golf Course** Brady Ave., Salem. (603) 894-4653	Greens: $$ Carts: $	W T S

Nashua Area

DEAL	18 holes. Par 71/71. Yards: 6,249/5,056	Rating:	69.5/68.4	
	Apr.–Nov. High: July–Aug.	Slope:	120/114	
P	**Sagamore-Hampton Golf Club**	Greens:	$$	L
☺☺	North Rd., North Hampton. (603) 964-5341	Carts:	Inquire	
	18 holes. Par 71/71. Yards: 6,489/5,822	Rating:	70.5/67.1	
	Apr.–Dec. High: May–Sept.	Slope:	101/101	
SP	**Sky Meadow Country Club**	Greens:	$$$–$$$$$	
☺☺☺☺	Mtn. Laurels Dr., Nashua. (603) 888-3000	Carts:	Incl.	
STATE	18 holes. Par 72/72. Yards: 6,590/5,127	Rating:	73.3/71.2	
	Apr.–Nov. High: June–Sept.	Slope:	133/131	

New Jersey

The very best the Garden State has to offer includes a pair of very green and very challenging courses north of Philadelphia: the venerable **Hominy Hill** in Colts Neck, home of more than a hundred bunkers, and **Howell Park**, in Farmingdale. Hominy Hill also appears on the Econoguide Deals list.

Just outside of Atlantic City is the sandy new **Blue Heron Pines Golf Club**.

In northwest New Jersey, 50 miles west of New York City, there are the outstanding White and Blue courses of **Flanders Valley** in Flanders.

Some courses in southern New Jersey endeavor to stay open all year round, while others are limited to a season that runs from about March through early December. Peak season rates are in effect from about April through September.

Econoguide Leader Board: Best Public Courses in New Jersey

☺☺☺☺   Blue Heron Pines Golf Club
☺☺☺☺   Flanders Valley Golf Course (White, Blue)
☺☺☺☺   Hominy Hill Golf Course
☺☺☺☺   Howell Park Golf Course

Econoguide Leader Board: Best Deals in New Jersey

$$/☺☺☺   Buena Vista Country Club
$$/☺☺☺   Farmstead Golf and Country Club (Clubview, Lakeview, Valleyview)
$$/☺☺☺☺   Hominy Hill Golf Course
$$/☺☺☺   Ocean County Golf Course at Atlantis
$$/☺☺☺   Rancocas Golf Club
$$/☺☺☺   Sunset Valley Golf Course

Northern New Jersey/Newark Area

P	**Ash Brook Golf Course**	Greens:	$$	W
☺☺	Raritan Rd., Scotch Plains. (908) 668-8503	Carts:	$	
	18 holes. Par 72/72. Yards: 6,916/6,373	Rating:	NA	
	Year-round. High: Mar.–Oct.	Slope:	115/121	
SP	**Beaver Brook Country Club**	Greens:	$$–$$$	T
☺☺☺	Rte. 31 South, Clinton. (908) 735-4022	Carts:	$$	
	18 holes. Par 72/72. Yards: 6,546/5,283	Rating:	71.6/70.4	
	Mar.–Dec. High: June–Aug.	Slope:	122/112	

New Jersey Golf Guide

Northern New Jersey/Newark Area

SP ☺☺☺	**Bowling Green Golf Club** Schoolhouse Rd., Milton. (201) 697-8688 18 holes. Par 72/72. Yards: 6,689/4,966 Mar.–Dec. High: Apr.–Sept.	Greens: Carts: Rating: Slope:	$$–$$$ W T $ 73.0/68.4 136/116
SP ☺☺☺	**Crystal Springs Golf Club** Crystal Springs Rd., Hamburg. (201) 827-1444 18 holes. Par 72/72. Yards: 6,857/5,131 Apr.–Nov. High: May–Sept.	Greens: Carts: Rating: Slope:	$$–$$$$ W T Incl. 73.3/70.5 133/123
P ☺☺☺ DEAL	**Farmstead Golf and Country Club** Lawrence Rd., Lafayette. (201) 383-1666 *Clubview/Lakeview/Valleyview* 27 holes. Par 71/69/68. Yards: 6,680/6,221/6,161 Apr.–Nov. High: May–Oct.	Greens: Carts: Rating: Slope:	$$ T S Inquire 71.3/69.3/68.9 118/117/116
P ☺☺☺	**Flanders Valley Golf Course** Pleasant Hill Rd., Flanders. (201) 584-5382 *Red/Gold* 18 holes. Par 72/73. Yards: 6,770/5,540 Apr.–Nov. High: May–Aug.	Greens: Carts: Rating: Slope:	$–$$$ W T S $$ 72.6/72.0 126/121
☺☺☺☺ STATE	*White/Blue* 18 holes. Par 72/72. Yards: 6,765/5,534	Rating: Slope:	72.7/72.6 126/122
P ☺☺☺	**Great Gorge Country Club** Rte. 517, McAfee. (201) 827-5757 *Lake/Quarry/Rail* 27 holes. Par 71/71/72. Yards: 6,819/6,826/6,921 Mar.–Nov. High: May–Oct.	Greens: Carts: Rating: Slope:	$$$–$$$$ W L R T S Incl. 73.3/72.7/73.4 131/126/128
P ☺☺	**Green Knoll Golf Course** Garretson Rd., Bridgewater. (908) 722-1301 18 holes. Par 71/72. Yards: 6,443/5,349 Mar.–Nov. High: May–Sept.	Greens: Carts: Rating: Slope:	$$ S J $$ 70.9/73.0 117/121
SP ☺☺	**High Mountain Golf Club** Ewing Ave., Franklin Lakes. (201) 891-4653 18 holes. Par 71/71. Yards: 6,347/5,426 Apr.–Nov. High: May–Oct.	Greens: Carts: Rating: Slope:	$$ W T Incl. 69.5/70.0 118/117
SP ☺☺	**Jumping Brook Golf and Country Club** Jumping Brook Rd., Neptune. (908) 922-6140 18 holes. Par 72/72. Yards: 6,591/5,316 Year-round. High: May–Sept.	Greens: Carts: Rating: Slope:	$$ W T S J $ 71.4/71.2 122/118
SP ☺☺	**Old Orchard Country Club** Monmouth Rd., Eatontown. (908) 542-7666 18 holes. Par 72/72. Yards: 6,588/5,575 Year-round. High: May–Sept.	Greens: Carts: Rating: Slope:	$–$$ W L T S $$ 70.5/70.8 116/115
P ☺☺	**Paramus Golf Club** Paramus Rd., Paramus. (201) 440-6079 18 holes. Par 71/70. Yards: 6,212/5,241 Year-round. High: Apr.–Nov.	Greens: Carts: Rating: Slope:	$$ W S $$ 69.1/72.0 118/117
P ☺☺	**Quail Brook Golf Course** New Brunswick Rd., Somerset. (908) 560-9528 18 holes. Par 71/72. Yards: 6,591/5,385 Year-round. High: May–Sept.	Greens: Carts: Rating: Slope:	$$ S J $$ 70.8/69.9 119/115
P ☺☺☺	**River Vale Country Club** Rivervale Rd., River Vale. (201) 391-2300 18 holes. Par 72/74. Yards: 6,470/5,293 Mar.–Nov. High: June–Sept.	Greens: Carts: Rating: Slope:	$$$–$$$$$ L T Incl. 70.1/68.6 116/107

New Jersey Golf Guide

Northern New Jersey/Newark Area

P	**Spooky Brook Golf Course**	Greens:	$$ S J
◎◎	Elizabeth Ave., Somerset. (908) 873-2242	Carts:	$$
	18 holes. Par 71/72. Yards: 6,612/5,376	Rating:	70.5/73.5
	Year-round. High: May–Sept.	Slope:	113/120

P	**Sunset Valley Golf Course**	Greens:	$–$$ T S
◎◎◎	W. Sunset Rd., Pompton Plains. (201) 835-1515	Carts:	$$
DEAL	18 holes. Par 72/72. Yards: 6,483/5,274	Rating:	71.7/70.8
	Apr.–Dec. High: May–Sept.	Slope:	129/123

SP	**Woodlake Golf and Country Club**	Greens:	$$–$$$ W L T
◎◎◎	New Hampshire Ave., Lakewood. (908) 367-4500	Carts:	Incl.
	18 holes. Par 72/74. Yards: 6,766/5,557	Rating:	72.5/72.2
	Year-round. High: May–Aug.	Slope:	126/120

Trenton Area

SP	**Cranbury Golf Club**	Greens:	$$ W L T J
◎◎	Southfield Rd., Cranbury. (609) 799-0341	Carts:	$
	18 holes. Par 71/72. Yards: 6,312/5,545	Rating:	70.0/72.0
	Year-round. High: May–Sept.	Slope:	117/118

SP	**Cream Ridge Golf Club**	Greens:	$–$$ W L T S J
◎◎	Rte. 539, Cream Ridge. (609) 259-2849	Carts:	$$
	18 holes. Par 71/71. Yards: 6,630/5,101	Rating:	72.3/72.3
	Year-round. High: May–Sept.	Slope:	119/119

P	**Spring Meadow Golf Course**	Greens:	$ W T S
◎◎	Atlantic Ave., Farmingdale. (908) 449-0806	Carts:	$$
	18 holes. Par 72/76. Yards: 5,953/5,310	Rating:	68.1/69.7
	Year-round. High: Apr.–Oct.	Slope:	113/114

Cherry Hill/Philadelphia Suburbs

P	**Buena Vista Country Club**	Greens:	$$ W L T
◎◎◎	Rte. 40, Buena. (609) 697-3733	Carts:	$
DEAL	18 holes. Par 72/72. Yards: 6,869/5,651	Rating:	73.5/72.2
	Year-round. High: May–Oct.	Slope:	131/128

SP	**Golden Pheasant Golf Club**	Greens:	$–$$ W T S
◎◎	Eayrestown Rd., Medford. (609) 267-4276	Carts:	$
	18 holes. Par 72/72. Yards: 6,273/5,105	Rating:	68.1/68.4
	Year-round. High: Apr.–Oct.	Slope:	119/114

P	**Hominy Hill Golf Course**	Greens:	$–$$ W T S J
◎◎◎◎	Mercer Rd., Colts Neck. (908) 462-9222	Carts:	$$
DEAL	18 holes. Par 72/72. Yards: 7,056/5,794	Rating:	74.4/73.9
STATE	Mar.–Dec. High: May–Oct.	Slope:	132/128

P	**Howell Park Golf Course**	Greens:	$$–$$$ W T
◎◎◎◎	Yellow Brook Rd., Farmingdale. (908) 938-4771	Carts:	Inquire
STATE	18 holes. Par 72/72. Yards: 6,885/5,693	Rating:	73.0/72.5
	Mar.–Dec. High: Apr.–Oct.	Slope:	128/125

P	**Ramblewood Country Club**	Greens:	$$$ W L T S
	Mt. Laurel. (609) 235-2118	Carts:	Inquire
◎◎	*Red/White/Blue*	Rating:	72.9/71.1/72.1
	27 holes. Par 72/72/72. Yards: 6,883/6,624/6,723	Slope:	130/129/130
	Year-round. High: Apr.–Oct.		

P	**Rancocas Golf Club**	Greens:	$–$$ W L T S J
◎◎◎	Willingboro. (609) 877-5344	Carts:	Incl.
DEAL	18 holes. Par 71/72. Yards: 6,634/5,284	Rating:	73.0/73.0
	Year-round. High: Apr.–Nov.	Slope:	130/127

SP	**Ron Jaworski's Eagles' Nest Country Club**	Greens:	$–$$ W L T S
◎◎	Woodbury-Glassboro Rd., Sewell. (609) 468-3542	Carts:	$

New Jersey Golf Guide

Cherry Hill/Philadelphia Suburbs

	18 holes. Par 71/71. Yards: 6,376/5,210	Rating: 71.3/71.2	
	Year-round. High: Apr.–Oct.	Slope: 130/125	

SP	**Willow Brook Country Club**	Greens: $$	W L T S
◎◎	Bridgeboro Rd., Moorestown. (609) 461-0131	Carts: $	
	18 holes. Par 72/72. Yards: 6,457/5,028	Rating: 71.2/68.3	
	Year-round. High: May–Sept.	Slope: 125/110	

Jersey Shore

SP	**Ocean Acres Country Club**	Greens: $–$$	L T
◎◎	Buccaneer Lane, Manahawkin. (609) 597-9393	Carts: $$	
	18 holes. Par 72/72. Yards: 6,548/5,412	Rating: 70.5/70.7	
	Year-round. High: June–Aug.	Slope: 120/118	

Atlantic City Area

SP	**Avalon Country Club**	Greens: $$–$$$	W L T J
◎◎	Rte. 9N, Cape May Court House. (609) 465-4653	Carts: Incl.	
	18 holes. Par 71/72. Yards: 6,325/4,924	Rating: 70.3/70.7	
	Year-round. High: May–Sept.	Slope: 122/122	

P	**Blue Heron Pines Golf Club**	Greens: $$$–$$$$$	W L T
◎◎◎◎	Galloway. (609) 965-4653	Carts: Incl.	
STATE	18 holes. Par 72/72. Yards: 6,777/5,053	Rating: 71.6/70.4	
	Year-round. High: May–Oct.	Slope: 122/112	

P	**Brigantine Golf Links**	Greens: $$$	L R T
◎◎	Roosevelt Blvd., Brigantine. (609) 266-1388	Carts: Incl.	
	18 holes. Par 72/72. Yards: 6,520/6,233	Rating: NA	
	Year-round. High: May–Sept.	Slope: 123/120	

SP	**Cape May National Golf Club**	Greens: $$–$$$$	W L T J
◎◎◎	Rte. 9, Cape May. (609) 884-1563	Carts: Incl.	
	18 holes. Par 71/71. Yards: 6,857/4,696	Rating: 72.9/68.8	
	Year-round. High: May–Oct.	Slope: 136/115	

P	**Cedar Creek Golf Course**	Greens: $–$$	W T S J
◎◎	Tilton Blvd., Bayville. (908) 269-4460	Carts: $$	
	18 holes. Par 72/72. Yards: 6,325/5,173	Rating: 71.2/72.5	
	Year-round. High: May–Sept.	Slope: 115/116	

R	**Greate Bay Resort and Country Club**	Greens: $$$$	L R T
◎◎◎	Mays Landing Rd., Somers Point. (609) 927-0066	Carts: Incl.	
	18 holes. Par 71/71. Yards: 6,750/5,495	Rating: NA	
	Year-round. High: May–Sept.	Slope: 130/126	

R	**Marriott's Seaview Resort**	Greens: $$–$$$$$	L T
	S. New York Rd., Absecon. (609) 748-7680	Carts: Incl.	
◎◎◎	*Bay Course*	Rating: 69.0/70.7	
	18 holes. Par 71/72. Yards: 6,263/5,586	Slope: 113/115	
	Year-round.		

◎◎◎	*Pines Course*	Rating: 73.0/73.2	
	18 holes. Par 71/75. Yards: 6,885/5,837	Slope: 132/128	

P	**Ocean County Golf Course at Atlantis**	Greens: $–$$	T S J
◎◎◎	Tuckerton. (609) 296-2444	Carts: $$	
DEAL	18 holes. Par 72/72. Yards: 6,845/5,579	Rating: 73.6/71.8	
	Year-round. High: Aug.	Slope: 134/124	

P	**Pinelands Golf Club**	Greens: $–$$	W L T
◎	S. Mays Landing Rd., Winslow. (609) 561-8900	Carts: $	
	18 holes. Par 71/71. Yards: 6,224/5,375	Rating: 69.7/70.4	
	Year-round. High: May–Nov.	Slope: 114/119	

New Jersey Golf Guide

Southern New Jersey

P	**Centerton Golf Club**	Greens:	$	W L T
◎◎	Almond Rd., Elmer. (609) 358-2220	Carts:	$$	
	18 holes. Par 71/71. Yards: 6,725/5,525	Rating:	69.2/71.5	
	Year-round. High: May–Aug.	Slope:	120/120	

P	**Holly Hills Golf Club**	Greens:	$$	W L T J
◎◎	Freisburg Rd., Alloway. (609) 455-5115	Carts:	$	
	18 holes. Par 72/72. Yards: 6,376/5,056	Rating:	70.8/68.0	
	Year-round. High: Apr.–Oct.	Slope:	120/114	

New York

The Empire State, despite the image of the concrete canyons of New York City, is actually a very green place with a lot of open space and mountain ranges.

The best of the public and resort courses of New York include the famed Adirondack Mountain courses at the **Sagamore Golf Club** in Bolton Landing, which have been restored to their original difficult 1928 Donald Ross design. There is also the memorable pine-lined **Saratoga Spa Golf Course** in Saratoga Springs.

Around Syracuse in central New York are the rolling forests and impossibly green lakes of **Green Lakes State Park Golf Club** in Fayetteville, and the **Radisson Greens Golf Club** in Baldwinsville.

Wayne Hills Country Club winds through the trees in Lyons, east of Rochester.

The Southern Tier around Binghamton features the **En-Joie Golf Club** in Endicott, home of the B.C. Open and a handsome challenge.

The rolling Catskill Mountains, about 100 miles from New York City, have a few memorable courses at the Borscht Belt resorts including the monstrous Monster Course at the **Concord Resort Hotel** in Kiamesha Lake, and the spectacular mountain Lake/Valley/Vista triumvirate at the **Grossinger Resort** in Liberty.

Courses near New York City can be very crowded, and very slow to play; come early, or drive out of the city a bit to save waiting at the course.

Finally, there are two notable courses on Long Island: the very difficult, hilly Black Course at **Bethpage State Park** in Farmingdale, and the rolling links-like beach challenge of **Montauk Downs State Park**, at the end of the island in Montauk, 100 miles east of New York City.

No fewer than seven courses coexist on the Econoguide Best and Econoguide Deals lists: Bethpage State Park, En-Joie, Green Lakes State Park, Montauk Downs State Park, Radisson Greens, Saratoga Spa, and Wayne Hills.

Adirondack and Catskill Mountain courses (and many in western New York in and around Buffalo and Niagara Falls) operate from about April through October, with peak rates in effect from about June through August.

Many courses elsewhere in the state attempt to operate year-round, while others are open from March through December. Peak rates are in effect likewise from June through August.

Econoguide Leader Board: Best Public Courses in New York

○○○○　Bethpage State Park Golf Courses (Black)
○○○○　Concord Resort Hotel (Monster)
○○○　En-Joie Golf Club
○○○　Green Lakes State Park Golf Club
○○○○　Grossinger Resort (Lake, Valley, Vista)
○○○○　Montauk Downs State Park Golf Course
○○○○　Radisson Greens Golf Club
○○○○　The Sagamore Golf Club
○○○　Saratoga Spa Golf Course
○○○○　Wayne Hills Country Club

Econoguide Leader Board: Best Deals in New York

$/○○○　　　　Amsterdam Municipal Golf Course
$/○○○　　　　Arrowhead Golf Course
$/○○○○　　　Bethpage State Park Golf Courses (Black, Blue, Green, Red)
$$/○○○　　　Blue Hill Golf Club
$$/○○○　　　Bluff Point Golf & Country Club
$$/○○○　　　Centerpointe Country Club
$$/○○○　　　Chautauqua Golf Course (Hill, Lake)
$$/○○○　　　Conklin Players Club
$$/○○○　　　Crab Meadow Golf Club
$/○○○　　　　Craig Wood Golf Course
$$/○○○　　　Deerfield Country Club
$$/○○○　　　Deerwood Golf Course
$/○○○　　　　Durand Eastman Golf Course
$/○○○　　　　Dutch Hollow Country Club
$/○○○　　　　Endwell Greens Golf Club
$$/○○○　　　En-Joie Golf Club
$$/○○○　　　Foxfire Golf Club
$/○○○　　　　Green Lakes State Park Golf Club
$$/○○○　　　Hiland Golf Club
$$/○○○　　　Malone Golf Club (East, West)
$/○○○　　　　Mark Twain Golf Club
$$/○○○○　　Montauk Downs State Park Golf Course
$$/○○○　　　Nevele Country Club
$$/○○○　　　Peek'n Peak Resort
$$/○○○○　　Radisson Greens Golf Club
$$/○○○　　　River Oaks Golf Club
$$/○○○　　　Rock Hill Country Club
$/○○○　　　　Saratoga Spa Golf Course
$$/○○○　　　Segalla Country Club
$$/○○○　　　Shadow Pines Golf Club
$/○○○　　　　Sheridan Park Golf Club
$$/○○○　　　Smithtown Landing Golf Club
$/○○○　　　　Soaring Eagles Golf Club

$$/◦◦◦	Spring Lake Golf Club
$$/◦◦◦	Swan Lake Golf Club
$$/◦◦◦	Tarry Brae Golf Club
$$/◦◦◦	Tennanah Lake Golf & Tennis Club
$/◦◦◦	Terry Hills Golf Course
$$/◦◦◦	Thendara Golf Club
$$/◦◦◦	Thomas Carvel Country Club
$$/◦◦◦	Town of Walkill Golf Club
$$/◦◦◦	Tri County Country Club
$$/◦◦◦	Watertown Golf Club
$$/◦◦◦◦	Wayne Hills Country Club
$$/◦◦◦	Whiteface Inn Resort Golf Club
$/◦◦◦	Willowbrook Country Club

New York Golf Guide

Buffalo Area

P ◦◦	**Beaver Island State Park Golf Club** Beaver Island SP, Grand Island. (716) 773-4668 18 holes. Par 72/72. Yards: 6,595/6,201 Apr.–Nov. High: July–Aug.	Greens: Carts: Rating: Slope:	$ $ 72.1 108	W S J
R ◦◦	**Byrncliff Golf Club** Rte. 20A, Varysburg. (716) 535-7300 18 holes. Par 72/73. Yards: 6,783/5,545 Apr.–Nov. High: June–Aug.	Greens: Carts: Rating: Slope:	$ $$ 73.1/75.1 115/119	L R T S
R ◦◦◦ DEAL	**Chautauqua Golf Course** Rte. 394, Chautauqua. (716) 357-6211 *Hill Course* 18 holes. Par 72/72. Yards: 6,412/5,076 Apr.–Nov. High: June–Aug.	Greens: Carts: Rating: Slope:	$–$$ $ 72.1/72.7 118/110	W L T
◦◦◦ DEAL	*Lake Course* 18 holes. Par 72/74. Yards: 6,462/5,423	Rating: Slope:	71.1/71.7 115/108	
P ◦◦◦ DEAL	**Deerwood Golf Course** Sweeney St., N. Tonawanda. (716) 695-8525 18 holes. Par 72/73. Yards: 6,948/6,150 Apr.–Dec. High: June–Aug.	Greens: Carts: Rating: Slope:	$–$$ $ 73.0/75.0 117/123	W T
R ◦◦	**Holiday Valley Resort** Rte. 219, Ellicottville. (716) 699-2346 18 holes. Par 72/73. Yards: 6,555/5,381 Apr.–Oct. High: June–Sept.	Greens: Carts: Rating: Slope:	$–$$ $ 71.3/74.0 125/115	L T
P ◦	**Hyde Park Golf Course** Porter Rd., Niagara Falls. (716) 297-2067 18 holes. Par 70/70. Yards: 6,400/5,700 Apr.–Nov. High: June–Sept.	Greens: Carts: Rating: Slope:	$ Inquire 70.0/72.0 110/110	S J
SP ◦◦◦ DEAL	**River Oaks Golf Club** Whitehaven Rd., Grand Island. (716) 773-3336 18 holes. Par 72/72. Yards: 7,389/5,747 Apr.–Nov. High: June–Sept.	Greens: Carts: Rating: Slope:	$–$$ $ 73.7/71.4 128/121	L R
P ◦◦	**Rothland Golf Course** Clarence Center Rd., Akron. (716) 542-4325 *Red/Gold/White* 27 holes. Par 72/72/72. Yards: 6,486/6,216/6,044 Apr.–Nov. High: June–Sept.	Greens: Carts: Rating: Slope:	$ $ 70.5/69.5/69.0 113/108/105	W L T S

New York Golf Guide

Buffalo Area

P ☺☺☺ DEAL	**Sheridan Park Golf Club** Center Park Dr., Tonawanda. (716) 875-1811 18 holes. Par 72/72. Yards: 6,534/5,656 Apr.–Nov. High: June–Aug.	Greens: $ Carts: $ Rating: 71.5/74.0 Slope: 116/116	W T
P ☺☺☺ DEAL	**Terry Hills Golf Course** Clinton St., Batavia. (716) 343-0860 18 holes. Par 72/72. Yards: 6,072/5,107 Mar.–Nov. High: June–Aug.	Greens: $ Carts: $ Rating: 68.7/68.0 Slope: 108/102	L T S
SP ☺☺☺ DEAL	**Tri County Country Club** Rte. 39, Forestville. (716) 965-9723 18 holes. Par 72/72. Yards: 6,639/5,574 Apr.–Oct. High: July–Aug.	Greens: $$ Carts: $ Rating: 69.2/72.6 Slope: 118/116	T
P ☺☺☺ DEAL	**Willowbrook Country Club** Lake Ave., Lockport. (716) 434-0111 18 holes. Par 71/71. Yards: 6,018/5,713 Apr.–Nov. High: June–Aug.	Greens: $ Carts: $ Rating: 68.9/67.7 Slope: 112/112	W L T S

Rochester Area

R ☺☺☺	**Bristol Harbour Golf Club** Senaca Point Rd., Canandaigua. (716) 396-2460 18 holes. Par 72/72. Yards: 6,700/5,500 Apr.–Nov. High: June–Sept.	Greens: $$–$$$ Carts: Incl. Rating: 72.6/73.0 Slope: 126/126	W L R T S J
SP ☺☺☺ DEAL	**Centerpointe Country Club** Brickyard Rd., Canandaigua. (716) 924-5346 18 holes. Par 71/71. Yards: 6,717/5,213 Apr.–Nov. High: June–Aug.	Greens: $–$$ Carts: $$ Rating: 70.7/68.3 Slope: 116/107	W L T S
SP ☺☺☺ DEAL	**Deerfield Country Club** Craig Hull Dr., Brockport. (716) 392-8080 18 holes. Par 72/72. Yards: 7,083/5,623 Apr.–Dec. High: June–Aug.	Greens: $–$$ Carts: $ Rating: 73.9/72.4 Slope: 138/123	L S J
P ☺☺☺ DEAL	**Durand Eastman Golf Course** Kings Hwy. N., Rochester. (716) 342-9810 18 holes. Par 70/72. Yards: 6,089/5,727 Apr.–Nov. High: June–Aug.	Greens: $ Carts: $ Rating: 68.8/71.7 Slope: 112/113	W L S J
P ☺☺	**Eagle Vale Golf Course** Nine Mile Point Rd., Fairport. (716) 377-5200 18 holes. Par 70/72. Yards: 6,524/5,787 Apr.–Dec. High: June–Aug.	Greens: $$ Carts: Incl. Rating: 70.9/72.8 Slope: 123/120	W L S J
P ☺	**Genesee Valley Golf Course** E. River Rd., Rochester. (716) 424-2920 *New Course* 18 holes. Par 72/72. Yards: 5,270/5,270 Apr.–Nov. High: June–July	Greens: $ Carts: $ Rating: NA/67.7 Slope: 93.0/100	L T S J
☺	*Old Course* 18 holes. Par 71/77. Yards: 6,374/5,561	Rating: 69.3/73.2 Slope: 104/102	
R ☺☺☺	**Glen Oak Golf Course** Smith Rd., E. Amherst. (716) 688-5454 18 holes. Par 72/72. Yards: 6,730/5,561 Apr.–Nov. High: June–Aug.	Greens: $$–$$$ Carts: Incl. Rating: 72.4/71.9 Slope: 129/118	W L T S
P ☺☺	**Lima Golf & Country Club** Plank Rd., Lima. (716) 624-1490 18 holes. Par 72/74. Yards: 6,338/5,624 Apr.–Oct. High: June–Sept.	Greens: $ Carts: $ Rating: 69.2/74.0 Slope: 115/117	W L S

New York Golf Guide

Rochester Area

R ☺☺☺ DEAL	**Peek'n Peak Resort** Olde Rd., Clymer. (716) 355-4141 18 holes. Par 72/72. Yards: 6,260/4,820 Apr.–Nov. High: June–Sept.	Greens: $$ Carts: $ Rating: 69.0/69.5 Slope: 115/112	W L S
P ☺☺	**Shadow Lake Golf & Raquet Club** Five Mile Line Rd., Penfield. (716) 385-2010 18 holes. Par 71/72. Yards: 6,164/5,498 Mar.–Dec. High: June–Aug.	Greens: $–$$ Carts: $ Rating: 68.5/70.5 Slope: 111/112	W L T S
P ☺☺☺ DEAL	**Shadow Pines Golf Club** Whalen Rd., Penfield. (716) 385-8550 18 holes. Par 72/72. Yards: 6,763/5,292 Apr.–Oct. High: June–Aug.	Greens: $–$$ Carts: $ Rating: 72.1/73.1 Slope: 121/124	W L T S
SP ☺☺☺☺ DEAL STATE	**Wayne Hills Country Club** Gannett Rd., Lyons. (315) 946-6944 18 holes. Par 72/72. Yards: 6,854/5,556 Apr.–Nov. High: May–Sept.	Greens: $$ Carts: $ Rating: 72.8/72.0 Slope: 125/116	
SP ☺☺	**Wild Wood Country Club** W. Rush Rd., Rush. (716) 334-5860 18 holes. Par 71/72. Yards: 6,431/5,368 Apr.–Oct. High: July–Aug.	Greens: $–$$ Carts: $$ Rating: 70.2/70.1 Slope: 120/116	L S
SP ☺☺	**Winged Pheasant Golf Links** Sand Hill Rd., Shortsville. (716) 289-8846 18 holes. Par 70/72. Yards: 6,400/5,835 Mar.–Nov. High: June–Aug.	Greens: $–$$ Carts: $$ Rating: 69.0/72.0 Slope: 118/119	W L R T S J

Syracuse/Central New York

P ☺☺☺ DEAL	**Arrowhead Golf Course** E. Taft Rd., E. Syracuse. (315) 656-7563 18 holes. Par 72/73. Yards: 6,700/5,156 Apr.–Nov. High: May–Sept.	Greens: $ Carts: $ Rating: 70.9/68.5 Slope: 113/109	S J
P ☺☺	**Battle Island Golf Course** Rte. 48, Battle Island State Park, Fulton. (315) 592-3361 18 holes. Par 72/72. Yards: 5,973/5,561 Apr.–Nov. High: Aug.–Sept.	Greens: $ Carts: $ Rating: 67.9/68.7 Slope: 109/NA	W S J
SP ☺☺	**Camillus Country Club** Bennets Corners Rd., Camillus. (315) 672-3770 18 holes. Par 73/73. Yards: 6,368/5,573 Apr.–Nov. High: June–Aug.	Greens: $ Carts: $ Rating: 70.1/71.4 Slope: 115/110	W L S J
P ☺☺☺ DEAL	**Conklin Players Club** Conklin Rd., Conklin. (607) 775-3042 18 holes. Par 72/72. Yards: 6,772/4,699 Apr.–Nov. High: May–Oct.	Greens: $–$$ Carts: $ Rating: 72.5/67.8 Slope: 127/116	W L S
P ☺	**Drumlins West Golf Club** Nottingham Rd., Syracuse. (315) 446-5580 18 holes. Par 70/70. Yards: 6,030/4,790 Apr.–Nov. High: May–Aug.	Greens: $ Carts: $$ Rating: 68.2/71.0 Slope: 111	S J
SP ☺☺☺ DEAL	**Dutch Hollow Country Club** Benson Rd., Owasco. (315) 784-5052 18 holes. Par 71/72. Yards: 6,400/5,045 Apr.–Nov. High: May–Sept.	Greens: $ Carts: $ Rating: 70.3/70.3 Slope: 120/113	W L T S J
P ☺☺	**Elm Tree Golf Course** State Rte. 13, Cortland. (607) 753-1341 18 holes. Par 72/72. Yards: 6,251/5,520 Apr.–Nov. High: June–Aug.	Greens: $ Carts: $ Rating: 66.4/66.3 Slope: 100/99	W L R T S J

New York Golf Guide

Syracuse/Central New York

P ☺☺☺ DEAL	**Foxfire Golf Club** Village Blvd., Baldwinsville. (315) 638-2930 18 holes. Par 72/72. Yards: 6,887/5,405 Mar.–Nov. High: June–Aug.	Greens: Carts: Rating: Slope:	$–$$ S J $ 72.8/71.5 127/115

P ☺☺☺ DEAL STATE	**Green Lakes State Park Golf Club** Green Lakes Rd., Fayetteville. (315) 637-0258 18 holes. Par 71/74. Yards: 6,212/5,481 Apr.–Nov. High: May–Sept.	Greens: Carts: Rating: Slope:	$ $$ 68.4/70.6 113/120

P ☺☺	**Liverpool Golf and Country Club** Morgan Rd., Liverpool. (315) 457-7170 18 holes. Par 71/69. Yards: 6,412/5,487 Year-round. High: Apr.–Nov.	Greens: Carts: Rating: Slope:	$ W L T S J $ 70.7/69.3 114/113

P ☺☺	**Massena Country Club** Rte. 131, Massena. (315) 769-2293 18 holes. Par 71/74. Yards: 6,602/5,361 May–Oct. High: June–Aug.	Greens: Carts: Rating: Slope:	$$ L T $$ 70.1/71.4 110/111

SP ☺☺☺☺ DEAL STATE	**Radisson Greens Golf Club** Potter Rd., Baldwinsville. (315) 638-0092 18 holes. Par 72/73. Yards: 7,010/5,543 Apr.–Nov. High: May–Sept.	Greens: Carts: Rating: Slope:	$–$$ S $$ 73.3/70.0 128/124

SP ☺☺☺☺	**Seven Oaks Golf Club** East Lake St., Hamilton. (315) 824-1432 18 holes. Par 72/72. Yards: 6,915/5,849 Apr.–Oct. High: June–Aug.	Greens: Carts: Rating: Slope:	$$–$$$ R $ NA 128/125

Utica-Rome Area

P ☺☺	**Domenico's Golf Course** Church Rd., Whitesboro. (315) 736-9812 18 holes. Par 72/75. Yards: 6,715/5,458 Mar.–Nov. High: May–Aug.	Greens: Carts: Rating: Slope:	$ W T $ 70.5/71.5 118/NA

SP ☺☺	**Rome Country Club** Rte. 69, Rome. (315) 336-6464 18 holes. Par 72/75. Yards: 6,775/5,505 Year-round. High: May–Aug.	Greens: Carts: Rating: Slope:	$–$$ W $$ 71.8/70.4 125/NA

SP ☺☺☺ DEAL	**Thendara Golf Club** Rte. 28, Thendara. (315) 369-3136 18 holes. Par 72/73. Yards: 6,435/5,757 May–Oct. High: July–Sept.	Greens: Carts: Rating: Slope:	$$ T Inquire 70.2/72.8 124/121

Adirondack Region

P ☺☺	**Adirondack Golf & Country Club** Peru. (518) 643-8403, (800) 346-1761 18 holes. Par 72/72. Yards: 6,851/5,069 Mar.–Dec. High: July–Aug.	Greens: Carts: Rating: Slope:	$–$$ W L T S J Inquire 71.9/67.9 123/115

SP ☺☺☺ DEAL	**Bluff Point Golf & Country Club** Bluff Point Dr., Plattsburgh. (518) 563-3420 18 holes. Par 72/72. Yards: 6,309/5,295 Apr.–Nov. High: June–Sept.	Greens: Carts: Rating: Slope:	$$ L T $ 70.6/71.0 122/121

P ☺☺☺ DEAL	**Craig Wood Golf Course** Rte. 73, Lake Placid. (518) 523-9811 18 holes. Par 72/72. Yards: 6,554/5,500 May–Oct. High: July–Aug.	Greens: Carts: Rating: Slope:	$ R T $ 70.6/70.2 114/118

R ☺☺	**Lake Placid Resort** Mirror Lake Dr., Lake Placid. (518) 523-4460 *Lower Course*	Greens: Carts: Rating:	$$$$ L R T J $$ 69.0/73.0

New York Golf Guide

Adirondack Region

	18 holes. Par 70/74. Yards: 6,235/5,658 May–Oct. High: July–Aug.	Slope:	115/113

☺☺	*Upper Course* 18 holes. Par 70/75. Yards: 5,852/5,463	Rating: Slope:	69.0/72.0 115/NA

SP	**Malone Golf Club** Country Club Rd., Malone. (518) 483-2926	Greens: Carts:	$$ $$	T
☺☺☺ DEAL	*East Course* 18 holes. Par 72/73. Yards: 6,545/5,224 Apr.–Oct. High: June–Aug.	Rating: Slope:	71.9/70.1 127/115	

☺☺☺ DEAL	*West Course* 18 holes. Par 71/71. Yards: 6,592/5,272	Rating: Slope:	71.3/70.0 126/119

R ☺☺	**Thousand Islands Golf Club** Cty. Rd. 100, Wellesley Island. (315) 482-9454 18 holes. Par 72/74. Yards: 6,302/5,240 Apr.–Nov. High: June–Sept.	Greens: Carts: Rating: Slope:	$$ $$ 69.2/68.5 118/114	W L R T J

SP ☺☺☺ DEAL	**Watertown Golf Club** Watertown. (315) 782-4040 18 holes. Par 72/73. Yards: 6,309/5,492 Apr.–Oct. High: June–Aug.	Greens: Carts: Rating: Slope:	$$ $ 69.4/67.9 113/114	T

R ☺☺☺ DEAL	**Whiteface Inn Resort Golf Club** Lake Placid. (518) 523-2551 18 holes. Par 72/74. Yards: 6,490/5,635 May–Oct. High: July–Aug.	Greens: Carts: Rating: Slope:	$$ $$ 70.6/73.9 123/113	W L R T J

Albany/Capital District

P ☺☺	**Alban Hills Country Club** Alban Hills Dr., Johnstown. (518) 762-3717 18 holes. Par 70/70. Yards: 5,819/5,015 Apr.–Nov. High: June–Aug.	Greens: Carts: Rating: Slope:	$ $ 66.3/67.6 103/105	W L T S J

P ☺☺☺ DEAL	**Amsterdam Municipal Golf Course** Upper Van Dyke Ave., Amsterdam. (518) 842-4265 18 holes. Par 71/74. Yards: 6,370/5,352 Apr.–Nov. High: July–Aug.	Greens: Carts: Rating: Slope:	$ $$ 70.2/70.2 120/110	S

SP ☺☺☺	**Ballston Spa Country Club** Rte. 67, Ballston Spa. (518) 885-7935 18 holes. Par 71/74. Yards: 6,215/5,757 Apr.–Nov. High: June–Sept.	Greens: Carts: Rating: Slope:	$$$ Incl. 69.3/69.4 124/122

SP ☺☺☺ DEAL	**Hiland Golf Club** Haviland Rd., Queensbury. (518) 761-4653 18 holes. Par 72/72. Yards: 6,632/5,677 Apr.–Nov. High: June–Sept.	Greens: Carts: Rating: Slope:	$$ $ 73.0/72.9 135/123	W L T

P ☺☺	**The New Course at Albany** O'Neil Rd., Albany. (518) 489-3526 18 holes. Par 71/71. Yards: 6,300/4,990 Apr.–Nov. High: June–Aug.	Greens: Carts: Rating: Slope:	$ $ 69.4/72.0 117/113	T

R ☺☺☺☺ STATE	**The Sagamore Golf Club** Sagamore Rd., Bolton Landing. (518) 644-9400 18 holes. Par 70/71. Yards: 6,890/5,261 Apr.–Nov. High: May–Oct.	Greens: Carts: Rating: Slope:	$$$$ Incl. 72.9/73.0 130/122

P ☺☺☺ DEAL STATE	**Saratoga Spa Golf Course** Saratoga Spa SP, Saratoga Springs. (518) 584-2006 18 holes. Par 72/72. Yards: 7,149/5,649 Apr.–Nov. High: June–Aug.	Greens: Carts: Rating: Slope:	$ Inquire 73.7/72.5 130/122	S J

New York Golf Guide

Albany/Capital District

| P
☺☺ | **Schenectady Golf Course**
Oregon Ave., Schenectady. (518) 382-5155
18 holes. Par 72/72. Yards: 6,570/5,275
Apr.–Nov. High: May–Aug. | Greens:
Carts:
Rating:
Slope: | $
$
71.1/68.1
123/115 | S J |

Catskill Region

| R

☺☺☺ | **Concord Resort Hotel**
Kiamesha Lake. (914) 794-4000
International Golf Course
18 holes. Par 71/71. Yards: 5,968/5,564
Apr.–Nov. High: June–Aug. | Greens:
Carts:
Rating:
Slope: | $$$–$$$$
Incl.
71.8/73.6
124/125 | W R T |

| ☺☺☺☺
BEST | *Monster Golf Course*
18 holes. Par 72/72. Yards: 7,471/6,548 | Greens:
Carts:
Rating:
Slope: | $$$$–$$$$$
Incl.
76.4/78.5
142/144 | W R T |

| R

☺☺☺☺
STATE | **Grossinger Resort**
Rte. 52 E., Liberty. (914) 292-9000
Lake/Valley/Vista
27 holes. Par 72/72/72. Yards: 6,839/6,750/6,625
Apr.–Nov. High: June–Sept. | Greens:
Carts:
Rating:
Slope: | $$–$$$$
Incl.
72.9/72.5/72.1
134/133/132 | W L R T |

| R
☺☺☺ | **Kutsher's Country Club**
Kutsher Rd., Monticello. (914) 794-6000
18 holes. Par 71/71. Yards: 7,001/5,676
Apr.–Nov. High: July–Aug. | Greens:
Carts:
Rating:
Slope: | $$$
Incl.
73.5/72.3
123/119 | R T |

| R
☺☺☺
DEAL | **Nevele Country Club**
Rte. 209, Ellenville. (800) 647-6000
18 holes. Par 70/70. Yards: 6,600/4,600
Apr.–Dec. High: May–Sept. | Greens:
Carts:
Rating:
Slope: | $$
Inquire
71.9/71.1
128/126 | W R T |

| P
DEAL
☺☺☺ | **Tarry Brae Golf Club**
Pleasant Valley Rd., S. Fallsburg. (914) 434-2620
18 holes. Par 72/72. Yards: 6,888/6,270
Apr.–Nov. High: June–Sept. | Greens:
Carts:
Rating:
Slope: | $–$$
$
73.1/72.1
128/123 | W L T |

| R
☺☺☺
DEAL | **Tennanah Lake Golf & Tennis Club**
Hankins Rd., Roscoe. (607) 498-5502
18 holes. Par 72/74. Yards: 6,769/5,797
May–Oct. High: June–Aug. | Greens:
Carts:
Rating:
Slope: | $$
$$
71.2/72.5
121/115 | W R T S J |

Binghamton/Southern Tier

| SP
☺☺ | **Canasawacta Country Club**
Norwich. (607) 336-2685
18 holes. Par 72/72. Yards: 6,271/5,166
Apr.–Oct. High: June–Aug. | Greens:
Carts:
Rating:
Slope: | $–$$
$
69.9/68.8
120/114 | L T J |

| P
☺☺☺
DEAL
STATE | **En-Joie Golf Club**
W. Main St., Endicott. (607) 785-1661
18 holes. Par 72/74. Yards: 7,016/5,205
Mar.–Dec. High: May–Sept. | Greens:
Carts:
Rating:
Slope: | $–$$
$
73.0/69.8
125/118 | W L S J |

| P
☺☺☺
DEAL | **Endwell Greens Golf Club**
Sally Piper Rd., Endwell. (607) 785-4653
18 holes. Par 72/76. Yards: 7,053/5,382
Apr.–Nov. High: May–Aug. | Greens:
Carts:
Rating:
Slope: | $
$
73.6/70.6
121/117 | W L S |

| P
☺☺ | **The Links at Hiawatha Landing**
Marshland Rd., Apalachin. (607) 687-6952
18 holes. Par 72/72. Yards: 7,067/5,101
Apr.–Nov. High: June–Sept. | Greens:
Carts:
Rating:
Slope: | $$–$$$
Incl.
73.5/68.4
131/113 | W L T |

| P
☺☺☺ | **Mark Twain Golf Club**
Corning Rd., Elmira. (607) 737-5770 | Greens:
Carts: | $
$ | W T S J |

New York Golf Guide

Binghamton/Southern Tier

DEAL			Rating:	73.6/72.3

18 holes. Par 72/76. Yards: 6,829/5,571
Apr.–Oct. High: June–Aug.
Slope: 123/121

P	**Soaring Eagles Golf Club**	Greens:	$	T S J

☺☺☺ Middle Rd., Horseheads. (607) 796-9350 Carts: $$
DEAL 18 holes. Par 72/72. Yards: 6,625/4,930 Rating: 71.6/67.5
Apr.–Nov. High: June–Sept. Slope: 117/108

New York City/Northern Suburbs

SP **Blue Hill Golf Club** Greens: $$ W T
☺☺☺ Blue Hill Rd., Pearl River. (914) 735-2094 Carts: $$
DEAL 18 holes. Par 72/72. Yards: 6,471/5,651 Rating: 70.6/70.6
Mar.–Dec. High: June–Sept. Slope: 116/117

P **Dunwoodie Golf Club** Greens: $$–$$$ T S J
☺☺ Wasylenko Lane, Yonkers. (914) 968-2771 Carts: $$
18 holes. Par 70/72. Yards: 5,815/4,511 Rating: 68.3/67.8
Apr.–Dec. High: Apr.–Nov. Slope: 117/117

SP **Garrison Golf Club** Greens: $$–$$$ W T S
☺☺☺ Rte. 9, Garrison. (914) 424-3605 Carts: $
18 holes. Par 72/70. Yards: 6,470/5,041 Rating: 71.3/69.3
Apr.–Nov. High: June–Aug. Slope: 130/122

R **Hanah Country Club** Greens: $$–$$$ W L R T S
☺☺☺ Rte. 30, Margaretville. (914) 586-4849 Carts: $
18 holes. Par 72/72. Yards: 7,033/5,294 Rating: 73.5/69.7
Apr.–Oct. High: June–July Slope: 133/123

SP **IBM Mid-Hudson Valley Golf Course** Greens: $$ W T J
☺☺ South Rd., Poughkeepsie. (914) 433-2222 Carts: $$
18 holes. Par 72/72. Yards: 6,691/4,868 Rating: 72.4/67.9
Mar.–Dec. High: Mar.–Dec. Slope: 130/117

P **James Baird State Park Golf Club** Greens: $ L T S J
☺☺ Freedom Plains Rd., Pleasant Valley. (914) 473-1052 Carts: $$
18 holes. Par 71/74. Yards: 6,616/5,541 Rating: 71.3/75.2
Apr.–Nov. High: May–Aug. Slope: 124/131

P **La Tourette Golf Club** Greens: $$ T S J
☺☺ Richmond Hill Rd., Staten Island. (718) 351-1889 Carts: $$
18 holes. Par 72/72. Yards: 6,692/5,493 Rating: 70.7/70.9
Year-round. High: May–Sept. Slope: 119/115

P **McCann Memorial Golf Club** Greens: $$ S J
☺☺ Wilbur Rd., Poughkeepsie. (914) 471-3917 Carts: $$
18 holes. Par 72/72. Yards: 6,524/5,354 Rating: 72.0/71.4
Mar.–Dec. High: Apr.–Oct. Slope: 128/123

P **Mohansic Golf Club** Greens: $$–$$$ W T S J
☺☺ Baldwin Rd., Yorktown Heights. (914) 962-4049 Carts: $$
18 holes. Par 70/75. Yards: 6,500/5,594 Rating: 69.9/75.2
Apr.–Dec. High: June–Aug. Slope: 120/127

P **Pelham–Split Rock Golf Course** Greens: $ W T S J
Shore Rd., Bronx. (718) 885-1258 Carts: $
☺ *Pelham Course* Rating: 69.6/NA
18 holes. Par 71/71. Yards: 6,991/5,634 Slope: 114/115
Year-round. High: May–Sept.

☺ *Split Rock Course* Rating: 71.9/71.7
18 holes. Par 71/71. Yards: 6,714/5,509 Slope: 125/122

SP **Putnam Country Club** Greens: $–$$ W T S J
☺☺ Hill St., Mahopac. (914) 628-4200 Carts: $

New York Golf Guide

New York City/Northern Suburbs

	18 holes. Par 71/73. Yards: 6,774/5,799	Rating:	72.1/73.7	
	Apr.–Nov. High: June–Sept.	Slope:	131/132	
P	**Saxon Woods Golf Course**	Greens:	$–$$$	W T S J
☺☺	Mamaroneck Ave., Scarsdale. (914) 725-3814	Carts:	$$	
	18 holes. Par 71/73. Yards: 6,397/5,617	Rating:	70.2/71.2	
	Apr.–Dec. High: June–Aug.	Slope:	119/120	
P	**Segalla Country Club**	Greens:	$$	L T S J
☺☺☺	Amenia. (914) 373-9200	Carts:	Inquire	
DEAL	18 holes. Par 72/72. Yards: 6,617/5,601	Rating:	72.0/72.3	
	Apr.–Nov. High: May–Sept.	Slope:	133/129	
P	**Spook Rock Golf Course**	Greens:	$$–$$$	T
☺☺	Suffern. (914) 357-3085	Carts:	$$	
	18 holes. Par 72/72. Yards: 6,894/4,953	Rating:	73.3/70.9	
	Apr.–Nov. High: May–Sept.	Slope:	129/118	
P	**Stony Ford Golf Club**	Greens:	$–$$	W L T S
☺☺	Rte. 416, Montgomery. (914) 457-1532	Carts:	$	
	18 holes. Par 72/72. Yards: 6,550/4,856	Rating:	72.4/72.4	
	Apr.–Nov. High: May–Sept.	Slope:	128/128	
P	**Thomas Carvel Country Club**	Greens:	$$	W L T S
☺☺☺	Ferris Rd., Pine Plains. (518) 398-7101	Carts:	Incl.	
DEAL	18 holes. Par 73/75. Yards: 7,025/5,066	Rating:	73.5/69.0	
	Apr.–Nov. High: June–Sept.	Slope:	127/115	
P	**Town of Walkill Golf Club**	Greens:	$$	W T S
☺☺☺	Sands Rd., Middletown. (914) 361-1022	Carts:	$	
DEAL	18 holes. Par 72/72. Yards: 6,437/5,171	Rating:	NA	
	Apr.–Nov. High: June–Aug.	Slope:	128/122	
P	**Van Cortlandt Golf Club**	Greens:	$–$$	T S J
☺	Van Cortlandt Park, Bronx. (718) 543-4595	Carts:	$$	
	18 holes. Par 70/70. Yards: 6,122/5,421	Rating:	68.9/73.0	
	Mar.–Dec. High: Apr.–Oct.	Slope:	112/120	
SP	**Villa Roma Country Club**	Greens:	$$–$$$	W R T S
☺☺☺	Villa Roma Rd., Callicoon. (914) 887-5097	Carts:	Incl.	
	18 holes. Par 71/72. Yards: 6,231/4,791	Rating:	70.6/68.3	
	Apr.–Nov. High: May–Sept.	Slope:	125/117	

Long Island

P	**Bergen Point Country Club**	Greens:	$–$$	W L T S J
☺☺	Bergen Ave., W. Babylon. (516) 661-8282	Carts:	$	
	18 holes. Par 71/71. Yards: 6,637/5,707	Rating:	71.4/71.8	
	Mar.–Dec. High: June–Oct.	Slope:	120/122	
P	**Bethpage State Park Golf Courses**	Greens:	$–$$	W L T S
	Farmingdale. (516) 293-8899	Carts:	$	
☺☺☺☺	*Black Course*	Rating:	75.4/78.9	
BEST	18 holes. Par 71/71. Yards: 7,065/6,556	Slope:	144/146	
DEAL				
☺☺☺	*Blue Course*	Rating:	72.2/75.5	
DEAL	18 holes. Par 72/72. Yards: 6,684/6,213	Slope:	126/130	
☺☺☺	*Green Course*	Rating:	69.8/73.3	
DEAL	18 holes. Par 71/71. Yards: 6,267/5,903	Slope:	121/125	
☺☺☺	*Red Course*	Rating:	73.0/76.0	
DEAL	18 holes. Par 70/70. Yards: 6,756/6,198	Slope:	127/131	
☺☺	*Yellow Course*	Rating:	70.1/67.2	
	18 holes. Par 71/71. Yards: 6,316/5,680	Slope:	121/115	

New York Golf Guide

Long Island

P ☺☺☺ DEAL	**Crab Meadow Golf Club** Waterside Ave., Northport. (516) 757-8800 18 holes. Par 72/72. Yards: 6,575/5,807 Mar.–Dec. High: Apr.–Sept.	Greens: Carts: Rating: Slope:	$$ $$ 70.2/72.6 116/116	T S J
P ☺	**Eisenhower Park Golf** Eisenhower Park, E. Meadow. (516) 542-0015 *Blue Course* 18 holes. Par 72/72. Yards: 6,026/5,800 Year-round. High: May–Oct.	Greens: Carts: Rating: Slope:	$–$$ $$ 68.7/74.1 112/122	W L S
☺☺	*Red Course* 18 holes. Par 72/72. Yards: 6,756/5,449	Rating: Slope:	71.5/69.8 119/115	
☺	*White Course* 18 holes. Par 72/72. Yards: 6,269/5,920	Rating: Slope:	69.5/71.4 115/117	
SP ☺☺	**Hauppauge Country Club** Veterans Memorial Hwy., Hauppauge. (516) 724-7500 18 holes. Par 72/74. Yards: 6,525/5,925 Mar.–Dec. High: May–Oct.	Greens: Carts: Rating: Slope:	$$ $ 71.0/75.5 122/131	W L T S J
P ☺☺	**Indian Island Country Club** Riverside Dr., Riverhead. (516) 727-7776 18 holes. Par 72/72. Yards: 6,353/5,524 Mar.–Dec. High: May–Sept.	Greens: Carts: Rating: Slope:	$ $ 71.0/72.8 124/126	L T S J
R ☺☺	**Marriott's Golf Club at Wind Watch** Vanderbilt Motor Pkwy., Hauppauge. (516) 232-9850 18 holes. Par 71/71. Yards: 6,425/5,135 Year-round. High: Apr.–Oct.	Greens: Carts: Rating: Slope:	$$–$$$$ Incl. 71.2/68.6 133/118	L R T J
P ☺☺	**Middle Island Country Club** Yapank Rd., Middle Island. (516) 924-5100 *Dogwood/Oaktree/Spruce* 27 holes. Par 72/72/72. Yards: 6,934/7,027/7,015 Year-round. High: Apr.–Oct.	Greens: Carts: Rating: Slope:	$$ $ 73.4/73.4/73.4 128/128/128	
P ☺☺☺☺ BEST DEAL	**Montauk Downs State Park Golf Course** S. Fairview Ave., Montauk. (516) 668-1100 18 holes. Par 72/72. Yards: 6,762/5,797 Apr.–Dec. High: July–Sept.	Greens: Carts: Rating: Slope:	$$ $ 73.3/75.9 133/135	T S
P ☺☺☺	**Oyster Bay Town Golf Course** Southwood Rd., Woodbury. (516) 364-3977 18 holes. Par 70/70. Yards: 6,351/5,109 Year-round. High: Apr.–Oct.	Greens: Carts: Rating: Slope:	$$$ Inquire 71.5/70.4 131/126	W L T S J
P ☺☺☺ DEAL	**Rock Hill Country Club** Clancy Rd., Manorville. (516) 878-2250 18 holes. Par 71/72. Yards: 7,050/5,390 Year-round. High: May–Sept.	Greens: Carts: Rating: Slope:	$$ $$ 73.7/71.4 128/121	W L T S J
P ☺☺☺ DEAL	**Smithtown Landing Golf Club** Landing Ave., Smithtown. (516) 360-7618 18 holes. Par 72/72. Yards: 6,114/5,263 Year-round. High: May–Sept.	Greens: Carts: Rating: Slope:	$–$$ $ 70.9/69.8 125/122	W L
P ☺☺☺ DEAL	**Spring Lake Golf Club** E. Bartlett Rd., Middle Island. (516) 924-5115 18 holes. Par 72/72. Yards: 7,048/5,732 Year-round. High: Apr.–Oct.	Greens: Carts: Rating: Slope:	$$ $ 73.2/70.0 128/120	W T
P ☺☺	**Sunken Meadow State Park Golf Club** Sunken Meadow SP, Kings Park. (516) 269-3838 *Blue/Red/Green*	Greens: Carts: Rating:	$ Inquire 73.2/73.6/73.2	S

Long Island

	27 holes. Par 71/72/71. Yards: 6,100/6,165/6,185	Slope:	120/120/119
	Apr.–Nov. High: Apr.–Sept.		

P	**Swan Lake Golf Club**	Greens:	$$	T
☺☺☺	River Rd., Manorville. (516) 369-1818	Carts:	$$	
DEAL	18 holes. Par 72/72. Yards: 7,011/5,245	Rating:	72.5/69.0	
	Year-round. High: Apr.–Oct.	Slope:	121/112	

P	**Timber Point Golf Course**	Greens:	$–$$	W L T S J
	Great River Rd., Great River. (516) 581-2401	Carts:	$$	
☺	*Red/White/Blue*	Rating:	72.9/71.9/70.6	
	27 holes. Par 72/72/72. Yards: 6,642/6,525/6,441	Slope:	121/116/116	
	Year-round. High: June–Aug.			

P	**West Sayville Golf Club**	Greens:	$	W L T S J
☺☺	Montauk Hwy., W. Sayville. (516) 567-1704	Carts:	$	
	18 holes. Par 72/72. Yards: 6,715/5,387	Rating:	72.5/71.2	
	Year-round. High: May–Sept.	Slope:	124/119	

Pennsylvania

Eagle Lodge in Lafayette Hill just west of Philadelphia offers a long, hilly challenge. In Oxford, 55 miles southwest of Philly, you'll find **Wyncote**, a very difficult links-style course.

Center Valley near Allentown offers an interesting course with contrasting front and back nines, the first set open and the last tight.

Some courses smell of pines, others of money; at the **Hershey Country Club** the prevailing odor is chocolate. It's an old-style club in Hershey near Harrisburg, with modern amenities and maintenance. The West Course is the better of two courses, with the East just slightly behind. In Lebanon, about 15 miles east of Hershey, is **Royal Oaks**, a challenging links course in superb shape.

In State College is the **Toftrees Resort**, where every very wooded hole presents a different challenge and view.

Near Pittsburgh are the very tight **Champion Lakes** in Bolivar, and **Tom's Run** in Blairsville, home of nearly 100 sand traps.

Residents of both the Econoguide Best and the Econoguide Deals list are Center Valley, Champion Lakes, and Royal Oaks.

Many courses in Pennsylvania are open year-round, with peak rates in effect from about March to September.

Mountain-region courses and those in and around Lake Erie have a season from March to November, with peak rates usually charged from April to September.

Econoguide Leader Board: Best Public Courses in Pennsylvania

- ☺☺☺☺ Center Valley Club
- ☺☺☺☺ Champion Lakes Golf Course
- ☺☺☺☺ Eagle Lodge Country Club
- ☺☺☺☺ Hershey Country Club (West)
- ☺☺☺☺ Royal Oaks Golf Course
- ☺☺☺☺ Toftrees Resort

○○○○ Tom's Run Golf Course
○○○○ Wyncote Golf Club

Econoguide Leader Board: Best Deals in Pennsylvania

$/○○○	Bavarian Hills Golf Course
$$/○○○	Bucknell Golf Club
$$/○○○	Butler's Golf Course
$$/○○○	Carroll Valley Golf Resort (Mountain View, Carroll Valley)
$$/○○○	Cedarbrook Golf Course (Gold)
$$/○○○○	Center Valley Club
$$/○○○○	Champion Lakes Golf Course
$$/○○○	Chestnut Ridge Golf Club
$/○○○	Downing Golf Course
$/○○○	Downriver Golf Club
$/○○○	Edgewood in the Pines Golf Course
$/○○○	Emporium Country Club
$$/○○○	Fairview Golf Course
$/○○○	Flying Hills Golf Course
$$/○○○	Foxchase Golf Club
$$/○○○	Greencastle Greens Golf Club
$$/○○○	Hawk Valley Golf Club
$$/○○○	Heritage Hills Golf Resort
$$/○○○	Honey Run Golf and Country Club
$$/○○○	Iron Masters Country Club
$$/○○○	Locust Valley Golf Club
$$/○○○	Mayfield Golf Club
$/○○○	Mill Race Golf Course
$/○○○	Mohawk Trails Golf Course
$/○○○	North Hills Golf Club
$$/○○○	Penn National Golf Club
$$/○○○	Pennsylvania State University Golf Course (Blue)
$$/○○○	Pine Acres Country Club
$$/○○○	Riverside Golf Course
$$/○○○○	Royal Oaks Golf Course
$$/○○○	South Hills Golf Club
$$/○○○	State College Elks Country Club
$$/○○○	Stone Hedge Country Club
$/○○○	Sugarloaf Golf Club
$/○○○	Tam O'Shanter Golf Club
$$/○○○	Tamiment Resort and Conference Center
$$/○○○	Upper Perk Golf Course
$/○○○	White Deer Park and Golf Course (Challenge)
$$/○○○	White Tail Golf Club
$$/○○○	Wilkes-Barre Golf Club

Pennsylvania Golf Guide

Erie Area

P	**Cross Creek Resort** Titusville. (814) 827-9611	Greens: **$$** Carts: **$**	W L

Pennsylvania Golf Guide

Erie Area

☺☺	*North Course* 18 holes. Par 70/70. Yards: 6,495/5,285 Apr.–Oct. High: June–Aug.	Rating: Slope:	68.6 112/108	

P ☺☺☺ DEAL	**Downing Golf Course** Troupe Rd., Harborcreek. (814) 899-5827 18 holes. Par 72/74. Yards: 7,175/6,259 Year-round. High: Mar.–Nov.	Greens: Carts: Rating: Slope:	$ $ 73.0/74.4 114/115	L T

P ☺☺	**Erie Golf Club** Old Zuck Rd., Erie. (814) 866-0641 18 holes. Par 69/72. Yards: 5,682/4,977 Mar.–Nov. High: Apr.–Oct.	Greens: Carts: Rating: Slope:	$ $ 67.2/68.2 111/109	T

P ☺☺☺ DEAL	**North Hills Golf Club** N. Center St., Corry. (814) 664-4477 18 holes. Par 71/72. Yards: 6,800/5,146 Apr.–Oct. High: July–Aug.	Greens: Carts: Rating: Slope:	$ $ 71.0/71.4 115/119	W L T

P ☺☺☺ DEAL	**Riverside Golf Course** Cambridge Springs. (814) 398-4537 18 holes. Par 72/72. Yards: 6,113/5,232 Mar.–Oct. High: June–Sept.	Greens: Carts: Rating: Slope:	$$ Incl. 69.3/70.2 116/117	W L T

Scranton/Wilkes-Barre Area

P ☺☺☺ DEAL	**Edgewood in the Pines Golf Course** Edgewood Rd., Drums. (717) 788-1101 18 holes. Par 72/72. Yards: 6,721/5,184 Apr.–Nov. High: May–Aug.	Greens: Carts: Rating: Slope:	$$ Incl. 71.9/69.9 NA	W L T

P ☺☺	**Glen Brook Country Club** Glenbrook Rd., Stroudsburg. (717) 421-3680 18 holes. Par 72/72. Yards: 6,536/5,234 Apr.–Nov. High: May–Oct.	Greens: Carts: Rating: Slope:	$$ Incl. 71.4/69.4 123/117	W L R T S

R ☺☺☺ DEAL	**Mill Race Golf Course** Benton. (717) 925-2040 18 holes. Par 70/71. Yards: 6,096/4,791 Mar.–Nov. High: May–Aug.	Greens: Carts: Rating: Slope:	$ $ 68.6/68.3 126/122	W S J

R ☺☺☺	**Mount Airy Lodge Golf Course** Woodland Rd., Mount Pocono. (717) 839-8811 18 holes. Par 72/73. Yards: 7,123/5,771 Apr.–Nov. High: May–Sept.	Greens: Carts: Rating: Slope:	$$$ $ 74.3/73.3 138/122	W R T

P ☺☺	**Pocono Manor Inn and Golf Club** Pocono Manor. (717) 839-7111 *East Course* 18 holes. Par 72/72. Yards: 6,480/6,113 Apr.–Nov. High: May–Oct.	Greens: Carts: Rating: Slope:	$$–$$$ Incl. 71 NA	W R T

R ☺☺	**Shawnee Inn and Golf Resort** River Rd., Shawnee-on-Delaware. (717) 421-1500 *Blue/Red/White* 27 holes. Par 72/72/72. Yards: 6,589/6,665/6,800 Apr.–Nov. High: May–Aug.	Greens: Carts: Rating: Slope:	$$–$$$$ Incl. 72.4/72.8/72.2 131/129/132	W L R T

R ☺☺	**Skytop Lodge Golf Club** Skytop. (717) 595-8910 18 holes. Par 71/75. Yards: 6,256/5,683 Apr.–Oct. High: June–Sept.	Greens: Carts: Rating: Slope:	$$–$$$ $ 70.2/72.8 121/122	R

P ☺☺☺ DEAL	**Stone Hedge Country Club** Tunkhannock. (717) 836-5108 18 holes. Par 71/71. Yards: 6,506/4,992 Apr.–Dec. High: May–Sept.	Greens: Carts: Rating: Slope:	$–$$ $ 71.9/69.7 124/122	W L T S

Pennsylvania Golf Guide

Scranton/Wilkes-Barre Area

P ☺☺☺ DEAL	**Sugarloaf Golf Club** Sugarloaf. (717) 384-4097 18 holes. Par 72/72. Yards: 6,845/5,620 Mar.–Nov. High: July–Aug.	Greens: Carts: Rating: Slope:	$ T $$ 73.0/72.8 122/120
R ☺☺☺ DEAL	**Tamiment Resort and Conference Center** Bushkill Falls Rd., Tamiment. (717) 588-6652 18 holes. Par 72/72. Yards: 6,858/5,598 Apr.–Nov. High: May–Sept.	Greens: Carts: Rating: Slope:	$$ W L R T J $ 72.7/71.9 130/124
SP ☺☺	**Water Gap Golf Club** Mtn. Rd., Delaware Water Gap. (717) 476-0200 18 holes. Par 72/72. Yards: 6,186/5,175 Mar.–Nov. High: July–Sept.	Greens: Carts: Rating: Slope:	$$–$$$ W Incl. 70.0 125/114
P ☺☺☺ DEAL	**Wilkes-Barre Golf Club** Wilkes-Barre. (717) 472-3590 18 holes. Par 72/74. Yards: 6,912/5,690 Apr.–Nov. High: June–Aug.	Greens: Carts: Rating: Slope:	$$ W L T S J $ 72.8/73.2 125/115

North Central Pennsylvania

P ☺☺☺ DEAL	**Bavarian Hills Golf Course** Mulligan Rd., St. Mary's. (814) 834-3602 18 holes. Par 71/73. Yards: 6,290/4,845 Year-round. High: June–Aug.	Greens: Carts: Rating: Slope:	$ T J $ NA NA
SP ☺☺	**Corey Creek Golf Club** U.S. Rte. 6 E., Mansfield. (717) 662-3520 18 holes. Par 72/72. Yards: 6,571/4,920 Apr.–Nov. High: May–Oct.	Greens: Carts: Rating: Slope:	$–$$ W L T $ 71.1/66.0 120/110
SP ☺☺☺ DEAL	**Emporium Country Club** Cameron Rd., Emporium. (814) 486-7715 18 holes. Par 72/72. Yards: 6,032/5,233 Mar.–Nov. High: Apr.–Sept.	Greens: Carts: Rating: Slope:	$ W T J $ 68.5/69.0 118/115
SP ☺☺☺ DEAL	**Pine Acres Country Club** W. Warren Rd., Bradford. (814) 362-2005 18 holes. Par 72/72. Yards: 6,700/5,600 Apr.–Oct. High: June–Aug.	Greens: Carts: Rating: Slope:	$–$$ W L S J $ 70.3/72.3 120/120
P ☺☺☺ DEAL	**White Deer Park and Golf Course** Montgomery. (717) 547-2186 *Challenge Course* 18 holes. Par 72/72. Yards: 6,605/4,742 Year-round. High: May–Sept.	Greens: Carts: Rating: Slope:	$ W L S J $ 71.6/68.4 133/125
☺☺	*Vintage Course* 18 holes. Par 72/72. Yards: 6,405/4,843	Rating: Slope:	69.7/68.5 122/120

Pittsburgh Area

P ☺☺☺ DEAL	**Butler's Golf Course** Rock Run Rd., Elizabeth. (412) 751-9121 18 holes. Par 72/NA. Yards: 6,616/NA Year-round. High: Apr.–Oct.	Greens: Carts: Rating: Slope:	$–$$ W L T S J $ 70.3/NA 115/NA
P ☺☺	**Castle Hills Golf Course** W. Oakwood Way, New Castle. (412) 652-8122 18 holes. Par 72/73. Yards: 6,415/5,784 Mar.–Dec. High: May–Sept.	Greens: Carts: Rating: Slope:	$ L S J $ 69.7/73.3 118/113
P ☺☺☺ DEAL	**Cedarbrook Golf Course** Belle Vernon. (412) 929-8300 *Gold Course* 18 holes. Par 72/72. Yards: 6,701/5,211 Year-round. High: Apr.–Sept.	Greens: Carts: Rating: Slope:	$–$$ L S J $ 71.6/68.6 135/123

Pennsylvania Golf Guide

Pittsburgh Area

◎◎	*Red Course* 18 holes. Par 71/71. Yards: 6,100/4,600	Rating: Slope:	67.2/64.6 118/107

P ◎◎◎◎ DEAL STATE	**Champion Lakes Golf Course** Bolivar. (412) 238-5440 18 holes. Par 71/74. Yards: 6,608/5,556 Apr.–Dec. High: May–Sept.	Greens: Carts: Rating: Slope:	$$ $ 69.0/72.1 128/127	W L

P ◎◎◎ DEAL	**Chestnut Ridge Golf Club** Blairsville. (412) 459-7188 18 holes. Par 72/72. Yards: 6,321/5,130 Apr.–Nov. High: May–Sept.	Greens: Carts: Rating: Slope:	$$ $ 70.7/70.2 129/119	W

R ◎◎	**Conley's Resort Inn** Pittsburgh Rd., Butler. (412) 586-7711 18 holes. Par 72/72. Yards: 6,200/5,625 Year-round. High: Apr.–Oct.	Greens: Carts: Rating: Slope:	$–$$ $ 69.0/69.0 110/110	W L R T S

P ◎◎	**Donegal Highlands Golf Club** Donegal. (412) 423-7888 18 holes. Par 72/72. Yards: 121/113 Mar.–Nov. High: June–Aug.	Greens: Carts: Rating: Slope:	$–$$ $$ 69.6/65.7 121/113	W L S J

P ◎◎	**Fox Run Golf Course** River Rd., Beaver Falls. (412) 847-3568 18 holes. Par 70/72. Yards: 6,488/5,337 Year-round. High: May–Sept.	Greens: Carts: Rating: Slope:	$ Inquire 69.6/72.2 113/117	L S

R ◎◎◎	**Golf Club at Hidden Valley** Craighead Dr., Hidden Valley. (814) 443-6454 18 holes. Par 72/72. Yards: 6,579/5,097 Apr.–Nov. High: June–Aug.	Greens: Carts: Rating: Slope:	$$–$$$ $ 73.5/69.2 142/129	W L R T

P ◎◎	**Hickory Heights Golf Club** Hickory Heights Dr., Bridgeville. (412) 257-0300 18 holes. Par 72/72. Yards: 6,504/5,057 Year-round. High: Apr.–Oct.	Greens: Carts: Rating: Slope:	$$ Inquire 71.8/69.6 132/126	W L T S J

P ◎◎	**Lenape Heights Golf Course** Ford City. (412) 763-2201 18 holes. Par 71/71. Yards: 6,145/4,869 Mar.–Nov. High: Apr.–Sept.	Greens: Carts: Rating: Slope:	$ $ 69.0/67.4 120/114	W

R ◎◎	**Linden Hall Golf Club** Dawson. (412) 529-2366 18 holes. Par 72/77. Yards: 6,675/5,900 Year-round. High: Mar.–Nov.	Greens: Carts: Rating: Slope:	$–$$ $$ 71.2/NA NA	W L R S J

P ◎◎◎ DEAL	**Mayfield Golf Club** Rte. 68, Clarion. (814) 226-8888 18 holes. Par 72/72. Yards: 6,990/5,439 Apr.–Oct. High: June–Aug.	Greens: Carts: Rating: Slope:	$–$$ $ 73.0/71.0 117/118	W

P ◎◎	**Meadowlink Golf Club** Bulltown Rd., Murrysville. (412) 327-8243 18 holes. Par 72/72. Yards: 6,139/5,103 Year-round. High: Apr.–Sept.	Greens: Carts: Rating: Slope:	$ $ 68.2/66.9 125/118	W L S

P ◎◎◎ DEAL	**Mohawk Trails Golf Course** New Castle. (412) 667-8570 18 holes. Par 72/NA. Yards: 6,324/NA Mar.–Dec. High: May–Sept.	Greens: Carts: Rating: Slope:	$ $ 70.3/NA 108/NA	W L S

P ◎◎	**Mount Odin Park Golf Club** Mt. Odin Park Dr., Greensburg. (412) 834-2640	Greens: Carts:	$ $

Pennsylvania Golf Guide

Pittsburgh Area

	18 holes. Par 70/72. Yards: 5,395/4,733	Rating:	65.0/68.0	
	Year-round. High: Apr.–Sept.	Slope:	108/104	

R
☺☺☺

Nemacolin Woodlands Resort
Rte. 40E, Farmington. (412) 329-6111
The Links Golf Club
18 holes. Par 71/71. Yards: 6,814/4,825
Apr.–Nov. High: May–Oct.

Greens: $$$–$$$$ W L T
Carts: Incl.
Rating: 73.0/68.1
Slope: 131/115

☺☺

Mystic Rock Golf Club
18 holes. Par 72/72. Yards: 7,196/4,991

Greens: $$$$$ L
Carts: Incl.
Rating: 73.7/69.9
Slope: 146

SP
☺☺

North Fork Golf and Tennis Club
Johnstown. (814) 288-2822
18 holes. Par 72/72. Yards: 6,470/5,762
Apr.–Oct. High: June–Aug.

Greens: $ S J
Carts: $
Rating: 71.1/72.0
Slope: 124/114

P
☺☺

Oakbrook Golf Course
Stoystown. (814) 629-5892
18 holes. Par 71/73. Yards: 5,935/5,530
Apr.–Nov. High: June–Aug.

Greens: $
Carts: Inquire
Rating: 67.4/70.4
Slope: 109/113

P
☺☺

Pittsburgh North Golf Club
Bakerstown Rd., Bakerstown. (412) 443-3800
18 holes. Par 72/73. Yards: 7,021/5,075
Year-round. High: June–Aug.

Greens: $–$$ L S J
Carts: $
Rating: 68.8/68.3
Slope: 128/114

P
☺☺☺

Quicksilver Golf Club
Quicksilver Rd., Midway. (412) 796-1811
18 holes. Par 72/74. Yards: 7,120/5,067
Mar.–Dec. High: May–Oct.

Greens: $$$$ L T S J
Carts: Incl.
Rating: 75.7/68.6
Slope: 145/115

R
☺☺☺

Seven Springs Mountain Resort Golf Course
Champion. (814) 352-7777
18 holes. Par 71/72. Yards: 6,360/4,934
Apr.–Oct. High: July–Aug.

Greens: $$$–$$$$ W L R T
Carts: Incl.
Rating: 70.6/68.3
Slope: 116/111

P
☺☺

Springdale Golf Club
Uniontown. (412) 439-4400
18 holes. Par 70/71. Yards: 6,100/5,350
Year-round. High: July–Aug.

Greens: $ W L S
Carts: $
Rating: 67.5/68.5
Slope: 115/115

P
☺☺☺
DEAL

Tam O'Shanter Golf Club
Rte. 18 M, Hermitage. (412) 981-3552
18 holes. Par 72/76. Yards: 6,537/5,385
Mar.–Nov. High: June–Sept.

Greens: $ W L R S J
Carts: $
Rating: 69.4/70.2
Slope: 121/113

P
☺☺☺☺
STATE

Tom's Run Golf Course
Blairsville. (412) 459-7188
18 holes. Par 72/72. Yards: 6,705/5,363
Apr.–Nov. High: Apr.–Nov.

Greens: $$$ W
Carts: $
Rating: 72.9/71.2
Slope: 134/126

Allentown/Reading/Bethlehem Area

P
☺☺

Allentown Municipal Golf Course
Tilghman St., Allentown. (610) 395-9926
18 holes. Par 73/73. Yards: 7,085/5,635
Year-round. High: May–Sept.

Greens: $ L T S J
Carts: $$
Rating: 72.0/71.3
Slope: 127/123

P
☺☺

Arrowhead Golf Course
Weavertown Rd., Douglassville. (610) 582-4258
Red/White
18 holes. Par 71/71. Yards: 6,002/6,002
Year-round.

Greens: $ W L T
Carts: $
Rating: 68.9/73.4
Slope: 116/124

Pennsylvania Golf Guide

Allentown/Reading/Bethlehem Area

P ⊙⊙	**Bethlehem Municipal Golf Club** Illicks Mills Rd., Bethlehem. (610) 691-9393 18 holes. Par 72/72. Yards: 6,830/5,119 Year-round. High: Mar.–Oct.	Greens: Carts: Rating: Slope:	$–$$ $ 70.6/69.1 112/NA	W T S J
P ⊙⊙	**Blackwood Golf Course** Red Corner Rd., Douglassville. (610) 385-6922 18 holes. Par 70/70. Yards: 6,403/4,826 Year-round. High: May–Sept.	Greens: Carts: Rating: Slope:	$ Inquire 68.6/62.0 115/95	W L T S
SP ⊙⊙⊙	**Buck Hill Golf Club** Buck Hill Falls. (717) 595-7730 *White/Blue/Red* 27 holes. Par 72/70/70. Yards: 6,450/6,150/6,300 Apr.–Nov. High: June–Sept.	Greens: Carts: Rating: Slope:	$$–$$$ $ 71.0/69.8/70.4 126/120/122	T
P ⊙⊙⊙⊙ DEAL STATE	**Center Valley Club** Center Valley Pkwy., Center Valley. (610) 791-5580 18 holes. Par 72/72. Yards: 6,904/4,932 Year-round. High: May–Oct.	Greens: Carts: Rating: Slope:	$$ $ 74.1/70.6 135/123	T
P ⊙⊙⊙ DEAL	**Fairview Golf Course** Rte. 72, Quentin. (717) 273-3411 18 holes. Par 71/73. Yards: 6,227/5,221 Year-round. High: May–Sept.	Greens: Carts: Rating: Slope:	$–$$ $ 69.2/72.9 106/115	W L T S J
P ⊙⊙⊙ DEAL	**Flying Hills Golf Course** Village Center Dr., Reading. (610) 775-4063 18 holes. Par 70/70. Yards: 6,023/5,176 Year-round. High: Mar.–Sept.	Greens: Carts: Rating: Slope:	$ $ 68.2/68.8 118/118	W L
P ⊙⊙	**Macoby Run Golf Course** McLeans Station Rd., Green Lane. (215) 541-0161 18 holes. Par 72/NA. Yards: 6,319/NA Year-round. High: May–Sept.	Greens: Carts: Rating: Slope:	$ $ 69.5/NA 118/NA	L T S J
P ⊙⊙	**Rich Maiden Golf Course** Fleetwood. (610) 926-1606 18 holes. Par 69/70. Yards: 5,635/5,145 Year-round. High: Apr.–Sept.	Greens: Carts: Rating: Slope:	$ $ 63.7/65.1 97/99	L T S
P ⊙⊙	**Wedgewood Golf Club** Limeport Pike, Coopersburg. (610) 797-4551 18 holes. Par 71/72. Yards: 6,162/5,622 Year-round. High: Apr.–Sept.	Greens: Carts: Rating: Slope:	$–$$ Incl. 68.8/65.8 122/108	W L T S
P ⊙⊙⊙ DEAL	**White Tail Golf Club** Klein Rd., Bath. (610) 837-9626 18 holes. Par 72/72. Yards: 6,432/5,228 Apr.–Dec. High: May–Sept.	Greens: Carts: Rating: Slope:	$–$$ $ 70.1/NA 113/NA	W T S J
P ⊙⊙	**Willow Hollow Golf Course** Prison Rd., Leesport. (610) 373-1505 18 holes. Par 70/70. Yards: 5,810/4,435 Year-round. High: May–Sept.	Greens: Carts: Rating: Slope:	$ $ 67.1/NA 105/90	W T S J

Altoona Area

P ⊙⊙⊙ DEAL	**Downriver Golf Club** Everett. (814) 652-5193 18 holes. Par 72/73. Yards: 6,855/5,513 Apr.–Nov. High: June–Sept.	Greens: Carts: Rating: Slope:	$ $ 70.5/71.6 115/118	W T J
SP ⊙⊙⊙ DEAL	**Iron Masters Country Club** Roaring Spring. (814) 224-2915 18 holes. Par 72/75. Yards: 6,644/5,683 Apr.–Dec. High: June–Aug.	Greens: Carts: Rating: Slope:	$$ $ 72.2/73.6 130/119	W

Pennsylvania Golf Guide

Harrisburg/York Area

P	**Blue Mountain View Golf Course**	Greens:	$	W L S J
⊙⊙	Blue Mtn. Dr., Fredericksburg. (717) 865-4401	Carts:	$$	
	18 holes. Par 71/73. Yards: 6,010/4,520	Rating:	68.2/64.9	
	Year-round. High: Apr.–Sept.	Slope:	110/101	

P	**Briarwood Golf Club**	Greens:	$–$$	W L R T S
	W. Market St., York. (717) 792-9776	Carts:	$	
⊙⊙	*East Course*	Rating:	69.7/67.8	
	18 holes. Par 72/72. Yards: 6,550/5,120	Slope:	116/112	
	Year-round. High: Mar.–Oct.			

| ⊙⊙ | *West Course* | Rating: | 69.7/67.3 | |
| | 18 holes. Par 70/70. Yards: 6,300/4,820 | Slope: | 119/112 | |

SP	**Bucknell Golf Club**	Greens:	$$	
⊙⊙⊙	Rte. 1, Lewisburg. (717) 523-8193	Carts:	$	
DEAL	18 holes. Par 70/71. Yards: 6,268/5,387	Rating:	70.3/71.2	
	Mar.–Nov. High: June–Aug.	Slope:	128/122	

P	**Carroll Valley Golf Resort**	Greens:	$–$$	W L R
⊙⊙⊙	*Mountain View Course.* Fairfield. (717) 642-5848	Carts:	$	
DEAL	18 holes. Par 71/70. Yards: 6,343/5,024	Rating:	70.2/68.2	
	Mar.–Nov. High: Apr.–Oct.	Slope:	122/113	

⊙⊙⊙	*Carroll Valley Course.* Fairfield. (717) 642-8252	Greens:	$$	L R
DEAL	18 holes. Par 71/72. Yards: 6,633/5,005	Carts:	$	
	Year-round. High: Apr.–Oct.	Rating:	71.2/67.6	
		Slope:	120/114	

P	**Cedar Ridge Golf Course**	Greens:	$	L T
⊙⊙	Barlow Two Taverns Rd., Gettysburg. (717) 359-4480	Carts:	$	
	18 holes. Par 72/NA. Yards: 6,132/5,546	Rating:	69.5/69.3	
	Year-round. High: Apr.–Nov.	Slope:	114/114	

P	**Greencastle Greens Golf Club**	Greens:	$–$$	W L T S J
⊙⊙⊙	Castlegreen Dr., Greencastle. (717) 597-1188	Carts:	$	
DEAL	18 holes. Par 72/74. Yards: 6,908/5,315	Rating:	72.6/70.3	
	Year-round. High: Apr.–Oct.	Slope:	129/124	

P	**Grandview Golf Club**	Greens:	$–$$	W L R T
⊙⊙	Carlisle Rd., York. (717) 764-2674	Carts:	$	
	18 holes. Par 72/73. Yards: 6,639/5,578	Rating:	70.5/71.1	
	Year-round. High: Apr.–Oct.	Slope:	119/120	

R	**Heritage Hills Golf Resort**	Greens:	$$	L T S
⊙⊙⊙	Mt. Rose Ave., York. (717) 755-4653	Carts:	$	
DEAL	18 holes. Par 71/71. Yards: 6,330/5,075	Rating:	70.6/69.5	
	Year-round. High: Apr.–Sept.	Slope:	120/116	

R	**Hershey Country Club**	Greens:	$$$$	W T
	E. Derry Rd., Hershey. (717) 533-2464	Carts:	Incl.	
⊙⊙⊙	*East Course*	Rating:	73.6/71.6	
	18 holes. Par 71/71. Yards: 7,061/5,645	Slope:	128/127	
	Year-round. High: May–Oct.			

⊙⊙⊙⊙	*West Course*	Greens:	$$$$$	W T
STATE	18 holes. Par 73/76. Yards: 6,860/5,908	Carts:	Incl.	
		Rating:	73.1/74.7	
		Slope:	131/127	

P	**Hershey Parkview Golf Course**	Greens:	$$–$$$	W T
⊙⊙⊙	West Derry Rd., Hershey. (717) 534-3450	Carts:	Inquire	
	18 holes. Par 70/71. Yards: 6,103/4,817	Rating:	69.8/69.6	
	Year-round. High: May–Oct.	Slope:	121/107	

Pennsylvania Golf Guide

Harrisburg/York Area

SP ☺☺☺ DEAL	**Honey Run Golf and Country Club** S. Salem Church Rd., York. (717) 792-9771 18 holes. Par 72/72. Yards: 6,797/5,948 Year-round. High: May–Aug.	Greens: Carts: Rating: Slope:	$$ $ 72.4/74.0 123/125	W L R T S J

P ☺	**Manada Golf Club** Grantville. (717) 469-2400 18 holes. Par 72/72. Yards: 6,705/5,276 Year-round. High: Apr.–Sept.	Greens: Carts: Rating: Slope:	$ $ 70.7/68.8 117/111	W L T S J

SP ☺☺☺ DEAL	**Penn National Golf Club** Fayetteville. (717) 352-3000 18 holes. Par 72/72. Yards: 6,919/5,331 Year-round. High: May–Oct.	Greens: Carts: Rating: Slope:	$–$$ $ 73.2/70.1 129/116	L T S J

P ☺☺☺ DEAL	**Pennsylvania State University Golf Course** W. College Ave., State College. (814) 865-4653 *Blue Course* 18 holes. Par 72/72. Yards: 6,525/5,128 Mar.–Nov. High: June–Sept.	Greens: Carts: Rating: Slope:	$–$$ $ 72.0/69.8 128/118	T

☺☺	*White Course* 18 holes. Par 70/70. Yards: 6,008/5,212	Rating: Slope:	68.2/69.4 115/116	

P ☺☺☺☺ DEAL STATE	**Royal Oaks Golf Course** W. Oak St., Lebanon. (717) 274-2212 18 holes. Par 71/71. Yards: 6,542/4,687 Year-round. High: Apr.–Nov.	Greens: Carts: Rating: Slope:	$–$$ $ 71.3/66.6 118/108	W L

P ☺☺☺ DEAL	**South Hills Golf Club** Westminster Ave., Hanover. (717) 637-7500 18 holes. Par 71/71. Yards: 6,575/5,749 Year-round. High: May–Oct.	Greens: Carts: Rating: Slope:	$–$$ $ 71.0/72.0 121/119	W L T

SP ☺☺☺ DEAL	**State College Elks Country Club** Rte. 322, Boalsburg. (814) 466-6451 18 holes. Par 71/72. Yards: 6,358/5,125 Apr.–Nov. High: May–Sept.	Greens: Carts: Rating: Slope:	$$ $$ 70.9/70.2 123/119	

R ☺☺☺☺ STATE	**Toftrees Resort** State College. (814) 238-7600 18 holes. Par 72/72. Yards: 7,018/5,555 Apr.–Nov. High: June–Sept.	Greens: Carts: Rating: Slope:	$$–$$$ Incl. 74.3/71.8 134/126	W L T J

SP ☺☺	**Towanda Country Club** Towanda. (717) 265-6939 18 holes. Par 71/76. Yards: 6,100/5,600 Apr.–Dec. High: May–Sept.	Greens: Carts: Rating: Slope:	$ $$ 68.0/67.0 119/102	S J

P ☺	**Valley Green Golf Course** Valley Green Rd., Etters. (717) 938-4200 18 holes. Par 71/71. Yards: 6,000/5,500 Mar.–Nov. High: Apr.–Oct.	Greens: Carts: Rating: Slope:	$ $ 67.0/67.0 110/109	W L T S J

Philadelphia Area

SP ☺☺	**Center Square Golf Club** Rte. 73, Center Square. (610) 584-5700 18 holes. Par 71/73. Yards: 6,296/5,598 Year-round. High: Apr.–Oct.	Greens: Carts: Rating: Slope:	$–$$ $$ 69.6/70.6 119/114	L T S

P ☺☺	**Cool Creek Country Club** Cool Creek Rd., Wrightsville. (717) 252-3691 18 holes. Par 71/71. Yards: 6,521/5,703 Year-round. High: Apr.–Oct.	Greens: Carts: Rating: Slope:	$–$$ $ 71.1/72.6 118/118	W L R T S J

Pennsylvania Golf Guide

Philadelphia Area

R	**Eagle Lodge Country Club**	Greens: $$$$$	L
☺☺☺☺	Ridge Pike and Manor Rd., Lafayette. (610) 825-9198	Carts: Incl.	
STATE	18 holes. Par 71/71. Yards: 6,759/5,260	Rating: 72.8/70.4	
	Year-round. High: Apr.–Oct.	Slope: 130/123	
P	**Five Ponds Golf Club**	Greens: $–$$	W L T S
☺☺	W. St. Rd., Warminster. (215) 956-9727	Carts: $	
	18 holes. Par 71/71. Yards: 6,760/5,430	Rating: 71.0/70.1	
	Year-round. High: Apr.–Sept.	Slope: 121/117	
P	**Fox Hollow Golf Club**	Greens: $–$$	W L T S J
☺☺	Trumbauersville Rd., Quakertown. (215) 538-1920	Carts: $	
	18 holes. Par 71/71. Yards: 6,595/5,411	Rating: 70.2/67.0	
	Year-round. High: May–Sept.	Slope: 117/106	
P	**Foxchase Golf Club**	Greens: $–$$	W L T S J
☺☺☺	Stevens Rd., Stevens. (717) 336-3673	Carts: Incl.	
DEAL	18 holes. Par 72/72. Yards: 6,689/4,690	Rating: 72.7/66.9	
	Year-round. High: May–Oct.	Slope: 124/116	
P	**General Washington Golf Course**	Greens: $–$$	L T S J
☺☺	Egypt Rd., Audubon. (610) 666-7602	Carts: $	
	18 holes. Par 70/72. Yards: 6,300/5,300	Rating: 67.5/67.4	
	Year-round. High: Apr.–Oct.	Slope: NA	
P	**Hawk Valley Golf Club**	Greens: $–$$	J
☺☺☺	Crestview Dr., Denver. (717) 445-5445	Carts: $	
DEAL	18 holes. Par 72/72. Yards: 6,628/5,661	Rating: 70.3/70.2	
	Year-round. High: Apr.–Nov.	Slope: 132/119	
P	**Limekiln Golf Club**	Greens: $$	T S
	Limekiln Pike, Ambler. (215) 643-0643	Carts: $	
☺☺	*Red/White/Blue*	Rating: 67.8/68.7/NA	
	27 holes. Par 70/70/70. Yards: 6,213/6,415/6,176	Slope: 114/114/NA	
	Year-round. High: May–July		
P	**Locust Valley Golf Club**	Greens: $–$$	L T S
☺☺☺	Locust Valley Rd., Coopersburg. (610) 282-4711	Carts: $	
DEAL	18 holes. Par 72/74. Yards: 6,451/5,444	Rating: 71.0/71.3	
	Mar.–Dec. High: May–Sept.	Slope: 132/121	
P	**Moccasin Run Golf Course**	Greens: $–$$	W L T S J
☺☺	Schoff Rd., Atglen. (610) 593-7341	Carts: $	
	18 holes. Par 72/72. Yards: 6,336/5,275	Rating: 69.0/67.7	
	Year-round. High: Apr.–Oct.	Slope: 113/113	
R	**Mountain Laurel Golf Club**	Greens: $$$	L R T S
☺☺☺	Rte. 534 and 180, White Haven. (717) 443-7424	Carts: Incl.	
	18 holes. Par 72/72. Yards: 6,798/5,631	Rating: 72.3/71.9	
	Apr.–Nov. High: June–Aug.	Slope: 113/113	
SP	**Mountain Manor Inn and Golf Club**	Greens: $–$$	W L R T
	Creek Rd., Marshall's Creek. (717) 223-1290	Carts: $$	
☺☺	*Blue/Yellow*	Rating: 68.5/68.5	
	18 holes. Par 71/71. Yards: 6,233/5,079	Slope: 115/115	
	Apr.–Oct.		
☺☺	*Orange/Silver*	Rating: 71.0/71.5	
	18 holes. Par 72/72. Yards: 6,426/5,146	Slope: 132/124	
SP	**Northampton Valley Country Club**	Greens: $–$$	W T S
☺☺	Rte. 232, Richboro. (215) 355-2234	Carts: $	
	18 holes. Par 71/76. Yards: 6,377/5,586	Rating: 69.2/70.0	
	Year-round. High: Apr.–Oct.	Slope: 123/118	

Pennsylvania Golf Guide

Philadelphia Area

P	**Overlook Golf Course**	Greens:	$–$$	L S
⊙⊙	Lititz Pike, Lancaster. (717) 569-9551	Carts:	$	
	18 holes. Par 70/71. Yards: 6,100/4,962	Rating:	69.2/68.4	
	Year-round. High: May–Aug.	Slope:	110/113	

P	**Pickering Valley Golf Club**	Greens:	$–$$	W T S
⊙⊙	S. White Horse Rd., Phoenixville. (610) 933-2223	Carts:	Incl.	
	18 holes. Par 72/72. Yards: 6,530/5,235	Rating:	70.3/64.5	
	Year-round. High: Apr.–Oct.	Slope:	122/111	

P	**Upper Perk Golf Course**	Greens:	$–$$	W L T S J
⊙⊙⊙	Rte. 663 and Ott Rd., Pennsburg. (215) 679-5594	Carts:	$$	
DEAL	18 holes. Par 71/71. Yards: 6,381/5,249	Rating:	70.0/69.6	
	Mar.–Dec. High: May–Sept.	Slope:	117/113	

P	**Valley Forge Golf Club**	Greens:	$–$$	
⊙	N. Gulf Rd., King of Prussia. (610) 337-1776	Carts:	$	
	18 holes. Par 71/73. Yards: 6,200/5,668	Rating:	68.9/71.1	
	Mar.–Nov. High: June–July	Slope:	107	

SP	**Wyncote Golf Club**	Greens:	$$–$$$	W T S J
⊙⊙⊙⊙	Wyncote Dr., Oxford. (610) 932-8900	Carts:	$	
STATE	18 holes. Par 72/72. Yards: 7,012/5,454	Rating:	73.8/71.6	
	Mar.–Dec. High: May–Oct.	Slope:	128/126	

Rhode Island

The small state of Rhode Island is limited in public golf course offerings, but visitors can count on at least three memorable places to play. The **North Kingstown Municipal Golf Course** lies alongside a Navy air base and the ocean, making for plenty of man-made and natural challenges. The **Richmond Country Club** feels like a very different place, stretching deep into the pines.

The **Triggs Memorial** course dates back to a Donald Ross design of 1927. It is a difficult challenge with a wee bit of a Scottish feel.

All three—North Kingstown, Richmond, and Triggs—also win spots on the Econoguide Deals list.

Courses in Rhode Island are generally open from March through November, with peak rates in effect in the summer months from June to September.

Econoguide Leader Board: Best Public Courses in Rhode Island

⊙⊙⊙   North Kingstown Municipal Golf Course
⊙⊙⊙   Richmond Country Club
⊙⊙⊙   Triggs Memorial Golf Course

Econoguide Leader Board: Best Deals in Rhode Island

$$/⊙⊙⊙   Exeter Country Club
$$/⊙⊙⊙   North Kingstown Municipal Golf Course
$$/⊙⊙⊙   Richmond Country Club
$$/⊙⊙⊙   Triggs Memorial Golf Course

Rhode Island Golf Guide

Providence/Newport Area

| P | **Country View Golf Club** | Greens: | $–$$ | W L T S |
| ⊙⊙ | Colwell Rd., Harrisville. (401) 568-7157 | Carts: | $$ | |

Rhode Island Golf Guide

Providence/Newport Area

	18 holes. Par 70/70. Yards: 6,067/4,755	Rating:	69.2/67.0	
	Mar.–Nov. High: June–Sept.	Slope:	119/105	
P ◎◎	**Cranston Country Club** Burlingame Rd., Cranston. (401) 826-1683 18 holes. Par 71/72. Yards: 6,750/5,499 Mar.–Dec. High: May–Sept.	Greens: Carts: Rating: Slope:	$$ $ 72.4/NA 124/NA	T S
P ◎◎◎ DEAL	**Exeter Country Club** Ten Rod Rd., Exeter. (401) 295-1178 18 holes. Par 72/72. Yards: 6,919/5,733 Mar.–Nov. High: June–Sept.	Greens: Carts: Rating: Slope:	$$ $ NA 123/115	L T
SP ◎◎	**Foster Country Club** Johnson Rd., Foster. (401) 397-7750 18 holes. Par 72/74. Yards: 6,200/5,500 Apr.–Nov. High: May–Aug.	Greens: Carts: Rating: Slope:	$–$$ $ 69.5/70.0 114/112	
SP ◎◎	**Green Valley Country Club** Union St., Portsmouth. (401) 849-2162 18 holes. Par 71/71. Yards: 6,830/5,459 Mar.–Dec. High: May–Sept.	Greens: Carts: Rating: Slope:	$$ $$ 72.0/69.5 126/120	W T
SP ◎◎	**Laurel Lane Golf Course** Laurel Lane, W. Kingston. (401) 783-3844 18 holes. Par 71/70. Yards: 5,806/5,381 Mar.–Dec. High: June–Sept.	Greens: Carts: Rating: Slope:	$ Inquire 68.1/70.8 113/115	T
P ◎◎◎ DEAL STATE	**North Kingstown Municipal Golf Course** Callahan Rd., N. Kingstown. (401) 294-4051 18 holes. Par 70/70. Yards: 6,161/5,227 Apr.–Nov. High: May–Oct.	Greens: Carts: Rating: Slope:	$–$$ $$ 69.7/69.5 119/115	W L T
P ◎◎◎ DEAL STATE	**Richmond Country Club** Sandy Pond Rd., Richmond. (401) 364-9200 18 holes. Par 71/71. Yards: 6,826/4,974 Apr.–Nov. High: June–Sept.	Greens: Carts: Rating: Slope:	$$ $$ 72.1/NA 121/NA	W T
P ◎◎◎ DEAL STATE	**Triggs Memorial Golf Course** Chalkstone Ave., Providence. (401) 521-8460 18 holes. Par 72/73. Yards: 6,596/5,598 Year-round. High: June–Aug.	Greens: Carts: Rating: Slope:	$$ $$ 71.9/NA 126/NA	L S
SP ◎◎	**Winnapaug Country Club** Shore Rd., Westerly. (401) 596-1237 18 holes. Par 72/72. Yards: 6,337/5,113 Year-round. High: June–Sept.	Greens: Carts: Rating: Slope:	$$ $ 68.9/69.0 113/110	T

Vermont

You'll find a very green mountain challenge at **Gleneagles Golf Course** in Manchester Village in southern Vermont's ski region. A bit farther east is the **Mount Snow Golf Club** in West Dover, a hilly challenge in the ski area.

The **Stratton Mountain Resort** is a bit farther north, home of the handsome and well-maintained Lake/Mountain/Forest nines, which feature views of the green off-season ski runs above.

In the central part of the state is the **Rutland Country Club**, an attractive course at the base of the mountains. In the north-central region is the **Sugarbush Golf Course** in Warren, set at the base of Sugarbush Mountain and surrounded by spectacular forest and hills.

East of Rutland, in lovely covered-bridge country, is the **Woodstock**

Courtesy of Killington Ski & Summer Resort, Killington, Vermont.
Photo © Bob Perry.

Country Club, a sandy course situated just behind the picturesque Woodstock Inn in the Kedron Valley.

Most courses in Vermont operate on a snow-country schedule. Expect peak rates from about June to August.

For a classic taste of New England, golf packages are available at the traditional Equinox Hotel or the elegant Charles Orvis Inn at The Equinox in Manchester Center. The golfing high season in snow country runs from about May to November; the rest of the year is high season for skiing. Rates that include golf start at about $205 per person for double-occupancy rooms.

One advantage to golfing in snow country, though, is the abundance of off-season hotels and guest houses near the ski areas. Look for nightly rates, not including golf, of $50–$100.

Another option is to stay in a ski chalet at one of Vermont's winter resorts. For example, the Killington Resort offers golf packages from mid-May to mid-October. Rates, including motel room, breakfast, and golf, are as low as $79 per person for double-occupancy rooms, with deluxe suites about $100 per person. Luxury condos with kitchens rent for as little as $95 for a one-bedroom unit, to about $200 for a three- or four-bedroom unit.

Econoguide Leader Board: Best Public Courses in Vermont

☺☺☺	Gleneagles Golf Course
☺☺☺	Mount Snow Golf Club
☺☺☺☺	Rutland Country Club
☺☺☺	Stratton Mountain Resort (Lake, Mountain, Forest)
☺☺☺	Sugarbush Golf Course
☺☺☺	Woodstock Country Club

Econoguide Leader Board: Best Deals in Vermont

$$/○○○	Country Club of Barre
$$/○○○	Crown Point Country Club
$$/○○○	Killington Golf Course
$$/○○○	Proctor-Pittsford Country Club

Vermont Golf Guide

St. Albans

SP ○○	**Champlain Country Club** St. Albans. (802) 527-1187 18 holes. Par 70/70. Yards: 6,145/5,217 Apr.–Oct. High: July–Aug.	Greens: $$ Carts: $$ Rating: 69.6/69.4 Slope: 120/106	W T J

Burlington Area

R ○○	**Basin Harbor Golf Club** Basin Harbor Rd., Vergennes. (802) 475-2309 18 holes. Par 72/72. Yards: 6,513/5,745 May–Oct. High: July–Aug.	Greens: $$ Carts: $$ Rating: 71.5/74.8 Slope: 122/125	W L R T J
SP ○○	**Kwiniaska Golf Club** Spear St., Shelburne. (802) 985-3672 18 holes. Par 72/72. Yards: 7,067/5,670 Apr.–Nov. High: June–Aug.	Greens: $$ Carts: $$ Rating: 72.5/72.6 Slope: 128/119	T
SP ○○	**Newport Country Club** Pine Hill Rd., Newport. (802) 334-2391 18 holes. Par 72/72. Yards: 6,117/5,312 Apr.–Oct. High: July–Aug.	Greens: $$ Carts: $ Rating: NA Slope: 120/111	T
SP ○○	**Rocky Ridge Golf Club** Ledge Rd., Burlington. (802) 482-2191 18 holes. Par 72/72. Yards: 6,000/5,230 Apr.–Nov. High: July–Aug.	Greens: $ Carts: $$ Rating: 69.1/68.7 Slope: 124/110	T
R ○○	**Stowe Golf Course** Cape Cod Rd., Stowe. (802) 253-4893 18 holes. Par 72/72. Yards: 6,206/5,346 May–Oct. High: July–Sept.	Greens: $$$ Carts: $ Rating: 70.4/66.5 Slope: 122/115	T
R ○○○ STATE	**Sugarbush Golf Course** Warren. (802) 583-2722 18 holes. Par 72/72. Yards: 6,524/5,187 May–Oct. High: July–Oct.	Greens: $$–$$$ Carts: $ Rating: 71.7/70.4 Slope: 128/119	W L R T J

Montpelier/Barre Area

P ○○○ DEAL	**Country Club of Barre** Plainfield Rd., Barre. (802) 476-7658 18 holes. Par 71/71. Yards: 6,191/5,515 Apr.–Oct. High: June–Aug.	Greens: $$ Carts: $ Rating: 70.2/72.0 Slope: 123/116	

Rutland Area

R ○○○ DEAL	**Killington Golf Course** Killington Rd., Killington. (802) 422-6700 18 holes. Par 72/72. Yards: 6,326/5,108 May–Oct.	Greens: $$ Carts: $ Rating: 70.6/71.2 Slope: 126/123	T J
P ○○○ DEAL	**Proctor-Pittsford Country Club** Corn Hill Rd., Pittsford. (802) 483-9379 18 holes. Par 70/72. Yards: 6,052/5,446 Apr.–Nov. High: July–Aug.	Greens: $$ Carts: $ Rating: 69.4/66.1 Slope: 121/115	T J
SP ○○○○ STATE	**Rutland Country Club** North Grove St., Rutland. (802) 773-7061 18 holes. Par 70/71. Yards: 6,100/5,446 Apr.–Oct. High: June–Aug.	Greens: $$$ Carts: $$ Rating: 69.7/71.6 Slope: 125/125	

Vermont Golf Guide

Rutland Area

R	**Stratton Mountain Resort**	Greens:	$$$–$$$$ W L R J
	Stratton Mountain. (802) 297-4114	Carts:	$
☺☺☺	*Lake/Mountain/Forest*	Rating:	71.2/71.2/72.0
STATE	27 holes. Par 72/72/72. Yards: 6,526/6,478/6,602	Slope:	125/126/125
	May–Oct. High: July–Aug.		

R	**Woodstock Country Club**	Greens:	$$$ W L R T
☺☺☺	The Green, Woodstock. (802) 457-6674	Carts:	$
STATE	18 holes. Par 69/71. Yards: 6,001/4,924	Rating:	69.0/67.0
	May–Nov. High: July–Aug.	Slope:	121/113

Southern Vermont

SP	**Crown Point Country Club**	Greens:	$$ W T J
☺☺☺	Weathersfield Center Rd., Springfield. (802) 885-1010	Carts:	$$
DEAL	18 holes. Par 72/72. Yards: 6,572/5,542	Rating:	72.0/71.3
	Apr.–Oct. High: May–Sept.	Slope:	123/117

R	**Gleneagles Golf Course**	Greens:	$$$$–$$$$$ T
☺☺☺	Rte. 7A, Manchester Village. (802) 362-3223	Carts:	$
STATE	18 holes. Par 71/71. Yards: 6,423/5,082	Rating:	71.3/65.2
	May–Oct.	Slope:	129/117

SP	**Haystack Golf Club**	Greens:	$$–$$$ W L R J
☺☺☺☺	Mann Rd., Wilmington. (802) 464-8301	Carts:	$
	18 holes. Par 72/74. Yards: 6,549/5,471	Rating:	71.5/71.3
	May–Nov. High: July–Aug.	Slope:	125/120

R	**Mount Snow Golf Club**	Greens:	$$$ L R T J
☺☺☺	West Dover. (802) 464-5642	Carts:	$
STATE	18 holes. Par 72/72. Yards: 6,894/5,839	Rating:	72.4/72.5
	May–Oct. High: July–Aug.	Slope:	130/118

Virginia

The Cascades Course at the **Homestead Resort** in far western Virginia at the base of the Allegheny Mountains is a famous but still-hidden mountain gem, probably the best course in the state. In Wintergreen, west of Charlottesville, is the Stoney Creek at Wintergreen Course at the **Wintergreen Resort**, a superior challenge at the foot of the Blue Ridge Mountains. Its front nine are located in a former cornfield and the back nine in a deep forest; also at Wintergreen is the Devil's Knob Golf Club, a well-regarded mountain course.

In Williamsburg, the Gold Course at the **Golden Horseshoe Golf Club** is an exceptional challenge in the historic colonial town, with a more modern island green at No. 16. The Blue/Gold Course at **Ford's Colony** in Williamsburg is a handsome test of golfing skills. Another excellent, tricky challenge is the River Course at the **Kingsmill Resort** in Williamsburg near the Busch Gardens theme park; it includes several watery challenges, including the sometimes foggy James River on the way home.

The Golden Eagle Course at the **Tides Inn** near Chesapeake Bay in Irvington has a lot of water, including a pair of long carries and some 120 bunkers.

Most courses in temperate Virginia are open year-round, with peak rates usually in effect from April to October. Mountain-region resorts, including the Homestead Resort in Hot Springs, are open from April to October, with peak rates in effect for much of the operating year.

The Kingsmill Resort in Williamsburg, a rolling green golfing heaven, has off-season pricing on its rooms and suites from December through April.

The famed Golden Horseshoe at the Williamsburg Inn has value-season pricing in January and February; leisure prices in March, June, September, and early November; summer rates in July and August; and highest peak rates in April, May, and October, and at Thanksgiving. Rates per person for rooms and unlimited golf vary from $176 during value season to $351 at peak times. To save more money, you can stay at the not-quite-as-posh Williamsburg Woodlands or the Governor's Inn, where golf and room deals run from a high season (mid-March to mid-November) of about $150 per person to about $120 in other months.

Econoguide Leader Board: Best Public Courses in Virginia

⊙⊙⊙⊙   Ford's Colony Country Club (Blue, Gold)
⊙⊙⊙⊙   Golden Horseshoe Golf Club (Gold)
⊙⊙⊙⊙   The Homestead Resort (Cascades)
⊙⊙⊙⊙   Kingsmill Resort (River)
⊙⊙⊙⊙   The Tides Inn (Golden Eagle)
⊙⊙⊙⊙   Wintergreen Resort (Devil's Knob, Stoney Creek)

Econoguide Leader Board: Best Deals in Virginia

$$/⊙⊙⊙	Bristow Manor Golf Club
$$/⊙⊙⊙	Bryce Resort Golf Course
$$/⊙⊙⊙	Caverns Country Club
$$/⊙⊙⊙	Draper Valley Golf Club
$/⊙⊙⊙	The Hamptons Golf Course
$$/⊙⊙⊙	Hanging Rock Golf Club
$/⊙⊙⊙	Lakeview Golf Course
$$/⊙⊙⊙	Lee's Hill Golfer's Club
$$/⊙⊙⊙	Meadows Farms Golf Course
$/⊙⊙⊙	Newport News Golf Club at Deer Run (Cardinal, Deer Run)
$$/⊙⊙⊙	Olde Mill Golf Course
$$/⊙⊙⊙	Pohick Bay Regional Golf Course
$$/⊙⊙⊙	Reston National Golf Course
$$/⊙⊙⊙	River's Bend Golf and Country Club
$$/⊙⊙⊙	Royal Virginia Golf Club
$$/⊙⊙⊙	Shenandoah Crossing Resort and Country Club
$/⊙⊙⊙	Sleepy Hole Golf Course
$/⊙⊙⊙	Suffolk Golf Course
$$/⊙⊙⊙	Sycamore Creek Golf Course
$/⊙⊙⊙	Wolf Creek Golf and Country Club

Virginia Golf Guide

Washington, D.C., Area

P ⊙⊙	**Algonkian Regional Park Golf Course** Sterling. (703) 450-4655 18 holes. Par 72/72. Yards: 7,015/5,795 Year-round. High: May–Dec.	Greens: $–$$ Carts: $$ Rating: 73.5/74.0 Slope: 125/113	W R S J
P ⊙⊙⊙	**Bristow Manor Golf Club** Valley View Dr., Bristow. (703) 368-3558	Greens: $$ Carts: $	W L T S J

Virginia Golf Guide

Washington, D.C., Area

DEAL	18 holes. Par 72/74. Yards: 7,102/5,527 Year-round. High: Mar.–Nov.	Rating: 72.9/73.4 Slope: 129/128

R ☺☺☺ DEAL	**Bryce Resort Golf Course** Basye. (703) 856-2124 18 holes. Par 72/72. Yards: 6,261/5,240 Mar.–Dec. High: May–Aug.	Greens: $–$$ W L R T Carts: $ Rating: 68.8/70.1 Slope: 122/120

R ☺☺☺ DEAL	**Caverns Country Club** Airport Rd., Luray. (703) 743-7111 18 holes. Par 72/72. Yards: 6,499/5,499 Year-round. High: Apr.–June, Sept.–Oct.	Greens: $–$$ Carts: $ Rating: 71.2/72.4 Slope: 117/120

P ☺☺	**The Greens of Fredericksburg** Plank Rd., Fredericksburg. (703) 786-8385 18 holes. Par 72/72. Yards: 6,921/5,486 Year-round. High: Mar.–June, Nov.	Greens: $$–$$$ W L R T Carts: Incl. Rating: 72.9/72.1 Slope: 135/124

P ☺☺	**Herndon Centennial Golf Club** Ferndale Ave., Herndon. (703) 471-5769 18 holes. Par 71/71. Yards: 6,445/5,025 Year-round. High: May–Sept.	Greens: $$ W S J Carts: $$ Rating: 68.7/69.0 Slope: 116/121

R ☺☺☺	**Lansdowne Golf Club** Woodridge Pkwy., Lansdowne. (703) 729-4071 18 holes. Par 72/72. Yards: 7,057/5,213 Year-round. High: Apr.–Nov.	Greens: $$$$$ L R J Carts: Incl. Rating: 73.3/75.0 Slope: 126/134

P ☺☺☺ DEAL	**Lee's Hill Golfer's Club** Old Dominion Pkwy., Fredericksburg. (703) 891-0111 18 holes. Par 72/72. Yards: 6,805/5,064 Year-round. High: Apr.–Oct.	Greens: $–$$ W L T S J Carts: $ Rating: 72.4/69.2 Slope: 128/115

P ☺☺☺ DEAL	**Meadows Farms Golf Course** Flat Run Rd., Locust Grove. (703) 854-9890 18 holes. Par 72/72. Yards: 7,005/4,541 Year-round. High: Apr.–Sept.	Greens: $$ L T S Carts: Incl. Rating: 73.2/65.2 Slope: 129/110

P ☺☺☺ DEAL	**Pohick Bay Regional Golf Course** Gunston Rd., Lorton. (703) 339-8585 18 holes. Par 72/72. Yards: 6,405/5,897 Year-round. High: Apr.–Nov.	Greens: $–$$ W L Carts: $ Rating: NA Slope: 131/126

P ☺☺☺ DEAL	**Reston National Golf Course** Sunrise Valley Dr., Reston. (703) 620-9333 18 holes. Par 71/72. Yards: 6,871/5,936 Year-round. High: Apr.–Oct.	Greens: $$ W L T S J Carts: $ Rating: 72.9/74.3 Slope: 126/132

P ☺☺	**South Wales Golf Course** Jeffersonton. (703) 451-1344 18 holes. Par 71/73. Yards: 7,077/5,020 Year-round. High: Apr.–Oct.	Greens: $–$$ W L T S Carts: $$ Rating: 73.2/68.5 Slope: 123/104

SP ☺☺	**Stoneleigh Golf Club** Prestwick Court, Round Hill. (703) 589-1402 18 holes. Par 72/71. Yards: 6,903/5,014 Year-round. High: Apr.–Oct.	Greens: $$$ Carts: Incl. Rating: 73.4/69.8 Slope: 132/119

P ☺☺	**Twin Lakes Golf Course** Clifton Rd., Clifton. (703) 631-9099 18 holes. Par 73/73. Yards: 7,010/5,935 Year-round. High: May–Sept.	Greens: $$ W S J Carts: $$ Rating: 73.0/72.6 Slope: 121/118

Northern Virginia

SP ☺☺☺	**Shenandoah Valley Golf Club** Rte. 2, Front Royal. (703) 636-4653	Greens: $–$$$ W L T Carts: Incl.

Virginia Golf Guide

Northern Virginia

	27 holes. Par 71/71/72. Yards: 6,121/6,330/6,399	Rating:	69.0/70.2/70.0
	Year-round. High: Mar.–Oct.	Slope:	115/117/116

R	**The Shenvale**	Greens:	$–$$	L R T
◐◐	New Market. (703) 740-9930	Carts:	$	
	27 holes. Par 71/71/71. Yards: 6,595/6,297/6,358	Rating:	71.1/70.1/70.1	
	Year-round. High: Apr.–Oct.	Slope:	120/119/117	

Charlottesville Area

SP	**Birdwood Golf Course**	Greens:	$–$$$	W L R T S J
◐◐◐	Rte. 250 W., Charlottesville. (804) 293-4653	Carts:	$	
	18 holes. Par 72/72. Yards: 6,820/5,041	Rating:	72.8/65.2	
	Year-round. High: Apr.–Oct.	Slope:	132/116	

SP	**Lakeview Golf Course**	Greens:	$	T
	Rte. 11, Harrisonburg. (703) 434-8937	Carts:	$	
◐◐◐	*Lake/Peak/Spring*	Rating:	71.0/71.3/70.9	
DEAL	27 holes. Par 72/72/72. Yards: 6,517/6,640/6,303	Slope:	119/121/120	
	Year-round. High: Apr.–Oct.			

P	**Royal Virginia Golf Club**	Greens:	$–$$	W L T S
◐◐◐	Dukes Rd., Hadensville. (804) 457-2041	Carts:	$	
DEAL	18 holes. Par 72/NA. Yards: 7,106/NA	Rating:	73.4/NA	
	Year-round. High: Dec.–Feb.	Slope:	131/NA	

R	**Shenandoah Crossing Resort and Country Club**	Greens:	$$	W L T S J
◐◐◐	Rte. 2, Gordonsville. (703) 832-9543	Carts:	Incl.	
DEAL	18 holes. Par 72/72. Yards: 6,192/4,713	Rating:	69.8/66.5	
	Year-round. High: May–Sept.	Slope:	119/111	

R	**Wintergreen Resort**	Greens:	$$$–$$$$	W L R
	Wintergreen. (804) 325-8240	Carts:	$	
◐◐◐◐	*Devil's Knob Golf Club*	Rating:	72.4/68.6	
STATE	18 holes. Par 70/70. Yards: 6,576/5,101	Slope:	126/118	
	Apr.–Nov. High: May–Oct.			

◐◐◐◐	*Stoney Creek at Wintergreen*	Rating:	74.0/72.0
BEST	18 holes. Par 72/72. Yards: 7,003/5,500	Slope:	132/125

Richmond Area

P	**Belmont Golf Course**	Greens:	$–$$	S J
◐◐	Hilliard Rd., Richmond. (804) 266-4929	Carts:	$	
	18 holes. Par 72/72. Yards: 6,350/5,418	Rating:	70.6/72.6	
	Year-round. High: Apr.–Oct.	Slope:	126/130	

SP	**Birkdale Golf and Country Club**	Greens:	$$	W L R T S J
◐◐	Royal Birkdale Dr., Chesterfield. (804) 739-8800	Carts:	Incl.	
	18 holes. Par 71/71. Yards: 6,544/4,459	Rating:	71.1/NA	
	Year-round. High: May–Oct.	Slope:	122/NA	

P	**The Crossings Golf Club**	Greens:	$$–$$$	W L S J
◐◐◐	Virginia Center Pkwy., Glen Allen. (804) 261-0000	Carts:	Incl.	
	18 holes. Par 72/72. Yards: 6,619/5,625	Rating:	70.7/73.2	
	Year-round.	Slope:	126/128	

P	**Glenwood Golf Club**	Greens:	$–$$	W T S J
◐◐	Creighton Rd., Richmond. (804) 226-1793	Carts:	$	
	18 holes. Par 71/75. Yards: 6,464/5,197	Rating:	70.0/72.1	
	Year-round. High: May–Oct.	Slope:	114/120	

SP	**Mill Quarter Plantation Golf Course**	Greens:	$–$$	W L R T S J
◐◐	Mill Quarter Dr., Powhatan. (804) 598-4221	Carts:	Inquire	
	18 holes. Par 72/72. Yards: 6,970/5,280	Rating:	73.2/NA	
	Year-round. High: Apr.–Sept.	Slope:	127/109	

Virginia Golf Guide

Richmond Area

SP ☺☺☺ DEAL	**River's Bend Golf and Country Club** Hogans Alley, Chester. (804) 530-1000 18 holes. Par 71/71. Yards: 6,671/4,932 Year-round. High: Apr.–Sept.	Greens: $–$$ W T S J Carts: $ Rating: 71.9/67.8 Slope: 132/117
P ☺☺☺ DEAL	**Sycamore Creek Golf Course** Manakin Rd., Manakin Sabot. (804) 784-3544 18 holes. Par 70/70. Yards: 6,256/5,149 Year-round. High: Apr.–Oct.	Greens: $$ W L T S J Carts: Incl. Rating: 69.7/64.6 Slope: 124/114

Southwest Virginia

SP ☺☺☺ DEAL	**Wolf Creek Golf and Country Club** Rte. 1, Bastian. (703) 688-4610 18 holes. Par 71/71. Yards: 6,215/4,788 Year-round. High: Apr.–Oct.	Greens: $ W L R T S J Carts: $ Rating: 68.7/71.0 Slope: 107/128

Roanoke Area

P ☺☺☺ DEAL	**Draper Valley Golf Club** Rte. 1, Draper. (703) 980-4653 18 holes. Par 72/72. Yards: 7,046/4,793 Year-round. High: Mar.–Nov.	Greens: $–$$ W L Carts: $ Rating: 73.3/65.6 Slope: 125/113
P ☺☺☺ DEAL	**Hanging Rock Golf Club** Red Lane, Salem. (703) 389-7275 18 holes. Par 72/72. Yards: 6,828/4,463 Year-round. High: Apr.–Oct.	Greens: $–$$ W L R T S J Carts: $ Rating: 72.3/62.6 Slope: 125/106
R ☺☺☺☺ BEST	**The Homestead Resort** Hot Springs. *Cascades Course.* (703) 839-7994 18 holes. Par 70/71. Yards: 6,566/5,448 Apr.–Oct. High: Apr.–Oct.	Greens: $$$$–$$$$$ L R T J Carts: $ Rating: 72.9/72.9 Slope: 136/137
☺☺☺	*Homestead Course.* (703) 839-7740 18 holes. Par 72/72. Yards: 6,200/5,150	Greens: $$$–$$$$ L R T J Carts: $ Rating: 70.1/70.0 Slope: 121/117
☺☺☺	*Lower Cascades Course.* (703) 839-7995 18 holes. Par 72/72. Yards: 6,619/4,726	Greens: $$$$ L R T J Carts: $ Rating: 72.2/65.5 Slope: 127/116
R ☺☺☺ DEAL	**Olde Mill Golf Course** Rte. 1, Laurel Fork. (703) 398-2211 18 holes. Par 72/72. Yards: 6,833/4,876 Year-round. High: Apr.–Oct.	Greens: $$ W L R T Carts: $ Rating: 72.7/70.4 Slope: 127/134

Williamsburg Area

R ☺☺☺☺ STATE	**Ford's Colony Country Club** Ford's Colony Dr., Williamsburg. (804) 258-4130 *Blue/Gold Course* 18 holes. Par 71/71. Yards: 6,769/5,424 Year-round. High: Apr.–Oct.	Greens: $$$–$$$$$ W L R T Carts: Incl. Rating: 72.3/NA Slope: 124/109
☺☺☺	*Red/White Course* 18 holes. Par 72/72. Yards: 6,755/5,614	Rating: 72.3/73.2 Slope: 126/132
R ☺☺☺☺ BEST	**Golden Horseshoe Golf Club** S. England St., Williamsburg. (804) 220-7696 *Gold Course* 18 holes. Par 71/71. Yards: 6,700/5,159 Year-round. High: Apr.–Oct.	Greens: $$$$$–$$$$$$ L R T Carts: Incl. Rating: 73.1/66.2 Slope: 137/120
☺☺☺☺	*Green Course* 18 holes. Par 72/72. Yards: 7,120/5,348	Rating: 73.4/69.3 Slope: 134/109

Virginia Golf Guide

Williamsburg Area

R	**Kingsmill Resort**	Greens:	$$$–$$$$$$	L R T
	Kingsmill Rd., Williamsburg. (804) 253-3906	Carts:	Incl.	
☺☺☺	*Plantation Course*	Rating:	72.1/69.2	
	18 holes. Par 72/72. Yards: 6,605/4,880	Slope:	126/122	
	Year-round. High: Apr.–Oct.			
☺☺☺☺	*River Course*	Rating:	73.3/67.4	
STATE	18 holes. Par 71/71. Yards: 6,797/4,606	Slope:	137/109	
☺☺	*Woods Course*	Rating:	72.7/68.7	
	18 holes. Par 72/72. Yards: 6,784/5,140	Slope:	125/120	

Newport/Norfolk/Virginia Beach Area

P	**The Hamptons Golf Course**	Greens:	$	W L S J
☺☺☺	Butler Farm Rd., Hampton. (804) 766-9148	Carts:	$	
DEAL	27 holes. Par 71/71/70. Yards: 6,401/6,283/5,940	Rating:	69.9/69.4/67.8	
	Year-round. High: Mar.–Sept.	Slope:	110/110/106	
P	**Hell's Point Golf Course**	Greens:	$$–$$$	W L R T
☺☺☺	Atwoodtown Rd., Virginia Beach. (804) 721-3400	Carts:	Incl.	
	18 holes. Par 72/72. Yards: 6,966/5,003	Rating:	73.3/71.2	
	Year-round. High: May–Aug.	Slope:	130/116	
SP	**Honey Bee Golf Club**	Greens:	$$–$$$	W L T S J
☺☺☺	S. Indian Blvd., Virginia Beach. (804) 471-2768	Carts:	Incl.	
	18 holes. Par 72/72. Yards: 6,705/4,929	Rating:	69.6/67.0	
	Year-round. High: Mar.–Oct.	Slope:	123/104	
SP	**Kiln Creek Golf and Country Club**	Greens:	$$–$$$	W L
☺☺☺	Brick Kiln Blvd., Newport News. (804) 988-3220	Carts:	Incl.	
	18 holes. Par 72/72. Yards: 6,889/5,313	Rating:	73.4/69.5	
	Year-round. High: Apr.–Oct.	Slope:	130/119	
P	**Newport News Golf Club at Deer Run**	Greens:	$	W L S J
	Jefferson Ave., Newport News. (804) 886-7925	Carts:	$	
☺☺☺	*Cardinal Course*	Rating:	70.9/65.7	
DEAL	18 holes. Par 72/72. Yards: 6,624/5,603	Slope:	119/98	
	Year-round. High: Apr.–Nov.			
☺☺☺	*Deer Run Course*	Rating:	73.7/70.0	
DEAL	18 holes. Par 72/72. Yards: 7,081/6,322	Slope:	133/113	
P	**Red Wing Lake Golf Course**	Greens:	$$	S J
☺☺	Prosperity Rd., Virginia Beach. (804) 437-4845	Carts:	$	
	18 holes. Par 72/72. Yards: 7,080/5,285	Rating:	73.7/68.1	
	Year-round. High: Apr.–Oct.	Slope:	125/102	
P	**Sleepy Hole Golf Course**	Greens:	$	W S J
☺☺☺	Sleepy Hole Rd., Suffolk. (804) 538-4100	Carts:	$	
DEAL	18 holes. Par 71/72. Yards: 6,695/5,121	Rating:	71.7/64.8	
	Year-round. High: Apr.–Oct.	Slope:	122/108	
P	**Stumpy Lake Golf Club**	Greens:	$	W L T S J
☺☺	E. Indian River Rd., Virginia Beach. (804) 467-6119	Carts:	$	
	18 holes. Par 72/72. Yards: 6,800/5,200	Rating:	72.2/67.1	
	Year-round. High: Apr.–Oct.	Slope:	119/97	
P	**Suffolk Golf Course**	Greens:	$	S J
☺☺☺	Holland Rd., Suffolk. (804) 539-6298	Carts:	$	
DEAL	18 holes. Par 72/72. Yards: 6,340/5,561	Rating:	70.3/71.1	
	Year-round. High: May–Sept.	Slope:	121/112	
R	**The Tides Inn**	Greens:	$$–$$$$	W L R
	Golden Eagle Dr., Irvington. (804) 438-5501	Carts:	$	
☺☺☺☺	*Golden Eagle Golf Course*	Rating:	73.0/69.9	

Newport/Norfolk/Virginia Beach Area

STATE	18 holes. Par 72/72. Yards: Year-round. High: Apr.–Oct.		Slope:	130/121
R ☺☺☺	**The Tides Lodge Resort and Country Club** St. Andrews Lane, Irvington. (804) 438-6200 *The Tartan Course* 18 holes. Par 72/72. Yards: 6,586/5,121 Mar.–Dec. High: May–Oct.	Greens: Carts: Rating: Slope:	$$–$$$ $ 71.5/69.2 124/116	W L R T
P ☺☺	**Woodlands Golf Course** Woodland Rd., Hampton. (804) 727-1195 18 holes. Par 69/69. Yards: 5,482/4,399 Year-round. High: Apr.–Sept.	Greens: Carts: Rating: Slope:	$ $ 64.6/64.8 99/100	S J

Washington, D.C.

It's hard to believe that there are a handful of golf courses within the tight confines of the District of Columbia—none are so lavish as to warrant a congressional investigation, but at least you can air out your bag of clubs while on a business or tourist visit.

The best of the courses is probably the **Langston Golf Course**, which also wins a spot on the Econoguide Deals list. The Blue Course at the **East Potomac Park Golf Course** has great views of the city skyline, although the course has become a bit bedraggled. Finally, there is the **Rock Creek Park Golf Course**, a short, tight challenge in the city's best-known greensward.

You can expect courses to stay open year-round, although weather and conditions can be pretty grim in the winter and wiltingly hot in the summer. High season runs from late spring through the end of summer.

Econoguide Leader Board: Best Public Course in Washington, D.C.

☺ Langston Golf Course

Econoguide Leader Board: Best Deals in Washington, D.C.

$/☺   East Potomac Park Golf Course
$/☺   Langston Golf Course
$/☺   Rock Creek Park Golf Course

P ☺	**East Potomac Park Golf Course** Ohio Dr., Washington. (202) 554-7600 *Blue Course* 18 holes. Par: 72/72. Yards: 6,305/5,761 Year-round. High: May–Sept.	Greens: Carts: Rating: Slope:	$ $ 68.5/NA 109/NA	W S
P ☺ STATE	**Langston Golf Course** Benning Rd. N.E., Washington. (202) 397-8638 18 holes. Par: 72/NA. Yards: 6,340/NA Year-round. High: Mar.–Oct.	Greens: Carts: Rating: Slope:	$ $ 69.6/NA 112/NA	W
P ☺	**Rock Creek Park Golf Course** 16th & Rittenhouse St. N.W., Washington. (202) 882-7332 18 holes. Par: 65/65. Yards: 4,715/NA Year-round. High: June–Aug.	Greens: Carts: Rating: Slope:	$ $ 62.5/65.5 112/102	W S

The Central States

Illinois	Missouri
Indiana	Nebraska
Iowa	North Dakota
Kansas	Ohio
Kentucky	South Dakota
Michigan	West Virginia
Minnesota	Wisconsin

Illinois

The best of the public courses in the Land of Lincoln is probably No. 4 at **Cog Hill Golf Club** in Lemont, southwest of Chicago. Players say they need every club in their bag to survive its numerous sand and water hazards.

Two attractive courses are the tree-lined Woodside and Lakeside nines at **Cantigny Golf** in Wheaton, west of Chicago. Other Illinois courses of note include **Kemper Lakes** in Long Grove, north of Chicago, a woods-meadow-lake combination with some very technically demanding holes; **Pine Meadow** in Mundelein, also to the north; and the **George W. Dunne**, another woodsy wonderland.

All the way over in the northwest corner near Dubuque in the Mississippi River Valley are the winning North and South courses of **Eagle Ridge**. The ridge overlooks Lake Galena.

The best of our Econoguide Deals include the **Aldeen Golf Club**, **Balmoral Woods**, and **Heritage Bluffs**.

Some of the courses in Illinois operate year-round, especially those in the southern part of the state, particularly those near St. Louis. Elsewhere expect courses to be open from about April through November. Statewide peak rates are in effect during late spring and summer months.

Econoguide Leader Board: Best Public Courses in Illinois

☺☺☺☺	Cantigny Golf (Woodside, Lakeside, Hillside)
☺☺☺☺	Cog Hill Golf Club (No. 4)
☺☺☺☺	Eagle Ridge Inn and Resort (North, South)
☺☺☺	George W. Dunne National Golf Course
☺☺☺☺	Kemper Lakes Golf Course
☺☺☺☺	Pine Meadow Golf Club

Econoguide Leader Board: Best Deals in Illinois

$$/☺☺☺☺	Aldeen Golf Club
$$/☺☺☺	Balmoral Woods Country Club
$$/☺☺☺	Belk Park Golf Club
$$/☺☺☺	Big Run Golf Club
$$/☺☺☺	Blackberry Oaks Golf Course
$$/☺☺☺	Bonnie Brook Golf Club
$$/☺☺☺	Bon Vivant Country Club
$$/☺☺☺	Cog Hill Golf Club (No. 2)

$$/◎◎◎	Edgebrook Country Club
$$/◎◎◎	Fox Bend Golf Course
$$/◎◎◎	Fox Creek Golf Club
$$/◎◎◎	Glenwoodie Country Club
$$/◎◎◎◎	Heritage Bluffs Golf Course
$/◎◎◎	Hickory Point Golf Club
$$/◎◎◎	The Ledges Golf Club
$/◎◎◎	Lick Creek Golf Course
$$/◎◎◎	Marengo Ridge Golf Club
$$/◎◎◎	Naperbrook Golf Course
$/◎◎◎	Newman Golf Course
$$/◎◎◎	The Oak Club of Genoa
$$/◎◎◎	The Orchards Golf Club
$/◎◎◎	Park Hills Golf Club (West)
$$/◎◎◎	Pinecrest Golf & Country Club
$/◎◎◎◎	Prairie Vista Golf Course
$$/◎◎◎	Prairieview Golf Course
$$/◎◎◎	The Rail Golf Club
$$/◎◎◎	Rend Lake Golf Course
$$/◎◎◎	Sandy Hollow Golf Course
$$/◎◎◎	Schaumburg Golf Course
$$/◎◎◎	Silver Lake Country Club (South)
$$/◎◎◎	Springbrook Golf Course
$$/◎◎◎	Steeple Chase Golf Club
$$/◎◎◎	Timber Trails Country Club
$$/◎◎◎	Village Greens of Glen Ellyn
$$/◎◎◎	Wedgewood Golf Course
$/◎◎◎	Westview Golf Course

Illinois Golf Guide

Dubuque Area

R	**Eagle Ridge Inn and Resort**	Greens:	$$$$–$$$$$	L R T
	Galena. (815) 777-5200	Carts:	$	
◎◎◎◎	*North Course*	Rating:	73.4/72.3	
BEST	18 holes. Par 72/72. Yards: 6,836/5,578	Slope:	134/127	
	Apr.–Nov. High: May–Oct.			
◎◎◎◎	*South Course*	Rating:	72.9/72.4	
BEST	18 holes. Par 72/72. Yards: 6,762/5,609	Slope:	133/128	
P	**Lacoma Golf Course**	Greens:	$	
	Timmerman Rd., E. Dubuque. (815) 747-3874	Carts:	$	
◎◎	*Blue Course*	Rating:	71.5/70.9	
	18 holes. Par 72/72. Yards: 6,705/5,784	Slope:	118/117	
	Mar.–first snow. High: May–Sept.			
P	**The Ledges Golf Club**	Greens:	$–$$	W L T S J
◎◎◎	McCurry Rd., Roscoe. (815) 389-0979	Carts:	$	
DEAL	18 holes. Par 72/72. Yards: 6,740/5,881	Rating:	72.5/74.1	
	Apr.–Oct. High: May–Aug.	Slope:	129/129	
P	**Prairieview Golf Course**	Greens:	$–$$	W T S J
◎◎◎	N. River Rd., Byron. (815) 234-4653	Carts:	Inquire	

Illinois Golf Guide

Dubuque Area

DEAL	18 holes. Par 72/72. Yards: 6,893/5,658		Rating:	72.3/71.6
	Apr.–Oct. High: June–Aug.		Slope:	123/117

Rock Island

P	**Highland Springs Golf Course**		Greens:	$	W T S J
☺☺	35th St. W., Rock Island. (309) 787-5814		Carts:	Inquire
	18 holes. Par 72/72. Yards: 6,884/5,875		Rating:	73.0/69.0
	Apr.–Oct. High: June–Aug.		Slope:	118/NA

Chicago Area

P	**Aldeen Golf Club**		Greens:	$$	W T
☺☺☺☺	Reid Farm Rd., Rockford. (815) 282-4653		Carts:	$$
DEAL	18 holes. Par 72/72. Yards: 7,058/5,038		Rating:	73.6/69.1
	Apr.–Oct. High: June–Aug.		Slope:	126/115

P	**Arboretum Golf Club**		Greens:	$$	W L
☺☺	Half Day Rd., Buffalo Grove. (847) 913-1112		Carts:	Inquire
	18 holes. Par 72/72. Yards: 6,477/5,039		Rating:	71.1/68.7
	Mar.–Dec. High: June–Aug.		Slope:	132/118

P	**Balmoral Woods Country Club**		Greens:	$$	W L T S
☺☺☺	Crete. (708) 672-7448		Carts:	Incl.
DEAL	18 holes. Par 72/72. Yards: 6,683/5,282		Rating:	72.6/71.8
	Mar.–Nov. High: June–Aug.		Slope:	131/117

P	**Bartlett Hills Golf Course**		Greens:	$–$$	W L T S J
☺☺	W. Oneida, Bartlett. (630) 837-2741		Carts:	$
	18 holes. Par 71/71. Yards: 6,482/5,488		Rating:	71.2/71.8
	Year-round. High: Apr.–Sept.		Slope:	124/121

P	**Big Run Golf Club**		Greens:	$$	L T J
☺☺☺	W. 135th St., Lockport. (815) 838-1057		Carts:	$
DEAL	18 holes. Par 72/74. Yards: 6,980/6,090		Rating:	73.9/75.4
	Apr.–Nov. High: June–Aug.		Slope:	139/133

P	**Blackberry Oaks Golf Course**		Greens:	$$	T S J
☺☺☺	Kennedy Rd., Bristol. (630) 553-7170		Carts:	$$
DEAL	18 holes. Par 72/72. Yards: 6,258/5,230		Rating:	69.8/70.1
	Apr.–Nov. High: June–Aug.		Slope:	121/119

P	**Bonnie Brook Golf Club**		Greens:	$–$$	T S
☺☺☺	N. Lewis Ave., Waukegan. (847) 360-4730		Carts:	Inquire
DEAL	18 holes. Par 72/73. Yards: 6,701/5,559		Rating:	72.4/72.2
	Apr.–Nov. High: May–Sept.		Slope:	126/124

P	**The Burr Hill Club**		Greens:	$–$$	W L T
☺☺	Burr Rd., St. Charles. (630) 584-8236		Carts:	$
	18 holes. Par 72/72. Yards: 6,640/5,111		Rating:	72.5/70.9
	Year-round. High: May–Aug.		Slope:	128/120

P	**Cantigny Golf**		Greens:	$$$	S J
	Mack Rd., Wheaton. (630) 668-3323		Carts:	$
☺☺☺☺	*Woodside/Lakeside/Hillside*		Rating:	72.4/71.1/72.2
BEST	27 holes. Par 72/72/72. Yards: 6,709/6,625/6,760		Slope:	130/126/125
	Apr.–Oct. High: June–Aug.		

P	**Carillon Golf Club**		Greens:	$$–$$$	W L T S
☺☺☺	S. Carillon, Plainfield. (815) 886-2132		Carts:	Incl.
	18 holes. Par 71/71. Yards: 6,607/5,194		Rating:	71.1/68.4
	Mar.–Nov. High: June–Sept.		Slope:	121/108

P	**Cog Hill Golf Club**		Greens:	$–$$	W L
	Archer Ave., Lemont. (630) 257-5872		Carts:	$$
☺☺	*No. 1*		Rating:	69.9/71.3
	18 holes. Par 71/72. Yards: 6,329/5,594		Slope:	117/118
	Year-round. High: Apr.–Oct.		

Illinois Golf Guide

Chicago Area

☺☺☺ DEAL	*No. 2* 18 holes. Par 72/72. Yards: 6,268/5,564	Rating: 69.4/72.3 Slope: 120/120	
☺☺	*No. 3* 18 holes. Par 72/72. Yards: 6,437/5,321	Rating: 70.1/69.9 Slope: 117/114	
☺☺☺☺ BEST	*No. 4* 18 holes. Par 72/72. Yards: 6,930/5,874	Greens: $$$$$ Carts: Incl. Rating: 75.6/76.7 Slope: 142/134	W L
P ☺☺	**Deer Creek Golf Club** University Park. (708) 672-6667 18 holes. Par 72/72. Yards: 6,755/5,835 Year-round. High: May–Sept.	Greens: $–$$ Carts: $ Rating: 72.4/73.2 Slope: 124/120	W T S J
SP ☺☺☺ DEAL	**Edgebrook Country Club** Sudyam Rd., Sandwich. (815) 786-3058 18 holes. Par 72/72. Yards: 6,100/5,134 Year-round. High: June–Aug.	Greens: $$ Carts: $$ Rating: 69.1/69.5 Slope: 119/114	L
P ☺☺☺ DEAL	**Fox Bend Golf Course** Rte. 34, Oswego. (630) 554-3939 18 holes. Par 72/72. Yards: 6,800/5,600 Mar.–Dec. High: May–Sept.	Greens: $$ Carts: $ Rating: 71.4/72.5 Slope: 118/120	W L T S J
P ☺☺	**Fox Run Golf Links** Plum Grove Rd., Elk Grove Village. (847) 980-4653 18 holes. Par 70/70. Yards: 6,287/5,288 Apr.–Nov. High: June–Aug.	Greens: $$ Carts: $$ Rating: 70.5/70.2 Slope: 119/116	W T
P ☺☺☺ BEST	**George W. Dunne National Golf Course** S. Central, Oak Forest. (708) 535-3377 18 holes. Par 72/72. Yards: 7,170/5,535 Mar.–Dec. High: May–Aug.	Greens: $$–$$$ Carts: Inquire Rating: 75.1/71.4 Slope: 135/121	W T S J
P ☺☺	**Gleneagles Golf Club** McNulty Rd., Lemont. (630) 257-5466 *Red Course* 18 holes. Par 70/74. Yards: 6,090/6,090 Mar.–Dec. High: June–Aug.	Greens: $$ Carts: Inquire Rating: 67.6/71.3 Slope: 112/111	L T S
☺☺	*White Course* 18 holes. Par 70/75. Yards: 6,080/6,080	Rating: 68.7/72.3 Slope: 116/114	
P ☺☺☺ DEAL	**Glenwoodie Country Club** 193rd and State, Glenwood. (708) 758-1212 18 holes. Par 72/72. Yards: 6,715/5,176 Year-round. High: Apr.–Sept.	Greens: $–$$ Carts: Inquire Rating: 71.8/68.4 Slope: 120/108	W L T S J
R ☺☺	**The Golf Club at Oak Brook Hills** Midwest Rd., Oak Brook. (630) 850-5530 18 holes. Par 70/69. Yards: 6,372/5,152 Mar.–Nov. High: Apr.–Sept.	Greens: $$$–$$$$ Carts: Inquire Rating: 70.4/69.2 Slope: 122/114	W L T S
P ☺☺☺	**Golf Club of Illinois** Edgewood Rd., Algonquin. (847) 658-4400 18 holes. Par 71/71. Yards: 7,011/4,896 Mar.–Nov. High: May–Sept.	Greens: $$–$$$ Carts: $ Rating: 74.6/68.6 Slope: 133/115	W L T S J
P ☺☺☺☺ DEAL	**Heritage Bluffs Golf Course** W. Bluff Rd., Channahon. (815) 467-7888 18 holes. Par 72/72. Yards: 7,106/4,967 Apr.–Oct. High: May–Sept.	Greens: $$ Carts: $ Rating: 73.9/68.4 Slope: 132/112	W T S J

Illinois Golf Guide

Chicago Area

P	**Highland Park Country Club**	Greens: $$$	W L T
☺☺	Park Ave. W., Highland Park. (847) 433-9015	Carts: $	
	18 holes. Par 70/70. Yards: 6,522/5,353	Rating: 72.1/71.8	
	Apr.–Nov. High: May–Sept.	Slope: 130/122	
P	**Highland Woods Golf Course**	Greens: $$	W T
☺☺	N. Ela Rd., Hoffman Estates. (847) 202-0340	Carts: $$	
	18 holes. Par 72/72. Yards: 6,995/5,895	Rating: 72.5/72.0	
	Mar.–Dec. High: May–Sept.	Slope: 129/125	
P	**Hilldale Golf Club**	Greens: $$	W L T S
☺☺	Ardwick Dr., Hoffman Estates. (847) 310-1100	Carts: $	
	18 holes. Par 71/72. Yards: 6,432/5,409	Rating: 71.3/72.1	
	Apr.–Nov. High: June–Aug.	Slope: 125/121	
P	**Hughes Creek Golf Club**	Greens: $–$$	W L T S J
☺	Spring Valley Dr., Elburn. (630) 365-9200	Carts: $	
	18 holes. Par 72/72. Yards: 6,506/5,561	Rating: 70.9/71.7	
	Apr.–Nov. High: June–Aug.	Slope: 117/115	
R	**Indian Lakes Resort**	Greens: $$$	W L T
	W. Schick Rd., Bloomingdale. (630) 529-6466	Carts: Incl.	
☺	*Iroquois Course*	Rating: 72.4/NA	
	18 holes. Par 72/72. Yards: 6,923/6,239	Slope: 120/NA	
	Apr.–Nov. High: June–Sept.		
☺	*Sioux Course*	Rating: 72.1/NA	
	18 holes. Par 72/72. Yards: 6,803/6,225	Slope: 123/NA	
P	**Ingersoll Memorial Golf Club**	Greens: $–$$	T
☺☺	Daisyfield Rd., Rockford. (815) 987-8834	Carts: $$	
	18 holes. Par 71/74. Yards: 5,991/5,140	Rating: 68.2/73.3	
	Apr.–Oct.	Slope: 108/108	
P	**Kemper Lakes Golf Course**	Greens: $$$$$$	
☺☺☺☺	Old McHenry Rd., Long Grove. (847) 320-3450	Carts: Incl.	
BEST	18 holes. Par 72/72. Yards: 7,217/5,638	Rating: 75.7/67.9	
	Apr.–Nov. High: June–Aug.	Slope: 140/125	
P	**Klein Creek Golf Club**	Greens: $$$–$$$$	W
☺☺☺	Pleasant Hill Rd., Winfield. (630) 690-0101	Carts: Incl.	
	18 holes. Par 72/72. Yards: 6,673/4,509	Rating: 71.9/66.2	
	Apr.–Nov. High: June–Sept.	Slope: 127/110	
P	**Marengo Ridge Golf Club**	Greens: $–$$	W L T S J
☺☺☺	Harmony Hill Rd., Marengo. (815) 923-2332	Carts: $	
DEAL	18 holes. Par 72/73. Yards: 6,636/5,659	Rating: 71.4/72.2	
	Mar.–Dec. High: May–Sept.	Slope: 122/120	
R	**Marriott's Lincolnshire Resort**	Greens: $$–$$$	L T
☺☺	Lincolnshire. (847) 634-5935	Carts: Incl.	
	18 holes. Par 72/72. Yards: 6,313/4,892	Rating: 71.1/68.9	
	Apr.–Oct. High: May–Sept.	Slope: 129/117	
P	**Midlane Country Club**	Greens: $$–$$$	W L T S
☺☺☺	W. Yorkhouse Rd., Wadsworth. (847) 244-1990	Carts: Inquire	
	18 holes. Par 72/72. Yards: 7,073/5,635	Rating: 74.4/72.7	
	Mar.–Nov. High: June–Sept.	Slope: 132/124	
P	**Naperbrook Golf Course**	Greens: $$	W L T S J
☺☺☺	111th St., Plainfield. (630) 378-4215	Carts: $$	
DEAL	18 holes. Par 72/72. Yards: 6,755/5,381	Rating: 71.2/69.5	
	Mar.–Dec. High: June–Aug.	Slope: 120/112	
P	**Oak Brook Golf Club**	Greens: $$	T
☺☺	York Rd., Oak Brook. (630) 990-3032	Carts: $	

Illinois Golf Guide

Chicago Area

	18 holes. Par 72/72. Yards: 6,541/5,341	Rating:	71.2/70.9
	Mar.–Dec. High: Apr.–Sept.	Slope:	121/120

P
○○○
DEAL

The Oak Club of Genoa
Ellwood Greens Rd., Genoa. (815) 784-5678
18 holes. Par 72/72. Yards: 7,032/5,556
Mar.–Dec. High: May–Sept.

Greens: $$ W L T S
Carts: Incl.
Rating: 74.1/72.5
Slope: 135/127

P
○○○

Odyssey Golf Course
S. Ridgeland, Tinley Park. (708) 429-7400
18 holes. Par 72/72. Yards: 7,095/5,554
Apr.–Nov. High: June–Aug.

Greens: $–$$$ W L T
Carts: Incl.
Rating: 72.6/68.9
Slope: 128/112

P
○○

Old Oak Country Club
S. Parker Rd., Lockport. (708) 301-3344
18 holes. Par 71/72. Yards: 6,535/5,274
Apr.–Dec. High: June–Sept.

Greens: $$ W L T S J
Carts: $
Rating: 70.1/NA
Slope: 124/NA

P
○○○○

Orchard Valley Golf Club
W. Illinois Ave., Aurora. (630) 907-0500
18 holes. Par 72/72. Yards: 6,745/5,162
Apr.–Oct. High: June–Sept.

Greens: $$–$$$ T S J
Carts: $
Rating: 72.2/70.1
Slope: 132/118

P
○○

Palatine Hills Golf Course
W. Northwest Hwy., Palatine. (847) 359-4020
18 holes. Par 72/72. Yards: 6,800/5,975
Apr.–Nov. High: June–Aug.

Greens: $$–$$$ W L T
Carts: $
Rating: 71.6/73.1
Slope: 120/119

P

○○○
DEAL

Park Hills Golf Club
W. Stephenson, Freeport. (815) 235-3611
West Course
18 holes. Par 72/73. Yards: 6,622/5,940
Apr.–Nov. High: June–Aug.

Greens: $ W J
Carts: $
Rating: 71.3/76.2
Slope: 121/127

P
○○○○
BEST

Pine Meadow Golf Club
Mundelein. (847) 566-4653
18 holes. Par 72/72. Yards: 7,141/5,412
Mar.–Dec. High: Apr.–Nov.

Greens: $$$ T J
Carts: $
Rating: 74.4/70.9
Slope: 131/121

P
○○○
DEAL

Pinecrest Golf & Country Club
Algonquin Rd., Huntley. (847) 669-3111
18 holes. Par 72/72. Yards: 6,636/5,061
Mar.–Dec. High: June–Aug.

Greens: $$ T S J
Carts: $
Rating: 71.4/68.9
Slope: 119/112

P
○○○

Plum Tree National Golf Club
Lembcke Rd., Harvard. (815) 943-7474
18 holes. Par 72/72. Yards: 6,648/5,954
Apr.–Dec. High: June–Aug.

Greens: $$–$$$ L T S
Carts: Incl.
Rating: 72.9/74.9
Slope: 128/132

P
○○

Poplar Creek Country Club
Hoffman Estates. (847) 884-0219
18 holes. Par 72/72. Yards: 6,108/5,386
Mar.–Nov. High: June–Aug.

Greens: $$ T S J
Carts: $
Rating: 69.6/69.9
Slope: 124/118

P
○○○○

Prairie Landing Golf Course
W. Chicago. (630) 208-7600
18 holes. Par 72/72. Yards: 6,862/4,859
Apr.–Nov. High: May–Sept.

Greens: $$$$ L T J
Carts: Incl.
Rating: NA
Slope: NA

P
○○

Randall Oaks Golf Club
Binnie Rd., Dundee. (847) 428-5661
18 holes. Par 71/71. Yards: 6,160/5,379
Apr.–Nov. High: June–Aug.

Greens: $–$$ W T S J
Carts: $
Rating: 67.7/70.3
Slope: 113/110

SP
○○○

Ruffled Feathers Golf Club
Lemont. (630) 257-1000

Greens: $$$–$$$$$ W L T
Carts: Incl.

Illinois Golf Guide

Chicago Area

	18 holes. Par 72/72. Yards: 6,878/5,273 Mar.–Nov. High: Apr.–Oct.	Rating: 73.1/65.7 Slope: 134/110	
P ◎◎	**St. Andrews Golf and Country Club** W. Chicago. (630) 231-3100 *Lakewood Course* 18 holes. Par 72/72. Yards: 6,666/5,353 Year-round. High: May–Sept.	Greens: $$ Carts: $$ Rating: 71.1/69.4 Slope: 121/114	W L T J
◎◎	*St. Andrews Course* 18 holes. Par 71/71. Yards: 6,759/5,138	Rating: 71.2/68.2 Slope: 118/110	
P ◎◎◎ DEAL	**Sandy Hollow Golf Course** Rockford. (815) 987-8836 18 holes. Par 71/76. Yards: 6,228/5,883 Apr.–Oct. High: June–Aug.	Greens: $–$$ Carts: $$ Rating: 69.4/72.8 Slope: 113/113	T
P ◎◎◎ DEAL	**Schaumburg Golf Course** N. Roselle Rd., Schaumburg. (847) 885-9000 18 holes. Par 72/72. Yards: 6,522/4,885 Apr.–Dec. High: June–Aug.	Greens: $$ Carts: $ Rating: 70.6/67.2 Slope: 117/114	W T S J
P ◎◎◎	**Seven Bridges Golf Club** Woodridge. (630) 964-7777 18 holes. Par 72/72. Yards: 7,118/5,277 Apr.–Nov. High: May–Oct.	Greens: $$$–$$$$ Carts: Incl. Rating: 74.4/69.8 Slope: 132/118	
P ◎◎	**Silver Lake Country Club** 82nd Ave., Orland Park. (708) 349-6940 *North Course* 18 holes. Par 72/77. Yards: 6,826/5,659 Mar.–Jan. High: Apr.–Oct.	Greens: $$ Carts: $ Rating: 71.9/71.5 Slope: 116/116	W L T S J
◎◎◎ DEAL	*South Course* 18 holes. Par 70/72. Yards: 5,948/5,138	Rating: 67.9/69.3 Slope: 108/109	
P ◎◎	**Spartan Meadows Golf Club** Elgin. (847) 931-5950 18 holes. Par 72/72. Yards: 6,853/5,353 Apr.–Nov. High: May–Sept.	Greens: $–$$ Carts: $$ Rating: 72.7/70.3 Slope: 123/116	W L T S J
P ◎◎◎ DEAL	**Springbrook Golf Course** 83rd St., Naperville. (630) 420-4215 18 holes. Par 72/73. Yards: 6,896/5,850 Mar.–Dec.	Greens: $–$$ Carts: $$ Rating: 72.6/72.7 Slope: 124/125	W L T S J
P ◎◎◎ DEAL	**Steeple Chase Golf Club** N. La Vista Dr., Mundelein. (847) 949-8900 18 holes. Par 72/72. Yards: 6,827/4,831 Apr.–Nov. High: May–Sept.	Greens: $$ Carts: $ Rating: 73.1/68.1 Slope: 129/113	W T S J
P ◎◎	**Sunset Valley Golf Club** Sunset Rd., Highland Park. (847) 432-7140 18 holes. Par 72/72. Yards: 6,458/5,465 Mar.–Nov. High: Mar.–Aug.	Greens: $$ Carts: $ Rating: 70.5/71.6 Slope: 121/119	W L T S J
SP ◎◎	**Tamarack Golf Club** Royal Worlington Dr., Naperville. (630) 904-4004 18 holes. Par 70/70. Yards: 6,955/5,016 Mar.–Nov. High: June–Sept.	Greens: $$–$$$ Carts: Incl. Rating: 74.2/68.8 Slope: 131/114	W L T S
P ◎◎◎ DEAL	**Timber Trails Country Club** Plainfield Rd., La Grange. (708) 246-0275 18 holes. Par 71/73. Yards: 6,197/5,581 Mar.–Dec. High: May–Oct.	Greens: $$ Carts: $ Rating: 68.7/71.1 Slope: 113/116	L T S

Illinois Golf Guide

Chicago Area

P ☺☺	**Urban Hills Country Club** Crawford Ave., Richton Park. (708) 747-0306 18 holes. Par 71/71. Yards: 6,650/5,266 Year-round. High: Apr.–Oct.	Greens: $ Carts: $ Rating: 71.1/69.1 Slope: 114/110	W L T S J
P ☺☺	**Village Greens of Woodridge** W. 75th St., Woodridge. (630) 985-3610 18 holes. Par 72/73. Yards: 6,650/5,847 Mar.–Nov. High: May–Sept.	Greens: $$ Carts: $ Rating: 71.2/72.2 Slope: 121/119	W L T S J
P ☺☺☺ DEAL	**Village Greens of Glen Ellyn** Winchell Way, Glen Ellyn. (630) 469-8180 18 holes. Par 71/73. Yards: 6,933/5,753 Mar.–Nov. High: May–Sept.	Greens: $$ Carts: $ Rating: 73.5/73.3 Slope: 120/127	W L S J
P ☺☺☺ DEAL	**Wedgewood Golf Course** Rte. 59, Joliet. (815) 741-7270 18 holes. Par 72/72. Yards: 6,519/5,792 Apr.–Oct. High: June–Aug.	Greens: $–$$ Carts: $ Rating: 72.0/72.4 Slope: 119/123	W T S J
P ☺☺	**White Pines Golf Club** W. Jefferson, Bensenville. (630) 766-0304 *East Course* 18 holes. Par 71/74. Yards: 6,412/5,415 Year-round. High: May–Oct.	Greens: $$ Carts: $$ Rating: 71.1/71.4 Slope: 126/122	W L T
☺☺	*West Course* 18 holes. Par 72/74. Yards: 6,601/5,998	Rating: 71.5/73.4 Slope: 119/121	
P ☺☺	**Winnetka Golf Course** Oak St., Winnetka. (847) 501-2050 18 holes. Par 71/72. Yards: 6,458/5,857 Apr.–Dec. High: May–Aug.	Greens: $$ Carts: NA Rating: 70.9/73.3 Slope: 125/124	W L T

Kankakee Area

P ☺☺☺ DEAL	**Bon Vivant Country Club** Career Center Rd., Bourbonnais. (815) 935-0403 18 holes. Par 72/75. Yards: 7,498/5,979 Apr.–Nov. High: May–Sept.	Greens: $–$$ Carts: $ Rating: 76.2/74.7 Slope: 128/123	

Peoria Area

P ☺☺	**Bunker Links Municipal Golf Course** Lincoln Park Dr., Galesburg. (309) 344-1818 18 holes. Par 71/73. Yards: 5,934/5,354 Mar.–Nov. High: Apr.–Sept.	Greens: $ Carts: $ Rating: 67.4/69.4 Slope: 106/108	T
P ☺☺	**Illinois State University Golf Course** W. Gregory St., Normal. (309) 438-8065 18 holes. Par 71/73. Yards: 6,533/5,581 Mar.–Dec. High: May–Aug.	Greens: $ Carts: $ Rating: 71.1/71.8 Slope: 120/119	T S J
P ☺☺	**Kellogg Golf Course** N. Radnor Rd., Peoria. (309) 691-0293 18 holes. Par 72/72. Yards: 6,735/5,675 Mar.–Nov. High: June–Aug.	Greens: $ Carts: $ Rating: 70.9/71.5 Slope: 117/120	W T J
P ☺☺☺	**Lick Creek Golf Course** N. Parkway Dr., Pekin. (309) 346-0077 18 holes. Par 72/72. Yards: 6,909/5,729 Apr.–Nov. High: June–Sept.	Greens: $ Carts: $ Rating: 72.8/72.9 Slope: 128/125	W T S J
P ☺☺☺ DEAL	**Newman Golf Course** W. Nebraska, Peoria. (309) 674-1663 18 holes. Par 71/74. Yards: 6,838/5,933 Mar.–Nov. High: Apr.–Aug.	Greens: $ Carts: Inquire Rating: 71.8/74.2 Slope: 119/120	W T J

Illinois Golf Guide

Peoria Area

P	**Prairie Vista Golf Course**	Greens: $	T S J
○○○○	Sale Barn Rd., Bloomington. (309) 823-4217	Carts: Inquire	
DEAL	18 holes. Par 72/71. Yards: 6,748/5,224	Rating: 71.8/68.9	
	Mar.–Nov. High: May–July	Slope: 128/114	

P	**Railside Golf Club**	Greens: $	T S J
○○	W. 19th St., Gibson City. (217) 784-5000	Carts: $	
	18 holes. Par 72/72. Yards: 6,801/5,367	Rating: 71.8/70.2	
	Year-round. High: May–Sept.	Slope: 122/115	

Quincy

P	**Westview Golf Course**	Greens: $	L T
○○○	S. 36th St., Quincy. (217) 223-7499	Carts: $	
DEAL	18 holes. Par 71/71. Yards: 5,841/5,898	Rating: 70.1/70.2	
	Jan.–Dec. High: May–Aug.	Slope: 116/114	

Springfield/Decatur/Champaign Area

P	**Bunn Golf Course**	Greens: $	S J
○○	S. 11th, Springfield. (217) 522-2633	Carts: $	
	18 holes. Par 72/73. Yards: 6,104/5,355	Rating: 68.7/68.4	
	Mar.–Nov. High: June–July	Slope: 118/119	

R	**Eagle Creek Resort Golf Course**	Greens: $$–$$$	W L R T J
○○○	Eagle Creek State Park, Findlay. (217) 756-3456	Carts: Incl.	
	18 holes. Par 72/72. Yards: 6,908/4,978	Rating: 73.5/69.1	
	Year-round. High: May–Oct.	Slope: 132/115	

P	**Hickory Point Golf Club**	Greens: $	T S J
○○○	Weaver Rd., Decatur. (217) 421-7444	Carts: Inquire	
DEAL	18 holes. Par 72/72. Yards: 6,855/5,896	Rating: 71.4/NA	
	Mar.–Nov. High: June–Aug.	Slope: 121/NA	

P	**Lake of the Woods Golf Club**	Greens: $	S J
○○	Mahomet. (217) 586-2183	Carts: $	
	18 holes. Par 72/72. Yards: 6,520/5,187	Rating: 70.8/69.1	
	Mar.–Dec. High: June–Aug.	Slope: 118/112	

St. Louis Area

P	**Annbriar Golf Course**	Greens: $$$	L
○○○○	Waterloo. (618) 939-4653	Carts: Incl.	
	18 holes. Par 72/72. Yards: 6,841/4,792	Rating: 72.3/66.4	
	Year-round. High: Apr.–Oct.	Slope: 141/110	

P	**Belk Park Golf Club**	Greens: $$	L T J
○○○	Wood River. (618) 251-3115	Carts: $$	
DEAL	18 holes. Par 72/73. Yards: 6,761/5,726	Rating: 71.5/70.8	
	Year-round. High: May–Sept.	Slope: 121/118	

P	**Fox Creek Golf Club**	Greens: $$	W L T S
○○○	Fox Creek Dr., Edwardsville. (618) 692-9400	Carts: Incl.	
DEAL	18 holes. Par 72/72. Yards: 7,027/5,185	Rating: 74.9/72.1	
	Year-round. High: May–Sept.	Slope: 144/132	

P	**Lincoln Greens Golf Course**	Greens: $–$$	W T S J
○○	E. Lake Dr., Springfield. (217) 786-4000	Carts: $	
	18 holes. Par 72/72. Yards: 6,582/5,625	Rating: 70.3/70.9	
	Mar.–Dec. High: June–Aug.	Slope: 112/114	

P	**The Orchards Golf Club**	Greens: $–$$	W L T S J
○○○	Belleville. (618) 233-8921	Carts: $	
DEAL	18 holes. Par 71/71. Yards: 6,405/5,001	Rating: 69.0/70.1	
	Year-round. High: Apr.–Oct.	Slope: 121/120	

P	**The Rail Golf Club**	Greens: $$	S J
○○○	Springfield. (217) 525-0365	Carts: $	

St. Louis Area

DEAL	18 holes. Par 72/72. Yards: 6,583/5,406	Rating:	71.1/70.6	
	Mar.–Dec. High: May–Sept.	Slope:	120/116	
P	**Rend Lake Golf Course**	Greens:	$$	W S
⊙⊙⊙	Marcum Branch Rd., Benton. (618) 629-2353	Carts:	$	
DEAL	27 holes. Par 72/72/72. Yards: 6,861/6,812/6,835	Rating:	72.2/71.8/73.0	
	Mar.–Nov. High: May–Oct.	Slope:	130/131/133	
P	**Spencer T. Olin Community Golf Course**	Greens:	$$–$$$	W L T J
⊙⊙⊙⊙	College Ave., Alton. (618) 465-3111	Carts:	Incl.	
	18 holes. Par 72/72. Yards: 6,941/5,049	Rating:	73.8/68.5	
	Year-round. High: Apr.–Oct.	Slope:	135/117	

Indiana

The **Brickyard Crossing**, with four of its holes within auto racing's magic brick shrine in Indianapolis, is a challenging newer course. Near Louisville, Kentucky, is **Covered Bridge**, ranked as a bit less difficult but exceptionally beautiful.

Other winners near Indianapolis include **The Legends of Indiana, Otter Creek, Eagle Creek**, and the **Golf Club of Indiana**. Near Terre Haute is **Hulman Links**; in West Lafayette is the hilly South Course of **Purdue University**. Another hilly spot in this mostly flat state is the Hill Course at the **French Lick Springs Resort**, an old Donald Ross course.

The French Lick Springs Resort, the Golf Club of Indiana, Hulman Links, The Legends of Indiana, and Purdue University also appear on our Econoguide Deals list.

Many courses in Indiana are open year-round, although the best golfing— and the highest prices—can be found from spring through the end of summer.

Econoguide Leader Board: Best Public Courses in Indiana

⊙⊙⊙⊙	Brickyard Crossing Golf Club
⊙⊙⊙⊙	Covered Bridge Golf Club
⊙⊙⊙	Eagle Creek Golf Club
⊙⊙⊙	French Lick Springs Resort (Hill)
⊙⊙⊙	Golf Club of Indiana
⊙⊙⊙	Hulman Links Golf Course
⊙⊙⊙	The Legends of Indiana Golf Course
⊙⊙⊙	Otter Creek Golf Club
⊙⊙⊙	Purdue University Golf Course (South)

Econoguide Leader Board: Best Deals in Indiana

$$/⊙⊙⊙	Autumn Ridge Golf Club
$/⊙⊙⊙	Brookwood Golf Club
$/⊙⊙⊙	Elbel Park Golf Course
$/⊙⊙⊙	Erskine Park Golf Club
$$/⊙⊙⊙	Fox Prairie Golf Club
$$/⊙⊙⊙	French Lick Springs Resort (Hill)
$/⊙⊙⊙	Geneva Hills Golf Club

$$/☺☺☺	Golf Club of Indiana
$$/☺☺☺	Grand Oak Golf Club
$/☺☺☺	Green Acres Golf Club
$/☺☺☺	Hidden Creek Golf Club
$$/☺☺☺	Honeywell Golf Course
$$/☺☺☺	Hulman Links Golf Course
$/☺☺☺	Indiana University Golf Club
$$/☺☺☺	Juday Creek Golf Course
$$/☺☺☺	The Legends of Indiana Golf Course
$$/☺☺☺	The Links Golf Club
$/☺☺☺	Otis Park Golf Club
$$/☺☺☺	Pheasant Valley Golf Club
$/☺☺☺	Purdue University Gold Course (South)
$$/☺☺☺☺	Rock Hollow Golf Club
$$/☺☺☺	Royal Hylands Golf Club
$$/☺☺☺	Salt Creek Golf Club
$$/☺☺☺	Sultan's Run Golf Course
$/☺☺☺	Swan Lake Golf Club (East)
$/☺☺☺	Valley View Golf Club (Floyds Knobs)
$/☺☺☺	Valley View Golf Club (Middletown)
$/☺☺☺	Wabash Valley Golf Club
$/☺☺☺	Walnut Creek Golf Course
$/☺☺☺	Winchester Golf Club
$/☺☺☺	Zollner Golf Course at Tri-State University

Indiana Golf Guide

Gary Area

P ☺☺	**Black Squirrel Golf Club** Hwy. 119 S., Goshen. (219) 533-1828 18 holes. Par 72/72. Yards: 6,483/5,018 Mar.–Nov. High: June–Aug.	Greens: Carts: Rating: Slope:	$ $ 69.8/67.8 115/110	W L
P ☺☺☺☺	**Blackthorn Golf Club** Nimitz Pkwy., South Bend. (219) 232-4653 18 holes. Par 72/72. Yards: 7,105/5,036 Apr.–Nov. High: May–Sept.	Greens: Carts: Rating: Slope:	$$–$$$ $ 75.2/71.0 135/120	
P ☺☺	**Dykeman Park Golf Course** Eberts Rd., Logansport. (219) 753-0222 18 holes. Par 70/73. Yards: 6,185/5,347 Mar.–Dec. High: Apr.–Aug.	Greens: Carts: Rating: Slope:	$ $ 69.4/69.8 118/102	T S J
P ☺☺☺ DEAL	**Elbel Park Golf Course** Auten Rd., South Bend. (219) 271-9180 18 holes. Par 72/73. Yards: 6,700/5,750 Mar.–Dec. High: June–Aug.	Greens: Carts: Rating: Slope:	$ $ 70.7/71.4 113/114	W L T S J
P ☺☺☺ DEAL	**Erskine Park Golf Club** Miami St., South Bend. (219) 291-3216 18 holes. Par 70/76. Yards: 6,100/5,882 Mar.–Nov. High: Apr.–Sept.	Greens: Carts: Rating: Slope:	$ $ 69.0/69.1 121/121	T S J
P ☺☺	**Forest Park Golf Course** Sheffield Dr., Valparaiso. (219) 462-5144 18 holes. Par 70/72. Yards: 5,731/5,339 Apr.–Dec. High: June–Sept.	Greens: Carts: Rating: Slope:	$ $ 67.4/70.7 114/111	T J

Indiana Golf Guide

Gary Area

P ☺☺☺ DEAL	**Juday Creek Golf Course** Lindy Dr., Granger. (219) 277-4653 18 holes. Par 72/72. Yards: 6,940/5,000 Mar.–Oct. High: June–Sept.	Greens: $–$$ Carts: $ Rating: 73.3/67.1 Slope: 133/116	T S J
SP ☺☺	**Maxwelton Golf Club** E. Elkhart County Line Rd., Syracuse. (219) 457-3504 18 holes. Par 72/72. Yards: 6,490/5,992 Mar.–Nov. High: May–Sept.	Greens: $ Carts: $ Rating: 70.1/73.4 Slope: 124/128	
P ☺☺	**Michigan City Municipal Golf Course** E. Michigan Blvd., Michigan City. (219) 873-1516 18 holes. Par 72/74. Yards: 6,169/5,363 Apr.–Nov. High: June–Aug.	Greens: $ Carts: $ Rating: 67.6/68.6 Slope: 113/113	W L J
SP ☺☺	**Palmira Golf and Country Club** W. 109th St., St. John. (219) 365-4331 18 holes. Par 71/73. Yards: 6,421/5,863 Year-round. High: May–Sept.	Greens: $–$$ Carts: $$ Rating: 70.9/74.2 Slope: 118/117	W L T S J
SP ☺☺☺ DEAL	**Pheasant Valley Golf Club** W. 141st Ave., Crown Point. (219) 663-5000 18 holes. Par 72/73. Yards: 6,869/6,166 Apr.–Dec. High: May–Oct.	Greens: $–$$ Carts: $$ Rating: 72.3/72.6 Slope: 126/NA	W L T S J
P ☺☺☺☺ DEAL	**Rock Hollow Golf Club** County Rd., 250 W., Peru. (317) 473-6100 18 holes. Par 72/72. Yards: 6,994/4,967 Mar.–Oct. High: June–Sept.	Greens: $$ Carts: $ Rating: 74.0/64.8 Slope: 132/112	
P ☺☺	**Scherwood Golf Course** E. Joliet St., Schererville. (219) 865-2554 18 holes. Par 72/72. Yards: 6,710/5,053 Apr.–Dec. High: May–Sept.	Greens: $–$$ Carts: $ Rating: 72.0/67.3 Slope: 127/108	W L
P ☺☺☺ DEAL	**Swan Lake Golf Club** Plymouth LaPorte Trail, Plymouth. (219) 936-9798 *East Course* 18 holes. Par 72/72. Yards: 6,345/5,289 Mar.–Oct. High: Apr.–June	Greens: $ Carts: $ Rating: 69.9/69.4 Slope: 120/109	W T S
☺☺	*West Course* 18 holes. Par 72/72. Yards: 6,507/5,545	Rating: 70.5/71.7 Slope: 117/106	
P ☺☺	**Wicker Memorial Park Golf Course** Indianapolis Blvd., Highland. (219) 838-9809 18 holes. Par 72/73. Yards: 6,515/5,301 Year-round. High: May–Sept.	Greens: $ Carts: $ Rating: 70.8/69.3 Slope: 106/107	W L T S J

Fort Wayne Area

SP ☺☺☺ DEAL	**Autumn Ridge Golf Club** Old Auburn Rd., Fort Wayne. (219) 637-8727 18 holes. Par 72/72. Yards: 7,035/5,273 Mar.–Dec. High: May–Sept.	Greens: $$ Carts: $ Rating: 73.9/70.9 Slope: 134/122	L T S
P ☺☺☺ DEAL	**Brookwood Golf Club** Bluffton Rd., Fort Wayne. (219) 747-3136 18 holes. Par 72/73. Yards: 6,700/6,250 Mar.–Dec. High: Apr.–Sept.	Greens: $ Carts: $ Rating: 70.3/67.9 Slope: 123/111	
P ☺☺☺ DEAL	**Honeywell Golf Course** W. Division Rd., Wabash. (219) 563-8663 18 holes. Par 72/72. Yards: 6,550/5,650 Year-round. High: Mar.–Oct.	Greens: $–$$ Carts: $ Rating: 69.4/70.4 Slope: 120/124	W L
P ☺☺	**Riverbend Golf Course** St. Joe Rd., Fort Wayne. (219) 485-2732	Greens: $–$$ Carts: $	W L T S J

Indiana Golf Guide

Fort Wayne Area

	18 holes. Par 72/72. Yards: 6,702/5,633	Rating:	72.5/72.5
	Mar.–Oct. High: May–Sept.	Slope:	127/124

P	**Wabash Valley Golf Club**	Greens:	$
☺☺☺	North Dr., Geneva. (219) 368-7388	Carts:	$
DEAL	18 holes. Par 71/71. Yards: 6,375/5,018	Rating:	70.5/69.8
	Mar.–Nov. High: June–Aug.	Slope:	117/106

P	**Walnut Creek Golf Course**	Greens:	$
☺☺☺	E. 400 S., Marion. (317) 998-7651	Carts:	$
DEAL	18 holes. Par 72/72. Yards: 6,880/5,154	Rating:	72.1/68.5
	Apr.–Dec. High: June–Aug.	Slope:	121/109

P	**Zollner Golf Course at Tri-State University**	Greens:	$
☺☺☺	W. Park St., Angola. (219) 665-4269	Carts:	$
DEAL	18 holes. Par 72/73. Yards: 6,628/5,259	Rating:	71.1/69.4
	Mar.–Dec. High: May–Sept.	Slope:	124/117

Indianapolis Area

SP	**Bear Slide Golf Club**	Greens:	$$$	
☺☺☺☺	E. 231 St., Cicero. (317) 984-3837	Carts:	$	
	18 holes. Par 71/71. Yards: 7,041/4,831	Rating:	74.6/69.5	
	Mar.–Dec. High: May–Oct.	Slope:	136/117	

R	**Brickyard Crossing Golf Club**	Greens:	$$$$	
☺☺☺☺	W. 16th St., Indianapolis. (317) 484-6572	Carts:	Incl.	
STATE	18 holes. Par 72/72. Yards: 6,994/5,038	Rating:	74.4/68.3	
	Apr.–Oct. High: May–Aug.	Slope:	137/116	

SP	**Brookshire Golf Club**	Greens:	$$	W T J
☺☺	Brookshire Pkwy., Carmel. (317) 846-7431	Carts:	Incl.	
	18 holes. Par 72/75. Yards: 6,651/5,635	Rating:	71.8/74.4	
	Year-round. High: May–Oct.	Slope:	123/129	

P	**Coffin Golf Club**	Greens:	$	T S J
☺☺	Cold Springs Rd., Indianapolis. (317) 327-7845	Carts:	$	
	18 holes. Par 72/72. Yards: 6,709/5,135	Rating:	73.7/NA	
	Mar.–Dec.	Slope:	129/NA	

P	**Eagle Creek Golf Club**	Greens:	$	W L T S J
☺☺☺	W. 56th St., Indianapolis. (317) 297-3366	Carts:	$	
STATE	18 holes. Par 72/72. Yards: 7,159/5,800	Rating:	74.6/68.2	
	Feb.–Dec. High: June–Aug.	Slope:	139/116	

P	**Forest Park Golf Course**	Greens:	$	L T
☺☺	Brazil. (812) 442-5681	Carts:	$	
	18 holes. Par 71/73. Yards: 6,012/5,647	Rating:	68.0/69.8	
	Year-round. High: Mar.–Nov.	Slope:	110/112	

P	**Fox Prairie Golf Club**	Greens:	$–$$	W T
☺☺☺	E. 196th St., Noblesville. (317) 776-6357	Carts:	$	
DEAL	18 holes. Par 72/75. Yards: 6,946/5,533	Rating:	72.6/71.4	
	Mar.–Nov. High: June–Aug.	Slope:	118/114	

P	**Geneva Hills Golf Club**	Greens:	$	W L T S J
☺☺☺	R.R. 3, Clinton. (317) 832-8384	Carts:	$	
DEAL	18 holes. Par 72/72. Yards: 6,768/4,785	Rating:	70.2/67.3	
	Year-round. High: Apr.–Oct.	Slope:	118/115	

P	**Golf Club of Indiana**	Greens:	$$	L T
☺☺☺	Exit 30, Interstate 65, Lebanon. (317) 769-6388	Carts:	$	
BEST	18 holes. Par 72/72. Yards: 7,084/5,498	Rating:	73.2/72.7	
DEAL	Feb.–Dec. High: May–Sept.	Slope:	140/122	

P	**Green Acres Golf Club**	Greens:	$	L S J
☺☺☺	Green Acres Dr., Kokomo. (317) 883-5771	Carts:	$	

Indiana Golf Guide

Indianapolis Area

DEAL	18 holes. Par 72/76. Yards: 6,798/5,653	Rating:	72.8/72.7
	Mar.–Dec. High: May–Oct.	Slope:	128/122

SP
○○
Greenfield Country Club
S. Morristown Pike, Greenfield. (317) 462-2706
18 holes. Par 72/73. Yards: 6,773/5,501
Mar.–Nov. High: May–Sept.

Greens: $–$$ W
Carts: $
Rating: 71.2/73.5
Slope: 119/120

SP
○○○
Hanging Tree Golf Club
W. 161st St., Westfield. (317) 896-2474
18 holes. Par 71/71. Yards: 6,519/5,151
Year-round. High: Apr.–Nov.

Greens: $$–$$$ W L T
Carts: Incl.
Rating: 72.6/70.6
Slope: 130/122

P
○○○
BEST
DEAL
Hulman Links Golf Course
N. Chamberlain St., Terre Haute. (812) 877-2096
18 holes. Par 72/72. Yards: 7,225/5,775
Mar.–Dec. High: Mar.–Dec.

Greens: $–$$ L
Carts: $
Rating: 74.9/73.4
Slope: 144/134

P
○○○
DEAL
Indiana University Golf Club
State Road 46 Bypass, Bloomington. (812) 855-7543
18 holes. Par 71/72. Yards: 6,891/5,661
Mar.–Dec. High: Apr.–Oct.

Greens: $
Carts: $
Rating: 72.4/73.1
Slope: 129/123

P
○○○
DEAL
STATE
The Legends of Indiana Golf Course
Hurricane Rd., Franklin. (317) 736-8186
18 holes. Par 72/72. Yards: 7,044/5,244
Mar.–Dec. High: May–Oct.

Greens: $$ T
Carts: $
Rating: 74.0/71.1
Slope: 132/121

P
○○○
DEAL
The Links Golf Club
N. Shelby 700 W., New Palestine. (317) 861-4466
18 holes. Par 72/72. Yards: 7,054/5,018
Year-round. High: May–Sept.

Greens: $–$$ W L T
Carts: $
Rating: 73.3/68.4
Slope: 122/100

P
○○○
DEAL
Otis Park Golf Club
Tunnelton Rd., Bedford. (812) 279-9092
18 holes. Par 72/72. Yards: 6,308/5,184
Mar.–Dec. High: May–Oct.

Greens: $
Carts: $
Rating: 70.0/69.3
Slope: 128/122

P
○○○
BEST
Otter Creek Golf Club
E. 50 N., Columbus. (812) 579-5227
18 holes. Par 72/72. Yards: 7,258/5,690
Mar.–Nov. High: May–Sept.

Greens: $$$–$$$$ W L
Carts: Incl.
Rating: 74.2/72.1
Slope: 137/116

P

○○
Pebble Brook Golf and Country Club
Westfield Rd., Noblesville. (317) 896-5596
South Course
18 holes. Par 72/72. Yards: 6,557/5,261
Mar.–Dec. High: May–Sept.

Greens: $$ W
Carts: $
Rating: 70.5/71.9
Slope: 121/115

○○
North Course
18 holes. Par 70/70. Yards: 6,392/5,806

Rating: 70.5/74.1
Slope: 118/115

R
○○
The Pointe Golf and Tennis Resort
E. Pointe Rd., Bloomington. (812) 824-4040
18 holes. Par 71/71. Yards: 6,604/5,186
Year-round. High: May–Sept.

Greens: $$–$$$ W L T
Carts: Incl.
Rating: 73.0/71.2
Slope: 140/126

P

○
Purdue University Golf Course
Cherry Lane, West Lafayette. (317) 494-3139
North Course
18 holes. Par 72/72. Yards: 6,852/5,961
Mar.–Nov. High: May–Oct.

Greens: $ W L T S J
Carts: $
Rating: 72.4/NA
Slope: 116/NA

○○○
DEAL
STATE
South Course
18 holes. Par 71/72. Yards: 6,428/5,382

Rating: 70.5/NA
Slope: 122/NA

Indiana Golf Guide

Indianapolis Area

P ☺☺☺ DEAL	**Royal Hylands Golf Club** S. Greensboro Pike, Knightstown. (317) 345-2123 18 holes. Par 71/71. Yards: 6,452/4,590 Mar.–Dec. High: May–Aug.	Greens: $–$$ Carts: $ Rating: 71.9/68.8 Slope: 130/122	W L J
P ☺☺☺ DEAL	**Salt Creek Golf Club** Hwy. 46 E. and Salt Creek Rd., Nashville. (812) 988-7888 18 holes. Par 72/72. Yards: 6,407/5,001 Mar.–Nov. High: May–Aug.	Greens: $$ Carts: $ Rating: 71.2/68.8 Slope: 132/122	
P ☺☺	**Shady Hills Golf Course** W. Chapel Pike, Marion. (317) 668-8256 18 holes. Par 71/72. Yards: 6,513/5,595 Mar.–Nov. High: June–Aug.	Greens: $ Carts: $ Rating: 71.6/71.6 Slope: 123/110	S J
P ☺☺	**Smock Golf Course** S. County Line Rd. E., Indianapolis. (317) 888-0036 18 holes. Par 72/72. Yards: 7,055/6,230 Year-round. High: May–Sept.	Greens: $ Carts: $ Rating: 73.7/75.7 Slope: 125/127	T S J
P ☺☺☺ DEAL	**Sultan's Run Golf Course** N. Meridian Rd., Jasper. (812) 482-1009 18 holes. Par 72/72. Yards: 7,060/5,343 Year-round. High: Apr.–Oct.	Greens: $$ Carts: Incl. Rating: 72.8/68.1 Slope: 132/120	W L T J
P ☺☺	**Valle Vista Golf Club** E. Main St., Greenwood. (317) 888-5313 18 holes. Par 70/74. Yards: 6,306/5,680 Year-round. High: May–Sept.	Greens: $–$$ Carts: $ Rating: 70.0/73.1 Slope: 117/113	W L
SP ☺☺☺ DEAL	**Valley View Golf Club** W. County Rd. 850 N., Middletown. (317) 354-2698 18 holes. Par 72/72. Yards: 6,421/5,281 Mar.–Nov. High: May–Sept.	Greens: $ Carts: $ Rating: 70.3/69.9 Slope: 114/109	S
P ☺☺☺ DEAL	**Winchester Golf Club** Simpson Dr., Winchester. (317) 584-5151 18 holes. Par 72/74. Yards: 6,540/5,023 Year-round. High: Apr.–Oct.	Greens: $ Carts: $ Rating: 70.4/67.6 Slope: 115/106	W L

Southwest Indiana

R ☺☺☺ DEAL STATE	**French Lick Springs Resort** Hwy. 56, French Lick. (812) 936-9300, (800) 457-4042 *Hill Course* 18 holes. Par 70/71. Yards: 6,650/5,927 Mar.–Nov. High: May–Oct.	Greens: $$ Carts: $ Rating: 71.6/70.3 Slope: 119/116	L R
P ☺☺	**Helfrich Golf Course** Mesker Park Dr., Evansville. (812) 435-6075 18 holes. Par 71/74. Yards: 6,306/5,506 Year-round. High: Apr.–Oct.	Greens: $ Carts: $ Rating: 69.8/71.4 Slope: 124/117	
P ☺☺☺ DEAL	**Valley View Golf Club** Lawrence Banet Rd., Floyds Knobs. (812) 923-7291 18 holes. Par 71/76. Yards: 6,523/5,488 Year-round. High: Apr.–Sept.	Greens: $ Carts: $ Rating: 71.0/71.0 Slope: 125/122	W T S

Southeast Indiana

SP ☺☺☺☺ STATE	**Covered Bridge Golf Club** Covered Bridge Rd., Sellersburg. (812) 246-8880 18 holes. Par 72/72. Yards: 6,832/5,943 Year-round. High: Apr.–Oct.	Greens: $$$ Carts: Incl. Rating: 73.0/74.7 Slope: 128/126	W L
SP ☺☺☺	**Grand Oak Golf Club** Grand Oak Dr., W. Harrison. (812) 637-3943	Greens: $–$$ Carts: $	L S J

Southeast Indiana

DEAL	18 holes. Par 71/71. Yards: 6,363/4,842	Rating:	70.5/69.9
	Feb.–Dec. High: Apr.–Oct.	Slope:	125/127
P	**Hidden Creek Golf Club**	Greens: $	L T
⊙⊙⊙	Utica Sellersburg Rd., Sellersburg. (812) 246-2556	Carts: $	
DEAL	18 holes. Par 71/71. Yards: 6,756/5,245	Rating:	73.0/70.6
	Year-round. High: Mar.–Oct.	Slope:	133/123
SP	**Liberty Country Club**	Greens: $	T
⊙⊙	N. U.S. 27, Liberty. (317) 458-5664	Carts: $	
	18 holes. Par 72/72. Yards: 6,203/4,544	Rating:	70.5/69.3
	Year-round. High: June–Aug.	Slope:	120/115

Iowa

The **Amana Colonies** course north of Cedar Rapids is a forested, hilly challenge. South of Cedar Rapids is **Finkbine**, a venerable older course that calls for long, straight shooting; it's an Econoguide Deal, too.

Near Des Moines, the **Bos Landen** club is one of the prettiest places to play golf in Iowa, and it's also an Econoguide Deal. In the northwest corner of the state is **Spencer**, another long straight-shot course.

The typical season in Iowa runs from April through October or November, with the best conditions and highest prices from May through early September.

Econoguide Leader Board: Best Public Courses in Iowa

⊙⊙⊙   Amana Colonies Golf Course
⊙⊙⊙⊙   Bos Landen Golf Club
⊙⊙⊙   Finkbine Golf Course
⊙⊙⊙⊙   Spencer Golf and Country Club

Econoguide Leader Board: Best Deals in Iowa

$$/⊙⊙⊙⊙	Bos Landen Golf Club
$$/⊙⊙⊙	Emerald Hills Golf Club
$$/⊙⊙⊙	Finkbine Golf Course
$/⊙⊙⊙	Gates Park Golf Course
$/⊙⊙⊙	Glynns Creek Golf Course
$/⊙⊙⊙	Jester Park Golf Course
$$/⊙⊙⊙	Lake Panorama National Golf Course
$/⊙⊙⊙	Muscatine Municipal Golf Course
$/⊙⊙⊙	Pheasant Ridge Municipal Golf Course
$/⊙⊙⊙	Pleasant Valley Golf Club
$/⊙⊙⊙	Sheaffer Golf Course
$$/⊙⊙⊙⊙	Spencer Golf and Country Club
$/⊙⊙⊙	Valley Oaks Golf Club
$/⊙⊙⊙	Veenker Memorial Golf Course
$/⊙⊙⊙	Waveland Golf Course

Iowa Golf Guide

Sioux City Area

SP ☺☺☺ DEAL	**Emerald Hills Golf Club** Hwy. 71, Arnolds Park. (712) 332-5672 18 holes. Par 72/72. Yards: 6,600/5,956 Apr.–Oct. High: May–Sept.	Greens: Carts: Rating: Slope:	$$ $ 70.6/NA 118/NA	W L T J
P ☺☺	**Okoboji View Golf Course** Hwy. 86, Spirit Lake. (712) 337-3372 18 holes. Par 70/73. Yards: 6,051/5,441 Apr.–Oct. High: June–Aug.	Greens: Carts: Rating: Slope:	$$ $ 68.5/70.1 113/113	L T
SP ☺☺☺☺ DEAL STATE	**Spencer Golf and Country Club** W. 18th St., Spencer. (712) 262-2028 18 holes. Par 72/73. Yards: 6,888/5,760 Mar.–Oct. High: June–Sept.	Greens: Carts: Rating: Slope:	$$ $ 73.0/74.5 127/124	

Fort Dodge Area

P ☺☺	**Briggs Wood Golf Course** Webster City. (515) 832-9572 18 holes. Par 72/71. Yards: 6,502/5,267 Apr.–Oct. High: Apr.–Sept.	Greens: Carts: Rating: Slope:	$ $ 72.0/70.0 128/118	W L T J

Des Moines Area

P ☺☺	**A.H. Blank Golf Course** County Line Rd., Des Moines. (515) 285-0864 18 holes. Par 72/72. Yards: 6,815/5,617 Mar.–Oct. High: May–Aug.	Greens: Carts: Rating: Slope:	$ $ 72.0/NA 119/115	L T S J
P ☺☺	**Beaver Run Golf Course** N.W. Towner Dr., Grimes. (515) 986-3221 18 holes. Par 72/73. Yards: 6,550/5,383 Mar.–Nov. High: May–Aug.	Greens: Carts: Rating: Slope:	$ $ 70.6/70.0 118/112	W S J
P ☺☺☺☺ DEAL STATE	**Bos Landen Golf Club** Pella. (515) 628-4625 18 holes. Par 72/72. Yards: 6,932/5,155 Apr.–Nov. High: Apr.–Sept.	Greens: Carts: Rating: Slope:	$–$$ $ 73.5/70.9 133/122	W L T S J
P ☺☺☺ DEAL STATE	**Finkbine Golf Course** W. Melrose Ave., Iowa City. (319) 335-9556 18 holes. Par 72/72. Yards: 6,989/5,645 Apr.–Nov. High: June–Aug.	Greens: Carts: Rating: Slope:	$–$$ $$ 72.7/73.1 130/123	T
P ☺☺☺ DEAL	**Jester Park Golf Course** Granger. (515) 999-2903 18 holes. Par 72/73. Yards: 6,801/6,062 Mar.–Oct. High: June–Aug.	Greens: Carts: Rating: Slope:	$ $ 72.7/NA 125/NA	L T S J
R ☺☺☺ DEAL	**Lake Panorama National Golf Course** Clover Ridge Rd., Panora. (515) 755-2024 18 holes. Par 72/72. Yards: 7,015/5,765 Apr.–Nov. High: June–Aug.	Greens: Carts: Rating: Slope:	$$ Incl. 73.2/73.2 131/121	L
P ☺☺	**Otter Creek Golf Club** N.E. 36th, Ankeny. (515) 965-6464 18 holes. Par 71/73. Yards: 6,473/5,889 Apr.–Oct. High: Apr.–Oct.	Greens: Carts: Rating: Slope:	$ $ 71.0/73.1 117/119	W T
P ☺☺	**Ottumwa Municipal Golf Course** Angle Rd., Ottumwa. (514) 683-0646 18 holes. Par 70/70. Yards: 6,335/4,954 Mar.–Nov. High: June–Aug.	Greens: Carts: Rating: Slope:	$ $ 70.4/66.7 118/102	
P ☺☺☺ DEAL	**Pleasant Valley Golf Club** S.E. Sand Rd., Iowa City. (319) 337-7209 18 holes. Par 72/72. Yards: 6,472/4,754 Apr.–Oct. High: June–July	Greens: Carts: Rating: Slope:	$ $ 71.0/NA 119/NA	W S J

Iowa Golf Guide

Des Moines Area

P	**Veenker Memorial Golf Course**	Greens:	$	W J
☺☺☺	Stange Rd., Ames. (515) 294-6727	Carts:	$	
DEAL	18 holes. Par 72/73. Yards: 6,543/5,357	Rating:	71.3/70.6	
	Mar.–Nov. High: June–Aug.	Slope:	124/120	

P	**Waveland Golf Course**	Greens:	$	L T S J
☺☺☺	University Ave., Des Moines. (515) 242-2911	Carts:	$	
DEAL	18 holes. Par 72/71. Yards: 6,419/5,295	Rating:	71.4/69.4	
	Mar.–Nov. High: May–Aug.	Slope:	126/116	

P	**Willow Creek Golf Club**	Greens:	$	
☺☺	Army Post Rd., Des Moines. (515) 285-4558	Carts:	$	
	18 holes. Par 71/74. Yards: 6,465/5,758	Rating:	70.2/71.4	
	Apr.–Oct. High: June–Sept.	Slope:	116/112	

Waterloo Area

P	**Gates Park Golf Course**	Greens:	$	S J
☺☺☺	E. Donald St., Waterloo. (319) 291-4485	Carts:	$	
DEAL	18 holes. Par 72/72. Yards: 6,833/5,635	Rating:	70.0/69.5	
	Apr.–Dec. High: June–Aug.	Slope:	105/105	

P	**Pheasant Ridge Municipal Golf Course**	Greens:	$	L S J
☺☺☺	W. 12th St., Cedar Falls. (319) 273-8647	Carts:	$$	
DEAL	18 holes. Par 72/70. Yards: 6,730/5,179	Rating:	72.5/68.4	
	Apr.–Nov. High: Apr.–Sept.	Slope:	122/101	

P	**South Hills Golf Course**	Greens:	$	S J
☺☺	Campbell, Waterloo. (319) 291-4268	Carts:	$	
	18 holes. Par 72/72. Yards: 6,698/5,818	Rating:	71.4/NA	
	Apr.–Dec. High: June–Aug.	Slope:	108/NA	

Cedar Rapids Area

P	**Amana Colonies Golf Course**	Greens:	$$$	W L T
☺☺☺	27th Ave., Amana. (319) 622-6222	Carts:	Incl.	
STATE	18 holes. Par 72/72. Yards: 6,824/5,228	Rating:	73.3/69.7	
	Mar.–Nov. High: June–Sept.	Slope:	136/115	

P	**Ellis Park Municipal Golf Course**	Greens:	$	W T S J
☺☺	Zika Ave. N.W., Cedar Rapids. (319) 398-5180	Carts:	$	
	18 holes. Par 72/72. Yards: 6,648/5,210	Rating:	72.0/70.8	
	Apr.–Nov. High: June–Aug.	Slope:	124/111	

Davenport Area

P	**Duck Creek Golf Club**	Greens:	$	S J
☺☺	Locust and Marlow, Davenport. (319) 326-7824	Carts:	$	
	18 holes. Par 70/74. Yards: 5,900/5,500	Rating:	67.9/72.0	
	Apr.–Nov. High: Apr.–Sept.	Slope:	115/120	

P	**Emeis Golf Club**	Greens:	$	S J
☺☺	W. Central Park, Davenport. (319) 326-7825	Carts:	$	
	18 holes. Par 72/74. Yards: 6,500/5,549	Rating:	71.9/74.0	
	Apr.–Oct. High: May–Aug.	Slope:	120/115	

P	**Glynns Creek Golf Course**	Greens:	$	W L T S J
☺☺☺	290th St., Long Grove. (319) 285-6444	Carts:	$	
DEAL	18 holes. Par 72/72. Yards: 7,036/5,435	Rating:	73.5/70.4	
	Apr.–Oct. High: June–Aug.	Slope:	131/124	

P	**Muscatine Municipal Golf Course**	Greens:	$	S J
☺☺☺	Hwy. 38 N, Muscatine. (319) 263-4735	Carts:	$	
DEAL	18 holes. Par 72/72. Yards: 6,471/5,471	Rating:	69.7/72.5	
	Mar.–Nov. High: May–June	Slope:	117/108	

P	**Palmer Hills Municipal Golf Course**	Greens:	$	W T S J
☺☺	Middle Rd., Bettendorf. (319) 332-8296	Carts:	$	

Iowa Golf Guide

Davenport Area

		Rating:	71.5/74.0
	18 holes. Par 71/71. Yards: 6,535/5,923	Slope:	124/130
	Apr.–Dec. High: Apr.–Sept.		

SP	**Valley Oaks Golf Club**	Greens: $	W J
☺☺☺	Harts Mill Rd., Clinton. (319) 242-7221	Carts: $	
DEAL	18 holes. Par 72/73. Yards: 6,855/5,325	Rating: 72.5/70.3	
	Apr.–Oct. High: Apr.–Oct.	Slope: 124/121	

Southeast Iowa

P	**Sheaffer Golf Course**	Greens: $	W T S J
☺☺☺	308th Ave., Fort Madison. (319) 528-6214	Carts: $	
DEAL	18 holes. Par 72/73. Yards: 6,303/5,441	Rating: 69.9/69.9	
	Mar.–Nov. High: June–Aug.	Slope: 118/113	

Kansas

Alvamar, southwest of Kansas City, is a public course that seems more like a country club in atmosphere. Not far away is **Deer Creek**, an interesting challenge in which the creek plays a role on almost every hole.

Terradyne Resort, east of Wichita, is set within a sea of tall prairie grass for a prairie links-style challenge.

Way out west is **Buffalo Dunes** in Garden City, which, as its name suggests, is built in and around dunes.

Alvamar and Buffalo Dunes also earn a place on the Econoguide Deals list.

Most courses in Kansas operate year-round, although you'll find the best conditions and the peak prices from March through October.

Econoguide Leader Board: Best Public Courses in Kansas

☺☺☺☺ Alvamar Golf Club
☺☺☺☺ Buffalo Dunes Golf Club
☺☺☺☺ Deer Creek Golf Club
☺☺☺☺ Terradyne Resort Hotel and Country Club

Econoguide Leader Board: Best Deals in Kansas

$$/☺☺☺☺   Alvamar Golf Club
$/☺☺☺☺   Buffalo Dunes Golf Club
$$/☺☺☺   Dub's Dread Golf Club
$$/☺☺☺   Heritage Park Golf Course
$/☺☺☺   Hesston Municipal Golf Park
$/☺☺☺   Lake Shawnee Golf Course
$/☺☺☺   Mariah Hills Golf Course
$/☺☺☺   Quail Ridge Golf Course
$/☺☺☺   Rolling Meadows Golf Course
$/☺☺☺   Sunflower Hills Golf Club
$/☺☺☺   Turkey Creek Golf Course

Kansas Golf Guide

Dodge City

P	**Mariah Hills Golf Course**	Greens: $	T J
☺☺☺	Dodge City. (316) 225-8182	Carts: $	

Kansas Golf Guide

Dodge City

DEAL	18 holes. Par 71/73. Yards: 6,868/5,559	Rating: 72.4/71.5
	Year-round. High: Apr.–Oct.	Slope: 118/112

Garden City

P	**Buffalo Dunes Golf Club**	Greens: $ T
☺☺☺☺	Garden City. (316) 276-1210	Carts: $
DEAL	18 holes. Par 72/72. Yards: 6,767/5,598	Rating: 72.5/72.0
STATE	Year-round. High: Apr.–Oct.	Slope: 124/114

Wichita Area

SP	**Braeburn Golf Club at Wichita State University**	Greens: $ W L T S J
☺	E. 21st, Wichita. (316) 685-6601	Carts: $
	18 holes. Par 70/71. Yards: 6,320/5,301	Rating: 71.6/71.4
	Year-round. High: Mar.–Oct.	Slope: 129/121

P	**Hesston Municipal Golf Park**	Greens: $ S
☺☺☺	Hesston. (316) 327-2331	Carts: Inquire
DEAL	18 holes. Par 71/71. Yards: 6,526/5,475	Rating: 71.4/66.7
	Year-round. High: May–Sept.	Slope: 125/118

P	**Hidden Lakes Golf Course**	Greens: $ W T S J
☺☺	S. Greenwich Rd., Derby. (316) 788-2855	Carts: $
	18 holes. Par 72/71. Yards: 6,523/5,212	Rating: 70.8/72.2
	Year-round. High: Mar.–Oct.	Slope: 122/120

P	**L.W. Clapp Golf Course**	Greens: $ W T S J
☺☺	E. Harry, Wichita. (316) 688-9341	Carts: $
	18 holes. Par 70/70. Yards: 6,087/4,965	Rating: 70.0/69.7
	Year-round. High: May–Aug.	Slope: 120/110

P	**Quail Ridge Golf Course**	Greens: $ W R S J
☺☺☺	Winfield. (316) 221-5645	Carts: $
DEAL	18 holes. Par 72/72. Yards: 6,826/5,328	Rating: 73.0/71.4
	Year-round. High: Apr.–Oct.	Slope: 130/130

P	**Sim Park Golf Course**	Greens: $ T
☺☺	W. Murdock, Wichita. (316) 337-9100	Carts: $
	18 holes. Par 72/72. Yards: 6,330/5,048	Rating: 70.5/67.9
	Year-round. High: Apr.–Sept.	Slope: 119/103

R	**Terradyne Resort Hotel and Country Club**	Greens: $$–$$$$ R
☺☺☺☺	Terradyne, Andover. (316) 733-5851	Carts: $
STATE	18 holes. Par 71/71. Yards: 6,704/5,048	Rating: 74.3/70.2
	Year-round. High: Apr.–Oct.	Slope: 139/121

P	**Turkey Creek Golf Course**	Greens: $ W
☺☺☺	Fox Run, McPherson. (316) 241-8530	Carts: $
DEAL	18 holes. Par 70/69. Yards: 6,241/4,723	Rating: 71.3/66.7
	Year-round. High: Apr.–Sept.	Slope: 125/112

P	**Wellington Golf Club**	Greens: $ W T
☺☺	W. Harvey, Wellington. (316) 326-7904	Carts: $
	18 holes. Par 70/70. Yards: 6,201/5,384	Rating: 70.5/70.9
	Year-round. High: Apr.–Sept.	Slope: 135/113

Topeka Area

P	**Lake Shawnee Golf Course**	Greens: $ W T S J
☺☺☺	S.E. Edge Rd., Topeka. (913) 267-2295	Carts: $
DEAL	18 holes. Par 69/69. Yards: 6,013/5,459	Rating: 68.3/70.8
	Year-round. High: May–Sept.	Slope: 107/113

P	**Rolling Meadows Golf Course**	Greens: $ W T
☺☺☺	Old Milford Rd., Milford. (913) 238-4303	Carts: $
DEAL	18 holes. Par 72/72. Yards: 6,879/5,515	Rating: 74.0/70.7
	Year-round. High: Apr.–Oct.	Slope: 134/116

Kansas Golf Guide

Topeka Area

		Greens:	$	J
SP	**Western Hills Golf Club**	Greens:	$	J
☺☺	S.W. 21st St., Topeka. (913) 478-4000	Carts:	$	
	18 holes. Par 70/70. Yards: 6,089/4,728	Rating:	69.2/66.1	
	Year-round. High: Apr.–Sept.	Slope:	121/110	

Kansas City Area

SP	**Alvamar Golf Club**	Greens:	$–$$	W L R T S J
☺☺☺☺	Crossgates Dr., Lawrence. (913) 842-1907	Carts:	$	
BEST	18 holes. Par 72/72. Yards: 7,096/5,489	Rating:	75.0/NA	
DEAL	Year-round. High: May–Sept.	Slope:	135/NA	

SP	**Deer Creek Golf Club**	Greens:	$$–$$$	W L T
☺☺☺☺	W. 133rd St., Overland Park. (913) 681-3100	Carts:	Inquire	
STATE	18 holes. Par 72/72. Yards: 6,870/5,120	Rating:	74.5/68.5	
	Year-round. High: 6,870/5,120	Slope:	137/113	

P	**Dub's Dread Golf Club**	Greens:	$$	T S J
☺☺☺	Hollingsworth Rd., Kansas City. (913) 721-1333	Carts:	$	
DEAL	18 holes. Par 72/72. Yards: 6,987/5,454	Rating:	73.6/70.4	
	Year-round. High: Apr.–Oct.	Slope:	131/121	

P	**Heritage Park Golf Course**	Greens:	$–$$	W T S J
☺☺☺	Lackman Rd., Olathe. (913) 829-4653	Carts:	$$	
DEAL	18 holes. Par 71/71. Yards: 6,876/5,797	Rating:	72.6/72.3	
	Year-round. High: Mar.–Oct.	Slope:	131/121	

P	**Overland Park Golf Club**	Greens:	$	T S J
	Quivira Rd., Overland Park. (913) 897-3809	Carts:	$	
☺☺	*South/North/West*	Rating:	69.9/69.7/69.9	
	27 holes. Par 70/70/70. Yards: 6,446/6,455/6,367	Slope:	113/119/115	
	Year-round. High: Apr.–Sept.			

P	**St. Andrew's Golf Course**	Greens:	$	T S J
☺☺	W. 135 St., Overland Park. (913) 897-3804	Carts:	$	
	18 holes. Par 70/70. Yards: 6,205/4,713	Rating:	69.5/67.7	
	Year-round. High: June–July	Slope:	109/108	

P	**Stagg Hill Golf Club**	Greens:	$	
☺☺	Ft. Riley Blvd., Manhattan. (913) 539-1041	Carts:	$	
	18 holes. Par 72/72. Yards: 6,697/5,642	Rating:	70.3/72.1	
	Year-round. High: Apr.–Oct.	Slope:	112/117	

P	**Sunflower Hills Golf Club**	Greens:	$	W T S J
☺☺☺	Riverview, Bonner Springs. (913) 721-2727	Carts:	$	
DEAL	18 holes. Par 72/73. Yards: 7,001/5,850	Rating:	73.3/72.6	
	Year-round. High: Apr.–Sept.	Slope:	124/124	

Kentucky

Lassing Pointe, a newer course located south of Cincinnati, was an immediate hit when it opened. A bit farther south is **Kearney Hill** in Lexington, with a lot of open and windy fairways and plenty of sand and grass bunkers. To make things even better, both courses are also on the Econoguide Deals list.

Most golf courses in Kentucky are open year-round, although a few close up in the bleak month of January. You'll find the best conditions and peak rates from April through September.

Econoguide Leader Board: Best Public Courses in Kentucky

☺☺☺☺   Kearney Hill Golf Links
☺☺☺☺   Lassing Pointe Golf Club

Econoguide Leader Board: Best Deals in Kentucky

$/ooo	Barren River State Park Golf Course
$$/ooo	Crooked Creek Golf Club
$$/ooo	Doe Valley Golf Club
$/ooo	Frances E. Miller Golf Course
$/ooo	Gibson Bay Golf Course
$$/ooo	The Golf Courses at Kenton County (Fox Run, Willows)
$$/oooo	Kearney Hill Golf Links
$/ooo	Kentucky Dam Village State Resort Park
$/oooo	Lassing Pointe Golf Club
$$/ooo	Nevel Meade Golf Course
$/ooo	Quail Chase Golf Club
$/ooo	Western Hills Golf Course

Kentucky Golf Guide

Paducah Area

P ooo DEAL	**Frances E. Miller Golf Course** Rte. 6, Murray. (502) 762-2238 18 holes. Par 71/71. Yards: 6,592/5,058 Year-round. High: May–Aug.	Greens: Carts: Rating: Slope:	$ $ 71.6/68.9 125/117	T S J
R ooo DEAL	**Kentucky Dam Village State Resort Park** Hwy. 641, Gilbertsville. (502) 362-8658 18 holes. Par 72/72. Yards: 6,704/5,094 Year-round. High: Mar.–Oct.	Greens: Carts: Rating: Slope:	$ Inquire 73.0/70.0 135/124	T

Bowling Green Area

P ooo DEAL	**Barren River State Park Golf Course** State Park Rd., Lucas. (502) 646-4653 18 holes. Par 72/72. Yards: 6,440/4,919 Year-round. High: Apr.–Sept.	Greens: Carts: Rating: Slope:	$ $ 69.1/66.6 118/106	T
P oo	**Hartland Municipal Golf Course** Wilkinson Trace, Bowling Green. (502) 843-5559 18 holes. Par 71/72. Yards: 6,512/5,044 Year-round. High: July–Aug.	Greens: Carts: Rating: Slope:	$ $ 69.9/68.3 119/113	W L T S J
P ooo DEAL	**Western Hills Golf Course** Russellville Rd., Hopkinsville. (502) 885-6023 18 holes. Par 72/72. Yards: 6,907/3,921 Year-round. High: May–Sept.	Greens: Carts: Rating: Slope:	$ Inquire 73.8/64.0 134/109	W S J

Louisville Area

P oo	**Charlie Vettiner Golf Course** Mary Dell Lane, Jeffersontown. (502) 267-9958 18 holes. Par 72/73. Yards: 6,914/5,388 Year-round. High: Apr.–Sept.	Greens: Carts: Rating: Slope:	$ $ 72.3/70.0 123/116	T S
SP ooo DEAL	**Doe Valley Golf Club** Doe Valley Pkwy., Brandenburg. (502) 422-3397 18 holes. Par 71/72. Yards: 6,471/5,519 Year-round. High: Apr.–Sept.	Greens: Carts: Rating: Slope:	$–$$ $ 69.8/70.3 119/118	T S
P oo	**Iroquois Golf Course** Rundill Rd., Louisville. (502) 363-9520 18 holes. Par 71/73. Yards: 6,138/5,004 Year-round. High: Apr.–Nov.	Greens: Carts: Rating: Slope:	$ $ 67.3/70.2 106/112	T S J
P oo	**Lincoln Homestead State Park Golf Course** Lincoln Park Rd., Springfield. (606) 336-7461	Greens: Carts:	$ $	W L T

Kentucky Golf Guide

Louisville Area

	18 holes. Par 71/73. Yards: 6,359/5,472	Rating:	70.0/71.0
	Year-round. High: Apr.–Oct.	Slope:	119/118

P	**My Old Kentucky Home State Park Golf Club**	Greens:	$ W
◯◯	Hwy. 49, Bardstown. (502) 349-6542	Carts:	$
	18 holes. Par 70/71. Yards: 6,065/5,239	Rating:	69.5/70.2
	Year-round.	Slope:	119/118

P	**Nevel Meade Golf Course**	Greens:	$–$$ L T S J
◯◯◯	Nevel Meade Dr., Prospect. (502) 228-9522	Carts:	$
DEAL	18 holes. Par 72/72. Yards: 6,956/5,616	Rating:	72.2/70.4
	Year-round. High: Mar.–Oct.	Slope:	122/117

R	**Pine Valley Country Club & Resort**	Greens:	$
◯◯	Pine Valley Dr., Elizabethtown. (502) 737-8300	Carts:	$
	18 holes. Par 70/74. Yards: 6,613/5,357	Rating:	71.3/69.6
	Year-round. High: Apr.–June	Slope:	119/114

SP	**Quail Chase Golf Club**	Greens:	$ W L T S J
◯◯◯	Cooper Chapel Rd., Louisville. (502) 239-2110	Carts:	Inquire
DEAL	27 holes. Par 72/72/72. Yards: 6,728/6,715/6,493	Rating:	71.7/72.0/70.5
	Year-round. High: June–Aug.	Slope:	127/133/124

P	**Seneca Golf Course**	Greens:	$ W T S J
◯◯	Seneca Park Rd., Louisville. (502) 458-9298	Carts:	$
	18 holes. Par 72/73. Yards: 7,034/5,469	Rating:	73.7/71.5
	Year-round. High: Apr.–Sept.	Slope:	130/122

P	**Shawnee Golf Course**	Greens:	$ T
◯◯	Northwestern Pkwy., Louisville. (502) 776-9389	Carts:	Inquire
	18 holes. Par 70/70. Yards: 6,072/5,476	Rating:	65.1/68.5
	Year-round. High: May–Oct.	Slope:	100/105

P	**Tanglewood Golf Course**	Greens:	$ W L R T S J
◯◯	Tanglewood Dr., Taylorsville. (502) 477-2468	Carts:	$
	18 holes. Par 72/72. Yards: 6,626/5,275	Rating:	70.2/68.8
	Year-round. High: May–Sept.	Slope:	121/115

P	**Weissinger Hills Golf Course**	Greens:	$ W L T J
◯◯	Mt. Eden Rd., Shelbyville. (502) 633-7332	Carts:	$
	18 holes. Par 72/73. Yards: 6,534/5,165	Rating:	70.8/69.0
	Year-round. High: Apr.–Sept.	Slope:	118/112

Lexington Area

SP	**Crooked Creek Golf Club**	Greens:	$$ W L T J
◯◯◯	Crooked Creek Dr., London. (606) 877-1993	Carts:	$
DEAL	18 holes. Par 72/72. Yards: 7,007/5,087	Rating:	73.4/71.3
	Year-round. High: Mar.–Oct.	Slope:	134/122

SP	**Eagle's Nest Country Club**	Greens:	$$
◯◯	Hwy. 39 N., Somerset. (606) 679-7754	Carts:	$
	18 holes. Par 71/72. Yards: 6,404/5,010	Rating:	69.8/67.9
	Feb.–Dec. High: May–Oct.	Slope:	117/109

P	**Gibson Bay Golf Course**	Greens:	$ W T S J
◯◯◯	Gibson Bay Dr., Richmond. (606) 623-0225	Carts:	$
DEAL	18 holes. Par 72/72. Yards: 7,113/5,069	Rating:	74.1/69.1
	Year-round.	Slope:	128/115

P	**Juniper Hills Golf Course**	Greens:	$ T
◯◯	Louisville Rd., Frankfort. (502) 875-8559	Carts:	$
	18 holes. Par 70/74. Yards: 6,200/5,904	Rating:	68.7/67.7
	Year-round. High: Apr.–Oct.	Slope:	111/106

P	**Kearney Hill Golf Links**	Greens:	$$ T S J
◯◯◯◯	Kearney Rd., Lexington. (606) 253-1981	Carts:	Inquire

Kentucky Golf Guide

Lexington Area

DEAL	18 holes. Par 72/72. Yards: 6,987/5,362	Rating:	73.5/70.1
STATE	Year-round. High: Apr.–Oct.	Slope:	128/118

R	**Marriott's Griffin Gate Resort Golf Club**	Greens:	$$–$$$$ W L T
☺☺☺	Newtown Pike, Lexington. (606) 254-4101	Carts:	Incl.
	18 holes. Par 72/72. Yards: 6,801/4,979	Rating:	73.3/69.3
	Year-round. High: Apr.–Oct.	Slope:	132/119

R	**Woodson Bend Resort**	Greens:	$–$$ L J
☺☺	Woodson Bend, Bronston. (606) 561-5316	Carts:	Incl.
	18 holes. Par 72/75. Yards: 6,189/5,155	Rating:	69.2/72.0
	Feb.–Dec. High: May–Sept.	Slope:	117/113

Covington/Florence Area

P	**Boone Links**	Greens:	$ S J
☺☺	Florence. (606) 371-7550	Carts:	$
	27 holes. Par 70/72/70. Yards: 5,950/6,634/6,110	Rating:	68.4/72.1/69.2
	Feb.–Dec. High: May–Aug.	Slope:	118/128/122

P	**The Golf Courses at Kenton County**	Greens:	$$
	Richardson Rd., Independence. (606) 371-3200	Carts:	Incl.
☺☺☺	*Fox Run Course*	Rating:	74.8/68.1
DEAL	18 holes. Par 72/72. Yards: 7,055/4,707	Slope:	143/123
	Apr.–Oct. High: May–Aug.		

☺☺	*The Pioneer Course*	Greens:	$ W S J
	18 holes. Par 70/71. Yards: 6,059/5,336	Carts:	$
		Rating:	67.9/69.5
		Slope:	114/115

☺☺☺	*The Willows Course*	Greens:	$ S J
DEAL	18 holes. Par 72/72. Yards: 6,791/5,669	Carts:	$
		Rating:	72.5/74.0
		Slope:	130/129

P	**Lassing Pointe Golf Club**	Greens:	$ S J
☺☺☺☺	Double Eagle Dr., Union. (606) 384-2266	Carts:	$
DEAL	18 holes. Par 71/71. Yards: 6,724/5,153	Rating:	72.2/69.5
STATE	Apr.–Oct. High: May–Aug.	Slope:	132/122

Michigan

The stars of northern Michigan include the scenic but difficult **Dunmaglas** in Charlevoix, the little bit of Scotland on the Gailes Course at **Lakewood Shores** in Oscoda, the woodsy charm of **Elk Ridge** in Atlanta, and the Black Forest Course at **Wilderness Valley** in Gaylord. The Ross and Heather courses at **Boyne Highlands Resort** in Harbor Springs are among the best anywhere; the Ross Course re-creates many of Donald Ross's most famous holes.

The better resorts near Traverse City include the spectacular Legend Course at the **Shanty Creek Resort** in Bellaire. It's situated among the trees around Lake Bellaire, with narrow fairways and diabolically placed water. Also worth visiting is the Bear Course (named after Jack Nicklaus, responsible for the design) at the **Grand Traverse Resort**, and the **High Pointe Golf Club**. And there is the Traverse City golfing supermall: the impressive **Treetops Sylvan Resort** with its top-rated Jones, Smith, and Fazio courses.

Near Grand Rapids you'll find the heavily forested **Grand Haven**. And don't miss the challenging **Thoroughbred** in Rothbury north of Muskegon.

The **Timber Ridge** club is the pride of the Lansing area.

The Detroit region has three local champions: **The Orchards**, **Rattle Run**, and the **University of Michigan Golf Course**.

Three courses share positions on both the Econoguide Best and Econoguide Deals lists: Grand Haven Golf Club, High Pointe Golf Club, and Wilderness Valley Golf Club.

Most golf courses in Michigan are open from March through November, with high-season rates in effect from spring through early September. The northern latitude of the upper courses allows play late into the evening.

The popular Boyne Mountain and Boyne Highlands resorts offer low-season rates of as much as 40 percent off for the first half of May and the entire month of October. At Boyne Highlands, midseason rates are in effect from mid-May through early June and from the last week of August through late September. High-season rates are in effect from mid-June through late August. A golf package is priced at $75 in low season for a standard room and as high as $125 in the summer. A luxury condo ranges in price from $105 to $226 across the seasons.

Econoguide Leader Board: Best Public Courses in Michigan

☻☻☻☻	Boyne Highlands Resort (Donald Ross, Heather)
☻☻☻☻	Dunmaglas Golf Club
☻☻☻☻	Elk Ridge Golf Course
☻☻☻	Grand Haven Golf Club
☻☻☻☻	Grand Traverse Resort (Bear)
☻☻☻	High Pointe Golf Club
☻☻☻☻	Lakewood Shores Resort (Gailes)
☻☻☻☻	The Orchards Golf Club
☻☻☻	Rattle Run Golf Course
☻☻☻☻	Shanty Creek Resort (Schuss Mountain)
☻☻☻☻	Thoroughbred Golf Club
☻☻☻	Timber Ridge Golf Course
☻☻☻☻	Treetops Sylvan Resort (Jones, Smith, Fazio)
☻☻☻	University of Michigan Golf Course
☻☻☻☻	Wilderness Valley Golf Club (Black Forest)

Econoguide Leader Board: Best Deals in Michigan

$$/☻☻☻	Bedford Valley Golf Course
$/☻☻☻	Binder Park Golf Course
$$/☻☻☻	Candlestone Golf Club
$/☻☻☻	Cascades Golf Course
$$/☻☻☻	Clearbrook Golf Club
$$/☻☻☻	Eagle Glen Golf Course
$$/☻☻☻	Faulkwood Shores Golf Club
$$/☻☻☻	Fox Run Country Club
$$/☻☻☻	Grand Haven Golf Club
$/☻☻☻	Grand View Golf Course
$$/☻☻☻	Gull Lake View Golf Club (East, West)

$$/○○○	Heather Highlands Golf Club
$$/○○○	High Pointe Golf Club
$$/○○○	Huron Breeze Golf and Country Club
$$/○○○	Huron Golf Club
$$/○○○	Indian River Golf Club
$$/○○○	Katke Golf Course
$$/○○○	Lake Doster Golf Club
$$/○○○	The Links of Novi (East, South, West)
$/○○○	Maple Leaf Golf Course
$$/○○○	The Meadows Golf Club
$/○○○	Milham Park Municipal Golf Course
$$/○○○	Mistwood Golf Course
$$/○○○	Pine River Golf Club
$/○○○	Pleasant Hills Golf Club
$/○○○	Saskatoon Golf Club (Blue, White)
$$/○○○	Salem Hills Golf Club
$$/○○○	Scott Lake Country Club
$/○○○	Springfield Oaks Golf Course
$$/○○○	Sycamore Hills Golf Club (North, South, West)
$$/○○○	Tanglewood Golf Club (North, South, West)
$$/○○○	Taylor Meadows Golf Club
$$/○○○	Thornapple Creek Golf Club
$$/○○○	Wallinwood Springs Golf Course
$$/○○○○	Wilderness Valley Golf Club

Michigan Golf Guide

Northern Michigan

P ○○○	**Antrim Dells Golf Club** Rte. 1, Ellsworth. (616) 599-2679 18 holes. Par 72/72. Yards: 6,606/5,493 Apr.–Oct. High: July–Sept.	Greens: $$$ Carts: Incl. Rating: NA Slope: 125/121	L T
R ○○○○	**Boyne Highlands Resort** 600 Highland Dr., Harbor Springs. (616) 526-3029 *Donald Ross Memorial Course* 18 holes. Par 72/72. Yards: 6,840/4,977 May–Oct. High: June–Aug.	Greens: $$$–$$$$ Carts: $ Rating: 73.4/68.5 Slope: 132/119	L R
○○○○	*Heather Course* 18 holes. Par 72/72. Yards: 7,210/5,245 May–Oct. High: June–Aug.	Rating: 74.0/67.8 Slope: 131/111	
○○○	*Moor Course* 18 holes. Par 72/72. Yards: 7,179/5,459 May–Oct. High: June–Aug.	Greens: $$$ Carts: $ Rating: 74.0/70.0 Slope: 131/118	
SP ○○○○	**Dunmaglas Golf Club** Boyne City Rd., Charlevoix. (616) 547-1022 18 holes. Par 72/74. Yards: 6,897/5,334 May–Oct. High: July–Aug.	Greens: $$$ Carts: $ Rating: 74.0/70.9 Slope: 142/127	L T
P ○○○○	**Elk Ridge Golf Course** 9400 Rouse Rd., Atlanta. (517) 785-2275 18 holes. Par 72/72. Yards: 7,058/5,261 May–Oct. High: June–Aug.	Greens: $$$ Carts: $ Rating: 75.0/73.1 Slope: 144/135	W L T S J

Michigan Golf Guide

Northern Michigan

P ☺☺☺ DEAL	**Fox Run Country Club** 5825 W. Four Mile Rd., Grayling. (517) 348-4343 18 holes. Par 72/72. Yards: 6,268/4,809 Apr.–Oct. High: June–Sept.	Greens: Carts: Rating: Slope:	$$ $ 70.4/68.5 126/117	T

R ☺☺☺	**Grand Traverse Resort** U.S. 31 N., Acme. (616) 938-1620 *Spruce Run Course* 18 holes. Par 72/73. Yards: 6,741/5,139 Apr.–Oct. High: June–Aug.	Greens: Carts: Rating: Slope:	$$$$ Incl. 73.7/70.7 137/131	W L R T

☺☺☺☺ BEST	*The Bear* 18 holes. Par 72/72. Yards: 7,065/5,281	Greens: Carts: Rating: Slope:	$$$$$ Incl. 75.8/72.0 149/131

R ☺☺☺	**Hidden Valley Resort and Club** Gaylord. (517) 732-4653 18 holes. Par 71/71. Yards: 6,305/5,591 Apr.–Oct. High: June–Aug.	Greens: Carts: Rating: Slope:	$$$ Incl. NA 121/113	W L R T

P ☺☺☺ DEAL	**High Pointe Golf Club** 5555 Arnold Rd., Williamsburg. (616) 267-9900 18 holes. Par 71/72. Yards: 6,849/5,101 Apr.–Oct. High: June–Aug.	Greens: Carts: Rating: Slope:	$$ $ 72.9/69.6 135/121	W L R T S J

SP ☺☺☺ DEAL	**Indian River Golf Club** 6460 Chippewa Beach Rd., Indian River. (616) 238-7011 18 holes. Par 72/72. Yards: 6,718/5,277 May.–Oct. High: July–Aug.	Greens: Carts: Rating: Slope:	$$ $ 72.4/71.3 124/119	W L T J

R ☺☺☺☺	**Lakewood Shores Resort** 7751 Cedar Lake Rd., Oscoda. (517) 739-2073 *Gailes Course* 18 holes. Par 72/73. Yards: 6,954/5,246 Apr.–Oct. High: June–Sept.	Greens: Carts: Rating: Slope:	$$$ $ 74.6/72.0 137/132	W L R T

☺☺☺	*Resort Course* 18 holes. Par 72/74. Yards: 6,806/5,295 Apr.–Oct. High: June–Sept.	Rating: Slope:	72.9/70.9 120/115

P ☺☺☺ DEAL	**Maple Leaf Golf Course** 158 N. Mackinaw Rd., Linwood. (517) 697-3531 *East/North/West* 27 holes. Par 71/71/70. Yards: 5,762/5,997/5,697 Apr.–Nov. High: June–Aug.	Greens: Carts: Rating: Slope:	$ $ 67.6/68.3/66.4 116/114/109	W L S J

R ☺☺☺☺	**Shanty Creek Resort** Bellaire. (616) 533-8621 *Schuss Mountain Course* 18 holes. Par 72/72. Yards: 6,922/5,423 Apr.–Oct. High: July–Aug.	Greens: Carts: Rating: Slope:	$$$$ $ 73.4/71.2 127/126	R T

☺☺☺	*Shanty Creek Course* 18 holes. Par 71/71. Yards: 6,276/4,545 Apr.–Oct. High: July–Aug.	Rating: Slope:	71.7/70.7 120/116

R ☺☺☺☺	**Treetops Sylvan Resort** 3962 Wilkinson Rd., Gaylord. (517) 732-6711 *Robert Trent Jones Masterpiece Course* 18 holes. Par 71/71. Yards: 7,060/4,972 Apr.–Oct. High: June–Sept.	Greens: Carts: Rating: Slope:	$$$$ $ 75.8/70.2 146/124	W L T S J

☺☺☺☺	*Rick Smith Signature Course* 18 holes. Par 70/70. Yards: 6,653/4,604 Apr.–Oct. High: June–Sept.	Rating: Slope:	72.7/66.8 137/118

Michigan Golf Guide

Northern Michigan

⊘⊘⊘⊘	Tom Fazio Premier Course 18 holes. Par 72/72. Yards: 6,832/5,039 Apr.–Oct. High: June–Sept.	Rating: Slope:	73.2/70.2 135/123	

R	**Wilderness Valley Golf Club** 7519 Mancelona Rd., Gaylord. (616) 585-7090	Greens: $$ Carts: $	W L R T S J
⊘⊘⊘⊘ DEAL	Black Forest Course 18 holes. Par 73/74. Yards: 7,044/5,282 Apr.–Oct. High: July–Aug.	Rating: Slope:	75.3/71.8 145/131
⊘⊘⊘	Valley Course 18 holes. Par 71/71. Yards: 6,485/4,889 Apr.–Oct. High: July–Aug.	Rating: Slope:	70.6/67.8 126/115

Grand Rapids Area

R ⊘⊘⊘ DEAL	**Candlestone Golf Club** 8100 N. Storey, Belding. (616) 794-1580 18 holes. Par 72/74. Yards: 6,692/5,547 Mar.–Oct. High: May–Sept.	Greens: $$ Carts: $ Rating: 72.8/73.1 Slope: 129/126	W L R T J
SP ⊘⊘⊘ DEAL	**Clearbrook Golf Club** 6494 Clearbrook Dr., Saugatuck. (616) 857-2000 18 holes. Par 72/74. Yards: 6,453/5,153 Apr.–Oct. High: June–Aug.	Greens: $–$$ Carts: $ Rating: 72.8/70.0 Slope: 132/127	L
SP ⊘⊘⊘ DEAL	**Grand Haven Golf Club** 17000 Lincoln St., Grand Haven. (616) 842-4040 18 holes. Par 72/72. Yards: 6,789/5,536 Mar.–Nov. High: June–Aug.	Greens: $$ Carts: $ Rating: 71.9/71.4 Slope: 124/119	
P ⊘⊘⊘ DEAL	**Grand View Golf Course** S. 68th Ave., New Era. (616) 861-6616 18 holes. Par 71/71. Yards: 6,258/4,737 Apr.–Oct. High: June–Aug.	Greens: $ Carts: $ Rating: NA Slope: NA	W S
P ⊘⊘⊘ DEAL	**Gull Lake View Golf Club** 7417 N. 38th St., Augusta. (616) 731-4148 East Course 18 holes. Par 70/70. Yards: 6,002/4,918 Apr.–Nov. High: May–Aug.	Greens: $$ Carts: $ Rating: 69.4/68.5 Slope: 124/118	W L R T J
⊘⊘⊘	West Course 18 holes. Par 71/72. Yards: 6,300/5,218 Apr.–Nov. High: May–Aug.	Rating: 70.6/69.0 Slope: 123/114	
P ⊘⊘⊘ DEAL	**Katke Golf Course** 1003 Perry St., Big Rapids. (616) 592-2213 18 holes. Par 72/72. Yards: 6,729/5,344 Apr.–Nov. High: May–Sept.	Greens: $$ Carts: $ Rating: 72.5/70.8 Slope: 124/119	W L R S J
SP ⊘⊘⊘ DEAL	**Lake Doster Golf Club** Plainwell. (616) 685-5308 18 holes. Par 72/72. Yards: 6,570/5,530 Apr.–Oct. High: June–Aug.	Greens: $$ Carts: $ Rating: 72.7/72.8 Slope: 134/128	
P ⊘⊘⊘ DEAL	**The Meadows Golf Club** 4645 W. Campus Dr., Allendale. (616) 895-1000 18 holes. Par 71/72. Yards: 7,034/4,777 Apr.–Oct. High: June–Sept.	Greens: $$ Carts: $ Rating: 74.5/67.4 Slope: 133/117	W L T J
P ⊘⊘⊘ DEAL	**Milham Park Municipal Golf Course** 4200 Lovers Lane, Kalamazoo. (616) 344-7639 18 holes. Par 73/72. Yards: 6,578/5,582 Mar.–Dec. High: June–Aug.	Greens: $ Carts: NA Rating: 71.3/71.8 Slope: 120/120	S J
P	**Saskatoon Golf Club** 9038 92nd St., Alto. (616) 891-9229	Greens: $ Carts: $	S

Michigan Golf Guide

Grand Rapids Area

☺☺☺ DEAL	Blue/White 18 holes. Par 73/73. Yards: 6,750/6,125 Mar.–Dec. High: May–July	Rating: Slope:	70.7/71.7 123/122

SP ☺☺☺ DEAL	Scott Lake Country Club 911 Hayes Rd., Comstock Park. (616) 784-1355 18 holes. Par 72/72. Yards: 6,333/4,794 Apr.–Nov. High: May–Sept.	Greens: Carts: Rating: Slope:	$$ $ 70.8/67.6 122/110	W L S J

P ☺☺☺ DEAL	Thornapple Creek Golf Club 6415 W. F Ave., Kalamazoo. (616) 344-0040 18 holes. Par 72/72. Yards: 6,960/4,948 Apr.–Nov. High: June–Aug.	Greens: Carts: Rating: Slope:	$$ $$ 73.7/68.9 137/121	W L

R ☺☺☺☺ STATE	Thoroughbred Golf Club 6886 Water Rd., Rothbury. (616) 893-4653 18 holes. Par 72/72. Yards: 6,900/4,851 Apr.–Nov. High: June–Sept.	Greens: Carts: Rating: Slope:	$$$ Incl. 74.4/69.5 147/126	L R T

SP ☺☺☺ DEAL	Wallinwood Springs Golf Course 8152 Weatherwax, Jenison. (616) 457-9920 18 holes. Par 72/72. Yards: 6,751/5,067 Apr.–Nov. High: June–Aug.	Greens: Carts: Rating: Slope:	$$ $ 72.4/69.1 128/115	W

East-Central Michigan

P ☺☺☺ DEAL	Bedford Valley Golf Course 23161 Waubascon Rd., Battle Creek. (616) 965-3384 18 holes. Par 71/72. Yards: 6,876/5,104 Apr.–Nov. High: May–Aug.	Greens: Carts: Rating: Slope:	$$ $ 73.8/70.0 135/119	W L R T J

P ☺☺☺ DEAL	Binder Park Golf Course 6723 B Drive S., Battle Creek. (616) 966-3459 18 holes. Par 72/75. Yards: 6,328/4,965 Apr.–Oct. High: June–Aug.	Greens: Carts: Rating: Slope:	$ $ 69.6/68.4 114/109	S J

P ☺☺☺ DEAL	Cascades Golf Course 1922 Warren Ave., Jackson. (517) 788-4323 18 holes. Par 72/73. Yards: 6,614/5,282 Mar.–Oct. High: July–Sept.	Greens: Carts: Rating: Slope:	$ NA 71.8/70.5 122/117	W L T S J

P ☺☺☺ DEAL	Eagle Glen Golf Course Farwell. (517) 588-9357 18 holes. Par 72/72. Yards: 6,602/5,119 Apr.–Oct. High: June–Oct.	Greens: Carts: Rating: Slope:	$$ $ 71.1/69.2 123/116	W L R S J

P ☺☺	Firefly Golf Links S. Clare Ave., Clare. (517) 386-3510 18 holes. Par 72/72. Yards: 5,658/4,470 Apr.–Oct. High: June–Aug.	Greens: Carts: Rating: Slope:	$–$$ $ NA NA	W L S

P ☺☺☺ DEAL	Huron Breeze Golf and Country Club 5200 Huron Breeze Dr., Au Gres. (517) 876-6868 18 holes. Par 72/72. Yards: 6,806/5,075 Apr.–Oct. High: June–Sept.	Greens: Carts: Rating: Slope:	$$ $ 73.1/69.4 133/123	W L T S J

P ☺☺☺ BEST	Timber Ridge Golf Course 16339 Park Lake Rd., East Lansing. (517) 339-8000 18 holes. Par 72/72. Yards: 6,497/5,048 Mar.–Nov. High: May–Sept.	Greens: Carts: Rating: Slope:	$$$ $ 72.7/70.4 137/129	W L T S

Detroit/Ann Arbor Area

P ☺☺☺ DEAL	Faulkwood Shores Golf Club 300 S. Hughes Rd., Howell. (517) 546-4180 18 holes. Par 72/72. Yards: 6,828/5,341 Apr.–Nov. High: June–Sept.	Greens: Carts: Rating: Slope:	$$ Incl. 74.3/71.8 140/128	W L T S J

Michigan Golf Guide

Detroit/Ann Arbor Area

P ☺☺☺ DEAL	**Heather Highlands Golf Club** 11450 E. Holly Rd., Holly. (810) 634-6800 18 holes. Par 72/72. Yards: 6,845/5,764 Apr.–Nov. High: May–Sept.	Greens: $$　　　L Carts: $ Rating: 72.4/72.6 Slope: 121/120
R ☺☺☺ DEAL	**Huron Golf Club** 1275 Huron St., Ypsilanti. (313) 487-2441 18 holes. Par 72/72. Yards: 6,750/5,185 Mar.–Nov. High: June–Aug.	Greens: $$　　　W L T S J Carts: Incl. Rating: 73.6/69.7 Slope: 138/124
P ☺☺☺ DEAL	**The Links of Novi** 50395 Ten Mile Rd., Novi. (810) 380-9595 *East/South/West* 27 holes. Par 69/70/71. Yards: 5,795/5,899/6,358 Apr.–Dec. High: June–Aug.	Greens: $$　　　T S J Carts: $ Rating: 67.9/68.3/71.2 Slope: 118/119/127
P ☺☺☺ DEAL	**Mistwood Golf Course** 7568 Sweet Lake Rd., Lake Ann. (616) 275-5500 18 holes. Par 71/71. Yards: 6,715/5,070 Apr.–Nov. High: June–Aug.	Greens: $$　　　W L T S J Carts: $ Rating: 72.4/69.6 Slope: 130/120
P ☺☺☺☺ STATE	**The Orchards Golf Club** 62900 Campgrounds Rd., Washington. (810) 786-7200 18 holes. Par 72/72. Yards: 7,026/5,158 Apr.–Oct. High: May–Sept.	Greens: $$$　　　L T Carts: Incl. Rating: 73.9/70.1 Slope: 133/122
P ☺☺☺ DEAL	**Pine River Golf Club** 2244 Pine River Rd., Standish. (517) 846-6819 18 holes. Par 71/74. Yards: 6,250/5,156 Apr.–Oct. High: June–Aug.	Greens: $–$$　　　W S J Carts: $ Rating: 70.8/70.7 Slope: 126/126
P ☺☺☺ DEAL	**Pleasant Hills Golf Club** 4452 E. Millbrook Rd., Mt. Pleasant. (517) 772-0487 18 holes. Par 72/72. Yards: 6,012/4,607 Mar.–Dec. High: June–Aug.	Greens: $　　　W L T S J Carts: $ Rating: 68.2/65.9 Slope: 110/107
P ☺☺	**Raisin River Country Club** N. Dixie Hwy., Monroe. (313) 289-3700 *East Course* 18 holes. Par 71/71. Yards: 6,930/5,580 Mar.–Nov. High: May–Sept.	Greens: $　　　L R Carts: $ Rating: 73.1/68.4 Slope: NA
☺☺	*West Course* 18 holes. Par 72/72. Yards: 6,255/5,880	Rating: 68.5/NA　　R S J Slope: NA
P ☺☺☺ BEST	**Rattle Run Golf Course** St. Clair Hwy., China Twnshp. (810) 329-2070 18 holes. Par 72/75. Yards: 6,891/5,085 Apr.–Nov. High: May–Sept.	Greens: $$–$$$　　L T S J Carts: Incl. Rating: 75.1/70.4 Slope: 139/124
P ☺☺	**Reddeman Farms Golf Course** S. Dancer Rd., Chelsea. (313) 475-3020 18 holes. Par 72/72. Yards: 6,513/5,813 Apr.–Nov. High: June–Sept.	Greens: $$　　　W L T S J Carts: $ Rating: 71.4/73.4 Slope: 122/126
P ☺☺☺ DEAL	**Salem Hills Golf Club** W. Six Mile Rd., Northville. (810) 437-2152 18 holes. Par 72/76. Yards: 6,966/5,874 Apr.–Nov. High: May–Sept.	Greens: $–$$　　　T S J Carts: $ Rating: 72.9/73.4 Slope: 121/119
P ☺☺☺ DEAL	**Springfield Oaks Golf Course** Andersonville Rd., Davisburg. (810) 625-2540 18 holes. Par 71/71. Yards: 6,235/5,372 Mar.–Nov. High: June–Aug.	Greens: $　　　W L T S J Carts: $ Rating: 69.4/70.3 Slope: 115/114
P ☺☺☺	**Stonebridge Golf Club** Stonebridge Dr. S., Ann Arbor. (313) 429-8383	Greens: $$–$$$　　L T S J Carts: $

Michigan Golf Guide

Detroit/Ann Arbor Area

	18 holes. Par 72/72. Yards: 6,932/5,075	Rating:	74.2/71.0
	Mar.–Dec. High: June–Aug.	Slope:	139/128

P	**Sycamore Hills Golf Club**	Greens:	$$	W L T S J
	Mt. Clemens. (810) 598-9500	Carts:	$	
☺☺☺	*North/South/West*	Rating:	70.3/70.7/70.2	
DEAL	27 holes. Par 72/72/72. Yards: 6,255/6,305/6,205	Slope:	123/130/132	
	Mar.–Dec. High: May–Sept.			

P	**Tanglewood Golf Club**	Greens:	$$	L T S J
	W. Ten Mile Rd., S. Lyon. (810) 486-3355	Carts:	$	
☺☺☺	*North/South/West*	Rating:	70.3/70.7/70.2	
DEAL	27 holes. Par 72/72/72. Yards: 7,077/6,922/7,117	Slope:	123/130/132	
	Mar.–Nov. High: May–Aug.			

P	**Taylor Meadows Golf Club**	Greens:	$–$$	W L T S J
☺☺☺	Ecorse Rd., Taylor. (313) 295-0506	Carts:	$$	
DEAL	18 holes. Par 71/71. Yards: 6,075/5,118	Rating:	67.8/67.6	
	Mar.–Dec. High: May–Oct.	Slope:	114/111	

SP	**University of Michigan Golf Course**	Greens:	$$$	
☺☺☺	E. Stadium Blvd., Ann Arbor. (313) 663-5005	Carts:	$$	
STATE	18 holes. Par 71/75. Yards: 6,687/5,331	Rating:	72.5/71.0	
	Apr.–Oct. High: May–Sept.	Slope:	135/125	

P	**Warren Valley Golf Course**	Greens:	$	W L T S J
	W. Warren, Dearborn Heights. (313) 561-1040	Carts:	$$	
☺☺	*East Course*	Rating:	69.1/70.0	
	18 holes. Par 72/72. Yards: 6,189/5,328	Slope:	114/113	
	Mar.–Nov. High: May–Oct.			

☺☺	*West Course*	Rating:	68.5/69.2
	18 holes. Par 71/71. Yards: 6,066/5,150	Slope:	115/114

Minnesota

The Land of 10,000 Lakes has quite a few golf courses that use the plentiful water to great advantage.

The spectacular **Edinburgh USA** club in Brooklyn Park, north of Minneapolis, is among the best public courses anywhere, with some especially challenging sand and water hazards. Even better, it's also on the Econoguide Deals list.

Also just outside of Minneapolis is the Platinum Course at **Majestic Oaks** in Ham Lake, another Econoguide Deal.

In north central Minnesota is the acclaimed **Grand View Lodge** in Nisswa, well worth the trip away from civilization.

Minnesota has some tremendous extremes in weather, with an average temperature in Minneapolis of 12°F in January and a balmy 74°F in July. Most, but not all, courses in the state operate from April through November, with high-season conditions and rates in effect from June through early September.

Econoguide Leader Board: Best Public Courses in Minnesota

☺☺☺☺ Edinburgh USA Golf Club
☺☺☺☺ Grand View Lodge
☺☺☺ Majestic Oaks Golf Club (Platinum)

Econoguide Leader Board: Best Deals in Minnesota

$$/○○○	Baker National Golf Course
$$/○○○	Braemar Golf Course (Red, White, Blue)
$/○○○	Brooktree Municipal Golf Course
$$/○○○○	Bunker Hills Golf Course
$$/○○○	Cannon Golf Club
$/○○○	Cedar River Country Club
$$/○○○	Detroit Country Club
$$/○○○○	Edinburgh USA Golf Club
$$/○○○	Fox Hollow Golf Club
$$/○○○	Headwaters Country Club
$$/○○○	Inverwood Golf Course
$/○○○	Keller Golf Course
$$/○○○	The Links at Northfork
$$/○○○	Little Crow Country Club
$$/○○○	Majestic Oaks Golf Club (Platinum)
$/○○○	Maple Valley Golf and Country Club
$$/○○○	Marshall Golf Club
$$/○○○	Mississippi National Golf Links
$$/○○○	Monticello Country Club
$$/○○○	New Prague Golf Club
$$/○○○	North Links Golf Course
$/○○○	Northern Hills Golf Course
$$/○○○	Northfield Golf Club
$$/○○○	Oak Glen Golf Club
$/○○○	Oaks Country Club
$$/○○○○	Pebble Creek Country Club
$$/○○○	Pebble Lake Golf Club
$$/○○○	Perham Lakeside Country Club
$$/○○○	Pine Meadows Golf Course
$$/○○○	Pokegama Golf Club
$$/○○○	Purple Hawk Golf Club
$$/○○○	Southern Hills Golf Club
$$/○○○	Stonebrooke Golf Club
$$/○○○	Tianna Country Club
$$/○○○	Wedgewood Golf Club
$$/○○○	Wildflower at Fair Hills
$$/○○○○	Willinger's Golf Club
$/○○○	Willow Creek Golf Club

Minnesota Golf Guide

Northern Minnesota

R	**Grand View Lodge**	Greens:	$$–$$$ W L R T
	Nisswa. (218) 963-3146	Carts:	$
○○○○	*The Pines-Lakes/Woods/Marsh*	Rating:	74.2/73.3/73.7
STATE	27 holes. Par 72/72/72. Yards: 6,874/6,883/6,837	Slope:	137/132/134
	Apr.–Oct. High: June–Sept.		
SP	**Headwaters Country Club**	Greens:	$–$$ L T J
○○○	Cty. Rd. 99, Park Rapids. (218) 732-4832	Carts:	$$

Minnesota Golf Guide

Northern Minnesota

DEAL	18 holes. Par 72/72. Yards: 6,455/5,362 Mar.–Nov. High: June–Aug.		Rating: Slope:	70.9/71.0 120/118

R ☺☺	**Madden's on Gull Lake** Pine Beach Peninsula, Brainerd. (218) 829-7118 *Pine Beach East Course* 18 holes. Par 72/72. Yards: 5,956/5,352 Apr.–Oct. High: July–Aug.	Greens: Carts: Rating: Slope:	$$ $$ 67.9/70.9 119/116	W R T

☺☺	*Pine Beach West Course* 18 holes. Par 67/67. Yards: 5,049/4,662	Rating: Slope:	64.0/66.7 103/107

P ☺☺☺ DEAL	**Pine Meadows Golf Course** Brainerd. (218) 829-5733 18 holes. Par 72/72. Yards: 6,200/5,538 Apr.–Oct. High: June–Aug.	Greens: Carts: Rating: Slope:	$$ $ 70.7/72.7 129/133	W L R T S J

R ☺☺☺	**Ruttger's Bay Lake Lodge** Rte. 2, Deerwood. (218) 678-2885 *The Lakes Course* 18 holes. Par 72/72. Yards: 6,750/5,100 Apr.–Oct. High: May–Sept.	Greens: Carts: Rating: Slope:	$$–$$$ $ 72.5/69.3 132/125	L R T

SP ☺☺☺ DEAL	**Tianna Country Club** Walker. (218) 547-1712 18 holes. Par 72/74. Yards: 6,550/5,681 May–Oct. High: June–Aug.	Greens: Carts: Rating: Slope:	$$ $$ 70.7/73.5 127/127	T

Duluth Area

P ☺☺	**Enger Park Golf Club** W. Skyline Blvd., Duluth. (218) 723-3451 27 holes. Par 72/72/72. Yards: 6,434/6,325/6,499 Apr.–Nov. High: June–Aug.	Greens: Carts: Rating: Slope:	$ $ 70.9/70.3/71.0 124/121/121	L T S J

P ☺	**Lester Park Golf Club** Lester River Rd., Duluth. (218) 525-1400 *Front/Back/Lake* 27 holes. Par 72/72/72. Yards: 6,371/6,606/6,599 Apr.–Nov. High: June–July	Greens: Carts: Rating: Slope:	$ $ 70.8/71.7/71.7 118/126/125	L T S J

P ☺☺☺ DEAL	**Pokegama Golf Club** Grand Rapids. (218) 326-3444 18 holes. Par 71/72. Yards: 6,481/4,979 Apr.–Oct. High: June–Aug.	Greens: Carts: Rating: Slope:	$–$$ $ 70.3/67.7 121/116	W R T J

Central Minnesota

R ☺☺☺ DEAL	**Detroit Country Club** Rte. 5, Detroit Lakes. (218) 847-5790 18 holes. Par 71/72. Yards: 5,941/5,508 May–Oct. High: June–Aug.	Greens: Carts: Rating: Slope:	$$ $$ 69.5/71.8 124/127	

P ☺☺☺☺ DEAL	**Pebble Creek Country Club** Becker. (612) 261-4653 27 holes. Par 72/72/72. Yards: 6,820/6,649/6,769 Apr.–Nov. High: June–Sept.	Greens: Carts: Rating: Slope:	$–$$ $ 73.2/72.2/72.4 129/126/129	S J

P ☺☺☺ DEAL	**Pebble Lake Golf Club** Cty. Rd. 82 S., Fergus Falls. (218) 736-7404 18 holes. Par 72/74. Yards: 6,711/5,531 Apr.–Oct. June–Aug.	Greens: Carts: Rating: Slope:	$$ $ 72.3/72.1 128/126	L T S J

P ☺☺☺ DEAL	**Perham Lakeside Country Club** Perham. (218) 346-6070 18 holes. Par 72/72. Yards: 6,575/5,312 Apr.–Nov. High: June–Aug.	Greens: Carts: Rating: Slope:	$$ $ 72.5/71.1 128/122	W L R T J

P ☺☺☺	**Wildflower at Fair Hills** Detroit Lakes. (218) 439-3357	Greens: Carts:	$$ $$	W L R T S J

Minnesota Golf Guide

Central Minnesota

DEAL	18 holes. Par 72/72. Yards: 6,965/5,250	Rating:	74.8/71.8	
	May–First snow. High: June–Aug.	Slope:	136/124	

Minneapolis/St. Paul Area

P	**Baker National Golf Course**	Greens:	$$	S J
☺☺☺	Parkview Dr., Medina. (612) 473-0800	Carts:	$$	
DEAL	18 holes. Par 72/74. Yards: 6,762/5,395	Rating:	74.2/72.7	
	Apr.–Oct. High: June–Aug.	Slope:	133/129	

P	**Bellwood Oaks Golf Course**	Greens:	$	S
☺☺	210th St., Hastings. (612) 437-4141	Carts:	$	
	18 holes. Par 73/74. Yards: 6,775/5,707	Rating:	71.3/71.2	
	Apr.–Nov. High: May–Sept.	Slope:	115/115	

R	**Bemidji Town and Country Club**	Greens:	$–$$	L R T
☺☺	Birchmont Dr. N.E., Bemidji. (218) 751-9215	Carts:	$	
	18 holes. Par 72/72. Yards: 6,535/5,058	Rating:	71.8/69.1	
	Year-round. High: June–Aug.	Slope:	127/120	

P	**Braemar Golf Course**	Greens:	$$	L J
	John Harris Dr., Edina. (612) 941-2072	Carts:	$$	
☺☺☺	*Red/White/Blue*	Rating:	71.8/71.6/73.0	
DEAL	27 holes. Par 71/71/72. Yards: 6,739/6,377/6,692	Slope:	124/129/134	
	Apr.–Oct. High: May–Sept.			

P	**Brooktree Municipal Golf Course**	Greens:	$	
☺☺☺	Cherry St., Owatonna. (507) 451-0730	Carts:	$	
DEAL	18 holes. Par 71/72. Yards: 6,648/5,534	Rating:	71.9/71.3	
	Apr.–Oct. High: June–Aug.	Slope:	121/121	

P	**Brookview Golf Course**	Greens:	$$	
☺☺	Golden Valley. (612) 544-8446	Carts:	$$	
	18 holes. Par 72/72. Yards: 6,369/5,436	Rating:	70.2/71.2	
	Apr.–Oct. High: June–Sept.	Slope:	122/121	

P	**Bunker Hills Golf Course**	Greens:	$$	S J
	Foley Blvd., Coon Rapids. (612) 755-4141	Carts:	$$	
☺☺☺☺	*North/East/West*	Rating:	72.7/73.1/73.4	
DEAL	27 holes. Par 72/72/72. Yards: 6,799/6,938/6,901	Slope:	130/135/133	
	Apr.–Nov. High: June–Aug.			

SP	**Cannon Golf Club**	Greens:	$–$$	W S
☺☺☺	295th St. E., Cannon Falls. (507) 263-3126	Carts:	$$	
DEAL	18 holes. Par 71/71. Yards: 6,200/5,011	Rating:	67.4/68.9	
	Apr.–Oct.	Slope:	121/121	

P	**Columbia Golf Course**	Greens:	$	T S J
☺☺	Central Ave., Minneapolis. (612) 789-2627	Carts:	$$	
	18 holes. Par 71/71. Yards: 6,385/5,489	Rating:	70.0/71.9	
	Apr.–Nov. High: May–Aug.	Slope:	121/123	

P	**Dahlgreen Golf Club**	Greens:	$$	W L S J
☺☺	Dahlgreen Rd., Chaska. (612) 448-7463	Carts:	$$	
	18 holes. Par 72/72. Yards: 6,887/5,850	Rating:	72.5/72.1	
	Mar.–Nov. High: June–Aug.	Slope:	124/120	

P	**Deer Run Golf Club**	Greens:	$$	T S J
☺☺	Vistoria. (612) 443-2351	Carts:	$$	
	18 holes. Par 71/71. Yards: 6,265/5,541	Rating:	70.5/72.1	
	Mar.–Nov. High: June–Aug.	Slope:	122/121	

P	**Edinburgh USA Golf Club**	Greens:	$$	T S J
☺☺☺☺	Edinbrook Crossing, Brooklyn Park. (612) 424-7060	Carts:	$$	
BEST	18 holes. Par 72/72. Yards: 6,701/5,255	Rating:	73.0/71.4	
DEAL	Apr.–Oct. High: June–Aug.	Slope:	133/128	

SP	**Fox Hollow Golf Club**	Greens:	$$	W L S J
☺☺☺	Palmgren Lane N.E., Rogers. (612) 428-4468	Carts:	$$	

Minnesota Golf Guide

Minneapolis/St. Paul Area

DEAL	18 holes. Par 72/72. Yards: 6,726/5,161	Rating: 72.7/70.8	
	Apr.–Nov. High: June–Aug.	Slope: 129/122	

P	**Francis A. Gross Golf Course**	Greens: $	W T S J
◎◎	St. Anthony Blvd., Minneapolis. (612) 789-2542	Carts: $$	
	18 holes. Par 71/71. Yards: 6,575/5,824	Rating: 70.1/73.2	
	Apr.–Nov. High: June–Aug.	Slope: 120/121	

P	**Hidden Greens Golf Club**	Greens: $	W S
◎◎	200th St. E., Hastings. (612) 437-3085	Carts: $	
	18 holes. Par 72/72. Yards: 5,954/5,599	Rating: 68.8/72.2	
	Apr.–Nov. High: July–Aug.	Slope: 114/127	

P	**Inverwood Golf Course**	Greens: $$	J
◎◎◎	Inver Grove Heights. (612) 457-3667	Carts: $$	
DEAL	18 holes. Par 72/72. Yards: 6,724/5,175	Rating: 72.5/70.3	
	Apr.–Oct. High: May–Aug.	Slope: 135/124	

R	**Izaty's Golf and Yacht Club**	Greens: $$–$$$	W R T
◎◎◎	Rte. 1, Onamia. (612) 532-4575	Carts: $$	
	18 holes. Par 72/72. Yards: 6,481/4,939	Rating: 72.1/69.7	
	Apr.–Oct. High: June–Sept.	Slope: 132/127	

P	**Keller Golf Course**	Greens: $	L T S J
◎◎◎	Maplewood Dr., St. Paul. (612) 484-3011	Carts: $$	
DEAL	18 holes. Par 72/73. Yards: 6,566/5,373	Rating: 71.7/71.4	
	Mar.–Nov. High: May–Sept.	Slope: 127/124	

P	**The Links at Northfork**	Greens: $$	W L T S J
◎◎◎	153rd Ave., Ramsey. (612) 241-0506	Carts: $$	
DEAL	18 holes. Par 72/72. Yards: 6,989/5,242	Rating: 73.7/70.5	
	Apr.–Oct. High: June–Aug.	Slope: 127/117	

P	**Majestic Oaks Golf Club**	Greens: $–$$	W L T S J
	Bunker Lake Blvd., Ham Lake. (612) 755-2142	Carts: $$	
◎◎	*Gold Course*	Rating: NA	
	18 holes. Par 72/72. Yards: 6,396/4,848	Slope: 122/118	
	Apr.–Oct. High: June–Aug.		

◎◎◎	*Platinum Course*	Rating: 73.9/71.1	
BEST	18 holes. Par 72/72. Yards: 7,013/5,268	Slope: 132/124	
DEAL			

P	**Manitou Ridge Golf Course**	Greens: $	S J
◎◎	N. McKnight Rd., White Bear Lake. (612) 777-2987	Carts: $	
	18 holes. Par 71/71. Yards: 6,422/5,556	Rating: 70.5/71.5	
	Apr.–Oct. High: Apr.–Oct.	Slope: 120/119	

P	**Meadowbrook Golf Course**	Greens: $	L T S J
◎◎	Meadowbrook Rd., Hopkins. (612) 929-2077	Carts: $$	
	18 holes. Par 72/72. Yards: 6,593/5,610	Rating: 69.6/71.1	
	Apr.–Nov. High: May–Aug.	Slope: 113/122	

P	**Monticello Country Club**	Greens: $–$$	W L S
◎◎◎	Monticello. (612) 295-4653	Carts: $$	
DEAL	18 holes. Par 71/72. Yards: 6,390/5,298	Rating: 70.4/70.8	
	Apr.–Oct. High: June–Aug.	Slope: 118/119	

P	**New Prague Golf Club**	Greens: $$	L S J
◎◎◎	Lexington Ave. S., New Prague. (612) 758-3126	Carts: $$	
DEAL	18 holes. Par 72/72. Yards: 6,335/5,032	Rating: 69.5/68.3	
	Apr.–Oct. High: May–Aug.	Slope: 121/116	

SP	**Northfield Golf Club**	Greens: $$	
◎◎◎	Prairie St., Northfield. (507) 645-4026	Carts: $$	
DEAL	18 holes. Par 69/71. Yards: 5,856/5,103	Rating: 68.7/70.4	
	Apr.–Oct. High: Apr.–Sept.	Slope: 128/126	

Minnesota Golf Guide

Minneapolis/St. Paul Area

P ☺☺☺ DEAL	**Oak Glen Golf Club** McKusick Rd., Stillwater. (612) 439-6963 18 holes. Par 72/72. Yards: 6,550/5,626 Apr.–Nov. High: June–Aug.	Greens: $$ Carts: $ Rating: 72.4/73.4 Slope: 131/130	T
P ☺☺	**Phalen Park Golf Course** Phalen Dr., St. Paul. (612) 778-0413 18 holes. Par 70/71. Yards: 6,101/5,439 Mar.–Nov. High: June–Aug.	Greens: $ Carts: $$ Rating: 68.7/70.7 Slope: 121/121	T S J
P ☺☺	**Pheasant Run Golf Club** Cty. Rd., 116, Rogers. (612) 428-8244 18 holes. Par 71/72. Yards: 6,400/5,200 Apr.–Nov. High: June–Sept.	Greens: $–$$ Carts: $$ Rating: 69.9/68.7 Slope: 117/115	W L T S J
SP ☺☺☺ DEAL	**Purple Hawk Golf Club** Cambridge. (612) 689-3800 18 holes. Par 72/74. Yards: 6,679/5,748 Apr.–Oct. High: June–Aug.	Greens: $–$$ Carts: $$ Rating: 72.3/73.5 Slope: 132/131	T S J
SP ☺☺	**Rich Spring Golf Course** Cold Spring. (612) 685-8810 18 holes. Par 72/72. Yards: 6,542/5,347 Apr.–Oct. High: June–Aug.	Greens: $ Carts: $ Rating: 69.7/70.0 Slope: 119/110	S
P ☺☺	**Rum River Hills Golf Club** St. Francis Blvd., Anoka. (612) 753-3339 18 holes. Par 71/71. Yards: 6,338/5,095 Mar.–Nov. High: June–Aug.	Greens: $–$$ Carts: $$ Rating: 71.3/70.1 Slope: 122/119	T S J
SP ☺☺	**Sawmill Golf Club** McKusick Rd., Stillwater. (612) 439-7862 18 holes. Par 70/71. Yards: 6,300/5,300 Apr.–Nov. High: May–Sept.	Greens: $–$$ Carts: $ Rating: 70.2/69.5 Slope: 125/122	L T S J
P ☺☺☺ DEAL	**Southern Hills Golf Club** Chippendale Ave., Farmington. (612) 463-4653 18 holes. Par 71/71. Yards: 6,314/4,970 Apr.–Oct. High: June–July	Greens: $–$$ Carts: $ Rating: 70.4/68.3 Slope: 123/116	W L T S J
SP ☺☺☺ DEAL	**Stonebrooke Golf Club** Cty. Rd., 79, Shakopee. (612) 496-3171 18 holes. Par 71/71. Yards: 6,604/5,033 Apr.–Oct. High: June–July	Greens: $$ Carts: $$ Rating: 71.7/69.3 Slope: 133/118	
P ☺☺	**Theodore Wirth Golf Course** Minneapolis. (612) 522-4584 18 holes. Par 72/72. Yards: 6,408/5,639 Apr.–Nov. High: June–Aug.	Greens: $ Carts: $ Rating: 71.7/72.8 Slope: 129/123	W L T S J
SP ☺☺☺ DEAL	**Wedgewood Golf Club** Wedgewood Dr., Woodbury. (612) 731-4779 18 holes. Par 72/72. Yards: 6,717/5,267 Mar.–Nov. High: Apr.–Sept.	Greens: $$ Carts: $ Rating: 72.3/70.1 Slope: 120/121	W T J

Rochester Area

P ☺☺	**Eastwood Golf Club** Eastwood Rd., S.E., Rochester. (507) 281-6173 18 holes. Par 72/72. Yards: 6,178/5,289 Apr.–Nov. High: May–Aug.	Greens: $ Carts: $ Rating: 69.9/71.0 Slope: 120/121	
SP ☺☺☺ DEAL	**Maple Valley Golf and Country Club** Maple Valley Rd., S.E., Rochester. (507) 285-9100 18 holes. Par 71/71. Yards: 6,270/5,330 Mar.–Nov. High: July–Aug.	Greens: $ Carts: Inquire Rating: 68.9/68.5 Slope: 108/108	
P ☺☺☺	**North Links Golf Course** Cty. Rd., 66, N. Mankato. (507) 947-3355	Greens: $–$$ Carts: $	T S J

Minnesota Golf Guide

Rochester Area

DEAL	18 holes. Par 72/72. Yards: 6,073/4,659		Rating:	69.5/66.9	
	Apr.–Nov. High: June–Aug.		Slope:	117/114	

P	**Northern Hills Golf Course**		Greens:	$	
☺☺☺	N.W. 41st Ave., Rochester. (507) 281-6170		Carts:	$	
DEAL	18 holes. Par 72/72. Yards: 6,315/5,456		Rating:	70.4/71.6	
	Apr.–Oct. High: May–Sept.		Slope:	123/123	

SP	**Oaks Country Club**		Greens:	$	L
☺☺☺	Hayfield. (507) 477-3233		Carts:	$	
DEAL	18 holes. Par 72/72. Yards: 6,404/5,663		Rating:	69.7/71.7	
	Apr.–Oct. High: June–Aug.		Slope:	114/118	

P	**Willinger's Golf Club**		Greens:	$$	T S J
☺☺☺☺	Canby Trail, Northfield. (612) 440-7000		Carts:	$$	
DEAL	18 holes. Par 72/72. Yards: 6,711/5,166		Rating:	73.3/71.6	
	Apr.–Oct. High: June–Aug.		Slope:	140/130	

SP	**Willow Creek Golf Club**		Greens:	$	
☺☺☺	1700 S.W. 48th St., Rochester. (507) 285-0305		Carts:	$	
DEAL	18 holes. Par 70/70. Yards: 6,053/5,293		Rating:	69.1/70.5	
	Mar.–Nov. High: June–Aug.		Slope:	117/121	

Southern Minnesota

P	**Cedar River Country Club**		Greens:	$	L
☺☺☺	Hwy. 56 W., Adams. (507) 582-3595		Carts:	$	
DEAL	18 holes. Par 72/74. Yards: 6,211/5,517		Rating:	70.3/72.0	
	Mar.–Nov. High: June–Aug.		Slope:	124/124	

SP	**Little Crow Country Club**		Greens:	$–$$	W L
☺☺☺	Hwy. 23, Spicer. (612) 354-2296		Carts:	$	
DEAL	18 holes. Par 72/72. Yards: 6,765/5,757		Rating:	72.3/73.1	
	Apr.–Nov. High: June–Aug.		Slope:	123/125	

SP	**Marshall Golf Club**		Greens:	$$	
☺☺☺	Marshall. (507) 537-1622		Carts:	$$	
DEAL	18 holes. Par 72/72. Yards: 6,565/5,136		Rating:	71.6/69.5	
	Apr.–Oct. High: May–Sept.		Slope:	123/120	

P	**Mississippi National Golf Links**		Greens:	$$	W
	Red Wing. (612) 388-1874		Carts:	$	
☺☺☺	*Lowlands/Midlands/Highlands*		Rating:	70.0/71.5/71.1	
DEAL	18 holes. Par 72/72. Yards: 6,035/6,488/6,215		Slope:	125/128/130	
	Apr.–Oct. High: June–Aug.				

P	**Mount Frontenac Golf Course**		Greens:	$	W T S
☺☺	Hwy. 61, Frontenac. (612) 388-5826		Carts:	$	
	18 holes. Par 70/70. Yards: 6,050/4,832		Rating:	69.2/67.7	
	Apr.–Oct. High: June–Aug.		Slope:	119/117	

P	**Ramsey Golf Club**		Greens:	$	L
☺☺	Autin. (507) 433-9098		Carts:	$	
	18 holes. Par 71/72. Yards: 5,987/5,426		Rating:	68.2/70.7	
	Apr.–Nov. High: May–Sept.		Slope:	120/117	

Missouri

Foremost among the gems of Missouri public courses are the venerable **Shirkey Golf Club** near Kansas City, and the newer **Tapawingo National Golf Club**, outside of St. Louis. Shirkey also has a spot on the Econoguide Deals list.

Half a notch below are the lush fairways of **Eagle Lake**, in Farmington south of St. Louis, and the hilly Osage Course at the **North Port National Golf Course**. Eagle Lake is an Econoguide Deal.

Golf courses in Missouri are generally open year-round. Look for peak rates from April through late September at most courses.

Econoguide Leader Board: Best Public Courses in Missouri

☺☺☺	Eagle Lake Golf Club
☺☺☺	North Port National Golf Club (Osage)
☺☺☺☺	Shirkey Golf Club
☺☺☺☺	Tapawingo National Golf Club

Econoguide Leader Board: Best Deals in Missouri

$$/☺☺☺	Bent Creek Golf Course
$$/☺☺☺	Crystal Highlands Golf Club
$$/☺☺☺	Eagle Lake Golf Club
$/☺☺☺	Honey Creek Golf Club
$/☺☺☺	Longview Lake Golf Course
$$/☺☺☺	Paradise Pointe Golf Club (Outlaw)
$$/☺☺☺☺	Shirkey Golf Club
$/☺☺☺	Swope Memorial Golf Course

Missouri Golf Guide

Northern Missouri

| SP ☺☺ | **Kirksville Country Club**
State Hwy. 63, Kirksville. (816) 665-5335
18 holes. Par 71/71. Yards: 6,418/5,802
Mar.–Dec. High: June–Aug. | Greens: $
Carts: $
Rating: 70.9/71.6
Slope: 118/114 | |

Kansas City Area

SP ☺☺	**Bent Oak Golf Club** S.E. 30th, Oak Grove. (816) 690-3028 18 holes. Par 72/73. Yards: 6,855/5,500 Year-round. High: May–Sept.	Greens: $ Carts: $$ Rating: 73.1/71.0 Slope: 134/119	W S J
P ☺☺	**Excelsior Springs Golf Club** Excelsior Springs. (816) 630-3731 18 holes. Par 72/72. Yards: 6,650/5,450 Year-round. High: May–Sept.	Greens: $ Carts: $ Rating: 69.5/67.9 Slope: 116/110	W T
P ☺☺	**Hodge Park Golf Course** N.E. Barry Rd., Kansas City. (816) 781-4152 18 holes. Par 71/71. Yards: 6,181/5,707 Year-round. High: Apr.–Oct.	Greens: $ Carts: Incl. Rating: NA Slope: 117/110	T
P ☺☺☺ DEAL	**Longview Lake Golf Course** View High Dr., Kansas City. (816) 761-9445 18 holes. Par 72/72. Yards: 6,835/5,534 Year-round. High: May–Aug.	Greens: $ Carts: $$ Rating: 71.9/70.8 Slope: 121/113	W S J
R ☺☺☺	**Marriott's Tan-Tar** Osage Beach. (314) 348-8521 *The Oaks Course* 18 holes. Par 71/70. Yards: 6,442/3,943 Year-round. High: May–Oct.	Greens: $$$–$$$$ Carts: Incl. Rating: 72.1/62.5 Slope: 143/103	W L T
P ☺☺☺ DEAL	**Paradise Pointe Golf Club** Smithville. (816) 532-4100 *Outlaw Course* 18 holes. Par 72/72. Yards: 6,988/5,322 Year-round. High: May–Oct.	Greens: $–$$ Carts: $ Rating: 73.8/67.0 Slope: 138/118	W L S
☺☺	*Posse Course* 18 holes. Par 72/73. Yards: 6,663/5,600	Rating: 71.8/70.0 Slope: 125/115	

Missouri Golf Guide

Kansas City Area

SP ◎◎◎◎ DEAL STATE	**Shirkey Golf Club** Wollard Blvd., Richmond. (816) 776-9965 18 holes. Par 71/74. Yards: 6,907/5,516 Year-round. High: May–Oct.	Greens: $–$$ Carts: $$ Rating: 71.3/73.1 Slope: 136/129	W S
P ◎◎◎ DEAL	**Swope Memorial Golf Course** Kansas City. (816) 523-9081 18 holes. Par 72/72. Yards: 6,274/4,517 Year-round. High: Apr.–Oct.	Greens: $ Carts: $ Rating: 70.9/65.9 Slope: 128/107	T S J

St. Louis Area

P ◎◎◎	**Cherry Hills Golf Club** Manchester Rd., Grover. (314) 458-4113 18 holes. Par 71/72. Yards: 6,450/5,491 Year-round. High: May–Aug.	Greens: $$–$$$ Carts: Incl. Rating: 71.1/72.6 Slope: 132/120	L T S
P ◎◎◎ DEAL	**Crystal Highlands Golf Club** U.S. Hwy. 61, Festus/Crystal City. (314) 931-3880 18 holes. Par 72/72. Yards: 6,480/4,946 Year-round. High: Apr.–Oct.	Greens: $$ Carts: $ Rating: 71.6/68.0 Slope: 135/109	W L T J
P ◎◎	**Eagle Springs Golf Course** Redman Rd., St. Louis. (314) 355-7277 18 holes. Par 72/72. Yards: 6,679/5,533 Year-round. High: May–Sept.	Greens: $–$$ Carts: $ Rating: 71.4/72.3 Slope: 122/121	W L S J
P ◎◎◎	**Quail Creek Golf Club** Wells Rd., St. Louis. (314) 487-1988 18 holes. Par 72/72. Yards: 6,984/5,244 Year-round. High: Apr.–Oct.	Greens: $$$ Carts: Incl. Rating: NA Slope: 141/109	W L T
P ◎◎◎◎ STATE	**Tapawingo National Golf Club** W. Watson Rd., St. Louis. (314) 349-3100 18 holes. Par 72/72. Yards: 7,151/5,566 Year-round. High: Apr.–Oct.	Greens: $$$ Carts: Incl. Rating: 75.1/72.2 Slope: 144/121	W T S J
P ◎◎◎	**Whitmoor Country Club** Whitmoor Dr., St. Charles. (314) 926-9622 18 holes. Par 71/71. Yards: 6,646/4,658 Year-round. High: Apr.–Sept.	Greens: $$$ Carts: Incl. Rating: NA Slope: 132/110	L T

Springfield Area

P ◎◎	**Bill and Payne Stewart Golf Course** E. Norton, Springfield. (417) 833-9962 18 holes. Par 70/72. Yards: 6,043/5,693 Year-round. High: Mar.–Oct.	Greens: $ Carts: $ Rating: 68.4/71.3 Slope: 113/117	W S J
P ◎◎	**Carthage Municipal Golf Course** Oak St., Carthage. (417) 358-8724 18 holes. Par 71/73. Yards: 6,402/5,469 Year-round. High: Apr.–Aug.	Greens: $ Carts: $ Rating: 69.4/70.5 Slope: 124/115	W J
SP ◎◎	**Cassville Golf Club** Hwy. 112 S., Cassville. (417) 847-2399 18 holes. Par 72/72. Yards: 6,620/5,802 Year-round. High: Apr.–Oct.	Greens: $ Carts: Inquire Rating: 71.3/79.8 Slope: 118/117	
P ◎◎	**Hidden Valley Golf Links** Rte. 1, Clever. (417) 743-2860 18 holes. Par 73/75. Yards: 6,611/5,288 Year-round. High: May–Sept.	Greens: $ Carts: $ Rating: 71.9/NA Slope: 118/NA	S
P ◎◎◎ DEAL	**Honey Creek Golf Club** Aurora. (417) 678-3353 18 holes. Par 71/79. Yards: 6,732/5,972 Year-round. High: Apr.–Oct.	Greens: $ Carts: $ Rating: 71.9/NA Slope: 118/NA	

Missouri Golf Guide

Springfield Area

P ☺☺☺	**Lake Valley Golf Club** Camdenton. (314) 346-7218 18 holes. Par 72/74. Yards: 6,430/5,320 Year-round. High: Apr.–Oct.	Greens: Carts: Rating: Slope:	$$–$$$ L R T J Inquire 71.1/70.5 121/118
P ☺☺	**Schifferdecker Golf Course** Schifferdecker, Joplin. (417) 624-3533 18 holes. Par 71/72. Yards: 6,123/5,251 Year-round. High: Apr.–Sept.	Greens: Carts: Rating: Slope:	$ T S J $ 68.7/69.7 108/117

Southern Missouri

SP ☺☺☺ DEAL	**Bent Creek Golf Course** Jackson. (314) 243-6060 18 holes. Par 72/72. Yards: 6,958/5,148 Year-round. High: May–Sept.	Greens: Carts: Rating: Slope:	$$ W L T S J Incl. 72.5/69.8 136/112
SP ☺☺☺ DEAL STATE	**Eagle Lake Golf Club** Hunt Rd., Farmington. (314) 756-6660 18 holes. Par 72/72. Yards: 7,093/5,648 Year-round. High: Apr.–Oct.	Greens: Carts: Rating: Slope:	$–$$ L T S $ 73.9/NA 130/NA
R ☺☺☺ STATE	**North Port National Golf Club** Osage Hills Rd., Lake Ozark. (314) 365-1100 *Osage* 18 holes. Par 72/72. Yards: 7,150/5,252 Year-round. High: Apr.–Oct.	Greens: Carts: Rating: Slope:	$$$ W L R T S J Incl. 75.6/70.5 145/122
R ☺☺☺	**The Lodge of Four Seasons** State Rd. HH, Lake Ozark. (314) 365-8544 *Robert Trent Jones Course* 18 holes. Par 71/71. Yards: 6,567/5,238 Year-round. High: May–Oct.	Greens: Carts: Rating: Slope:	$$$–$$$$ W L T Incl. 71.4/70.8 136/124

Nebraska

Shadow Ridge in Omaha is a spectacular, well-maintained semiprivate gem. **Heritage Hills** in McCook (southwestern Nebraska) is a hidden gem, a linkslike rolling prairie that is worth the hike from civilization. **Woodland Hills** in Eagle, outside of Lincoln, is an interesting challenge in the piney woods. Both Heritage Hills and Woodland Hills are also Econoguide Deals.

Some courses in Nebraska manage to stay open year-round, but most operate from March through October. Peak rates are in effect from about May through early September.

Econoguide Leader Board: Best Public Courses in Nebraska

☺☺☺☺   Heritage Hills Golf Course
☺☺☺☺   Shadow Ridge Country Club
☺☺☺☺   Woodland Hills Golf Course

Econoguide Leader Board: Best Deals in Nebraska

$/☺☺☺	Grand Island Municipal Golf Course
$$/☺☺☺☺	Heritage Hills Golf Course
$/☺☺☺	Highlands Golf Course
$/☺☺☺	Himark Golf Course
$/☺☺☺	Holmes Park Golf Course
$$/☺☺☺	Indian Creek Golf Course

$/☺☺☺	Meadowlark Hills Golf Course
$$/☺☺☺	The Pines Country Club
$/☺☺☺	Pioneers Golf Course
$/☺☺☺	Quail Run Golf Course
$$/☺☺☺	Tiburon Golf Club
$$/☺☺☺☺	Woodland Hills Golf Course

Nebraska Golf Guide

McCook and Kearney

SP ☺☺☺☺ DEAL STATE	**Heritage Hills Golf Course** McCook. (308) 345-5032 18 holes. Par 72/72. Yards: 6,715/5,475 Year-round. High: May–Sept.	Greens: $$ Carts: $ Rating: 72.7/71.1 Slope: 130/127	T J
SP ☺☺☺ DEAL	**Meadowlark Hills Golf Course** 30th Ave., Kearney. (308) 233-3265 18 holes. Par 71/72. Yards: 6,485/4,967 Year-round. High: May–Aug.	Greens: $ Carts: $ Rating: 70.4/68.2 Slope: 119/112	L T S J

Grand Island Area

P ☺☺☺ DEAL	**Grand Island Municipal Golf Course** Shady Bend Rd., Grand Island. (308) 385-5340 18 holes. Par 72/72. Yards: 6,752/5,487 Year-round. High: Apr.–Sept.	Greens: $ Carts: $ Rating: 71.3/70.8 Slope: 118/112	S J
P ☺☺	**Indianhead Golf Course** Husker Hwy., Grand Island. (308) 381-4653 18 holes. Par 72/72. Yards: 6,597/5,664 Year-round. High: May–Sept.	Greens: $ Carts: $ Rating: 70.9/71.9 Slope: 122/117	W T S J

Lincoln Area

P ☺☺☺ DEAL	**Highlands Golf Course** N.W. 12th St., Lincoln. (402) 441-6081 18 holes. Par 72/72. Yards: 7,021/5,280 Year-round. High: Apr.–Oct.	Greens: $ Carts: $ Rating: 72.5/69.4 Slope: 119/111	S J
P ☺☺☺ DEAL	**Himark Golf Course** Pioneers Blvd., Lincoln. (402) 488-7888 18 holes. Par 72/70. Yards: 6,700/4,900 Mar.–Nov. High: June–Aug.	Greens: $ Carts: $ Rating: 71.3/67.1 Slope: 120/111	W L T S J
P ☺☺☺ DEAL	**Holmes Park Golf Course** S. 70th St., Lincoln. (402) 441-8960 18 holes. Par 72/74. Yards: 6,805/6,054 Mar.–Dec. High: July	Greens: $ Carts: $$ Rating: 72.2/73.8 Slope: 120/126	W S J
P ☺☺	**Mahoney Golf Course** Adams St., Lincoln. (402) 441-8969 18 holes. Par 72/72. Yards: 6,300/5,607 Apr.–Nov. High: June–Aug.	Greens: $ Carts: $ Rating: 72.3/70.3 Slope: 125/118	S J
P ☺☺☺ DEAL	**Pioneers Golf Course** W. Van Dorn, Lincoln. (402) 441-8966 18 holes. Par 71/74. Yards: 6,478/5,771 Year-round. High: June–Aug.	Greens: $ Carts: $$ Rating: 69.2/73.2 Slope: 110/114	W S J
P ☺☺☺☺ DEAL STATE	**Woodland Hills Golf Course** Eagle. (402) 475-4653 18 holes. Par 71/71. Yards: 6,592/4,945 Year-round. High: July–Aug.	Greens: $–$$ Carts: $ Rating: 71.3/69.8 Slope: 125/121	W L R T S J

Omaha Area

P ☺☺	**Applewood Golf Course** S. 99th St., Omaha. (402) 444-4656	Greens: $ Carts: $	W S J

Omaha Area

	18 holes. Par 72/72. Yards: 6,916/6,014	Rating:	72.4/74.6
	Year-round. High: May–Sept.	Slope:	121/126

SP	**Ashland Country Club**	Greens:	$–$$
☺☺	Ashland. (402) 944-3388	Carts:	$
	18 holes. Par 70/74. Yards: 6,337/5,606	Rating:	70.0/69.8
	Mar.–Oct. High: June–Sept.	Slope:	112/112

P	**Benson Park Golf Course**	Greens:	$	S J
☺☺	N. 72nd St., Omaha. (402) 444-4626	Carts:	$	
	18 holes. Par 72/78. Yards: 6,814/6,085	Rating:	72.1/73.4	
	Mar.–Dec. High: May–Sept.	Slope:	120/121	

P	**Indian Creek Golf Course**	Greens:	$–$$	S
☺☺☺	W. Maple Rd., Elkhorn. (402) 289-0900	Carts:	$	
DEAL	18 holes. Par 72/72. Yards: 7,236/5,149	Rating:	75.5/68.9	
	Mar.–Nov. High: June–July	Slope:	129/112	

P	**The Knolls Golf Course**	Greens:	$	T S J
☺☺	Sahler St., Omaha. (402) 493-1740	Carts:	$	
	18 holes. Par 71/71. Yards: 6,300/5,111	Rating:	69.8/69.8	
	Year-round. High: Apr.–Oct.	Slope:	123/NA	

P	**Miracle Hill Golf and Tennis Center**	Greens:	$–$$	T S
☺☺	N. 120th St., Omaha. (402) 498-0220	Carts:	$	
	18 holes. Par 70/70. Yards: 6,412/5,069	Rating:	71.0/69.0	
	Year-round. High: May–Aug.	Slope:	129/117	

SP	**The Pines Country Club**	Greens:	$–$$	W S J
☺☺☺	N. 286th St., Valley. (402) 359-4311	Carts:	$	
DEAL	18 holes. Par 72/72. Yards: 6,650/5,370	Rating:	69.9/70.2	
	Mar.–Oct. High: May–Aug.	Slope:	117/117	

P	**Quail Run Golf Course**	Greens:	$	W T S J
☺☺☺	South 5th St., Columbus. (402) 564-1313	Carts:	$	
DEAL	18 holes. Par 72/72. Yards: 7,024/5,147	Rating:	75.1/70.7	
	Apr.–Oct. High: June–Aug.	Slope:	140/125	

SP	**Shadow Ridge Country Club**	Greens:	$$–$$$	T
☺☺☺☺	S. 188th Plaza, Omaha. (402) 333-0500	Carts:	$	
STATE	18 holes. Par 72/72. Yards: 7,013/5,176	Rating:	74.6/69.8	
	Mar.–Oct. High: May–Sept.	Slope:	137/116	

SP	**Tiburon Golf Club**	Greens:	$–$$	W S J
☺☺☺	S. 168th St., Omaha. (402) 895-2688	Carts:	$	
DEAL	27 holes. Par 72/72/72. Yards: 6,887/6,932/7,005	Rating:	73.4/73.4/74.2	
	Mar.–Nov. High: June–Sept.	Slope:	131/131/137	

North Dakota

The best of North Dakota includes **Edgewood** in Fargo, a course that dates back to 1915 and provides the polished experience of a successful old-timer.

In Minot, the **Minot Country Club** is another venerable beauty, much greener than the prairies that surround it. In Bismarck, the **Riverwood Golf Club**, with its river and woods, is a tight challenge.

Edgewood and Riverwood both also appear on the Econoguide Deals list.

Most golf courses in North Dakota are open from April through October or November. Peak rates are typically in effect from June through early September.

Econoguide Leader Board: Best Public Courses in North Dakota

⊚⊚⊚   Edgewood Golf Course
⊚⊚⊚   Minot Country Club
⊚⊚⊚   Riverwood Golf Club

Econoguide Leader Board: Best Deals in North Dakota

$/⊚⊚⊚   Bois de Sioux Golf Club
$/⊚⊚⊚   Edgewood Golf Course
$/⊚⊚⊚   Prairie West Golf Course
$/⊚⊚⊚   Riverwood Golf Club
$/⊚⊚⊚   Souris Valley Golf Club

North Dakota Golf Guide

Eastern North Dakota

P	**Bois de Sioux Golf Club**	Greens:	$	W
⊚⊚⊚	North 4th St., Wahpeton. (701) 642-3673	Carts:	$	
DEAL	18 holes. Par 72/72. Yards: 6,675/5,500	Rating:	71.3/71.4	
	Apr.–Nov. High: Apr.–Sept.	Slope:	122/119	

P	**Edgewood Golf Course**	Greens:	$	T S J
⊚⊚⊚	2nd St. N., Fargo. (701) 232-2824	Carts:	$	
DEAL	18 holes. Par 72/72. Yards: 6,369/5,176	Rating:	68.4/68.9	
STATE	Apr.–Nov. High: July–Aug.	Slope:	122/115	

P	**Manvel Golf Course**	Greens:	$	J
	County Rd., 5, Manvel. (701) 696-8268	Carts:	$	
⊚⊚	*Pioneer/Settler's*	Rating:	70.6/69.1	
	18 holes. Par 72/72. Yards: 6,357/5,146	Slope:	126/118	
	Apr.–Oct. High: Apr.–June			

P	**Rose Creek Golf Course**	Greens:	$	T S J
⊚⊚	Rose Creek Pkwy., Fargo. (701) 235-5100	Carts:	$	
	18 holes. Par 72/72. Yards: 6,616/5,062	Rating:	71.4/68.8	
	Apr.–Nov. High: May–Aug.	Slope:	123/114	

Western North Dakota

P	**Heart River Golf Course**	Greens:	$	J
⊚⊚	Dickinson. (701) 225-9412	Carts:	$	
	18 holes. Par 72/71. Yards: 6,652/5,583	Rating:	70.8/71.0	
	Mar.–Oct. High: June–Aug.	Slope:	125/116	

SP	**Minot Country Club**	Greens:	$$	W
⊚⊚⊚	Hwy. 15 W., Minot. (701) 839-6169	Carts:	$	
STATE	18 holes. Par 72/72. Yards: 6,667/6,217	Rating:	NA	
	Apr.–Nov. High: June–Aug.	Slope:	124/121	

P	**Prairie West Golf Course**	Greens:	$	S J
⊚⊚⊚	Long Spur Trail, Mandan. (701) 667-3222	Carts:	$	
DEAL	18 holes. Par 72/72. Yards: 6,681/5,452	Rating:	71.6/70.1	
	Apr.–Oct. High: July–Aug.	Slope:	127/118	

P	**Riverwood Golf Club**	Greens:	$	S J
⊚⊚⊚	Bismarck Dr., Bismarck. (701) 222-6462	Carts:	$	
DEAL	18 holes. Par 72/72. Yards: 6,941/5,196	Rating:	70.0/68.6	
STATE	Apr.–Oct. High: June–Sept.	Slope:	130/112	

P	**Souris Valley Golf Club**	Greens:	$	T S J
⊚⊚⊚	14th Ave. S.W., Minot. (701) 838-4112	Carts:	$	
DEAL	18 holes. Par 72/72. Yards: 6,815/5,474	Rating:	72.5/71.2	
	Apr.–Sept. High: June–Aug.	Slope:	126/118	

Western North Dakota

P	Tom O'Leary Golf Course	Greens:	$	S J
☺	N. Washington St., Bismarck. (701) 222-6462	Carts:	$	
	18 holes. Par 68/68. Yards: 5,800/4,026	Rating:	65.0/62.3	
	Apr.–Oct. High: June–Sept.	Slope:	110/97	

Ohio

There are 14 courses at 12 clubs on the Econoguide Best list for public courses in Ohio.

Five of the favorites are in and around Cleveland: **Avalon, Fowler's, Pine Hills, Quail Hollow,** and **Windmill Lakes**. In nearby Akron are **Hawks Nest** and **Yankee Run**. Near Toledo is **Maumee Bay State Park**. In central Ohio near Columbus, golfers in search of the best should consider **Eagle Sticks** and **Indian Springs**.

Down south near Cincinnati are **Shaker Run** and **The Vineyard**, which is built on the rolling ground of a former vineyard.

The courses that also earn a spot on the Econoguide Deals list are Eagle Sticks, Hawks Nest, Indian Springs, Maumee Bay State Park, Pine Hills, The Vineyard, Windmill Lakes, and Yankee Run.

Many courses in Ohio are open year-round, with peak rates and conditions from about May to October. Other courses, including many in the snowbelts near Cleveland, operate from March through November, with peak rates in the summer.

Econoguide Leader Board: Best Public Courses in Ohio

☺☺☺☺	Avalon Lakes Golf Course
☺☺☺☺	Eagle Sticks Golf Course
☺☺☺☺	Fowler's Mill Golf Club (Blue, White, Red)
☺☺☺☺	Hawks Nest Golf Club
☺☺☺☺	Indian Springs Golf Club
☺☺☺☺	Maumee Bay State Park Golf Course
☺☺☺☺	Pine Hills Golf Club
☺☺☺☺	Quail Hollow Resort
☺☺☺☺	Shaker Run Golf Course
☺☺☺☺	The Vineyard Golf Course
☺☺☺☺	Windmill Lakes Golf Club
☺☺☺☺	Yankee Run Golf Course

Econoguide Leader Board: Best Deals in Ohio

$/☺☺☺	Apple Valley Golf Club
$/☺☺☺	Beaver Creek Meadows Golf Course
$/☺☺☺	Blackhawk Golf Club
$/☺☺☺	Blacklick Woods Golf Course (Gold)
$/☺☺☺	Blue Ash Golf Course
$$/☺☺☺	Champions Golf Course
$$/☺☺☺	Chardon Lakes Golf Club
$/☺☺☺	Chippewa Golf Club

$/○○○	Country Acres Golf Club
$$/○○○○	Eagle Sticks Golf Course
$$/○○○	Fox Den Golf Club
$/○○○	Foxfire Golf Club
$$/○○○	Glenview Golf Course
$$/○○○	Granville Golf Club
$$/○○○○	Hawks Nest Golf Club
$$/○○○	Heatherwoode Golf Club
$/○○○	Hemlock Springs Golf Club
$/○○○	Hilliard Lakes Golf Club
$$/○○○	Hinckley Hills Golf Course
$$/○○○	Hueston Woods State Park Golf Resort
$$/○○○○	Indian Springs Golf Club
$/○○○	Ironwood Golf Club
$/○○○	J.E. Good Park Golf Club
$/○○○	Manakiki Golf Club
$$/○○○○	Maumee Bay State Park Golf Course
$/○○○	Miami Whitewater Forest Golf Course
$/○○○	Mill Creek Park Golf Course (North, South)
$/○○○	Mohican Hills Golf Club
$$/○○○	Orchard Hills Golf and Country Club
$/○○○	Pebble Creek Golf Club
$/○○○○	Pine Hills Golf Club
$$/○○○	Pipestone Golf Club
$$/○○○	Raintree Country Club
$/○○○	Reid Park Memorial Golf Course (North)
$$/○○○	Royal American Links Golf Club
$/○○○	Salem Hills Golf and Country Club
$/○○○	Sharon Woods Golf Course
$/○○○	Shelby Oaks Golf Club
$$/○○○	Skyland Pines Golf Club
$/○○○	Sleepy Hollow Golf Course
$$/○○○	Tam O'Shanter Golf Course (Dales, Hills)
$/○○○	Thunderbird Hills Golf Club
$$/○○○	Turnberry Golf Course
$$/○○○	Valleywood Golf Club
$$/○○○○	The Vineyard Golf Course
$/○○○	Weatherwax Golf Course (Valleyview, Highlands, Woodside, Meadows)
$$/○○○○	Windmill Lakes Golf Club
$$/○○○	Woodland Golf Club
$$/○○○○	Yankee Run Golf Course
$/○○○	Zoar Village Golf Club

Ohio Golf Guide

Toledo Area

SP	**Ironwood Golf Club**	Greens: $	W
○○○	W. Leggett, Wauseon. (419) 335-0587	Carts: $	

Ohio Golf Guide

Toledo Area

DEAL	18 holes. Par 72/74. Yards: 6,965/5,306	Rating:	72.2/69.2
	Mar.–Nov. High: June–Aug.	Slope:	112/106

P	**Maumee Bay State Park Golf Course**	Greens:	$$ W L T S
☺☺☺☺	Park Rd., 2, Oregon. (419) 836-9009	Carts:	$
DEAL	18 holes. Par 72/72. Yards: 6,941/5,221	Rating:	73.3/70.5
STATE	Apr.–Oct. High: May–Aug.	Slope:	129/118

SP	**Sycamore Hills Golf Club**	Greens:	$ W L S J
☺☺	W. Hayes Ave., Fremont. (419) 332-5716	Carts:	$
	18 holes. Par 70/72. Yards: 6,221/5,076	Rating:	67.3/66.3
	Mar.–Dec. High: Apr.–Sept.	Slope:	110/107

SP	**Valleywood Golf Club**	Greens:	$–$$ S
☺☺☺	Airport Hwy., Swanton. (419) 826-3991	Carts:	$
DEAL	18 holes. Par 71/73. Yards: 6,364/5,588	Rating:	68.4/71.6
	Feb.–Dec.	Slope:	115/121

Cleveland Area

R	**Avalon Lakes Golf Course**	Greens:	$$$ W L T
☺☺☺☺	Warren. (216) 856-8898	Carts:	Incl.
STATE	18 holes. Par 71/71. Yards: 6,868/5,324	Rating:	73.4/70.9
	Year-round. High: June–Aug.	Slope:	128/116

P	**Big Met Golf Club**	Greens:	$ L S J
☺☺	Valley Pkwy., Fairview Park. (216) 331-1070	Carts:	$
	18 holes. Par 72/74. Yards: 6,125/5,870	Rating:	68.0/72.0
	Year-round. High: May–Aug.	Slope:	108/113

P	**Briarwood Golf Course**	Greens:	$–$$ W L T S J
	Edgerton Rd., Broadview Heights. (216) 237-5271	Carts:	$
☺☺	*Ben/Glens/Lochs*	Rating:	70.1/72.8/70.8
	27 holes. Par 71/72/71. Yards: 6,405/6,985/6,500	Slope:	117/125/117
	Year-round. High: May–Sept.		

P	**Chapel Hills Golf Course**	Greens:	$ W S J
☺☺	Austinburg Rd., Ashtabula. (216) 997-3791	Carts:	$
	18 holes. Par 72/72. Yards: 5,971/4,507	Rating:	68.6/65.7
	Year-round. High: June–Sept.	Slope:	112/104

P	**Chardon Lakes Golf Club**	Greens:	$–$$ L S J
☺☺☺	South St., Chardon. (216) 285-4653	Carts:	$
DEAL	18 holes. Par 71/73. Yards: 6,789/5,077	Rating:	73.1/66.6
	Apr.–Nov. High: June–Sept.	Slope:	135/111

P	**Deer Track Golf Club**	Greens:	$ L S
☺☺	Leavitt Rd., Elyria. (216) 986-5881	Carts:	$
	18 holes. Par 71/71. Yards: 6,410/5,191	Rating:	70.3/68.7
	Year-round. High: Apr.–Oct.	Slope:	104/115

P	**Dorlon Park Golf Course**	Greens:	$ S
☺☺	18000 Station Rd., Columbus. (216) 236-8234	Carts:	$
	18 holes. Par 72/74. Yards: 7,154/5,691	Rating:	74.0/67.4
	Apr.–Nov. High: May–Sept.	Slope:	131/118

P	**The Elms Country Club**	Greens:	$ W L T S J
☺☺	Manchester Rd. S.W., N. Lawrence. (216) 833-2668	Carts:	$$
	27 holes. Par 72/71/73. Yards: 6,545/6,054/6,633	Rating:	69.9/67.7/70.1
	Feb.–Dec. High: May–Sept.	Slope:	110/104/108

P	**Fowler's Mill Golf Club**	Greens:	$$–$$$ W L T S J
	Rockhaven Rd., Chesterland. (216) 729-7569	Carts:	$
☺☺☺☺	*Blue/White/Red*	Rating:	74.7/70.7/72.1
STATE	27 holes. Par 72/72/72. Yards: 7,002/6,385/6,595	Slope:	136/125/128
	Mar.–Oct. High: June–Aug.		

P	**Hemlock Springs Golf Club**	Greens:	$ W L T S J
☺☺☺	Cold Springs Rd., Geneva. (216) 466-4044	Carts:	$

Ohio Golf Guide

Cleveland Area

DEAL	18 holes. Par 72/72. Yards: 6,812/5,453	Rating:	72.8/73.8
	Apr.–Nov. High: June–Aug.	Slope:	123/115

P	**Hilliard Lakes Golf Club**	Greens: $	W S J
☺☺☺	Hilliard Rd., Westlake. (216) 871-9578	Carts: $$	
DEAL	18 holes. Par 72/75. Yards: 6,680/5,636	Rating: 70.7/74.0	
	Mar.–Nov. High: May–Sept.	Slope: 124/118	

P	**Hinckley Hills Golf Course**	Greens: $$	
☺☺☺	Hinckley. (216) 278-4861	Carts: $	
DEAL	18 holes. Par 73/72. Yards: 6,704/5,478	Rating: 73.6/70.1	
	Apr.–Nov. High: May–Sept.	Slope: 125	

P	**Manakiki Golf Club**	Greens: $	L S J
☺☺☺	Eddy Rd., Willoughby. (216) 942-2500	Carts: $	
DEAL	18 holes. Par 72/72. Yards: 6,302/5,739	Rating: 71.4/72.8	
	Mar.–Dec. High: May–Sept.	Slope: 128/121	

P	**Maple Ridge Golf Course**	Greens: $	S J
☺☺	Rte. 45, Austinburg. (216) 969-1368	Carts: $	
	18 holes. Par 70/70. Yards: 6,001/5,400	Rating: 68.5/69.0	
	Mar.–Nov. High: June–Aug.	Slope: 118/118	

SP	**Orchard Hills Golf and Country Club**	Greens: $–$$	
☺☺☺	Caves Rd., Chesterland. (216) 729-1963	Carts: $$	
DEAL	18 holes. Par 72/72. Yards: 6,409/5,651	Rating: 71.1/72.6	
	Apr.–Nov. High: May–Sept.	Slope: 126/122	

P	**Pine Brook Golf Course**	Greens: $	W S J
☺	N. Durkee Rd., Grafton. (216) 748-2939	Carts: $	
	18 holes. Par 70/70. Yards: 6,062/5,225	Rating: 66.8/68.9	
	Year-round. High: June–Aug.	Slope: 110/109	

P	**Pine Hills Golf Club**	Greens: $$	
☺☺☺☺	W. 130th St., Hinckley. (216) 225-4477	Carts: $	
DEAL	18 holes. Par 72/73. Yards: 6,482/5,685	Rating: 71.2/74.3	
STATE	Apr.–Nov. High: Apr.–Nov.	Slope: 124/126	

P	**Powderhorn Golf Course**	Greens: $	W L T S J
☺☺	Bates Rd., Madison. (216) 428-5951	Carts: $	
	18 holes. Par 70/70. Yards: 6,004/4,881	Rating: 68.5/67.6	
	Year-round. High: Apr.–Oct.	Slope: 117/113	

R	**Quail Hollow Resort**	Greens: $$$$–$$$$$	W L T J
☺☺☺☺	Concord Hambden Rd., Concord.	Carts: Incl.	
STATE	18 holes. Par 72/72. Yards: 6,712/4,389	Rating: 72.2/65.7	
	Apr.–Nov. High: June–Aug.	Slope: 130/107	

P	**Ridge Top Golf Course**	Greens: $	W L S J
☺☺	Tower Rd., Medina. (216) 725-5500	Carts: $	
	18 holes. Par 71/71. Yards: 6,211/4,968	Rating: 70.0/67.9	
	Mar.–Nov. High: June–Aug.	Slope: 109/106	

R	**Sawmill Creek Golf and Racquet Club**	Greens: $$$	L
☺☺☺	Cleveland Rd., W. Huron. (419) 433-3789	Carts: $$	
	18 holes. Par 71/74. Yards: 6,813/5,416	Rating: 72.3/70.6	
	Apr.–Oct. High: June–Sept.	Slope: 128/120	

P	**Shawnee Hills Golf Course**	Greens: $	L S J
☺☺	Egbert Rd., Bedford. (216) 232-7184	Carts: $	
	18 holes. Par 71/73. Yards: 6,160/6,029	Rating: 68.7/72.5	
	Mar.–Dec. High: May–Sept.	Slope: 112/116	

P	**Sleepy Hollow Golf Course**	Greens: $	W L S J
☺☺☺	Brecksville Rd., Brecksville. (216) 526-4285	Carts: $	

Ohio Golf Guide

Cleveland Area

DEAL	18 holes. Par 71/73. Yards: 6,630/5,715	Rating:	71.9/73.5	
	Mar.–Dec. High: May–Sept.	Slope:	124/128	

P	**Sweetbriar Golf**	Greens:	$	L T S J
	Jaycox Rd., Avon Lake. (216) 933-9001	Carts:	$	
◎◎	*First/Second/Third*	Rating:	68.7/67.5/66.3	
	27 holes. Par 72/72/70. Yards: 6,491/6,292/6,075	Slope:	106/104/100	
	Year-round. High: May–Oct.			

P	**Tam O'Shanter Golf Course**	Greens:	$$	W L R S J
	Hills and Dales Rd. N.W., Canton. (216) 478-6501	Carts:	$	
◎◎◎	*Dales Course*	Rating:	70.4/69.7	
DEAL	18 holes. Par 70/75. Yards: 6,569/5,384	Slope:	110/109	
	Mar.–Dec. High: Apr.–Oct.			

◎◎◎	*Hills Course*	Rating:	69.1/67.4	
DEAL	18 holes. Par 70/75. Yards: 6,385/5,076	Slope:	104/102	

P	**Thunder Hill Golf Club**	Greens:	$$	L S J
◎◎	Griswold Rd., S. Madison. (216) 298-3473	Carts:	Incl.	
	18 holes. Par 72/72. Yards: 7,223/5,524	Rating:	78.0/NA	
	Apr.–Dec. High: May–Sept.	Slope:	151/127	

P	**Thunderbird Hills Golf Club**	Greens:	$	W L S
	Mudbrook Rd., Huron. (419) 433-4552	Carts:	$	
◎◎◎	*North Course*	Rating:	70.3/74.0	
DEAL	18 holes. Par 72/74. Yards: 6,464/5,993	Slope:	109/121	
	Year-round. High: Apr.–Nov.			

P	**Windmill Lakes Golf Club**	Greens:	$–$$	L T S J
◎◎◎◎	St. Rte. 14, Ravenna. (216) 297-0440	Carts:	$	
DEAL	18 holes. Par 70/70. Yards: 6,936/5,368	Rating:	73.8/70.4	
STATE	Mar.–Nov. High: May–Sept.	Slope:	128/115	

Akron Area

R	**Atwood Resort Golf Course**	Greens:	$	W L R S J
◎◎	Lodge Rd., Dellroy. (216) 735-2211	Carts:	$	
	18 holes. Par 70/70. Yards: 6,152/4,188	Rating:	65.7/62.0	
	Year-round. High: June–Sept.	Slope:	102/91	

P	**Brandywine Country Club**	Greens:	$$	W T S
◎◎	Akron Peninsula Rd., Peninsula. (216) 657-2525	Carts:	$$	
	18 holes. Par 72/75. Yards: 7,100/5,625	Rating:	70.2/70.5	
	Year-round. High: May–Sept.	Slope:	113/113	

P	**Chippewa Golf Club**	Greens:	$	W L S J
◎◎◎	Shank Rd., Doylestown. (216) 658-6126	Carts:	$	
DEAL	18 holes. Par 72/72. Yards: 6,273/4,877	Rating:	69.1/67.0	
	Year-round. High: Apr.–Oct.	Slope:	109/103	

P	**Fox Den Golf Club**	Greens:	$–$$	W L S J
◎◎◎	Call Rd., Stow. (216) 673-3443	Carts:	$	
DEAL	18 holes. Par 72/72. Yards: 6,468/5,431	Rating:	70.4/69.0	
	Mar.–Nov. High: May–Sept.	Slope:	115/114	

P	**Hawks Nest Golf Club**	Greens:	$–$$	S
◎◎◎◎	E. Pleasant Home Rd., Creston. (216) 435-4611	Carts:	$	
DEAL	18 holes. Par 72/72. Yards: 6,670/4,767	Rating:	71.5/67.9	
STATE	Apr.–Dec. High: May–Oct.	Slope:	124/110	

P	**J.E. Good Park Golf Club**	Greens:	$	L S J
◎◎◎	Nome Ave., Akron. (216) 864-0020	Carts:	$	
DEAL	18 holes. Par 71/71. Yards: 6,663/4,926	Rating:	72.0/69.1	
	Mar.–Dec. High: May–Oct.	Slope:	123/115	

Ohio Golf Guide

Akron Area

| P ⊙⊙ | **Maplecrest Golf Course**
Tallmadge Rd., Kent. (216) 673-2722
18 holes. Par 71/72. Yards: 6,412/5,285
Mar.–Oct. High: May–Aug. | Greens:
Carts:
Rating:
Slope: | $–$$
$
69.2/67.8
108/113 | W S |

| P ⊙⊙⊙ DEAL | **Mohican Hills Golf Club**
Cty. Rd. 1950, Jeromesville. (419) 368-3303
18 holes. Par 72/72. Yards: 6,536/4,976
Apr.–Dec. High: June–Aug. | Greens:
Carts:
Rating:
Slope: | $
$
71.1/67.9
122/112 | W |

| P

⊙⊙ | **Oak Knolls Golf Club**
St. Rte. 43, Kent. (216) 673-6713
High Course
18 holes. Par 71/72. Yards: 6,483/5,279
Mar.–Nov. High: May–Sept. | Greens:
Carts:
Rating:
Slope: | $–$$
$
70.5/69.7
111/107 | W L S J |

| ⊙⊙ | *West Course*
18 holes. Par 72/72. Yards: 6,373/5,681 | Rating:
Slope: | 69.0/71.4
112/112 | |

| P ⊙⊙ | **Pine Valley Golf Club**
Reimer Rd., Wadsworth. (216) 335-3375
18 holes. Par 72/74. Yards: 6,097/5,268
Mar.–Nov. High: May–Oct. | Greens:
Carts:
Rating:
Slope: | $
$
68.5/67.9
109/107 | W S J |

| P ⊙⊙ | **Raccoon Hill Golf Course**
Judson Rd., Kent. (216) 673-2111
18 holes. Par 71/71. Yards: 6,068/4,650
Mar.–Nov. High: May–Sept. | Greens:
Carts:
Rating:
Slope: | $–$$
$
69.2/67.0
115/106 | W L T S |

| SP ⊙⊙⊙ DEAL | **Raintree Country Club**
Mayfair Rd., Uniontown. (216) 699-3232
18 holes. Par 72/72. Yards: 6,811/5,030
Year-round. High: Apr.–Oct. | Greens:
Carts:
Rating:
Slope: | $–$$
$
73.0/68.5
127/114 | W L T S J |

| SP ⊙⊙⊙ DEAL | **Skyland Pines Golf Club**
Columbus Rd. N.E., Canton. (216) 454-5131
18 holes. Par 72/72. Yards: 6,467/5,279
Feb.–Dec. High: Apr.–Nov. | Greens:
Carts:
Rating:
Slope: | $–$$
$
69.6/69.6
113/113 | L |

| P ⊙⊙ | **Sunnyhill Golf Club**
Sunnybrook Rd., Kent. (216) 673-1785
18 holes. Par 71/72. Yards: 6,289/5,083
Mar.–Jan. High: May–Aug. | Greens:
Carts:
Rating:
Slope: | $
Incl.
68.4/68.4
110/107 | W L S J |

| P ⊙⊙ | **Tannenhauf Golf Club**
McCallum Ave., Alliance. (216) 823-4402
18 holes. Par 72/72. Yards: 6,666/5,455
Apr.–Oct. High: June–Aug. | Greens:
Carts:
Rating:
Slope: | $
$
71.0/70.8
111/109 | W L S J |

| P ⊙⊙ | **Valley View Golf Club**
Cuyahoga St., Akron. (216) 928-9034
27 holes. Par 72/72/72. Yards: 6,293/6,183/6,168
Mar.–Nov. High: May–Sept. | Greens:
Carts:
Rating:
Slope: | $
$
68.7/68.2/68.2
111/111/109 | W S |

| P ⊙⊙⊙⊙ DEAL STATE | **Yankee Run Golf Course**
Warren Sharon Rd., Brookfield. (216) 448-8096
18 holes. Par 70/73. Yards: 6,501/5,140
Mar.–Nov. High: May–Sept. | Greens:
Carts:
Rating:
Slope: | $$
Incl.
70.7/69.0
119/109 | W L S J |

| P ⊙⊙⊙ DEAL | **Zoar Village Golf Club**
Zoar. (216) 874-4653
18 holes. Par 72/72. Yards: 6,535/5,235
Mar.–Dec. High: July–Aug. | Greens:
Carts:
Rating:
Slope: | $
$
70.7/69.7
117/115 | W S |

Youngstown Area

| P ⊙⊙⊙ | **Beaver Creek Meadows Golf Course**
St. Rte. 7, Lisbon. (216) 385-3020 | Greens:
Carts: | $
$ | W L |

Ohio Golf Guide

Youngstown Area

DEAL	18 holes. Par 72/72. Yards: 6,500/5,500	Rating:	68.7/68.5	
	Year-round. High: June–Aug.	Slope:	NA	

P	**Countryside Golf Course**	Greens:	$	W L S J
☺	Struthers Colt Rd., Lowellville. (216) 755-0016	Carts:	$	
	18 holes. Par 71/71. Yards: 6,461/5,399	Rating:	70.5/70.1	
	Mar.–Nov. High: May–Aug.	Slope:	NA	

P	**Mill Creek Park Golf Course**	Greens:	$	L S J
	Boardman. (216) 758-7926	Carts:	$	
☺☺☺	*North Course*	Rating:	71.9/74.4	
DEAL	18 holes. Par 70/74. Yards: 6,412/5,889	Slope:	124/117	
	Apr.–Nov. High: June–Sept.			

☺☺☺	*South Course*	Rating:	71.8/74.9	
DEAL	18 holes. Par 70/75. Yards: 6,511/6,102	Slope:	129/118	

SP	**Salem Hills Golf and Country Club**	Greens:	$	W S J
☺☺☺	Salem-Warren Rd., Salem. (216) 337-8033	Carts:	$	
DEAL	18 holes. Par 72/72. Yards: 7,146/5,597	Rating:	74.3/69.7	
	Apr.–Nov. High: June–Aug.	Slope:	126/114	

P	**Tamer Win Golf and Country Club**	Greens:	$	L S J
☺	Niles Cortland Rd. N.E., Cortland. (216) 637-2881	Carts:	$	
	18 holes. Par 71/74. Yards: 6,275/5,623	Rating:	68.8/68.8	
	Apr.–Nov. High: May–Sept.	Slope:	112/112	

Northwest Ohio

SP	**Country Acres Golf Club**	Greens:	$	S J
☺☺☺	St. Rte. 694, Ottawa. (419) 532-3434	Carts:	$	
DEAL	18 holes. Par 72/72. Yards: 6,464/4,961	Rating:	69.9/67.9	
	Year-round. High: June–Sept.	Slope:	126/113	

P	**Hickory Grove Golf Club**	Greens:	$	W T
☺☺	St. Rte. 294, Harpster. (614) 496-2631	Carts:	$$	
	18 holes. Par 72/76. Yards: 6,874/5,376	Rating:	71.0/69.1	
	Mar.–Nov. High: June–Aug.	Slope:	108/105	

P	**Miami Shores Golf Course**	Greens:	$	
☺	Rutherford Dr., Troy. (513) 335-4457	Carts:	$	
	18 holes. Par 72/73. Yards: 6,200/5,417	Rating:	67.6/68.5	
	Mar.–Dec. High: June–Aug.	Slope:	97/101	

P	**Shelby Oaks Golf Club**	Greens:	$	T
☺☺☺	Sidney Freyburg Rd., Sidney. (513) 492-2883	Carts:	$	
DEAL	27 holes. Par 72/72/72. Yards: 6,651/6,650/6,561	Rating:	71.2/60.9/70.5	
	Mar.–Nov. High: May–Oct.	Slope:	115/115/115	

Dayton Area

P	**Heatherwoode Golf Club**	Greens:	$$	S J
☺☺☺	Heatherwoode Blvd., Springboro. (513) 748-3222	Carts:	$	
DEAL	18 holes. Par 71/71. Yards: 6,730/5,069	Rating:	72.9/70.3	
	Mar.–Dec. High: June–Aug.	Slope:	142/129	

P	**Kitty Hawk Golf Club**	Greens:	$	L S J
	Chuck Wagner Lane, Dayton. (513) 237-5424	Carts:	$	
☺	*Eagle Course*	Rating:	72.8/74.3	
	18 holes. Par 72/75. Yards: 7,115/5,887	Slope:	120/123	
	Year-round. High: Apr.–Oct.			

P	**Larch Tree Golf Course**	Greens:	$	L J
☺☺	N. Snyder Rd., Trotwood. (513) 854-1951	Carts:	$	
	18 holes. Par 72/74. Yards: 6,982/5,912	Rating:	71.5/72.7	
	Year-round. High: May–Aug.	Slope:	107/107	

P	**Pipestone Golf Club**	Greens:	$$	T
☺☺☺	Benner Rd., Miamisburg. (513) 866-4653	Carts:	$	

Ohio Golf Guide

Dayton Area

| DEAL | | 18 holes. Par 72/72. Yards: 6,939/5,207 | Rating: | 72.1/69.2 | |
| | | Mar.–Dec. High: June–Aug. | Slope: | 137/121 | |

P	**Sugar Isle Golf Country**	Greens:	$	W S
☺☺	Dayton-Lakeview Rd., New Carlisle. (513) 845-8699	Carts:	$	
	18 holes. Par 72/72. Yards: 6,743/5,651	Rating:	70.2/71.1	
	Year-round. High: June–Sept.	Slope:	107/110	

Columbus Area

P	**Apple Valley Golf Club**	Greens:	$	S
☺☺☺	Howard. (617) 397-7664	Carts:	$	
DEAL	18 holes. Par 72/75. Yards: 6,946/6,116	Rating:	72.4/74.9	
	Year-round. High: June–Aug.	Slope:	116/120	

P	**Bent Tree Golf Club**	Greens:	$$$	L T S
☺☺☺	Bent Tree Rd., Sunbury. (614) 965-5140	Carts:	Incl.	
	18 holes. Par 72/72. Yards: 6,805/5,280	Rating:	72.1/69.2	
	Year-round. High: May–Oct.	Slope:	122/113	

P	**Blackhawk Golf Club**	Greens:	$	L T S
☺☺☺	Dustin Rd., Galena. (614) 965-1042	Carts:	$	
DEAL	18 holes. Par 71/71. Yards: 6,550/4,726	Rating:	70.6/66.0	
	Year-round. High: May–Oct.	Slope:	115/106	

P	**Blacklick Woods Golf Course**	Greens:	$	W L T
	E. Livingston Ave., Reynoldsburg. (614) 861-3193	Carts:	$	
☺☺☺	*Gold Course*	Rating:	72.2/70.9	
DEAL	18 holes. Par 72/72. Yards: 7,069/5,633	Slope:	120/116	
	Year-round. High: May–Aug.			

P	**Champions Golf Course**	Greens:	$$	W L T S J
☺☺☺	Westerville Rd., Columbus. (614) 645-7111	Carts:	$	
DEAL	18 holes. Par 70/72. Yards: 6,555/5,427	Rating:	71.2/71.2	
	Year-round. High: May–Oct.	Slope:	127/127	

SP	**Cherokee Hills Golf Course**	Greens:	$	W L J
☺☺	Bellfontaine. (513) 599-3221	Carts:	$	
	18 holes. Par 72/72. Yards: 6,448/5,327	Rating:	70.8/70.3	
	Mar.–Dec. High: May–Sept.	Slope:	115/108	

P	**Darby Creek Golf Course**	Greens:	$–$$	W T S
☺☺	Orchard Rd., Marysville. (513) 349-7491	Carts:	$	
	18 holes. Par 72/72. Yards: 7,054/5,245	Rating:	72.7/68.1	
	Year-round. High: May–Oct.	Slope:	124/114	

R	**Deer Creek State Park Golf Course**	Greens:	$	W L R T S J
☺☺	Waterloo Rd., Mt. Sterling. (614) 869-3088	Carts:	$	
	18 holes. Par 72/72. Yards: 7,134/5,611	Rating:	73.7/71.7	
	Year-round. High: May–Sept.	Slope:	113/113	

P	**Eagle Sticks Golf Course**	Greens:	$$	W L T S J
☺☺☺☺	Maysville Pike, Zanesville. (614) 454-4900	Carts:	$	
DEAL	18 holes. Par 70/70. Yards: 6,412/4,137	Rating:	70.1/63.7	
STATE	Apr.–Dec. High: June–Aug.	Slope:	120/96	

P	**Estate Club Golf Course**	Greens:	$	W T S J
☺	Tschopp Rd., Lancaster. (614) 654-4444	Carts:	$	
	18 holes. Par 71/72. Yards: 6,405/5,680	Rating:	69.9/NA	
	Year-round. High: June–Sept.	Slope:	115/113	

P	**Flagstone Golf Club**	Greens:	$	W L T S
☺☺	St. Rte. 38, Marysville. (513) 642-1816	Carts:	$	
	18 holes. Par 72/72. Yards: 6,323/5,111	Rating:	69.6/68.9	
	Year-round. High: May–Sept.	Slope:	115/113	

Ohio Golf Guide

Columbus Area

P	**Foxfire Golf Club**	Greens: $	L
	St. Rte. 104, Lockbourne. (614) 224-3694	Carts: $	
☺☺☺	*The Foxfire Course*	Rating: 71.1/69.1	
DEAL	18 holes. Par 72/72. Yards: 6,891/5,175	Slope: 118/112	
	Year-round. High: June–Sept.		

P	**Granville Golf Club**	Greens: $$	
☺☺☺	Neward Rd., Granville. (614) 587-4653	Carts: $	
DEAL	18 holes. Par 72/72. Yards: 6,612/5,413	Rating: 71.3/70.6	
	Year-round. High: Apr.–Nov.	Slope: 126/121	

P	**Hiawatha Golf Course**	Greens: $	W L T S J
☺☺	Beech St., Mt. Vernon. (614) 393-2886	Carts: $	
	18 holes. Par 72/74. Yards: 6,721/5,100	Rating: 71.5/68.5	
	Year-round. High: 6,721/5,100	Slope: 104	

P	**Indian Springs Golf Club**	Greens: $$	W L T
☺☺☺☺	St. Rte. 161, Mechanicsburg. (513) 834-2111	Carts: $	
DEAL	18 holes. Par 72/72. Yards: 7,123/5,733	Rating: 73.8/72.6	
STATE	Mar.–Oct. High: June–Aug.	Slope: 126/122	

SP	**Kings Mill Golf Course**	Greens: $	L J
☺☺	Berringer Rd., Waldo. (614) 726-2626	Carts: $	
	18 holes. Par 70/74. Yards: 6,099/5,318	Rating: 68.1/68.8	
	Mar.–Dec. High: May–Oct.	Slope: 106/109	

P	**Licking Springs Trout and Golf Club**	Greens: $	L S
☺☺	Horns Hill Rd., Newark. (614) 366-2770	Carts: $	
	18 holes. Par 72/72. Yards: 6,400/5,035	Rating: 70.0/68.7	
	Year-round. High: May–Sept.	Slope: 116/107	

SP	**Mill Creek Golf Club**	Greens: $	W L S J
☺☺	Penn Rd., Ostrander. (614) 666-7711	Carts: $	
	18 holes. Par 72/72. Yards: 6,300/5,100	Rating: 69.0/70.0	
	Mar.–Dec. High: June–Sept.	Slope: 111/111	

P	**Oxbow Golf and Country Club**	Greens: $	S J
☺☺	Cty. Rd. 85, Belpre. (614) 423-6771	Carts: $	
	18 holes. Par 71/72. Yards: 6,558/4,858	Rating: 70.9/68.8	
	Year-round. High: May–July	Slope: 117/109	

P	**Pebble Creek Golf Club**	Greens: $	W S J
☺☺☺	Algire Rd., Lexington. (419) 884-3434	Carts: $	
DEAL	18 holes. Par 72/72. Yards: 6,554/5,195	Rating: 70.8/69.1	
	Mar.–Oct.	Slope: 117/113	

P	**Raccoon International Golf Club**	Greens: $	W L
☺☺	Worthington Rd. S.W., Granville. (614) 587-0921	Carts: Incl.	
	18 holes. Par 72/72. Yards: 6,586/6,094	Rating: NA	
	Year-round. High: Mar.–Oct.	Slope: 125/116	

P	**Reid Park Memorial Golf Course**	Greens: $	T
	Bird Rd., Springfield. (513) 324-7725	Carts: $	
☺☺☺	*North Course*	Rating: 72.5/69.2	
DEAL	18 holes. Par 72/72. Yards: 6,760/5,035	Slope: 130/118	
	Year-round. High: May–Oct.		

☺☺	*South Course*	Rating: 69.0/66.5	
	18 holes. Par 72/72. Yards: 6,500/4,895	Slope: 110/102	

SP	**Rickenbacker Golf Club**	Greens: $	W L T S J
☺☺	Airbase Rd., Groveport. (614) 491-5000	Carts: $	
	18 holes. Par 72/72. Yards: 7,003/5,476	Rating: 72.6/71.2	
	Year-round. High: June–Aug.	Slope: 117/117	

Ohio Golf Guide

Columbus Area

SP ☺☺☺ DEAL	**Royal American Links Golf Club** Miller Paul Rd., Galena. (614) 965-1215 18 holes. Par 72/72. Yards: 6,809/5,171 Mar.–Dec. High: June–Sept.	Greens: **$$** Carts: **$** Rating: 72.7/70.1 Slope: 126/111	W L T S J
P ☺☺	**St. Albans Golf Club** Northridge Rd. N.W., Alexandria. (614) 924-8885 18 holes. Par 71/71. Yards: 6,717/5,498 Mar.–Dec. High: May–Aug.	Greens: **$** Carts: **$$** Rating: 71.6/71.1 Slope: 112/112	L S
P ☺☺	**Table Rock Golf Club** Wilson Rd., Centerburg. (614) 625-6859 18 holes. Par 72/72. Yards: 6,694/5,565 Year-round. High: May–Sept.	Greens: **$** Carts: **$** Rating: 70.7/71.3 Slope: 113/NA	W L T S
P ☺☺☺ DEAL	**Turnberry Golf Course** Pickerington. (614) 645-2582 27 holes. Par 72/73. Yards: 6,636/5,440 Year-round. High: Apr.–Oct.	Greens: **$–$$** Carts: **$** Rating: 71.1/68.8 Slope: 114/110	W L T S J
P ☺☺	**Whetstone Golf and Swim Club** Marion Mt. Gilead Rd., Caledonia. (614) 383-4343 18 holes. Par 72/72. Yards: 6,674/5,023 Apr.–Oct. High: Apr.–Oct.	Greens: **$** Carts: **$$** Rating: 71.7/73.6 Slope: 120/111	W S
P ☺☺☺ DEAL	**Woodland Golf Club** Swisher Rd., Cable. (513) 653-8875 18 holes. Par 71/71. Yards: 6,407/4,965 Year-round. High: Mar.-Sept.	Greens: **$–$$** Carts: **$** Rating: 70.1/67.7 Slope: 116/110	W L T S J

Cincinnati Area

P ☺☺☺ DEAL	**Blue Ash Golf Course** Cooper Rd., Cincinnati. (513) 745-8577 18 holes. Par 72/72. Yards: 6,643/5,125 Year-round. High: May–Sept.	Greens: **$** Carts: **$** Rating: 72.6/70.3 Slope: 127/124	L S J
P ☺☺	**California Golf Course** Kellogg Ave., Cincinnati. (513) 231-4734 18 holes. Par 70/71. Yards: 6,216/5,626 Year-round. High: Apr.–Sept.	Greens: **$** Carts: **$** Rating: 70.0/71.4 Slope: 116/113	L
P ☺☺	**Fairfield Golf Club** John Gray Rd., Fairfield. (513) 867-5385 18 holes. Par 70/70. Yards: 6,250/4,900 Mar.–Dec. High: June–Aug.	Greens: **$** Carts: **$$** Rating: 69.5/68.8 Slope: 123/113	S J
P ☺☺☺ DEAL	**Glenview Golf Course** Springfield Pike, Cincinnati. (513) 771-1747 18 holes. Par 72/72. Yards: 6,965/5,091 Year-round. High: May–Sept.	Greens: **$$** Carts: **$$** Rating: 72.3/69.9 Slope: 132/110	L S J
R ☺☺☺	**The Golf Center at Kings Island** Mason. (513) 398-7700 *The Grizzly Course* 18 holes. Par 71/72. Yards: 6,731/5,256 Mar.–Dec. High: May–Sept.	Greens: **$$–$$$** Carts: **$** Rating: 72.6/68.5 Slope: 131/115	W L T
P ☺☺	**Hickory Woods Golf Course** Hickory Woods Dr., Loveland. (513) 575-3900 18 holes. Par 70/71. Yards: 6,105/5,115 Year-round. High: Apr.–Aug.	Greens: **$–$$** Carts: **$** Rating: 70.1/69.4 Slope: 119/113	L S J
R ☺☺☺	**Hueston Woods State Park Golf Resort** Brown Rd., Oxford. (513) 523-8081	Greens: **$–$$** Carts: **$$**	W T S

Ohio Golf Guide

Cincinnati Area

DEAL	18 holes. Par 72/72. Yards: 7,005/5,176	Rating:	73.1/68.9
	Apr.–Oct. High: June–Sept.	Slope:	132/NA

P	**Miami Whitewater Forest Golf Course**	Greens:	$	S J
☺☺☺	Mt. Hope Rd., Harrison. (513) 367-4627	Carts:	$
DEAL	18 holes. Par 72/72. Yards: 6,780/5,093	Rating:	71.9/68.8
	Mar.–Dec. High: June–Aug.	Slope:	120/104

P	**Neumann Golf Course**	Greens:	$	L S J
	Bridgetown Rd., Cincinnati. (513) 574-1320	Carts:	$
☺☺	*White/Blue/Red*	Rating:	69.0/68.5/68.4
	27 holes. Par 71/70/71. Yards: 6,218/6,115/5,989	Slope:	109/109/111
	Year-round. High: Mar.–Nov.		

P	**Pleasant Hill Golf Club**	Greens:	$	W L S J
☺☺	Hankins Rd., Middletown. (513) 539-7220	Carts:	$
	18 holes. Par 71/71. Yards: 6,586/4,723	Rating:	70.2/65.6
	Year-round. High: June–July	Slope:	111/101

P	**Shaker Run Golf Course**	Greens:	$$$	L T S J
☺☺☺☺	Greentree Rd., Lebanon. (513) 727-0007	Carts:	Incl.
STATE	18 holes. Par 72/72. Yards: 6,965/5,075	Rating:	75.4/68.8
	Mar.–Dec. High: May–Oct.	Slope:	141/121

P	**Sharon Woods Golf Course**	Greens:	$	S J
☺☺☺	Cincinnati. (513) 769-4325	Carts:	$
DEAL	18 holes. Par 70/70. Yards: 6,652/5,288	Rating:	72.3/69.7
	Mar.–Dec. High: Apr.–Sept.	Slope:	127/114

P	**The Vineyard Golf Course**	Greens:	$$	S J
☺☺☺☺	Nordyke Rd., Cincinnati. (513) 474-3007	Carts:	$
DEAL	18 holes. Par 71/71. Yards: 6,789/4,747	Rating:	73.0/65.7
STATE	Mar.–Nov. High: May–Sept.	Slope:	129/113

P	**Weatherwax Golf Course**	Greens:	$	S J
	Mosiman Rd., Middletown. (513) 425-7886	Carts:	$
☺☺☺	*Valleyview/Highlands*	Rating:	72.0/69.8
DEAL	18 holes. Par 72/72. Yards: 6,756/5,253	Slope:	120/114
	Year-round. High: Apr.–Nov.		

☺☺☺	*Woodside/Meadows*	Rating:	73.4/71.5
DEAL	18 holes. Par 72/72. Yards: 7,174/5,669	Slope:	116/112

P	**Winton Woods Golf Club**	Greens:	$	S J
☺☺	W. Sharon Rd., Cincinnati. (513) 825-3770	Carts:	$
	18 holes. Par 72/72. Yards: 6,376/4,554	Rating:	70.0/66.6
	Mar.–Dec. High: May–Sept.	Slope:	120/108

South Dakota

The best of South Dakota's public courses may be the **Meadowbrook Golf Course** in Rapid City. It boasts flat fairways, the meandering Rapid Creek, and views of Mount Rushmore.

In Sioux Falls is **Willow Run**, where every hole presents a different challenge. In Yankton, about 50 miles to the southwest, is the worthy **Hillcrest**.

Up north in Aberdeen is **Moccasin Creek**, fair but challenging with lots of trees.

The good news is that four all of South Dakota's best also reside on the Econoguide Deals list.

Courses in South Dakota are generally open from April to November, with peak rates in effect in the summer months. Some courses are open year-round.

Econoguide Leader Board: Best Public Courses in South Dakota

◎◎◎◎ Hillcrest Golf and Country Club
◎◎◎◎ Meadowbrook Golf Course
◎◎◎◎ Moccasin Creek Country Club
◎◎◎◎ Willow Run Golf Course

Econoguide Leader Board: Best Deals in South Dakota

$/◎◎◎ Fox Run Golf Course
$$/◎◎◎◎ Hillcrest Golf and Country Club
$/◎◎◎ Meadowbrook Golf Course
$$/◎◎◎◎ Moccasin Creek Country Club
$/◎◎◎ Two Rivers Golf Course
$/◎◎◎◎ Willow Run Golf Course

South Dakota Golf Guide

Rapid City and Western South Dakota

P ◎◎	**Hillsview Golf Club** Hwy. 34, Pierre. (605) 224-6191 18 holes. Par 72/72. Yards: 6,828/5,470 Apr.–Oct. High: June–Aug.	Greens: $ Carts: $ Rating: 71.4/73.9 Slope: 122/119	J
P ◎◎◎ BEST DEAL	**Meadowbrook Golf Course** Jackson Blvd., Rapid City. (605) 394-4191 18 holes. Par 72/72. Yards: 7,054/5,603 Year-round. High: Apr.–Oct.	Greens: $ Carts: $ Rating: 73.0/71.1 Slope: 138/130	L T S J

Sioux City and Eastern South Dakota

P ◎◎	**Elmwood Golf Course** W. Russell, Sioux Falls. (605) 367-7092 18 holes. Par 72/72. Yards: 6,850/5,750 Apr.–Oct. High: May–Aug.	Greens: $ Carts: $ Rating: 72.1/72.0 Slope: 129/125	
P ◎◎◎ DEAL	**Fox Run Golf Course** W. 27th St., Yankton. (605) 665-8456 18 holes. Par 72/72. Yards: 6,696/5,209 Mar.–Oct. High: May–Aug.	Greens: $ Carts: $ Rating: 70.8/68.6 Slope: 122/115	W
SP ◎◎◎◎ DEAL STATE	**Hillcrest Golf and Country Club** Mulberry, Yankton. (605) 665-4621 18 holes. Par 72/72. Yards: 6,874/5,726 Apr.–Nov. High: June–Aug.	Greens: $$ Carts: $ Rating: 72.2/72.2 Slope: 130/126	W
P ◎◎	**Lakeview Golf Course** N. Ohlman, Mitchell. (605) 996-1424 18 holes. Par 72/73. Yards: 6,670/5,808 Apr.–Oct. High: June–Aug.	Greens: $ Carts: $ Rating: 71.3/72.6 Slope: 124/125	J
SP ◎◎◎◎ DEAL STATE	**Moccasin Creek Country Club** 40th Ave. N.E., Aberdeen. (605) 226-0989 18 holes. Par 72/73. Yards: 7,125/5,416 Apr.–Nov. High: June–Aug.	Greens: $$ Carts: $ Rating: 72.5/69.4 Slope: 138/127	
P ◎◎	**Prairie Green Golf Course** E. 69th St., Sioux Falls. (605) 339-6076 18 holes. Par 72/72. Yards: 7,179/5,250 Apr.–Oct. High: May–Sept.	Greens: $–$$ Carts: $ Rating: 74.2/70.2 Slope: 134/122	W T

Souix City and Eastern South Dakota

P	**Two Rivers Golf Course**	Greens: $	L
☺☺☺	S. Oak Tree Lane, Dakota Dunes. (605) 232-3241	Carts: $	
DEAL	18 holes. Par 72/72. Yards: 6,181/5,603	Rating: 69.0/71.0	
	Apr.–Oct. High: June–Sept.	Slope: 120/112	
P	**Watertown Municipal Golf Course**	Greens: $	T
☺☺	S. Lake Dr., Watertown. (605) 886-3618	Carts: $	
	18 holes. Par 72/78. Yards: 5,220/5,858	Rating: 67.4 71.3	
	Apr.–Oct. High: May–Sept.	Slope: 106/114	
P	**Willow Run Golf Course**	Greens: $	W T S J
☺☺☺☺	E. Hwy. 38/42, Sioux Falls. (605) 335-5900	Carts: $	
DEAL	18 holes. Par 71/71. Yards: 6,505/4,855	Rating: 71.1/68.7	
STATE	Mar.–Nov. High: May–Oct.	Slope: 127/119	

West Virginia

The gem of West Virginia is the spectacular **Greenbrier** in White Sulphur Springs; the Greenbrier Course is the best of three there, although the venerable Old White Course, designed in 1910, is still a major favorite.

In second place in the state is the **Hawthorn Valley Golf Course**, a hilly newer course near the ski mountain at Snowshoe. The **Glade Springs Resort** in Daniels, south of Beckley, is a wide-open course, especially difficult in the wind.

The **Lakeview Resort** in Morgantown lies next to the Greenbrier and has its own woodsy, narrow challenge along Cheat Lake.

Mountain-region and snowbelt courses in West Virginia usually operate from April to November, with peak rates in the summer months. Elsewhere in the state many courses are open year-round, also with summertime peak rates.

The lovely Greenbrier in White Sulphur Springs operates year-round with room rates (including breakfast and dinner) as high as $301 per person in the high season of April 1 through October 31; that same superior room drops in price to $236 from November 1 through March 31. Less-opulent accommodations are available from a high-season rate of $183 per person to a low-season rate of about $150 per night.

Golf greens fees are free to guests in December, January, and February. In March and November, greens fees are about $45, and in the high season—April through October—it'll cost you $90 to tee it up at the Greenbrier.

Econoguide Leader Board: Best Public Courses in West Virginia

☺☺☺☺ Glade Springs Resort

☺☺☺☺ The Greenbrier (Greenbrier, Old White)

☺☺☺☺ Hawthorne Valley Golf Course

☺☺☺ Lakeview Resort & Conference Center (Lakeview)

Econoguide Leader Board: Best Deals in West Virginia

$$/☺☺☺ Cacapon State Park Resort Golf Course

$$/☺☺☺ Canaan Valley State Park Resort Golf Course

$/☺☺☺ Greenhills Country Club

$$/☺☺☺	Lakeview Resort & Conference Center (Lakeview)
$$/☺☺☺	Locust Hill Golf Course
$$/☺☺☺	Oglebay Park (Speidel)
$$/☺☺☺	The Woods Resort

West Virginia Golf Guide

Wheeling

P	**Oglebay Park**	Greens:	$$	W R
	Oglebay Park, Wheeling. (304) 243-4050	Carts:	$	
☺	*Crispin Course*	Rating:	66.6/68.4	
	18 holes. Par 71/71. Yards: 5,760/5,100	Slope:	103/108	
	Mar.–Nov. High: May–Aug.			

| ☺☺☺ | *Speidel Course* | Rating: | 72.7/72.0 | |
| DEAL | 18 holes. Par 71/71. Yards: 7,000/5,515 | Slope: | 126/120 | |

Clarksburg Area

R	**Canaan Valley State Park Resort Golf Course**	Greens:	$$	S
☺☺☺	Rte. 1, Davis. (304) 866-4121	Carts:	$$	
DEAL	18 holes. Par 72/72. Yards: 6,982/5,820	Rating:	73.4/71.8	
	Apr.–Nov. High: June–Aug.	Slope:	125/115	

R	**Lakeview Resort & Conference Center**	Greens:	$$	W L R J
	Rte. 6, Morgantown. (304) 594-2011	Carts:	$	
☺☺☺	*Lakeview Course*	Rating:	72.8/71.8	
DEAL	18 holes. Par 72/72. Yards: 6,800/5,432	Slope:	130/118	
STATE	Year-round. High: June–Sept.			

| ☺☺ | *Mountainview Course* | Rating: | 70.7/69.4 | |
| | 18 holes. Par 72/72. Yards: 6,447/5,242 | Slope: | 119/122 | |

SP	**Locust Hill Golf Course**	Greens:	$–$$	W L T
☺☺☺	St. Andrews Dr., Charles Town. (304) 728-7300	Carts:	$	
DEAL	18 holes. Par 72/72. Yards: 7,005/5,112	Rating:	73.5/72.0	
	Year-round. High: May–Oct.	Slope:	128/120	

R	**The Woods Resort**	Greens:	$$	W L T S J
	Mtn. Lake Road, Hedgesville. (304) 754-7222	Carts:	$	
☺☺☺	*Mountain View Golf Course*	Rating:	72.2/68.5	
DEAL	18 holes. Par 72/71. Yards: 6,608/4,900	Slope:	121/107	
	Year-round. High: Apr.–Sept.			

Berkeley Springs/Northeast Region

R	**Cacapon State Park Resort Golf Course**	Greens:	$–$$	L S
☺☺☺	Rte. 1, Berkeley Springs. (304) 258-1022	Carts:	$	
DEAL	18 holes. Par 72/72. Yards: 6,940/5,510	Rating:	72.4/72.1	
	Year-round. High: Apr.–Oct.	Slope:	121/116	

Charleston Area

SP	**Greenhills Country Club**	Greens:	$	W L R
☺☺☺	Rte. 56, Ravenswood. (304) 273-3396	Carts:	$	
DEAL	18 holes. Par 72/74. Yards: 6,056/5,018	Rating:	68.6/69.0	
	Year-round. High: Apr.–Oct.	Slope:	119/108	

P	**Lavalette Golf Club**	Greens:	$	
☺☺	Lynn Oak Dr., Lavalette. (304) 525-7405	Carts:	$	
	18 holes. Par 71/71. Yards: 6,262/5,257	Rating:	69.5/72.6	
	Year-round. High: May–Sept.	Slope:	118/120	

SP	**Scarlet Oaks Country Club**	Greens:	$$	
☺☺	Dair Rd., Poca. (304) 755-8079	Carts:	Incl.	
	18 holes. Par 72/72. Yards: 6,700/5,036	Rating:	72.3/69.3	
	Mar.–Dec. High: June–July	Slope:	129/109	

Beckley Area

| R | **Glade Springs Resort** | Greens: | $$$ | W L R T J |
| ☺☺☺☺ | Lake Dr., Daniels. (304) 763-2050 | Carts: | Incl. | |

West Virginia Golf Guide

Beckley Area

STATE	18 holes. Par 72/72. Yards: 6,941/4,884		Rating:	73.5/67.6
	Year-round. High: May–Oct.		Slope:	135/118
R	**The Greenbrier**		Greens:	$$$–$$$$$ L
	White Sulphur Springs. (304) 536-7851		Carts:	$$
⊙⊙⊙⊙	*Greenbrier Course*		Rating:	73.7/71.5
BEST	18 holes. Par 72/72. Yards: 6,681/5,280		Slope:	136/123
	Mar.–Nov. High: Apr.–Oct.			
⊙⊙⊙	*Lakeside Course*		Rating:	70.4/69.9
	18 holes. Par 70/70. Yards: 6,336/5,175		Slope:	121/115
⊙⊙⊙⊙	*Old White Course*		Rating:	72.7/73.7
STATE	18 holes. Par 70/70. Yards: 6,640/5,658		Slope:	128/126
R	**Hawthorne Valley Golf Course**		Greens:	$$$ W L R
⊙⊙⊙⊙	Snowshoe Dr., Snowshoe. (304) 572-1000		Carts:	Incl.
STATE	18 holes. Par 72/72. Yards: 7,045/4,363		Rating:	72.1/64.3
	May–Nov. High: July–Sept.		Slope:	130/103
P	**Twin Falls State Park Golf Course**		Greens:	$–$$ W L S
⊙⊙	Mullens. (304) 294-4044		Carts:	Inquire
	18 holes. Par 71/71. Yards: 6,382/5,202		Rating:	70.1/69.5
	Year-round. High: June–Oct.		Slope:	122/112

Wisconsin

Although few are national names, Wisconsin has more than its share of fine golf courses.

Among the best are the River Course at the **Blackwolf Run Golf Club** in Kohler, about 50 miles north of Milwaukee, and **Brown Deer** in Milwaukee proper. Also worth a trip are the Palmer and Trevino courses at **Geneva National Golf Club** in Lake Geneva, about 50 miles southwest of Milwaukee, and the Briar Patch Course and the Brute Course at the **Grand Geneva Resort and Spa** in Lake Geneva.

The tight woods challenge of **Old Hickory** is in Beaver Dam, about 30 miles north of Madison. The **Brown County Golf Course** is in Oneida, about seven miles west of Green Bay.

Courses in and around Oshkosh include the acclaimed Links Course and the almost-as-wonderful Woodlands at **The Golf Courses of Lawsonia** in Green Lake, some 35 miles southwest of Oshkosh. There's also the **Lake Arrowhead Golf Course** in Nekoosa, south of Wisconsin Rapids.

In the northern portion of the state there are the superb sand traps and the famed "Flower Hole" No. 16 (with nearly 100,000 flowers planted in beds around the green) at **Sentryworld** in Stevens Point. Also worth a visit are the East and West pair at **Nemadji** in Superior, the **New Richmond Golf Club** in New Richmond, and the **Northwood Golf Course** in Rhinelander. Some 90 miles south of Duluth is the challenging **Turtleback Golf and Country Club** in Rice Lake.

Near Madison is the difficult **University Ridge Golf Course** in Verona, with rolling hills, lots of water, and plenty of woods.

Joint residents of the Econoguide Best and Econoguide Deals lists are Lake Arrowhead, New Richmond, Northwood, and Turtleback.

Courses in Wisconsin generally are open from April to October, with peak rates from June to early September.

Econoguide Leader Board: Best Public Courses in Wisconsin

ⓒⓒⓒⓒ   Blackwolf Run Golf Club (Meadow Valleys, River)
ⓒⓒⓒⓒ   Brown County Golf Course
ⓒⓒⓒⓒ   Brown Deer Golf Course
ⓒⓒⓒⓒ   Geneva National Golf Club (Palmer, Trevino)
ⓒⓒⓒⓒ   The Golf Courses of Lawsonia (Links, Woodlands)
ⓒⓒⓒⓒ   Grand Geneva Resort and Spa (Brute, Briar Patch)
ⓒⓒⓒⓒ   Lake Arrowhead Golf Course
ⓒⓒⓒⓒ   Nemadji Golf Course (East, West)
ⓒⓒⓒⓒ   New Richmond Golf Club
ⓒⓒⓒⓒ   Northwood Golf Course
ⓒⓒⓒⓒ   Old Hickory Golf Club
ⓒⓒⓒⓒ   Sentryworld Golf Course
ⓒⓒⓒⓒ   Turtleback Golf and Country Club
ⓒⓒⓒⓒ   University Ridge Golf Course

Econoguide Leader Board: Best Deals in Wisconsin

$$/ⓒⓒⓒⓒ   Brighton Dale Golf Club (Blue Spruce, White Birch)
$/ⓒⓒⓒ   Dretzka Park Golf Course
$$/ⓒⓒⓒ   Eagle River Golf Course
$$/ⓒⓒⓒ   Evergreen Golf Club
$/ⓒⓒⓒ   Ives Grove Golf Links
$/ⓒⓒⓒ   Johnson Park Golf Course
$$/ⓒⓒⓒ   Kettle Hills Golf Course (Ponds, Woods)
$$/ⓒⓒⓒⓒ   Lake Arrowhead Golf Course
$/ⓒⓒⓒ   Maplecrest Country Club
$$/ⓒⓒⓒ   Mascoutin Golf Club
$/ⓒⓒⓒ   Mill Run Golf Course
$/ⓒⓒⓒ   Naga-Waukee Golf Course
$/ⓒⓒⓒⓒ   Nemadji Golf Course (East, West)
$$/ⓒⓒⓒⓒ   New Richmond Golf Club
$$/ⓒⓒⓒⓒ   Northwood Golf Course
$/ⓒⓒⓒ   Oakwood Park Golf Course
$$/ⓒⓒⓒ   Petrifying Springs Golf Course
$$/ⓒⓒⓒ   Quit-Qui-Oc Golf Club
$$/ⓒⓒⓒ   Rainbow Springs Golf Club
$$/ⓒⓒⓒ   Reedsburg Country Club
$$/ⓒⓒⓒ   Riverside Golf Course
$$/ⓒⓒⓒ   Spooner Golf Club
$/ⓒⓒⓒ   Spring Valley Country Club
$/ⓒⓒⓒⓒ   Turtleback Golf and Country Club

Wisconsin Golf Guide

Duluth Area and Northern Wisconsin

P	**Eagle River Golf Course**	Greens:	$–$$	L R T S J
☺☺☺	McKinley Blvd., Eagle River. (715) 479-8111	Carts:	$	
DEAL	18 holes. Par 71/72. Yards: 6,103/5,167	Rating:	69.3/67.8	
	May–Oct. High: July–Aug.	Slope:	121/119	

P	**Mill Run Golf Course**	Greens:	$	S J
☺☺☺	Kane Rd., Eau Claire. (715) 834-1766	Carts:	$	
DEAL	18 holes. Par 70/71. Yards: 6,065/4,744	Rating:	68.7/66.6	
	Apr.–Oct.	Slope:	116/109	

P	**Nemadji Golf Course**	Greens:	$	L T J
	N. 58th St. E., Superior. (715) 394-9022	Carts:	$	
☺☺☺☺	*East/West*	Rating:	72.7/70.7	
DEAL	18 holes. Par 72/72. Yards: 6,701/5,252	Slope:	133/124	
STATE	Apr.–Oct. High: June–Aug.			

☺☺	*North/South*	Rating:	69.7/67.8	
	18 holes. Par 71/71. Yards: 6,362/4,983	Slope:	120/114	

SP	**New Richmond Golf Club**	Greens:	$$	W L S J
☺☺☺☺	180th Ave., New Richmond. (715) 246-6724	Carts:	$	
DEAL	18 holes. Par 72/73. Yards: 6,716/5,547	Rating:	72.5/71.7	
STATE	Apr.–Oct. High: June–Aug.	Slope:	136/129	

P	**Northwood Golf Course**	Greens:	$$	J
☺☺☺☺	Hwy. 8 W., Rhinelander. (715) 282-6565	Carts:	$$	
DEAL	18 holes. Par 72/72. Yards: 6,719/5,338	Rating:	72.8/71.0	
STATE	Apr.–Oct. High: June–Sept.	Slope:	135/127	

P	**Sentryworld Golf Course**	Greens:	$$$	L T J
☺☺☺☺	N. Michigan Ave., Stevens Point. (715) 345-1600	Carts:	Incl.	
BEST	18 holes. Par 72/72. Yards: 7,055/5,197	Rating:	74.5/71.6	
	Apr.–Oct. High: June–Aug.	Slope:	144/130	

SP	**Spooner Golf Club**	Greens:	$–$$	W T
☺☺☺	Spooner. (715) 635-3580	Carts:	$	
DEAL	18 holes. Par 71/72. Yards: 6,407/5,084	Rating:	70.1/68.7	
	Apr.–Oct. High: June–Aug.	Slope:	125/120	

P	**Turtleback Golf and Country Club**	Greens:	$	W
☺☺☺☺	W. Allen Rd., Rice Lake. (715) 234-7641	Carts:	$	
DEAL	18 holes. Par 71/72. Yards: 6,132/5,328	Rating:	68.6/69.6	
STATE	Apr.–Oct. High: June–Aug.	Slope:	116/115	

Green Bay Area

P	**Brown County Golf Course**	Greens:	$$	S J
☺☺☺☺	Riverdale Dr., Oneida. (414) 497-1731	Carts:	$	
BEST	18 holes. Par 72/73. Yards: 6,729/5,801	Rating:	72.1/72.7	
	Apr.–Oct. High: June–Aug.	Slope:	133/127	

R	**Cherry Hills Golf Course**	Greens:	$–$$	W L T S J
☺☺	Dunn Rd., Sturgeon Bay. (414) 743-3240	Carts:	$	
	18 holes. Par 72/72. Yards: 6,163/5,432	Rating:	69.2/71.0	
	Apr.–Oct. High: June–Aug.	Slope:	121/122	

P	**Idlewild Golf Course**	Greens:	$$	T S J
☺☺	Sturgeon Bay. (414) 743-3334	Carts:	$	
	18 holes. Par 72/76. Yards: 6,889/5,886	Rating:	72.7/73.4	
	Apr.–Oct. High: June–Sept.	Slope:	130/128	

P	**Shawano Lake Golf Club**	Greens:	$	W L R T S J
☺☺	Lake Dr., Shawano. (715) 524-4890	Carts:	$	
	18 holes. Par 71/75. Yards: 6,211/5,516	Rating:	72.9/70.4	
	Apr.–Nov. High: June–Sept.	Slope:	128/128	

Wisconsin Golf Guide

Oshkosh Area

P	**Chaska Golf Course**	Greens: $	T S J
☺☺	Hwys. 10 and 45, Appleton. (414) 757-5757	Carts: $$	
	18 holes. Par 72/72. Yards: 6,854/5,847	Rating: 72.5/73.1	
	Apr.–Nov. High: May–Aug.	Slope: 128/126	

R	**The Golf Courses of Lawsonia**	Greens: $$–$$$	L R T
	S. Valley View Dr., Green Lake. (414) 294-3320	Carts: Incl.	
☺☺☺☺	*Links Course*	Rating: 72.8/68.9	
BEST	18 holes. Par 72/71. Yards: 6,764/5,078	Slope: 130/114	
	Apr.–Nov. High: June–Aug.		

☺☺☺☺	*The Woodlands*	Rating: 71.5/69.1	
STATE	18 holes. Par 72/72. Yards: 6,618/5,106	Slope: 129/120	

P	**Lake Arrowhead Golf Course**	Greens: $$	L T
☺☺☺☺	Apache Lane, Nekoosa. (715) 325-2929	Carts: $	
DEAL	18 holes. Par 72/72. Yards: 6,624/5,213	Rating: 72.3/70.2	
STATE	Apr.–Oct. High: May–Sept.	Slope: 135/125	

P	**Lake Shore Golf Course**	Greens: $	S J
☺☺	Punhoqua St., Oshkosh. (414) 235-6200	Carts: Inquire	
	18 holes. Par 70/71. Yards: 6,030/5,162	Rating: 68.2/69.4	
	Apr.–Nov. High: June–Aug.	Slope: 120/119	

P	**Mascoutin Golf Club**	Greens: $$	W L T S J
☺☺☺	Berlin. (414) 361-2360	Carts: $	
DEAL	18 holes. Par 72/73. Yards: 6,821/5,133	Rating: 72.2/68.9	
	Apr.–Oct. High: May–Sept.	Slope: 123/114	

Madison Area

SP	**Baraboo Country Club**	Greens: $–$$	W L T
☺☺	Lake St., Baraboo. (608) 356-8195	Carts: $$	
	18 holes. Par 72/72. Yards: 6,570/5,681	Rating: 71.3/72.5	
	Apr.–Oct. High: June–Aug.	Slope: 124/124	

R	**Devil's Head Resort and Convention Center**	Greens: $$	L T
☺☺	Bluff Rd., Merrimac. (608) 493-2251	Carts: Incl.	
	18 holes. Par 73/73. Yards: 6,725/5,141	Rating: 71.6/64.4	
	Apr.–Oct. High: June–Aug.	Slope: 127/113	

P	**Evansville Country Club**	Greens: $	L J
☺☺	Cemetery Rd., Evansville. (608) 882-6524	Carts: $$	
	18 holes. Par 72/72. Yards: 6,559/5,366	Rating: 71.0/70.3	
	Apr.–Oct. High: June–Aug.	Slope: 127/122	

SP	**Reedsburg Country Club**	Greens: $$	T
☺☺☺	Hwy. 33, Reedsburg. (608) 524-6000	Carts: $	
DEAL	18 holes. Par 72/73. Yards: 6,300/5,324	Rating: 70.5/70.3	
	Mar.–Nov. High: June–Aug.	Slope: 129/124	

P	**Riverside Golf Course**	Greens: $–$$	W S J
☺☺☺	Janesville. (608) 757-3080	Carts: $	
DEAL	18 holes. Par 72/72. Yards: 6,508/5,147	Rating: 70.7/68.9	
	Apr.–Nov. High: June–Aug.	Slope: 123/116	

P	**Trappers Turn Golf Club**	Greens: $$–$$$	W L R T
☺☺☺	Wisconsin Dells. (608) 253-7000	Carts: Incl.	
	18 holes. Par 72/72. Yards: 6,550/5,013	Rating: 71.7/69.3	
	Apr.–Oct. High: July–Aug.	Slope: 129/119	

P	**University Ridge Golf Course**	Greens: $$–$$$	L T J
☺☺☺☺	City Trunk Rd., Verona. (608) 845-7700	Carts: $	
STATE	18 holes. Par 72/72. Yards: 6,825/5,005	Rating: 73.2/68.9	
	Apr.–Oct. High: May–Sept.	Slope: 142/121	

Wisconsin Golf Guide

Madison Area

P	**Yahara Hills Golf Course**	Greens:	$	L S J
	East Broadway, Madison. (608) 838-3126	Carts:	$$	
◎◎	*East Course*	Rating:	71.9/73.4	
	18 holes. Par 72/72. Yards: 7,200/6,115	Slope:	116/118	
	Apr.–Nov. High: Apr.–Aug.			

◎◎	*West Course*	Rating:	71.6/71.4	
	18 holes. Par 72/72. Yards: 7,000/5,705	Slope:	118/116	

Milwaukee Area

R	**Abbey Springs Golf Course**	Greens:	$$$$	L J
◎◎◎	Fontana on Geneva Lake. (414) 275-6111	Carts:	Incl.	
	18 holes. Par 72/72. Yards: 6,466/5439	Rating:	71.4/72.4	
	Apr.–Nov. High: June–Sept.	Slope:	133/129	

R	**Blackwolf Run Golf Club**	Greens:	$$$$	L T
	Riverside Dr., Kohler. (414) 457-4446	Carts:	$	
◎◎◎◎	*Meadow Valleys Course*	Rating:	74.7/69.5	
STATE	18 holes. Par 72/72. Yards: 7,142/5,065	Slope:	143/125	
	Apr.–Oct. High: June–Sept.			

◎◎◎◎	*River Course*	Greens:	$$$$$$	
BEST	18 holes. Par 72/72. Yards: 6,991/5,115	Carts:	$	
		Rating:	74.9/70.7	
		Slope:	151/128	

P	**Brighton Dale Golf Club**	Greens:	$–$$	W
	248th Ave., Kansasville. (414) 878-1440	Carts:	$	
◎◎◎	*White Birch Course*	Rating:	73.3/73.2	
DEAL	18 holes. Par 72/72. Yards: 6,977/6,206	Slope:	130/126	
	Apr.–Nov. High: May–Sept.			

◎◎◎◎	*Blue Spruce*	Rating:	72.0/72.1	
DEAL	18 holes. Par 72/72. Yards: 6,687/5,988	Slope:	129/125	

P	**Brown Deer Golf Course**	Greens:	$$$	
◎◎◎◎	N. Green Bay Rd., Milwaukee. (414) 352-8080	Carts:	$$	
STATE	18 holes. Par 71/71. Yards: 6,763/5,965	Rating:	NA	
	Year-round. High: June–Aug.	Slope:	130/131	

P	**Browns Lake Golf Course**	Greens:	$	S J
◎◎	Burlington. (414) 763-6065	Carts:	$	
	18 holes. Par 72/75. Yards: 6,449/6,206	Rating:	70.2/75.8	
	Mar.–Oct. High: June–Sept.	Slope:	122/132	

P	**Country Club of Wisconsin**	Greens:	$$–$$$	W T S J
◎◎◎	Grafton. (414) 375-2444	Carts:	$	
	18 holes. Par 72/72. Yards: 7,108/5,499	Rating:	74.7/67.4	
	Apr.–Nov. High: May–Sept.	Slope:	137/119	

P	**Dretzka Park Golf Course**	Greens:	$	T S J
◎◎◎	W. Bradley Rd., Milwaukee. (414) 354-7300	Carts:	$	
DEAL	18 holes. Par 72/72. Yards: 6,832/5,680	Rating:	70.8/74.6	
	Mar.–Nov. High: May–Sept.	Slope:	124/123	

P	**Evergreen Golf Club**	Greens:	$$	W L T J
	Hwys. 12 and 67 N., Elkhorn. (414) 723-5722	Carts:	$	
◎◎◎	*North/East/South*	Rating:	71.7/71.7/70.8	
DEAL	27 holes. Par 72/72/72. Yards: 6,431/6,501/6,280	Slope:	128/127/125	
	Mar.–Dec. High: May–Sept.			

R	**Geneva National Golf Club**	Greens:	$$$$–$$$$$	L R
	Lake Geneva. (414) 245-7000	Carts:	Incl.	
◎◎◎◎	*Palmer Course*	Rating:	74.8/68.7	
STATE	18 holes. Par 72/72. Yards: 7,171/4,904	Slope:	140/122	
	Mar.–Oct. High: May–Sept.			

Wisconsin Golf Guide

Milwaukee Area

◔◔◔◔ STATE	*Trevino Course* 18 holes. Par 72/72. Yards: 7,120/5,193		Rating: Slope:	74.5/70.1 137/124
R ◔◔◔ STATE	**Grand Geneva Resort and Spa** Hwys. 50 and 12, Lake Geneva. (414) 248-2556 *The Briar Patch Course* 18 holes. Par 71/71. Yards: 6,478/4,950 Apr.–Nov. High: May–Sept.	Greens: Carts: Rating: Slope:	$$$$–$$$$$ L T Incl. 71.7/65.0 133/117	
◔◔◔◔ STATE	*The Brute Course* 18 holes. Par 72/74. Yards: 6,997/5,408		Rating: Slope:	73.4/67.5 135/122
P ◔◔	**Grant Park Golf Course** Hawthorne Ave., S. Milwaukee. (414) 762-4646 18 holes. Par 67/71. Yards: 5,174/5,147 Year-round. High: June–Aug.	Greens: Carts: Rating: Slope:	$ W L T S J $$ 64.1/68.4 110/103	
SP ◔◔	**Hartford Golf Club** Lee Rd., Hartford. (414) 673-2710 18 holes. Par 72/74. Yards: 6,406/5,850 Apr.–Dec. High: May–Sept.	Greens: Carts: Rating: Slope:	$$ T $ 69.7/72.9 114/119	
P ◔◔	**Hawthorne Hills Golf Club** Hwy. 1, Saukville. (414) 692-2151 18 holes. Par 72/72. Yards: 6,595/5,307 Apr.–Oct.	Greens: Carts: Rating: Slope:	$ S J $$ 70.5/69.1 118/114	
SP ◔◔	**Hillmoor Golf Club** Hwy. 50, Lake Geneva. (414) 248-4570 18 holes. Par 72/72. Yards: 6,350/5,360 Mar.–Dec. High: May–Oct.	Greens: Carts: Rating: Slope:	$$ W L T J $ 71.0/65.3 123/113	
P ◔◔◔ DEAL	**Ives Grove Golf Links** Washington Ave., Sturtevant. (414) 878-3714 18 holes. Par 72/72. Yards: 6,915/5,410 Mar.–Nov. High: May–Sept.	Greens: Carts: Rating: Slope:	$ S J $$ 72.5/70.7 129/123	
P ◔◔◔ DEAL	**Johnson Park Golf Course** Northwestern Ave., Racine. (414) 637-2840 18 holes. Par 72/74. Yards: 6,683/5,732 Apr.–Nov. High: June–Aug.	Greens: Carts: Rating: Slope:	$ W L S J $ 70.8/73.0 117/120	
P ◔◔◔ DEAL	**Kettle Hills Golf Course** Hwy. 167 W., Richfield. (414) 255-2200 *Ponds/Woods* 18 holes. Par 72/72. Yards: 6,787/5,171 Apr.–Nov. High: May–Sept.	Greens: Carts: Rating: Slope:	$$ L T S J $ 72.5/69.6 128/123	
R ◔◔	**Lake Lawn Golf Course** Hwy. 50 E., Delavan. (414) 728-7950 18 holes. Par 70/70. Yards: 6,418/5,215 Apr.–Oct. High: June–Aug.	Greens: Carts: Rating: Slope:	$$$ W L R T S J Incl. 69.2/64.1 120/107	
P ◔◔	**Lake Park Golf Course** Mequon Rd., Germantown. (414) 255-4200 *Red/White/Blue* 27 holes. Par 72/72/72. Yards: 6,979/6,781/6,642 Apr.–Oct. High: May–Sept.	Greens: Carts: Rating: Slope:	$–$$ W L T S $ 73.4/72.7/71.9 131/126/126	
SP ◔◔◔ DEAL	**Maplecrest Country Club** 18th St., Kenosha. (414) 859-2887 18 holes. Par 70/70. Yards: 6,396/5,056 Mar.–Nov. High: May–Sept.	Greens: Carts: Rating: Slope:	$ L T S Inquire 70.9/71.0 121/124	
P ◔◔◔	**Naga-Waukee Golf Course** Maple Ave., Pewaukee. (414) 367-2153		Greens: Carts:	$–$$ W L T S J $

Wisconsin Golf Guide

Milwaukee Area

DEAL		Rating:	71.8/72.6
	18 holes. Par 72/72. Yards: 6,780/5,796		
	Apr.–Dec. High: May–Sept.	Slope:	125/125

P	**Oakwood Park Golf Course**	Greens:	$	W S J
☺☺☺	W. Oak Ridge Rd., Franklin. (414) 281-6700	Carts:	$$	
DEAL	18 holes. Par 72/72. Yards: 6,972/6,179	Rating:	71.4/74.4	
	Apr.–Oct. High: June–Aug.	Slope:	118/123	

SP	**Old Hickory Golf Club**	Greens:	$$$	L
☺☺☺☺	Hwy. 33 E., Beaver Dam. (414) 887-7577	Carts:	Incl.	
STATE	18 holes. Par 72/73. Yards: 6,688/5,644	Rating:	72.5/72.8	
	Apr.–Oct. High: June–Aug.	Slope:	129/127	

R	**Olympia Resort Golf Club**	Greens:	$$	L T S J
☺☺	Royale Mile Rd., Oconomowoc. (414) 567-2577	Carts:	$	
	18 holes. Par 72/71. Yards: 6,458/5,735	Rating:	70.5/72.4	
	Apr.–Nov. High: June–Sept.	Slope:	118/119	

P	**Petrifying Springs Golf Course**	Greens:	$–$$	
☺☺☺	7th St., Kenosha. (414) 552-9052	Carts:	$	
DEAL	18 holes. Par 71/72. Yards: 5,979/5,588	Rating:	67.8/70.9	
	Apr.–Oct. High: July	Slope:	119/122	

P	**Quit-Qui-Oc Golf Club**	Greens:	$–$$	W L T S J
☺☺☺	Elkhart Lake. (414) 876-2833	Carts:	$	
DEAL	18 holes. Par 70/71. Yards: 6,178/5,134	Rating:	69.6/64.9	
	Apr.–Nov. High: May–Sept.	Slope:	119/109	

SP	**Rainbow Springs Golf Club**	Greens:	$$	W L T S J
☺☺☺	Hwy. 99, Mukwonago. (414) 363-4550	Carts:	Incl.	
DEAL	18 holes. Par 72/72. Yards: 6,914/5,135	Rating:	73.4/69.8	
	Apr.–Nov. High: June–Sept.	Slope:	132/120	

SP	**Rivermoor Country Club**	Greens:	$$	L T S
☺☺	Waterford Dr., Waterford. (414) 534-2500	Carts:	$	
	18 holes. Par 70/72. Yards: 6,508/5,147	Rating:	68.7/72.7	
	Apr.–Nov. High: June–Aug.	Slope:	121/125	

P	**Spring Valley Country Club**	Greens:	$	W L T S
☺☺☺	23913 Wilmot Rd., Salem. (414) 862-2626	Carts:	$	
DEAL	18 holes. Par 70/70. Yards: 6,450/5,950	Rating:	69.8/69.5	
	Year-round. High: Apr.–Nov.	Slope:	123/114	

SP	**Tuscumbia Golf Club**	Greens:	$$	L T S J
☺☺	Illinois Ave., Green Lake. (414) 294-3240	Carts:	$$	
	18 holes. Par 71/71. Yards: 6,301/5,619	Rating:	70.1/73.2	
	Apr.–Oct. High: June–Sept.	Slope:	122/123	

P	**Whitnall Park Golf Course**	Greens:	$$	L T S J
☺☺	S. 92nd St., Hales Corners. (414) 425-7931	Carts:	$	
	18 holes. Par 71/74. Yards: 6,216/5,778	Rating:	69.9/72.1	
	Apr.–Nov. High: June–Sept.	Slope:	117/119	

The South

Alabama	North Carolina
Arkansas	Oklahoma
Florida	South Carolina
Georgia	Tennessee
Louisiana	Texas
Mississippi	

Alabama

Among the crown jewels of Alabama, and among America's premier golf tours open to the public, is the Robert Trent Jones Golf Trail, a collection of 18 superb courses in seven Alabama cities. The largest golf course construction project ever attempted, the trail was initiated in the late 1980s with funding from the state pension fund.

The courses include Cambrian Ridge in Greenville, Grand National in Opelika, Hampton Cove in Huntsville, Highland Oaks in Dothan, Magnolia Grove in Mobile, Oxmoor Valley in Birmingham, and Silver Lakes near Anniston.

The **Cambrian Ridge Golf Club** offers 27 holes of championship-level golf at public-course rates in Greenville, about 40 miles south of Montgomery. The Canyon and Sherling courses there are considered the best of the lot and also are Econoguide Deals.

The Grand National Golf Club in Opelika, east of Montgomery, is Alabama's golfing mall, with 54 holes of superior golf at the Lake, Links, and Short courses. And even better, they are on our list of Econoguide Deals. The Lake Course is considered one for the scrapbooks of traveling golfers. The Links Course is the toughest of the three at Grand National.

We also give high marks to the **Highland Oaks Golf Club** in Dothan, considered by some to be the most difficult challenge on the Jones Trail.

The Crossings and Falls courses at **Magnolia Grove Golf Club** in Semmes, west of Mobile, are both handsome and challenging courses and are Econoguide Deals.

Most golf courses and resorts in Alabama operate year-round, with high-season prices in effect from spring to fall. Some courses, though, may drop to a midseason rate for the hottest months of summer.

The Robert Trent Jones Golf Trail offers three-, five-, and seven-day passes and other special deals. Contact any of the courses for information.

Econoguide Leader Board: Best Public Courses in Alabama

⊚⊚⊚⊚	Cambrian Ridge Golf Club (Canyon, Sherling)
⊚⊚⊚⊚	Grand National Golf Club (Lake, Links)
⊚⊚⊚⊚	Highland Oaks Golf Club (Highland, Magnolia, Marshwood)
⊚⊚⊚	Lagoon Park Golf Course
⊚⊚⊚⊚	Magnolia Grove Golf Club (Crossings, Falls)
⊚⊚⊚	Rock Creek Golf Club
⊚⊚⊚⊚	Timbercreek Golf Club (Dogwood, Magnolia, Pines)

Econoguide Leader Board: Best Deals in Alabama

$$/⊚⊚⊚	Auburn Links
$$/⊚⊚⊚⊚	Cambrian Ridge Golf Club
$$/⊚⊚⊚	Eagle Point Golf Club
$$/⊚⊚⊚⊚	Grand National Golf Club
$$/⊚⊚⊚	Hampton Cove Golf Club
$/⊚⊚⊚	Lagoon Park Golf Course

$$/ⓄⓄⓄⓄ	Magnolia Grove Golf Club (Crossings, Falls)
$$/ⓄⓄⓄ	Silver Lakes Golf Course
$$/ⓄⓄⓄⓄ	Timbercreek Golf Club (Dogwood, Magnolia, Pines)

Alabama Golf Guide

Birmingham Area

R	**Alpine Bay Golf and Country Club**	Greens:	$–$$	W R T
Ⓞ	Renfore Rd., Alpine (205) 268-9410	Carts:	$	
	18 holes. Par 72/72. Yards: 6,518/5,518	Rating:	70.9/69.8	
	Year-round. High: May–Sept.	Slope:	129/120	

P	**Bent Brook Golf Course**	Greens:	$$	
ⓄⓄⓄ	Dickey Springs Rd., Bessemer. (205) 424-2368	Carts:	$	
	27 holes. Par 71/71/70. Yards: 6,934/7,053/6,847	Rating:	71.8/71.7/71.1	
	Year-round.	Slope:	119/121/121	

P	**Eagle Point Golf Club**	Greens:	$$	S
ⓄⓄⓄ	Eagle Point Dr., Birmingham. (205) 991-9070	Carts:	$	
	18 holes. Par 71/70. Yards: 6,470/4,691	Rating:	70.2/61.9	
	Year-round. High: Apr.–Sept.	Slope:	127/108	

P	**Oak Mountain State Park Golf Course**	Greens:	$	S
Ⓞ	Findley Dr., Pelham. (205) 620-2522	Carts:	$	
	18 holes. Par 72/72. Yards: 6,748/5,540	Rating:	71.5/NA	
	Year-round. High: May–Sept.	Slope:	127/124	

P	**Oxmoor Valley Golf Club**	Greens:	$$	W L T S J
	Sunbelt Pkwy., Birmingham. (205) 942-1177	Carts:	$	
ⓄⓄ	*Ridge Course*	Rating:	73.5/68.6	
	18 holes. Par 72/72. Yards: 7,053/4,869	Slope:	140/130	
	Year-round. High: Apr.–Nov.			

ⓄⓄ	*Valley Course*	Rating:	73.9/65.4	
	18 holes. Par 72/72. Yards: 7,240/4,866	Slope:	135/118	

P	**Silver Lakes Golf Course**	Greens:	$$	W L T S J
	Sunbelt Pkwy., Glencoe. (205) 892-3268	Carts:	$	
ⓄⓄⓄ	*Mindbreaker/Heartbreaker/Backbreaker*	Rating:	NA	
DEAL	27 holes. Par 72/72/72. Yards: 7,407/7,674/7,425	Slope:	NA	
	Year-round. High: Apr.–Oct.			

Huntsville Area

R	**Goose Pond Colony Golf Course**	Greens:	$–$$	W R S J
ⓄⓄ	Ed Hembree Dr., Scottsboro. (205) 574-5353	Carts:	$	
	18 holes. Par 72/72. Yards: 6,860/5,370	Rating:	71.7/70.0	
	Year-round. High: Apr.–Aug.	Slope:	125/115	

P	**Hampton Cove Golf Club**	Greens:	$$	W T J
	Old Hwy. 431 S., Owens Cross Roads. (205) 551-1818	Carts:	$	
ⓄⓄⓄ	*Highlands*	Rating:	74.1/66.0	
DEAL	18 holes. Par 72/72. Yards: 7,262/4,766	Slope:	134/118	
	Year-round High: July–Sept.			

ⓄⓄⓄ	*River Course*	Rating:	75.6/67.0	
	18 holes. Par 72/72. Yards: 7,507/5,283	Slope:	135/118	

R	**Joe Wheeler State Park Golf Club**	Greens:	$	R S
Ⓞ	Rte. 4, Rogersville. (205) 247-9308	Carts:	$	
	18 holes. Par 72/72. Yards: 7,251/6,055	Rating:	73.1/67.7	
	Year-round.	Slope:	120/109	

P	**Lake Guntersville Golf Club**	Greens:	$	S
ⓄⓄ	St. Hwy. 227. Guntersville. (205) 582-0379	Carts:	$	

Alabama Golf Guide

Huntsville Area

	18 holes. Par 72/72. Yards: 6,785/5,776	Rating:	71.2/70.3	
	Year-round. High: July–Aug.	Slope:	128/124	

P	**Point Mallard Golf Course**	Greens:	$	W L S J
☺☺	Point Mallard Dr., Decatur. (205) 351-7776	Carts:	$	
	18 holes. Par 72/73. Yards: 7,113/5,437	Rating:	73.7/NA	
	Year-round. High: Apr.–Sept.	Slope:	125/NA	

Mobile Area

P	**Azalea City Golf Club**	Greens:	$	T
☺☺	Gaillard Dr., Mobile. (334) 342-4221	Carts:	$	
	18 holes. Par 72/72. Yards: 6,765/6,491	Rating:	70.9/69.8	
	Year-round. High: Mar.–Oct.	Slope:	124/121	

SP	**Cotton Creek Club**	Greens:	$$$	W L
	Cotton Creek Blvd., Gulf Shores. (334) 968-7766	Carts:	$	
☺☺☺	*North/West/East*	Rating:	73.9/73.0/73.2	
	27 holes. Par 72/72/72. Yards: 7,028/6,971/6,975	Slope:	132/127/131	
	Year-round. High: Mar.–Oct.			

SP	**Glenlakes Country Club**	Greens:	$$	L R T J
	Foley. (334) 943-8000	Carts:	Incl.	
☺	*Dunes Course*	Rating:	69.1/70.5	
	18 holes. Par 72/72. Yards: 6,680/5,019	Slope:	126/120	
	Year-round. High: Jan.–Mar.			

P	**Gulf State Park Golf Course**	Greens:	$	R S
☺☺	20115 St. Hwy. 135, Gulf Shores. (334) 948-4653	Carts:	$	
	18 holes. Par 72/72. Yards: 6,563/5,310	Rating:	72.5/70.4	
	Year-round. High: Feb.–Apr., June–Aug.	Slope:	NA	

P	**Isle Dauphine Golf Club**	Greens:	$	W
☺	Orleand Dr., Dauphin Island. (334) 861-2433	Carts:	$	
	18 holes. Par 72/72. Yards: 6,620/5,619	Rating:	NA	
	Year-round. High: Feb.–May	Slope:	123/122	

P	**The Linksman Golf Club**	Greens:	$	W R T S J
☺	St. Andres Dr., Mobile. (334) 661-0018	Carts:	$	
	18 holes. Par 72/72. Yards: 6,275/5,416	Rating:	70.1/71.0	
	Year-round. High: Mar.–June	Slope:	123/121	

P	**Magnolia Grove Golf Club**	Greens:	$$	W L T S J
	Lamplighter Dr., Semmes. (334) 645-0075	Carts:	$	
☺☺☺☺	*Crossings Course*	Rating:	74.6/NA	
DEAL	18 holes. Par 72/72. Yards: 7,150/5,184	Slope:	134/NA	
STATE	Year-round. High: Feb.–Apr.			

☺☺☺☺	*Falls Course*	Rating:	75.1/NA	
DEAL	18 holes. Par 72/72. Yards: 7,240/5,253	Slope:	137/NA	
STATE				

R	**Marriott's Lakewood Golf Club**	Greens:	$$$$	J
	Hwy. 98, Point Clear. (334) 990-6312	Carts:	Incl.	
☺☺	*Azalea Course*	Rating:	72.5/71.3	
	18 holes. Par 72. Yards: 6,770/5,307	Slope:	128/118	
	Year-round.			

☺☺☺	*Dogwood Course*	Rating:	72.1/72.6	
	18 holes. Par 71/72. Yards: 6,676/5,532	Slope:	124/122	

P	**Quail Creek Golf Course**	Greens:	$	T
☺	Quail Creek Dr., Fairhope. (334) 990-0240	Carts:	$	
	18 holes. Par 72/72. Yards: 6,426/5,305	Rating:	70.1/69.6	
	Year-round. High: Jan.–Apr.	Slope:	112/114	

SP	**Rock Creek Golf Club**	Greens:	$$–$$$	T
☺☺☺	Fairhope. (334) 928-4223	Carts:	$	

Mobile Area

| STATE | 18 holes. Par 72/72. Yards: 6,920/5,135 | Rating: | 72.2/68.4 |
| | Year-round. High: Spring and Fall | Slope: | 129/117 |

P	**Timbercreek Golf Club**	Greens:	$$
	Timbercreek Blvd., Daphne. (334) 621-9900	Carts:	$
☺☺☺☺	*Dogwood/Magnolia/Pines*	Rating:	73.8/72.9/74.3
DEAL	27 holes. Par 72/72/72. Yards: 7,062/6,928/7,090	Slope:	144/137/143
STATE	Year-round.		

Montgomery Area

P	**Auburn Links**	Greens:	$$	L R S J
☺☺☺	Shell-Toomer Pkwy., Auburn. (334) 887-5151	Carts:	$	
DEAL	18 holes. Par 72/72. Yards: 7,145/5,320	Rating:	72.5/68.5	
	Year-round. High: June–Oct.	Slope:	129/118	

P	**Cambrian Ridge Golf Club**	Greens:	$$	W T S J
	Sunbelt Pkwy., Greenville. (334) 382-9787	Carts:	$	
☺☺☺☺	*Canyon/Sherling/Loblolly*	Rating:	75.4/74.6/73.9	
DEAL	27 holes. Par 72/71/71. Yards: 7,424/7,297/7,232	Slope:	142/140/133	
STATE	Year-round.			

P	**Grand National Golf Club**	Greens:	$$	W L T J
	Sunbelt Pkwy., Opelika. (334) 749-9042	Carts:	$	
☺☺☺☺	*Lake Course*	Rating:	74.9/67.4	
DEAL	18 holes. Par 72/72. Yards: 7,089/4,910	Slope:	138/123	
STATE	Year-round. High: Mar.–Oct.			

☺☺☺☺	*Links Course*	Rating:	74.9/66.8	W L T
DEAL	18 holes. Par 72/72. Yards: 7,311/4,843	Slope:	141/125	
STATE				

P	**Lagoon Park Golf Course**	Greens:	$	W L
☺☺☺	Lagoon Park Dr., Montgomery. (334) 271-7000	Carts:	$	
BEST	18 holes. Par 72/72. Yards: 6,773/5,342	Rating:	71.1/69.6	
DEAL	Year-round. High: Apr.–Oct.	Slope:	124/113	

R	**Still Waters Resort**	Greens:	$$	W L J
☺☺	Still Waters Dr., Dadeville. (205) 825-7021	Carts:	$	
	18 holes. Par 72/72. Yards: 6,407/5,287	Rating:	69.9/71.5	
	Year-round. High: Mar.–Oct.	Slope:	124/125	

Southern Alabama

P	**Highland Oaks Golf Club**	Greens:	$$–$$$	W L T J
	Royal Parkway, Dothan. (334) 712-2820	Carts:	$	
☺☺☺☺	*Highland/Magnolia/Marshwood*	Rating:	76.9/76.0/75.7	
STATE	27 holes. Par 72/72. Yards: 7,704/7,591/7,511	Slope:	138/135/133	
	Year-round. High: Mar.–Oct.			

R	**Lakepoint Resort Golf Course**	Greens:	$	S
☺☺	Hwy. 431, Eufala. (334) 687-6677	Carts:	$	
	18 holes. Par 72/72. Yards: 6,752/5,363	Rating:	73.6/69.2	
	Year-round. High: Mar.–June	Slope:	123	

SP	**Olympia Spa Golf Resort**	Greens:	$	T
☺	Hwy. 231 S., Dothan. (334) 677-3326	Carts:	$	
	18 holes. Par 72/72. Yards: 7,242/5,470	Rating:	74.5/71.1	
	Year-round. High: Mar.–June	Slope:	123/113	

Arkansas

Not known as a golf state, Arkansas nevertheless has a decent collection of courses of varying quality. The best of the lot available to the public is probably **Mountain Ranch Golf Club**, a resort in Fairfield Bay, way north of Little Rock. It's hidden away in the hills, and features more than its share of water and sand hazards.

Also worthy are the mountain and meadow South Course at **Cherokee Village** and the **Prairie Creek Country Club** in Rogers, a tough hilltop challenge.

Most courses in Arkansas operate year-round. Expect to find peak prices during the summer, with the best deals in the fall through spring.

Econoguide Leader Board: Best Public Courses in Arkansas

☺☺☺	Cherokee Village (South)
☺☺☺☺	Mountain Ranch Golf Club
☺☺☺	Prairie Creek Country Club

Econoguide Leader Board: Best Deals in Arkansas

$$/☺☺☺	Cherokee Village (South)
$$/☺☺☺	Quapaw Golf Links
$$/☺☺☺	Prairie Creek Country Club
$$/☺☺☺☺	Mountain Ranch Golf Club

Arkansas Golf Guide

Fayetteville Area

R ☺☺	**Dawn Hill Golf Club** Dawn Hill Rd., Siloam Springs. (501) 524-4838 18 holes. Par 72/73. Yards: 6,852/5,330 Year-round. High: May–Oct.	Greens: Carts: Rating: Slope:	$–$$ Inquire 71.3/69.1 114/110	T
SP ☺☺☺ DEAL STATE	**Prairie Creek Country Club** Hwy. 12 E., Rogers. (501) 925-2414 18 holes. Par 72/72. Yards: 6,707/5,921 Year-round. High: Apr.–Sept.	Greens: Carts: Rating: Slope:	$ $ 73.4/76.3 130/127	W R T

Fort Smith

P ☺☺	**Ben Green Regional Park Golf Course** S. Zero, Fort Smith. (501) 646-5301 18 holes. Par 72/73. Yards: 6,782/5,023 Year-round. High: Apr.–Oct.	Greens: Carts: Rating: Slope:	$ $$ 71.7/67.7 120/109	W T S J

Little Rock Area

P ☺☺	**DeGray State Park Golf Course** Bismarck. (501) 865-2807 18 holes. Par 72/72. Yards: 6,930/5,731 Year-round. High: Apr.–Sept.	Greens: Carts: Rating: Slope:	$ $ 60.7/67.0 134/123	S
P ☺☺	**Hindman Park Golf Course** Brookview Dr., Little Rock. (501) 565-6450 18 holes. Par 72/72. Yards: 6,393/4,349 Year-round. High: May–Aug.	Greens: Carts: Rating: Slope:	$ $ 68.9/NA 109/NA	L T S J
R ☺☺☺	**Hot Springs Country Club** Malvern Ave., Hot Springs. (501) 624-2661 *Arlington Course* 18 holes. Par 72/74. Yards: 6,646/6,206 Year-round. High: Mar.–Oct.	Greens: Carts: Rating: Slope:	$$$$ Incl. 72.0/75.6 127/137	W R
☺☺	*Majestic Course* 18 holes. Par 72/72. Yards: 6,715/5,541	Greens: Carts: Rating: Slope:	$$$ Incl. 72.7/70.9 131/121	W R

Arkansas Golf Guide

Little Rock Area

SP	**Longhills Golf Club**	Greens:	$	J
⊙⊙	Hwy. 5 N., Benton. (501) 794-9907	Carts:	$	
	18 holes. Par 72/73. Yards: 6,539/5,350	Rating:	69.9/69.5	
	Year-round. High: Apr.–Sept.	Slope:	110/110	
P	**Quapaw Golf Links**	Greens:	$–$$	W L T S J
⊙⊙⊙	St. Hwy. 391 N., North Little Rock. (501) 945-0945	Carts:	$	
DEAL	18 holes. Par 72/72. Yards: 6,972/5,118	Rating:	72.4/70.3	
	Year-round. High: Mar.–Oct.	Slope:	119/120	
R	**The Red Apple Inn and Country Club**	Greens:	$$	
⊙⊙	Heber Springs. (501) 362-3131	Carts:	$	
	18 holes. Par 72/72. Yards: 6,402/5,137	Rating:	70.0/69.0	
	Year-round. High: Apr.–Nov.	Slope:	121/110	

Northern Arkansas

R	**Cherokee Village**	Greens:	$–$$	
	Laguna Dr., Cherokee Village. (501) 257-2555	Carts:	Inquire	
⊙⊙⊙	*South*	Rating:	73.5/70.4	
DEAL	18 holes. Par 72/72. Yards: 7,058/5,270	Slope:	128/116	
STATE	Year-round. High: May–Sept.			
R	**Mountain Ranch Golf Club**	Greens:	$$	W L R T J
⊙⊙⊙⊙	Lost Creek Pkwy., Fairfield Bay. (501) 884-3400	Carts:	$	
DEAL	18 holes. Par 72/72. Yards: 6,780/5,134	Rating:	71.8/69.8	
STATE	Year-round. High: May–Oct.	Slope:	129/121	

Florida

The Sunshine State is probably best known for beaches, Mickey Mouse's home away from home, and golf. And if you really want to, you can combine all three on a single visit. In fact, the **Walt Disney World** megaresort near Orlando has turned into a golf factory, with five major first-class resorts located on the grounds of the sprawling theme park. There are at least that many superb courses at hotels and resorts outside of the park.

All told, there are more than 1,000 courses of all kinds in the state; about half of them are open to the public.

Orlando and Walt Disney World

Some of the best courses in Florida—or anywhere else—are in and around Orlando, but that's not the best reason to go there. No, the best reasons to play golf in the area are all of the other things to do: Walt Disney World's rides, water sports, entertainment, and more; Universal Studios Florida; Sea World Orlando; and so much more. If these things don't appeal to you, they may still offer you the chance to take the spouse and kids with you on a golf vacation and not worry about whether they'll be able to entertain themselves.

Walt Disney World's Magic Linkdom includes no fewer than five fabulous 18-hole courses—any one of which would be among the best in any other state. The best of the best is generally acknowledged to be the Osprey Ridge Golf Course, a long, difficult challenge with elevated tees. The circulating layout features holes that play in all possible directions.

Close behind in challenge level is the Palm Golf Course, one of the most difficult resort courses in the country, with lots of sand and water, and an 18th hole rated among the most challenging on the PGA Tour.

Other winners at Disney World include Eagle Pines Golf Course, a Pete Dye design with deep-dish fairways that keep the ball at tree level.

The Magnolia Golf Course is named for the more than 1,500 magnolia trees on the land; it is used as the setting for the final round of the Walt Disney World/Oldsmobile Golf Classic held each mid-October. It features elevated tees and greens, and a real Mickey Mouse of a hazard on the 6th hole.

Disney's Lake Buena Vista Golf Course is considered the easiest of the bunch, but it nevertheless is one of the few golfing sites that play host to a PGA Tour event, an LPGA event, *and* a USGA event. The course wanders through dense pine forests and around condos.

There's even the Oak Trail 9-hole "executive" course nearby to the Magnolia, featuring some of the most challenging holes at the resort and a miniature-golf course. Oh, and we're told there are a couple of big theme parks nearby.

Non-Disney resorts worth noting include **Arnold Palmer's Bay Hill Club**, one of the top resorts in Florida and the nation.

There are 45 superb holes (18 at the New Course and 9 holes each at the North and South courses are the best of the lot) at the **Grand Cypress Resort** in Orlando. The New Course is a near-replica of the Old Course at St. Andrews (including 145 bunkers). Grand Cypress is a palatial resort, sort of an art museum–cum–golf course and hotel . . . or is it the other way around? In any case, this is a five-star hotel with a four-star golf course (and a private trolley system that runs between the two).

The **Grenelefe Golf and Tennis Resort**, about 25 miles south of Walt Disney World in Haines City, has 54 holes of golf, including the top-rated and very long West Course near and along Lake Marion.

Some 75 miles north of Orlando is the **Golden Ocala Golf Course**, which includes eight replicas of famous holes, including samples of St. Andrews, Muirfield, Baltusrol, and Augusta National.

Miami

The **Doral Golf Resort and Spa** offers no fewer than 72 superb holes created out of the swamps near Miami, including the top-rated Blue Course, better known as the Blue Monster, the home of the Doral Ryder Open on the PGA Tour. It is a long, difficult course with lots of sand and water. The killer hole is the 18th, a dogleg left with water at the tee and on the approach. More than 30 years ago, Doral was built in the middle of nowhere on land that was considered wasted; what exists today is a showplace with some of the most beautifully manicured lawns anywhere, including more than 1,000 bunkers, 100 acres of water, and some sumptuous resort and spa amenities.

The **Links at Key Biscayne** is a challenging course along the waterfront, a bit more difficult when the wind blows through the coconut palms.

The **Golf Club of Miami**, a close contender for an Econoguide Best rating, deserves mention for something else: the club was one of the first to equip many of its golf carts with specialized Global Positioning System receivers that tell golfers the distance, within four feet, from the cart to the pin. How did we ever get along without this?

West Palm Beach

The **PGA National Resort and Spa** has 90 holes of superb golf, topped by the Champion Course in Palm Beach Gardens. This is the home of the PGA of America itself (along with the U.S. Croquet Association, in case you were wondering where *that* was). The Champion was originally designed by George and Tom Fazio, and was redesigned by Jack Nicklaus in 1990; it stretches more than 7,000 yards.

Among West Palm Beach's best is the **Emerald Dunes Golf Club**, a plush though pricey course that includes all sorts of grass, dunes, and water hazards.

The **Palm Beach Polo and Country Club** has water on 14 holes of its Dunes Course. Note the order of the sports in the club's name, by the way. The resort is the center of the universe for the sport of polo; over the last decade the resort has expanded to offer golf challenges that entertain the horsey crowd. The acclaimed Cypress Course is a Pete Dye design, a 7,116-yard monster; the Dunes, laid out by Rong Garl and Jerry Pate, is a slightly shorter, slightly easier world-class links challenge.

Tampa

There are two top-rated courses at the **Innisbrook Hilton Resort** in Palm Harbor, northwest of Tampa: the challenging Copperhead Course and the gorgeous Island Course. Copperhead is practically mountainous (by Florida standards); well, it does go up and down a lot more than other challenges in the state. The Island Course, as befits its name, has more than 50 sand bunkers and a dozen water hazards.

About 60 miles north of Tampa are a pair of outstanding courses that are greener and more manicured than most other Florida courses: the Pine Barrens Course and the Rolling Oaks Course at **World Woods Golf Club** in Brooksville.

The **Eastwood Golf Course** is an exceptionally attractive municipal course in Fort Myers that includes an abundance of wildlife and some long-distance over-water calls. Also in Fort Myers is the **Gateway Golf and Country Club**, a links-type course in the marshes and trees.

Jacksonville

By most rankings the Stadium Course at the famed **Tournament Players Club at Sawgrass** in Ponte Vedra Beach is among the top 10 resorts nationwide; the difficult course includes treacherous greens, huge bunkers, and its famed 17th-hole island—shades of a similar challenge at the TPC Stadium Course at PGA West Resort in California. Water comes into play on all 18 holes.

The famed **Amelia Island Plantation** near Jacksonville offers a quartet of memorable challenges, including the Oceanside, which runs along and amidst the dunes; the Oakmarsh, which plunges deep into the oak and palmetto woods; the marshy Oysterbay; and the Long Point, which combines forests and dunes. The courses are known for tight fairways, small greens, and spectacular beachside links.

The Panhandle

Water, water everywhere—that's the unofficial motto at **Marriott's Bay Point Resort** near Panama City beach, and The Lagoon Legend is considered among the most difficult in the nation. In fact, it has the highest slope rating—152— of any public course listed in this book. If the water or the sand doesn't get you, the marsh and the Tai Tai Swamp will. The front nine is somewhat easier, but we're only speaking in relative terms here.

Florida offers year-round golfing; its high season is in the winter when temperatures are moderate and the snowbirds (northerners) are in town. Expect to pay peak rates from about December through April, including spring break. You can find deep discounts during the heat of the summer; be aware, though, that in and around Orlando, hotel rooms may be at peak or near-peak levels in the summer, too, because of young people on school vacation.

Winter rates for the 1995–96 season at the Doral Golf Resort and Spa— including a room, 18 holes of golf with a cart, breakfast, a clinic, and other amenities—start at $195 per person for a double room. You can also sign on for an "ultimate" package that includes tennis and spa facilities, beginning at $295 per person.

Rates for the basic package drop to $139 per person for spring and fall. In 1996, the resort offered summer packages from late May through the end of September, including a $79 per-person (double-occupancy) unlimited-golf program that delivered room, breakfast, free golf clinic, free cart, unlimited driving range, and advance tee times.

At the Walt Disney World golf complex there are many more golfers than tee-off times available from Christmas through late spring. But the links are much less crowded from May through December. In the golfing off-season you can purchase a Classic Badge for about $50 that permits deeply discounted rounds after 10 A.M. each day—as low as $35 for 18 holes and a cart. It also includes admission to the four championship rounds of the Walt Disney World/Oldsmobile Golf Classic in October if you're there at that time. In 1996, other specials at the Disney complex included reduced rates from June 1 to August 31, twilight golf after 3 P.M. all summer and into the early fall, and a summertime junior special that allowed one junior to play for free with an adult.

Econoguide Leader Board: Best Public Courses in Florida

☺☺☺	Amelia Island Plantation (Oakmarsh, Oysterbay, Oceanside, Long Point)
☺☺☺☺	Arnold Palmer's Bay Hill Club
☺☺☺☺	Baytree National Golf Links
☺☺☺	Cimarrone Golf and Country Club
☺☺☺	The Country Club at Jacaranda West
☺☺☺	Doral Golf Resort and Spa (Blue)
☺☺☺	Doral Park Golf and Country Club (Silver)
☺☺☺	Eastwood Golf Course
☺☺☺☺	Emerald Dunes Golf Club
☺☺☺	Gateway Golf and Country Club

◎◎◎ Golden Ocala Golf Course
◎◎◎ The Golf Club at Cypress Creek
◎◎◎ The Golf Club at Marco
◎◎◎ Golf Club of Jacksonville
◎◎◎◎ Grand Cypress Resort (New, North, South, East)
◎◎◎◎ Grenelefe Golf and Tennis Resort (West)
◎◎◎ Hunter's Creek Golf Course
◎◎◎◎ Innisbrook Hilton Resort (Copperhead, Island)
◎◎◎◎ Links at Key Biscayne
◎◎◎◎ Marriott's Bay Point Resort (The Lagoon Legend)
◎◎◎◎ Palm Beach Polo and Country Club (Dunes)
◎◎◎◎ PGA National Resort and Spa (Champion)
◎◎◎◎ Tournament Players Club at Sawgrass (Stadium)
◎◎◎◎ Walt Disney World Resort (Osprey Ridge)
◎◎◎ West Palm Beach Municipal Country Club
◎◎◎◎ World Woods Golf Club (Pine Barrens, Rolling Oaks)

Econoguide Leader Board: Best Deals in Florida

$$/◎◎◎ Bluewater Bay Resort (Magnolia, Marsh, Bay, Lake)
$$/◎◎◎ Cimarrone Golf and Country Club
$$/◎◎◎ Cocoa Beach Golf Course (River, Dolphin, Lakes)
$$/◎◎◎ The Country Club at Jacaranda West
$$/◎◎◎ The Country Club at Silver Springs Shores
$$/◎◎◎ DeBary Golf and Country Club
$$/◎◎◎ Delray Beach Golf Club
$$/◎◎◎ Fairwinds Golf Course
$$/◎◎◎ The Golf Club at Cypress Creek
$$/◎◎◎ The Golf Club at Marco
$$/◎◎◎ Golf Club of Jacksonville
$$/◎◎◎ Golf Club of Miami (East, West)
$/◎◎◎ Habitat Golf Course
$/◎◎◎ Halifax Plantation Golf Club
$$/◎◎◎ Killearn Country Club and Inn (South, East, North)
$/◎◎◎ Mangrove Bay Golf Course
$$/◎◎◎◎ Marcus Pointe Golf Club
$$/◎◎◎ Marriott at Sawgrass Resort (Oak Bridge Golf Club)
$$/◎◎◎ The Moors Golf Club
$$/◎◎◎ Oak Hills Golf Club
$$/◎◎◎ Pelican Bay Country Club (South)
$/◎◎◎ St. Johns Country Golf Club
$$/◎◎◎ Sandridge Golf Club (Dunes, Lakes)
$$/◎◎◎ Seven Hills Golfers Club
$$/◎◎◎ Seville Golf and Country Club
$$/◎◎◎ Sherman Hills Golf Club
$$/◎◎◎ Summerfield Golf Club
$$/◎◎◎ Tatum Ridge Golf Links

| $$/☺☺☺ | Viera East Golf Club |
| $$/☺☺☺ | West Palm Beach Municipal Country Club |

Florida Golf Guide

Pensacola Area

R	**Bluewater Bay Resort**	Greens:	$$	L R
	Bluewater Blvd., Niceville. (904) 897-3241	Carts:	$	
☺☺☺	*Magnolia/Marsh*	Rating:	72.2/68.4	
DEAL	18 holes. Par 72/72. Yards: 6,669/5,048	Slope:	131/117	
	Year-round. High: Feb.–May			

| ☺☺☺ | *Bay/Lake* | Rating: | 73.0/70.6 | |
| DEAL | 18 holes. Par 72/72. Yards: 6,803/5,415 | Slope: | 140/124 | |

SP	**The Club at Hidden Creek**	Greens:	$$–$$$	W L T J
☺☺☺☺	PGA Blvd., Navarre. (904) 939-4604	Carts:	Incl.	
	18 holes. Par 72/72. Yards: 6,862/5,213	Rating:	73.2/70.1	
	Year-round. High: Jan.–Apr.	Slope:	139/124	

SP	**Emerald Bay Golf Course**	Greens:	$$$–$$$$	W L R J
☺☺☺☺	Emerald Coast Pkwy., Destin. (904) 837-5197	Carts:	Incl.	
	18 holes. Par 72/72. Yards: 6,802/5,184	Rating:	73.1/70.1	
	Year-round. High: Mar.–Nov.	Slope:	135/122	

P	**Fort Walton Beach Municipal Golf Course**	Greens:	$	T
	Fort Walton Beach. (904) 862-3922	Carts:	$	
☺☺	*Oaks Course.* 1909 Lewis Turner Blvd.	Rating:	70.2/67.8	
	18 holes. Par 72/72. Yards: 6,409/5,366	Slope:	119/107	
	Year-round. High: Feb.–Aug.			

| ☺☺ | *Pines Course.* 699 Country Club Dr. | Rating: | 69.9/69.1 | |
| | 18 holes. Par 72/72. Yards: 6,802/5,320 | Slope: | 110/107 | |

P	**Hilaman Park Municipal Golf Course**	Greens:	$	W T S J
☺☺	Blairstone Rd., Tallahassee. (904) 891-3935	Carts:	$	
	18 holes. Par 72/72. Yards: 6,364/5,365	Rating:	70.1/70.8	
	Year-round. High: Mar.–June	Slope:	121/116	

SP	**Hombre Golf Club**	Greens:	$$$$	L R T J
☺☺☺	Coyote Pass, Panama City Beach. (904) 234-3673	Carts:	Incl.	
	18 holes. Par 72/74. Yards: 6,820/4,793	Rating:	73.4/67.2	
	Year-round. High: Mar.–Apr., June–July	Slope:	136/118	

SP	**Indian Bayou Golf and Country Club**	Greens:	$$–$$$	
	Destin. (904) 837-6191	Carts:	Inquire	
☺☺☺	*Seminole/Choctaw/Creek*	Rating:	73.3/73.1/73.7	
	27 holes. Par 72/72/72. Yards: 6,958/6,893/7,016	Slope:	126/129/128	
	Year-round. High: Feb.–Aug.			

R	**Killearn Country Club and Inn**	Greens:	$$	W T J
	Tyron Circle, Tallahassee. (904) 893-2144, (800) 476-4101	Carts:	Inquire	
☺☺☺	*South/East/North*	Rating:	73.9/73.1/73.3	
DEAL	27 holes. Par 72/72. Yards: 7,025/6,760/6,899	Slope:	133/131/132	
	Year-round. High: Mar.–Aug.			

P	**Marcus Pointe Golf Club**	Greens:	$$	W L T J
☺☺☺☺	Oak Pointe Dr., Pensacola. (904) 484-9770	Carts:	$	
DEAL	18 holes. Par 72/72. Yards: 6,737/5,252	Rating:	72.3/69.6	
	Year-round. High: Feb.–May	Slope:	129/119	

SP	**Marriott's Bay Point Resort**	Greens:	$$$$	L R J
	Dellwood Beach Rd., Panama City Beach. (904) 235-6937	Carts:	Incl.	
☺☺☺	*Club Meadows Course*	Rating:	73.3/68.0	
	18 holes. Par 72/72. Yards: 6,913/4,999	Slope:	126/118	
	Year-round. High: Feb.–June			

| P | **The Lagoon Legend** | Greens: | $$$$ | L R T J |
| ☺☺☺ | Marriott Dr., Panama City Beach. (904) 234-3307 | Carts: | Incl. | |

Florida Golf Guide

Pensacola Area

BEST	18 holes. Par 72/72. Yards: 6,885/4,942 Year-round. High: June–Oct.	Rating: Slope:	75.3/69.8 152/127	

P ☺☺☺ DEAL	**The Moors Golf Club** Avalon Blvd., Milton. (904) 995-4653 18 holes. Par 71/71. Yards: 6,956/5,340 Year-round. High: Apr.–May, Sept.–Oct.	Greens: Carts: Rating: Slope:	$$ $ 73.3/70.3 126/117	W R J

R ☺☺☺	**Perdido Bay Golf Club** Doug Ford Dr., Pensacola. (904) 492-1223 18 holes. Par 72/72. Yards: 7,154/5,478 Year-round. High: Jan.–Apr.	Greens: Carts: Rating: Slope:	$$–$$$ Incl. 73.6/71.4 125/121	R T J

R ☺☺☺	**Sandestin Beach Hilton Golf and Tennis Resort** Hwy. 98 W., Destin *Baytowne: Troon/Dunes/Harbor.* (904) 267-8155 27 holes. Par 72/72/72. Yards: 7,185/6,890/6,891 Year-round. High: Mar.–Apr., Sept.–Oct.	Greens: Carts: Rating: Slope:	$$$–$$$$$ $ 74.6/73.4/73.9 128/127/127	L R T

☺☺☺	*Burnt Pines Golf Course.* (904) 267-6500 18 holes. Par 72/72. Yards: 7,046/5,950	Rating: Slope:	74.1/68.7 135/124	R

☺☺☺	*The Links Course.* (904) 267-6500 18 holes. Par 72/72. Yards: 6,710/4,969	Rating: Slope:	72.8/69.2 124/115	L R T

P ☺☺	**Scenic Hills Country Club** Burning Tree Rd., Pensacola. (904) 476-0611 18 holes. Par 71/71. Yards: 6,689/5,187 Year-round. High: Feb.–Apr.	Greens: Carts: Rating: Slope:	$$ Incl. NA 135/116	W L R T

R ☺☺☺	**Seascape Resort** Seascape Dr., Destin. (904) 654-7888 18 holes. Par 71/71. Yards: 6,488/5,029 Year-round. High: Mar.–Oct.	Greens: Carts: Rating: Slope:	$$–$$$ Incl. 71.5/70.3 120/113	L R J

P ☺☺	**Seminole Golf Club** Pottsdamer St., Tallahassee. (904) 644-2582 18 holes. Par 72/72. Yards: 7,033/5,930 Year-round.	Greens: Carts: Rating: Slope:	$ $ 73.4/73.0 121/111	W R T J

SP ☺☺	**Shalimar Pointe Golf and Country Club** Shalimar. (904) 651-1416 18 holes. Par 72/72. Yards: 6,765/5,427 Year-round. High: Jan.–Apr.	Greens: Carts: Rating: Slope:	$$–$$$ Incl. 72.9/70.7 125/115	W L R T

P ☺☺	**Tanglewood Golf and Country Club** Tanglewood Dr., Milton. (904) 623-6176 18 holes. Par 72/72. Yards: 6,455/5,295 Year-round. High: Apr.–Nov.	Greens: Carts: Rating: Slope:	$–$$ $ 70.0/69.9 115/118	L S

SP ☺☺☺	**Tiger Point Golf and Country Club** Gulf Breeze. (904) 932-1333 *East Course* 18 holes. Par 72/72. Yards: 7,033/5,217 Year-round. High: Feb.–Apr., Oct.–Nov.	Greens: Carts: Rating: Slope:	$$–$$$ Incl. 73.8/70.2 132/125	W L T

☺☺	*West Course* 18 holes. Par 72/72. Yards: 6,715/5,314	Greens: Carts: Rating: Slope:	$$ Incl. 72.2/70.2 119/121	

Jacksonville Area

R ☺☺☺	**Amelia Island Plantation** 1st Coast Hwy., Amelia Island. (904) 277-5907 (800) 874-6878 *Oakmarsh/Oysterbay/Oceanside*	Greens: Carts: Rating: Slope:	$$$$–$$$$$ Incl. 70.7/68.6/69.3 127/117/120	L R T J

Florida Golf Guide

Jacksonville Area

STATE	27 holes. Par 72/71/71. Yards: 6,502/6,026/6,140 Year-round. High: Apr.–May	

☺☺☺ BEST	*Long Point Golf Club* 18 holes. Par 72/72. Yards: 6,775/4,927	Greens: $$$$$–$$$$$$ Carts: Incl. Rating: 72.9/69.1 Slope: 129/121

SP ☺☺	**Baymeadows Golf Club** Baymeadows Circle W., Jacksonville. (904) 731-5701 18 holes. Par 72/72. Yards: 7,002/5,309 Year-round. High: Year-round	Greens: $$ T Carts: Incl. Rating: 73.7/72.2 Slope: 130/130

SP ☺☺	**Champions Club at Julington Creek** Durbin Creek Blvd., Jacksonville. (904) 287-4653 18 holes. Par 72/72. Yards: 6,872/4,994 Year-round. High: Mar.–May, Oct.–Dec.	Greens: $$ W T S J Carts: Incl. Rating: 72.8/68.6 Slope: 126/114

SP ☺☺☺ DEAL STATE	**Cimarrone Golf and Country Club** Cimarrone Blvd., Jacksonville. (904) 287-2000 18 holes. Par 72/72. Yards: 6,891/4,707 Year-round. High: Apr.–May, Sept.–Oct.	Greens: $$ W T Carts: Incl. Rating: NA Slope: 128

P ☺☺	**Deerfield Lakes Golf Course** Lem Turner Rd., Callahan. (904) 879-1210 18 holes. Par 72/74. Yards: 6,700/5,266 Year-round. High: Oct.–Mar.	Greens: $$ W Carts: Incl. Rating: 70.2/69.0 Slope: 114/102

SP ☺☺☺☺	**Eagle Harbor Golf Club** Eagle Harbor Pkwy., Orange Park. (904) 269-9300 18 holes. Par 72/72. Yards: 6,840/4,980 Year-round. High: Apr.–June	Greens: $$–$$$ W T J Carts: Incl. Rating: 72.6/68.2 Slope: 133/121

P ☺☺	**Fernandina Beach Municipal Golf Course** Bill Melton Rd., Fernandina Beach. (904) 227-7370 *North/West/South* 27 holes. Par 72/71/73. Yards: 6,806/6,412/7,027 Year-round.	Greens: $ W J Carts: $ Rating: 71.5/69.7/72.6 Slope: 118/121/123

R ☺☺☺	**The Golf Club of Amelia Island** Amelia Island Pkwy., Amelia Island. (904) 277-8015 18 holes. Par 72/72. Yards: 6,681/5,039 Year-round. High: May–Sept.	Greens: $$$$$ L R T S J Carts: Incl. Rating: 71.7/70.6 Slope: 127/122

P ☺☺☺ DEAL STATE	**Golf Club of Jacksonville** Jacksonville. (904) 779-0800 18 holes. Par 71/71. Yards: 6,620/5,021 Year-round. High: Mar.–June	Greens: $$ W T S J Carts: Incl. Rating: 70.7/68.0 Slope: 120/115

P ☺☺	**Jacksonville Beach Golf Course** S. Penman Rd., Jacksonville. (904) 249-8600 18 holes. Par 72/72. Yards: 6,510/5,245 Year-round. High: Spring and Fall	Greens: $ W L T J Carts: Inquire Rating: 70.5/69.2 Slope: 119/114

SP ☺☺☺☺	**Marriott at Sawgrass Resort** Marsh Landing Golf Club TPC Blvd., Ponte Vedra Beach. (904) 273-3720 18 holes. Par 72/72. Yards: 6,841/6,001 Year-round. High: Mar.–May	Greens: $$$$$ L Carts: Incl. Rating: NA Slope: 131/120

R ☺☺☺ DEAL	**Oak Bridge Golf Club** Alta Mar Dr., Ponte Vedra Beach. (904) 285-0204 18 holes. Par 70/70. Yards: 6,383/4,869 Year-round. High: Feb.–May	Greens: $$ Carts: $ Rating: 70.3/67.8 Slope: 126/116

Florida Golf Guide

Jacksonville Area

SP ⊙⊙	**Meadowbrook Golf Club** N.W. 37th Place, Gainesville. (904) 332-0577 18 holes. Par 72/72. Yards: 6,289/4,720 Year-round. High: Jan.–Apr.	Greens: Carts: Rating: Slope:	$ Inquire 69.9/66.7 119/117	W T
P ⊙⊙	**Mill Cove Golf Club** Monument Rd., Jacksonville. (904) 646-4653 18 holes. Par 71/71. Yards: 6,671/4,719 Year-round.	Greens: Carts: Rating: Slope:	$–$$ $ 71.7/66.3 129/112	W L T S J
R ⊙⊙	**Ponce de Leon Golf and Conference Resort** U.S. Hwy. 1 N., St. Augustine. (904) 829-5314 18 holes. Par 72/72. Yards: 6,823/5,308 Year-round. High: Feb.–May, Oct.–Nov.	Greens: Carts: Rating: Slope:	$$–$$$ $ 72.9/70.7 131/125	L R T
R ⊙⊙⊙	**Ponte Vedra Inn and Club** Ponte Vedra Blvd., Ponte Vedra Beach. (904) 285-1111 *Lagoon Course* 18 holes. Par 70/70. Yards: 5,574/4,641	Greens: Carts: Rating: Slope:	$$$–$$$$ Incl. 66.2/66.9 110/113	L
⊙⊙⊙	*Ocean Course* 18 holes. Par 72/72. Yards: 6,573/5,237	Rating: Slope:	71.3/69.6 120/119	
SP ⊙⊙⊙	**Ravines Golf and Country Club** Ravines Rd., Middleburg. (904) 282-7888 18 holes. Par 72/70. Yards: 6,733/4,817 Year-round. High: Mar.–May	Greens: Carts: Rating: Slope:	$$–$$$ Incl. 72.4/67.4 133/120	
P ⊙⊙⊙ DEAL	**St. Johns Country Golf Club** Cypress Links Blvd., Ecton. (904) 825-4900 18 holes. Par 72/72. Yards: 6,926/5,173 Year-round. High: Jan.–Apr.	Greens: Carts: Rating: Slope:	$ $ 72.9/68.8 130/117	T
R ⊙⊙⊙⊙ BEST	**Tournament Players Club at Sawgrass** TPC Blvd., Ponte Vedra Beach. (904) 273-3235 *Stadium Course* 18 holes. Par 72/72. Yards: 6,857/5,034 Year-round. High: Mar.–May	Greens: Carts: Rating: Slope:	$$$$$–$$$$$$ Incl. 74.0/64.7 135/123	L J
⊙⊙⊙⊙	*Valley Course* 18 holes. Par 72/72. Yards: 6,864/5,126	Greens: Carts: Rating: Slope:	$$$$–$$$$$ Incl. 72.6/63.8 129/117	
P ⊙⊙⊙	**Windsor Parke Golf Club** Hodges Blvd., Jacksonville. (904) 223-4653 18 holes. Par 72/72. Yards: 6,740/5,206 Year-round. High: Mar.–May	Greens: Carts: Rating: Slope:	$$$ Incl. 71.9/69.4 133/123	W T S J

Daytona Area

SP ⊙⊙	**Cypress Knoll Golf Club** E. Hampton Blvd., Palm Coast. (904) 437-5807 18 holes. Par 72/72. Yards: 6,591/5,386 Year-round. High: Nov.–Apr.	Greens: Carts: Rating: Slope:	$$–$$$ Incl. 71.6/69.3 130/117	W L
P ⊙	**Daytona Beach Golf Course** Wilder Blvd., Daytona Beach. (904) 258-3119 *North Course* 18 holes. Par 72/72. Yards: 6,567/5,247 Year-round. High: Nov.–May	Greens: Carts: Rating: Slope:	$ $ 71.0/69.1 111/111	W L T
⊙	*South Course* 18 holes. Par 71/71. Yards: 6,229/5,346	Rating: Slope:	69.7/69.6 106/106	
P ⊙⊙⊙	**The Golf Club at Cypress Head** Palm Vista St., Port Orange. (904) 756-5449	Greens: Carts:	$$ Incl.	R T J

Florida Golf Guide

Daytona Area

DEAL	18 holes. Par 72/72. Yards: 6,814/4,909 Year-round. High: Feb.–Apr.	Rating: Slope:	72.4/68.3 133/116

SP ☺☺☺ DEAL	**Halifax Plantation Golf Club** Old Dixie Hwy., Ormond Beach. (904) 676-9600 18 holes. Par 72/72. Yards: 7,128/4,971 Year-round. High: Nov.–Apr.	Greens: $ Carts: $ Rating: 73.9/67.6 Slope: 129/113	W L R T

SP ☺☺☺	**Indigo Lakes Golf Club** Indigo Dr., Daytona Beach. (904) 254-3607 18 holes. Par 72/72. Yards: 7,168/5,159 Year-round. High: Jan.–May	Greens: $$–$$$ Carts: Incl. Rating: 73.5/69.1 Slope: 128/123	W L T

P ☺☺	**LPGA International** Daytona Beach. (904) 274-3880 18 holes. Par 72/72. Yards: 7,088/5,131 Year-round. High: Nov.–Dec.	Greens: $$–$$$$ Carts: Incl. Rating: 74.0/68.9 Slope: 134/122	L T

SP ☺☺☺	**Matanzas Woods Golf Club** Lakeview Dr., Palm Coast. (904) 446-6360 18 holes. Par 72/72. Yards: 6,985/5,336 Year-round. High: Jan.–Apr.	Greens: $$–$$$ Carts: Incl. Rating: 73.3/71.2 Slope: 132/126	L R T J

SP ☺☺	**Palm Harbor Golf Club** Palm Harbor Pkwy., Palm Coast. (904) 445-0845 18 holes. Par 72/72. Yards: 6,572/5,346 Year-round. High: Jan.–May	Greens: $$–$$$ Carts: Incl. Rating: 71.8/71.2 Slope: 127/128	L R T J

P ☺☺☺ DEAL	**Pelican Bay Country Club** Sea Duck Dr., Daytona Beach. (904) 788-6496 *South Course* 18 holes. Par 72/72. Yards: 6,630/5,278 Year-round. High: Dec.–Apr.	Greens: $$ Carts: Incl. Rating: NA Slope: 123/126	W L T

SP ☺☺	**Pine Lakes Country Club** Pine Lakes Pkwy., Palm Coast. (904) 445-0852 18 holes. Par 72/72. Yards: 7,074/5,166 Year-round. High: Jan.–Apr.	Greens: $$–$$$ Carts: Incl. Rating: 73.5/71.4 Slope: 126/124	L R T J

SP ☺☺☺	**River Bend Golf Club** Airport Rd., Ormond Beach. (904) 673-6000 18 holes. Par 72/72. Yards: 6,821/5,112 Year-round. High: Jan.–Apr.	Greens: $$–$$$ Carts: Incl. Rating: 72.3/69.6 Slope: 126/120	W L T J

SP ☺☺	**Spruce Creek Country Club** Daytona Beach. (904) 756-6114 18 holes. Par 72/72. Yards: 6,751/5,157 Year-round. High: Jan.–Apr.	Greens: $$ Carts: Incl. Rating: 72.2/70.3 Slope: 125/121	L R T J

SP ☺☺☺	**Sugar Mill Country Club** New Smyrna Beach. (904) 426-5210 *Red/White/Blue* 27 holes. Par 72/72/72. Yards: 6,766/6,695/6,749 Year-round. High: Jan.–Apr.	Greens: $$–$$$$ Carts: Incl. Rating: 72.1/72.4/72.6 Slope: 125/128/129	L

Orlando Area

R ☺☺☺☺ BEST	**Arnold Palmer's Bay Hill Club** Bay Hill Blvd., Orlando. (407) 876-2429, ext. 630 *Challenger/Champion* 18 holes. Par 72/NA. Yards: 7,114/5,192 Year-round. High: Jan.–Apr.	Greens: $$$$$$ Carts: $ Rating: 74.6/70.3 Slope: 141/120	R J

SP ☺☺☺☺ STATE	**Baytree National Golf Links** National Dr., Melbourne. (407) 259-9060 18 holes. Par 72/72. Yards: 7,043/4,803 Year-round. High: Jan.–Mar.	Greens: $$–$$$$ Carts: Incl. Rating: 73.7/67.5 Slope: 129/109	L R T J

Florida Golf Guide

Orlando Area

SP ☺☺	**Bella Vista Golf and Yacht Club** Hwy. 48, Howey In The Hills. (904) 324-3233 (800) 955-7001 18 holes. Par 71/71. Yards: 6,321/5,386 Year-round. High: Sept.–Apr.	Greens: Carts: Rating: Slope:	$–$$$ W L R T S J Incl. 68.4/71.9 119/123
P ☺☺☺ DEAL	**Cocoa Beach Golf Course** Tom Warriner Blvd., Cocoa Beach. (407) 868-3351 *River/Dolphin/Lakes* 27 holes. Par 71/71/72. Yards: 6,363/6,393/6,714 Year-round. High: Dec.–Apr.	Greens: Carts: Rating: Slope:	$–$$ W L T J $ 69.9/70.1/71.7 116/115/119
SP ☺☺☺ DEAL	**The Country Club at Silver Springs Shores** Silver Rd., Ocala. (904) 687-2828 18 holes. Par 72/72. Yards: 6,857/5,188 Year-round. High: Dec.–Apr.	Greens: Carts: Rating: Slope:	$–$$ L T Incl. 73.7/70.2 131/120
SP ☺☺☺	**Country Club of Mount Dora** Mount Dora. (904) 735-2263 18 holes. Par 72/72. Yards: 6,612/4,689 Year-round. High: Jan.–Mar.	Greens: Carts: Rating: Slope:	$$–$$$ W L R T J Incl. 71.5/67.8 121/118
SP ☺☺☺ DEAL	**DeBary Golf and Country Club** Plantation Dr., DeBary. (407) 668-2061 18 holes. Par 72/72. Yards: 6,776/5,060 Year-round. High: Feb.–Apr.	Greens: Carts: Rating: Slope:	$$ L J Incl. 72.3/68.8 128/122
SP ☺☺☺	**Deltona Hills Golf and Country Club** Elkcam Blvd., Deltona. (904) 789-4911 18 holes. Par 72/73. Yards: 6,892/5,668 Year-round. High: Jan.–Apr.	Greens: Carts: Rating: Slope:	$$–$$$ W L R T J Incl. 72.7/72.5 125/125
P ☺☺☺ BEST	**Eastwood Golf Club** Golfway Blvd., Orlando. (407) 281-4653 18 holes. Par 72/72. Yards: 7,176/5,393 Year-round. High: Jan.–Apr.	Greens: Carts: Rating: Slope:	$$–$$$ W L R T J Incl. 73.9/70.5 124/117
SP ☺☺☺	**Ekana Golf Club** Ekana Dr., Oviedo. (407) 366-1211 18 holes. Par 72/72. Yards: 6,683/5,544 Year-round. High: Jan.–Apr.	Greens: Carts: Rating: Slope:	$$–$$$ W L T Incl. 72.0/72.1 130/128
P ☺☺☺	**Falcon's Fire Golf Club** Seralago Blvd., Kissimmee. (407) 239-5445 18 holes. Par 72/72. Yards: 6,901/5,417 Year-round. High: Jan.–Apr.	Greens: Carts: Rating: Slope:	$$$–$$$$ L J Incl. 72.5/70.4 125/118
P ☺☺☺ STATE	**Golden Ocala Golf Course** U.S. Hwy. 27 N.W., Ocala. (904) 622-0198 18 holes. Par 72/72. Yards: 6,735/5,595 Year-round. High: Nov.–Apr.	Greens: Carts: Rating: Slope:	$$$ L T Incl. 72.2/72.2 132/124
SP ☺☺	**Golf Hammock Country Club** Golf Hammock Dr., Sebring. (813) 382-2151 18 holes. Par 72/72. Yards: 6,431/5,352 Year-round. High: Oct.–Apr.	Greens: Carts: Rating: Slope:	$$ L R T J Incl. 71.0/70.2 127/118
R ☺☺☺☺ BEST	**Grand Cypress Resort** N. Jacaranda, Orlando. (407) 239-1904 *New Course* 18 holes. Par 72/72. Yards: 6,773/5,314	Greens: Carts: Rating: Slope:	$$$$$–$$$$$$ L T J Incl. 72.1/69.8 126/117
☺☺☺☺ BEST	*North/South/East* 27 holes. Par 72/72/72. Yards: 6,993/6,906/6,955	Rating: Slope:	73.9/74.4/73.9 130/132/130

Florida Golf Guide

Orlando Area

SP	**Grenelefe Golf and Tennis Resort**	Greens:	$$–$$$$$$ W L R T
	State Rd., 546, Haines City. (813) 422-7511	Carts:	Incl.
☺☺☺	*South Course*	Rating:	72.6/69.5
	18 holes. Par 71/71. Yards: 6,869/5,174	Slope:	124/115
	Year-round. High: Jan.–Apr.		

☺☺☺☺	*East Course*	Rating:	72.5/69.2
	18 holes. Par 72/72. Yards: 6,802/5,114	Slope:	123/114

☺☺☺☺	*West Course*	Rating:	75.0/70.9
STATE	18 holes. Par 72/72. Yards: 7,325/5,398	Slope:	130/118

P	**Habitat Golf Course**	Greens:	$　　　　W L R J
☺☺☺	Fairgreen St., Valkaria. (407) 952-6312	Carts:	$
DEAL	18 holes. Par 72/72. Yards: 6,836/4,969	Rating:	72.9/68.2
	Year-round. High: Dec.–Mar.	Slope:	129/115

P	**Harder Hall Country Club**	Greens:	$–$$　　L
☺☺	Golfview Dr., Sebring. (813) 382-0500	Carts:	Incl.
	18 holes. Par 72/72. Yards: 6,300/5,003	Rating:	70.0/68.5
	Year-round. High: Jan.–Apr.	Slope:	116/114

P	**Hunter's Creek Golf Course**	Greens:	$$–$$$　W L T
☺☺☺	Sports Club Way, Orlando. (407) 240-4653	Carts:	Incl.
STATE	18 holes. Par 72/72. Yards: 7,432/5,755	Rating:	75.2/72.5
	Year-round. High: Jan.–Mar.	Slope:	127/120

SP	**Kissimmee Bay Country Club**	Greens:	$$–$$$$　W L T
☺☺	Kissimmee Bay Blvd., Kissimmee. (407) 348-4653	Carts:	Incl.
	18 holes. Par 71/71. Yards: 6,846/5,171	Rating:	70.1/71.0
	Year-round. High: Jan.–Apr.	Slope:	119/109

SP	**Kissimmee Golf Club**	Greens:	$$–$$$　L R T
☺☺	Florida Coach Dr., Kissimmee. (407) 847-2816	Carts:	Incl.
	18 holes. Par 72/72. Yards: 6,537/5,083	Rating:	71.4/68.6
	Year-round. High: Dec.–Apr.	Slope:	119/109

R	**Marriott's Orlando World Center**	Greens:	$$$$–$$$$$$ R T J
☺☺	World Center Dr., Orlando. (407) 238-8660	Carts:	Incl.
	18 holes. Par 71/71. Yards: 6,307/4,988	Rating:	69.8/68.5
	Year-round. High: Jan.–Apr.	Slope:	121/115

SP	**Metrowest Country Club**	Greens:	$$$–$$$$　L T J
☺☺☺	S. Hiawasee Rd., Orlando. (407) 299-1099	Carts:	Incl.
	18 holes. Par 72/72. Yards: 7,051/5,325	Rating:	73.1/69.6
	Year-round. High: Jan.–May	Slope:	126/117

SP	**Mission Inn Golf and Tennis Resort**	Greens:	$$–$$$$　W L T S J
	County Road 48, Howie-in-the-Hills. (904) 324-3885	Carts:	Incl.
☺☺☺	*El Campeon Course*	Rating:	73.5/68.0
	18 holes. Par 72/73. Yards: 6,852/4,709	Slope:	134/122
	Year-round. High: Feb.–Apr.		

☺☺☺	*Las Colinas Course*	Rating:	72.7/65.2
	18 holes. Par 72/71. Yards: 6,867/4,500	Slope:	128/109

R	**Orange Lake Country Club**	Greens:	$$–$$$$　W L R T J
☺☺	W. Irlo Bronson Mem. Blvd., Kissimmee. (407) 239-1050	Carts:	Incl.
	27 holes. Par 72/72/72. Yards: 6,531/6,670/6,571	Rating:	72.6/72.6/72.3
	Year-round. High: Jan.–Apr.	Slope:	132/131/131

SP	**Palisades Golf Club**	Greens:	$$–$$$　W L R T S J
☺☺☺	Palisades Blvd., Clermont. (904) 394-0085	Carts:	Incl.
	18 holes. Par 72/72. Yards: 6,988/5,528	Rating:	73.8/72.1
	Year-round. High: Jan.–Apr.	Slope:	127/122

Orlando Area

R ⊙⊙	**Plantation Inn and Golf Resort** West Fort Island Trail, Crystal River. (904) 795-7211 *Championship Course* 18 holes. Par 72/72. Yards: 6,502/5,395 Year-round. High: Feb.–Apr.	Greens: Carts: Rating: Slope:	$–$$ Incl. 71.6/71.1 126/117	W L R T J
R ⊙⊙	**Poinciana Golf and Racquet Resort** E. Cypress Pkwy., Kissimmee. (407) 933-5300 18 holes. Par 72/72. Yards: 6,700/4,938 Year-round. High: Jan.–Apr.	Greens: Carts: Rating: Slope:	$$–$$$ Incl. 72.2/68.4 125/118	L R T J
SP ⊙⊙⊙	**Ridgewood Lakes Golf Club** Eagle Ridge Dr., Davenport. (813) 424-8688 18 holes. Par 72/72. Yards: 7,016/5,217 Year-round. High: Nov.–Apr.	Greens: Carts: Rating: Slope:	$–$$$ Incl. 73.7/69.9 129/116	
SP ⊙⊙	**Royal Oak Golf Course** Titusville. (407) 268-1550 18 holes. Par 71/72. Yards: 6,709/5,471 Year-round. High: Jan.–Mar.	Greens: Carts: Rating: Slope:	$–$$$ Incl. 72.3/71.5 126/128	W L R T S J
SP ⊙⊙	**Sabal Point Country Club** Sabal Club Way, Longwood. (407) 869-4622 18 holes. Par 72/72. Yards: 6,603/5,278 Year-round. High: Jan.–Apr.	Greens: Carts: Rating: Slope:	$$–$$$ Incl. 71.6/70.0 129/119	W L T J
P ⊙⊙	**Sebastian Municipal Golf Course** E. Airport Dr., Sebastian. (407) 589-6801 18 holes. Par 72/72. Yards: 6,717/4,579 Year-round. High: Dec.–Apr.	Greens: Carts: Rating: Slope:	$–$$ Incl. 71.0/64.6 112/101	L T J
P ⊙⊙⊙⊙	**Southern Dunes Golf and Country Club** Southern Dunes Blvd., Haines City. (813) 421-4653 18 holes. Par 72/72. Yards: 7,200/5,200 Year-round. High: Oct.–Apr.	Greens: Carts: Rating: Slope:	$$–$$$ Incl. 74.7/72.4 135/126	W L J
R ⊙⊙	**Spring Lake Golf and Tennis Resort** Sebring. (813) 655-1276 *Osprey/Hawk/Eagle* 27 holes. Par 71/71/72. Yards: 6,531/6,398/6,673 Year-round. High: Jan.–Mar.	Greens: Carts: Rating: Slope:	$–$$ Incl. 71.3/70.1/71.8 127/116/125	R T
SP ⊙⊙⊙	**Timacuan Golf and Country Club** Timacuan Blvd., Lake Mary. (407) 321-0010 18 holes. Par 72/72. Yards: 7,019/5,401 Year-round. High: Jan.–Apr.	Greens: Carts: Rating: Slope:	$$–$$$$$ Incl. 73.5/72.1 137/123	W L R T J
P ⊙⊙	**Turtle Creek Golf Club** Admiralty Blvd., Rockledge. (407) 632-2520 18 holes. Par 72/72. Yards: 6,709/4,880 Year-round. High: Jan.–Apr.	Greens: Carts: Rating: Slope:	$$–$$$ Incl. 70.1/68.8 129/113	W L T J
P ⊙⊙⊙ DEAL	**Viera East Golf Club** Viera. (407) 639-6500 18 holes. Par 72/72. Yards: 6,720/5,428 Year-round. High: Dec.–Apr.	Greens: Carts: Rating: Slope:	$$ Incl. NA NA	L R J
R ⊙⊙⊙⊙	**Walt Disney World Resort** Lake Buena Vista *Eagle Pines Golf Course.* (407) 824-2675 18 holes. Par 72/72. Yards: 6,772/4,838 Year-round. High: Jan.–Apr.	Greens: Carts: Rating: Slope:	$$$$$–$$$$$$ Incl. 72.3/68.0 131/111	L R T
⊙⊙⊙	*Lake Buena Vista Golf Course.* (407) 828-3741 18 holes. Par 72/73. Yards: 6,819/5,194	Greens: Carts:	$$$$$ Incl.	

Florida Golf Guide

Orlando Area

Year-round. High: Jan.–Apr.

Rating: 72.7/69.4
Slope: 128/120

◎◎◎◎ *Magnolia Golf Course.* (407) 824-2288
18 holes. Par 72/72. Yards: 7,190/5,232
Year-round. High: Jan.–Apr.

Greens: $$$$$
Carts: Incl.
Rating: 73.9/70.5
Slope: 133/123

◎◎◎◎ *Osprey Ridge Golf Course.* (407) 824-2675
STATE 18 holes. Par 72/72. Yards: 7,101/5,402
Year-round. High: Jan.–Apr.

Greens: $$$$$–$$$$$$
Carts: Incl.
Rating: 73.9/70.5
Slope: 135/122

◎◎◎◎ *Palm Golf Course.* (407) 824-2288
18 holes. Par 72/72. Yards: 6,957/5,311
Year-round. High: Jan.–Apr.

Greens: $$$$$
Carts: Incl.
Rating: 73.0/70.4
Slope: 133/124

SP **Zellwood Station Country Club**
◎◎ Spillman Dr., Zellwood. (407) 886-3303
18 holes. Par 72/74. Yards: 6,400/5,377
Year-round. High: Nov.–Apr.

Greens: $$ L T
Carts: Incl.
Rating: 70.5/71.1
Slope: 122/122

Tampa Area

P **Apollo Beach Golf and Sea Club**
◎◎ Golf & Sea Blvd., Apollo Beach. (813) 645-6212
18 holes. Par 72/72. Yards: 7,040/4,831
Year-round. High: Nov.–Mar.

Greens: $$ L T S J
Carts: Incl.
Rating: 73.9/69.1
Slope: 130/115

P **Bardmoor North Golf Club**
◎◎ Bardmoor Blvd., Largo. (813) 397-0483
18 holes. Par 72/72. Yards: 6,960/5,269
Year-round. High: Dec.–Apr.

Greens: $$–$$$$ W L T J
Carts: Incl.
Rating: 72.4/71.8
Slope: 126/118

R **Belleview Mido Country Club**
◎◎ Indian Rocks Rd., Belleair. (813) 581-5498
18 holes. Par 72/74. Yards: 6,655/5,703
Year-round. High: Jan.–Apr.

Greens: $$–$$$$ L R
Carts: $
Rating: 70.7/72.1
Slope: 118/119

SP **Bloomingdale Golfer's Club**
◎◎◎ Nature's Way Blvd., Valrico. (813) 685-4105
18 holes. Par 72/73. Yards: 7,165/5,506
Year-round. High: Dec.–Apr.

Greens: $$–$$$
Carts: $
Rating: 74.4/71.6
Slope: 137/129

P **Bobby Jones Golf Complex**
Azinger Way, Sarasota. (813) 955-8097
◎ *American Course*
18 holes. Par 71/71. Yards: 6,009/4,453
Year-round. High: Dec.–Apr.

Greens: $ L T J
Carts: $
Rating: 68.4/65.1
Slope: 117/107

◎ *British Course*
18 holes. Par 72/72. Yards: 6,468/5,695

Rating: 70.0/71.8
Slope: 111/115

SP **Capri Isles Golf Club**
◎ Capri Isles Blvd., Venice. (813) 485-3371
18 holes. Par 72/72. Yards: 6,472/5,480
Year-round. High: Jan.–Apr.

Greens: $$–$$$ L T
Carts: Incl.
Rating: 70.0/69.8
Slope: 123/113

SP **Citrus Hills Golf and Country Club**
E. Hartford St., Hernando. (904) 746-4425
◎◎ *Meadows Course*
18 holes. Par 70/70. Yards: 5,885/4,585

Greens: $$ L T
Carts: NA
Rating: NA
Slope: 115/112

◎◎◎ *Oaks Course*
18 holes. Par 70/70. Yards: 6,323/4,647
Year-round. High: Dec.–Apr.

Rating: NA
Slope: 120/114

Florida Golf Guide

Tampa Area

P	**The Club at Oak Ford**	Greens:	$$	L
	Palm View Rd., Sarasota. (813) 371-3680	Carts:	Incl.	
☺☺☺	*Myrtle/Palms/Live Oaks*	Rating:	NA	
	27 holes. Par NA. Yards: NA	Slope:	NA	
	Year-round. High: Jan.–Apr.			

SP	**The Country Club at Jacaranda West**	Greens:	$$	L T J
☺☺☺	Jacaranda Blvd., Venice. (813) 493-2664	Carts:	Incl.	
DEAL	18 holes. Par 72/72. Yards: 6,602/5,321	Rating:	71.9/70.7	
STATE	Year-round. High: Jan.–Apr.	Slope:	126/120	

SP	**Dunedin Country Club**	Greens:	$$–$$$	L T
☺☺	Palm Blvd., Dunedin. (813) 733-7836	Carts:	Incl.	
	18 holes. Par 72/73. Yards: 6,565/5,726	Rating:	70.3/73.1	
	Year-round. High: Dec.–Apr.	Slope:	115/121	

SP	**The Eagles Golf Club**	Greens:	$$–$$$	W L T
	Nine Eagles Dr., Odessa. (813) 920-6681	Carts:	Incl.	
☺☺☺	*Forest/Lakes/Oaks*	Rating:	70.3/70.3/70.3	
	27 holes. Par 72/72/72. Yards: 7,134/7,194/7,068	Slope:	130/130/130	
	Year-round. High: Jan.–Apr.			

P	**Fox Hollow Golf Club**	Greens:	$$–$$$	W L J
☺☺☺	Robert Trent Jones Pkwy., New Port Richey	Carts:	Incl.	
	(813) 376-6333	Rating:	74.3/65.7	
	18 holes. Par 71/71. Yards: 7,138/4,454	Slope:	137/112	
	Year-round. High: Jan.–Mar.			

SP	**The Golf Club at Cypress Creek**	Greens:	$$	W L R T S
☺☺☺	Cypress Village Blvd., Ruskin. (813) 634-8888	Carts:	Incl.	
DEAL	18 holes. Par 72/72. Yards: 6,839/NA	Rating:	74.0/66.0	
STATE	Year-round. High: Feb.–Apr.	Slope:	133/114	

R	**The Golf Club at Marco**	Greens:	$$	
☺☺☺	Marriott Club Dr., Naples. (813) 793-6060	Carts:	Incl.	
DEAL	18 holes. Par 72/72. Yards: 6,898/5,416	Rating:	73.4/70.9	
STATE	Year-round. High: Jan.–Apr.	Slope:	137/122	

SP	**Huntington Hills Golf and Country Club**	Greens:	$$	W L T
☺☺☺	Duff Rd., Lakeland. (813) 859-3689	Carts:	Incl.	
	18 holes. Par 72/72. Yards: 6,631/5,011	Rating:	72.5/68.7	
	Year-round. High: Dec.-Mar.	Slope:	122/115	

SP	**Imperial Lakes Golf Club**	Greens:	$–$$	W L T J
☺☺	Buffalo Rd., Palmetto. (813) 747-4653	Carts:	Incl.	
	18 holes. Par 72/72. Yards: 6,658/5,270	Rating:	71.5/69.7	
	Year-round. High: Nov.–Apr.	Slope:	123/117	

R	**Innisbrook Hilton Resort**	Greens:	$$$–$$$$$$	L R J
	Hwy. 19 N., Palm Harbor. (813) 942-2000	Carts:	Incl.	
☺☺☺☺	*Copperhead Course*	Rating:	74.4/72.0	
BEST	18 holes. Par 71/71. Yards: 7,087/5,506	Slope:	140/128	
	Year-round. High: Nov.–Apr.			

☺☺☺☺	*Island Course*	Rating:	73.2/74.1
BEST	18 holes. Par 72/72. Yards: 6,999/5,795	Slope:	133/130

☺☺☺☺	*Sandpiper Course: Palmetto/Palms/Pines*	Rating:	68.7/69.8/69.8
	27 holes. Par 70/70/70. Yards: 5,969/6,200/6,245	Slope:	122/125/119

SP	**Lansbrook Golf Club**	Greens:	$$–$$$	W L T
☺☺	Village Center Dr., Palm Harbor. (813) 784-7333	Carts:	Incl.	
	18 holes. Par 72/72. Yards: 6,719/5,264	Rating:	71.6/69.3	
	Year-round. High: Dec.–Apr.	Slope:	126/119	

SP	**The Links of Lake Bernadette**	Greens:	$$	W L T
☺☺	Links Lane, Zephyr Hills. (813) 788-4653	Carts:	Incl.	

Florida Golf Guide

Tampa Area

	18 holes. Par 71/71. Yards: 6,392/5,031		Rating:	70.0/68.0	
	Year-round. High: Jan.–Apr.		Slope:	117/118	

R	**Longboat Key Club**		Greens:	$$$$$	L
	Gulf of Mexico Dr., Longboat Key. (813) 383-0781		Carts:	Incl.	
☺☺☺	*Islandside Course*		Rating:	NA	
	18 holes. Par 72/72. Yards: 6,792/5,198		Slope:	138/121	
	Year-round. High: Dec.–May				

P	**Mangrove Bay Golf Course**		Greens:	$	L T
☺☺☺	62nd Ave. N.E., St. Petersburg. (813) 893-7800		Carts:	Inquire	
DEAL	18 holes. Par 72/72. Yards: 6,779/5,204		Rating:	71.5/68.5	
	Year-round. High: Nov.–Feb., Apr.–May		Slope:	120/112	

SP	**Northdale Golf Club**		Greens:	$$	T
☺☺	Northdale Blvd., Tampa. (813) 962-0428		Carts:	Incl.	
	18 holes. Par 72/72. Yards: 6,791/5,397		Rating:	72.1/71.0	
	Year-round. High: Dec.–Apr.		Slope:	119/113	

P	**Oak Hills Golf Club**		Greens:	$–$$	T
☺☺☺	Northcliff Blvd., Spring Hill. (904) 683-6830		Carts:	Incl.	
DEAL	18 holes. Par 72/72. Yards: 6,791/5,397		Rating:	72.1/71.0	
	Year-round. High: Dec.–Mar.		Slope:	119/113	

SP	**Plantation Golf and Country Club**		Greens:	$$–$$$	L R
	Rockley Blvd., Venice. (813) 493-2000		Carts:	$	
☺☺☺	*Bobcat Course*		Rating:	73.0/70.6	
	18 holes. Par 72/72. Yards: 6,840/5,023		Slope:	130/121	
	Year-round. High: Oct.–Apr.				

☺☺☺	*Panther Course*		Rating:	71.6/71.1	
	18 holes. Par 72/72. Yards: 6,311/4,751		Slope:	124/117	

P	**The River Club**		Greens:	$$	L T
☺☺☺	River Club Blvd., Bradenton. (813) 751-4211		Carts:	Incl.	
	18 holes. Par 72/72. Yards: 7,004/5,252		Rating:	NA	
	Year-round. High: Jan.–Apr.		Slope:	133	

SP	**River Hills Country Club**		Greens:	$$–$$$	
☺☺☺	New River Hills Pkwy., Valrico. (813) 653-3323		Carts:	$	
	18 holes. Par 72/72. Yards: 7,004/5,236		Rating:	74.0/70.4	
	Year-round. High: Jan.–Apr.		Slope:	132/124	

SP	**Riverwood Golf Club**		Greens:	$$–$$$$	L R T
☺☺☺☺	Riverwood Dr., Port Charlotte. (813) 764-6661		Carts:	Incl.	
	18 holes. Par 72/72. Yards: 6,938/4,695		Rating:	73.2/67.1	
	Year-round. High: Dec.–Apr.		Slope:	131/111	

P	**Rogers Park Golf Course**		Greens:	$$	W L T S J
☺☺	N. 30th St., Tampa. (813) 234-1911		Carts:	$	
	18 holes. Par 72/72. Yards: 6,500/5,900		Rating:	71.0/67.0	
	Year-round. High: Jan.–Apr.		Slope:	120/114	

SP	**Rosedale Golf and Country Club**		Greens:	$$–$$$	L R T
☺☺☺	87th St. E., Bradenton. (813) 756-0004		Carts:	Incl.	
	18 holes. Par 72/72. Yards: 6,779/5,169		Rating:	72.6/69.7	
	Year-round. High: Oct.–May		Slope:	130/120	

R	**Saddlebrook Resort**		Greens:	$$–$$$$$	L R
	Saddlebrook Way, Wesley Chapel. (813) 973-1111		Carts:	Incl.	
☺☺☺	*Palmer Course*		Rating:	71.0/70.2	
	18 holes. Par 71/71. Yards: 6,469/5,212		Slope:	126/121	
	Year-round. High: Nov.–Apr.				

☺☺☺	*Saddlebrook Course*		Rating:	72.0/70.8	
	18 holes. Par 70/70. Yards: 6,603/5,183		Slope:	124/124	

Florida Golf Guide

Tampa Area

SP ⊙⊙	**Sandpiper Golf and Country Club** Sandpipers Dr., Lakeland. (813) 859-5461 18 holes. Par 70/70. Yards: 6,442/5,024 Year-round. High: Jan.–Mar.	Greens: Carts: Rating: Slope:	$$ Incl. 70.4/67.7 120/109	W L T
SP ⊙⊙	**Sarasota Golf Club** N. Leewynn Dr., Sarasota. (813) 371-3431 18 holes. Par 72/72. Yards: 7,066/5,004 Year-round. High: Jan.–Apr.	Greens: Carts: Rating: Slope:	$$ Incl. 73.0/67.4 120/106	L R T S J
SP ⊙⊙	**Schalamar Creek Golf and Country Club** U.S. Hwy. 92 E., Lakeland. (813) 666-1623 18 holes. Par 72/72. Yards: 6,399/4,363 Year-round. High: Jan.–Apr.	Greens: Carts: Rating: Slope:	$-$$ $ 70.9/64.8 124/106	W L T
SP ⊙⊙⊙ DEAL	**Seven Hills Golfers Club** Fairchild Rd., Spring Hill. (904) 688-8888 18 holes. Par 72/72. Yards: 6,715/4,902 Year-round. High: Dec.–Apr.	Greens: Carts: Rating: Slope:	$$ Incl. 70.5/66.5 126/109	W L T
SP ⊙⊙⊙	**Seven Springs Golf and Country Club** Trophy Blvd., New Port Richey. (813) 376-0035 *Championship Course* 18 holes. Par 72/72. Yards: 6,566/5,250 Year-round. High: Jan.–Apr.	Greens: Carts: Rating: Slope:	$$ Incl. NA 123/112	L T
P ⊙⊙⊙ DEAL	**Seville Golf and Country Club** Weeki Wachee. (904) 596-7888 18 holes. Par 72/72. Yards: 7,140/5,236 Year-round. High: Jan.–Apr.	Greens: Carts: Rating: Slope:	$-$$ Incl. 74.9/70.8 138/126	W L T
P ⊙⊙⊙ DEAL	**Sherman Hills Golf Club** Eagle Falls Dr., Brooksville. (904) 544-0990 18 holes. Par 72/72. Yards: 6,778/4,959 Year-round. High: Oct.–Apr.	Greens: Carts: Rating: Slope:	$-$$ Incl. 72.1/68.2 118/110	W L T
SP ⊙⊙	**Silver Oaks Golf and Country Club** Zephyr Hills. (813) 788-1225 18 holes. Par 72/72. Yards: 6,632/5,147 Year-round. High: Dec.–May	Greens: Carts: Rating: Slope:	$-$$ Incl. 71.1/68.8 120/109	W L R T S J
R ⊙⊙	**Stouffer Vinoy Golf Club** Snell Isle Blvd. N.E., St. Petersburg. (813) 896-8000 18 holes. Par 70/71. Yards: 6,267/4,818 Year-round. High: Jan.–Apr.	Greens: Carts: Rating: Slope:	$$$$ Inquire 70.0/67.3 118/111	T
SP ⊙⊙⊙ DEAL	**Summerfield Golf Club** Summerfield Blvd., Riverview. (813) 671-3311 18 holes. Par 71/71. Yards: 6,883/5,139 Year-round. High: Jan.–Apr.	Greens: Carts: Rating: Slope:	$-$$ Incl. 73.0/69.6 125/114	
SP ⊙⊙	**Tarpon Woods Golf and Country Club** Tarpon Woods Blvd., Palm Harbor. (813) 784-2273 18 holes. Par 72/72. Yards: 6,466/5,205 Year-round. High: Jan.–May	Greens: Carts: Rating: Slope:	$$-$$$ Incl. 71.2/69.5 128/115	W L T
SP ⊙⊙⊙ DEAL	**Tatum Ridge Golf Links** North Tatum Rd., Sarasota. (813) 378-4211 18 holes. Par 72/72. Yards: 6,757/5,149 Year-round. High: Nov.–May	Greens: Carts: Rating: Slope:	$-$$ Incl. 71.9/68.9 124/114	L S
SP ⊙⊙	**Tournament Players Club of Tampa Bay** Terrain de Golf Dr., Lutz. (813) 949-0091 18 holes. Par 71/71. Yards: 6,898/5,036 Year-round. High: Jan.–Apr.	Greens: Carts: Rating: Slope:	$$$-$$$$ Incl. 73.4/69.1 130/119	W L T J

Florida Golf Guide

Tampa Area

P ☺☺	**University of South Florida Golf Course** 46th St., Tampa. (813) 974-2071 18 holes. Par 72/72. Yards: 6,942/5,393 Year-round. High: Nov.–Apr.	Greens: $ Carts: Inquire Rating: 73.1/69.8 Slope: 131/115	W L T S J
SP ☺☺☺☺	**University Park Country Club** Park Blvd., University Park. (813) 359-9999 18 holes. Par 72/72. Yards: 6,951/5,511 Year-round. High: Nov.–Apr.	Greens: $$$–$$$$$ Carts: Incl. Rating: 73.4/71.3 Slope: 132/120	W L T
P ☺☺☺	**Waterford Golf Club** Gleneagles Dr., Venice. (813) 484-6621 18 holes. Par 72/72. Yards: 6,601/5,242 Year-round. High: Jan.–Apr.	Greens: $$$ Carts: Incl. Rating: NA Slope: 124/116	L
SP ☺☺	**Wedgewood Golf and Country Club** Carpenter's Way, Lakeland. (813) 858-4451 18 holes. Par 72/72. Yards: 6,401/4,885 Year-round. High: Nov.–May	Greens: $–$$ Carts: Incl. Rating: 69.1/68.1 Slope: 115/113	L T
P ☺☺☺	**Westchase Golf Club** Radcliffe Dr., Tampa. (813) 854-2331 18 holes. Par 72/72. Yards: 6,710/5,205 Year-round. High: Jan.–Apr.	Greens: $$–$$$ Carts: Incl. Rating: 71.8/69.1 Slope: 130/121	W L T J
R ☺☺☺☺ STATE	**World Woods Golf Club** Ponce De Leon Blvd., Brooksville. (904) 796-5500 *Pine Barrens Course* 18 holes. Par 71/71. Yards: 6,902/5,301 Year-round. High: Jan.–Apr.	Greens: $$$–$$$$ Carts: Incl. Rating: 73.7/70.9 Slope: 140/132	W L
☺☺☺☺ STATE	*Rolling Oaks Course* 18 holes. Par 72/72. Yards: 6,985/5,245	Rating: 73.5/70.7 Slope: 136/128	

Fort Myers Area

P ☺☺	**Cape Coral Golf and Tennis Resort** Palm Tree Blvd., Cape Coral. (813) 542-7879 18 holes. Par 72/72. Yards: 6,649/5,464 Year-round. High: Jan.–Mar.	Greens: $–$$$ Carts: Incl. Rating: 71.6/71.2 Slope: 122/119	L R T J
P ☺☺	**Coral Oaks Golf Course** N.W. 28th Ave., Cape Coral. (813) 283-4100 18 holes. Par 72/72. Yards: 6,623/4,803 Year-round. High: Dec.–Apr.	Greens: $$ Carts: Incl. Rating: 71.7/68.9 Slope: 123/117	
P ☺☺☺	**Eastwood Golf Course** Bruce Herd Lane, Fort Myers. (813) 275-4848 18 holes. Par 72/72. Yards: 6,772/5,116 Year-round. High: Dec.–Mar.	Greens: $$–$$$ Carts: Incl. Rating: 73.3/68.9 Slope: 130/120	W L T
P ☺☺	**Fort Myers Country Club** McGregor Blvd., Fort Myers. (813) 936-2457 18 holes. Par 71/71. Yards: 6,414/5,135 Year-round. High: Dec.–Apr.	Greens: $$ Carts: $ Rating: NA Slope: 118/117	W L T
SP ☺☺☺ STATE	**Gateway Golf and Country Club** Fort Myers. (813) 561-1010 18 holes. Par 72/72. Yards: 6,974/5,323 Year-round. High: Jan.–Mar.	Greens: $$$$–$$$$$ Carts: Incl. Rating: 73.7/70.6 Slope: 130/120	L T
P ☺☺☺☺	**Lely Flamingo Island Club** Lely Resort Blvd., Naples. (813) 793-2223 18 holes. Par 72/72. Yards: 7,171/5,377 Year-round. High: Nov.–Apr.	Greens: $$–$$$$$ Carts: Incl. Rating: 73.9/70.6 Slope: 135/126	L T

Florida Golf Guide

Fort Myers Area

SP ◉◉	**Lochmoor Country Club** Orange Grove Blvd., North Fort Myers. (813) 995-0501 18 holes. Par 72/72. Yards: 7,908/5,152 Year-round. High: Jan.–Apr.	Greens: Carts: Rating: Slope:	$$–$$$ L T Incl. 73.1/69.1 128/116
P ◉◉	**Marco Shores Country Club** Mainsail Dr., Naples. (813) 394-2581 18 holes. Par 72/72. Yards: 6,879/5,634 Year-round. High: Jan.–Apr.	Greens: Carts: Rating: Slope:	$$–$$$$ L T J Incl. 73.0/72.3 125/121
SP ◉◉	**Naples Beach Hotel and Golf Club** Gulf Shore Blvd. N., Naples. (813) 261-2222 18 holes. Par 72/72. Yards: 6,500/5,300 Year-round. High: Jan.–Apr.	Greens: Carts: Rating: Slope:	$$–$$$$$ R Incl. 71.2/70.1 122/115
P ◉◉◉◉	**Pelican's Nest Golf Club** Pelican's Nest Dr., Bonita Springs. (813) 947-4600 *Hurricane/Gator/Seminole/Panther* 36 holes. Par 72/72. Yards: 7,016/5,201 Year-round. High: Jan.–Mar.	Greens: Carts: Rating: Slope:	$$–$$$$$$$ L T J Incl. 74.8/69.2 140/122

Palm Beach Area

R ◉◉◉	**Atlantis Country Club** Atlantis Blvd., Atlantis. (407) 968-1300 18 holes. Par 72/72. Yards: 6,510/5,258 Year-round. High: Oct.–Mar.	Greens: Carts: Rating: Slope:	$$–$$$ W L R $ 71.2/70.9 126/123
SP ◉◉◉	**Binks Forest Golf Course** Binks Forest Dr., Wellington. (407) 795-0595 18 holes. Par 72/72. Yards: 7,065/5,599 Year-round. High: Nov.–Apr.	Greens: Carts: Rating: Slope:	$$–$$$$ W L R T Incl. 75.0/71.9 138/127
R ◉	**Boca Raton Resort and Club** E. Camino Real, Boca Raton. (407) 395-3000, ext. 3076 *Country Club Course* 18 holes. Par 72/72. Yards: 6,564/5,565 Year-round. High: Oct.–May	Greens: Carts: Rating: Slope:	$$$$ L T Incl. NA 126/124
◉◉	*Resort Course* 18 holes. Par 71/71. Yards: 6,682/5,518	Rating: Slope:	NA 122/124
P ◉◉	**Boynton Beach Municipal Golf Course** Jog Rd., Boynton Beach. (407) 969-2201 *Red/White/Blue* 27 holes. Par 71/66/65. Yards: 6,316/5,290/5,062	Greens: Carts: Rating: Slope:	$ L J $ 70.1/65.0/63.9 129/NA/NA
R ◉◉	**The Breakers Club** South County Rd., Palm Beach. (407) 659-8407 18 holes. Par 70/72. Yards: 6,017/5,582 Year-round. High: Dec.–Mar.	Greens: Carts: Rating: Slope:	$$$$ R T J Incl. 69.3/72.6 121/122
SP ◉◉◉	**Breakers West Country Club** Flagler Pkwy., W. Palm Beach. (407) 653-6320 18 holes. Par 71/71. Yards: 6,905/5,197 Year-round. High: Nov.–Apr.	Greens: Carts: Rating: Slope:	$$$$–$$$$$ Incl. 73.9/71.1 135/123
P ◉◉◉	**The Champions Club at Summerfield** S.E. Summerfield Way, Stuart. (407) 283-1500 18 holes. Par 72/72. Yards: 6,809/5,014 Year-round. High: Nov.–Apr.	Greens: Carts: Rating: Slope:	$$–$$$ L T J Incl. 72.8/69.4 131/116
P ◉◉◉ DEAL	**Delray Beach Golf Club** Highland Ave., Delray Beach. (407) 243-7380 18 holes. Par 72/72. Yards: 6,907/5,189 Year-round. High: Dec.–Mar.	Greens: Carts: Rating: Slope:	$–$$ L J Incl. 73.0/69.8 126/117
SP ◉◉	**Dodger Pines Country Club** 26th St., Vero Beach. (407) 569-4400	Greens: Carts:	$–$$$ $

Florida Golf Guide

Palm Beach Area

	18 holes. Par 73/74. Yards: 6,692/5,776	Rating: 71.2/72.3
	Year-round. High: Jan.–Apr.	Slope: 122/124

SP
◎◎◎◎
STATE

Emerald Dunes Golf Club
Emerald Dunes Dr., W. Palm Beach. (407) 684-4653
18 holes. Par 72/72. Yards: 7,006/4,676
Year-round. High: Nov.–Apr.

Greens: $$$$–$$$$$$ L T J
Carts: Incl.
Rating: 73.8/67.1
Slope: 133/115

P
◎◎◎
DEAL

Fairwinds Golf Course
Fairwinds Dr., Fort Pierce. (407) 466-4653
(800) 894-1781
18 holes. Par 72/72. Yards: 6,783/5,392
Year-round. High: Jan.–Apr.

Greens: $$ L J
Carts: Incl.
Rating: 71.1/68.5
Slope: 119/112

P
◎◎

Lake Worth Golf Club
7th Ave. N., Lake Worth. (407) 582-9713
18 holes. Par 70/70. Yards: 6,113/5,413
Year-round. High: Jan.–Mar.

Greens: $–$$ W T J
Carts: Inquire
Rating: 68.6/69.6
Slope: 116/113

P

◎◎

Martin County Golf and Country Club
S.E. Saint Lucie Blvd., Stuart. (407) 287-3747
Blue/Gold
18 holes. Par 72/72. Yards: 5,900/5,236
Year-round. High: Dec.–Apr.

Greens: $–$$ L J
Carts: Inquire
Rating: 67.5/69.1
Slope: 120/120

◎◎

Red/White
18 holes. Par 72/73. Yards: 6,200/5,400

Rating: 69.1/70.4
Slope: 116/120

P
◎◎

North Palm Beach Country Club
U.S. Hwy. 1, N. Palm Beach. (407) 626-4344
18 holes. Par 72/72. Yards: 6,275/5,055
Year-round. High: Nov.–May

Greens: $$–$$$ L J
Carts: Incl.
Rating: 70.0/69.0
Slope: 117/115

P
◎◎

Palm Beach Gardens Municipal Golf Course
Northlake Blvd., Palm Beach Gardens. (407) 775-2556
18 holes. Par 72/72. Yards: 6,375/4,663
Year-round. High: Dec.–Apr.

Greens: $$ W L T S J
Carts: Incl.
Rating: 71.1/66.5
Slope: 125/110

R

◎◎◎

Palm Beach Polo and Country Club
Polo Club Rd., W. Palm Beach. (407) 798-7401
The Cypress Course
18 holes. Par 72/72. Yards: 7,116/5,172
Year-round. High: Dec.–Apr.

Greens: $$$$–$$$$$$ R T
Carts: $
Rating: 74.4/69.8
Slope: 138/121

◎◎◎◎
BEST

The Dunes Course
18 holes. Par 72/72. Yards: 7,050/5,516

Rating: 73.6/71.4
Slope: 132/122

R

◎◎◎◎
BEST

PGA National Resort and Spa
Ave. of Champions, Palm Beach Gardens. (407) 627-1800
Champion Course
18 holes. Par 72/72. Yards: 7,022/5,377
Year-round. High: Jan.–Apr.

Greens: $$$$$$ L
Carts: $
Rating: 74.7/71.1
Slope: 142/123

◎◎◎

Estate Course
18 holes. Par 72/72. Yards: 6,784/4,903

Greens: $$$$$
Carts: $
Rating: 73.4/68.4
Slope: 131/118

◎◎◎

General Course
18 holes. Par 72/72. Yards: 6,768/5,324

Greens: $$$$$
Carts: $
Rating: 73.0/71.0
Slope: 130/122

◎◎◎

Haig Course
18 holes. Par 72/72. Yards: 6,806/5,645

Greens: $$$$$
Carts: $
Rating: 73.0/72.5
Slope: 130/121

Florida Golf Guide

Palm Beach Area

☺☺☺	Squire Course	Greens:	$$$$$	
	18 holes. Par 72/72. Yards: 6,478/4,982	Carts:	$	
		Rating:	71.3/69.8	
		Slope:	127/123	

SP ☺☺☺☺	**St. Lucie West Country Club**	Greens:	$$–$$$	L T J
	S.W. Country Club Dr., Port St. Lucie. (407) 340-1911	Carts:	Incl.	
	18 holes. Par 72/72. Yards: 6,801/5,054	Rating:	72.7/69.8	
	Year-round. High: Jan.–Mar.	Slope:	130/121	

P ☺☺☺ DEAL	**Sandridge Golf Club**	Greens:	$–$$	W L T J
	73rd St., Vero Beach. (407) 770-5000	Carts:	Incl.	
	Dunes Course	Rating:	72.2/68.8	
	18 holes. Par 72/72. Yards: 6,900/4,922	Slope:	123/109	
	Year-round. High: Jan.–Mar.			

☺☺☺ DEAL	*Lakes Course*	Rating:	69.3/66.6	
	18 holes. Par 72/72. Yards: 6,200/4,625	Slope:	120/109	

P ☺☺☺ DEAL STATE	**West Palm Beach Municipal Country Club**	Greens:	$–$$	L T J
	Parker Ave., West Palm Beach. (407) 582-2019	Carts:	$	
	18 holes. Par 72/72. Yards: 6,789/5,884	Rating:	72.8/73.3	
	Year-round. High: Dec.–Apr.	Slope:	124/126	

SP ☺☺☺	**Westchester Golf and Country Club**	Greens:	$$–$$$	W L R
	Westchester Club Dr., Boynton Beach. (407) 734-6300	Carts:	Incl.	
	18 holes. Par 72/72. Yards: 6,760/4,886	Rating:	72.0/67.5	
	Year-round. High: Nov.–Apr.	Slope:	128/111	

P ☺☺☺	**Winston Trails Golf Club**	Greens:	$$–$$$$	W L T
	Winston Trails Blvd., Lake Worth. (407) 439-3700	Carts:	Incl.	
	18 holes. Par 72/72. Yards: 6,835/5,405	Rating:	72.8/71.1	
	Year-round. High: Mar.–Nov.	Slope:	123/117	

Fort Lauderdale Area

P ☺☺	**Crystal Lake Country Club**	Greens:	$$–$$$	L T
	Crystal Lake Dr., Pompano Beach. (305) 942-1900	Carts:	Incl.	
	Tam O'Shanter North Course	Rating:	71.0/70.0	
	18 holes. Par 70/72. Yards: 6,390/5,205	Slope:	121/118	
	Year-round. High: Nov.–Apr.			

☺☺	*South Course*	Rating:	71.7/71.5	
	18 holes. Par 72/72. Yards: 6,610/5,458	Slope:	112/109	

SP ☺☺☺	**Deer Creek Golf Club**	Greens:	$$–$$$$$$	W L R J
	Deerfield Beach. (305) 421-5550	Carts:	Incl.	
	18 holes. Par 72/72. Yards: 7,038/5,319	Rating:	74.8/71.6	
	Year-round. High: Dec.–Apr.	Slope:	133/120	

R ☺☺	**Grand Palms Golf and Country Club Resort**	Greens:	$$–$$$	W L R T
	Grand Palms Dr., Pembroke Pines. (305) 437-3334	Carts:	Incl.	
	Grand/Royal/Sabal	Rating:	71.6/71.9/71.5	
	27 holes. Par 72/73/71. Yards: 6,757/6,736/6,653	Slope:	127/128/124	
	Year-round. High: Dec.–Apr.			

P ☺☺☺	**Jacaranda Golf Club**	Greens:	$$$–$$$$	W L T
	W. Broward Blvd., Plantation. (305) 472-5836	Carts:	Incl.	
	East Course	Rating:	NA	
	18 holes. Par 72/72. Yards: 7,170/5,668	Slope:	130/121	
	Year-round. High: Nov.–May			

☺☺☺	*West Course*	Rating:	NA	
	18 holes. Par 72/72. Yards: 6,729/5,314	Slope:	135/129	

R ☺☺	**Palm Aire Spa Resort and Country Club**	Greens:	$$–$$$	
	Palm Aire Dr. N., Pompano Beach. (305) 974-7699	Carts:	$	
	Palms Course	Rating:	73.7/70.9	

Florida Golf Guide

Fort Lauderdale Area

	18 holes. Par 72/72. Yards: 6,932/5,434	Slope:	128/120
	Year-round. High: May–Sept.		

R	**Palm Aire Spa Resort and Country Club**	Greens:	$$–$$$
	Pompano Beach. (305) 978-1737	Carts:	$
☺☺	*The Oaks*	Rating:	72.2/70.4
	18 holes. Par 72/72. Yards: 6,747/5,402	Slope:	122/114
	Year-round. High: May–Sept.		

☺☺	*The Cypress*	Rating:	73.3/70.8
	18 holes. Par 72/72. Yards: 6,868/5,447	Slope:	128/118

P	**Pompano Beach Golf Course**	Greens:	$$
	N. Federal Hwy., Pompano Beach. (954) 781-0426	Carts:	NA
☺☺	*Palms Course*	Rating:	69.4/70.2
	18 holes. Par 72/72. Yards: 6,356/5,426	Slope:	113/114
	Year-round. High: Jan.–Apr.		

☺☺	*Pines Course*	Rating:	69.4/70.2
	18 holes. Par 72/74. Yards: 6,886/5,980	Slope:	113/114

R	**Raintree Golf Course**	Greens: $$–$$$	W L R T S J
☺☺☺	S. Hiatus Rd., Pembroke Pines. (305) 432-4400	Carts: Incl.	
	18 holes. Par 72/72. Yards: 6,461/5,382	Rating: 70.8/70.2	
	Year-round. High: Nov.–Apr.	Slope: 126/122	

R	**Rolling Hills Hotel and Golf Resort**	Greens: $$–$$$	W L R T
☺☺	W. Rolling Hills Circle, Fort Lauderdale. (305) 475-3010	Carts: Incl.	
	18 holes. Par 72/72. Yards: 6,905/5,630	Rating: 72.7/71.7	
	Year-round. High: Jan.–Apr.	Slope: 124/121	

R	**Turnberry Isle Resort and Club**	Greens: $$$–$$$$$	L
	W. Country Club Dr., Aventura. (305) 933-6929	Carts: Incl.	
☺☺	*North Course*	Rating: 70.3/67.9	
	18 holes. Par 70/70. Yards: 6,348/4,991	Slope: 127/107	
	Year-round. High: Nov.–Apr.		

☺☺☺	*South Course*	Rating:	73.7/71.3
	18 holes. Par 72/72. Yards: 7,003/5,581	Slope:	136/116

Miami Area

P	**The Biltmore Golf Course**	Greens:	$$$
☺☺	Anastasia Ave., Coral Gables. (305) 460-5364	Carts:	Incl.
	18 holes. Par 71/74. Yards: 6,642/5,237	Rating:	71.5/70.1
	Year-round. High: Nov.–Apr.	Slope:	119/115

P	**Colony West Country Club**	Greens: $$–$$$$	W L T
	N.W. 88th Ave., Tamarac. (305) 726-8430	Carts: Incl.	
☺☺☺	*Championship Course*	Rating: 75.8/71.6	
	18 holes. Par 71/71. Yards: 7,271/5,422	Slope: 138/127	
	Year-round. High: Dec.–Apr.		

P	**Don Shula's Golf Club**	Greens: $$–$$$	W L R T
☺☺	Miami Lakes Dr., Miami Lake. (305) 821-1150	Carts: $	
	18 holes. Par 72/72. Yards: 7,055/5,639	Rating: 73.0/70.5	
	Year-round. High: Jan.–Apr.	Slope: 124/120	

R	**Doral Golf Resort and Spa**	Greens: $$$–$$$$$$	L R T
	N.W. 87th Ave., Miami. (305) 592-2000	Carts: Incl.	
☺☺☺	*Blue Course*	Rating: 73.2/73.0	
BEST	18 holes. Par: 72/72. Yards: 6,935/5,786	Slope: 127/124	
	Year-round. High: Oct.–Apr.		

☺☺☺	*Gold Course*	Rating:	70.6/71.4
	18 holes. Par: 70/70. Yards: 6,361/5,422	Slope:	127/123
	(Under restoration in 1996.)		

Miami Area

☺☺☺	*Red Course* 18 holes. Par: 71/71. Yards: 6,210/5,254	Rating: Slope:	69.9/70.6 118/118	
☺☺☺	*White Course* 18 holes. Par: 72/72. Yards: 6,208/5,286	Rating: Slope:	69.7/70.1 117/116	
SP ☺☺☺ STATE	**Doral Park Golf and Country Club** N.W. 104th Ave., Miami. (305) 594-0954 *Silver Course* 18 holes. Par 71/71. Yards: 6,614/4,661 Year-round. High: Jan.–Apr.	Greens: Carts: Rating: Slope:	$$$–$$$$ Incl. 72.0/66.6 129/113	W L R
P ☺	**Fontainebleau Golf Course** Fontainebleau Blvd., Miami. (305) 221-5181 *East Course* 18 holes. Par 72/72. Yards: 7,035/5,586 Year-round. High: Nov.–Apr.	Greens: Carts: Rating: Slope:	$$ Incl. 73.3/71.5 122/119	W L
☺	*West Course* 18 holes. Par 72/72. Yards: 6,944/5,565	Rating: Slope:	72.5/71.0 120/118	
P ☺☺☺ DEAL	**Golf Club of Miami** Miami Gardens Dr., Miami. (305) 829-4700 *East Course* 18 holes. Par 70/70. Yards: 6,553/5,025 Year-round. High: Feb.–Nov.	Greens: Carts: Rating: Slope:	$$ Incl. 70.3/68.8 124/117	L T
☺☺☺ DEAL	*West Course* 18 holes. Par 72/72. Yards: 7,017/5,298	Rating: Slope:	73.5/70.1 130/123	
P ☺☺☺☺ BEST	**Links at Key Biscayne** Crandon Blvd., Key Biscayne. (305) 361-9129 18 holes. Par 72/72. Yards: 7,070/5,662 Year-round. High: Dec.–May	Greens: Carts: Rating: Slope:	$$$–$$$$ Incl. 75.2/73.1 139/129	W L T
SP ☺☺☺	**The Links at Polo Trace** Hagen Ranch Rd., Delray Beach. (407) 459-5300 18 holes. Par 72/72. Yards: 7,096/5,314 Year-round. High: Dec.–Apr.	Greens: Carts: Rating: Slope:	$$–$$$$$ Incl. 73.4/71.0 134/124	W L T J
SP ☺☺	**Miami Shores Country Club** Biscayne Blvd., Miami Shores. (305) 795-2366 18 holes. Par 71/72. Yards: 6,400/5,400 Year-round. High: Dec.–Apr.	Greens: Carts: Rating: Slope:	$$–$$$ Incl. 70.6/71.3 121/126	W L T
P ☺☺	**Normandy Shores Golf Course** Biarritz Dr., Miami Beach. (305) 868-6502 18 holes. Par 71/73. Yards: 6,402/5,527 Year-round. High: Nov.–Apr.	Greens: Carts: Rating: Slope:	$$–$$$ Incl. 70.5/71.0 120/119	W L T
P ☺☺	**Palmetto Golf Course** S.W. 152nd St., Miami. (305) 238-2922 18 holes. Par 70/73. Yards: 6,713/5,725 Year-round. High: Jan.–Mar.	Greens: Carts: Rating: Slope:	$–$$ $ 72.7/73.4 128/125	W L T J

Georgia

The most famous of the more than 300 courses in Georgia is the Augusta
National Golf Club, site of the Masters; alas, it is not open to the public. You
can, though, practice your skills to prepare for the PGA Tour yourself at several hundred other interesting courses.

Atlanta Area

The Boulders Course at Lake Acworth is a tough lakeside course with an especially challenging back nine.

There are two topflight choices at **Reynold's Plantation** in Eatonton, in the rural countryside between Macon and Atlanta: the superb Nicklaus-designed Great Waters Course, which runs along a lake, and the lush Plantation Course.

The Stonemont and Woodmont courses at **Stone Mountain Park Golf Course** in Stone Mountain east of Atlanta are both ranked among the best public courses in the nation, with some demanding and very scenic holes.

The **Stouffer Renaissance PineIsle Resort** is a memorable course that juts out on a peninsula into Lake Lanier and includes eight holes along the water and at least one that tempts the golfer into trying to cut the corner with two water carries to an island green.

Another handsome challenge is at the **Port Armor Club** in Greensboro, with rolling terrain, tall pines, and marshes along Lake Oconee.

Augusta Area

The **Jones Creek Golf Club** in Evans is a fine public course that also earns a spot on the Econoguide Deals list.

Columbus Area

The Mountain View Course at the **Callaway Gardens Resort** in Pine Mountain is home to a PGA event. It features a long-distance call from tee to green on many of its holes.

The West Course at **Bull Creek Golf Course** near Columbus is considered one of the nation's best public courses, with heavy woods, a wandering creek, and some unusual challenges.

Southern Georgia

One of the highlights of St. Simons Island is the Seaside/Plantation pair at the **Sea Island Golf Club**. This place was built on the site of the former Retreat Plantation. Its grounds also feature the posh Cloister Hotel. Seaside, designed by Bobby Jones, has one of golf's memorable holes at No. 4, a shot across an open marsh.

The **Osprey Cove Golf Club** in St. Marys, on the state's southern border near Jacksonville, Florida, is a gem of an oceanside links-style course through the woods, across marshlands, and along several small lakes.

Georgia on Your Mind

Most courses in Georgia operate year-round. Expect off-peak prices in the winter, with highest prices from late spring through midfall.

Econoguide Leader Board: Best Public Courses in Georgia

⊙⊙⊙⊙   The Boulders Course at Lake Acworth
⊙⊙⊙   Bull Creek Golf Course (West)

○○○○   Callaway Gardens Resort (Mountain View)
○○○   Jones Creek Golf Club
○○○○   Osprey Cove Golf Club
○○○   Port Armor Golf and Country Club
○○○○   Reynold's Plantation (Great Waters, Plantation)
○○○○   Sea Island Golf Club (Seaside, Plantation)
○○○   Stone Mountain Park Golf Course (Lakemont, Woodmont, Stonemont)
○○○   Stouffer Renaissance PineIsle Resort

Econoguide Leader Board: Best Deals in Georgia

$$/○○○   Barrington Hall Golf Club
$$/○○○   Bull Creek Golf Course (East, West)
$$/○○○   Chattahoochee Golf Club
$$/○○○   Chicopee Woods Golf Course
$$/○○○   Fields Ferry Golf Club
$$/○○○   Forest Hills Golf Club
$$/○○○   Foxfire Golf Club
$$/○○○   Georgia Veterans State Park Golf Course
$$/○○○   Jekyll Island Golf Resort (Indian Mound, Oleander, Pine Lakes)
$$/○○○   Jones Creek Golf Club
$$/○○○   Landings Golf Club (Trestle, Bluff, Creek)
$$/○○○   Lane Creek Golf Club
$/○○○   Maple Ridge Golf Club
$/○○○   Nob North Golf Course
$/○○○   Oak Grove Island Golf Club
$$/○○○   The Oaks Golf Course
$$/○○○   Orchard Hills Golf Club
$$/○○○○   Osprey Cove Golf Club
$$/○○○   Port Armor Golf and Country Club
$$/○○○   Southbridge Golf Club
$$/○○○   Stone Mountain Park Golf Course (Lakemont, Woodmont, Stonemont)
$$/○○○   University of Georgia Golf Club
$$/○○○   Wallace Adams Golf Course
$$/○○○   Windstone Golf Club

Georgia Golf Guide

Atlanta Area

SP	**Barrington Hall Golf Club**	Greens:	$–$$	W
○○○	Zebulon Rd., Macon. (912) 757-8358	Carts:	$	
DEAL	18 holes. Par 72/72. Yards: 7,062/5,012	Rating:	73.8/69.3	
	Year-round. High: Apr.–May	Slope:	138/118	

P	**The Boulders Course at Lake Acworth**	Greens:	$$–$$$	W L T
○○○○	Nance Rd., Acworth. (404) 917-5151	Carts:	$	
STATE	18 holes. Par 72/72. Yards: 6,759/5,400	Rating:	73.1/71.5	
	Year-round. High: Mar.–Oct.	Slope:	140/129	

P	**Browns Mill Golf Course**	Greens:	$–$$	W T S J
○○	Cleveland Ave., Atlanta. (404) 366-3573	Carts:	$	
	18 holes. Par 72/72. Yards: 6,539/5,545	Rating:	71.0/71.4	
	Year-round. High: Mar.–Oct.	Slope:	123/118	

Georgia Golf Guide

Atlanta Area

P ◔◔	**Centennial Golf Club** Woodstock Rd., Acworth. (404) 975-1000 18 holes. Par 72/72. Yards: 6,850/5,095 Year-round. High: June–Oct.	Greens: $$–$$$ Carts: Incl. Rating: 73.1/69.5 Slope: 134/122	T S J
SP ◔◔◔	**The Champions Club of Atlanta** Hopewell Rd., Alpharetta. (404) 343-9700 18 holes. Par 72/72. Yards: 6,725/4,470 Year-round. High: Mar.–Dec.	Greens: $$$ Carts: Incl. Rating: 72.9/65.2 Slope: 131/108	T
R ◔◔◔	**Chateau Elan Golf Club** Braselton. (404) 271-6050 18 holes. Par 71/71. Yards: 7,030/5,092 Year-round. High: Apr.–Oct.	Greens: $$$–$$$$ Carts: Incl. Rating: 73.5/70.8 Slope: 136/124	
P ◔◔◔ DEAL	**Chattahoochee Golf Club** Tommy Aaron Dr., Gainesville. (404) 532-0066 18 holes. Par 71/71. Yards: 6,700/5,000 Year-round. High: Apr.–Oct.	Greens: $–$$ Carts: $ Rating: 72.1/64.5 Slope: 125/110	T S J
P ◔◔◔ DEAL	**Chicopee Woods Golf Course** Atlanta Hwy., Gainesville. (404) 534-7322 18 holes. Par 72/72. Yards: 7,040/5,001 Year-round. High: Apr.–Sept.	Greens: $$ Carts: $ Rating: 74.0/69.0 Slope: 135/117	T
SP ◔◔◔	**Eagle Watch Golf Club** Eagle Watch Dr., Woodstock. (404) 591-1000 18 holes. Par 72/72. Yards: 6,900/5,243 Year-round. High: June–Aug.	Greens: $$$–$$$$ Carts: Incl. Rating: 72.6/68.9 Slope: 136/126	W L R T S J
P ◔◔	**Georgia National Golf Club** Lake Dow Rd., McDonough. (404) 914-9994 18 holes. Par 71/71. Yards: 6,874/5,741 Year-round. High: Apr.–Sept.	Greens: $$–$$$ Carts: Incl. Rating: 73.3/73.0 Slope: 132/130	S J
SP ◔◔	**Harbor Club** Greensboro. (706) 453-4414 18 holes. Par 72/72. Yards: 6,988/5,207 Year-round. High: Mar.–Oct.	Greens: $$–$$$$ Carts: Inquire Rating: 73.7/70.2 Slope: 135/123	T S J
P ◔◔	**Hard Labor Creek State Park Golf Course** Knox Chapel Rd., Rutledge. (706) 557-3006 18 holes. Par 72/75. Yards: 6,437/4,854 Year-round. High: Mar.–Oct.	Greens: $ Carts: $ Rating: 71.5/68.8 Slope: 129/123	T S J
P ◔◔	**Innsbruck Resort and Golf Club** Bahn Innsbruck, Helen. (706) 878-2100, (800) 642-2709 18 holes. Par 72/72. Yards: 6,748/5,174 Year-round. High: Apr.–Oct.	Greens: $$–$$$ Carts: Incl. Rating: 72.4/NA Slope: 136/118	L R T S J
R ◔◔◔	**Lake Lanier Islands Hilton Resort** Holiday Rd., Lake Lanier. (404) 945-8787 18 holes. Par 72/72. Yards: 6,341/4,935 Year-round. High: Apr.–Sept.	Greens: $$$ Carts: Incl. Rating: 70.1/68.3 Slope: 124/117	W L T
P ◔◔	**Lakeside Country Club** Old Fairburn Rd., Atlanta. (404) 344-3629 18 holes. Par 71/71. Yards: 6,522/5,279 Year-round. High: Mar.–May	Greens: $$ Carts: Incl. Rating: 71.4/70.7 Slope: 127/121	W L T S
P ◔◔◔ DEAL	**Lane Creek Golf Club** Cole Springs Rd., Bishop. (706) 769-6699 18 holes. Par 72/72. Yards: 6,725/5,195 Year-round. High: Year-round	Greens: $$ Carts: Incl. Rating: 72.6/68.4 Slope: 134/115	W T S J
SP ◔◔◔	**Metropolitan Golf Club** Fairington Pkwy., Lithonia. (404) 981-7976	Greens: $$–$$$ Carts: Incl.	W T

Atlanta Area

	18 holes. Par 72/72. Yards: 6,030/5,966	Rating:	74.2/74.8
	Year-round. High: Apr.–Sept.	Slope:	138/131

P	**Mystery Valley Golf Course**	Greens:	$	W S J
◎◎	Shadowrock Dr., Lithonia. (404) 469-6913	Carts:	$	
	18 holes. Par 72/75. Yards: 6,705/5,928	Rating:	71.5/67.9	
	Year-round. High: Mar.–Sept.	Slope:	124/115	

P	**Nob North Golf Course**	Greens:	$	S J
◎◎◎	Nob North Dr., Cohutta. (706) 694-8505	Carts:	Inquire	
DEAL	18 holes. Par 72/72. Yards: 6,573/5,448	Rating:	71.7/71.7	
	Year-round. High: Mar.–Nov.	Slope:	128/126	

P	**North Fulton Golf Course**	Greens:	$	W L T S J
◎◎	W. Wieuca Rd., Atlanta. (404) 255-0723	Carts:	Inquire	
	18 holes. Par 71/71. Yards: 6,570/5,120	Rating:	71.8/69.5	
	Year-round. High: July	Slope:	126/118	

P	**The Oaks Golf Course**	Greens:	$$	W L R T S J
◎◎◎	Brown Bridge Rd., Covington. (404) 221-0200	Carts:	Incl.	
DEAL	18 holes. Par 70/70. Yards: 6,420/4,600	Rating:	69.5/64.5	
	Year-round. High: Apr.–Sept.	Slope:	118/107	

SP	**Olde Atlanta Golf Club**	Greens:	$$–$$$	T S
◎◎◎	Olde Atlanta Pkwy., Suwanee. (404) 497-0097	Carts:	Incl.	
	18 holes. Par 71/71. Yards: 6,800/5,147	Rating:	73.1/69.3	
	Year-round. High: Apr.–Sept.	Slope:	132/120	

P	**Orchard Hills Golf Club**	Greens:	$$	W L T S J
◎◎◎	E. Hwy. 16, Newnan. (404) 251-5683	Carts:	$$	
DEAL	18 holes. Par 72/72. Yards: 7,100/5,304	Rating:	73.7/69.5	
	Year-round. High: Apr.–May	Slope:	132/116	

R	**Port Armor Golf and Country Club**	Greens:	$$	L R
◎◎◎	Port Armor Pkwy., Greensboro. (706) 453-4564	Carts:	$	
DEAL	18 holes. Par 72/72. Yards: 6,926/5,177	Rating:	74.0/72.8	
STATE	Year-round. High: Apr.–Oct.	Slope:	140/131	

SP	**River's Edge Golf Course**	Greens:	$$–$$$	W T S J
◎◎◎	Fayetteville. (404) 460-1098	Carts:	Incl.	
	18 holes. Par 71/71. Yards: 6,810/5,641	Rating:	72.9/69.9	
	Year-round. High: Mar.–Oct.	Slope:	135/121	

P	**Riverpines Golf Club**	Greens:	$$$	J
◎◎◎	Old Alabama Rd., Alpharetta. (404) 442-5960	Carts:	Incl.	
	18 holes. Par 70/70. Yards: 6,511/4,279	Rating:	71.3/64.7	
	Year-round. High: Apr.–Sept.	Slope:	126/107	

SP	**Royal Lakes Golf and Country Club**	Greens:	$$–$$$	W T J
◎◎◎	Royal Lakes Dr., Flowery Branch. (404) 535-8800	Carts:	Incl.	
	18 holes. Par 72/72. Yards: 6,871/5,325	Rating:	72.0/70.4	
	Year-round. High: Mar.–Sept.	Slope:	131/125	

SP	**Royal Oaks Golf Club**	Greens:	$$	W L T S J
◎◎	Summit Ridge Dr., Cartersville. (404) 382-3999	Carts:	$	
	18 holes. Par 71/75. Yards: 6,309/4,890	Rating:	70.0/71.0	
	Year-round. High: Apr.–Oct.	Slope:	124/121	

P	**St. Marlo Golf Club**	Greens:	$$$–$$$$	W J
◎◎	St. Marlo Country Club Pkwy., Duluth. (404) 495-7725	Carts:	$	
	18 holes. Par 71/75. Yards: 6,900/5,300	Rating:	73.6/70.3	
	Year-round. High: Apr.–Oct.	Slope:	137/121	

R	**Sconti Golf Club**	Greens:	$$–$$$	W L
	Big Canoe. (706) 268-3323	Carts:	Incl.	
◎◎◎	*Choctaw/Cherokee/Creek*	Rating:	71.0/70.2/70.4	

Georgia Golf Guide

Atlanta Area

	27 holes. Par 72/72/72. Yards: 6,371/6,276/6,247	Slope:	136/132/134	
	Year-round. High: Apr.–Oct.			

SP	**Southerness Golf Club**	Greens:	$$–$$$	T
☺☺☺	Flat Bridge Rd., Stockbridge. (404) 808-6000	Carts:	Incl.	
	18 holes. Par 72/72. Yards: 6,766/4,956	Rating:	72.2/69.0	
	Year-round. High: Apr.–Sept.	Slope:	127/119	

R	**Stone Mountain Park Golf Course**	Greens:	$$
	Stone Mountain. (404) 498-5715	Carts:	Incl.
☺☺☺	*Lakemont/Woodmont*	Rating:	71.6/69.4
BEST	18 holes. Par 72/72. Yards: 6,595/5,231	Slope:	130/120
DEAL	Year-round. High: Apr.–Oct.		

☺☺☺	*Stonemont*	Rating:	72.6/69.1
BEST	18 holes. Par 72/72. Yards: 6,683/5,020	Slope:	133/121
DEAL			

R	**Stouffer Renaissance Pinelsle Resort**	Greens:	$$$
☺☺☺	Holiday Rd., Lake Lanier Islands. (404) 945-8922	Carts:	Incl.
STATE	18 holes. Par 72/72. Yards: 6,527/5,297	Rating:	71.6/70.6
	Year-round. High: Apr.–Oct.	Slope:	132/127

P	**Sugar Hill Golf Club**	Greens:	$$–$$$	L T S J
☺	Suwanee Dam Rd., Sugar Hill. (404) 271-0519	Carts:	Incl.	
	18 holes. Par 72/72. Yards: 6,423/4,207	Rating:	70.7/65.3	
	Year-round. High: Apr.–Oct.	Slope:	127/112	

P	**Towne Lake Hills Golf Club**	Greens:	$$–$$$	L T
☺☺	Towne Lake Hills E., Woodstock. (404) 592-9969	Carts:	Incl.	
	18 holes. Par 72/72. Yards: 6,757/4,984	Rating:	72.3/69.0	
	Year-round. High: May–Oct.	Slope:	133/116	

P	**University of Georgia Golf Club**	Greens:	$–$$	W T
☺☺☺	Riverbend Rd., Athens. (706) 369-5739	Carts:	$	
DEAL	18 holes. Par 72/73. Yards: 6,890/5,713	Rating:	73.4/74.0	
	Year-round. High: Mar.–June	Slope:	133/128	

P	**White Columns Golf Club**	Greens:	$$$$–$$$$$
☺☺	White Columns Dr., Alpharetta. (404) 343-9025	Carts:	Incl.
	18 holes. Par 72/72. Yards: 6,739/4,909	Rating:	72.3/68.2
	Year-round. High: Mar.–Oct.	Slope:	133/123

SP	**Windstone Golf Club**	Greens:	$–$$
☺☺☺	Windstone Dr., Ringgold. (615) 894-1231	Carts:	$
DEAL	18 holes. Par 72/72. Yards: 6,626/4,956	Rating:	71.1/66.8
	Year-round. High: Apr.–Oct.	Slope:	119/108

Augusta Area

P	**Belle Meade Country Club**	Greens:	$–$$	W S
☺☺	Twin Pine Rd. N.W., Thomson. (706) 595-4511	Carts:	Inquire	
	18 holes. Par 72/73. Yards: 6,212/5,362	Rating:	69.9/68.6	
	Year-round. High: May–Aug.	Slope:	120/113	

SP	**The Fields Golf Club**	Greens:	$	W L T S
☺☺	S. Smith Rd., LaGrange. (706) 845-7425	Carts:	$	
	18 holes. Par 72/72. Yards: 6,650/5,000	Rating:	71.4/67.4	
	Year-round. High: Mar.–Oct.	Slope:	128/113	

P	**Forest Hills Golf Club**	Greens:	$–$$	J
☺☺☺	Comfort Rd., Augusta. (706) 733-0001	Carts:	$	
DEAL	18 holes. Par 72/72. Yards: 6,780/4,875	Rating:	72.8/69.8	
	Year-round. High: Mar.–Oct.	Slope:	124/117	

SP	**Goshen Plantation Country Club**	Greens:	$$	W L T S J
☺☺	Augusta. (706) 793-1168	Carts:	Incl.	

Georgia Golf Guide

Augusta Area

	18 holes. Par 72/72. Yards: 6,902/5,688	Rating:	72.6/70.9
	Year-round. High: Mar.–Oct.	Slope:	130/125

P
☺☺☺
BEST
DEAL

Jones Creek Golf Club
Hammond's Ferry Rd., Evans. (706) 860-4228
18 holes. Par 72/72. Yards: 7,008/5,430
Year-round. High: Apr.–Aug.

Greens: $$ S J
Carts: $
Rating: 73.8/72.4
Slope: 137/130

Macon/Warner Robins Area

P
☺☺☺
DEAL

Georgia Veterans State Park Golf Course
Hwy. 280 W., Cordel. (912) 276-2377
18 holes. Par 72/72. Yards: 7,088/5,171
Year-round. High: Apr.–Sept.

Greens: $–$$ W T S J
Carts: $
Rating: 72.1/73.5
Slope: 130/124

SP

☺☺☺
DEAL

Landings Golf Club
Statham's Way, Warner Robins. (912) 923-5222
Trestle/Bluff/Creek
27 holes. Par 72/72/72. Yards: 6,998/6,671/6,819
Year-round. High: Mar.–Dec.

Greens: $–$$
Carts: $
Rating: 73.1/71.9/72.6
Slope: 133/130/131

R

☺☺☺☺
STATE

Reynold's Plantation
Wood Crest Dr. N.E., Eatonton. (706) 485-0235
Great Waters Course
18 holes. Par 72/72. Yards: 7,058/5,057
Year-round. High: Apr.–Oct.

Greens: $$$$–$$$$$ W R
Carts: Inquire
Rating: 73.8/69.2
Slope: 135/114

☺☺☺☺
STATE

Plantation Course
18 holes. Par 71/72. Yards: 6,656/5,641
Year-round. High: Apr.–Aug.

Greens: $$$
Carts: $
Rating: 71.2/69.1
Slope: 125/117

P
☺☺☺
DEAL

Wallace Adams Golf Course
Hwy. 441 N., McRae. (912) 868-6651
18 holes. Par 72/72. Yards: 6,625/5,001
Year-round. High: Spring/Fall

Greens: $–$$ R S
Carts: Inquire
Rating: 70.8/69.1
Slope: 128/120

Columbus Area

P
☺☺☺
DEAL

Bull Creek Golf Course
Lynch Rd., Columbus. (706) 561-1614
East Course
18 holes. Par 72/74. Yards: 6,705/5,430
Year-round. High: Apr.–Aug.

Greens: $ W S J
Carts: $
Rating: 71.2/69.8
Slope: 124/114

☺☺☺
BEST
DEAL

West Course
18 holes. Par 72/74. Yards: 6,921/5,385

Rating: 72.5/69.9
Slope: 130/121

R

☺☺☺

Callaway Gardens Resort
U.S. Hwy. 27, Pine Mountain. (706) 663-2281, (800) 282-8181
Garden View Course
18 holes. Par 72/72. Yards: 6,921/5,385
Year-round. High: Feb.–Mar, June–Aug.

Greens: $$$–$$$$ L T
Carts: Incl.
Rating: 70.7/72.7
Slope: 121/123

☺☺☺

Lake View Course
18 holes. Par 70/71. Yards: 6,006/5,452

Greens: $$$–$$$$
Carts: Incl.
Rating: 69.4/70.3
Slope: 115/122

☺☺☺☺
BEST

Mountain View Course
18 holes. Par 70/71. Yards: 7,057/5,848

Greens: $$$–$$$$$
Carts: Incl.
Rating: 74.1/73.2
Slope: 138/122

P
☺☺☺

Fields Ferry Golf Club
Fields Ferry Dr., Calhoun. (706) 625-5666

Greens: $–$$ W T S J
Carts: $

Georgia Golf Guide

Columbus Area

DEAL	18 holes. Par 72/72. Yards: 6,824/5,355	Rating:	71.8/70.5
	Year-round. High: Apr.–Oct.	Slope:	123/120

P	**Maple Ridge Golf Club**	Greens:	$	W L T S J
☺☺☺	Maple Ridge Trail, Columbus. (706) 569-0966	Carts:	Inquire	
DEAL	18 holes. Par 71/71. Yards: 6,652/5,030	Rating:	72.2/68.9	
	Year-round. High: Apr.–July	Slope:	123/127	

R	**Sky Valley Golf Club**	Greens:	$$–$$$	L R T
☺☺☺	Sky Valley. (706) 746-5303	Carts:	Incl.	
	18 holes. Par 72/72. Yards: 6,452/5,017	Rating:	71.7/69.0	
	Year-round. High: Apr.–Oct.	Slope:	128/118	

Savannah Area

SP	**Foxfire Golf Club**	Greens:	$$	W S J
☺☺☺	Foxfire Dr., Vidalia. (912) 538-8670	Carts:	Incl.	
DEAL	18 holes. Par 72/71. Yards: 6,118/4,757	Rating:	69.3/65.4	
	Year-round. High: Mar.–Sept.	Slope:	125/116	

SP	**Oak Grove Island Golf Club**	Greens:	$	W R T S J
☺☺☺	Clipper Bay, Brunswick. (912) 262-9575	Carts:	Inquire	
DEAL	18 holes. Par 72/72. Yards: 6,910/4,855	Rating:	73.2/67.6	
	Year-round. High: Apr.–Sept.	Slope:	132/116	

R	**Sheraton Savannah Resort & Country Club**	Greens:	$$–$$$	W L R T S J
☺☺☺	Wilmington Island Rd., Savannah. (912) 897-1612	Carts:	Incl.	
	18 holes. Par 72/72. Yards: 6,876/5,328	Rating:	73.5/70.6	
	Year-round. High: Apr.–Oct.	Slope:	137/128	

SP	**Southbridge Golf Club**	Greens:	$$	W L S
☺☺☺	Southbridge Blvd., Savannah. (912) 651-5455	Carts:	Incl.	
DEAL	18 holes. Par 72/72. Yards: 6,990/5,181	Rating:	73.4/69.2	
	Year-round. High: Apr.–May	Slope:	136/118	

Southern Georgia

P	**Francis Lake Golf Course**	Greens:	$–$$	W R T J
☺☺	Lake Park. (912) 559-7961	Carts:	Incl.	
	18 holes. Par 72/72. Yards: 6,458/5,709	Rating:	71.4/70.1	
	Year-round. High: Mar.–Aug.	Slope:	124/117	

SP	**Hampton Club**	Greens:	$$$$	R J
☺☺☺	Tabbystone, St. Simons Island. (912) 634-0255	Carts:	$	
	18 holes. Par 72/72. Yards: 6,400/5,233	Rating:	71.4/71.0	
	Year-round. High: Mar.–Apr.	Slope:	130/123	

R	**Jekyll Island Golf Resort**	Greens:	$$	T
	Captain Wylly Rd., Jekyll Island. (912) 635-2368	Carts:	$	
☺☺☺	*Indian Mound Course*	Rating:	71.1/NA	
DEAL	18 holes. Par 72/72. Yards: 6,596/5,345	Slope:	127/122	
	Year-round. High: Feb.–Apr.			

☺☺☺	*Oleander Course*	Rating:	72.0/72.6
DEAL	18 holes. Par 72/72. Yards: 6,679/5,654	Slope:	128/124

☺☺☺	*Pine Lakes Course*	Rating:	71.9/71.9
DEAL	18 holes. Par 72/72. Yards: 6,802/5,742	Slope:	130/124

SP	**Osprey Cove Golf Club**	Greens:	$$	J
☺☺☺☺	Osprey Dr., St. Marys. (912) 882-5575	Carts:	$	
DEAL	18 holes. Par 72/72. Yards: 6,791/5,263	Rating:	73.0/71.1	
STATE	Year-round. High: Feb.–July	Slope:	130/120	

P	**St. Simons Island Club**	Greens:	$$$	L R T J
☺☺☺	Kings Way, St. Simons Island. (912) 638-5130	Carts:	$	
	18 holes. Par 72/72. Yards: 6,490/5,361	Rating:	71.8/70.0	
	Year-round. High: Mar.–Apr.	Slope:	133/124	

Southern Georgia

R	**Sea Island Golf Club**	Greens:	$$$$–$$$$$ L R T J
	Retreat Ave., St. Simons Island. (912) 638-5118	Carts:	$
☺☺☺	*Retreat/Marshside*	Rating:	71.2/69.5
	18 holes. Par 72/72. Yards: 6,518/5,056	Slope:	130/111
	Year-round. High: Apr.–Oct.		

☺☺☺☺	*Seaside/Plantation*	Rating:	73.2/69.1
BEST	18 holes. Par 72/72. Yards: 6,900/5,178	Slope:	134/115

R	**Sea Palms Resort**	Greens:	$$–$$$ W L R T J
	Frederica Rd., St. Simons Island. (912) 638-9041	Carts:	$
☺☺	*Tall Pines/Great Oaks/Sea Palms*	Rating:	71.3/71.1/69.7
	27 holes. Par 72/72/72. Yards: 6,658/6,350/6,198	Slope:	128/126/124
	Year-round. High: Feb.–May		

Louisiana

The distinguishing feature of many of the courses in Louisiana is water: open water, swamp, and bayou.

The best public resort course in Louisiana is the surprisingly up-and-down challenge of the **Bluffs on Thompson Creek** in St. Francisville, located to the north of Baton Rouge.

Louisiana's Econoguide Deals include the swampy bayou course at **Belle Terre Country Club**, west of New Orleans, and the long and hard **Mallard Cove** in Lake Charles.

Down south in Louisiana the courses generally are open all year long. Peak rates usually are in effect from April through September. Off-season covers the fall through spring, and some courses also reduce prices slightly in the hottest months of summer.

Econoguide Leader Board: Best Public Course in Louisiana

☺☺☺☺   Bluffs on Thompson Creek Golf Club

Econoguide Leader Board: Best Deals in Louisiana

$/☺☺☺	Bayou Oaks Golf Courses (Championship)
$$/☺☺☺	Belle Terre Country Club
$/☺☺☺	Mallard Cove Golf Course
$$/☺☺☺	Santa Maria Golf Course

Shreveport Area

P	**Huntington Park Golf Course**	Greens:	$ W T S J
☺☺	Pines Rd., Shreveport. (318) 673-7765	Carts:	$
	18 holes. Par 72/74. Yards: 7,294/6,171	Rating:	73.3/74.7
	Year-round. High: May–Sept.	Slope:	NA

R	**Toro Hills Lodge**	Greens:	$–$$ W
☺☺	Florien. (318) 586-4661	Carts:	$
	18 holes. Par 72/72. Yards: 6,550/6,300	Rating:	NA
	Year-round. High: Apr.–Sept.	Slope:	120/118

Lake Charles

P	**Mallard Cove Golf Course**	Greens:	$ W T S J
☺☺☺	Chennault Air Base, Lake Charles. (318) 491-1204	Carts:	$

Louisiana Golf Guide

Lake Charles

DEAL	18 holes. Par 72/72. Yards: 6,903/5,294	Rating:	72.4/70.1
	Year-round. High: Apr.–Oct.	Slope:	125/117

Baton Rouge Area

R	**Bluffs on Thompson Creek Golf Club**	Greens:	$$–$$$	W L R T
☺☺☺☺	Hwy. 965, St. Francisville. (504) 634-5551	Carts:	$	
STATE	18 holes. Par 72/72. Yards: 7,143/4,813	Rating:	74.6/69.0	
	Year-round. High: Spring/Fall	Slope:	143/123	
P	**Santa Maria Golf Course**	Greens:	$–$$	T S J
☺☺☺	Old Perkins Rd., Baton Rouge. (504) 752-9667	Carts:	$	
DEAL	18 holes. Par 72/72. Yards: 7,051/5,267	Rating:	72.9/69.6	
	Year-round. High: Apr.–Oct.	Slope:	124/120	

New Orleans Area

P	**Bayou Oaks Golf Courses**	Greens:	$	T S J
	Filmore, New Orleans. (504) 483-9396	Carts:	$	
☺	*Lakeside Course*	Rating:	68.5/70.5	
	18 holes. Par 70/70. Yards: 6,054/5,872	Slope:	110/103	
	Year-round. High: Apr.–June, Sept.–Oct.			
☺☺☺	*Championship Course*	Rating:	71.5/73.3	
DEAL	18 holes. Par 72/72. Yards: 7,061/6,013	Slope:	116/118	
☺☺	*Wisner Course*	Rating:	70.5/71.8	
	18 holes. Par 72/72. Yards: 6,465/5,707	Slope:	111/116	
SP	**Belle Terre Country Club**	Greens:	$$	W
☺☺☺	La Place. (504) 652-5000	Carts:	Incl.	
DEAL	18 holes. Par 72/72. Yards: 6,840/5,510	Rating:	72.2/71.6	
	Year-round. High: Apr.–Oct.	Slope:	130/113	
P	**Oak Harbor Golf Club**	Greens:	$$–$$$	T J
☺☺☺	Oak Harbor Blvd., Slidell. (504) 646-0110	Carts:	Incl.	
	18 holes. Par 72/72. Yards: 6,896/5,305	Rating:	72.7/70.0	
	Year-round. High: Apr.–July	Slope:	132/118	

Mississippi

The best public course in Mississippi may be **Timberton** in Hattiesburg; the fact that it is an Econoguide Deal makes it even better.

Other recommended courses include **Kirkwood National** in Holly Springs in the northern reach of the state, and **Windance Country Club** in Gulfport on the Gulf of Mexico.

Courses in Mississippi generally are open year-round. Expect peak rates and conditions from about February through April at most courses; some, though, extend their peak through the hot summer as well.

Econoguide Leader Board: Best Public Courses in Mississippi

☺☺☺☺ Kirkwood National Golf Club
☺☺☺☺ Timberton Golf Club
☺☺☺☺ Windance Country Club

Econoguide Leader Board: Best Deals in Mississippi

$$/☺☺☺ Diamondhead Country Club (Cardinal, Pine)
$$/☺☺☺ Mississippi National Golf Club
$/☺☺☺ Mississippi State University Golf Course
$/☺☺☺ Ole Miss Golf Club

$$/☺☺☺	Plantation Golf Course
$$/☺☺☺☺	Timberton Golf Club
$$/☺☺☺	Wedgewood Golf Course

Mississippi Golf Guide

Northern Mississippi

SP ☺☺☺☺ STATE	**Kirkwood National Golf Club** Holly Springs. (601) 252-4888 18 holes. Par 72/72. Yards: 7,129/4,898 Year-round. High: June–Aug.	Greens: Carts: Rating: Slope:	$$–$$$　　L Incl. NA NA
P ☺☺☺ DEAL	**Ole Miss Golf Club** College Hill Rd., Oxford. (601) 234-4816 18 holes. Par 72/72. Yards: 6,682/5,276 Year-round. High: May–Aug.	Greens: Carts: Rating: Slope:	$ $ 72.8/70.9 129/120
SP ☺☺☺ DEAL	**Plantation Golf Course** Plantation Rd., Olive Branch. (601) 895-3530 18 holes. Par 72/72. Yards: 6,773/5,055 Year-round. High: Mar.–Sept.	Greens: Carts: Rating: Slope:	$–$$　　W L T S J Inquire 72.0/64.4 122/109
SP ☺☺☺ DEAL	**Wedgewood Golf Course** Olive Branch. (901) 521-8275 18 holes. Par 72/72. Yards: 6,863/5,627 Year-round. High: May–Sept.	Greens: Carts: Rating: Slope:	$$　　W L R T S J $ 72.8/69.1 127/118

Tupelo Area

SP ☺☺	**Natchez Trace Golf Club** Beech Springs Rd., Saltillo. (601) 869-2166 18 holes. Par 72/72. Yards: 6,841/4,791 Year-round. High: June–Aug.	Greens: Carts: Rating: Slope:	$–$$　　W $ 72.3/69.3 116/108

Columbus Area

P ☺☺☺ DEAL	**Mississippi State University Golf Course** Old Hwy. 82 E., Starkville. (601) 325-3028 18 holes. Par 72/72. Yards: 6,926/5,443 Year-round. High: Mar.–Sept.	Greens: Carts: Rating: Slope:	$　　W J $ 73.5/71.8 130/121

Jackson Area

P ☺☺	**Eagle Ridge Golf Course** Hwy. 18 S., Raymond. (601) 857-5993 18 holes. Par 70.5/NA. Yards: 6,500/5,135 Year-round. High: Mar.–Aug.	Greens: Carts: Rating: Slope:	$　　W S $ 70.5/NA 113/NA

Hattiesburg Area

P ☺☺☺☺ DEAL STATE	**Timberton Golf Club** Hattiesburg. (601) 584-4653 18 holes. Par 72/72. Yards: 7,028/5,439 Year-round. High: Mar.–Apr.	Greens: Carts: Rating: Slope:	$$ Incl. 73.1/71.4 131/128
P ☺	**USM Van Hook Golf Course** Hattiesburg. (601) 264-1872 18 holes. Par 72/73. Yards: 6,660/5,226 Year-round. High: May–June	Greens: Carts: Rating: Slope:	$　　W L T S J Inquire 69.0/70.0 NA

Gulfport/Biloxi Area

R ☺☺	**Broadwater Resort** Beach Dr., Gulfport. (601) 385-4085 *Sea Course* 18 holes. Par 72/72. Yards: 6,214/5,403 Year-round. High: Feb.–May	Greens: Carts: Rating: Slope:	$$$　　L Incl. 70.0/72.0 118/113
☺☺	*Sun Course* Beauvoir, Biloxi. (601) 385-4081 18 holes. Par 72/72. Yards: 7,168/5,485	Rating: Slope:	72.0/72.0 126/120

Mississippi Golf Guide

Gulfport/Biloxi Area

R	**Diamondhead Country Club**	Greens:	$$	L R J
	Diamondhead. (601) 255-3910	Carts:	Incl.	
☺☺☺	*Cardinal Course*	Rating:	72.7/68.9	
DEAL	18 holes. Par 72/72. Yards: 6,831/5,065	Slope:	132/117	
	Year-round. High: Feb.–May			
☺☺☺	*Pine Course*	Rating:	73.6/71.1	
DEAL	18 holes. Par 72/72. Yards: 6,817/5,313	Slope:	133/118	
P	**Mississippi National Golf Club**	Greens:	$–$$	L
☺☺☺	Hickory Hill Dr., Gautier. (601) 497-2372	Carts:	$	
DEAL	18 holes. Par 72/72. Yards: 7,003/5,229	Rating:	73.1/69.6	
	Year-round. High: Feb.–Apr.	Slope:	128/113	
SP	**Pass Christian Isles Golf Club**	Greens:	$$	
☺☺	Pass Christian. (601) 452-3830	Carts:	$	
	18 holes. Par 72/72. Yards: 6,438/5,428	Rating:	69.7/71.6	
	Year-round. High: Feb.–Apr.	Slope:	124/120	
SP	**Pine Island Golf Club**	Greens:	$–$$	W L R T
☺	Beachview Dr., Ocean Springs. (601) 875-1674	Carts:	$	
	18 holes. Par 71/71. Yards: 6,369/4,915	Rating:	70.9/67.8	
	Year-round. High: Feb.–Apr.	Slope:	129/109	
SP	**St. Andrews Country Club**	Greens:	$–$$	
☺☺	Ocean Springs. (601) 875-7730	Carts:	$	
	18 holes. Par 72/72. Yards: 6,460/4,960	Rating:	69.7/67.8	
	Year-round. High: Feb.–Mar.	Slope:	119/111	
SP	**Southwind Country Club**	Greens:	$$	
☺☺	Dismuke Dr., Biloxi. (601) 392-0400	Carts:	$	
	18 holes. Par 72/72. Yards: 6,202/5,577	Rating:	65.0/66.0	
	Year-round. High: Feb.–Apr.	Slope:	113/113	
R	**Sunkist Country Club**	Greens:	$$	W L T
☺☺	Sunkist Country Club Rd., Biloxi. (601) 388-3961	Carts:	Incl.	
	18 holes. Par 72/72. Yards: 6,000/5,300	Rating:	69.0/71.0	
	Year-round. High: Feb.–Apr.	Slope:	117/121	
P	**Tramark Golf Course**	Greens:	$	J
☺☺	Gulfport. (601) 863-7808	Carts:	$	
	18 holes. Par 72/72. Yards: 6,350/5,800	Rating:	68.5/69.5	
	Year-round. High: Feb.–Apr.	Slope:	116/109	
SP	**Windance Country Club**	Greens:	$$$$	
☺☺☺☺	Champion Circle, Gulfport. (601) 832-4871	Carts:	Incl.	
STATE	18 holes. Par 72/72. Yards: 6,678/5,179	Rating:	72.1/70.1	
	Year-round. High: Feb.–Apr.	Slope:	129/120	

North Carolina

North Carolina sometimes seems like one big, beautiful golf course, interrupted by a few towns, roads, and mountains. And that is the way many golfers think of the Tarheel State.

There is something for just about everyone in this state, which features spectacular courses chiseled out of the Great Smoky Mountains and the Blue Ridge Mountains, sprawling across the improbably green heartland, or hugging the coast and barrier islands. Among the nearly 500 courses in North Carolina is one of the game's meccas, Pinehurst.

North Carolina is, of course, one of the temples of golf in this country, and this is proved by the fact there are 19 Econoguide Best–rated courses at 17 clubs around the state. And in a state where some of the courses are among the priciest anywhere, there are nevertheless four Best–rated courses on the Econoguide Deals list.

The most famous of the North Carolina courses are at **Pinehurst Plantation** and **Pinehurst Resort,** located in the center of the state, east of Charlotte. Pinehurst was created around the turn of the century when a Boston soda-fountain inventor used some of his riches to purchase 5,000 acres of sandy barrens left behind by timber harvesters. The original intent was to create a winter haven for frozen northerners. For that purpose, the impressive Pinehurst Hotel was erected in 1901.

The Pinehurst Resort boasts no fewer than 144 championship holes, including the all-but-incomparable No. 2, first designed by Donald Ross in 1907 and adjusted by him for decades afterward. It rolls through tall pines with mounds and bunkers that offer a touch of Scotland. Ross also created numbers 1, 3, and 4, although the last one has been updated by someone else. In 1996, the spectacular No. 8 joined the ranks and was an immediate goal for visitors. Pinehurst No. 2 will be the site of the 1999 U.S. Open.

Also worth checking out in the area is **Pine Needles,** another Donald Ross design in the tall pines, this one dating from 1927; if Pinehurst weren't such a close neighbor, this one might be famous.

Also nearby is **The Pit Golf Links,** an unusual challenge that sends golfers down into the pit of a former sand mine for the front nine, only to make them work back alongside and across a lake.

Near Winston-Salem is **Tanglewood Park.** Around Greensboro is **Bryan Park,** a superb public course carved out of the forest and running along Lake

The Pit Golf Links, Pinehurst, North Carolina
Courtesy of the North Carolina Division of Travel and Tourism.

Townsend; it is in regular use for tournaments. Also in Greensboro is **Oak Hollow**. In the Raleigh-Durham area are fine courses at **Duke University**, **Keith Hills**, and **Porters Neck**. All the way west near Asheville is the mountain course at **Linville**.

Along the southern coast of Cape Fear near Wilmington is the well-regarded **North Shore Country Club**. Also of note is **Bald Head Island**, the southernmost point of North Carolina, served by a private passenger ferry. Bald Head has some 14 miles of nearly untouched beach, a seaside forest, and a superb, difficult course that uses the ocean as a backdrop and more than a dozen marshes and creeks as punishment for letting your mind wander.

Oyster Bay features an island green built from oyster shells. The **Marsh Harbour Golf Links** sits on the border between North Carolina and South Carolina, almost floating above marshes and wetlands.

At **Sandpiper Bay**, the course features marshes, numerous lakes, alligators, sandpipers, and the occasional eagle of the bird variety.

Joint members of the Econoguide Best and Econoguide Deals lists are Bryan Park, Keith Hills, Linville, and Oak Hollow.

A great collection of courses also lies along and nearby the spectacular Blue Ridge Parkway that cuts through the Appalachian Mountains in the western portion of the state. The road itself dates back to a rough passage cut by Daniel Boone; in 1934 nearly 500 miles of paved road was developed as a link between two national parks, the Great Smoky Mountains in North Carolina and Shenandoah in Virginia. Courses along the "golfway" are located in and near Asheville, Waynesville, Morganton, and up to Roanoke in Virginia.

The off-peak season for courses in North Carolina is generally mid-November through mid-March and June through August; peak season runs from mid-March through May, and mid-September through mid-November.

At the Pinehurst Resort and Country Club, peak prices are in effect from early March through early June and again from early September to mid-November. Midseason summer rates run from early June to early September. Off-season rates are in effect from late November through early March. Luxury golfing packages, including breakfast and dinner and daily golf, range from a low of about $270 per person to a high of about $360 per person.

Econoguide Leader Board: Best Public Courses in North Carolina

◎◎◎◎   Bald Head Island Club
◎◎◎◎   Bryan Park and Golf Club (Champions)
◎◎◎   Duke University Golf Club
◎◎◎◎   Keith Hills Country Club
◎◎◎◎   Linville Golf Course
◎◎◎   Marsh Harbour Golf Links
◎◎◎◎   North Shore Country Club
◎◎◎   Oak Hollow Golf Course
◎◎◎   Oyster Bay Golf Links
◎◎◎◎   Pine Needles Golf Club
◎◎◎◎   Pinehurst Plantation Golf Club

◎◎◎◎   Pinehurst Resort and Country Club (No. 2, No. 7, No. 8)
◎◎◎   The Pit Golf Links
◎◎◎   Porters Neck Country Club
◎◎◎   Sandpiper Bay Golf and Country Club
◎◎◎◎   Talamore Resort
◎◎◎◎   Tanglewood Park Golf Courses (Championship)

Econoguide Leader Board: Best Deals in North Carolina

$$/◎◎◎   Boone Golf Club
$$/◎◎◎◎   Bryan Park and Golf Club (Champions, Players)
$/◎◎◎   Carolina Lakes Golf Club
$$/◎◎◎   Cleghorn Plantation Golf and Country Club
$$/◎◎◎   Devil's Ridge Golf Club
$$/◎◎◎   Etowah Valley Country Club (South, West, North)
$/◎◎◎   Jamestown Park Golf Club
$$/◎◎◎   Jefferson Landing Club
$$/◎◎◎◎   Keith Hills Country Club
$$/◎◎◎   Lane Tree Golf Course
$$/◎◎◎◎   Linville Golf Course
$$/◎◎◎   Maggie Valley Resort Golf Club
$$/◎◎◎   Mount Mitchell Golf Club
$$/◎◎◎   The Neuse Golf Club
$/◎◎◎   Oak Hollow Golf Course
$/◎◎◎   River Bend Golf Club
$$/◎◎◎   Stoney Creek Golf Club
$$/◎◎◎   Woodbridge Golf Links

North Carolina Golf Guide

Asheville Area

R	**Etowah Valley Country Club**	Greens:	$$ L
	Brickyard Rd., Etowah. (704) 891-7141	Carts:	$
◎◎◎	*South/West/North*	Rating:	73.3/73.1/72.4
DEAL	27 holes. Par 72/73/73. Yards: 7,108/7,005/6,911	Slope:	125/125/125
	Year-round. High: Apr.–Oct.		
R	**Fairfield Mountains**	Greens:	$$$ L
	Blvd. of the Mountains, Lake Lure. (704) 625-2888	Carts:	Incl.
◎◎◎	*Apple Valley Golf Club*	Rating:	72.6/66.3
	18 holes. Par 72/72. Yards: 6,726/4,661	Slope:	138/114
	Year-round. High: Apr.–Oct.		
◎◎	*Bald Mountain Golf Club*	Greens:	$$ L
	18 holes. Par 72/72. Yards: 6,575/4,808	Carts:	Incl.
		Rating:	70.9/66.9
		Slope:	127/118
R	**Foxfire Resort and Country Club**	Greens:	$$–$$$$ L R J
	Jackson Springs. (910) 295-4563	Carts:	Incl.
◎◎	*East Course*	Rating:	6,851/5,256
	18 holes. Par 72/72. Yards: 6,851/5,256	Slope:	131/119
	Year-round. High: Mar.–June, Sept.		
◎◎◎	*West Course*	Rating:	72.4/70.3
	18 holes. Par 72/72. Yards: 6,742/5,273	Slope:	129/115
SP	**Glen Cannon Country Club**	Greens:	$$–$$$ L T
◎◎◎	Wilson Rd., Brevard. (704) 884-9160	Carts:	Incl.

North Carolina Golf Guide

Asheville Area

	18 holes. Par 72/72. Yards: 6,548/5,172	Rating:	71.7/69.1
	Year-round. High: Apr.–Oct.	Slope:	124/117

R	**The Grove Park Inn Resort**	Greens:	$$–$$$ L T
☺☺	Macon Ave., Asheville. (704) 252-2711	Carts:	Inquire
	18 holes. Par 72/72. Yards: 6,520/4,687	Rating:	71.7/68.6
	Year-round. High: Apr.–Nov.	Slope:	125/111

R	**High Hampton Inn and Country Club**	Greens:	$–$$ L R T
☺☺	Hwy. 107 S., Cashiers. (704) 743-2450	Carts:	$
	18 holes. Par 72/72. Yards: 6,012	Rating:	68.5
	Year-round. High: June–Aug.	Slope:	120

R	**Holly Forest Country Club**	Greens:	$$$ L
☺☺☺	Hwy. 64 W., Sapphire. (704) 743-1174	Carts:	Incl.
	18 holes. Par 70/70. Yards: 6,147/5,690	Rating:	NA
	Year-round. High: May–Sept.	Slope:	119/118

SP	**Hound Ears Club**	Greens:	$$–$$$$
☺☺☺	Blowing Rock. (704) 963-5831	Carts:	$
	18 holes. Par 72/73. Yards: 6,165/4,959	Rating:	73.3/70.1
	Apr.–Nov. High: June–Sept.	Slope:	133/128

R	**Linville Golf Course**	Greens:	$$
☺☺☺☺	Linville Ave., Linville. (704) 733-4363	Carts:	$
DEAL	18 holes. Par 72/72. Yards: 6,780/5,086	Rating:	72.7/69.3
STATE	Year-round. High: May–Oct.	Slope:	135/119

R	**Maggie Valley Resort Golf Club**	Greens:	$–$$ W L T J
☺☺☺	Maggie Valley. (704) 926-6013	Carts:	$
DEAL	18 holes. Par 72/73. Yards: 6,336/5,195	Rating:	69.8/69.4
	Year-round. High: Mar.–Nov.	Slope:	121/117

P	**Mount Mitchell Golf Club**	Greens:	$$–$$ W L R
☺☺☺	Hwy. 80 S., Burnsville. (704) 675-5454	Carts:	Incl.
DEAL	18 holes. Par 72/72. Yards: 6,475/5,455	Rating:	70.0/69.5
	Year-round. High: May–Oct.	Slope:	121/117

SP	**Reems Creek Golf Club**	Greens:	$$–$$$ W L R
☺☺☺	Pink Fox Cove Rd., Weaverville. (704) 645-4393	Carts:	Incl.
	18 holes. Par 72/72. Yards: 6,477/4,605	Rating:	71.6/66.9
	Year-round. High: Mar.–Oct.	Slope:	133/114

SP	**Springdale Country Club**	Greens:	$$ T
☺☺☺	Rte. 2, Canton. (704) 235-8451	Carts:	Incl.
	18 holes. Par 72/72. Yards: 6,812/5,421	Rating:	NA
	Year-round. High: Apr.–May	Slope:	126/113

R	**Waynesville Country Club Inn**	Greens:	$–$$ L R
☺☺	Ninevah Rd., Waynesville. (704) 452-4617	Carts:	$
	27 holes. Par 70/70/70. Yards: 5,798/5,803/5,943	Rating:	66.4/66.4/66.8
	Year-round. High: Mar.–Oct.	Slope:	103/105/104

Charlotte Area

P	**Charlotte Golf Links**	Greens:	$–$$ L T S J
☺☺	Providence Rd., Charlotte. (704)0 846-7990	Carts:	$
	18 holes. Par 71/72. Yards: 6,700/5,279	Rating:	71.5/70.3
	Year-round. High: Apr.–Nov.	Slope:	121/117

P	**Highland Creek Golf Club**	Greens:	$$$ W
☺☺☺	Highland Creek Pkwy., Charlotte. (704) 875-9000	Carts:	Incl.
	18 holes. Par 72/72. Yards: 7,008/5,005	Rating:	73.3/70.1
	Year-round. High: Apr.–Sept.	Slope:	133/128

P	**Monroe Country Club**	Greens:	$ W
☺☺	Hwy. 601 S., Monroe. (704) 282-4661	Carts:	$

North Carolina Golf Guide

Charlotte Area

	18 holes. Par 72/72. Yards: 6,759/4,964	Rating:	71.8/68.6
	Year-round. High: May–Aug.	Slope:	118/117

P
☺☺☺
DEAL

River Bend Golf Club
Longwood Dr., Shelby. (704) 482-4286
18 holes. Par 72/72. Yards: 6,610/4,920
Year-round. High: May–Oct.

Greens: $ S J
Carts: $
Rating: 71.0/66.0
Slope: 130/102

P
☺☺☺
DEAL

Woodbridge Golf Links
Kings Mountain. (704) 482-0353
18 holes. Par 72/72. Yards: 6,743/5.151
Year-round. High: Apr.–Oct.

Greens: $$
Carts: Incl.
Rating: 71.9/69.3
Slope: 131/116

Winston-Salem Area

P
☺☺☺
DEAL

Boone Golf Club
Boone. (704) 264-8760
18 holes. Par 71/75. Yards: 6,401/5,172
Apr.–Nov. High: June–Aug.

Greens: $$ W L T
Carts: $
Rating: 70.1/69.1
Slope: 120/113

P
☺☺☺
DEAL

Jefferson Landing Club
Jefferson. (910) 246-5555
18 holes. Par 72/72. Yards: 7,111/4,960
Mar.–Nov. High: June–Sept.

Greens: $$ W L R T
Carts: Incl.
Rating: NA
Slope: 121/103

P
☺☺

Mountain Aire Golf Club
W. Jefferson. (910) 877-4716
18 holes. Par 71/71. Yards: 6,107/4,143
Year-round. High: June–Aug.

Greens: $ W L T J
Carts: $
Rating: 71.0/66.0
Slope: 113/113

P

☺☺☺☺
BEST

Tanglewood Park Golf Courses
Hwy. 158 W., Clemmons. (910) 766-5082
Championship Course
18 holes. Par 72/74. Yards: 7,022/5,119
Year-round. High: Spring/Fall

Greens: $–$$$ W L R T S J
Carts: $
Rating: 74.5/70.9
Slope: 140/130

☺☺☺

Reynolds Course
18 holes. Par 72/72. Yards: 6,469/5,432

Rating: 71.0/70.2
Slope: 125/120

Greensboro Area

P

☺☺☺☺
DEAL
STATE

Bryan Park and Golf Club
Bryan Park Rd., Brown Summit. (910) 375-2200
Champions Course
18 holes. Par 72/72. Yards: 7,135/5,395
Year-round. High: Apr.–Sept.

Greens: $–$$ L T S J
Carts: $
Rating: 74.0/72.0
Slope: 130/123

☺☺☺
DEAL

Players Course
18 holes. Par 72/72. Yards: 7,076/5,260

Rating: 73.0/70.5
Slope: 128/120

P
☺☺☺
DEAL

Cleghorn Plantation Golf and Country Club
Rutherfordton. (704) 286-9117
18 holes. Par 72/73. Yards: 6,903/4,751
Year-round. High: Apr.–Sept.

Greens: $$ W
Carts: Incl.
Rating: 74.6/68.1
Slope: 134/111

P
☺☺☺
DEAL

Jamestown Park Golf Club
E. Fork Rd., Jamestown. (910) 584-7871
18 holes. Par 72/72. Yards: 6,665/5,298
Year-round. High: May–Sept.

Greens: $ W S J
Carts: $
Rating: 72.6/70.7
Slope: 126/118

P
☺☺☺
BEST
DEAL

Oak Hollow Golf Course
Oakview Rd., High Point. (910) 883-3260
18 holes. Par 72/72. Yards: 6,483/4,796
Year-round. High: Apr.–Aug.

Greens: $ S J
Carts: $
Rating: 71.6/67.4
Slope: 124/114

P
☺☺☺

Stoney Creek Golf Club
E. Stoney Creek. (910) 449-5688

Greens: $–$$ W L T S J
Carts: $

North Carolina Golf Guide

Greensboro Area

DEAL	18 holes. Par 72/72. Yards: 7,063/4,737	Rating:	74.1/69.8
	Year-round. High: Spring/Fall	Slope:	144/123

Raleigh-Durham Area

SP	**Devil's Ridge Golf Club**	Greens:	$$	W L T S J
☺☺☺	Linksland Dr., Holly Springs. (919) 557-6100	Carts:	$	
DEAL	18 holes. Par 72/72. Yards: 7,002/5,244	Rating:	73.7/69.8	
	Year-round. High: June–Aug.	Slope:	138/121	

R	**Duke University Golf Club**	Greens:	$$–$$$	W L R T S J
☺☺☺	Rte. 741, Durham. (919) 681-2288	Carts:	$	
STATE	18 holes. Par 72/73. Yards: 7,045/5,505	Rating:	73.9/71.2	
	Year-round. High: Mar.–Sept.	Slope:	137/124	

SP	**Keith Hills Country Club**	Greens:	$–$$	J
☺☺☺☺	Blues Creek. (910) 893-5051	Carts:	Inquire	
DEAL	18 holes. Par 72/72. Yards: 6,660/5,225	Rating:	71.6/69.6	
STATE	Year-round. High: Mar.–June	Slope:	129/120	

SP	**Lane Tree Golf Course**	Greens:	$–$$	W L R
☺☺☺	Salem Church Rd., Goldsboro. (919) 734-1245	Carts:	$	
DEAL	18 holes. Par 72/72. Yards: 6,962/5,168	Rating:	72.4/68.9	
	Year-round. High: Apr.–Sept.	Slope:	131/120	

SP	**The Neuse Golf Club**	Greens:	$–$$	W L T S J
☺☺☺	Birkdale Dr., Clayton. (919) 550-0550	Carts:	$	
DEAL	18 holes. Par 72/72. Yards: 7,010/5,478	Rating:	73.5/72.2	
	Year-round. High: Apr.–Oct.	Slope:	136/126	

SP	**Porters Neck Country Club**	Greens:	$$–$$$$	W L R T
☺☺☺	Porters Neck Rd., Wilmington. (910) 686-1177	Carts:	Incl.	
STATE	18 holes. Par 72/72. Yards: 7,209/5,268	Rating:	74.4/70.1	
	Year-round. High: Feb.–May	Slope:	130/115	

SP	**Quail Ridge Golf Course**	Greens:	$$	W L T S J
☺☺	Quail Ridge Dr., Sanford. (919) 776-6623	Carts:	Incl.	
	18 holes. Par 72/72. Yards: 6,875/5,280	Rating:	73.2/70.8	
	Year-round. High: Spring/Fall	Slope:	125/117	

P	**Reedy Creek Golf Club**	Greens:	$–$$	W R T S J
☺☺	Reedy Creek Rd., Four Oaks. (919) 934-7502	Carts:	$	
	18 holes. Par 72/72. Yards: 6,401/5,115	Rating:	70.5/68.5	
	Year-round. High: Apr.–Sept.	Slope:	117/115	

R	**Woodlake Country Club**	Greens:	$$–$$$$	W L R T
	Vass. (910) 245-4686	Carts:	Incl.	
☺☺☺	*Lake Shore/Cypress Creek*	Rating:	73.4/71.4	
	18 holes. Par 72/72. Yards: 7,012/5,255	Slope:	134/128	
	Year-round. High: Mar.–May			

Fayetteville/Pinehurst Area

P	**Carolina Lakes Golf Club**	Greens:	$	W L R T S J
☺☺☺	Rte. 6, Sanford. (919) 499-5421	Carts:	$	
DEAL	18 holes. Par 70/70. Yards: 6,397/5,010	Rating:	70.7/67.0	
	Year-round. High: Mar.–May	Slope:	117/110	

SP	**The Club at Longleaf**	Greens:	$$–$$$	L R T J
☺☺☺	Midland Rd., Southern Pines. (910) 692-6100	Carts:	Incl.	
	18 holes. Par 71/71. Yards: 6,600/4,719	Rating:	69.7/65.7	
	Year-round. High: Mar.–May, Oct.	Slope:	117/108	

SP	**Country Club of Whispering Pines**	Greens:	$$$	L R J
	Whispering Pines. (910) 949-2311	Carts:	$	
☺☺☺	*East Course*	Rating:	73.9/72.0	
	18 holes. Par 72/72. Yards: 7,138/5,542	Slope:	125/123	
	Year-round. High: Mar.–Oct.			

North Carolina Golf Guide

Fayetteville/Pinehurst Area

☺☺☺   *West Course*
18 holes. Par 71/71. Yards: 6,363/5,135

Rating: 70.3/69.8
Slope: 128/121

P
☺☺   **Cypress Lakes Golf Course**
Rte. 1, Hope Mills. (910) 483-0359
18 holes. Par 72/74. Yards: 7,240/5,685
Year-round. High: Spring/Fall

Greens: $ W
Carts: Inquire
Rating: 74.2/72.1
Slope: 126/116

SP
☺☺☺   **Deercroft Golf and Country Club**
Deercroft Dr., Wagram. (910) 369-3107
18 holes. Par 72/72. Yards: 6,745/5,443
Year-round. High: Spring/Fall

Greens: $$$–$$$$ W L T S J
Carts: Incl.
Rating: 72.2/67.0
Slope: 125/113

SP
☺☺☺   **Gates Four Country Club**
Irongate Dr., Fayetteville. (910) 425-2176
18 holes. Par 72/72. Yards: 6,865/5,368
Year-round. High: Spring/Fall

Greens: $–$$ W L R
Carts: $
Rating: 73.4/70.5
Slope: 122/115

P
☺☺   **Hyland Hills Golf Club**
U.S. 1 N., Southern Pines. (910) 692-3752
18 holes. Par 72/72. Yards: 6,726/4,677
Year-round. High: Mar.–May, Oct.

Greens: $–$$
Carts: $
Rating: 70.4/66.8
Slope: 124/109

P
☺☺☺   **Legacy Golf Links**
U.S. 15, Aberdeen. (910) 944-8825
18 holes. Par 72/72. Yards: 6,989/4,948
Year-round. High: Spring/Fall

Greens: $$–$$$$ L R J
Carts: Incl.
Rating: 73.2/68.3
Slope: 132/120

R
☺☺☺   **Mid Pines Golf Club**
Midland Rd., Southern Pines. (910) 692-9362
18 holes. Par 72/75. Yards: 6,515/5,592
Year-round.

Greens: $$–$$$$ L R T
Carts: $
Rating: 71.4/72.3
Slope: 127/128

R
☺☺☺☺
STATE   **Pine Needles Golf Club**
Midland Rd., Southern Pines. (910) 692-8611
18 holes. Par 71/71. Yards: 6,708/5,039
Year-round. High: Spring/Fall

Greens: $$$$ L R
Carts: $
Rating: 72.2/68.4
Slope: 131/118

SP
☺☺☺☺
STATE   **Pinehurst Plantation Golf Club**
Midland Rd., Pinehurst. (910) 695-3193
18 holes. Par 72/72. Yards: 7,135/5,046
Year-round. High: Apr.–May, Oct.

Greens: $$$–$$$$$$
Carts: Incl.
Rating: 74.5/68.8
Slope: 140/125

R   **Pinehurst Resort and Country Club**
Carolina Vista St., Pinehurst. (910) 295-8141
☺☺☺   *Pinehurst No. 1*
18 holes. Par 70/73. Yards: 5,780/5,329
Year-round. High: Spring/Fall

Greens: $$$–$$$$ L T
Carts: $$
Rating: 67.4/70.1
Slope: 114/117

☺☺☺☺
BEST   *Pinehurst No. 2*
18 holes. Par 72/74. Yards: 7,020/5,966

Greens: $$$$$$+   L T
Carts: $$
Rating: 74.1/74.2
Slope: 131/135

☺☺☺   *Pinehurst No. 3*
18 holes. Par 72/72. Yards: 6,827/5,658

Greens: $$–$$$$ L T
Carts: $$
Rating: 67.2/71.1
Slope: 112/114

☺☺☺   *Pinehurst No. 4*
18 holes. Par 72/73. Yards: 6,919/5,696

Greens: $$–$$$$ L T
Carts: $$
Rating: 73.3/74.7
Slope: 126/119

☺☺☺   *Pinehurst No. 5*
18 holes. Par 72/73. Yards: 6,827/5,658

Greens: $$–$$$$ L T
Carts: $$

North Carolina Golf Guide

Fayetteville/Pinehurst Area

		Rating: 73.4/74.7
		Slope: 130/131

☺☺☺	*Pinehurst No. 6* 18 holes. Par 72/72. Yards: 7,157/5,430	Greens: $$–$$$$ L T Carts: $$ Rating: 75.6/71.2 Slope: 139/125
☺☺☺☺ BEST	*Pinehurst No. 7* 18 holes. Par 72/72. Yards: 7,114/4,924	Greens: $$$$$–$$$$$$ L T Carts: $$ Rating: 75.6/69.7 Slope: 145/124
☺☺☺☺ BEST	*Pinehurst No. 8: Centennial Course* 18 holes. Par 72/72. Yards: 7,092/5,805	Greens: Resort packages only Carts: Inquire Rating: NA Slope: NA
P BEST ☺☺☺	**The Pit Golf Links** Hwy. 5, Pinehurst. (910) 944-1600 18 holes. Par 72/72. Yards: 6,600/4,759 Year-round. High: Mar., May–Oct.	Greens: $$–$$$$ L T J Carts: $ Rating: 72.3/68.4 Slope: 139/121
SP ☺☺☺	**Rock Barn Club of Golf** Conover. (704) 459-9279 18 holes. Par 72/72. Yards: 6,778/4,812 Year-round. High: Apr.–Oct.	Greens: $$ W S Carts: $ Rating: 72.2/67.7 Slope: 132/117
SP ☺☺☺	**Seven Lakes Country Club** West End. (910) 673-1092 18 holes. Par 72/73. Yards: 6,927/5,192 Year-round. High: Spring/Fall	Greens: $$–$$$ L J Carts: $ Rating: 74.4/70.6 Slope: 133/123
SP ☺☺☺	**Southern Pines Golf Course** Southern Pines. (910) 692-6551 18 holes. Par 71/74. Yards: 6,500/5,400 Year-round. High: Mar.–Oct.	Greens: $$–$$$ W L R T Carts: $ Rating: 70.3/70.9 Slope: 124/118
SP ☺☺	**Star Hill Golf and Country Club** Cape Carteret. (919) 393-8111 *Sands/Pines/Lakes* 27 holes. Par 72/71/71. Yards: 6,301/6,448/6,361 Year-round. High: June–Aug.	Greens: $–$$ L R T Carts: $ Rating: 70.5/70.2/70.9 Slope: 115/113/118
P ☺☺☺☺ STATE	**Talamore Resort** Midland Rd., Southern Pines. (910) 692-5884 18 holes. Par 72/72. Yards: 7,020/4,945 Year-round. High: Spring/Fall	Greens: $$$–$$$$ L T Carts: Incl. Rating: 72.9/69.0 Slope: 142/125
SP ☺☺	**Whispering Woods Golf Club** Sandpiper Dr., Whispering Pines. (910) 949-4653 18 holes. Par 72/72. Yards: 6,334/4,924 Year-round. High: Spring/Fall	Greens: $$–$$$ L T S J Carts: $ Rating: 70.5/68.7 Slope: 122/122

North Carolina Shore

R ☺☺☺☺ STATE	**Bald Head Island Club** Bald Head Island. (910) 457-7310 18 holes. Par 72/72. Yards: 6,855/4,810 Year-round. High: Mar.–Nov.	Greens: $$–$$$ L R J Carts: $ Rating: 74.2/69.5 Slope: 143/121
SP ☺☺	**Brandywine Bay Golf & Country Club** Hwy. 70 W., Morehead City. (919) 247-2541 18 holes. Par 71/71. Yards: 6,609/5,191 Year-round. High: Mar.–Oct.	Greens: $–$$ L T Carts: $ Rating: 72.2/68.5 Slope: 119/119

North Carolina Golf Guide

North Carolina Shore

R ◎◎	**Brick Landing Plantation** Goose Creek Rd., Ocean Isle Beach. (910) 754-5545 18 holes. Par 72/71. Yards: 6,752/4,707 Year-round. High: Mar.–Apr., Oct.	Greens: Carts: Rating: Slope:	$$–$$$$ T J Incl. 72.1/67.0 141/116
R ◎◎◎	**Brunswick Plantation Golf Links** Hwy. 17 N., Calabash. (910) 287-7888 18 holes. Par 72/72. Yards: 6,779/5,210 Year-round. High: Mar.–Apr., Oct.	Greens: Carts: Rating: Slope:	$$–$$$ Incl. 72.7/70.4 131/115
SP ◎◎	**Duck Woods Country Club** Dogwood Trail, Kitty Hawk. (919) 261-2609 18 holes. Par 72/72. Yards: 6,650/5,407 Year-round. High: May–Sept.	Greens: Carts: Rating: Slope:	$$–$$$ $ 71.3/70.7 132/127
R ◎◎◎	**Lion's Paw Golf Links** Ocean Ridge Pkwy., Sunset Beach. (910) 287-1717 18 holes. Par 72/72. Yards: 7,003/5,363 Year-round. High: Spring/Fall	Greens: Carts: Rating: Slope:	$$–$$$$ W L R T J $ 74.6/69.1 138/118
P ◎◎◎ BEST	**Marsh Harbour Golf Links** Hwy. 179, Calabash. (910) 579-3161 18 holes. Par 71/71. Yards: 6,690/4,795 Year-round. High: Mar.–Apr., Oct.	Greens: Carts: Rating: Slope:	$$–$$$$ L R $ 72.4/67.7 134/115
R ◎◎◎	**Nags Head Golf Links** S. Seachase Dr., Nags Head. (919) 441-8073 18 holes. Par 72/72. Yards: 6,200/5,800 Year-round. High: June–Aug.	Greens: Carts: Rating: Slope:	$$–$$$$ W L R T S J Incl. 68.8/66.9 130/126
P ◎◎	**Ocean Isle Beach Golf Course** Ocean Isle Beach. (910) 579-2610 18 holes. Par 72/72. Yards: 6,626/5,075 Year-round. High: Mar.–May, Sept.–Nov.	Greens: Carts: Rating: Slope:	$$ T Incl. NA 126/116
P ◎◎◎ BEST	**Oyster Bay Golf Links** Hwy. 179, Sunset Beach. (910) 579-7391 18 holes. Par 71/71. Yards: 6,785/4,825 Year-round. High: Mar.–Apr., Oct.	Greens: Carts: Rating: Slope:	$$–$$$$ L R $ 74.1/67.7 137/117
P ◎◎◎	**The Pearl Golf Links** Pearl Blvd., S.W., Sunset Beach. (910) 579-8132 *East Course* 18 holes. Par 72/72. Yards: 6,749/5,125 Year-round. High: Spring/Fall	Greens: Carts: Rating: Slope:	$$–$$$$ T J Incl. 73.1/73.9 135/129
◎◎◎	*West Course* 18 holes. Par 72/72. Yards: 7,000/5,188	Rating: Slope:	73.2/73.4 132/127
P ◎◎◎ STATE	**Sandpiper Bay Golf and Country Club** Sandpiper Bay Dr., Sunset Beach. (910) 579-9120 18 holes. Par 72/72. Yards: 6,503/4,869 Year-round. High: Spring/Fall	Greens: Carts: Rating: Slope:	$–$$$ W L $ 71.6/68.3 119/113
R ◎◎	**Sea Scape Golf Course** Eckner St., Kitty Hawk. (919) 261-2158 18 holes. Par 72/72. Yards: 6,409/5,536 Year-round. High: May–Oct.	Greens: Carts: Rating: Slope:	$$–$$$$ L R T J Incl. 70.4/70.9 120/115
R ◎◎◎	**Sea Trail Plantation and Golf Links** Sunset Beach. (910) 287-1122 *Willard Byrd Course* 18 holes. Par 72/72. Yards: 6,750/4,697 Year-round. High: Mar.–Apr., Oct.	Greens: Carts: Rating: Slope:	$–$$$ R J $ 72.1/69.1 128/121

North Carolina Golf Guide

North Carolina Shore

☺☺☺	*Dan Maples Course* 18 holes. Par 72/72. Yards: 6,751/5,090	Rating: Slope:	71.7/68.5 121/108
☺☺☺	*Rees Jones Course* 18 holes. Par 72/72. Yards: 6,761/4,912	Rating: Slope:	72.4/68.5 132/115

Wilmington Area

SP ☺☺	**Beau Rivage Plantation Country Club** Carolina Beach Rd., Wilmington. (910) 392-9022 18 holes. Par 72/72. Yards: 6,709/4,612 Year-round. High: Mar.–Sept.	Greens: Carts: Rating: Slope:	$$–$$$ Incl. 72.5/69.0 136/114	W L R T S J
P ☺☺	**Belvedere Plantation Golf and Country Club** Hampstead. (910) 270-2703 18 holes. Par 71/72. Yards: 6,401/4,992 Year-round. High: Mar.–May	Greens: Carts: Rating: Slope:	$$–$$$ Incl. 128/113 71.2/68.5	L R
SP ☺☺	**Brierwood Golf Club** Hwy. 179, Shallotte. (910) 754-4550 18 holes. Par 72/72. Yards: 6,607/4,810 Year-round. High: Apr.–Oct.	Greens: Carts: Rating: Slope:	$–$$ Incl. 6,607/4,812 129/114	W L T S
SP ☺☺	**Cape Golf and Racquet Club** The Cape Blvd., Wilmington. (910) 799-3110 18 holes. Par 72/72. Yards: 6,790/4,948 Year-round. High: Apr.	Greens: Carts: Rating: Slope:	$–$$$ Incl. 73.1/69.3 133/118	W L T S
SP ☺☺	**Echo Farms Golf and Country Club** Echo Farms Blvd., Wilmington. (910) 791-9318 18 holes. Par 72/72. Yards: 7,014/5,142 Year-round. High: Apr.–Oct.	Greens: Carts: Rating: Slope:	$$ Incl. 74.2/70.7 132/121	L R
SP ☺☺☺	**The Emerald Golf Club** New Bern. (919) 633-4440 18 holes. Par 72/72. Yards: 6,924/5,287 Year-round. High: Mar.–May, Oct.	Greens: Carts: Rating: Slope:	$$–$$$ Incl. 74.0/71.3 125/119	
SP ☺☺	**Fairfield Harbour Country Club** Pelican Dr., New Bern. (919) 514-0050 *Harbour Pointe Course* 18 holes. Par 72/72. Yards: 6,650/5,100 Year-round. High: Spring/Fall	Greens: Carts: Rating: Slope:	$$ $ 71.8/68.6 125/111	L T
SP ☺☺☺	**The Gauntlet at St. James Plantation** Hwy. 211, Southport. (910) 253-3008 18 holes. Par 72/72. Yards: 7,022/5,048 Year-round. High: Mar.–May	Greens: Carts: Rating: Slope:	$$$–$$$$ Incl. 75.0/69.7 142/119	L T S
SP ☺☺☺	**Lockwood Golf Links** Supply. (910) 842-5666 18 holes. Par 72/72. Yards: 6,836/5,524 Year-round. High: Spring/Fall	Greens: Carts: Rating: Slope:	$$–$$$$ Incl. 73.5/70.0 135/121	L R J
SP ☺	**Magnolia Country Club** Magnolia Lane, Magnolia. (910) 289-2126 18 holes. Par 71/71. Yards: 6,400/4,600 Year-round. High: June–Aug.	Greens: Carts: Rating: Slope:	$ $ 69.8/68.3 116/109	W R T S J
SP ☺☺☺☺ STATE	**North Shore Country Club** N. Shore Dr., Sneads Ferry. (910) 327-2410 18 holes. Par 72/72. Yards: 6,866/5,039 Year-round. High: Mar.–Nov.	Greens: Carts: Rating: Slope:	$$–$$$ Incl. 72.8/68.7 134/122	W L T J
P ☺☺	**Oak Island Golf and Country Club** Caswell Beach Rd., Caswell Beach. (910) 278-5275	Greens: Carts:	$$ Incl.	W L

North Carolina Golf Guide

Wilmington Area

	18 holes. Par 72/72. Yards: 6,608/5,437	Rating:	NA
	Year-round. High: June–Oct.	Slope:	128

SP	**Olde Point Country Club**	Greens:	$$–$$$	W L
○○○	Hwy. 17 N., Hampstead. (910) 270-2403	Carts:	Incl.	
	18 holes. Par 72/72. Yards: 6,913/5,133	Rating:	72.5/69.0	
	Year-round. High: Mar.–May	Slope:	136/115	

Oklahoma

The cream of the public golf course crop in Oklahoma is the **Karsten Creek Golf Course** in Stillwater, about 50 miles northeast of Oklahoma City. Also a worthy course is **Forest Ridge** in Broken Arrow, southeast of Tulsa.

Beyond these, there is an unusually large number of Econoguide Deals in Oklahoma, good deals for quality golf.

Golf courses in Oklahoma generally are open year-round. Expect peak rates from late spring through early fall.

Econoguide Leader Board: Best Public Courses in Oklahoma

○○○○   Forest Ridge Golf Club
○○○○   Karsten Creek Golf Course

Econoguide Leader Board: Best Deals in Oklahoma

$$/○○○	Bailey Golf Ranch
$/○○○	Boiling Springs Golf Club
$/○○○	Cedar Valley Golf Club (Augusta)
$/○○○	Cimarron National Golf Club (Cimarron)
$$/○○○	Coffee Creek Golf Course
$/○○○	Earlywine Park Golf Course
$$/○○○	Falconhead Ranch and Country Club
$/○○○	Heritage Hills Golf Course
$/○○○	John Conrad Regional Golf Course
$/○○○	Kickingbird Golf Course
$/○○○	Lake Hefner Golf Club (North)
$/○○○	Lakeview Golf Course
$/○○○	Lew Wentz Memorial Golf Course
$/○○○	Page Belcher Golf Course (Old Page, Stone Creek)
$$/○○○	Silverhorn Golf Club
$/○○○	Sunset Hills Golf Course

Oklahoma Golf Guide

Western Oklahoma

P	**Boiling Springs Golf Club**	Greens:	$	W L T S J
○○○	Woodward. (405) 256-1206	Carts:	$	
DEAL	18 holes. Par 71/75. Yards: 6,454/4,944	Rating:	69.6/68.6	
	Year-round. High: Apr.–Oct.	Slope:	117/117	

R	**Quartz Mountain Golf Course**	Greens:	$	R T S J
○○	Lone Wolf. (405) 563-2520	Carts:	$	

Oklahoma Golf Guide

Western Oklahoma

18 holes. Par 71/71. Yards: 6,595/5,706	Rating:	NA
Year-round. High: May–Aug.	Slope:	NA

Oklahoma City Area

P	**Cedar Valley Golf Club**	Greens:	$	W
	Guthrie. (405) 282-4800	Carts:	$	
☺☺☺	*Augusta Course*	Rating:	70.3/69.1	
DEAL	18 holes. Par 70/72. Yards: 6,602/5,170	Slope:	108/117	
	Year-round. High: May–Aug.			

☺☺	*International Course*	Rating:	71.1/68.4
	18 holes. Par 70/72. Yards: 6,520/4,955	Slope:	112/115

P	**Cimarron National Golf Club**	Greens:	$	W L S
	Duffy's Way, Guthrie. (405) 282-7888	Carts:	$	
☺☺	*Aqua Canyon Course*	Rating:	69.6/66.4	
	18 holes. Par 70/71. Yards: 6,515/5,439	Slope:	114/110	
	Year-round. High: May–Sept.			

☺☺☺	*Cimarron Course*	Rating:	68.1/66.1
DEAL	18 holes. Par 70/70. Yards: 6,653/5,559	Slope:	120/113

P	**Coffee Creek Golf Course**	Greens:	$–$$	W T S J
☺☺☺	N. Kelly, Edmond. (405) 340-4653	Carts:	$	
DEAL	18 holes. Par 70/70. Yards: 6,700/5,559	Rating:	71.5/70.5	
	Year-round. High: May–Sept.	Slope:	129/122	

P	**Earlywine Park Golf Course**	Greens:	$	W L T S J
	S. Portland, Oklahoma City. (405) 691-1727	Carts:	$	
☺☺☺	*South Course*	Rating:	69.5/71.6	
DEAL	18 holes. Par 71/71. Yards: 6,728/5,388	Slope:	107/117	
	Year-round. High: Mar.–Nov.			

P	**Fire Lake Golf Course**	Greens:	$	W T S J
☺☺	S. Gordon Cooper, Shawnee. (405) 275-4471	Carts:	$	
	18 holes. Par 70/71. Yards: 6,335/4,992	Rating:	69.6/NA	
	Year-round. High: May–July	Slope:	121/NA	

P	**John Conrad Regional Golf Course**	Greens:	$	T S J
☺☺☺	S. Douglas Blvd., Midwest City. (405) 732-2209	Carts:	$	
DEAL	18 holes. Par 72/74. Yards: 6,854/5,511	Rating:	72.0/70.8	
	Year-round. High: Apr.–Oct.	Slope:	115/119	

SP	**Karsten Creek Golf Course**	Greens:	$$$$$$+	
☺☺☺☺	Stillwater. (405) 743-1658	Carts:	Incl.	
BEST	18 holes. Par 72/72. Yards: 7,095/4,906	Rating:	74.8/70.1	
	Year-round. High: Apr.–Sept.	Slope:	142/127	

P	**Kickingbird Golf Course**	Greens:	$	T S J
☺☺☺	E. Danforth Rd., Edmond. (405) 341-5350	Carts:	$	
DEAL	18 holes. Par 71/72. Yards: 6,816/4,801	Rating:	71.4/68.5	
	Year-round. High: May–Sept.	Slope:	127/117	

P	**Lake Hefner Golf Club**	Greens:	$	T S J
	S. Lake Hefner Dr., Oklahoma City. (405) 843-1565	Carts:	$	
☺☺☺	*North Course*	Rating:	74.2/69.6	
DEAL	18 holes. Par 72/72. Yards: 6,970/5,169	Slope:	128/117	
	Year-round. High: Mar.–Sept.			

☺☺	*South Course*	Rating:	68.9/71.2
	18 holes. Par 70/73. Yards: 6,305/5,393	Slope:	111/115

R	**Lake Texoma Golf Resort**	Greens:	$	W L R T S J
☺☺	Kingston. (405) 564-3333	Carts:	$	
	18 holes. Par 71/74. Yards: 6,145/5,145	Rating:	67.8/68.7	
	Year-round. High: Apr.–Oct.	Slope:	112/108	

Oklahoma Golf Guide

Oklahoma City Area

P	**Lincoln Park Golf Course**	Greens: $	W T S J
	N.E. Grand Blvd., Oklahoma City. (405) 424-1421	Carts: Inquire	
◎◎	*East Course*	Rating: 70.0/66.2	
	18 holes. Par 70/71. Yards: 6,508/5,467	Slope: 120/112	
	Year-round. High: Apr.–Sept.		
◎◎	*West Course*	Rating: 70.7/68.4	
	18 holes. Par 70/71. Yards: 6,508/5,587	Slope: 121/115	
SP	**Silverhorn Golf Club**	Greens: $$	W L T S J
◎◎◎	N. Kelley Ave., Oklahoma City. (405) 752-1181	Carts: $	
DEAL	18 holes. Par 71/71. Yards: 6,800/4,943	Rating: 73.4/71.0	
	Year-round. High: Apr.–Sept.	Slope: 128/113	
P	**University of Oklahoma Golf Course**	Greens: $	T S J
◎◎	Norman. (405) 325-6716	Carts: $	
	18 holes. Par 72/72. Yards: 6,941/5,394	Rating: 72.9/70.7	
	Year-round. High: Apr.–Oct.	Slope: 123/116	
P	**Westwood Park Golf Course**	Greens: $	W T S
◎◎	Westport Dr., Norman. (405) 321-0433	Carts: $	
	18 holes. Par 72/72. Yards: 6,015/5,525	Rating: 67.7/71.0	
	Year-round. High: Apr.–Sept.	Slope: 108/120	

Tulsa Area

P	**Adams Municipal Golf Course**	Greens: $	W T S J
◎◎	E. Tuxedo Blvd., Bartlesville. (918) 337-5313	Carts: $	
	18 holes. Par 72/74. Yards: 6,819/5,655	Rating: 72.0/71.8	
	Year-round. High: Mar.–Oct.	Slope: 119/117	
P	**Bailey Golf Ranch**	Greens: $–$$	W L T S J
◎◎◎	Larkin Bailey Blvd., Owasso. (918) 272-9339	Carts: $	
DEAL	18 holes. Par 72/72. Yards: 6,752/4,898	Rating: 73.1/68.4	
	Year-round. High: Apr.–Oct.	Slope: 132/115	
P	**Forest Ridge Golf Club**	Greens: $$$–$$$$	W L T
◎◎◎◎	E. Kenosha, Broken Arrow. (918) 357-2282	Carts: Incl.	
STATE	18 holes. Par 72/72. Yards: 7,069/5,341	Rating: 74.0/70.5	
	Year-round. High: Mar.–Oct.	Slope: 134/112	
P	**Fountainhead State Park Golf Course**	Greens: $	T S J
◎◎	Checotah. (918) 689-3209	Carts: $	
	18 holes. Par 72/72. Yards: 6,919/4,864	Rating: 71.3/67.3	
	Year-round. High: Mar.–Oct.	Slope: 116/98	
P	**Heritage Hills Golf Course**	Greens: $	W T S J
◎◎◎	Claremore. (918) 341-0055	Carts: $	
DEAL	18 holes. Par 71/72. Yards: 6,760/5,324	Rating: 72.6/71.0	
	Year-round. High: Apr.–Sept.	Slope: 120/NA	
P	**Lafortune Park Golf Club**	Greens: $	T S J
◎◎	S. Yale Ave., Tulsa. (918) 596-8627	Carts: $	
	18 holes. Par 72/73. Yards: 6,970/5,780	Rating: 71.4/68.5	
	Year-round. High: Mar.–Aug.	Slope: 127/117	
P	**Lew Wentz Memorial Golf Course**	Greens: $	W S J
◎◎◎	Cann Dr., Ponca City. (405) 767-0433	Carts: $	
DEAL	18 holes. Par 71/70. Yards: 6,400/5,450	Rating: 70.0/71.8	
	Year-round. High: Apr.–Oct.	Slope: 125/123	
P	**Mohawk Park Golf Club**	Greens: $	T S J
	E. 41st St. N., Tulsa. (918) 425-6871	Carts: $	
◎◎	*Woodbine Course*	Rating: 71.0/73.9	
	18 holes. Par 72/76. Yards: 6,898/6,202	Slope: 115/127	
	Year-round. High: June–July		

Oklahoma Golf Guide

Tulsa Area

☺	*Pecan Valley Course* 18 holes. Par 70/70. Yards: 6,499/5,130	Rating: 71.6/69.6 Slope: 124/119	

P ☺☺☺ DEAL	**Page Belcher Golf Course** S. Union Ave., Tulsa. (918) 446-1529 *Old Page Course* 18 holes. Par 71/71. Yards: 6,826/5,532 Year-round. High: Apr.–Oct.	Greens: $ Carts: $ Rating: 72.0/71.5 Slope: 121/118	W T S J

☺☺☺ DEAL	*Stone Creek Course* 18 holes. Par 71/71. Yards: 6,539/5,144	Rating: 72.3/69.9 Slope: 126/127	

P ☺☺	**Sand Springs Municipal Golf Course** N. McKinley, Sand Springs. (918) 245-7551 18 holes. Par 71/70. Yards: 6,113/4,692 Year-round. High: Apr.–Oct.	Greens: $ Carts: $ Rating: 68.9/68.4 Slope: 115/118	W L T S J

R ☺☺☺	**Shangri-La Golf Resort** Afton. (918) 257-4204 *Blue Course* 18 holes. Par 72/73. Yards: 7,012/5,892 Year-round. High: Apr.–Oct.	Greens: $$$–$$$$ Carts: Incl. Rating: 74.0/74.8 Slope: 132/126	W L R

☺☺☺	*Gold Course* 18 holes. Par 70/71. Yards: 6,800/4,943	Rating: 66.8/66.8 Slope: 123/112	

P ☺☺	**South Lakes Golf Course** S. Elwood, Jenks. (918) 746-3760 18 holes. Par 71/71. Yards: 6,340/5,242 Year-round. High: Apr.–Sept.	Greens: $ Carts: $ Rating: 68.6/70.4 Slope: 113/116	T S J

SP ☺☺	**Spunky Creek Country Club** Catoosa. (918) 266-2207 18 holes. Par 71/74. Yards: 6,732/5,748 Year-round. High: Mar.–Oct.	Greens: $ Carts: $ Rating: 71.5/72.9 Slope: 124/127	W L T S J

SP ☺☺	**White Hawk Golf Club** S. York Ave., Bixby. (918) 366-4653 18 holes. Par 72/72. Yards: 6,982/5,148 Year-round. High: May–Oct.	Greens: $$ Carts: $ Rating: 74.1/NA Slope: 134/NA	W L T S J

Southern Oklahoma

R ☺☺	**Cedar Creek Golf Course** Broken Bow. (405) 494-6456 18 holes. Par 72/72. Yards: 6,724/5,762 Year-round. High: Apr.–Oct.	Greens: $ Carts: $ Rating: 72.1/NA Slope: 132/NA	W L R T S J

SP ☺☺☺ DEAL	**Falconhead Ranch and Country Club** Burneyville. (405) 276-9284 18 holes. Par 72/71. Yards: 6,400/5,280 Year-round. High: Apr.–Oct.	Greens: $–$$ Carts: $ Rating: 69.9/70.3 Slope: 118/120	S

P ☺☺☺ DEAL	**Lakeview Golf Course** N. Commerce, Ardmore. (405) 223-4260 18 holes. Par 71/72. Yards: 6,881/5,032 Year-round. High: Apr.–Sept.	Greens: $ Carts: $ Rating: 71.2/67.5 Slope: 114/113	W T S J

P ☺☺☺ DEAL	**Sunset Hills Golf Course** Guymon. (405) 338-7404 18 holes. Par 71/74. Yards: 6,732/5,780 Year-round. High: June–Aug.	Greens: $ Carts: $ Rating: 67.5/68.0 Slope: 108/112	T

South Carolina

The Palmetto State has a collection of some of the best oceanside courses anywhere.

On and nearby Hilton Head Island, a large barrier island at the southern end of the state's coastline, are three of the best of the best. The breathtaking **Harbour Town** is on the island. So too is the Arthur Hills Course at **Palmetto Hall Plantation**, a superb melding of woods and water, located near its corporate cousin, the renowned Palmetto Dunes Resort.

The namesake **Hilton Head National Golf Club** is a traditional course with a varying cast of traps and challenges that will reward the accurate shooter.

Hilton Head, about 42 square miles, has become a year-round destination and home; parts of the island look a bit like the worst of tourist America, with fast-food outlets and miniature golf, while other sections feature near-pristine beaches, marshes, and forests. The island has 12 miles of beaches, more than 20 golf courses, and dozens of superb resorts. The commercial center is Harbour Town.

In nearby Beaufort is the **Callawassie Island Club**, a bit less well known but no less beautiful or challenging.

The **Kiawah Island Resort** near Charleston has three great courses in one location. The Ocean Course there is one of the most spectacular and difficult in the country, stretching nearly three miles along the beach, with views of the ocean at every hole, and 10 holes directly on the water. Some say it is the best course anywhere. The Osprey Point Course is beautiful but not quite as hard; a huge new clubhouse opened late in 1996. The Turtle Point Course is right along the sea, featuring beaches, bikinis, and the occasional alligator. For those times when you aren't holding a club, the posh resort facilities on the island offer tennis, boating, fishing, and much more.

Nearby in Isle of Palms is the **Wild Dunes Resort**, which has one of the nation's best links courses, with the last two holes oceanside and spectacular. The resort there and its courses were all but erased by Hurricane Hugo in 1989, but the restoration has polished this gem even brighter.

At Myrtle Beach is the intriguingly named **The Witch**, a lovely, isolated beach-and-wetlands course that uses bridges and walkways to cross marshlands; your ball will have to take the aerial route to the greens.

Another Myrtle Beach favorite is the Heathland Course at **Legends**, which re-creates a links feeling on its treeless rolling land and has its own version of the famed clubhouse at St. Andrews.

Finally, **Cedar Creek** at Aiken, 25 miles west of Augusta, presents a deceptively difficult inland challenge. Cedar Creek is also South Carolina's only joint member of the Econoguide Best and Econoguide Deals lists.

Most courses in South Carolina are open year-round; look for peak rates from spring through fall. Some courses offer discounts during the hottest months of the summer.

The Kiawah Island Resort offers value-season rates from the end of October through about March 30. Peak season includes Easter and spring-break periods and mid-June through mid-August. In 1996 a basic room with a scenic (not ocean) view sold for $145 at peak rates and $95 in value season; a luxury oceanfront two-bedroom villa on the ocean sold for a high of $255 per night and a low of $135 per night.

Econoguide Leader Board: Best Public Courses in South Carolina

⊙⊙⊙⊙	Caledonia Golf and Fish Club
⊙⊙⊙⊙	Callawassie Island Club (Palmetto, Dogwood, Magnolia)
⊙⊙⊙⊙	Cedar Creek Golf Club
⊙⊙⊙⊙	Harbour Town Golf Links
⊙⊙⊙⊙	Heather Glen Golf Links
⊙⊙⊙⊙	Heritage Club
⊙⊙⊙	Hilton Head National Golf Club
⊙⊙⊙⊙	Kiawah Island Resort (Osprey Point, Ocean, Turtle Point)
⊙⊙⊙⊙	Legends (Heathland)
⊙⊙⊙⊙	The Long Bay Club
⊙⊙⊙⊙	Palmetto Hall Plantation (Arthur Hills)
⊙⊙⊙⊙	Tidewater Golf Club
⊙⊙⊙⊙	Wild Dunes Resort (Links)
⊙⊙⊙⊙	Wild Wing Plantation (Avocet, Wood Stork)
⊙⊙⊙⊙	The Witch

Econoguide Leader Board: Best Deals in South Carolina

$$/⊙⊙⊙⊙	Cedar Creek Golf Club
$$/⊙⊙⊙	Cobb's Glen Country Club
$$/⊙⊙⊙	Crowfield Golf and Country Club
$/⊙⊙⊙	Fox Creek Golf Club
$/⊙⊙⊙	Hickory Knob Golf Club
$$/⊙⊙⊙	Northwoods Golf Club
$/⊙⊙⊙	Persimmon Hill Golf Club
$$/⊙⊙⊙	River Falls Plantation
$/⊙⊙⊙	Stoney Point Golf Club
$$/⊙⊙⊙	Timberlake Plantation Golf Club
$$/⊙⊙⊙	The Wellman Club

South Carolina Golf Guide

Greenville/Anderson Area

SP	**Carolina Springs Country Club**	Greens:	$–$$ W L T S J
	Scuffletown Rd., Fountain Inn. (803) 862-3551	Carts:	$
⊙⊙	*Willows/Pines/Cedar*	Rating:	71.7/72.1/71.2
	27 holes. Par 72/72/72. Yards: 6,676/6,815/6,643	Slope:	125/121/121
	Year-round. High: Apr.–Sept.		

SP	**Cobb's Glen Country Club**	Greens:	$$ W S J
⊙⊙⊙	Cobb's Way, Anderson. (803) 226-7688	Carts:	$
DEAL	18 holes. Par 72/72. Yards: 7,005/5,312	Rating:	72.3/72.0
	Year-round. High: Apr.–Oct.	Slope:	129/121

SP	**Falcon's Lair Golf Course**	Greens:	$$ W L T S J
⊙	Falcon Dr., Walhalla. (803) 638-0000	Carts:	$
	18 holes. Par 72/72. Yards: 6,955/5,238	Rating:	72.1/70.6
	Year-round. High: Mar.–Oct.	Slope:	124/123

South Carolina Golf Guide

Greenville/Anderson Area

P	**The Gauntlet at Laurel Valley**	Greens:	$$–$$$ W L T S J
☺☺	Chinquapin Rd., Tigerville. (803) 895-6758	Carts:	Incl.
	18 holes. Par 72/72. Yards: 6,713/4,545	Rating:	72.1/69.7
	Year-round. High: Mar.–Oct.	Slope:	135/119

P	**River Falls Plantation**	Greens:	$$ L R S J
☺☺☺	Duncan. (803) 433-9192	Carts:	Incl.
DEAL	18 holes. Par 72/72. Yards: 6,734/4,928	Rating:	72.1/68.2
	Year-round. High: Apr.–Aug.	Slope:	127/125

SP	**Saluda Valley Country Club**	Greens:	$ W
☺☺	Beaver Dam Rd., Williamston. (803) 847-7102	Carts:	$
	18 holes. Par 72/72. Yards: 6,430/5,126	Rating:	70.8/69.4
	Year-round. High: Apr.–Sept.	Slope:	119/114

SP	**Stoney Point Golf Club**	Greens:	$ T S J
☺☺☺	Swing About Rd., Greenwood. (803) 942-0900	Carts:	$
DEAL	18 holes. Par 72/72. Yards: 6,760/5,060	Rating:	72.1/70.3
	Year-round. High: Spring/Fall	Slope:	125/120

R	**Verdae Greens Golf Club**	Greens:	$$–$$$ L R S J
☺☺☺	Verdae Blvd., Greenville. (803) 676-1500	Carts:	Incl.
	18 holes. Par 72/72. Yards: 6,773/5,012	Rating:	71.9/68.1
	Year-round. High: Mar.–Nov.	Slope:	126/116

Columbia Area

SP	**Calhoun Country Club**	Greens:	$–$$ W T S J
☺☺	Rte. 3, St. Matthews. (803) 823-2465	Carts:	Incl.
	18 holes. Par 71/71. Yards: 6,339/4,812	Rating:	70.0/66.4
	Year-round. High: Mar.–Apr.	Slope:	119/110

SP	**Coldstream Country Club**	Greens:	$$ W L R T S J
☺☺	Hwy. 60, Irmo. (803) 781-0114	Carts:	Incl.
	18 holes. Par 71/71. Yards: 6,155/5,097	Rating:	70.1/68.7
	Year-round. High: Apr.–Oct.	Slope:	122/NA

P	**Hillcrest Golf Club**	Greens:	$ L
☺☺	Orangeburg. (803) 533-6030	Carts:	$
	18 holes. Par 72/72. Yards: 6,722/5,208	Rating:	70.5/67.8
	Year-round. High: Mar.–May	Slope:	119/107

P	**Lake Marion Golf Club**	Greens:	$$–$$$ J
☺☺☺	Santee. (803) 854-2554	Carts:	Incl.
	18 holes. Par 72/72. Yards: 6,670/5,254	Rating:	71.6/69.8
	Year-round. High: Mar.–May	Slope:	117/112

SP	**Linrick Golf Course**	Greens:	$ S J
☺☺	Campground Rd., Columbia. (803) 754-6331	Carts:	$
	18 holes. Par 73/73. Yards: 6,919/5,243	Rating:	72.2/69.4
	Year-round. High: Mar.–Sept.	Slope:	125/NA

P	**Northwoods Golf Club**	Greens:	$–$$ W L T S J
☺☺☺	Powell Rd., Columbia. (803) 786-9242	Carts:	$
DEAL	18 holes. Par 72/72. Yards: 6,800/5,000	Rating:	71.9/67.8
	Year-round. High: May–Oct.	Slope:	122/116

P	**Oak Hills Golf Club**	Greens:	$$ W L T S J
☺☺	Fairfield Rd., Columbia. (803) 735-9830	Carts:	Incl.
	18 holes. Par 72/72. Yards: 6,894/4,574	Rating:	NA
	Year-round. High: Apr.–Aug.	Slope:	122/110

SP	**Timberlake Plantation Golf Club**	Greens:	$–$$ W L R T S J
☺☺☺	Amicks Ferry Rd., Chapin. (803) 345-9909	Carts:	$
DEAL	18 holes. Par 72/72. Yards: 6,703/5,111	Rating:	73.2/69.8
	Year-round. High: Apr.–May, Aug.–Nov.	Slope:	132/118

South Carolina Golf Guide

Florence Area

P ☺☺☺	**Cheraw State Park Golf Course** Cheraw. (803) 537-2215 18 holes. Par 72/72. Yards: 6,900/5,408 Year-round. High: Mar.–June	Greens: $ Carts: $ Rating: NA Slope: 130/120	W T
SP ☺☺☺ DEAL	**Fox Creek Golf Club** Hwy. 15 S., Lydia. (803) 332-0613 18 holes. Par 72/72. Yards: 6,903/5,271 Year-round. High: Feb.–May, Sept.–Nov.	Greens: $ Carts: $ Rating: 72.3/67.9 Slope: 123/106	W R S J

Myrtle Beach Region

P ☺☺☺	**Arcadian Shores Golf Club** Hilton Rd., Myrtle Beach. (803) 449-5217 18 holes. Par 72/72. Yards: 6,938/5,229 Year-round. High: Mar.–May, Oct.	Greens: $$$–$$$$$ Carts: Incl. Rating: 73.2/69.9 Slope: 136/117	L R
P ☺☺☺	**Arrowhead Golf Club** Burcal Rd., Myrtle Beach. (803) 236-3243 18 holes. Par 72/72. Yards: 6,666/4,812 Year-round. High: Spring/Fall	Greens: $$–$$$$$ Carts: Incl. Rating: 71.1/NA Slope: 130/NA	
P ☺☺	**Azalea Sands Golf Club** Hwy. 17 S., N. Myrtle Beach. (803) 272-6191 18 holes. Par 72/72. Yards: 6,902/5,172 Year-round. High: Spring/Fall	Greens: $$–$$$ Carts: Incl. Rating: 72.5/70.2 Slope: 123/119	L R T
P ☺☺	**Bay Tree Golf Plantation** N. Myrtle Beach. (803) 249-1487 *Gold Course* 18 holes. Par 72/72. Yards: 6,942/5,264 Year-round. High: Mar.–Apr.	Greens: $–$$$ Carts: $ Rating: 72.0/69.7 Slope: 135/117	L
☺☺	*Green Course* 18 holes. Par 72/72. Yards: 7,044/5,362	Rating: 72.5/69.0 Slope: 135/118	
☺☺	*Silver Course* 18 holes. Par 72/72. Yards: 6,871/5,417	Rating: 70.5/69.0 Slope: 131/116	
R ☺☺☺	**Blackmoor Golf Club** Longwood Rd., Murrells Inlet. (803) 650-5555 18 holes. Par 72/72. Yards: 6,614/4,807 Year-round. High: Apr.–Oct.	Greens: $$–$$$$ Carts: $ Rating: 71.1/67.9 Slope: 126/115	L R J
P ☺☺	**Buck Creek Golf Plantation** Bucks Trail, Hwy. 9, Longs. (803) 249-5996 *Meadow/Cypress/Tupelo* 27 holes. Par 72/72/72. Yards: 6,751/6,865/6,726 Year-round. High: Spring/Fall	Greens: $$–$$$$ Carts: $ Rating: 71.1/72.4/71.6 Slope: 126/132/128	L T J
R ☺☺	**Burning Ridge Golf Club** Hwy. 501 W., Conway. (803) 247-0538 *East Course* 18 holes. Par 72/72. Yards: 6,780/4,524 Year-round. High: Feb.–Oct.	Greens: $$$ Carts: Incl. Rating: 72.8/65.4 Slope: 128/111	W L T
☺☺	*West Course* 18 holes. Par 72/72. Yards: 6,714/4,831	Rating: 71.8/67.2 Slope: 122/118	
P ☺☺☺☺ STATE	**Caledonia Golf and Fish Club** Caledonia Dr., Pawleys Island. (803) 237-3675 18 holes. Par 70/70. Yards: 6,503/4,968 Year-round. High: Spring/Fall	Greens: $$$$$ Carts: Incl. Rating: 70.8/68.2 Slope: 130/113	
P ☺☺☺	**Colonial Charters Golf Club** Charter Dr., Longs. (803) 249-8809 18 holes. Par 72/72. Yards: 6,901/6,372 Year-round. High: Spring/Fall	Greens: $$$$ Carts: Incl. Rating: NA Slope: 124	

South Carolina Golf Guide

Myrtle Beach Region

R	**Deer Track Golf Resort**	Greens:	$–$$ W L R T J
	Platt Blvd., Surfside Beach. (803) 650-2146	Carts:	$
◎◎	*North Course*	Rating:	73.5/69.6
	18 holes. Par 72/72. Yards: 7,203/5,353	Slope:	121/119
	Year-round. High: Spring/Fall		
◎◎	*South Course*	Rating:	73.5/69.6
	18 holes. Par 71/71. Yards: 6,916/5,226	Slope:	119/120
R	**Eagle Nest Golf Club**	Greens:	$–$$$ R T
◎◎◎	Hwy. 17 N., N. Myrtle Beach. (803) 249-1449	Carts:	$
	18 holes. Par 72/72. Yards: 6,901/5,105	Rating:	73.0/69.8
	Year-round. High: Mar.–Apr., Oct.	Slope:	120/116
P	**Eastport Golf Club**	Greens:	$–$$ W
◎◎	Hwy. 17, N. Myrtle Beach. (803) 249-3997	Carts:	$
	18 holes. Par 72/72. Yards: 6,047/4,560	Rating:	66.2/65.7
	Year-round. High: Mar.–May	Slope:	116/114
P	**Gator Hole Golf Course**	Greens:	$$–$$$ T J
◎◎◎	Hwy. 17, N. Myrtle Beach. (803) 249-3543	Carts:	Incl.
	18 holes. Par 70/70. Yards: 6,000/4,685	Rating:	69.8/65.9
	Year-round. High: Mar.–May	Slope:	116/112
R	**Heather Glen Golf Links**	Greens:	$$–$$$$$
	Hwy. 17 N., Little River. (803) 249-9000	Carts:	Incl.
◎◎◎◎	*Red/White/Blue*	Rating:	72.4/72.4/72.4
BEST	27 holes. Par 72/72/72. Yards: 6,769/6,808/6,771	Slope:	130/130/127
	Year-round. High: Mar.–May, Oct.		
P	**Heritage Club**	Greens:	$$–$$$$$ W L R T S J
◎◎◎◎	Hwy. 17 S., Pawleys Island. (803) 237-3424	Carts:	Incl.
BEST	18 holes. Par 71/71. Yards: 7,100/5,325	Rating:	74.2/71.0
	Year-round. High: Mar.–Apr., Oct.	Slope:	137/125
P	**Heron Point Golf Club**	Greens:	$$ W L R T S J
◎◎	Blue Heron Blvd., Myrtle Beach. (803) 650-6664	Carts:	Incl.
	18 holes. Par 72/72. Yards: 6,477/4,734	Rating:	71.0/69.2
	Year-round. High: Spring/Fall	Slope:	120/121
P	**Indian Wells Golf Club**	Greens:	$–$$$ L R T J
◎◎	Woodlake Dr., Garden City. (803) 651-1505	Carts:	$
	18 holes. Par 72/72. Yards: 6,624/4,872	Rating:	71.9/68.2
	Year-round. High: Spring/Fall	Slope:	125/118
P	**Indigo Creek Golf Club**	Greens:	$$–$$$$ L T
◎◎	Surfside Beach. (803) 650-0381	Carts:	Incl.
	18 holes. Par 72/72. Yards: 6,750/4,921	Rating:	72.2/69.2
	Year-round. High: Spring/Fall	Slope:	128/120
R	**Legends Resorts**	Greens:	$$–$$$$ L R
	Hwy. 501, Myrtle Beach. (803) 236-9318	Carts:	$
◎◎◎◎	*Heathland at the Legends*	Rating:	74.5/71.0
STATE	18 holes. Par 71/71. Yards: 6,785/5,115	Slope:	127/121
	Year-round. High: Mar.–Apr., Oct.		
◎◎◎	*Moorland at the Legends*	Rating:	76.8/72.8
	18 holes. Par 72/72. Yards: 6,799/4,905	Slope:	140/127
◎◎◎	*Parkland at the Legends*	Rating:	74.3/72.9
	18 holes. Par 72/72. Yards: 7,170/5,570	Slope:	131/127
P	**The Links at Cypress Bay**	Greens:	$$–$$$ L R T J
◎◎	Little River. (803) 249-1025	Carts:	$
	18 holes. Par 72/72. Yards: 6,502/5,004	Rating:	70.0/69.0
	Year-round. High: Mar.–June, Sept.	Slope:	118/113

South Carolina Golf Guide

Myrtle Beach Region

R ⊙⊙⊙	**Litchfield Country Club** Hwy. 17, Pawleys Island. (803) 237-3411 18 holes. Par 72/72. Yards: 6,752/5,264 Year-round. High: Spring/Fall	Greens: Carts: Rating: Slope:	$$–$$$$ L J Incl. 72.6/70.8 130/119
R ⊙⊙⊙⊙ STATE	**The Long Bay Club** Hwy. 9, Longs. (803) 344-5590 18 holes. Par 72/72. Yards: 7,021/5,598 Year-round. High: Mar.–Apr., Oct.	Greens: Carts: Rating: Slope:	$$–$$$$ L R $ 74.3/72.1 137/127
R ⊙⊙⊙	**Myrtle Beach National Golf Club** National Dr., Myrtle Beach. (803) 448-2308 *North Course* 18 holes. Par 72/72. Yards: 6,759/5,047 Year-round. High: Mar.–Apr., Oct.	Greens: Carts: Rating: Slope:	$–$$$ L R $ 72.9/68.0 125/113
⊙⊙⊙	*Southcreek Course* 18 holes. Par 72/72. Yards: 6,416/4,723	Rating: Slope:	70.5/66.5 123/109
⊙⊙⊙	*West Course* 18 holes. Par 72/72. Yards: 6,866/5,307	Rating: Slope:	73.0/69.0 119/109
P ⊙⊙	**Myrtle West Golf Club** Hwy. 9 W., N. Myrtle Beach. (803) 249-1478 18 holes. Par 72/72. Yards: 6,787/4,859 Year-round. High: Spring/Fall	Greens: Carts: Rating: Slope:	$$–$$$ L Incl. 72.7/67.9 132/113
SP ⊙⊙⊙	**Myrtlewood Golf Club** Hwy. 17, Myrtle Beach. (803) 449-5134 *Palmetto Course* 18 holes. Par 72/72. Yards: 6,957/5,305 Year-round. High: Spring/Fall	Greens: Carts: Rating: Slope:	$–$$$ L R J $ 72.7/70.1 121/117
⊙⊙⊙	*Pinehills Course* 18 holes. Par 72/72. Yards: 6,640/4,906	Rating: Slope:	72.0/67.4 125/113
SP ⊙⊙⊙	**Pine Lakes International Country Club** Woodside Ave., Myrtle Beach. (803) 449-6459 18 holes. Par 72/72. Yards: 6,609/5,376 Year-round. High: Mar.–Apr.	Greens: Carts: Rating: Slope:	$$$–$$$$$ R $$ 71.5/71.6 125/122
R ⊙⊙	**Possum Trot Golf Club** N. Myrtle Beach. (803) 272-5341 18 holes. Par 72/72. Yards: 6,966/5,160 Year-round. High: Mar.–Apr., Sept.	Greens: Carts: Rating: Slope:	$$–$$$ W T Incl. 73.0/69.6 118/111
R ⊙⊙⊙	**The River Club** Hwy. 17 S., Pawley's Island. (803) 237-8755 18 holes. Par 72/72. Yards: 6,677/5,084 Year-round. High: Mar.–Apr., Oct.	Greens: Carts: Rating: Slope:	$$–$$$ L R $ 72.2/67.7 125/120
P ⊙⊙⊙	**River Hills Golf and Country Club** Cedar Creek Run, Little River. (803) 399-2100 18 holes. Par 72/72. Yards: 6,829/4,861 Year-round. High: Apr.–Oct.	Greens: Carts: Rating: Slope:	$–$$$ T $ 73.0/68.0 133/120
R ⊙⊙	**River Oaks Golf Plantation** River Oaks Dr., Myrtle Beach. (803) 236-2222 *Otter/Bear/Fox* 27 holes. Par 72/72/72. Yards: 6,877/6,778/6,791 Year-round. High: Mar.–Apr.	Greens: Carts: Rating: Slope:	$$–$$$ L R T J Incl. 72.5/72.0/71.7 125/126/125
P ⊙⊙	**Robbers Roost Golf Course** Hwy. 17 N., Myrtle Beach. (803) 249-1471 18 holes. Par 72/72. Yards: 7,148/5,387 Year-round. High: Mar.–Apr.	Greens: Carts: Rating: Slope:	$$–$$$ L T Incl. 74.4/70.2 137/116

South Carolina Golf Guide

Myrtle Beach Region

P ◎◎	**Rolling Hills Golf Course** Hwy. 501, Galavants Ferry. (803) 358-4653 18 holes. Par 72/72. Yards: 6,749/5,141 Year-round. High: Spring/Fall	Greens: $–$$ Carts: $ Rating: 71.4/86.3 Slope: 120/109	W L R T S J
P ◎◎	**Sea Gull Golf Club** Pawleys Island. (803) 448-5931 18 holes. Par 72/72. Yards: 6,910/5,250 Year-round. High: Spring/Fall	Greens: $$$ Carts: Incl. Rating: NA Slope: 128/115	L
SP ◎◎◎◎	**Surf Golf and Beach Club** Springland Lane, N. Myrtle Beach. (803) 249-1524 18 holes. Par 72/72. Yards: 6,842/5,178 Year-round. High: Spring/Fall	Greens: $–$$$ Carts: $ Rating: 72.6/68.2 Slope: 126/111	L
P ◎◎◎◎ STATE	**Tidewater Golf Club** Little River Neck Rd., N. Myrtle Beach. (803) 249-3829 18 holes. Par 72/72. Yards: 7,150/4,665 Year-round.	Greens: $$$–$$$$$ Carts: $ Rating: 73.7/67.5 Slope: 134/127	J
R ◎◎	**Waterway Hills Golf Club** Hwy. 17 N., Myrtle Beach. (803) 449-6488 *Oaks/Lakes/Ravines* 27 holes. Par 72/72/72. Yards: 6,461/6,339/6,470 Year-round. High: Mar.–Apr., Oct.	Greens: $–$$$ Carts: $ Rating: 71.0/70.6/70.8 Slope: 120/122/121	L R
SP ◎◎	**Wedgefield Plantation Country Club** Manor Dr., Georgetown. (803) 546-8587 18 holes. Par 72/73. Yards: 6,705/5,249 Year-round. High: Spring/Fall	Greens: $$–$$$ Carts: Incl. Rating: 72.2/69.9 Slope: 123/119	L T
SP ◎◎◎ DEAL	**The Wellman Club** Johnsonville. (803) 386-2521 18 holes. Par 72/72. Yards: 7,018/5,281 Year-round. High: Feb.–May	Greens: $–$$ Carts: $ Rating: 73.9/69.5 Slope: 129/105	W L R J
R ◎◎◎◎ STATE	**Wild Wing Plantation** Wild Wing Blvd., Conway. (803) 347-9464 *Avocet Course* 18 holes. Par 72/72. Yards: 7,127/5,298 Year-round. High: Apr.–Oct.	Greens: $$–$$$$$ Carts: $ Rating: 74.1/70.4 Slope: 128/118	W L R
◎◎◎	*Falcon Course* 18 holes. Par 72/72. Yards: 7,082/5,190	Greens: $$–$$$$$ Carts: $ Rating: NA Slope: NA	W L R
◎◎◎	*Hummingbird Course* 18 holes. Par 72/72. Yards: 6,853/5,168	Greens: $–$$$$ Carts: $ Rating: 73.0/69.5 Slope: 131/123	W L R
◎◎◎◎ STATE	*Wood Stork Course* 18 holes. Par 72/72. Yards: 7,004/5,409	Greens: $–$$$$ Carts: $ Rating: 71.8/67.9 Slope: 125/118	W L R
R ◎◎◎	**Willbrook Plantation Golf Course** Hwy. 17, Pawleys Island. (803) 237-4900 18 holes. Par 72/72. Yards: 6,704/4,963 Year-round. High: Mar.–Apr.	Greens: $$–$$$$ Carts: Incl. Rating: 71.8/67.9 Slope: 125/118	R
R ◎◎◎◎ STATE	**The Witch** Hwy. 544, Conway. (803) 448-1300 18 holes. Par 71/71. Yards: 6,702/4,812 Year-round. High: Feb.–May, Sept.–Nov.	Greens: $$–$$$$$ Carts: Incl. Rating: 71.2/69.0 Slope: 133/109	T

South Carolina Golf Guide

Augusta Area

SP	**Cedar Creek Golf Club**	Greens:	$$ R S
◐◐◐◐	Aiken. (803) 648-4206	Carts:	Incl.
DEAL	18 holes. Par 72/72. Yards: 7,206/5,231	Rating:	73.3/69.1
STATE	Year-round. High: Apr.–Sept.	Slope:	125/115

R	**Hickory Knob Golf Club**	Greens:	$ T S
◐◐◐	Hwy. 378, McCormick. (803) 391-2450	Carts:	$
DEAL	18 holes. Par 72/72. Yards: 6,560/4,905	Rating:	72.1/67.3
	Year-round. High: Apr.–Oct.	Slope:	119/120

P	**Persimmon Hill Golf Club**	Greens:	$ W L T
◐◐◐	Rte. 3, Saluda. (803) 275-3522	Carts:	$
DEAL	18 holes. Par 72/72. Yards: 6,925/5,449	Rating:	72.3/71.1
	Year-round. High: Mar.–May	Slope:	122/121

Charlotte Area

P	**Charleston Municipal Golf Course**	Greens:	$ T S J
◐◐	Maybank Hwy., Charleston. (803) 795-6517	Carts:	$
	18 holes. Par 72/72. Yards: 6,411/5,202	Rating:	70.2/69.2
	Year-round. High: Spring/Fall	Slope:	112/114

SP	**Charleston National Country Club**	Greens:	$$–$$$ W L T
◐◐◐	National Dr., Mt. Pleasant. (803) 884-7799	Carts:	Incl.
	18 holes. Par 72/72. Yards: 6,928/5,103	Rating:	73.5/70.8
	Year-round. High: Spring/Fall	Slope:	137/126

R	**The Club at Seabrook Island**	Greens:	$$$–$$$$
	Landfall Way, Seabrook Island. (803) 768-1000	Carts:	Incl.
◐◐◐	*Crooked Oaks Course*	Rating:	73.2/70.1
	18 holes. Par 72/72. Yards: 6,832/5,250	Slope:	126/119
	Year-round. High: Feb.–Aug.		

◐◐◐	*Ocean Winds Course*	Rating:	73.2/70.1
	18 holes. Par 72/72. Yards: 6,805/5,524	Slope:	126/119

SP	**Crowfield Golf and Country Club**	Greens:	$$ W L T
◐◐◐	Hamlet Circle, Goose Creek. (803) 764-4618	Carts:	$
DEAL	18 holes. Par 72/72. Yards: 7,003/5,682	Rating:	73.7/67.3
	Year-round. High: Spring	Slope:	134/NA

SP	**The Dunes West Golf Club**	Greens:	$$–$$$$ W L J
◐◐◐	Wando Plantation Way, Mt. Pleasant. (803) 856-9000	Carts:	Incl.
	18 holes. Par 72/72. Yards: 6,871/5,278	Rating:	73.4/69.2
	Year-round. High: Mar.–May, Oct.	Slope:	131/118

R	**Edisto Beach Golf Club**	Greens:	$$$ W L R J
◐◐	Edisto Island. (803) 869-1111	Carts:	Incl.
	18 holes. Par 71/72. Yards: 6,212/5,306	Rating:	69.5/70.3
	Year-round. High: Apr.–Oct.	Slope:	118/120

SP	**Fort Mill Golf Club**	Greens:	$
◐◐	Fort Mill. (803) 547-2044	Carts:	$$
	18 holes. Par 72/72. Yards: 6,865/5,448	Rating:	72.5/70.0
	Year-round. High: Apr.–Sept.	Slope:	123/123

R	**Kiawah Island Resort**	Greens:	$$$–$$$$ L R T J
	Kiawah Island.	Carts:	$
◐◐	*Marsh Point Course.* (803) 768-2121	Rating:	71.8/69.5
	18 holes. Par 71/71. Yards: 6,472/4,944	Slope:	126/122
	Year-round. High: Spring/Fall		

◐◐◐◐	*Osprey Point Course*	Greens:	$$$–$$$$$ L R T J
BEST	18 holes. Par 72/72. Yards: 6,678/5,122	Carts:	$
		Rating:	71.8/69.6
		Slope:	124/120

South Carolina Golf Guide

Charlotte Area

◎◎◎◎ BEST	*The Ocean Course.* (803) 768-7272 18 holes. Par 72/72. Yards: 7,371/5,327	Greens: $$$$$–$$$$$$ L R T J Carts: $ Rating: 76.9/72.9 Slope: 149/133
◎◎◎◎ BEST	*Turtle Point Course.* (803) 768-2121 18 holes. Par 72/72. Yards: 6,915/5,285	Greens: $$$–$$$$$ L R T J Carts: $ Rating: 73.5/69.8 Slope: 132/122
P ◎◎	**The Links at Stono Ferry** Forest Oaks Dr., Hollywood. (803) 763-1817 18 holes. Par 72/72. Yards: 6,606/4,928 Year-round. High: Mar.–May, Oct.	Greens: $–$$ W L T S Carts: Incl. Rating: 68.3/69.2 Slope: 115/119
P ◎◎◎	**Oak Point Golf Course** Bohicket Rd., Johns Island. (803) 768-7431 18 holes. Par 72/72. Yards: 6,759/4,671 Year-round. High: Apr.–Oct.	Greens: $$–$$$ W L T J Carts: Incl. Rating: 71.2/69.8 Slope: 132/121
P ◎◎	**Patriots Point Links** Mt. Pleasant. (803) 881-0042 18 holes. Par 72/72. Yards: 6,838/5,562 Year-round. High: Spring/Fall	Greens: $–$$ W L T Carts: $ Rating: 72.1/71.0 Slope: 118/115
SP ◎◎◎	**Pine Forest Country Club** Congressional Blvd., Summerville. (803) 851-1193 18 holes. Par 72/72. Yards: 6,905/5,007 Year-round. High: May–Sept.	Greens: $$–$$$ W L T J Carts: Incl. Rating: 73.0/67.7 Slope: 127/120
SP ◎◎	**Pinetuck Golf Club** Tuckaway Rd., Rock Hill. (803) 327-1141 18 holes. Par 72/72. Yards: 6,567/4,870 Year-round. High: Mar.–Oct.	Greens: $–$$ W T S Carts: $ Rating: 71.7/68.2 Slope: 127/111
R ◎◎	**Santee National Golf Club** Hwy. 6 W., Santee. (803) 854-3531 18 holes. Par 72/72. Yards: 6,858/4,748 Year-round. High: Mar.–Apr., Oct.	Greens: $$ R S J Carts: Incl. Rating: 72.1/68.2 Slope: 120/116
SP ◎◎	**Shadowmoss Plantation Golf Club** Dunvegan Dr., Charleston. (803) 556-8251 18 holes. Par 72/72. Yards: 6,700/5,200 Year-round. High: Mar.–May	Greens: $–$$ W L R T S J Carts: $ Rating: 72.4/70.2 Slope: 123/120
SP ◎◎	**Spring Lake Country Club** Spring Lake Rd., York. (803) 684-4898 18 holes. Par 72/72. Yards: 6,748/4,975 Year-round. High: May–Oct.	Greens: $–$$ W J Carts: $ Rating: 72.8/67.3 Slope: 126/108
R ◎◎◎	**Wild Dunes Resort** Palmetto Dr., Isle of Palms. (803) 886-2301 *Harbor Course* 18 holes. Par 70/70. Yards: 6,446/4,774 Year-round. High: Spring/Fall	Greens: $$–$$$$ W L R Carts: Incl. Rating: 70.9/68.1 Slope: 124/117
◎◎◎◎ BEST	*Links Course.* (803) 886-2180 18 holes. Par 72/72. Yards: 6,772/4,849	Greens: $$–$$$$$$ W L R Carts: Incl. Rating: 72.7/69.1 Slope: 131/121

Hilton Head

SP ◎◎◎◎ STATE	**Callawassie Island Club** Beaufort. (803) 521-1533 *Palmetto/Dogwood/Magnolia* 27 holes. Par 72/72/72. Yards: 6,936/6,956/7,070 Year-round. High: Spring/Fall	Greens: $$$–$$$$ Carts: Incl. Rating: 73.2/73.9/74.8 Slope: 130/132/138

South Carolina Golf Guide

Hilton Head

SP ☺☺	**Cat Island Golf Club** Waveland Ave., Beaufort. (803) 524-0300 18 holes. Par 71/71. Yards: 6,518/4,933 Year-round.	Greens: Carts: Rating: Slope:	$$ R T J Incl. 71.0/67.4 127/116
SP ☺☺	**Country Club of Beaufort** Barnwell Dr., Beaufort. (803) 522-1605 18 holes. Par 72/72. Yards: 6,506/4,880 Year-round. High: Spring/Fall	Greens: Carts: Rating: Slope:	$$ T $ 71.2/67.8 118/120
SP ☺☺☺	**Country Club of Hilton Head** Skull Creek Dr., Hilton Head Island. (803) 681-4653 18 holes. Par 72/72. Yards: 6,919/5,373 Year-round. High: Spring/Fall	Greens: Carts: Rating: Slope:	$$$–$$$$ L T Incl. 73.6/71.3 132/123
R ☺☺☺☺ BEST	**Harbour Town Golf Links** Lighthouse Lane, Hilton Head Island. (803) 363-4485 18 holes. Par 71/71. Yards: 6,916/5,019 Year-round. High: Spring/Fall	Greens: Carts: Rating: Slope:	$$$$–$$$$$$+ L R T J $ 74.0/69.0 136/117
P ☺☺☺ STATE	**Hilton Head National Golf Club** Hilton Head Island. (803) 842-5900 18 holes. Par 72/72. Yards: 6,779/5,589 Year-round. High: Spring/Fall	Greens: Carts: Rating: Slope:	$$$–$$$$ $ 69.9/NA 124/115
SP ☺☺	**Indigo Run Golf Club** Colonial Dr., Hilton Head Island. (803) 689-2200 18 holes. Par 72/72. Yards: 7,014/4,974 Year-round. High: Mar.–May, Oct.	Greens: Carts: Rating: Slope:	$$–$$$ L R T J $ 73.7/69.3 132/120
R ☺☺	**Island West Golf Club** U.S. Hwy. 278, Bluffton. (803) 689-6660 18 holes. Par 72/72. Yards: 6,803/4,938 Year-round. High: Mar.–Apr., Oct.	Greens: Carts: Rating: Slope:	$$–$$$ L R T J $ 72.1/66.5 129/116
P ☺☺☺	**Old South Golf Links** Buckingham Plantation Dr., Bluffton. (803) 785-5353 18 holes. Par 72/72. Yards: 6,772/4,776 Year-round. High: Mar.–Apr.	Greens: Carts: Rating: Slope:	$$–$$$$ L R T J Incl. 72.4/69.6 129/123
SP ☺☺☺	**Oyster Reef Golf Club** High Bluff Rd., Hilton Head Island. (803) 681-7717 18 holes. Par 72/72. Yards: 7,027/5,288 Year-round. High: Spring/Fall	Greens: Carts: Rating: Slope:	$$$–$$$$$ L R J Incl. 73.7/69.8 131/118
R ☺☺☺	**Palmetto Dunes Resort** Hilton Head Island. (803) 785-1140 *Arthur Hills Course* 18 holes. Par 72/72. Yards: 6,651/4,999 Year-round. High: Mar.–Oct.	Greens: Carts: Rating: Slope:	$$$–$$$$$ R Incl. 71.4/68.5 127/118
☺☺☺	*George Fazio Course* 18 holes. Par 72/72. Yards: 6,875/5,273	Greens: Carts: Rating: Slope:	$$$–$$$$ R Incl. 74.2/69.2 132/117
☺☺☺	*Robert Trent Jones Course* 18 holes. Par 72/72. Yards: 6,710/5,525	Greens: Carts: Rating: Slope:	$$$–$$$$ R Incl. 72.2/70.7 123/117
R ☺☺☺☺ STATE	**Palmetto Hall Plantation** Fort Howell Dr., Hilton Head Island. (803) 689-4100 *Arthur Hills Course* 18 holes. Par 72/72. Yards: 6,918/4,956 Year-round. High: Spring/Fall	Greens: Carts: Rating: Slope:	$$$–$$$$ R J Incl. 72.2/68.6 132/119

South Carolina Golf Guide

Hilton Head

☺☺	*Robert Cupp Course*	Rating:	74.8/71.1
	18 holes. Par 72/72. Yards: 7,079/5,220	Slope:	141/126
R	**Port Royal Golf Club**	Greens:	$$$–$$$$$ L R T J
	Glasslawn Ave., Hilton Head Island. (803) 686-8801	Carts:	Incl.
☺☺	*Barony Course*	Rating:	6,530/5,253
	18 holes. Par 72/72. Yards: 6,530/5,253	Slope:	124/115
	Year-round. High: Apr.–Sept., Mar.–May, Sept.		
☺☺	*Planter's Row Course*	Rating:	72.1/70.4
	18 holes. Par 72/72. Yards: 6,520/5,126	Slope:	134/114
☺☺☺	*Robber's Row Course*	Rating:	72.6/70.4
	18 holes. Par 72/72. Yards: 6,642/5,000	Slope:	134/114
R	**Sea Pines Sports and Conference Center**	Greens:	$$$$–$$$$$ L R T J
	Hilton Head Island. (803) 842-1894	Carts:	Incl.
☺☺☺	*Ocean Course*	Rating:	71.0/69.7
	18 holes. Par 72/72. Yards: 6,614/5,284	Slope:	125/111
	Year-round. High: Spring/Fall		
☺☺	*Sea Marsh Course*	Rating:	70.0/69.8
	18 holes. Par 72/72. Yards: 6,515/5,054	Slope:	120/123

Tennessee

The hills and dales of Tennessee have more than their share of golfing challenges.

In Fairfield Glade, 60 miles west of Knoxville, **Stonehenge Golf Club** is a mountain-and-forest challenge ranked as one of the best resort courses in the nation. The **Graysburg Hills Golf Course** is a hidden jewel. It's situated in a valley with three lakes in Chuckey, which is east of Knoxville and north of Greeneville—be sure to call for directions. The challenging and handsome course at **River Islands** is in Kodak, east of Knoxville.

Fall Creek Falls is a green hideaway in a state park with spectacular waterfalls in Pikeville, 70 miles north of Chattanooga.

In Franklin, south of Nashville, The North and South courses at the **Legends Club of Tennessee** are a pair of gems. The North Course is long and open; the South is more like a links challenge with mounding.

The **Springhouse Golf Club** in Nashville is a regular on the Senior PGA Tour; it is a tight and tricky course.

Fall Creek and Graysburg are also on the Econoguide Deals list.

Most courses in Tennessee are open year-round, with peak rates in effect from about April to September.

Econoguide Leader Board: Best Public Courses in Tennessee

☺☺☺	Fall Creek Falls State Park Golf Course
☺☺☺☺	Graysburg Hills Golf Course
☺☺☺☺	Legends Club of Tennessee (North, South)
☺☺☺☺	River Islands Golf Club
☺☺☺	Springhouse Golf Club
☺☺☺☺	Stonehenge Golf Club

Econoguide Leader Board: Best Deals in Tennessee

$$/○○○	Big Creek Golf Club
$$/○○○	Briarwood Golf Course
$/○○○	Eastland Green Golf Course
$/○○○	Fall Creek Falls State Park Golf Course
$$/○○○○	Graysburg Hills Golf Course
$/○○○	Henry Horton State Park Golf Course
$$/○○○	Hermitage Golf Course
$/○○○	Montgomery Bell State Park Golf Course
$$/○○○	Nashboro Village Golf Course
$/○○○	Orgill Park Golf Course
$$/○○○	Quail Ridge Golf Course
$$/○○○	Roan Valley Golf Estates
$$/○○○	Stonebridge Golf Course
$/○○○	Three Ridges Golf Course
$$/○○○	Willow Creek Golf Club

Tennessee Golf Guide

Memphis Area

SP ○○○ DEAL	**Big Creek Golf Club** Woodstock-Cuba Rd., Millington. (901) 353-1654 18 holes. Par 72/72. Yards: 7,052/5,086 Year-round. High: Apr.–Sept.	Greens: $–$$ Carts: $ Rating: 72.8/69.6 Slope: 121/111	W L T S J
SP ○○○	**Marriott's Golf Club at Shiloh Falls** Pickwick Dam. (901) 689-5050 18 holes. Par 72/72. Yards: 6,713/5,156 Year-round. High: Apr.–Oct.	Greens: $$–$$$ Carts: Incl. Rating: 73.1/71.3 Slope: 136/128	W L R J
P ○○○ DEAL	**Orgill Park Golf Course** Bethuel Rd., Millington. (901) 872-3610 18 holes. Par 72/72. Yards: 6,284/4,574 Year-round. High: Apr.–Sept.	Greens: $ Carts: Inquire Rating: 66.8/68.3 Slope: 109/108	W S J
P ○○○ DEAL	**Quail Ridge Golf Course** Altruria Rd., Bartlett. (901) 386-6951 18 holes. Par 72/72. Yards: 6,600/5,206 Year-round. High: Apr.–Oct.	Greens: $$ Carts: $ Rating: 71.8/NA Slope: 128/NA	W S J
P ○○○ DEAL	**Stonebridge Golf Course** Davies Plantation Rd., Memphis. (901) 382-1886 18 holes. Par 71/71. Yards: 6,788/5,012 Year-round. High: Apr.–Sept.	Greens: $$ Carts: $ Rating: 73.3/66.8 Slope: 133/113	W L
P ○○	**T.O. Fuller Golf Course** Pavilion Dr., Memphis. (901) 543-7771 18 holes. Par 72/73. Yards: 6,000/5,656 Year-round. High: May–Dec.	Greens: $ Carts: $ Rating: 71.0/72.0 Slope: 117/110	W L S

Nashville Area

P ○○	**Country Hills Golf Course** Saundersville Rd., Hendersonville. (615) 824-1100 18 holes. Par 72/72. Yards: 6,100/4,800 Year-round. High: Mar.–Oct.	Greens: $–$$ Carts: $ Rating: 71.2/67.8 Slope: 119/114	W L T S J
P ○○○ DEAL	**Eastland Green Golf Course** Clarksville. (615) 358-9051 18 holes. Par 72/72. Yards: 6,437/4,790 Year-round. High: July–Aug.	Greens: $ Carts: $ Rating: 71.5/68.4 Slope: 123/116	W T S J

Tennessee Golf Guide

Nashville Area

P ☺☺	**Forrest Crossing Golf Course** Riverview Dr., Franklin. (615) 794-9400 18 holes. Par 72/72. Yards: 6,968/5,011 Year-round. High: Apr.–Sept.	Greens: Carts: Rating: Slope:	$–$$ $ 73.6/69.1 125/114	W L T
P ☺☺	**Harpeth Hills Golf Course** Old Hickory Blvd., Nashville. (615) 862-8493 18 holes. Par 72/72. Yards: 6,900/5,200 Year-round. High: May–Sept.	Greens: Carts: Rating: Slope:	$ $ 73.1/71.2 126/124	
P ☺☺☺ DEAL	**Henry Horton State Park Golf Course** Nashville Hwy., Chapel Hill. (615) 364-2319 18 holes. Par 72/72. Yards: 7,060/5,625 Year-round. High: May–June	Greens: Carts: Rating: Slope:	$ $ 74.3/72.1 128/117	S J
P ☺☺☺ DEAL	**Hermitage Golf Course** Old Hickory Blvd., Old Hickory. (615) 847-4001 18 holes. Par 72/72. Yards: 6,775/5,475 Year-round. High: Apr.–Oct.	Greens: Carts: Rating: Slope:	$–$$ $ 71.9/70.8 122/120	T
P ☺☺	**Indian Hills Golf Club** Calumet Trace, Murfreesboro. (615) 898-0152 18 holes. Par 71/71. Yards: 6,495/5,686 Year-round. High: Apr.–Oct.	Greens: Carts: Rating: Slope:	$–$$ $ 72.8/70.3 125/118	W L T S J
SP ☺☺☺☺ STATE	**Legends Club of Tennessee** Franklin. (615) 790-1300 *North Course* 18 holes. Par 72/72. Yards: 7,190/5,333 Year-round. High: Apr.–Oct.	Greens: Carts: Rating: Slope:	$$$–$$$$ Incl. 75.0/70.9 132/119	W
☺☺☺☺ STATE	*South Course* 18 holes. Par 71/71. Yards: 7,113/5,290	Rating: Slope:	74.7/71.4 129/121	
P ☺☺☺ DEAL	**Montgomery Bell State Park Golf Course** Hotel Ave., Burns. (615) 797-2578 18 holes. Par 71/72. Yards: 6,091/4,961 Year-round. High: Apr.–Nov.	Greens: Carts: Rating: Slope:	$ $ 69.3/68.8 121/116	S J
P ☺☺☺ DEAL	**Nashboro Village Golf Course** Murfreesboro Rd., Nashville. (615) 367-2311 18 holes. Par 72/75. Yards: 6,887/5,485 Year-round. High: Apr.–Sept.	Greens: Carts: Rating: Slope:	$–$$ $ 73.5/72.3 134/121	W L R T J
R ☺☺☺ STATE	**Springhouse Golf Club** Springhouse Lane, Nashville. (615) 871-7759 18 holes. Par 72/72. Yards: 7,007/5,126 Year-round. High: Apr.–Oct.	Greens: Carts: Rating: Slope:	$$$ Incl. 74.0/70.2 133/118	S
P ☺☺	**Ted Rhodes Golf Course** Ed Temple Blvd., Nashville. (615) 862-8463 18 holes. Par 72/72. Yards: 6,660/5,732 Year-round. High: May–Sept.	Greens: Carts: Rating: Slope:	$ $ 71.8/68.3 120/115	S J
P ☺☺	**Two Rivers Golf Course** McGavock Pike, Nashville. (615) 889-2675 18 holes. Par 72/72. Yards: 6,595/5,336 Year-round. High: Apr.–Sept.	Greens: Carts: Rating: Slope:	$ Inquire 71.5/70.4 120/116	
P ☺☺	**Windtree Golf Course** Nonaville Rd., Mt. Juliet. (615) 754-4653 18 holes. Par 72/72. Yards: 6,557/5,126 Year-round. High: Apr.–Sept.	Greens: Carts: Rating: Slope:	$$ Inquire 71.1/69.6 124/117	T

Chattanooga Area

P ☺☺	**Brainerd Golf Course** Old Mission Rd., Chattanooga. (615) 855-2692	Greens: Carts:	$ $	W L

Tennessee Golf Guide

Chattanooga Area

18 holes. Par 72/72. Yards: 6,468/5,408	Rating: 69.8/69.9
Year-round. High: Apr.–Sept.	Slope: 119/118

P
☺☺☺
BEST
DEAL

Fall Creek Falls State Park Golf Course
Rte. 3, Pikeville. (615) 881-5706
18 holes. Par 72/72. Yards: 6,669/6,051
Year-round. High: May–Oct.

Greens: $ S J
Carts: $
Rating: 71.6/74.8
Slope: 127/126

P
☺☺

Moccasin Bend Golf Club
Moccasin Bend Rd., Chattanooga. (615) 267-3585
18 holes. Par 72/72. Yards: 6,469/5,290
Year-round. High: Apr.–Oct.

Greens: $ S J
Carts: $
Rating: 69.6/69.0
Slope: 111/109

Knoxville Area

R
☺☺

Bent Creek Golf Resort
E. Parkway, Gatlinburg. (615) 436-3947
18 holes. Par 72/72. Yards: 6,182/5,111
Year-round. High: Mar.–Nov.

Greens: $–$$ L R T
Carts: $
Rating: 70.3/69.2
Slope: 127/117

P
☺☺☺
DEAL

Briarwood Golf Course
Crab Orchard. (615) 484-5285
18 holes. Par 72/72. Yards: 6,689/5,021
Year-round. High: Apr.–Oct.

Greens: $$ W L
Carts: Incl.
Rating: 74.2/70.9
Slope: 132/123

P
☺☺☺

Egwani Farms Golf Course
Singleton Station Rd., Rockford. (615) 970-7132
18 holes. Par 72/72. Yards: 6,708/4,680
Year-round. High: Apr.–Oct.

Greens: $$$ J
Carts: Incl.
Rating: 71.9/66.1
Slope: 126/113

P
☺☺

Gatlinburg Golf Course
Dollywood Lane, Pigeon Forge. (615) 453-3912
18 holes. Par 71/72. Yards: 6,281/4,718
Year-round. High: May–Oct.

Greens: $$ T J
Carts: $
Rating: 72.3/68.9
Slope: 125/117

P

☺☺☺☺
DEAL
STATE

Graysburg Hills Golf Course
Graysburg Hills Rd., Chuckey. (615) 234-8061
Knobs/Fodderstack/Chimneytop
27 holes. Par 72/72/72. Yards: 6,834/6,875/6,743
Year-round. High: Apr.–Oct.

Greens: $$
Carts: $
Rating: 72.8/73.0/72.2
Slope: 128/134/133

SP
☺☺

Lambert Acres Golf Club
Tuckaleechee Park, Maryville. (615) 982-9838
18 holes. Par 72/72. Yards: 6,480/6,282/6,292
Year-round. High: May–Oct.

Greens: $
Carts: $
Rating: 70.8/70.1/69.6
Slope: 118/121/119

P
☺☺☺☺
STATE

River Islands Golf Club
Kodak Rd., Kodak. (615) 933-0100
18 holes. Par 72/72. Yards: 7,001/4,973
Year-round. High: Apr.–Oct.

Greens: $$–$$$ W L T
Carts: Incl.
Rating: 75.4/69.4
Slope: 133/118

R
☺☺☺☺
BEST

Stonehenge Golf Club
Fairfield Blvd., Fairfield Glade. (615) 484-3731
18 holes. Par 72/72. Yards: 6,549/5,000
Year-round. High: Apr.–Oct.

Greens: $$–$$$ L R T J
Carts: Incl.
Rating: 71.5/70.2
Slope: 131/124

P
☺☺☺
DEAL

Three Ridges Golf Course
Wise Springs Rd., Knoxville. (615) 687-4797
18 holes. Par 72/72. Yards: 6,825/5,225
Year-round. High: Apr.–Oct.

Greens: $ W T S J
Carts: $
Rating: 73.2/70.7
Slope: 128/121

R
☺☺

Thunder Hollow Golf Club
Tennessee Ave., Crossville. (615) 456-4060
18 holes. Par 72/72. Yards: 6,411/4,844
Year-round. High: Apr.–Sept.

Greens: $$
Carts: Incl.
Rating: 71.9/70.0
Slope: 124/121

Knoxville Area

P	**Warrior's Path State Park Golf Course**	Greens:	$	W L S J
☺☺	Kingsport. (615) 323-4990	Carts:	$	
	18 holes. Par 72/72. Yards: 6,581/5,328	Rating:	71.2/72.4	
	Year-round. High: July–Aug.	Slope:	115/117	

P	**Willow Creek Golf Club**	Greens:	$$	L J
☺☺☺	Kingston Pike, Knoxville. (615) 675-0100	Carts:	$	
DEAL	18 holes. Par 72/74. Yards: 7,266/5,557	Rating:	73.5/71.9	
	Year-round. High: Apr.–Oct.	Slope:	130/119	

Johnson City Area

P	**Elizabethton Municipal Golf Club**	Greens:	$–$$	
☺☺	Elizabethton. (615) 542-8051	Carts:	Incl.	
	18 holes. Par 72/72. Yards: 6,339/6,051	Rating:	71.2/67.7	
	Year-round. High: Apr.–Sept.	Slope:	129/118	

SP	**Roan Valley Golf Estates**	Greens:	$$	W L J
☺☺☺	Hwy. 421 S., Mountain City. (615) 727-7931	Carts:	Incl.	
DEAL	18 holes. Par 72/72. Yards: 6,736/4,370	Rating:	71.8/68.9	
	Apr.–Nov. High: May–Oct.	Slope:	120/107	

Texas

The **Barton Creek Resort** in Austin sports three superb courses, including two that are among the best in the state: the Fazio Course and the Palmer-Lakeside Course. The Lakeside Course is on high ground above Lake Travis.

Another triumvirate of golfing challenges can be found at **Horseshoe Bay Resort**. The Ram Rock Course there is a difficult beauty; the Applerock Course is a stunning challenge with lots of beach and water, and the Slick Rock Course is a bit easier but still picturesque, including a broad waterfall across the fairway of No. 14.

In Houston, the Masters Course at **Bear Creek Golf World** is tree-lined, full of sand and water . . . and long. In New Ulm, 60 miles west of Houston, **The Falls Country Club** is a tight challenge with all sorts of hazards.

One of the most unusual offerings in Texas or anywhere else is **Tour 18** in Humble, about 15 miles northeast of Houston. The club re-creates 18 holes from famous courses around the world.

Waterwood National Resort and Country Club in Huntsville, about 75 miles north of Houston, delivers water with Lake Livingston and wood from the neighboring Sam Houston National Forest. It all adds up to a very difficult but rewarding challenge.

There are two commendable courses at **The Woodlands Resort and Country Club**, located in The Woodlands, 25 miles north of Houston. The better of the two is TPC at the Woodlands, with unrelenting challenges on every hole. The North Course has enough sand to start its own beach.

Buffalo Creek is a rolling challenge in Rockwall, about 15 miles east of Dallas.

A very difficult, spectacular course is at **The Cliffs** in Graford, about 75 miles northwest of Fort Worth. The **Squaw Valley Golf Course** in Glen Rose, 60 miles southwest of Fort Worth, is full of tricks, with links out front and a tighter back nine.

The **Hill Country Golf Club** in San Antonio delivers hills and lots of trees and a good challenge. **The Quarry Golf Club** is set in an old quarry, which gives it some unusual fairways and tees. Another worthy course nearby is **Pecan Valley**; it's an older long course.

The **Painted Dunes Desert Golf Course** in El Paso is dry as, err, a desert, but it's an enjoyable challenge.

Painted Dunes and Squaw Valley also have positions on the Econoguide Deals list.

Most courses in Texas are open year-round, with peak rates in effect from about April to October. Some courses may offer lower rates during the hottest summer months.

Econoguide Leader Board: Best Public Courses in Texas

◐◐◐◐	Barton Creek Resort and Country Club (Fazio, Palmer-Lakeside)
◐◐◐	Bear Creek Golf World (Masters)
◐◐◐◐	Buffalo Creek Golf Club
◐◐◐◐	The Cliffs Golf Club
◐◐◐◐	The Falls Country Club
◐◐◐◐	Hill Country Golf Club
◐◐◐◐	Horseshoe Bay Resort (Ram Rock, Slick Rock)
◐◐◐◐	Painted Dunes Desert Golf Course
◐◐◐	Pecan Valley Golf Club
◐◐◐◐	The Quarry Golf Club
◐◐◐◐	Squaw Valley Golf Course
◐◐◐	Tour 18
◐◐◐	Waterwood National Resort and Country Club
◐◐◐◐	The Woodlands Resort and Country Club (TPC at the Woodlands)

Econoguide Leader Board: Best Deals in Texas

$/◐◐◐	Andrews County Golf Course
$/◐◐◐	Bay Forest Golf Course
$/◐◐◐	Cielo Vista Golf Course
$$/◐◐◐	Delaware Springs Golf Course
$$/◐◐◐	Firewheel Golf Park (Lakes, Old)
$$/◐◐◐	Flying L Ranch Golf Course
$$/◐◐◐	Galveston Island Municipal Golf Course
$/◐◐◐	Garden Valley Golf Resort (Hummingbird)
$/◐◐◐	Hidden Hills Public Golf Course
$$/◐◐◐	Indian Creek Golf Club (Creeks, Lakes)
$$/◐◐◐	Iron Horse Golf Club
$/◐◐◐	J.F. Sammons Park Golf Course
$/◐◐◐	Lady Bird Johnson Municipal Golf Course
$/◐◐◐	Mission del Lago Golf Course
$/◐◐◐◐	Painted Dunes Desert Golf Course
$$/◐◐◐	Peach Tree Golf Club (Oakhurst)
$$/◐◐◐	Rayburn Country Club and Resort
$$/◐◐◐	Rio Colorado Golf Course

$/ⓞⓞⓞ	San Saba Municipal Golf Course
$$/ⓞⓞⓞⓞ	Squaw Valley Golf Course
$$/ⓞⓞⓞ	Sugartree Golf Club
$$/ⓞⓞⓞ	Tanglewood Resort

Texas Golf Guide

Amarillo Area

| P
ⓞⓞ | **Comanche Trail Golf Club**
S. Grand, Amarillo. (806) 378-4281
18 holes. Par 72/72. Yards: 7,180/5,524
Year-round. High: Mar.–Sept. | Greens:
Carts:
Rating:
Slope: | $
$
72.9/70.0
117/108 | S J |

| P
ⓞⓞⓞ
DEAL | **Hidden Hills Public Golf Course**
N. Hwy. 70, Pampa. (806) 669-5866
18 holes. Par 71/71. Yards: 6,463/5,196
Year-round. High: May–Sept. | Greens:
Carts:
Rating:
Slope: | $
$
69.4/68.0
122/116 | W T S J |

El Paso

| P
ⓞⓞⓞ
DEAL | **Cielo Vista Golf Course**
Hawkins, El Paso. (915) 591-4927
18 holes. Par 71/71. Yards: 6,411/5,421
Year-round. High: Apr.–Oct. | Greens:
Carts:
Rating:
Slope: | $
$
69.4/69.4
122/113 | W T |

| P
ⓞⓞⓞⓞ
DEAL
STATE | **Painted Dunes Desert Golf Course**
McCombs, El Paso. (915) 821-2122
18 holes. Par 72/72. Yards: 6,925/5,717
Year-round. High: Apr.–May, Sept. | Greens:
Carts:
Rating:
Slope: | $
$
74.0/74.5
137/123 | T S J |

Odessa Area

| P
ⓞⓞⓞ
DEAL | **Andrews County Golf Course**
Andrews. (915) 524-1462
18 holes. Par 70/72. Yards: 6,300/5,331
Year-round. High: May–July | Greens:
Carts:
Rating:
Slope: | $
$
68.9/69.7
116/110 | |

San Antonio Area

| P
ⓞⓞⓞ | **Cedar Creek Golf Course**
Vista Colina, San Antonio. (210) 695-5050
18 holes. Par 72/72. Yards: 7,103/5,535
Year-round. | Greens:
Carts:
Rating:
Slope: | $–$$$
$
73.4/70.8
132/113 | W L T S J |

| R
ⓞⓞⓞ
DEAL | **Flying L Ranch Golf Course**
Bandera. (210) 460-3001
18 holes. Par 72/72. Yards: 6,635/5,442
Year-round. High: Apr.–Sept. | Greens:
Carts:
Rating:
Slope: | $$
$
71.0/69.9
123/109 | W L R T S J |

| R
ⓞⓞⓞⓞ
STATE | **Hill Country Golf Club**
Hyatt Resort Dr., San Antonio. (210) 520-4040
18 holes. Par 72/72. Yards: 6,913/4,781
Year-round. High: Mar.–Sept. | Greens:
Carts:
Rating:
Slope: | $$$$–$$$$$
Incl.
73.9/67.8
136/114 | W L T J |

| P
ⓞⓞⓞ
DEAL | **Lady Bird Johnson Municipal Golf Course**
Hwy. 16 S., Fredericksburg. (210) 997-4010
18 holes. Par 72/72. Yards: 6,432/5,092
Year-round. High: Mar.–Nov. | Greens:
Carts:
Rating:
Slope: | $
$
70.3/68.0
125/112 | W |

| P
ⓞⓞⓞ
DEAL | **Mission del Lago Golf Course**
Mission Grande, San Antonio. (210) 627-2522
18 holes. Par 72/72. Yards: 7,004/5,301
Year-round. High: Mar.–July, Oct.–Dec. | Greens:
Carts:
Rating:
Slope: | $
$
72.6/69.2
127/113 | W L R T S J |

| P
ⓞⓞⓞ
BEST | **Pecan Valley Golf Club**
San Antonio. (210) 333-9018
18 holes. Par 71/72. Yards: 7,071/5,621
Year-round. High: Spring/Fall | Greens:
Carts:
Rating:
Slope: | $$–$$$
Incl.
71.4/69.7
128/116 | W L T S J |

| P
ⓞⓞⓞⓞ | **The Quarry Golf Club**
E. Basse Rd., San Antonio. (210) 824-4500 | Greens:
Carts: | $$$–$$$$
Incl. | T |

Texas Golf Guide

San Antonio Area

STATE	18 holes. Par 71/71. Yards: 6,740/4,897	Rating:	71.0/67.0	
	Year-round. High: Mar.–Nov.	Slope:	122/110	

P	**Riverside Municipal Golf Course**	Greens:	$	W L R T S J
☺☺	McDonald, San Antonio. (210) 533-8371	Carts:	$	
	18 holes. Par 72/72. Yards: 6,729/5,730	Rating:	72.0/72.0	
	Year-round. High: Apr.–Sept.	Slope:	128/121	

R	**Tapatio Springs Resort and Conference Center**	Greens:	$$$$	R J
☺☺☺	West Johns Rd., Boerne. (210) 537-4197	Carts:	Incl.	
	18 holes. Par 72/72. Yards: 6,472/5,179	Rating:	70.9/69.5	
	Year-round. High: Spring/Fall	Slope:	122/118	

Austin Area

R	**Barton Creek Resort and Country Club**	Greens:	$$$$$	W
	Austin. (512) 329-4608	Carts:	$	
☺☺☺	*Crenshaw and Coore Course*	Rating:	71.0/67.2	
	18 holes. Par 72/72. Yards: 6,678/4,843	Slope:	124/110	
	Year-round. High: Spring/Fall			

☺☺☺☺	*Fazio Course*	Greens:	$$$$$$+	W
BEST	18 holes. Par 72/72. Yards: 6,956/5,207	Carts:	$	
		Rating:	74.0/69.4	
		Slope:	135/120	

☺☺☺☺	*Palmer-Lakeside Course*	Greens:	$$$$$	W
STATE	18 holes. Par 72/72. Yards: 6,657/5,067	Carts:	$	
		Rating:	71.0/74.0	
		Slope:	124/135	

P	**Bluebonnet Hill Golf Club**	Greens:	$	W T S J
☺☺	Decker Lane, Austin. (512) 272-4228	Carts:	$	
	18 holes. Par 72/72. Yards: 6,503/5,241	Rating:	70.0/68.2	
	Year-round. High: Mar.–Aug.	Slope:	113/107	

P	**Circle C Golf Club**	Greens:	$$–$$$	W L T J
☺☺☺	Austin. (512) 288-4297	Carts:	Incl.	
	18 holes. Par 72/72. Yards: 6,859/5,236	Rating:	72.7/69.9	
	Year-round. High: Spring/Fall	Slope:	122/120	

P	**Delaware Springs Golf Course**	Greens:	$$	T S J
☺☺☺	Hwy. 281 S., Burnet. (512) 756-8951	Carts:	$	
DEAL	18 holes. Par 72/71. Yards: 6,819/5,770	Rating:	72.0/66.5	
	Year-round. High: Mar.–Sept.	Slope:	121/107	

P	**Forest Creek Golf Club**	Greens:	$$–$$$	T S J
☺☺☺	Twin Ridge Pkwy., Round Rock. (512) 388-2874	Carts:	Incl.	
	18 holes. Par 72/72. Yards: 7,084/5,601	Rating:	72.8/71.9	
	Year-round. High: June–July	Slope:	130/124	

R	**Horseshoe Bay Resort**	Greens:	$$$$–$$$$$	W L R J
	Bay West Blvd., Horseshoe Bay. (210) 598-6561	Carts:	$	
☺☺☺☺	*Applerock Course*	Rating:	73.9/71.6	
	18 holes. Par 72/72. Yards: 6,999/5,509	Slope:	134/117	
	Year-round. High: Mar.–Nov.			

☺☺☺☺	*Ram Rock Course*	Rating:	73.9/71.4	
BEST	18 holes. Par 71/71. Yards: 6,946/5,306	Slope:	137/121	

☺☺☺☺	*Slick Rock Course*	Rating:	72.6/70.2	
STATE	18 holes. Par 72/72. Yards: 6,834/5,832	Slope:	125/115	

P	**J.F. Sammons Park Golf Course**	Greens:	$	W L T S J
☺☺☺	Temple. (817) 778-8282	Carts:	$	

Texas Golf Guide

Austin Area

DEAL	18 holes. Par 70/70. Yards: 6,100/4,450 Year-round. High: Mar.–Aug.	Rating: 69.8/65.8 Slope: 129/110	

P ☺☺	**Jimmy Clay Golf Course** Austin. (512) 444-0999 18 holes. Par 72/72. Yards: 6,857/5,036 Year-round. High: Aug.	Greens: $ Carts: $ Rating: 72.4/68.5 Slope: 124/110	W T S J

R ☺☺☺	**Lakeway Resort** Austin. (512) 261-7573 *Live Oak Course* 18 holes. Par 72/72. Yards: 6,643/5,472 Year-round. High: Spring/Fall	Greens: $$–$$$ Carts: $ Rating: NA Slope: 121/122	

☺☺☺	*Yaupon Course* 18 holes. Par 72/72. Yards: 6,565/5,032	Rating: NA Slope: 123/119	

P ☺☺	**Lions Municipal Golf Course** Enfield Rd., Austin. (512) 477-6963 18 holes. Par 72/72. Yards: 6,001/4,931 Year-round. High: June–Aug.	Greens: $ Carts: $ Rating: NA Slope: 118/NA	T

R ☺☺☺	**Mill Creek Golf and Country Club** Old Mill Rd., Salado. (817) 947-5698 18 holes. Par 71/73. Yards: 6,486/5,250 Year-round. High: Mar.–Oct.	Greens: $$–$$$ Carts: $ Rating: 72.1/69.6 Slope: 128/114	W R

SP ☺☺☺	**River Place Golf Club** Austin. (512) 346-6784 18 holes. Par 71/71. Yards: 6,611/4,878 Year-round. High: Mar.–Oct.	Greens: $$$ Carts: Incl. Rating: 72.0/65.5 Slope: 128/113	T S J

P ☺☺	**Riverside Golf Course** Grove Blvd., Austin. (512) 389-1070 18 holes. Par 71/71. Yards: 6,562/5,334 Year-round. High: May–Aug.	Greens: $ Carts: $ Rating: 70.3/69.6 Slope: 122/112	W T S J

P ☺☺☺ DEAL	**San Saba Municipal Golf Course** San Saba. (915) 372-3212 18 holes. Par 72/72. Yards: 6,904/5,246 Year-round. High: Mar.–Oct.	Greens: $ Carts: $ Rating: 72.5/69.0 Slope: 119/113	

Dallas/Fort Worth Area

SP ☺☺	**Briarwood Golf Club** Briarwood Dr., Tyler. (903) 593-7741 18 holes. Par 71/71. Yards: 6,512/4,735 Year-round. High: May–June	Greens: $–$$ Carts: $ Rating: 70.6/66.1 Slope: 118/111	L

P ☺☺☺☺ STATE	**Buffalo Creek Golf Club** Rockwall. (214) 771-4003 18 holes. Par 71/71. Yards: 7,018/5,209 Year-round. High: Mar.–June	Greens: $$–$$$$ Carts: Incl. Rating: 73.8/67.0 Slope: 133/113	L T S J

P ☺☺	**Cedar Crest Golf Course** Southerland, Dallas. (214) 670-7615 18 holes. Par 71/75. Yards: 6,550/5,594 Year-round. High: Apr.–Sept.	Greens: $ Carts: $ Rating: 71.0/76.0 Slope: 121/116	T S J

P ☺☺	**Chester W. Ditto Golf Club** Brown Blvd., Arlington. (817) 275-5941 18 holes. Par 72/72. Yards: 6,727/5,555 Year-round. High: Apr.–Sept.	Greens: $ Carts: $ Rating: 70.8/71.2 Slope: 117/116	W T S J

R ☺☺☺☺	**The Cliffs Golf Club** Graford. (817) 779-3926	Greens: $$$ Carts: $	W T J

Texas Golf Guide

Dallas/Fort Worth Area

STATE	18 holes. Par 71/71. Yards: 6,808/4,888	Rating:	73.8/69.5
	Year-round. High: Apr.–Sept.	Slope:	139/121

P
☺☺
Connally Golf Course
Concord Rd., Waco. (817) 799-6561
18 holes. Par 72/73. Yards: 6,975/5,950
Year-round. High: Apr.–Sept.

Greens: $ T S J
Carts: $
Rating: 72.5/73.8
Slope: 116/120

P
☺☺
Cottonwood Creek Golf Course
Bagby Dr., Waco. (817) 752-2474
18 holes. Par 72/72. Yards: 7,123/5,724
Year-round. High: Mar.–Oct.

Greens: $ W L S J
Carts: $
Rating: 73.3/71.9
Slope: 129/120

P
☺☺
Country View Golf Club
W. Beltline Rd., Lancaster. (214) 227-0995
18 holes. Par 71/71. Yards: 6,609/5,048
Year-round. High: Apr.–Oct.

Greens: $ L T S J
Carts: $$
Rating: 71.0/68.2
Slope: 120/114

P
☺☺☺
DEAL
Firewheel Golf Park
W. Blackburn Rd., Garland. (214) 205-2795
Lakes Course
18 holes. Par 71/71. Yards: 6,625/5,215
Year-round. High: June–Aug.

Greens: $–$$ T S
Carts: $
Rating: 72.0/69.1
Slope: 126/110

☺☺☺
DEAL
Old Course
18 holes. Par 72/72. Yards: 7,054/5,692

Rating: 74.1/71.7
Slope: 129/117

R
☺☺☺
Four Seasons Resort and Club
N. MacArthur Blvd., Irving. (214) 717-2530
TPC Course
18 holes. Par 70/70. Yards: 6,899/5,340
Year-round. High: Feb.–Oct.

Greens: $$$$–$$$$$$+   L R T
Carts: Incl.
Rating: 73.5/70.6
Slope: 135/116

R
☺☺☺
Garden Valley Golf Resort
Lindale. (903) 882-6107
Dogwood Course
18 holes. Par 72/72. Yards: 6,754/5,532
Year-round. High: Apr.–Oct.

Greens: $$$ W L T S
Carts: $
Rating: 72.4/72.5
Slope: 132/130

☺☺☺
DEAL
Hummingbird Course
18 holes. Par 71/71. Yards: 6,446/5,131

Greens: $
Carts: $
Rating: 71.0/69.0
Slope: NA

P
☺☺
Grand Prairie Municipal Golf Course
S.E. 14th St., Grand Prairie. (214) 263-0661
Blue/Red/White
27 holes. Par 72/71/71. Yards: 6,500/6,309/6,219
Year-round. High: May–Sept.

Greens: $ T S J
Carts: $
Rating: 71.0/69.5/69.5
Slope: 118/112/94

P
☺☺
Grapevine Golf Course
Grapevine. (817) 481-0421
18 holes. Par 72/72. Yards: 6,953/5,786
Year-round. High: Apr.–Sept.

Greens: $ T S J
Carts: $
Rating: 72.0/72.5
Slope: 113/113

P
☺☺
Grover C. Keaton Golf Course
Jim Miller Rd., Dallas. (214) 670-8784
18 holes. Par 72/72. Yards: 6,511/5,054
Year-round. High: Mar.–Aug.

Greens: $ W L T S J
Carts: $
Rating: 70.6/68.1
Slope: 113/113

P
☺☺☺
Hyatt Bear Creek Golf and Racquet Club
Bear Creek Court, DFW Airport. (214) 615-6800
East Course
18 holes. Par 72/72. Yards: 6,670/5,620
Year-round. High: Apr.–Nov.

Greens: $$$–$$$$ W L T S J
Carts: $
Rating: 72.5/72.4
Slope: 127/124

Texas Golf Guide

Dallas/Fort Worth Area

☺☺☺	*West Course* 18 holes. Par 72/72. Yards: 6,675/5,570	Rating: 72.7/72.5 Slope: 130/122	
P ☺☺☺ DEAL	**Indian Creek Golf Club** W. Frankford, Carrolton. (214) 492-3620 *Creeks Course* 18 holes. Par 72/72. Yards: 7,218/4,967 Year-round. High: Mar.–Oct.	Greens: $$ Carts: $ Rating: 74.7/68.2 Slope: 136/114	W T S J
☺☺☺ DEAL	*Lakes Course* 18 holes. Par 72/72. Yards: 7,060/5,367	Rating: 72.9/69.9 Slope: 135/114	
P ☺☺☺ DEAL	**Iron Horse Golf Club** Skylark Circle, N. Richland Hills. (817) 485-6666 18 holes. Par 70/70. Yards: 6,100/5,083 Year-round. High: Apr.–Aug.	Greens: $$ Carts: $ Rating: 71.8/69.6 Slope: 130/119	W T S J
P ☺☺☺	**Marriott's Golf Club at Fossil Creek** Fort Worth. (817) 847-1900 18 holes. Par 72/72. Yards: 6,865/5,066 Year-round. High: Mar.–June, Sept.	Greens: $$$ Carts: Incl. Rating: 73.6/68.5 Slope: 131/111	W T
SP ☺☺☺ DEAL	**Peach Tree Golf Club** Bullard. (903) 894-7079 *Oakhurst Course* 18 holes. Par 72/72. Yards: 6,813/5,086 Year-round. High: Apr.–Sept.	Greens: $–$$ Carts: $ Rating: 72.1/68.4 Slope: 126/113	W T S
P ☺☺	**Plantation Resort Golf Club** Frisco. (214) 335-4653 18 holes. Par 72/72. Yards: 6,382/5,945 Year-round.	Greens: $$–$$$ Carts: Incl. Rating: NA Slope: 122/117	W T
SP ☺☺☺	**The Ranch Country Club** Glen Oaks Dr., McKinney. (214) 529-5990 18 holes. Par 72/72. Yards: 7,087/5,053 Year-round. High: May–Sept.	Greens: $$–$$$ Carts: $ Rating: 73.8/69.4 Slope: 130/117	W L R T
P ☺☺	**Riverchase Golf Club** Coppell. (214) 462-8281 18 holes. Par 71/71. Yards: 6,593/6,041 Year-round. High: Apr.–Oct.	Greens: $$–$$$ Carts: Incl. Rating: NA Slope: 124/114	W L T
P ☺☺☺	**Riverside Golf Club** Riverside Pkwy., Grand Prairie. (817) 640-7800 18 holes. Par 72/72. Yards: 7,025/5,175 Year-round. High: Mar.–Oct.	Greens: $$$ Carts: Incl. Rating: 74.4/69.5 Slope: 132/113	W T S J
P ☺☺	**Sherill Park Golf Course** E. Lookout Dr., Richardson. (214) 234-1416 *Course No. 1* 18 holes. Par 72/72. Yards: 6,800/5,455 Year-round. High: May–Nov.	Greens: $ Carts: $ Rating: 72.6/72.0 Slope: 126/118	W L T S J
P ☺☺☺☺ DEAL STATE	**Squaw Valley Golf Course** Hwy. 67, Glen Rose. (817) 897-7956 18 holes. Par 72/72. Yards: 7,062/5,014 Year-round. High: Apr.–Oct.	Greens: $$ Carts: $$ Rating: 73.6/NA Slope: 130/NA	W T S
P ☺☺	**Stevens Park Golf Course** N. Montclair, Dallas. (214) 670-7506 18 holes. Par 71/71. Yards: 6,005/5,000 Year-round. High: Spring/Fall	Greens: $ Carts: $ Rating: 65.0/68.0 Slope: 98/118	W L T S J
SP ☺☺☺	**Sugartree Golf Club** Hwy. 1189, Dennis. (817) 441-8643	Greens: $–$$ Carts: $	W L T S J

Texas Golf Guide

Dallas/Fort Worth Area

DEAL	18 holes. Par 71/71. Yards: 6,775/5,254	Rating:	72.8/71.0
	Year-round. High: Mar.–Oct.	Slope:	138/125

R	**Tanglewood Resort**	Greens: $$	T
☺☺☺	Hwy. 120 N., Pottsboro. (903) 786-4140	Carts: $	
DEAL	18 holes. Par 72/72. Yards: 6,993/4,925	Rating: 73.7/67.5	
	Year-round. High: Spring/Fall	Slope: 128/104	

P	**Tenison Park Golf Course**	Greens: $	W L T S J
	Samuell, Dallas. (214) 670-1402	Carts: $	
☺☺	*East Course*	Rating: 72.0/70.2	
	18 holes. Par 72/75. Yards: 6,802/5,444	Slope: 123/113	
	Year-round. High: Apr.–Oct.		

☺☺	*West Course*	Rating: 72.0/72.2	
	18 holes. Par 72/72. Yards: 6,902/5,747	Slope: 121/118	

P	**Timarron Golf and Country Club**	Greens: $$$–$$$$	W
☺☺☺	Byron Nelson Pkwy., South Lake. (817) 481-7529	Carts: Incl.	
	18 holes. Par 72/72. Yards: 7,100/5,330	Rating: 74.2/71.3	
	Year-round. High: Mar.–Apr.	Slope: 137/120	

SP	**Western Oaks Country Club**	Greens: $	W L R T J
☺☺	Waco. (817) 772-8100	Carts: $	
	18 holes. Par 70/70. Yards: 6,400/5,040	Rating: 70.7/68.7	
	Year-round. High: Apr.–Nov.	Slope: 122/120	

SP	**White Bluff Golf Club**	Greens: $$$–$$$$$	T
☺☺☺	Whitney. (817) 694-3656	Carts: Incl.	
	18 holes. Par 72/72. Yards: 6.845/5,292	Rating: 73.3/72.4	
	Year-round. High: Apr.–Oct.	Slope: 132/128	

Houston Area

P	**Bay Forest Golf Course**	Greens: $	T S
☺☺☺	LaPorte. (713) 471-4653	Carts: $	
DEAL	18 holes. Par 72/72. Yards: 6,756/5,094	Rating: 72.4/69.0	
	Year-round. High: Apr.–Oct.	Slope: 126/113	

P	**Bayou Din Golf Club**	Greens: $	T S
	Rte. 2, Beaumont. (409) 796-1327	Carts: $	
☺☺	*Front/Back/New*	Rating: 68.5/70.6/72.1	
	27 holes. Par 71/71/72. Yards: 6,285/6,495/7,020	Slope: 108/118/116	
	Year-round. High: Mar.–Aug.		

P	**Bayou Golf Club**	Greens: $	T S
☺☺	Ted Dudley Dr., Texas City. (409) 643-5850	Carts: $	
	18 holes. Par 72/73. Yards: 6,665/5,448	Rating: 71.0/73.0	
	Year-round.	Slope: 114/118	

P	**Bear Creek Golf World**	Greens: $–$$$	W L T S J
	Clay Rd., Houston. (713) 855-4720	Carts: $	
☺☺	*Challenger Course*	Rating: 64.2/64.7	
	18 holes. Par 66/66. Yards: 5,295/4,432	Slope: 103/103	
	Year-round. High: Apr.–Oct.		

☺☺☺	*Masters Course*	Rating: 74.1/72.1	
BEST	18 holes. Par 72/72. Yards: 7,131/5,544	Slope: 133/125	

☺☺	*President's Course*	Rating: 69.1/70.6	
	18 holes. Par 72/72. Yards: 6,562/5,728	Slope: 110/111	

R	**Columbia Lakes Golf Club**	Greens: $$$	W L R
☺☺☺	Freeman Blvd., W. Columbia. (409) 345-5455	Carts: Incl.	
	18 holes. Par 72/72. Yards: 6,967/5,280	Rating: 75.7/71.7	
	Year-round. High: Apr.–June	Slope: 131/122	

Texas Golf Guide

Houston Area

P	**Cypresswood Golf Club**	Greens: $$–$$$	W T S J
	Cypresswood Dr., Spring. (713) 821-6300	Carts: $	
☺☺☺	*Creek Course*	Rating: 72.0/69.1	
	18 holes. Par 72/72. Yards: 6,937/5,549	Slope: 124/113	
	Year-round. High: Mar.–Oct.		
☺☺☺	*Cypress Course*	Rating: 71.8/67.6	
	18 holes. Par 72/72. Yards: 6,906/5,599	Slope: 123/111	
R	**Del Lago Resort**	Greens: $$–$$$	W R T
☺☺☺	Montgomery. (409) 582-6100	Carts: $	
	18 holes. Par 71/71. Yards: 6,907/6,467	Rating: NA	
	Year-round. High: May–Oct.	Slope: 122/113	
SP	**The Falls Country Club**	Greens: $$$	W R
☺☺☺☺	N. Falls Dr., New Ulm. (409) 992-3128	Carts: Incl.	
STATE	18 holes. Par 72/73. Yards: 6,757/5,326	Rating: 72.3/70.0	
	Year-round. High: Apr.–July	Slope: 133/123	
P	**Galveston Island Municipal Golf Course**	Greens: $–$$	W R T S J
☺☺☺	Sydnor Lane, Galveston. (409) 744-2366	Carts: $	
DEAL	18 holes. Par 72/73. Yards: 6,969/5,407	Rating: 73.0/71.4	
	Year-round. High: Apr.–Oct.	Slope: 131/121	
P	**Glenbrook Golf Course**	Greens: $	W L T S J
☺☺	N. Bayou Dr., Houston. (713) 649-8089	Carts: $	
	18 holes. Par 71/71. Yards: 6,427/5,258	Rating: 70.7/70.7	
	Year-round. High: Apr.–Oct.	Slope: 120/117	
P	**The Golf Club at Cinco Ranch**	Greens: $$–$$$	T S J
☺☺☺	Katy. (713) 395-4653	Carts: Incl.	
	18 holes. Par 72/72. Yards: 7,044/5,263	Rating: 73.7/70.3	
	Year-round. High: Apr.–June	Slope: 132/118	
P	**Greatwood Golf Club**	Greens: $$$	T
☺☺☺	Greatwood Pkwy., Sugar Land. (713) 343-9999	Carts: Incl.	
	18 holes. Par 72/72. Yards: 6,836/5,220	Rating: 72.6/70.0	
	Year-round. High: Mar.–Oct.	Slope: 130/125	
P	**Jersey Meadow Golf Course**	Greens: $$	W L T S J
	Rio Grande, Houston. (713) 896-0900	Carts: Incl.	
☺☺	*Red/White/Blue*	Rating: 70.5/70.4/68.9	
	27 holes. Par 72/72/72. Yards: 6,583/6,383/6,400	Slope: 120/118/118	
	Year-round. High: Apr.–Oct.		
P	**Kingwood Cove Golf Club**	Greens: $$	W L T S J
☺☺	Hamblen Rd., Kingwood. (713) 358-1155	Carts: $	
	18 holes. Par 71/71. Yards: 6,722/5,601	Rating: 71.9/73.2	
	Year-round. High: Spring/Fall	Slope: 118/114	
P	**Lake Houston Golf Club**	Greens: $$	W T S J
☺☺	Afton Way, Huffman. (713) 324-1841	Carts: Incl.	
	18 holes. Par 72/74. Yards: 6,850/5,759	Rating: 72.6/73.3	
	Year-round. High: Spring/Fall	Slope: 128/131	
P	**The Links at Tennwood**	Greens: $–$$	W T S J
☺☺	Magnolia Rd., Hockley. (713) 757-5465	Carts: $	
	18 holes. Par 72/73. Yards: 6,880/5,238	Rating: 70.8/68.3	
	Year-round. High: Spring/Fall	Slope: 120/109	
P	**Memorial Park Golf Course**	Greens: $	W T
☺☺	Memorial Loop Park E., Houston. (713) 862-4033	Carts: $	
	18 holes. Par 72/72. Yards: 7,380/6,140	Rating: NA	
	Year-round. High: Apr.–Aug.	Slope: 111	

Texas Golf Guide

Houston Area

P	**Old Orchard Golf Club**	Greens:	$$–$$$ T S J
	Richmond. (713) 277-3300	Carts:	Incl.
☺☺☺	*Stables/Barn/Range*	Rating:	73.5/73.6/71.7
	27 holes. Par 72/72/72. Yards: 6,888/6,927/6,687	Slope:	130/127/124
	Year-round. High: Spring/Fall		
R	**Rayburn Country Club and Resort**	Greens:	$$ W L T J
☺☺☺	Wingate Blvd., Sam Rayburn. (409) 698-2958	Carts:	$$
DEAL	27 holes. Par 72/72/72. Yards: 6,731/6,719/6,728	Rating:	71.3/72.5/72.2
	Year-round. High: Spring/Fall	Slope:	116/129/124
P	**Rio Colorado Golf Course**	Greens:	$–$$ L T S J
☺☺☺	Riverside Park, Bay City. (409) 244-2955	Carts:	$
DEAL	18 holes. Par 72/72. Yards: 6,824/5,020	Rating:	73.1/69.1
	Year-round. High: Apr.–Oct.	Slope:	127/116
P	**Southwyck Golf Club**	Greens:	$$–$$$ W L T S J
☺☺☺	Pearland. (713) 436-9999	Carts:	Incl.
	18 holes. Par 72/72. Yards: 7,015/5,211	Rating:	72.9/68.9
	Year-round. High: Spring/Fall	Slope:	123/112
☺☺☺	**Tour 18**	Greens:	$$$–$$$$ T J
BEST	Humble. (713) 540-1818	Carts:	Incl.
	18 holes. Par 72/72. Yards: 6,807/5,583	Rating:	72.2/66.6
	Year-round. High: Apr.–May	Slope:	126/113
R	**Waterwood National Resort and Country Club**	Greens:	$$–$$$ L T S
☺☺☺	Huntsville. (409) 891-5050	Carts:	$
STATE	18 holes. Par 71/73. Yards: 6,872/5,029	Rating:	73.7/68.0
	Year-round. High: Apr.–June	Slope:	142/117
P	**Wedgewood Golf Club**	Greens:	$–$$ W T S J
☺☺	Hwy. 105 W., Conroe. (409) 441-4653	Carts:	$
	18 holes. Par 72/72. Yards: 6,817/5,071	Rating:	73.7/69.6
	Year-round. High: Spring/Fall	Slope:	134/128
R	**The Woodlands Resort and Country Club**	Greens:	$$ W L T
	N. Millbend Dr., The Woodlands. (713) 367-1100	Carts:	$
☺☺☺☺	*North Course*	Rating:	NA
	18 holes. Par 72/72. Yards: 6,881/6,339	Slope:	126/122
	Year-round. High: Spring/Fall		
☺☺☺☺	*TPC at the Woodlands*	Rating:	73.6/70.3
STATE	18 holes. Par 72/72. Yards: 7,045/5,302	Slope:	135/120

The West, Alaska, and Hawaii

Alaska	Nevada
Arizona	New Mexico
California	Oregon
Colorado	Utah
Hawaii	Washington
Idaho	Wyoming
Montana	

Alaska

Let's be charitable here: Alaska is not the most hospitable location for golf-ing. The population is small and very spread out, and the tourists who come to the 49th state do not often arrive in search of the perfect 350-yard wooded dogleg. The courses may not be as fabulous as some you'll find in the lower 48 states, but some of the views—from mountains to moose—are incomparable.

The best course in Alaska may be the **Anchorage Golf Course**, set at the base of the Chugach Mountains with a view of Anchorage and, on clear days, distant vistas of Mount McKinley.

The state has about a dozen courses of various descriptions, including the **Eagleglen Golf Course** at Elmendorf Air Force Base in Anchorage. Yet another Robert Trent Jones course, it is a very scenic watery challenge.

We expect you already know that it gets cold and snowy in much of Alaska in the winter. Most courses are open from about May to October, with high-season rates in effect for the heart of the summer. Expect the best deals in the spring and fall. The summer days are longer than anywhere else in the nation, while winter days may not last much longer than 18 holes and lunch.

Econoguide Leader Board: Best Public Courses in Alaska

☺☺ Anchorage Golf Course

☺ Any course that is within a few hours of where you are and open

Econoguide Leader Board: Best Deal in Alaska

$$/☺☺   Anchorage Golf Course

Alaska Golf Guide

Anchorage Area

P	**Anchorage Golf Course**	Greens:	$$	R S J
☺☺	O'Malley Rd., Anchorage. (907) 522-3363	Carts:	$	
DEAL	18 holes. Par 72/72. Yards: 6,616/4,848	Rating:	72.1/68.2	
STATE	May–Oct. High: June–Aug.	Slope:	130/119	
P	**Eagleglen Golf Course**	Greens:	$–$$	L T S
☺☺	Elmendorf A.F.B., Anchorage. (907) 552-3821	Carts:	Inquire	
	18 holes. Par 72/72. Yards: 6,689/5,457	Rating:	71.6/70.4	
	May–Oct. High: June–Aug.	Slope:	128/123	
P	**Palmer Golf Course**	Greens:	$$	S J
☺	Lepak Ave., Palmer. (907) 745-4653	Carts:	$	
	18 holes. Par 72/73. Yards: 7,125/5,895	Rating:	74.5/74.6	
	May–Sept. High: May–July	Slope:	132/127	

Fairbanks

SP	**North Star Golf Course**	Greens:	$$	W R J
☺	Fairbanks. (907) 457-4653	Carts:	$	
	18 holes. Par 72/72. Yards: 6,852/5,995	Rating:	NA	
	May–Oct. High: June–Sept.	Slope:	NA	

Arizona

There are *a lot* of golf courses in the mostly arid and mountainous land of Arizona, proof positive of the state's lure to retirees and tourists. In fact, the state counts more than 225 courses. Some of the resort courses are kept quite green, but the lack of water in much of the state means you can expect to find a lot of sand and some unusual conditions including cactus, creosote bushes, and wildlife not common in cooler and wetter climes.

The state's best includes **The Boulders Club** in Carefree, north of Phoenix.

The North Course is a desert classic, and the South Course is equally challenging.

Another desert delight is the **Los Caballeros Golf Club** in Wickenburg, a bit farther north out of Phoenix.

In Sedona you'll find the **Sedona Golf Resort**, a breathtaking mountain course amidst the red rocks of Oak Creek Canyon.

And then there is **Troon North Golf Club** in Scottsdale, a national treasure with unreal greens in a desert setting.

The Stadium Course of the **Tournament Players Club** near Scottsdale is the site of the annual Phoenix Open, where some 400,000 fans squeeze onto the viewing mounds during tournament week.

Ventana Canyon Golf and Racquet Club offers a pair of memorable courses in Tucson. The Canyon Course is set at the base of the Catalina Mountains and plays into the Esperanto Canyon. The Mountain Course presents a high-desert challenge.

Also in Tucson is the superlative **Westin La Paloma**, with three nine-hole desert courses. They are so desertlike that not a splash of water is likely to interfere with your game; instead count on a lot of bunkers, mounds, and other dry natural obstructions.

At **Ocotillo** in Chandler, water is nearby on 23 of the 27 holes.

In the northern portion of the state, where there is a bit of green, the best golfing runs from late spring through the summer. In the desert around Phoenix and the rest of the southern portion of the state, golfing is best in the cooler fall and winter.

The posh **Wigwam Resort** in Litchfield Park, west of Phoenix, was built in 1918 as lodging for visiting executives of the Goodyear Tire and Rubber Company. Although it has undergone extensive renovation over the years, it still retains its old-time appeal, a five-star resort with 331 *casitas* for guests.

There are three courses at the resort, including a pair designed by Robert Trent Jones, Sr. The Gold Course is a huge course, sprawling across nearly twice the acreage of most modern courses.

High season includes the winter and spring, from early January through mid-May. In 1996 rooms rented for about $280–$430 per night. Fall rates (September through the end of the year) ranged from about $230 to $360 per night. Prices in the summer, from mid-May through early September, dropped to $120–$200. Golf packages, some including meals and other amenities, were also available. One example is a midweek high-season price of $570 per person for three nights and three rounds of golf; the same package drops to $438 per person in spring and fall, and $195 in the low summer season.

Econoguide Leader Board: Best Public Courses in Arizona

⊚⊚⊚⊚   The Boulders Club (North, South)
⊚⊚⊚⊚   Los Caballeros Golf Club
⊚⊚⊚⊚   Ocotillo Golf Club (Blue, White, Gold)
⊚⊚⊚⊚   Sedona Golf Resort
⊚⊚⊚⊚   Starr Pass Golf Club

⊝⊝⊝   Tonto Verde Golf Club
⊝⊝⊝⊝   Tournament Players Club of Scottsdale (Stadium)
⊝⊝⊝⊝   Troon North Golf Club
⊝⊝⊝⊝   Ventana Canyon Golf and Racquet Club (Mountain, Canyon)
⊝⊝⊝   Westin La Paloma Country Club (Ridge, Canyon, Hill)
⊝⊝⊝   Wigwam Golf and Country Club (Gold)

Econoguide Leader Board: Best Deals in Arizona

$$/⊝⊝⊝   Antelope Hills Golf Course
$/⊝⊝⊝   Desert Hills Golf Course
$$/⊝⊝⊝   Emerald Canyon Golf Course
$$/⊝⊝⊝   Happy Trails Golf Resort
$$/⊝⊝⊝   Papago Golf Course
$$/⊝⊝⊝   Pueblo El Mirage Country Club
$$/⊝⊝⊝   Silver Creek Golf Club
$$/⊝⊝⊝   Sun City Vistoso Golf Club

Arizona Golf Guide

Flagstaff Area

P ⊝⊝	**Elden Hills Golf Club** N. Oakmont Dr., Flagstaff. (520) 527-7999 18 holes. Par 73/73. Yards: 6,029/5,280 Mar.–Nov. High: May–Sept.	Greens: Carts: Rating: Slope:	$$ $ 66.6/70.5 115/120	W L T J
SP ⊝⊝⊝	**Oakcreek Country Club** Bell Rock Blvd., Sedona. (520) 284-1660 18 holes. Par 72/72. Yards: 6,854/5,555 Year-round. High: June–Oct.	Greens: Carts: Rating: Slope:	$$$ Incl. 71.0/71.6 129/130	T J
P ⊝⊝⊝⊝ STATE	**Sedona Golf Resort** Hwy. 179, Sedona. (520) 284-9355 18 holes. Par 71/71. Yards: 6,642/5,030 Year-round. High: Mar.–Nov.	Greens: Carts: Rating: Slope:	$$$–$$$$ Incl. 70.3/67.0 129/109	W L T

Lake Havasu City

P ⊝⊝	**London Bridge Golf Club** Lake Havasu City. (520) 855-2719 *London Bridge Course* 18 holes. Par 71/72. Yards: 6,618/5,756 Year-round. High: Jan.–Apr.	Greens: Carts: Rating: Slope:	$$–$$$ Incl. 70.4/73.5 122/133	L T S J
⊝⊝	*Stonebridge Course* 18 holes. Par 71/71. Yards: 6,166/5,045	Rating: Slope:	68.8/68.6 114/118	

Phoenix Area

SP ⊝⊝	**Ahwatukee Country Club** S. 48th St., Phoenix. (602) 893-1161 18 holes. Par 72/72. Yards: 6,713/5,506 Year-round. High: Jan.–Mar.	Greens: Carts: Rating: Slope:	$$$$ Incl. 71.5/70.3 124/118	W L T
P ⊝⊝⊝ DEAL	**Antelope Hills Golf Course** Perkins Dr., Prescott. (520) 776-7888 *North Course* 18 holes. Par 72/74. Yards: 6,778/6,097 Year-round. High: Apr.–Oct.	Greens: Carts: Rating: Slope:	$$ Inquire 71.4/74.3 131/126	L T J
⊝⊝	*South Course* 18 holes. Par 72/72. Yards: 7,014/5,560	Rating: Slope:	71.3/71.0 124/113	
R ⊝⊝	**Arizona Golf Resort** S. Power Rd., Mesa. (602) 832-1661	Greens: Carts:	$$$$ Incl.	W L R T

Arizona Golf Guide

Phoenix Area

	18 holes. Par 71/71. Yards: 6,574/6,195	Rating:	NA
	Year-round. High: Jan.–Mar.	Slope:	123/117

SP	**Arizona Biltmore Country Club**	Greens:	$$–$$$$$ L
	24th St. and Missouri, Phoenix. (602) 955-9655	Carts:	Incl.
☺☺☺	*Adobe Course*	Rating:	71.5/74.3
	18 holes. Par 72/73. Yards: 6,800/6,101	Slope:	121/123
	Year-round. High: Jan.–May		

☺☺☺	*Links Course*	Rating:	69.3/68.0
	18 holes. Par 71/71. Yards: 6,300/4,747	Slope:	122/107

R	**The Boulders Club**	Greens:	$$$$$$ L
	N. Tom Darlington Dr., Carefree. (602) 488-9028	Carts:	Incl.
☺☺☺☺	*North Course*	Rating:	NA
BEST	18 holes. Par 72/72. Yards: 6,731/4,893	Slope:	135/113
	Year-round. High: Feb.–May		

☺☺☺☺	*South Course*	Rating:	NA
STATE	18 holes. Par 71/71. Yards: 6,589/4,715	Slope:	137/107

P	**Club West Golf Club**	Greens:	$$–$$$$$ L T
☺☺☺	S. 14th Ave., Phoenix. (602) 460-4400	Carts:	Incl.
	18 holes. Par 72/72. Yards: 7,057/4,985	Rating:	73.1/63.5
	Year-round. High: Jan.–Apr.	Slope:	129/104

P	**Coyote Lakes Golf Club**	Greens:	$$–$$$ W L T J
☺☺☺	N. Coyote Lakes Pkwy., Surprise. (602) 566-2323	Carts:	Incl.
	18 holes. Par 72/72. Yards: 6,159/4,708	Rating:	68.9/68.0
	Year-round. High: Jan.–Apr.	Slope:	114/107

P	**Desert Hills Golf Course**	Greens:	$ L J
☺☺☺	Desert Hills Dr., Yuma. (520) 344-4653	Carts:	$
DEAL	18 holes. Par 72/74. Yards: 6,800/5,726	Rating:	71.1/72.4
	Year-round. High: Dec.–Apr.	Slope:	117/122

SP	**Eagle's Nest Country Club at Pebble Creek**	Greens:	$$–$$$ L T
☺☺	Goodyear. (602) 935-6750	Carts:	$
	18 holes. Par 72/72. Yards: 6,860/5,030	Rating:	72.6/68.0
	Year-round. High: Jan.–Mar.	Slope:	127/111

P	**Golf Club at El Dorado Lakes**	Greens:	$$–$$$$ W L R T
☺☺☺	W. Guadalupe, Gilbert. (602) 926-3589	Carts:	Incl.
	18 holes. Par 72/72. Yards: 6,716/4,992	Rating:	72.2/68.8
	Year-round. High: Jan.–Apr.	Slope:	132/120

P	**Emerald Canyon Golf Course**	Greens:	$–$$ W L T J
☺☺☺	Emerald Canyon Dr., Parker. (520) 667-3366	Carts:	Incl.
DEAL	18 holes. Par 72/71. Yards: 6,657/4,754	Rating:	71.5/66.2
	Year-round. High: Nov.–Mar.	Slope:	131/119

P	**Encanto Park Golf Course**	Greens:	$–$$ L T S J
☺☺	N. 15th Ave., Phoenix. (602) 253-3963	Carts:	$
	18 holes. Par 72/72. Yards: 6,386/5,731	Rating:	69.0/70.5
	Year-round. High: Feb.–Apr.	Slope:	111/111

P	**Estrella Mountain Golf Course**	Greens:	$–$$ L T S J
☺☺	Goodyear. (609) 932-3714	Carts:	Inquire
	18 holes. Par 71/73. Yards: 6,767/5,383	Rating:	71.2/71.2
	Year-round. High: Dec.–Apr.	Slope:	121/116

P	**The 500 Club**	Greens:	$$–$$$ W J
☺☺☺	W. Pinnacle Peak Rd., Glendale. (602) 492-9500	Carts:	$
	18 holes. Par 72/73. Yards: 6,543/5,557	Rating:	69/8/69.8
	Year-round. High: Nov.–Apr.	Slope:	116/112

Arizona Golf Guide

Phoenix Area

P ☺☺☺	**The Foothills Golf Club** Phoenix. (602) 460-4653 18 holes. Par 72/72. Yards: 6,958/5,438 Year-round. High: Jan.–Mar.	Greens: Carts: Rating: Slope:	$$–$$$$$ W L T J Incl. 72.3/70.1 122/114
SP ☺☺☺	**Fountain Hills Golf Club** Indian Wells Dr., Fountain Hills. (602) 837-1173 18 holes. Par 71/71. Yards: 6,087/5,035 Year-round. High: Jan.–Apr.	Greens: Carts: Rating: Slope:	$$–$$$$ L T J Inquire 68.9/68.9 119/112
R ☺☺	**Francisco Grande Resort and Golf Club** Gila Bend Hwy., Casa Grande. (520) 426-9205 18 holes. Par 72/72. Yards: 7,594/5,554 Year-round. High: Nov.–Apr.	Greens: Carts: Rating: Slope:	$$–$$$$ L J Incl. 74.9/69.9 126/112
R ☺☺☺	**Gainey Ranch Golf Club** Scottsdale. (602) 483-2582 *Dunes/Lakes/Arroyo* 27 holes. Par 72/72/72. Yards: 6,800/6,614/6,662 Year-round. High: Jan.–Apr.	Greens: Carts: Rating: Slope:	$$$$–$$$$$$ L Incl. 71.9/70.7 128/126/124
R ☺☺☺	**Gold Canyon Golf Club** S. Kings Rd., Apache Junction. (602) 982-9449 18 holes. Par 71/72. Yards: 6,398/4,876 Year-round. High: Jan.–Mar.	Greens: Carts: Rating: Slope:	$$–$$$$$ W L R T Incl. 69.8/67.5 135/112
P ☺☺	**Grayhawk Golf Club** N. Pima Rd., Scottsdale. (602) 502-1800 *Talon Course* 18 holes. Par 72/72. Yards: 7,001/5,143 Year-round. High: Oct.–May	Greens: Carts: Rating: Slope:	$$$$–$$$$$$+ L Incl. 74.3/70.0 141/121
☺☺	*Raptor Course* 18 holes. Par 71. Yards: 7,025	Greens: Carts: Rating: Slope:	$$$$$–$$$$$$+ L Incl. 74.0 136
SP ☺☺☺ DEAL	**Happy Trails Golf Resort** W. Bell Rd., Surprise. (602) 584-6000 18 holes. Par 72/72. Yards: 6,646/5,146 Year-round. High: Nov.–Apr.	Greens: Carts: Rating: Slope:	$–$$ W L R T J Incl. 72.1/68.7 124/113
P ☺☺☺	**Hillcrest Golf Club** Star Ridge Rd., Sun City West. (602) 584-1500 18 holes. Par 72/72. Yards: 6,960/5,880 Year-round. High: Nov.–May	Greens: Carts: Rating: Slope:	$$$ W L R T Incl. NA 127/119
P ☺☺☺	**Karsten Golf Course at ASU** E. Rio Salado Pkwy., Tempe. (602) 921-8070 18 holes. Par 72/72. Yards: 7.057/4,765 Year-round. High: Jan.–Apr.	Greens: Carts: Rating: Slope:	$$–$$$$$ W L J Incl. 74.3/63.4 133/110
P ☺☺	**Ken McDonald Golf Club** Tempe. (602) 350-5256 18 holes. Par 72/73. Yards: 6,743/5,872 Year-round. High: Nov.–Apr.	Greens: Carts: Rating: Slope:	$ T $ 70.8/70.8 115/112
P ☺☺☺	**The Legend Golf Resort at Arrowhead** N. 67th Ave., Glendale. (602) 561-1902 18 holes. Par 72/72. Yards: 7,005/5,233 Year-round. High: Jan.–Apr.	Greens: Carts: Rating: Slope:	$$–$$$$$ W L T Incl. 73.0/71.2 129/119
R ☺☺☺☺ STATE	**Los Caballeros Golf Club** S. Vulture Mine Rd., Wickenburg. (520) 684-2704 18 holes. Par 72/72. Yards: 6,962/5,690 Year-round. High: Feb.–Apr.	Greens: Carts: Rating: Slope:	$$$–$$$$$ L R Incl. 73.4/73.8 136/128

Arizona Golf Guide

Phoenix Area

R	**Marriott's Camelback Golf Club**	Greens:	$$–$$$$$ W L R T
	N. Mockingbird Lane, Scottsdale. (602) 948-6770	Carts:	Incl.
☺☺	*Indian Bend Course*	Rating:	71.9/72.0
	18 holes. Par 72/72. Yards: 7,014/5,917	Slope:	117/118
	Year-round. High: Jan.–Apr.		

☺☺	*Padre Course*	Rating:	70.3/71.1
	18 holes. Par 71/73. Yards: 6,559/5,626	Slope:	115/113

P	**Maryvale Golf Course**	Greens:	$–$$ W L T S J
☺☺	W. Indian School Rd., Phoenix. (602) 846-4022	Carts:	Inquire
	18 holes. Par 72/72. Yards: 6,539/5,656	Rating:	69.8/70.2
	Year-round. High: Nov.–Apr.	Slope:	115/113

R	**McCormick Ranch Golf Club**	Greens:	$$–$$$$$ W L R T
	E. McCormick Pkwy., Scottsdale. (602) 948-0260	Carts:	Incl.
☺☺☺	*Palm Course*	Rating:	73.7/70.2
	18 holes. Par 72/72. Yards: 7,032/5,210	Slope:	133/120
	Year-round. High: Jan.–June		

☺☺☺	*Pine Course*	Rating:	73.2/71.0
	18 holes. Par 72/72. Yards: 7,013/5,367	Slope:	133/120

P	**Ocotillo Golf Club**	Greens:	$$–$$$$$ L T
	Chandler. (602) 220-9000	Carts:	Incl.
☺☺☺☺	*Blue/White/Gold*	Rating:	70.8/71.3/71.4
STATE	27 holes. Par 71/72/71. Yards: 6,533/6,729/6,612	Slope:	128/131/128
	Year-round. High: Jan.–Apr.		

R	**Orange Tree Golf Club**	Greens:	$$–$$$$$
☺☺	N. 56th St., Scottsdale. (602) 948-3730	Carts:	Incl.
	18 holes. Par 72/72. Yards: 6,762/5,632	Rating:	71.3/71.8
	Year-round. High: Jan.–Mar.	Slope:	122/116

SP	**Palm Valley Golf Club**	Greens:	$–$$$ W L T J
☺☺☺	N. Litchfield Rd., Goodyear. (602) 935-2500	Carts:	$
	18 holes. Par 72/72. Yards: 7,015/5,300	Rating:	72.8/68.7
	Year-round. High: Jan.–Mar.	Slope:	130/109

P	**Papago Golf Course**	Greens:	$–$$ L T S J
☺☺☺	E. Moreland St., Phoenix. (602) 275-8428	Carts:	$
DEAL	18 holes. Par 72/72. Yards: 7,068/5,781	Rating:	73.3/72.4
	Year-round. High: Jan.–May	Slope:	132/119

R	**The Phoenician Golf Club**	Greens:	$$$$–$$$$$$+ L R
☺☺☺	E. Camelback Rd., Scottsdale. (602) 423-2449	Carts:	Incl.
	18 holes. Par 71/71. Yards: 6,487/5,058	Rating:	71.2/68.2
	Year-round. High: Oct.–May	Slope:	134/122

P	**Pohlcat Mountain View Golf Club**	Greens:	$–$$ W L T S J
	W. Baseline Rd., Laveen. (602) 237-4567	Carts:	$
☺	*East Course*	Rating:	71.7/72.3
	18 holes. Par 72/74. Yards: 6,875/5,945	Slope:	119/114
	Year-round. High: Dec.–Mar.		

☺	*West Course*	Greens:	$$ W L T S J
	18 holes. Par 71/71. Yards: 6,646/5,770	Carts:	$
		Rating:	70.9/71.6
		Slope:	121/116

R	**The Pointe Golf Club on Lookout Mountain**	Greens:	$$$–$$$$$$+ W L R T
☺☺☺	N. 7th St., Phoenix. (602) 866-6356	Carts:	Incl.
	18 holes. Par 72/72. Yards: 6,617/4,552	Rating:	71.7/65.3
	Year-round. High: Nov.–May	Slope:	131/113

Arizona Golf Guide

Phoenix Area

R ◐◐	**The Pointe Golf Club on South Mountain** S. Pointe Pkwy., Phoenix. (602) 431-6480 18 holes. Par 70/70. Yards: 6,003/4,550 Year-round. High: Jan.–Apr.	Greens: Carts: Rating: Slope:	$$–$$$$$ L T Incl. 68.1/66.2 117/107
SP ◐◐◐ DEAL	**Pueblo El Mirage Country Club** N. El Mirage Rd., El Mirage. (602) 583-0425 18 holes. Par 72/72. Yards: 6,521/5,563 Year-round. High: Nov.–Mar.	Greens: Carts: Rating: Slope:	$–$$ W L T J Incl. 70.0/71.0 119/117
SP ◐◐	**Rancho Mañana Golf Course** E. Rancho Mañana Blvd., Cave Creek. (602) 488-0398 18 holes. Par 72/73. Yards: 6,378/5,910 Year-round. High: Jan.–Apr.	Greens: Carts: Rating: Slope:	$$–$$$$ W L T Incl. NA/68.8 127/114
SP ◐◐◐	**Red Mountain Ranch Country Club** E. Teton, Mesa. (602) 985-0285 18 holes. Par 72/72. Yards: 6,797/4,982 Year-round. High: Jan.–Apr.	Greens: Carts: Rating: Slope:	$$–$$$$$$+ W L T Incl. 73.3/69.4 134/120
SP ◐◐◐	**San Marcos Golf & Country Club** N. Dakota St., Chandler. (602) 963-3358 18 holes. Par 72/72. Yards: 6,501/5,386 Year-round. High: Jan.–Apr.	Greens: Carts: Rating: Slope:	$$–$$$$ W L T Incl. 70.0/69.4 117/112
SP ◐◐	**Scottsdale Country Club** E. Shea Blvd., Scottsdale. (602) 948-6000 27 holes. Par 70/71/71. Yards: 6,085/6,335/6,292 Year-round. High: Jan.–Apr.	Greens: Carts: Rating: Slope:	$$–$$$$$ W L T Incl. 68.8/69.6/69.7 118/118/119
P ◐◐◐ DEAL	**Silver Creek Golf Club** Silver Lake Blvd., White Mountain Lake. (520) 537-2744 18 holes. Par 72/72. Yards: 6,813/5,193 Year-round. High: June–Sept.	Greens: Carts: Rating: Slope:	$–$$ W L T S J $ 71.5/68.0 131/120
SP ◐◐◐	**Stonecreek, The Golf Club** Paradise Valley. (602) 953-9111 18 holes. Par 71/71. Yards: 6,839/5,098 Year-round. High: Jan.–Apr.	Greens: Carts: Rating: Slope:	$$–$$$$$ W L J Incl. 72.6/68.4 134/118
R ◐◐◐	**Superstition Springs Golf Club** E. Baseline Rd., Mesa. (602) 985-5622 18 holes. Par 72/72. Yards: 7,005/5,328 Year-round. High: Oct.–Apr.	Greens: Carts: Rating: Slope:	$$–$$$$$ W L T Incl. 74.1/70.9 135/120
P ◐◐◐	**Tatum Ranch Golf Club** N. Tatum Ranch Dr., Cave Creek. (602) 585-2399 18 holes. Par 72/72. Yards: 6,870/5,609 Year-round. High: Nov.–Apr.	Greens: Carts: Rating: Slope:	$$–$$$$$ W L T J Incl. 73.4/71.5 128/116
SP ◐◐◐ STATE	**Tonto Verde Golf Club** El Circulo Dr., Rio Verde. (602) 471-2710 18 holes. Par 72/72. Yards: 6,736/5,376 Year-round. High: Dec.–Apr.	Greens: Carts: Rating: Slope:	$$–$$$$$ L Incl. 71.1/70.8 132/124
R ◐◐	**Tournament Players Club of Scottsdale** N. Hayden Rd., Scottsdale. (602) 585-3939 *Desert Course* 18 holes. Par 71/71. Yards: 6,552/4,715 Year-round. High: Oct.–Apr.	Greens: Carts: Rating: Slope:	$ L T S Inquire 71.4/66.3 112/109
◐◐◐◐ STATE	*Stadium Course* 18 holes. Par 71/71. Yards: 6,992/5,567	Greens: Carts: Rating: Slope:	$$–$$$$$ L T Inquire 73.9/71.6 131/122

Arizona Golf Guide

Phoenix Area

SP ☺☺☺☺ BEST	**Troon North Golf Club** E. Dynamite Blvd., Scottsdale. (602) 585-5300 18 holes. Par 72/72. Yards: 7,008/5,050 Year-round. High: Nov.–May	Greens: Carts: Rating: Slope:	$$$$–$$$$$$+ L J Incl. 73.1/69.0 146/116

R ☺☺☺	**The Wigwam Golf and Country Club** N. Litchfield Rd., Litchfield Park. (602) 272-4653 *Blue Course* 18 holes. Par 72/72. Yards: 6,130/5,235 Year-round. High: Jan.–May	Greens: Carts: Rating: Slope:	$$–$$$$$ L R Incl. 67.9/69.8 115/112

☺☺☺ STATE	*Gold Course* 18 holes. Par 72/72. Yards: 7,021/5,737	Rating: Slope:	73.6/72.2 129/120

☺☺☺	*Red Course* 18 holes. Par 72/72. Yards: 6,867/5,821	Rating: Slope:	71.8/71.9 118/115

Tucson Area

P ☺☺☺	**San Ignacio Golf Club** S. Camino Del Sol, Green Valley. (520) 648-3468 27 holes. Par 71/72. Yards: 6,704/5,200 Year-round. High: Jan.–Apr.	Greens: Carts: Rating: Slope:	$$–$$$ L $ 71.4/68.7 129/116

R ☺☺☺	**Sheraton El Conquistador Country Club** N. La Canada, Tucson. (520) 544-1800 *Sunrise Course* 18 holes. Par 72/72. Yards: 6,819/5,255 Year-round. High: Feb.–Apr.	Greens: Carts: Rating: Slope:	$$$–$$$$$$ L R Incl. 71.7/69.4 123/116

☺☺☺	*Sunset Course* 18 holes. Par 72/72. Yards: 6,763/5,323	Rating: Slope:	71.2/69.5 123/116

SP ☺☺☺☺ STATE	**Starr Pass Golf Club** W. Starr Pass Blvd., Tucson. (520) 670-0400 18 holes. Par 71/71. Yards: 6,910/5,071 Year-round. High: Jan.–May	Greens: Carts: Rating: Slope:	$$$–$$$$$ L R T Incl. 139/121 74.6/70.7

SP ☺☺☺ DEAL	**Sun City Vistoso Golf Club** E. Rancho Vistos Blvd., Tucson. (520) 825-3110 18 holes. Par 72/72. Yards: 6,723/5,109 Year-round. High: Nov.–Apr.	Greens: Carts: Rating: Slope:	$$ $ 71.8/68.3 137/114

R ☺☺☺	**Tucson National Resort and Conference Center** Tucson. (520) 575-7540 *Orange/Gold/Green* 27 holes. Par 73/73/72. Yards: 7,108/6,860/6,692 Year-round. High: Oct.–May	Greens: Carts: Rating: Slope:	$$$–$$$$$$+ R Incl. 74.8/74.7/74.6 136/135/134

R ☺☺☺ STATE	**Ventana Canyon Golf and Racquet Club** Tucson. (520) 577-4061 *Canyon Course* 18 holes. Par 72/72. Yards: 6,819/4,919 Year-round. High: Oct.–May	Greens: Carts: Rating: Slope:	$$$$–$$$$$$+ L R Incl. 72.7/68.3 141/114

☺☺☺☺ BEST	*Mountain Course* 18 holes. Par 72/72. Yards: 6,926/4,789	Rating: Slope:	74.2/68.3 146/117

R ☺☺☺☺ BEST	**Westin La Paloma Country Club** Tucson. (520) 299-1500 *Ridge/Canyon/Hill* 27 holes. Par 72/72/72. Yards: 7,088/7,017/6,997 Year-round. High: Jan.–May	Greens: Carts: Rating: Slope:	$$$$–$$$$$$ Incl. 75.3/74.2/74.8 152/150/151

California

Let's do lunch . . . at the club. There are some spectacular private and resort clubhouses in the Golden State . . . and more than a few fantastic golf courses too.

The state is so large that there are at least three regions that claim some sort of golf immortality: Pebble Beach in Monterey, the Palm Springs area, and the greater San Diego region. They may all be right; the only challenge may come from the fact that spotted around California are a number of other gems that would earn best-of-state ratings almost anywhere else.

In portions of the state—desert courses in and around Palm Springs among them—the summer climate can be brutal, with temperatures climbing well into triple digits. If you must play in the hot season, try to take advantage of early morning or late afternoon tee times; you can also expect to be rewarded with discounts of as much as 50 percent on hotels and greens fees for golfing between mid-May and mid-October.

The celebrity-filled history of California had a lot to do with the development of golf as we know it. Star golfer Bing Crosby is credited with launching much of the glitzy industry in 1946 when he hosted a tournament at Rancho Santa Fe, which is located north of San Diego; a year later, Crosby moved his party to the Monterey Peninsula, spreading the seeds of high-profile golf there. Another important figure in California golf was comedian Bob Hope, who helped establish the Coachella Valley and the Palm Springs area as two of the sport's meccas.

Pebble Beach/Monterey Area

The Monterey Peninsula on the central coast brings together the beauty of the sand, the green hills, the sea, the fog, and the golf.

Perhaps the most famous course in California and by some ratings the best in America is **Pebble Beach Golf Links** on the spectacular 17-Mile Drive. The course opened in 1919 and has been at or near the pinnacle of American golfing dreams ever since, serving as the site of three U.S. Opens. The course dates back to 1910, when the land was purchased from the Del Monte fruit company by businessman and artist Samuel F. B. Morse. Among the most difficult challenges is the 8th hole, which includes a nearly 200-yard carry over a deep chasm to a green surrounded by bunkers and backed up by a cliff; the finishing 18th hole brings you along the shores of Carmel Bay. Tee times can be difficult to obtain and, at around $200, difficult to rationalize, but few golfers complain about the experience.

Almost as wonderful is the **Spyglass Hill Golf Course**, a very difficult course with gorgeous ocean and forest views.

Also in the Pebble Beach area, there is **The Links at Spanish Bay**, a beach course not as famous as Pebble Beach itself, but considered by many to be almost as good and slightly less exorbitantly priced—expect to pay at least $125 for a round. Spanish Bay is considered one of the best classic links-style courses in America. It's a Robert Trent Jones, Jr., design that includes huge sand dunes, thick underbrush, and strong ocean winds.

Pebble Beach, Spyglass Hill, and Spanish Bay are all owned by the same company and are open to the public—although, as mentioned earlier, tee times can be very difficult to obtain.

The **Pasatiempo Golf Club** in Santa Cruz on the other side of Monterey Bay is a classic older course that is often compared to the Pebble Beach offerings. It includes the 395-yard 16th hole, a blind drive where you must trust in your skills—and the course map from the tee.

Other exceptional recreational opportunities include fishing and visiting the spectacular Monterey Bay Aquarium and the Carmel Mission, which dates back to 1771. Shopping opportunities abound near Cannery Row, a place immortalized by author John Steinbeck. An extraordinary visual entertainment is a car or bicycle tour along the gorgeous 17-Mile Drive, which goes down to the ocean, passing Pebble Beach, Cypress Point, and Spanish Bay.

Palm Springs/Coachella Valley Area

The self-proclaimed golf capital of the world in the Coachella Valley boasts some 90 courses in a 150-square-mile area. It features tracks by name designers including Jack Nicklaus, Arnold Palmer, Gary Player, Pete Dye, Robert Trent Jones, Jr., and others. Marquee tournaments at the courses are also likely to draw Hollywood stars.

To the north of Palm Springs, **Desert Dunes Golf Club** is a desert course considered an absolute pleasure except when the wind is blowing, which happens often. The Mountain Course at **La Quinta Resort and Club** about 15 miles east of Palm Springs is a spectacular desert track. The La Quinta Hotel, which dates back to 1926—making it a California antiquity—was an important extension of Hollywood in the 1930s and 1940s. The three golf courses, all designed by Pete Dye, were added in the 1970s and 1980s.

Another beauty in the area is the **Westin Mission Hills North Golf Course** in Rancho Mirage, a meticulously manicured challenge. The original course is a relatively forgiving Pete Dye design; the North Course, planned by Gary Player, wends its way among sand dunes, waterfalls, and rock formations set against the San Jacinto Mountains.

At the **PGA West Resort** in La Quinta there are two national stars: the Jack Nicklaus Resort Course and the TPC Stadium Course, which includes a famed island green on the 17th hole and the almost unbearably challenging Eternity 11th hole. The Stadium Course was designed to be as difficult as possible, and by most accounts that goal was met.

The **Ojai Valley Inn** is another link to old Hollywood, the setting for Frank Capra's famous 1937 film *Lost Horizon*. The old course there was reworked in the 1980s and is a regular stop on the tournament circuit.

By the way, if you want to mix with the horsey set, the polo season in Palm Springs runs from November through April.

Los Angeles Area

North of Los Angeles in Newport Coast, there is the **Pelican Hill Golf Club**, with its highly rated Links and Ocean courses, which have both been compared to the Pebble Beach standard. Also up the coast, above Santa Barbara, is the **Sandpiper Golf Course** on the sea cliffs in Goleta, one of the best and most spectacular public courses.

The **Redhawk Golf Club** is in Temecula, midway between Los Angeles and San Diego, and is considered a beautifully manicured destination from either direction. The Temecula Valley, a rich grape-growing region, benefits from cool ocean breezes most afternoons.

San Diego Area

San Diego has won the title of Sports Town USA, thanks to its more than 80 courses and its other outdoor appeals, including some 70 miles of Pacific Ocean beaches to the west and the Laguna and Palomar mountain ranges to the east.

San Diego won its golfing fame through the South Course at the **Torrey Pines Golf Course** in La Jolla, just north of San Diego, with its majestic coastal cliffs. The North Course is only slightly less wonderful. Torrey Pines is on the most-favored list of many golfers and the site of a PGA Tour tourney.

Other showplaces include **Aviara Golf Club**, the only Arnold Palmer–designed course in the area, located in Carlsbad, north of San Diego. The course sprawls across hills and valleys and on some holes overlooks Batiquitos Lagoon, a state environmental treasure. The lush hotel facilities are managed by Four Seasons Hotels and Resorts.

The annual Mercedes Championships are held each January on the PGA Championship Course at the **La Costa Resort and Spa** in Carlsbad, featuring the previous year's tour winners of the major tournaments, including the British Open, the Masters, the U.S. Open, and PGA Regular and Senior Championships. La Costa is open to guests and club members and includes some of the most sumptuous facilities of any golf resort in the world.

La Costa Resort and Spa's two PGA championship golf courses are home to the annual MONY Tournament of Champions golf classic.
Courtesy of the San Diego
Convention & Visitors Bureau.

California is a huge state, with widely varying climates and conditions. The northern California and mountain areas offer cool summers and cool-to-temperate winters. Central areas deliver hot summers and moderate winters. And desert and southern areas can be absolutely brutal in the summer, with midday temperatures reaching as high as 120°F with frightening regularity.

Because of this variation, the off-peak seasons around the state differ. Most courses are open year-round. Check the listings in this Econoguide for high seasons.

Econoguide Leader Board: Best Public Courses in California

○○	Ancil Hoffman Golf Course
○○○○	Aviara Golf Club
○○○○	Desert Dunes Golf Club
○○○○	La Quinta Resort and Club (Mountain)
○○○○	The Links at Spanish Bay
○○○○	Oak Valley Golf Club
○○○○	Ojai Valley Inn
○○○○	Pasatiempo Golf Club
○○○○	Pebble Beach Golf Links
○○○○	Pelican Hill Golf Club (Links, Ocean)
○○○○	PGA West Resort (Nicklaus, Stadium)
○○○○	Sandpiper Golf Course
○○○○	Spyglass Hill Golf Course
○○○○	Torrey Pines Golf Course (South, North)

Econoguide Leader Board: Best Deals in California

$$/○○○	Avila Beach Resort Golf Course
$$/○○○	Beau Pre Golf Club
$$/○○○	Canyon Oaks Golf Club
$$/○○○	Castle Oaks Golf Club
$$/○○○	Coronado Golf Course
$$/○○○	Delaveaga Golf Club
$$/○○○	Dry Creek Ranch Golf Course
$$/○○○	Elkins Ranch Golf Club
$$/○○○	El Rivino Country Club
$$/○○○○	Fall River Valley Golf and Country Club
$$/○○○	Graeagle Meadows Golf Course
$$/○○○	Horse Thief Country Club
$$/○○○	Hunter Ranch Golf Course
$$/○○○	La Contenta Golf Club
$$/○○○○	La Purisma Golf Course
$$/○○○	Lake Tahoe Golf Course
$$/○○○	Los Serranos Lakes Golf and Country Club (North, South)
$$/○○○	Morro Bay Golf Course
$$/○○○	Mountain Meadows Golf Club
$$/○○○	Oakmont Golf Club (West)
$$/○○○	Pacific Grove Municipal Golf Links

$$/○○○	Paradise Valley Golf Course
$$/○○○	Rancho Solano Golf Course
$$/○○○	Santa Teresa Golf Club
$$/○○○	Shandin Hills Golf Club
$$/○○○	Singing Hills Country Club (Oak Glen, Willow Glen)
$$/○○○	Soule Park Golf Course
$$/○○○	Tijeras Creek Golf Club

California Golf Guide

North and North Central California

SP ○○○ DEAL	**Beau Pre Golf Club** Norton Rd., McKinleyville. (707) 839-2342 18 holes. Par 72/72. Yards: 5,910/4,976 Year-round. High: May–Sept.	Greens: Carts: Rating: Slope:	$–$$ W T J $ 68.1/67.6 116/116
P ○○	**Bidwell Park Golf Course** Wildwood Ave., Chico. (916) 891-8417 18 holes. Par 72/72. Yards: 6,157 Year-round. High: June–July	Greens: Carts: Rating: Slope:	$ T S J $ 68.6/73.1 115/123
SP ○○○ DEAL	**Canyon Oaks Golf Club** Yosemite Dr., Chico. (916) 343-2582 18 holes. Par 72/72. Yards: 6,804/5,030 Year-round.	Greens: Carts: Rating: Slope:	$–$$ T S J Inquire 72.7/70.4 133/127
P ○○○○ DEAL	**Fall River Valley Golf and Country Club** Fall River Mills. (916) 336-5555 18 holes. Par 72/72. Yards: 7,365/6,200 Mar.–Nov. High: May–Sept.	Greens: Carts: Rating: Slope:	$–$$ W T S J Inquire 74.1/74.6 129/127
R ○○○ DEAL	**Graeagle Meadows Golf Course** Hwy. 89, Graeagle. (916) 836-2323 18 holes. Par 72/72. Yards: 6,680/5,640 Apr.–Nov. High: July–Aug.	Greens: Carts: Rating: Slope:	$$ T Inquire 70.7/71.3 118/118
R ○○○	**Lake Shastina Golf Resort** Weed. (916) 938-3205 *Championship Course* 18 holes. Par 72/72. Yards: 6,969/5,530 Year-round. High: May–Sept.	Greens: Carts: Rating: Slope:	$$–$$$ L R T J $ 72.6/NA 126/117
P ○○○ DEAL	**Morro Bay Golf Course** State Park Rd., Morro Bay. (805) 772-4341 18 holes. Par 71/72. Yards: 6,360/5,055 Year-round. High: Apr.–Aug.	Greens: Carts: Rating: Slope:	$$ T S J $ 70.4/69.5 118/117

Sacramento Area

SP ○○○	**Alta Sierra Golf and Country Club** Tammy Way, Grass Valley. (916) 273-2010 18 holes. Par 72/72. Yards: 6,537/5,984 Year-round. High: Apr.–June	Greens: Carts: Rating: Slope:	$$–$$$ W J $ 71.2/74.6 128/128
P ○○ STATE	**Ancil Hoffman Golf Course** Tarshes Dr., Carmichael. (916) 482-5660 18 holes. Par 72/73. Yards: 6,794/5,356 Year-round.	Greens: Carts: Rating: Slope:	$–$$ T S Inquire 72.5/73.4 123/123
P ○○○ DEAL	**Castle Oaks Golf Club** Castle Oaks Dr., Ione. (209) 274-0167 18 holes. Par 72/72. Yards: 6,739/4,953 Year-round. High: Spring/Fall	Greens: Carts: Rating: Slope:	$–$$ W T S J $ 72.3/67.3 129/114
P ○○	**Cherry Island Golf Course** Elverta Rd., Elverta. (916) 991-7293 18 holes. Par 72/72. Yards: 6,562/5,163 Year-round. High: Apr.–Nov.	Greens: Carts: Rating: Slope:	$–$$ L T S J $ 71.1/70.0 124/117

California Golf Guide

Sacramento Area

P	**Diamond Oaks Golf Club**	Greens:	$	W T S J
◎◎	Diamond Oaks Rd., Roseville. (916) 783-4947	Carts:	$	
	18 holes. Par 72/72. Yards: 6,283/5,608	Rating:	69.5/70.5	
	Year-round. High: Apr.–Oct.	Slope:	115/112	

P	**Dry Creek Ranch Golf Course**	Greens:	$–$$	W L T
◎◎◎	Crystal Way, Galt. (209) 745-4653	Carts:	$	
DEAL	18 holes. Par 72/74. Yards: 6,773/5,952	Rating:	72.7/73.9	
	Year-round. High: Apr.–July	Slope:	129/128	

P	**Green Tree Golf Club**	Greens:	$	T S J
◎◎	Leisure Town Rd., Vacaville. (707) 448-1420	Carts:	$	
	18 holes. Par 72/72. Yards: 6,017/5,318	Rating:	68.2/69.5	
	Year-round. High: Mar.–Nov.	Slope:	114/117	

P	**Haggin Oaks Golf Course**	Greens:	$	W T
	Fulton Ave., Sacramento. (916) 481-4507	Carts:	$	
◎	*North Course*	Rating:	71.4/71.7	
	18 holes. Par 72/72. Yards: 6,631/5,853	Slope:	115/111	
	Year-round. High: Apr.–Sept.			

◎◎	*South Course*	Rating:	70.6/71.4	
	18 holes. Par 72/72. Yards: 6,602/5,732	Slope:	113/113	

SP	**Rancho Murieta Country Club**	Greens:	$$$–$$$$	L R J
	Alameda Dr., Rancho Murieta. (916) 354-3440	Carts:	Incl.	
◎◎◎	*North Course*	Rating:	72.8/71.6	
	18 holes. Par 72/72. Yards: 6,839/5,608	Slope:	131/136	
	Year-round. High: Apr.–Oct.			

◎◎◎	*South Course*	Rating:	72.6/71.6	
	18 holes. Par 72/72. Yards: 6,886/5,527	Slope:	127/122	

P	**Rancho Solano Golf Course**	Greens:	$$	W T S J
◎◎◎	Rancho Solano Pkwy., Fairfield. (707) 429-4653	Carts:	Inquire	
DEAL	18 holes. Par 72/72. Yards: 7,011/5,624	Rating:	72.6/69.6	
	Year-round. High: June–Sept.	Slope:	127/117	

San Francisco Area

P	**Adobe Creek Golf Club**	Greens:	$–$$$$	W T S J
◎◎	Frates Rd., Petaluma. (707) 765-3000	Carts:	$	
	18 holes. Par 72/72. Yards: 6,825/5,027	Rating:	73.8/69.4	
	Year-round. High: May–Oct.	Slope:	131/120	

P	**Aptos Seascape Golf Course**	Greens:	$–$$$	W L R T S J
◎◎◎	Aptos. (408) 688-3213	Carts:	$$	
	18 holes. Par 72/72. Yards: 6,116/5,576	Rating:	69.8/72.6	
	Year-round. High: June–Oct.	Slope:	126/127	

P	**Bennett Valley Golf Course**	Greens:	$	W T S J
◎◎	Yulupa Ave., Santa Rosa. (707) 528-3673	Carts:	$	
	18 holes. Par 72/72. Yards: 6,600/5,958	Rating:	70.6/72.5	
	Year-round. High: May–Sept.	Slope:	112/123	

R	**Bodega Harbour Golf Links**	Greens:	$$–$$$$	W L R T
◎◎◎	Heron Dr., Bodega Bay. (707) 875-3538	Carts:	$	
	18 holes. Par 70/71. Yards: 6,260/4,749	Rating:	71.9/67.7	
	Year-round. High: Apr.–Oct.	Slope:	130/120	

P	**Canyon Lakes Country Club**	Greens:	$$$–$$$$	
◎◎◎	Bollinger Canyon Way, San Ramon. (510) 735-6511	Carts:	Incl.	
	18 holes. Par 70/71. Yards: 6,731/5,234	Rating:	70.9/69.9	
	Year-round. High: Feb.–Oct.	Slope:	124/121	

SP	**The Chardonnay Golf Club**	Greens:	$$$$–$$$$$$	W L T S J
	Jameson Canyon Rd., Napa. (707) 257-8950	Carts:	Incl.	
◎◎	*The Club Shakespeare*	Rating:	74.5/70.9	

California Golf Guide

San Francisco Area

	18 holes. Par 72/72. Yards: 6,811/5,200 Year-round. High: Apr.–Oct.	Slope:	137/125

☺☺☺	*The Vineyards Course* 18 holes. Par 71/71. Yards: 6,811/5,200	Greens: Carts: Rating: Slope:	$$$–$$$$ Incl. 73.7/70.1 133/126

P	**Chuck Corica Golf Complex**	Greens: $–$$	W T S J
	Alameda. (510) 522-4321	Carts: $	
☺☺	*Earl Fry Course*	Rating: 69.2/71.0	
	18 holes. Par 71/72. Yards: 6,141/5,560 Year-round. High: May–Oct.	Slope: 119/114	

☺☺	*Jack Clark South Course*	Rating: 70.8/70.0
	18 holes. Par 71/71. Yards: 6,559/5,473	Slope: 119/110

P	**Delaveaga Golf Club**	Greens: $$	W T
☺☺☺	Upper Park Rd., Santa Cruz. (408) 423-7214	Carts: Inquire	
DEAL	18 holes. Par 72/72. Yards: 6,010/5,331 Year-round.	Rating: 70.4/70.6 Slope: 133/125	

P	**Diablo Creek Golf Course**	Greens: $	W T S J
☺☺	Port Chicago Hwy., Concord. (510) 686-6262	Carts: $	
	18 holes. Par 71/72. Yards: 6,866/5,872 Year-round.	Rating: 72.2/72.5 Slope: 122/119	

SP	**Fountaingrove Resort and Country Club**	Greens: $$$–$$$$	W T
☺☺☺	Fountaingrove Pkwy., Santa Rosa. (707) 579-4653	Carts: Incl.	
	18 holes. Par 72/72. Yards: 6,797/5,644 Year-round. High: May–Oct.	Rating: 72.8/72.1 Slope: 132/128	

P	**Franklin Canyon Golf Course**	Greens: $$	W L T S J
☺☺	Hwy. 4, Rodeo. (510) 799-6191	Carts: $	
	18 holes. Par 72/72. Yards: 6,776/5,516 Year-round.	Rating: 70.9/71.2 Slope: 118/123	

R	**Half Moon Bay Golf Links**	Greens: $$$$$	W R T
☺☺☺	Half Moon Bay. (415) 726-4438	Carts: Incl.	
	18 holes. Par 72/72. Yards: 7,131/5,769 Year-round.	Rating: 74.5/73.3 Slope: 136/125	

P	**Harding Park Golf Club**	Greens: $$	W T S J
☺☺	Skyline Blvd., San Francisco. (415) 664-4690	Carts: $$	
	18 holes. Par 72/73. Yards: 6,743/6,205 Year-round. High: Apr.–Nov.	Rating: 72.1/74.1 Slope: 124/120	

SP	**La Contenta Golf Club**	Greens: $$	W R T S J
☺☺☺	Hwy. 26, Valley Springs. (209) 772-1081	Carts: $	
DEAL	18 holes. Par 71/72. Yards: 6,425/5,120 Year-round. High: Mar.–Oct.	Rating: 70.2/70.8 Slope: 125/120	

P	**Lincoln Park Golf Course**	Greens: $$	W T J
☺☺	34th Ave., San Francisco. (415) 221-9911	Carts: $$	
	18 holes. Par 68/70. Yards: 5,194/4,984 Year-round. High: Apr.–Nov.	Rating: 64.4/67.4 Slope: 106/108	

P	**Micke Grove Golf Links**	Greens: $–$$	W T S J
☺☺	Lodi. (209) 369-4410	Carts: $	
	18 holes. Par 72/72. Yards: 6,565/5,286 Year-round. High: Mar.–Nov.	Rating: 71.1/69.7 Slope: 118/111	

P	**Mountain Shadows Golf Course**	Greens: $$	W T S J
	Rohnert Park. (707) 584-7766	Carts: $	
☺☺	*North Course*	Rating: 72.1/70.5	
	18 holes. Par 72/72. Yards: 7,035/5,503 Year-round. High: Apr.–Oct.	Slope: NA	

California Golf Guide

San Francisco Area

☺	*South Course* 18 holes. Par 72/72. Yards: 6,720/5,805	Rating: Slope:	70.1/71.4 115/122

P
☺☺
Mountain Springs Golf Club
Sonora. (209) 532-1000
18 holes. Par 72/71. Yards: 6,665/5,195
Year-round. High: Apr.–Sept.

Greens: $–$$ T S J
Carts: $
Rating: 70.8/71.7
Slope: 124/120

P
☺☺
Napa Municipal Golf Club
Streblow Dr., Napa. (707) 255-4333
18 holes. Par 72/73. Yards: 6,730/5,956
Year-round. High: Apr.–Nov.

Greens: $–$$ W L T S J
Carts: $$
Rating: 71.7/76.8
Slope: 127/137

SP
☺☺☺
Oakhurst Country Club
Peacock Creek Dr., Clayton. (510) 672-9737
18 holes. Par 72/72. Yards: 6,739/5,285
Year-round.

Greens: $$$–$$$$ T S J
Carts: Incl.
Rating: 73.1/70.3
Slope: 132/123

SP

☺☺☺
DEAL
Oakmont Golf Club
Oakmont Dr., Santa Rosa. (707) 539-0415
West Course
18 holes. Par 72/72. Yards: 6,379/5,573
Year-round.

Greens: $$ T
Carts: $
Rating: 70.5/71.9
Slope: 121/128

P
☺☺☺
Paradise Valley Golf Course
Paradise Valley Dr., Fairfield. (707) 426-1600
18 holes. Par 72/72. Yards: 6,993/5,413
Year-round.

Greens: $$ W L R T
Carts: $
Rating: 74.1/71.1
Slope: 135/119

R

☺☺☺
Ridgemark Golf and Country Club
Airline Hwy., Hollister. (408) 637-1010
Diablo Course
18 holes. Par 72/72. Yards: 6,603/5,475
Year-round.

Greens: $$$ T
Carts: Incl.
Rating: 71.9/72.0
Slope: 123/123

☺☺
Gabilan Course
18 holes. Par 72/72. Yards: 6,781/5,683

Rating: 72.0/72.7
Slope: 124/124

P
☺☺
Riverside Golf Club
Monterey Rd., Coyote. (408) 463-0622
18 holes. Par 72/73. Yards: 6,881/5,942
Year-round.

Greens: $$ W L T S J
Carts: Inquire
Rating: 72.2/72.5
Slope: 127/118

SP
☺☺☺
San Geronimo Golf Club
Sir Francis Drake Blvd., San Geronimo. (415) 488-4030
18 holes. Par 72/72. Yards: 6,801/5,140
Year-round. High: Mar.–Oct.

Greens: $$–$$$ W T S J
Carts: Inquire
Rating: 73.3/69.9
Slope: 130/125

P
☺☺
San Jose Municipal Golf Course
Oakland Rd., San Jose. (408) 441-4653
18 holes. Par 72/72. Yards: 6,602/5,594
Year-round.

Greens: $$ W T S J
Carts: Inquire
Rating: 70.1/69.7
Slope: 108/112

SP
☺
San Ramon Royal Vista Golf Club
Fircrest Lane, San Ramon. (510) 828-6100
18 holes. Par 72/73. Yards: 6,560/5,770
Year-round. High: May–Sept.

Greens: $$ T S J
Carts: Inquire
Rating: 70.9/72.7
Slope: 115/119

P
☺☺☺
DEAL
Santa Teresa Golf Club
Bernal Rd., San Jose. (408) 225-2650
18 holes. Par 71/73. Yards: 6,742/6,032
Year-round. High: Apr.–Sept.

Greens: $$ W T S J
Carts: Inquire
Rating: 71.1/73.5
Slope: 121/125

R

☺☺☺
Silverado Country Club and Resort
Atlas Peak Rd., Napa. (707) 257-5460
South Course
18 holes. Par 72/72. Yards: 6,685/5,672
Year-round. High: Mar.–Nov.

Greens: $$$–$$$$$$ L R T
Carts: Incl.
Rating: 72.4/71.8
Slope: 129/123

California Golf Guide

San Francisco Area

☺☺☺	North Course 18 holes. Par 72/72. Yards: 6,900/5,857	Rating: Slope:	73.4/73.1 131/128

P ☺☺	**Skywest Golf Club** Hayward. (520) 278-6188 18 holes. Par 72/73. Yards: 6,930/6,171 Year-round.	Greens: Carts: Rating: Slope:	$–$$ S J Inquire 72.8/74.3 121/123

P ☺☺☺☺	**Sonoma Golf Club** Arnold Dr., Sonoma. (707) 996-0300 18 holes. Par 72/72. Yards: 7,069/5,519 Year-round. High: Apr.–Oct.	Greens: Carts: Rating: Slope:	$$$–$$$$ W L T Incl. 74.9/71.5 135/128

P ☺☺	**Sunol Valley Golf Course** Mission Rd., Sunol. *Palm Course.* (510) 862-0414 18 holes. Par 72/74. Yards: 6,843/5,997 Year-round. High: Apr.–Sept.	Greens: Carts: Rating: Slope:	$$$ T Incl. 72.2/74.4 118/124

☺☺	*Cypress Course.* (510) 862-2404 18 holes. Par 72/72. Yards: 6,195/5,458	Rating: Slope:	69.1/70.1 115/115

P ☺☺	**Tilden Park Golf Course** Shasta Rd., Berkeley. (510) 848-7373 18 holes. Par 72/72. Yards: 6,300/5,400 Year-round. High: Apr.–Oct.	Greens: Carts: Rating: Slope:	$–$$ W T S J $$ 69.9/69.2 120/116

P ☺☺	**Van Buskirk Park Golf Course** Houston Ave., Stockton. (209) 937-7357 18 holes. Par 72/74. Yards: 6,928/5,927 Year-round.	Greens: Carts: Rating: Slope:	$ T S J $$ 72.2/72.2 118/113

P ☺☺	**Willow Park Golf Club** Redwood Rd., Castro Valley. (510) 537-8989 18 holes. Par 71/71. Yards: 6,227/5,193 Year-round.	Greens: Carts: Rating: Slope:	$–$$ Inquire 67.4/69.2 110/117

P ☺☺☺	**Windsor Golf Club** Skylane Blvd., Windsor. (707) 838-7888 18 holes. Par 72/72. Yards: 6,650/5,116 Year-round.	Greens: Carts: Rating: Slope:	$$ W T S J Inquire 72.3/69.3 126/125

Modesto

P ☺☺	**Dryden Park Golf Course** Sunset Ave., Modesto. (209) 577-5359 18 holes. Par 72/74. Yards: 6,574/6,048 Year-round. High: May–Sept.	Greens: Carts: Rating: Slope:	$ W T S J $ 69.8/72.5 119/115

Monterey Area

P ☺☺☺	**Fort Ord Golf Course** McClure Way, Fort Ord. (408) 899-2351 *Bayonet Course* 18 holes. Par 72/72. Yards: 6,982/5,680 Year-round. High: Mar.–Nov.	Greens: Carts: Rating: Slope:	$–$$$ T $ 74.0/73.7 132/134

☺☺☺	*Blackhorse Course* 18 holes. Par 72/72. Yards: 6,396/5,613	Rating: Slope:	69.8/72.5 120/129

P ☺☺☺	**Laguna Seca Golf Club** York Rd., Monterey. (408) 373-3701 18 holes. Par 72/72. Yards: 6,125/5,186 Year-round. High: June–Aug.	Greens: Carts: Rating: Slope:	$$$ T $$ 70.4/70.2 123/119

R ☺☺☺☺ BEST	**The Links at Spanish Bay** 17 Mile Dr., Pebble Beach. (408) 647-7495 18 holes. Par 72/72. Yards: 6,820/5,309 Year-round. High: Sept.–Nov.	Greens: Carts: Rating: Slope:	$$$$$$+ R T $$ 74.6/70.6 142/129

California Golf Guide

Monterey Area

P ☺☺☺	**Old Del Monte Golf Course** Sylvan Rd., Monterey. (408) 373-2436 18 holes. Par 72/74. Yards: 6,278/5,431 Year-round. High: Apr.–Oct.	Greens: Carts: Rating: Slope:	$$$ R T S J $ 70.8/71.1 122/118
P ☺☺☺ DEAL	**Pacific Grove Municipal Golf Links** Asilomar Blvd., Pacific Grove. (408) 648-3175 18 holes. Par 70/72. Yards: 5,732/5,305 Year-round.	Greens: Carts: Rating: Slope:	$$ T J $ 67.5/70.5 117/114
P ☺☺☺	**Pajaro Valley Golf Club** Salinas Rd., Watsonville. (408) 724-3851 18 holes. Par 72/72. Yards: 6,234/5,694 Year-round. High: Apr.–Nov.	Greens: Carts: Rating: Slope:	$$–$$$ W T $$ 70.0/72.3 122/123
SP ☺☺☺☺ BEST	**Pasatiempo Golf Club** Santa Cruz. (408) 459-9155 18 holes. Par 71/72. Yards: 6,483/5,647 Year-round. High: June–Sept.	Greens: Carts: Rating: Slope:	$$$$$$ W T $$ 72.9/73.6 138/135
R ☺☺☺☺ BEST	**Pebble Beach Golf Links** 17 Mile Dr., Pebble Beach. (408) 624-3811 18 holes. Par 72/72. Yards: 6,799/5,197 Year-round. High: Sept.–Oct.	Greens: Carts: Rating: Slope:	$$$$$$+++ T Incl. 74.4/71.9 142/130
P ☺☺☺☺	**Poppy Hills Golf Course** Lopez Rd., Pebble Beach. (408) 625-2154 18 holes. Par 72/72. Yards: 6,861/5,473 Year-round. High: May–Aug.	Greens: Carts: Rating: Slope:	$$$–$$$$$ J Incl. 74.8/71.2 143/131
P ☺☺☺	**Rancho Canada Golf Club** Carmel Valley Rd., Carmel. (408) 624-0111 *East Course* 18 holes. Par 71/72. Yards: 6,113/5,279 Year-round. High: Apr.–Oct.	Greens: Carts: Rating: Slope:	$$$ T $ 70.1/69.5 124/118
☺☺☺	*West Course* 18 holes. Par 72/73. Yards: 6,338/5,574	Greens: Carts: Rating: Slope:	$$$$ T $ 71.1/71.6 126/121
R ☺☺☺☺ BEST	**Spyglass Hill Golf Course** Spyglass Hill Rd., Pebble Beach. (408) 625-8563 18 holes. Par 72/74. Yards: 6,859/5,642 Year-round. High: Aug.–Nov.	Greens: Carts: Rating: Slope:	$$$$$$+++ R T Incl. 75.9/73.7 143/133

Bakersfield Area

P ☺☺	**Kern River Golf Course** Rudal Rd., Bakersfield. (805) 872-5128 18 holes. Par 70/73. Yards: 6,458/5,971 Year-round.	Greens: Carts: Rating: Slope:	$ W T S $ 70.5/72.3 117/116
P ☺☺☺☺ BEST	**Sandpiper Golf Course** Hollister Ave., Goleta. (805) 968-1541 18 holes. Par 72/73. Yards: 7,068/5,725 Year-round. High: May–Oct.	Greens: Carts: Rating: Slope:	$$$–$$$$ W J $$ 74.5/73.3 134/125
P ☺☺	**Wasco Valley Rose Golf Course** N. Leonard Ave., Wasco. (805) 758-8301 18 holes. Par 72/72. Yards: 6,862/5,356 Year-round. High: Apr.–June, Oct.	Greens: Carts: Rating: Slope:	$ W L T S J $$ 72.5/70.5 121/119

Fresno Area

SP ☺☺	**Fig Garden Golf Club** N. Van Ness Blvd., Fresno. (209) 439-2928 18 holes. Par 72/72. Yards: 6,621/5,605 Year-round.	Greens: Carts: Rating: Slope:	$$ W T J $$ 70.6/71.9 113/120

California Golf Guide

Fresno Area

P ☺☺	**Fresno West Golf and Country Club** W. Whitesbridge Rd., Kerman. (209) 846-8655 18 holes. Par 72/72. Yards: 6,959/6,000 Year-round.	Greens: $ Carts: $$ Rating: 67.7/69.2 Slope: 103/111	W L T S J
P ☺☺	**Riverside of Fresno Golf Club** N. Josephine, Fresno. (209) 275-5900 18 holes. Par 72/72. Yards: 6,621/6,008 Year-round. High: Apr.–Oct.	Greens: $ Carts: $ Rating: 71.2/73.9 Slope: 122/125	T S J
P ☺☺	**Sherwood Forest Golf Club** N. Frankwood Ave., Sanger. (209) 787-2611 18 holes. Par 71/72. Yards: 6,205/5,605 Year-round. High: Apr.–June	Greens: $ Carts: Inquire Rating: 67.5/70.8 Slope: 110/115	J

Lake Tahoe Area

P ☺☺☺ DEAL	**Lake Tahoe Golf Course** Emerald Bay Rd., S. Lake Tahoe. (916) 577-0788 18 holes. Par 72/72. Yards: 6,685/5,654 Year-round. High: June–Sept.	Greens: $$ Carts: $ Rating: 70.9/70.1 Slope: 120/115	L T J
R ☺☺☺	**Northstar-at-Tahoe Resort Golf Course** Hwy. 267, Truckee. (916) 562-2490 18 holes. Par 72/72. Yards: 6,897/5,470 May–Oct. High: July–Aug.	Greens: $$$–$$$$ Carts: Incl. Rating: 72.0/71.2 Slope: 137/134	L R T S J
R ☺☺☺	**Resort at Squaw Creek** Squaw Creek Rd., Olympic Valley. (916) 583-6300 18 holes. Par 71/71. Yards: 6,931/5,097 May–Oct. High: July–Aug.	Greens: $$$$$$ Carts: Incl. Rating: 72.9/68.9 Slope: 140/127	W L T

Santa Barbara Area

R ☺☺☺	**The Alisal Ranch Golf Course** Alisal Rd., Solvang. (805) 688-4215 18 holes. Par 72/72. Yards: 6,396/5,709 Year-round. High: May–Oct.	Greens: $$$$ Carts: $$ Rating: 70.7/73.5 Slope: 121/127	
P ☺☺☺	**Avila Beach Resort Golf Course** Avila Beach. (805) 595-2307 18 holes. Par 72/72. Yards: 6,443/5,116 Year-round. High: Apr.–Nov.	Greens: $$ Carts: $ Rating: 70.9/69.9 Slope: 122/126	T S J
R ☺☺☺	**Black Lake Golf Club** Nipoma. (805) 343-1214 18 holes. Par 72/72. Yards: 6,412/5,614 Year-round. High: May–Sept.	Greens: $$$ Carts: $$ Rating: 70.3/71.8 Slope: 120/122	W L R T S J
P ☺☺☺ DEAL	**Elkins Ranch Golf Club** Chambersburg Rd., Fillmore. (805) 524-1440 18 holes. Par 71/73. Yards: 6,302/5,650 Year-round. High: Apr.–Oct.	Greens: $$ Carts: $ Rating: 69.9/72.6 Slope: 117/122	W T S J
R ☺☺☺	**Horse Thief Country Club** Stallion Spring, Tehachapi. (805) 822-5581 18 holes. Par 72/72. Yards: 6,678/5,677 Year-round. High: May–Sept.	Greens: $$ Carts: Inquire Rating: 72.1/72.1 Slope: 124/124	W T S J
P ☺☺☺ DEAL	**Hunter Ranch Golf Course** Hwy. 46 E., Paso Robles. (805) 237-7444 18 holes. Par 72/72. Yards: 6,741/5,629 Year-round. High: May–Oct.	Greens: $$ Carts: $$ Rating: 72.2/71.1 Slope: 128/125	J
P ☺☺☺☺ DEAL	**La Purisma Golf Course** St. Hwy. 246, Lompoc. (805) 735-8395 18 holes. Par 72/72. Yards: 7,105/5,762 Year-round. High: May–Oct.	Greens: $$ Carts: $$ Rating: 74.9/74.3 Slope: 143/131	J

California Golf Guide

Santa Barbara Area

P ◎◎	**Rancho Maria Golf Club** Casmalia Rd., Santa Maria. (805) 937-2019 18 holes. Par 72/73. Yards: 6,390/5,504 Year-round.	Greens: $–$$ Carts: $ Rating: 70.2/71.3 Slope: 119/123	W T S J
P ◎◎◎	**River Course at the Alisal** Alisal Rd., Solvang. (805) 688-6042 18 holes. Par 72/72. Yards: 6,820/5,815 Year-round. High: Jan.–Mar.	Greens: $$–$$$ Carts: $ Rating: 73.1/73.4 Slope: 126/127	W R S J
P ◎◎	**Santa Barbara Golf Club** McCaw Ave., Santa Barbara. (805) 687-7087 18 holes. Par 70/72. Yards: 6,014/5,541 Year-round. High: May–Sept.	Greens: $–$$ Carts: $ Rating: 67.6/71.9 Slope: 113/121	W T S J
P ◎◎◎ DEAL	**Soule Park Golf Course** E. Ojai Ave., Ojai. (805) 646-5633 18 holes. Par 72/72. Yards: 6,350/5,894 Year-round.	Greens: $–$$ Carts: Inquire Rating: 69.1/71.0 Slope: 107/115	W T S J

Los Angeles Area

P ◎◎	**Anaheim Hills Golf Course** Nohl Ranch Rd., Anaheim. (714) 748-8900 18 holes. Par 71/72. Yards: 6,218/5,356 Year-round.	Greens: $–$$ Carts: Rating: 70.0/70.0 Slope: 119/115	T S
P ◎◎	**Brookside Golf Club** N. Rosemont Ave., Pasadena. (818) 796-8151 *C.W. Koiner Course* 18 holes. Par 72/75. Yards: 7,037/6,104 Year-round. High: Apr.–Oct.	Greens: $–$$ Carts: $ Rating: 74.5/74.7 Slope: 134/128	W T S J
◎◎	*E.O. Nay Course* 18 holes. Par 70/71. Yards: 6,046/5,377	Rating: 68.4/70.5 Slope: 115/117	
P ◎◎	**Camarillo Springs Golf Course** Camarillo Springs Rd., Camarillo. (805) 484-1075 18 holes. Par 72/72. Yards: 6,375/5,297 Year-round. High: May–Aug.	Greens: $$–$$$$ Carts: Incl. Rating: 70.2/70.2 Slope: 115/116	W R T S J
P ◎◎◎	**Cypress Golf Club** Katella Ave., Los Alamitos. (714) 527-1800 18 holes. Par 71/71. Yards: 6,510/4,569 Year-round. High: Apr.–Oct.	Greens: $$$–$$$$$ Carts: Incl. Rating: 72.6/66.5 Slope: 140/117	W T S
P ◎◎	**Debell Golf Club** Walnut Ave., Burbank. (818) 845-0022 18 holes. Par 71/73. Yards: 5,610/5,412 Year-round.	Greens: $ Carts: $ Rating: 67.4/70.8 Slope: 108/118	W L T S J
P ◎◎	**El Prado Golf Courses** Pine Ave., Chino. (909) 597-1751 *Butterfield Stage Course* 18 holes. Par 72/73. Yards: 6,508/5,503 Year-round.	Greens: $–$$ Carts: $ Rating: 69.7/70.2 Slope: 108/118	W L T S J
◎◎	*Chino Creek Course* 18 holes. Par 72/73. Yards: 6,671/5,596	Rating: 71.0/70.8 Slope: 114/115	
P ◎◎◎ DEAL	**El Rivino Country Club** El Rivino Rd., Riverside. (909) 684-8905 18 holes. Par 73/73. Yards: 6,466/5,863 Year-round.	Greens: $–$$ Carts: $ Rating: NA Slope: 111/113	W T
P	**Green River Golf Course** Green River Rd., Corona. (909) 737-7393	Greens: $$ Carts: $	J

California Golf Guide

Los Angeles Area

☺☺	*Orange Course* 18 holes. Par 71/72. Yards: 6,416/5,744 Year-round.	Rating: Slope:	70.4/75.7 119/125	
☺☺	*Riverside Course* 18 holes. Par 71/71. Yards: 6,275/5,467	Rating: Slope:	69.2/73.9 117/121	T J
P ☺☺	**Griffith Park** Crystal Springs Dr., Los Angeles. (213) 664-2255 *Harding Course* 18 holes. Par 72/73. Yards: 6,536/6,028 Year-round. High: Mar.–Sept.	Greens: Carts: Rating: Slope:	$–$$ $ 70.4/72.5 112/118	W T S J
☺☺	*Wilson Course* 18 holes. Par 72/73. Yards: 6,942/6,330	Rating: Slope:	72.7/74.6 115/119	
SP ☺☺☺	**Hesperia Golf and Country Club** Bangor Ave., Hesperia. (619) 244-9301 18 holes. Par 72/72. Yards: 6,996/6,136 Year-round. High: Spring/Fall	Greens: Carts: Rating: Slope:	$–$$ $$ 74.6/73.9 133/124	J
P ☺☺	**Indian Hills Golf Course** Riverside. (909) 360-2090 18 holes. Par 70/72. Yards: 6,104/5,562 Year-round. High: Nov.–June	Greens: Carts: Rating: Slope:	$–$$ Inquire 70.0/70.7 126/118	W L T S J
R ☺☺☺	**Industry Hills Sheraton Resort** City of Industry. (818) 810-4653 *Eisenhower Course* 18 holes. Par 72/73. Yards: 7,181/5,589 Year-round. High: Apr.–July	Greens: Carts: Rating: Slope:	$$$ Incl. 76.6/73.1 149/135	W L T S J
☺☺☺	*Babe Didrikson Zaharias Course* 18 holes. Par 71/71. Yards: 6,778/5,363	Rating: Slope:	74.2/72.4 144/133	
P ☺☺	**Jurupa Hills Country Club** Morage Ave., Riverside. (909) 685-7214 18 holes. Par 70/71. Yards: 6,022/5,773 Year-round.	Greens: Carts: Rating: Slope:	$–$$ Incl. 68.2/73.4 112/121	W L T S J
P ☺☺	**La Mirada Golf Course** E. Alicante Rd., La Mirada. (310) 943-7123 18 holes. Par 72/72. Yards: 6,044/5,632 Year-round.	Greens: Carts: Rating: Slope:	$–$$ $ 67.2/71.7 109/115	W T S J
SP ☺	**Los Angeles Royal Vista Golf Course** E. Colima Rd., Walnut. (909) 595-7441 *North/South/East* 27 holes. Par 71/71/72. Yards: 6,381/6,071/6,182 Year-round. High: Apr.–Sept.	Greens: Carts: Rating: Slope:	$–$$ Incl. 69.0/67.6/68.5 115/110/112	W L R T S J
P ☺☺	**Los Robles Golf Club** S. Moorpark Rd., Thousand Oaks. (805) 495-6171 18 holes. Par 70/70. Yards: 6,274/5,333 Year-round.	Greens: Carts: Rating: Slope:	$–$$ $ 69.4/70.1 118/117	W T S J
P ☺☺☺ DEAL	**Los Serranos Lakes Golf and Country Club** Yorba Ave., Chino Hills. (909) 597-1711 *North Course* 18 holes. Par 72/74. Yards: 6,440/5,949 Year-round. High: Mar.–June	Greens: Carts: Rating: Slope:	$$ $ 70.4/74.5 120/118	W T S
☺☺☺ DEAL	*South Course* 18 holes. Par 74/74. Yards: 7,036/5,957	Rating: Slope:	74.3/73.5 133/123	

California Golf Guide

Los Angeles Area

P	**Los Verdes Golf Course**	Greens:	$-$$ W T S J
☺☺	Rancho Palos Verdes. (310) 377-0338	Carts:	$
	18 holes. Par 71/72. Yards: 6,651/5,738	Rating:	72.4/71.8
	Year-round. High: June–Sept.	Slope:	122/118

P	**Malibu Country Club**	Greens:	$$$-$$$$ S
☺☺☺	Encinal Canyon Rd., Malibu. (818) 889-6680	Carts:	Incl.
	18 holes. Par 72/72. Yards: 6,740/5,627	Rating:	72.3/71.4
	Year-round.	Slope:	130/120

SP	**Menifee Lakes Country Club**	Greens:	$$-$$$ W T J
☺☺☺	Menifee. (909) 672-3090	Carts:	Incl.
	18 holes. Par 72/72. Yards: 6,472/5,421	Rating:	71.2/71.3
	Year-round.	Slope:	128/119

P	**Mesquite Golf and Country Club**	Greens:	$$$$ W L T
☺☺☺	E. Mesquite Ave., Palm Springs. (619) 323-1502	Carts:	Incl.
	18 holes. Par 72/72. Yards: 6,328/5,244	Rating:	67.9/69.2
	Year-round. High: Nov.–May	Slope:	117/118

P	**Mile Square Golf Club**	Greens:	$$ T
☺☺	Warner Ave., Fountain Valley. (714) 968-4556	Carts:	$$
	18 holes. Par 72/72. Yards: 6,629/5,545	Rating:	71.4/70.5
	Year-round. High: Mar.–Sept.	Slope:	121/109

P	**Montebello Golf Club**	Greens:	$-$$
☺☺	Via San Clemente, Montebello. (213) 723-2971	Carts:	$$
	18 holes. Par 72/72. Yards: 6,671/5,979	Rating:	70.4/72.4
	Year-round. High: Apr.–Oct.	Slope:	114/117

P	**Moreno Valley Ranch Golf Club**	Greens:	$$-$$$ W L T S J
	JFK Dr., Moreno Valley. (909) 924-4444	Carts:	Incl.
☺☺☺	*Mountain/Lake/Valley*	Rating:	73.1/74.1/74.2
	27 holes. Par 72/72/72. Yards: 6,684/6,898/6,880	Slope:	139/138/140
	Year-round. High: Nov.–May		

P	**Mountain Meadows Golf Club**	Greens:	$-$$ W L T S J
☺☺☺	N. Fairplex Dr., Pomona. (909) 623-3704	Carts:	$
DEAL	18 holes. Par 72/72. Yards: 6,509/5,637	Rating:	71.5/71.5
	Year-round. High: May–Aug.	Slope:	125/117

P	**Oak Valley Golf Club**	Greens:	$$-$$$ W T
☺☺☺☺	14th St., Beaumont. (909) 769-7200	Carts:	Incl.
STATE	18 holes. Par 72/72. Yards: 7,003/5,494	Rating:	73.9/71.1
	Year-round. High: Mar.–June	Slope:	136/122

R	**Ojai Valley Inn**	Greens:	$$$$$ R T
☺☺☺☺	Ojai. (805) 646-2420	Carts:	$
STATE	18 holes. Par 70/71. Yards: 6,235/5,225	Rating:	70.6/70.2
	Year-round. High: Mar.–Oct.	Slope:	123/123

P	**Olivas Park Golf Course**	Greens:	$-$$ T J
☺☺	Ventura. (805) 642-4303	Carts:	$$
	18 holes. Par 72/72. Yards: 6,760/5,501	Rating:	71.3/71.3
	Year-round. High: May–Sept.	Slope:	119/117

SP	**Palos Verdes Golf Club**	Greens:	$$$$$ J
☺☺☺	Via Campesina, Palos Verdes Estates. (310) 375-2759	Carts:	Incl.
	18 holes. Par 72/72. Yards: 6,116/5,506	Rating:	70.4/73.3
	Year-round. High: June–Aug.	Slope:	131/128

R	**Pelican Hill Golf Club**	Greens:	$$$$$$++ R T
	Pelican Hill Rd., Newport Coast. (714) 759-5190	Carts:	Incl.
☺☺☺☺	*The Links Course*	Rating:	73.6/73.0
STATE	18 holes. Par 71/71. Yards: 6,856/5,800	Slope:	136/125
	Year-round.		

California Golf Guide

Los Angeles Area

○○○○ STATE	*The Ocean Course* 18 holes. Par 70/70. Yards: 6,634/5,409		Rating: 72.8/72.5 Slope: 138/124

P ○○○	**Recreation Park Golf Course** Deukmejian Dr., Long Beach. (310) 494-5000 18 holes. Par 72/74. Yards: 6,317/5,793 Year-round.
	Greens: $–$$ W T S J Carts: $ Rating: 69.0/72.6 Slope: 112/120

SP ○○○○	**Redhawk Golf Club** Redhawk Pkwy., Temecula. (909) 695-1424 18 holes. Par 72/72. Yards: 7,139/5,510 Year-round.
	Greens: $$$–$$$$ T J Carts: Incl. Rating: 75.7/72.0 Slope: 149/124

P ○○○	**Rio Hondo Golf Club** Old River School Rd., Downey. (310) 927-2329 18 holes. Par 72/72. Yards: 6,344/5,080 Year-round.
	Greens: $$ T S J Carts: Inquire Rating: 70.2/69.4 Slope: 119/117

P ○○	**San Bernardino Golf Club** S. Waterman, San Bernardino. (909) 885-2414 18 holes. Par 72/72. Yards: 5,782/5,226 Year-round. High: Apr.–May, Sept.–Oct.
	Greens: $–$$ W T S J Carts: $ Rating: 67.4/70.0 Slope: 112/112

P ○○	**San Dimas Canyon Golf Club** Terrebonne Ave., San Dimas. (909) 599-2313 18 holes. Par 72/72. Yards: 6,314/5,571 Year-round. High: Apr.–Sept.
	Greens: $–$$ W T S J Carts: Inquire Rating: 70.2/73.9 Slope: 118/123

P ○○	**Santa Anita Golf Course** S. Santa Anita Ave., Arcadia. (818) 447-7156 18 holes. Par 71/74. Yards: 6,368/5,908 Year-round.
	Greens: $–$$ T S J Carts: $$ Rating: 70.4/73.1 Slope: 122/121

P ○○○ DEAL	**Shandin Hills Golf Club** Little Mountain Dr., San Bernardino. (909) 886-0669 18 holes. Par 72/72. Yards: 6,517/5,592 Year-round. High: Oct.
	Greens: $–$$ W T S J Carts: $ Rating: 70.3/71.6 Slope: 120/122

P ○○○ DEAL	**Tijeras Creek Golf Club** Rancho Santa Margarita. (714) 589-9793 18 holes. Par 72/72. Yards: 6,601/5,400 Year-round. High: Apr.–Oct.
	Greens: $–$$ W T S J Carts: $$ Rating: 69.9/69.2 Slope: 120/116

P ○○○	**Tustin Ranch Golf Club** Tustin Ranch Rd., Tustin. (714) 730-1611 18 holes. Par 72/72. Yards: 6,736/5,204 Year-round. High: June–Oct.
	Greens: $$$$–$$$$$ W S J Carts: Incl. Rating: 72.9/70.3 Slope: 129/118

SP ○○	**Upland Hills Country Club** E. 16th St., Upland. (909) 946-4711 18 holes. Par 70/70. Yards: 5,827/4,813 Year-round.
	Greens: $–$$ Carts: $ Rating: 67.1/66.5 Slope: 111/106

SP ○○	**Victorville Municipal Golf Course** Green Tree Blvd., Victorville. (619) 245-4860 18 holes. Par 72/72. Yards: 6,640/5,878 Year-round. High: May–Sept.
	Greens: $–$$ W L R T S J Carts: $ Rating: 71.2/72.7 Slope: 121/118

Palm Springs Area

P ○○○○ BEST	**Desert Dunes Golf Club** Palm Dr., Desert Hot Springs. (619) 251-5367 18 holes. Par 72/72. Yards: 6,876/5,359 Year-round. High: Jan.–May
	Greens: $$–$$$$$$ W L R T S J Carts: Incl. Rating: 73.8/70.7 Slope: 142/122

SP ○○○	**Desert Falls Country Club** Desert Falls Pkwy., Palm Desert. (619) 341-4020
	Greens: $$–$$$$$$+ L T Carts: Incl.

California Golf Guide

Palm Springs Area

| | 18 holes. Par 72/72. Yards: 7,017/5,313 | Rating: | 75.0/71.7 |
| | Year-round. High: Nov.–Apr. | Slope: | 145/124 |

R
◎◎◎

Desert Princess Country Club and Resort
Landau Blvd., Cathedral City. (619) 322-2280
La Vista/El Cielo/Los Lagos
27 holes. Par 72/72/72. Yards: 6,764/6,587/6,667
Year-round. High: Nov.–May

Greens: $$$–$$$$$ W L R T
Carts: Incl.
Rating: 72.5/71.2/71.8
Slope: 126/121/123

R
◎◎◎

Golf Resort at Indian Wells
Indian Wells Lane, Indian Wells. (619) 346-4653
East Course
18 holes. Par 72/72. Yards: 6,157/5,408
Year-round. High: Jan.–May

Greens: $$$–$$$$$$ W L R T
Carts: Incl.
Rating: 70.3/70.0
Slope: 116/111

◎◎◎

West Course
18 holes. Par 72/72. Yards: 6,500/5,408

Rating: 70.3/70.0
Slope: 116/111

SP
◎◎◎◎
STATE

La Quinta Resort and Club
Vista Bonita, La Quinta. (619) 564-7686
Mountain Course
18 holes. Par 72/72. Yards: 6,758/5,010
Year-round. High: Nov.–Apr.

Greens: $$$$–$$$$$$ W L R T
Carts: Incl.
Rating: 74.1/68.4
Slope: 140/120

◎◎◎

Dunes Course
18 holes. Par 72/72. Yards: 6,747/5,005

Rating: 73.1/68.0
Slope: 137/114

SP
◎◎

Lawrence Welk's Desert Oasis Country Club
Cathedral Canyon Dr., Cathedral City. (619) 328-6571
Lakeview/Mountain/Resort
27 holes. Par 72/72/72. Yards: 6,505/6,477/6,366
Year-round. High: Jan.–Apr.

Greens: $$–$$$$$ W L T
Carts: Incl.
Rating: 71.6/70.9/70.3
Slope: 128/119/118

R
◎◎◎

Marriott's Desert Springs Resort and Spa
Palm Desert. (619) 341-1756
Palm Course
18 holes. Par 72/72. Yards: 6,761/5,492
Year-round. High: Oct.–May

Greens: $$$$–$$$$$$ W L R T
Carts: Incl.
Rating: 72.0/70.8
Slope: 124/116

◎◎◎

Valley Course
18 holes. Par 72/72. Yards: 6,679/5,330

Rating: 72.1/69.6
Slope: 124/110

R
◎◎

Marriott's Rancho Las Palmas Resort
Bob Hope Dr., Rancho Mirage. (619) 568-0955
North/South/West
27 holes. Par 71/69/70. Yards: 6,019/5,569/5,550
Year-round. High: Jan.–Apr.

Greens: $$$–$$$$$ W L R T
Carts: Inquire
Rating: 67.2/65.5/65.3
Slope: 115/106/105

P
◎◎◎◎

Mission Hills North Golf Course
Ramon Rd., Rancho Mirage. (619) 770-9496
18 holes. Par 72/72. Yards: 7,062/4,907
Year-round. High: Oct.–Apr.

Greens: $$$–$$$$$$+ W L R T
Carts: Incl.
Rating: 73.9/68.0
Slope: 134/118

SP
◎◎◎

Mission Lakes Country Club
Desert Hot Springs. (619) 329-8061
18 holes. Par 72/72. Yards: 6,737/5,390
Year-round. High: Jan.–May

Greens: $$–$$$$ W L R T J
Carts: Incl.
Rating: 72.8/71.2
Slope: 131/122

R
◎◎◎

Palm Desert Resort Country Club
Palm Desert. (619) 345-2791
18 holes. Par 72/72. Yards: 6,585/5,670
Nov.–Sept. High: Nov.–Apr.

Greens: $$$$–$$$$$ W L T
Carts: Incl.
Rating: 70.8/71.8
Slope: 117/123

R
◎◎◎◎

PGA West Resort
La Quinta. (619) 564-7170
Jack Nicklaus Resort Course

Greens: $$$$–$$$$$$+++ W L R T
Carts: Incl.
Rating: 75.5/69.0

California Golf Guide

Palm Springs Area

BEST	18 holes. Par 72/72. Yards: 7,126/5,043	Slope:	138/116
	Year-round. High: Jan.–Apr.		

◎◎◎◎	*TPC Stadium Course*	Greens:	$$$$–$$$$$$ W L R T
BEST	18 holes. Par 72/72. Yards: 7,261/5,087	Carts:	Incl.
		Rating:	77.3/70.3
		Slope:	151/124

SP	**Soboda Springs Country Club**	Greens:	$$–$$$ T J
◎◎◎	Soboda Rd., San Jacinto. (909) 654-9354	Carts:	Incl.
	18 holes. Par 73/74. Yards: 6,829/5,762	Rating:	73.5/73.2
	Year-round. High: Oct.–May	Slope:	135/131

R	**Sun City Palm Springs Golf Club**	Greens:	$$–$$$$ W L T
◎◎◎	Del Webb Blvd., Bermuda Dunes. (619) 772-2200	Carts:	Incl.
	18 holes. Par 72/72. Yards: 6,720/5,305	Rating:	73.0/70.3
	Year-round.	Slope:	131/118

SP	**Sun Lakes Country Club**	Greens:	$$$ T J
◎◎◎	Banning. (909) 845-2135	Carts:	$$$
	18 holes. Par 72/72. Yards: 7,035/5,516	Rating:	74.3/72.7
	Year-round. High: Apr.–Oct.	Slope:	132/118

R	**Tahquitz Creek Palm Springs Golf Course**	Greens:	$–$$ L T
	Palm Springs. (619) 328-1956	Carts:	$$
◎◎	*Old Course*	Rating:	69.5/72.6
	18 holes. Par 71/73. Yards: 6,040/5,800	Slope:	107/115
	Year-round. High: Jan.–May		

◎◎	*Resort Course*	Rating:	71.4/70.0
	18 holes. Par 72/72. Yards: 6,705/5,206	Slope:	120/119

R	**The Westin Mission Hills Resort**	Greens:	$$$–$$$$$$+ R
◎◎◎	Dinah Shore Dr., Rancho Mirage. (619) 328-3198	Carts:	Incl.
	18 holes. Par 70/70. Yards: 6,987/4,841	Rating:	73.7/67.4
	Year-round. High: Oct.–Apr.	Slope:	136/107

San Diego Area

R	**Aviara Golf Club**	Greens:	$$$$$–$$$$$$ W T
◎◎◎◎	Batiquitos Dr., Carlsbad. (619) 929-0077	Carts:	Incl.
STATE	18 holes. Par 72/72. Yards: 7,007/5,007	Rating:	74.9/69.1
	Year-round. High: Apr.–Aug.	Slope:	141/119

R	**Carlton Oaks Country Club**	Greens:	$$$–$$$$ R T
◎◎◎	Inwood Dr., Santee. (619) 448-8500	Carts:	Incl.
	18 holes. Par 72/72. Yards: 7,088/4,548	Rating:	75.7/62.1
	Year-round.	Slope:	144/114

R	**Carmel Highland Doubletree Resort**	Greens:	$$$ W L R T S J
◎◎	Penasquitos Dr., San Diego. (619) 672-9100	Carts:	Incl.
	18 holes. Par 72/72. Yards: 6,428/5,361	Rating:	70.7/71.9
	Year-round. High: Jan.–Apr.	Slope:	123/125

P	**Carmel Mountain Ranch Country Club**	Greens:	$$$–$$$$ T S J
◎◎◎	Carmel Ridge Rd., San Diego. (619) 487-9224	Carts:	Incl.
	18 holes. Par 72/72. Yards: 6,728/5,372	Rating:	71.9/71.0
	Year-round.	Slope:	131/122

SP	**Castle Creek Country Club**	Greens:	$$ W T
◎◎	Circle R Dr., Escondido. (619) 749-2422	Carts:	$
	18 holes. Par 72/72. Yards: 6,396/4,800	Rating:	70.8/67.4
	Year-round. High: Jan.–Apr.	Slope:	124/108

P	**Chula Vista Municipal Golf Course**	Greens:	$–$$ W T S J
◎◎	Bonita Rd., Bonita. (619) 479-4141	Carts:	$
	18 holes. Par 73/74. Yards: 6,759/5,776	Rating:	72.3/72.7
	Year-round. High: July–Sept.	Slope:	128/124

California Golf Guide

San Diego Area

P	**Coronado Golf Course**	Greens:	$$	T J
☺☺☺	Visalia Row, Coronado. (619) 435-3121	Carts:	$	
DEAL	18 holes. Par 72/72. Yards: 6,633/5,784	Rating:	71.8/73.7	
	Year-round.	Slope:	124/126	

P	**Eagle Crest Golf Club**	Greens:	$$–$$$	T S J
☺☺☺	Cloverdale Rd., Escondido. (619) 737-9762	Carts:	Incl.	
	18 holes. Par 72/72. Yards: 6,417/4,941	Rating:	71.6/69.6	
	Year-round. High: Jan.–Apr.	Slope:	136/123	

P	**Eastlake Country Club**	Greens:	$$$–$$$$	W S J
☺☺☺	Chula Vista. (619) 482-5757	Carts:	Incl.	
	18 holes. Par 72/72. Yards: 6,606/5,118	Rating:	70.7/68.8	
	Year-round. High: Jan.–June	Slope:	116/114	

P	**Fallbrook Golf Club**	Greens:	$–$$	W T J
☺☺	Gird Rd., Fallbrook. (619) 728-8334	Carts:	$	
	18 holes. Par 72/72. Yards: 6,223/5,597	Rating:	69.8/71.4	
	Year-round.	Slope:	117/119	

R	**La Costa Resort and Spa**	Greens:	$$$$$$++	W R T
	Costa Del Mar Rd., Carlsbad. (619) 438-9111	Carts:	Incl.	
☺☺☺	*North Course*	Rating:	74.8/74.0	
	18 holes. Par 72/73. Yards: 6,987/5,939	Slope:	137/127	
	Year-round.			

☺☺☺	*South Course*	Rating:	74.4/72.1
	18 holes. Par 72/74. Yards: 6,894/5,612	Slope:	138/123

SP	**Meadow Lake Country Club**	Greens:	$$	W R T J
☺☺	Meadow Glen Way, Escondido. (619) 749-1620	Carts:	$	
	18 holes. Par 72/74. Yards: 6,521/5,758	Rating:	72.5/72.8	
	Year-round.	Slope:	131/123	

R	**Monarch Beach Golf Links**	Greens:	$$$$–$$$$$$
☺☺☺	Stonehill Dr., Dana Point. (714) 240-8247	Carts:	Incl.
	18 holes. Par 70/70. Yards: 6,227/5,046	Rating:	69.2/68.5
	Year-round.	Slope:	128/120

SP	**Mt. Woodson Country Club**	Greens:	$$–$$$	W T J
☺☺☺	N. Woodson Dr., Ramona. (619) 788-3555	Carts:	Incl.	
	18 holes. Par 70/70. Yards: 6,180/4,441	Rating:	68.8/64.7	
	Year-round.	Slope:	130/108	

R	**Pala Mesa Resort**	Greens:	$$–$$$$	W L R T J
☺☺☺	S. Hwy. 395, Fallbrook. (619) 728-5881	Carts:	Incl.	
	18 holes. Par 72/72. Yards: 6,528/5,848	Rating:	72.0/74.5	
	Year-round. High: Jan.–May	Slope:	131/128	

R	**Rancho Bernardo Inn and Country Club**	Greens:	$$$–$$$$	W R T J
☺☺☺	Bernardo Oaks Dr., San Diego. (619) 675-8470	Carts:	Incl.	
	18 holes. Par 72/72. Yards: 6,458/5,448	Rating:	70.6/71.2	
	Year-round. High: Dec.–May	Slope:	122/119	

P	**The SCGA Members' Club at Rancho California**	Greens:	$$$	W T J
☺☺☺	Murrieta Hot Springs Rd., Murrieta. (909) 677-7446	Carts:	Incl.	
	18 holes. Par 72/72. Yards: 7,059/5,355	Rating:	73.9/70.5	
	Year-round. High: Jan.–May	Slope:	132/116	

P	**San Clemente Municipal Golf Club**	Greens:	$–$$	W T S J
☺☺	E. Magdalena, San Clemente. (714) 492-1997	Carts:	$	
	18 holes. Par 72/73. Yards: 5,782/5,226	Rating:	70.2/72.4	
	Year-round. High: June–Aug.	Slope:	118/117	

R	**San Luis Rey Downs Country Club**	Greens:	$$–$$$	T J
☺☺	Bonsall. (619) 758-9699	Carts:	Incl.	

San Diego Area

	18 holes. Par 72/72. Yards: 6,750/5,493	Rating:	72.6/71.4
	Year-round. High: Jan.–May	Slope:	128/124

SP	**San Vicente Golf Club**	Greens:	$$–$$$　　T
☺☺☺	San Vicente Rd., Ramona. (619) 789-3477	Carts:	Incl.
	18 holes. Par 72/72. Yards: 6,610/5,543	Rating:	71.5/72.8
	Year-round.	Slope:	123/128

R	**Singing Hills Country Club**	Greens:	$$　　　W T J
	Dehesa Rd., El Cajon. (619) 442-3425	Carts:	Inquire
☺☺☺	*Oak Glen Course*	Rating:	71.3/71.4
DEAL	18 holes. Par 72/72. Yards: 6,597/5,549	Slope:	122/124
	Year-round.		

☺☺☺	*Willow Glen Course*	Rating:	72.0/72.8
DEAL	18 holes. Par 72/72. Yards: 6,605/5,585	Slope:	124/122

P	**Steele Canyon Golf Club**	Greens:	$$$–$$$$ T S J
	Stonefield Dr., Jamul. (619) 441-6900	Carts:	Incl.
☺☺☺	*Canyon/Ranch/Meadow*	Rating:	72.7/74.0/72.2
	27 holes. Par 71/72/71. Yards: 6,741/7,001/6,672	Slope:	135/137/134
	Year-round. High: Dec.–May		

R	**Temecula Creek Inn**	Greens:	$$–$$$　W L R T J
	Rainbow Canyon Rd., Temecula. (909) 676-2405	Carts:	Inquire
☺☺☺	*Creek/Oaks/Stonehouse*	Rating:	72.6/72.6/71.8
	27 holes. Par 72/72/72. Yards: 6,784/6,693/6,605	Slope:	125/130/123
	Year-round.		

P	**Torrey Pines Golf Course**	Greens:	$$$$–$$$$$
	N. Torrey Pines Rd., La Jolla. (619) 452-3226	Carts:	Incl.
☺☺☺	*North Course*	Rating:	72.1/75.4
BEST	18 holes. Par 72/74. Yards: 6,647/6,118	Slope:	129/134
	Year-round.		

☺☺☺☺	*South Course*	Rating:	74.6/77.3
BEST	18 holes. Par 72/76. Yards: 7,055/6,457	Slope:	136/139

P	**The Vineyard at Escondido**	Greens:	$$–$$$　W L T S J
☺☺☺	San Pasqual Rd., Escondido. (619) 735-9545	Carts:	$
	18 holes. Par 70/70. Yards: 6,531/5,073	Rating:	70.3/70.3
	Year-round.	Slope:	125/117

SP	**Whispering Palms Lodge and Country Club**	Greens:	$$–$$$　　T
	Rancho Santa Fe. (619) 756-2471	Carts:	$
☺	*East/South/North*	Rating:	68.8/70.2/69.7
	27 holes. Par 71/72/71. Yards: 6,141/6,443/6,346	Slope:	110/112/112
	Year-round.		

Colorado

Colorado contains luxurious and interesting Rocky Mountain resorts *and* plains with surprisingly green greens. Whichever you choose, remember to check the operating season—mountain resorts may be open only from May to October, while some flatland courses operate year-round. With a bit of luck it may be possible to combine a golf and ski vacation in the same trip.

Rocky Mountain Highs

When skiers leave, golfers arrive to populate the condos and hotels at the base of the mountains and play on the lush courses that have come out from beneath their winter white. Among the best of the mountain tracks is the **Breckenridge Golf Club** at the ski resort of the same name. The **Keystone Ranch Golf Course** at Keystone is a handsome mountain challenge set in a former cattle ranch 9,300 feet above sea level. **Pole Creek Golf Club** is a gem at the base of the ski area at Winter Park.

The well-maintained **Sonnenalp Golf Club** is in Edwards, just west of Vail. The lovely **Tamarron Resort** in Durango is set among cliffs and canyons and high mountain meadows.

East of the Mountains

Among the best in the eastern foothills are the 54 holes at the **Broadmoor Golf Club**, on the grounds of the famed hotel of the same name in Colorado Springs. The East Course was designed in 1918 by Donald Ross; the West Course came half a century later, courtesy of Robert Trent Jones, Sr. And in 1976, Arnold Palmer and Ed Seay added the South Course, the toughest of the trio.

Also highly regarded is the **Arrowhead Golf Club** in Littleton south of Denver, which has some of the most spectacular geologic formations you'll ever find on the grounds of a golf course. Just west of Denver are the 27 holes of the **Fox Hollow at Lakewood Golf Course**, which are among the state jewels.

About 10 miles north of Denver is the challenging Dunes Course at the **Riverdale Golf Club**. Some 15 miles south of Denver is the **Plum Creek Golf and Country Club**, a links-type course designed as a stadium course with room for visitors, wide-open fairways, and views of the Rockies above.

All the way south, 45 miles below Pueblo, is the **Grandote Golf and Country Club** in La Veta, a hidden treasure and a great deal.

Most high-mountain courses and resorts in Colorado are closed for the winter; high season is the summer, with midlevel rates in the spring and fall. Plateau courses, mostly to the east of the Rockies, may be open year-round, with high-season rates in the summer and deepest discounts in the winter.

The renowned Broadmoor Hotel is a grand Colorado Springs resort built in 1918. This is a world of Italian Renaissance formality, with grand lobbies and staircases and works of art. There are 700 rooms and suites in the five-star hotel.

The Broadmoor overlooks a trio of 18-hole championship courses, including one designed by Donald Ross and a second by Robert Trent Jones, Sr.

Golf packages, including a room and greens fees, can range from a high-season (June 1 to mid-October) price of about $215 per person for double occupancy to about $150 per person in the spring and fall. The lowest rates are in November near the closing of the season; rates sometimes go as low as $82.50 per person.

Econoguide Leader Board: Best Public Courses in Colorado

❍❍❍	Arrowhead Golf Club
❍❍❍❍	Breckenridge Golf Club
❍❍❍❍	Broadmoor Golf Club (East, West, South)
❍❍❍	The Courses at Hyland Hills
❍❍❍❍	Fox Hollow at Lakewood Golf Course (Canyon, Meadow, Links)
❍❍❍	Keystone Ranch Golf Course
❍❍❍❍	Legacy Ridge Golf Course
❍❍❍	Plum Creek Golf and Country Club
❍❍❍❍	Pole Creek Golf Club
❍❍❍❍	Riverdale Golf Club (Dunes)
❍❍❍❍	Sonnenalp Golf Club
❍❍❍❍	Tamarron Resort

Econoguide Leader Board: Best Deals in Colorado

$$/❍❍❍	Battlement Mesa Golf Club
$/❍❍❍	Boomerang Links
$$/❍❍❍	Coal Creek Golf Course
$/❍❍❍	The Courses at Hyland Hills (Hyland Hills Gold)
$$/❍❍❍❍	Dalton Ranch Golf Club
$$/❍❍❍	Fairfield Pagosa Golf Club
$$/❍❍❍	Highland Hills Golf Course
$$/❍❍❍	Indian Peaks Golf Club
$$/❍❍❍❍	Legacy Ridge Golf Course
$$/❍❍❍	Loveland Golf Club
$$/❍❍❍❍	Mariana Butte Golf Course
$$/❍❍❍	The Meadows Golf Club
$$/❍❍❍	Pine Creek Golf Club
$/❍❍❍	Pueblo West Golf Course
$$/❍❍❍❍	Riverdale Golf Club (Dunes)
$/❍❍❍❍	Walking Stick Golf Course

Colorado Golf Guide

Grand Junction Area

P ❍❍	**Adobe Creek National Golf Course** Fruita. (303) 858-0521 18 holes. Par 72/72. Yards: 6,997/4,980 May–Dec. High: May–Sept.	Greens: Carts: Rating: Slope:	$–$$ $ 71.2/55.1 119/97	W L T S J

Rocky Mountain Region

P ❍❍	**Aspen Golf Course** E. Cooper, Aspen. (303) 925-2145 18 holes. Par 71/72. Yards: 7,165/5,591 Apr.–Oct. High: July–Sept.	Greens: Carts: Rating: Slope:	$$–$$$ $ 72.2/69.9 125/116	L S J
P ❍❍❍ DEAL	**Battlement Mesa Golf Club** N. Battlement Pkwy., Parachute. (303) 285-7274 18 holes. Par 72/72. Yards: 7,309/5,386 Mar.–Nov. High: June–Aug.	Greens: Carts: Rating: Slope:	$–$$ $ 73.9/69.9 132/112	W L S J
R ❍❍❍	**Beaver Creek Golf Club** Avon. (303) 845-5775 18 holes. Par 70/70. Yards: 6,752/5,200 May–Oct. High: May–June	Greens: Carts: Rating: Slope:	$$$$$$ Inquire 69.2/70.2 133/121	L R

Colorado Golf Guide

Rocky Mountain Region

P ☺☺☺☺ STATE	**Breckenridge Golf Club** Breckenridge. (303) 453-9104 18 holes. Par 72/72. Yards: 7,279/5,066 May–Oct. High: July–Sept.	Greens: $$$ Carts: $ Rating: 73.1/67.7 Slope: 146/118	L T
R ☺☺	**Copper Mountain Resort** Copper Creek Golf Club Wheeler Circle, Copper Mountain. (303) 968-2882 18 holes. Par 70/70. Yards: 6,094/4,374 June–Oct. High: July–Aug.	Greens: $$$–$$$$ Carts: Incl. Rating: 67.7/63.8 Slope: 124/100	L R T
P ☺☺☺	**Eagle Vail Golf Club** Eagle Dr., Avon. (303) 949-5267 18 holes. Par 72/72. Yards: 6,819/4,856 May–Oct. High: June–Sept.	Greens: $$$–$$$$ Carts: Incl. Rating: 70.9/67.3 Slope: 131/114	L T
P ☺☺	**Eagles Nest Golf Club** Golden Eagle Rd., Silverthorne. (303) 468-0681 18 holes. Par 72/72. Yards: 7,024/5,556 May–Oct. High: July–Sept.	Greens: $$–$$$$ Carts: Incl. Rating: 72.6/71.9 Slope: 141/126	W L T J
P ☺☺	**Estes Park Golf Course** S. Saint Vrain Ave., Estes Park. (303) 586-8146 18 holes. Par 71/72. Yards: 6,326/5,250 Apr.–Oct. High: June–Sept.	Greens: $$ Carts: $ Rating: 68.3/68.3 Slope: 118/115	L T
P ☺☺☺	**Grand Lake Golf Course** County Rd. 48, Grand Lake. (303) 627-8008 18 holes. Par 72/74. Yards: 6,542/5,685 May–Oct. High: July–Aug.	Greens: $$$ Carts: Inquire Rating: 70.5/70.9 Slope: 131/123	
R ☺☺☺ BEST	**Keystone Ranch Golf Course** Keystone. (303) 468-4250 18 holes. Par 72/72. Yards: 7,090/5,596 May–Oct. High: June–Sept.	Greens: $$$$$ Carts: Incl. Rating: 71.4/70.7 Slope: 130/129	L R T J
P ☺☺☺☺ BEST	**Pole Creek Golf Club** Winter Park. (303) 726-8847 18 holes. Par 72/72. Yards: 7,107/5,006 May–Oct. High: June–Sept.	Greens: $$–$$$$ Carts: $ Rating: 73.1/67.9 Slope: 135/119	W L T J
SP ☺☺	**Rifle Creek Golf Course** St. Hwy. 325, Rifle. (303) 625-1093 18 holes. Par 72/72. Yards: 6,241/5,131 Mar.–Nov. High: June–Sept.	Greens: $–$$ Carts: $ Rating: 69.3/68.5 Slope: 123/109	W S J
R ☺☺☺	**Sheraton Steamboat Resort** Steamboat Springs. (303) 879-1391 18 holes. Par 72/72. Yards: 6,906/5,647 May–Oct. High: June–Aug.	Greens: $$$–$$$$$ Carts: $ Rating: 71.7/72.6 Slope: 134/127	L R T S
SP ☺☺☺☺	**Skyland Mountain Golf Course** Crested Butte. (303) 349-6131 18 holes. Par 72/72. Yards: 7,208/5,702 May–Oct. High: July–Aug.	Greens: $$–$$$$ Carts: Incl. Rating: 72.6/72.4 Slope: 129/123	L R T
R ☺☺☺☺ BEST	**Sonnenalp Golf Club** Berry Creek Rd., Edwards. (303) 926-3533 18 holes. Par 71/71. Yards: 7,059/5,293 Apr.–Oct. High: June–Sept.	Greens: $$$$–$$$$$$ Carts: Incl. Rating: 72.3/70.0 Slope: 138/115	W L R T J
SP ☺☺☺	**The Club at Cordillera** Edwards. (303) 926-5100 18 holes. Par 72/72. Yards: 7,444/5,665 May–Oct.	Greens: $$$$$$++ Carts: Incl. Rating: 74.0/71.5 Slope: 145/138	
R ☺☺☺	**The Snowmass Club Golf Course** Snowmass Village. (303) 923-3148	Greens: $$$–$$$$$ Carts: Incl.	L R T J

Colorado Golf Guide

Rocky Mountain Region

	18 holes. Par 71/71. Yards: 6,894/5,008	Rating:	70.5/67.3
	May–Oct. High: June–Sept.	Slope:	134/114

P	**Vail Golf Club**	Greens:	$$$–$$$$$ L
☺☺☺	Vail Valley Dr., Vail. (303) 479-2260	Carts:	Incl.
	18 holes. Par 77/72. Yards: 7,100/5,291	Rating:	70.8/69.5
	May–Oct. High: June–Sept.	Slope:	121/114

Denver Area

P	**Applewood Golf Course**	Greens:	$–$$ W T S J
☺☺	W. 32nd Ave., Golden. (303) 279-3003	Carts:	$
	18 holes. Par 72/72. Yards: 6,229/5,374	Rating:	68.2/69.0
	Year-round. High: Apr.–Oct.	Slope:	122/118

P	**Arrowhead Golf Club**	Greens:	$$$–$$$$$ W L T S
☺☺☺	W. Sundown Trail, Littleton. (303) 973-9614	Carts:	Incl.
BEST	18 holes. Par 70/72. Yards: 6,682/5,465	Rating:	70.9/70.0
	Mar.–Nov. High: June–Sept.	Slope:	134/123

P	**Coal Creek Golf Course**	Greens:	$–$$ W L T S J
☺☺☺	S. Lark Ave., Louisville. (303) 666-7888	Carts:	$
DEAL	18 holes. Par 72/72. Yards: 6,957/5,168	Rating:	71.1/68.4
	Year-round. High: Apr.–Sept.	Slope:	130/114

P	**Flatirons Golf Course**	Greens:	$
☺☺	Arapahoe Rd., Boulder. (303) 442-7851	Carts:	$
	18 holes. Par 70/71. Yards: 6,765/5,615	Rating:	69.9/71.1
	Year-round. High: Mar.–Sept.	Slope:	125/115

P	**Foothills Golf Course**	Greens:	$
☺☺	S. Carr St., Denver. (303) 989-3901	Carts:	$
	18 holes. Par 72/74. Yards: 6,908/6,028	Rating:	71.1/73.4
	Year-round. High: Apr.–Oct.	Slope:	122/118

P	**Fox Hollow at Lakewood Golf Course**	Greens:	$$ S J
STATE	W. Morrison Rd., Lakewood. (303) 986-7888	Carts:	$
☺☺☺☺	*Canyon/Meadow/Links*	Rating:	71.2/71.1/72.3
	27 holes. Par 71/72/71. Yards: 6,806/6,888/7,030	Slope:	138/132/134
	Year-round. High: Apr.–Oct.		

P	**Indian Peaks Golf Club**	Greens:	$$ W
☺☺☺	Indian Peaks Trail, Lafayette. (303) 666-4706	Carts:	$
DEAL	18 holes. Par 72/72. Yards: 7,083/5,468	Rating:	72.5/69.9
	Year-round. High: May–Sept.	Slope:	134/116

P	**Indian Tree Golf Club**	Greens:	$
☺☺	Wadsworth Blvd., Arvada. (303) 423-3450	Carts:	$
	18 holes. Par 70/75. Yards: 6,742/5,850	Rating:	69.6/71.4
	Year-round. High: May–Sept.	Slope:	114/116

R	**Inverness Golf Course**	Greens:	$$$$ T
☺☺☺☺	Englewood. (303) 799-9660	Carts:	Incl.
	18 holes. Par 70/70. Yards: 6,948/6,407	Rating:	70.6
	Year-round. High: June–Aug.	Slope:	136/129

P	**John F. Kennedy Golf Club**	Greens:	$ S J
☺☺	E. Hampden Ave., Aurora. (303) 755-0105	Carts:	$$
	27 holes. Par 71/71/72. Yards: 6,868/6,753/7,009	Rating:	71.6/70.9/71.7
	Year-round. High: Apr.–Sept.	Slope:	131/125/118

SP	**Lake Valley Golf Club**	Greens:	$–$$ W T S J
☺☺	Lake Valley Dr., Longmont. (303) 444-2114	Carts:	$
	18 holes. Par 72/72. Yards: 6,725/5,713	Rating:	69.6/71.8
	Year-round. High: Apr.–Aug.	Slope:	121/119

Colorado Golf Guide

Denver Area

P	**Legacy Ridge Golf Course**	Greens: $$	W S J
☺☺☺☺	Westminster. (303) 438-8997	Carts: $	
DEAL	18 holes. Par 72/72. Yards: 7,251/5,383	Rating: 74.0/70.6	
STATE	Year-round. High: Apr.–Oct.	Slope: 134/122	

P	**Lone Tree Golf Club**	Greens: $$–$$$	S
☺☺	Sunningdale Blvd., Littleton. (303) 799-9940	Carts: $	
	18 holes. Par 72/72. Yards: 7,012/5,340	Rating: 72.1/70.6	
	Year-round. High: Apr.–Oct.	Slope: 127/120	

P	**Meadow Hills Golf Course**	Greens: $–$$	W T S J
☺☺☺	S. Dawson St., Aurora. (303) 690-2500	Carts: $	
	18 holes. Par 70/72. Yards: 6,717/5,481	Rating: 70.9/70.5	
	Year-round. High: May–Sept.	Slope: 133/117	

P	**Park Hill Golf Club**	Greens: $–$$
☺	E. 35th Ave., Denver. (303) 333-5411	Carts: $$
	18 holes. Par 71/72. Yards: 6,585/5,811	Rating: 69.4/73.4
	Year-round. High: May–Aug.	Slope: 120/124

SP	**Plum Creek Golf and Country Club**	Greens: $$$$–$$$$$	W L T
☺☺☺	Castle Rock. (303) 688-2611	Carts: Incl.	
STATE	18 holes. Par 72/72. Yards: 6,700/4,875	Rating: 70.1/68.3	
	Year-round. High: June–Sept.	Slope: 131/118	

P	**Riverdale Golf Club**	Greens: $$
	Riverdale Rd., Brighton. (303) 659-6700	Carts: $$
☺☺☺☺	*Dunes Course*	Rating: 72.1/67.5
BEST	18 holes. Par 72/72. Yards: 7,030/4,903	Slope: 129/109
DEAL	Year-round. High: May–Sept.	

☺☺	*Knolls Course*	Rating: 70.2/72.2
	18 holes. Par 71/73. Yards: 6,756/5,931	Slope: 118/117

P	**The Courses at Hyland Hills**	Greens: $
	Westminster. (303) 428-6526	Carts: $
☺☺☺	*Hyland Hills Gold Course*	Rating: 71.9/71.9
BEST	18 holes. Par 72/73. Yards: 7,021/5,654	Slope: 132/120
DEAL	Year-round. High: June–Aug.	

P	**The Meadows Golf Club**	Greens: $–$$	L S J
☺☺☺	S. Simms, Littleton. (303) 972-8831	Carts: $$	
DEAL	18 holes. Par 72/72. Yards: 6,995/5,416	Rating: 71.6/71.1	
	Year-round. High: May–Sept.	Slope: 130/123	

P	**Thorncreek Golf Club**	Greens: $$	T S J
☺☺	N. Washington St., Thornton. (303) 450-7055	Carts: $	
	18 holes. Par 72/72. Yards: 7,268/5,547	Rating: 73.7/70.5	
	Year-round. High: May–Sept.	Slope: 136/120	

P	**Wellshire Golf Course**	Greens: $–$$	W S J
☺☺	S. Colorado Blvd., Denver. (303) 757-1352	Carts: $$	
	18 holes. Par 71/73. Yards: 6,608/5,890	Rating: 70.1/69.3	
	Year-round. High: Apr.–Sept.	Slope: 124/121	

P	**West Woods Golf Club**	Greens: $$	J
☺☺	Quaker St., Arvada. (303) 424-3334	Carts: $	
	18 holes. Par 72/72. Yards: 7,035/5,197	Rating: 72.1/69.5	
	Year-round. High: Apr.–Aug.	Slope: 135/112	

Fort Collins Area

P	**Boomerang Links**	Greens: $	W L T S J
☺☺☺	W. 4th St., Greeley. (303) 351-8934	Carts: $	
DEAL	18 holes. Par 72/72. Yards: 7,214/5,285	Rating: 72.6/68.5	
	Year-round. High: June–Sept.	Slope: 131/113	

Colorado Golf Guide

Fort Collins Area

P	**Collindale Golf Club**	Greens: $	W L T S J
☺☺	E. Horsetooth Rd., Fort Collins. (303) 221-6651	Carts: $	
	18 holes. Par 71/73. Yards: 7,011/5,472	Rating: 71.5/69.9	
	Year-round. High: May–Sept.	Slope: 126/113	

P	**Fort Morgan Golf Course**	Greens: $	W
☺☺	Colorado Rd., Fort Morgan. (303) 867-5990	Carts: Inquire	
	18 holes. Par 73/74. Yards: 6,470/5,615	Rating: 69.7/70.1	
	Year-round. High: Apr.–Oct.	Slope: 117/113	

P	**Highland Hills Golf Course**	Greens: $–$$	W L T S J
☺☺☺	Greeley. (303) 330-7327	Carts: Inquire	
DEAL	18 holes. Par 71/75. Yards: 6,700/6,002	Rating: 71.4/72.8	
	Year-round. High: May–Oct.	Slope: 128/120	

P	**Loveland Golf Club**	Greens: $	W T J
☺☺☺	W. 29th St., Loveland. (303) 667-5256	Carts: Inquire	
DEAL	18 holes. Par 72/71. Yards: 6,827/5,498	Rating: 69.9/70.6	
	Year-round. High: May–Sept.	Slope: 120/117	

P	**Mariana Butte Golf Course**	Greens: $–$$	W L T
☺☺☺☺	Loveland. (303) 667-8308	Carts: $	
DEAL	18 holes. Par 72/72. Yards: 6,572/5,420	Rating: 70.6/70.2	
	Mar.–Nov. High: May–Sept.	Slope: 130/121	

SP	**Ptarmigan Country Club**	Greens: $$–$$$	W L T S J
☺☺☺	Vardon Way, Fort Collins. (303) 226-6600	Carts: $$	
	18 holes. Par 72/72. Yards: 7,201/5,327	Rating: 73.0/69.0	
	Year-round. High: May–Sept.	Slope: 135/116	

P	**Southridge Golf Club**	Greens: $	W L T S J
☺☺	S. Lemay Ave., Fort Collins, (303) 226-2828	Carts: $	
	18 holes. Par 71/71. Yards: 6,363/5,508	Rating: 69.1/69.3	
	Year-round. High: Apr.–Sept.	Slope: 122/118	

Colorado Springs Area

P	**Appletree Golf Course**	Greens: $–$$	W L S J
☺☺	Rolling Ridge Rd., Colorado Springs. (719) 382-3649	Carts: $$	
	18 holes. Par 72/72. Yards: 6,407/5,003	Rating: 68.6/66.9	
	Year-round. High: May–Sept.	Slope: 122/113	

R	**Broadmoor Golf Club**	Greens: $$$$$	
	Pourtales Dr., Colorado Springs. (719) 577-5790	Carts: $	
☺☺☺☺	*East Course*	Rating: 73.0/74.1	
BEST	18 holes. Par 72/73. Yards: 7,091/5,873	Slope: 129/126	
	Year-round. High: Apr.–Oct.		

☺☺☺	*South Course*	Rating: 72.1/68.4	
STATE	18 holes. Par 72/72. Yards: 6,781/4,834	Slope: 135/117	

☺☺☺☺	*West Course*	Rating: 73.0/71.6	
BEST	18 holes. Par 72/72. Yards: 6,937/5,505	Slope: 133/122	

P	**Pine Creek Golf Club**	Greens: $$	W L T S J
☺☺☺	Colorado Springs. (719) 594-9999	Carts: $$	
DEAL	18 holes. Par 72/72. Yards: 7,194/5,314	Rating: 72.6/69.0	
	Year-round. High: Apr.–Oct.	Slope: 139/113	

P	**Pueblo West Golf Course**	Greens: $	W S J
☺☺☺	S. McCulloch Blvd., Pueblo West. (719) 547-2280	Carts: $	
DEAL	18 holes. Par 72/72. Yards: 7,368/5,688	Rating: 73.3/71.4	
	Year-round. High: Apr.–Sept.	Slope: 125/117	

P	**Walking Stick Golf Course**	Greens: $	W T
☺☺☺☺	Pueblo. (719) 584-3400	Carts: $	

Colorado Golf Guide

Colorado Springs Area

| DEAL | 18 holes. Par 72/72. Yards: 7,147/5,181 | Rating: | 72.6/69.0 |
| | Year-round. High: May–Sept. | Slope: | 130/114 |

Southern Colorado

SP	**Dalton Ranch Golf Club**	Greens:	$$	L R T
☺☺☺☺	Rte. 252, Durango. (303) 247-8774	Carts:	$	
DEAL	18 holes. Par 72/72. Yards: 6,934/5,539	Rating:	72.4/71.7	
	Apr.–Nov. High: June–Sept.	Slope:	135/125	

R	**Fairfield Pagosa Golf Club**	Greens:	$$	L T J
	Pines Club Place, Pagosa Springs. (303) 731-4755	Carts:	$	
☺☺☺	*Pinon/Ponderosa/Meadows*	Rating:	69.4/72.9/70.9	
DEAL	27 holes. Par 71/72/71. Yards: 6,670/7,221/6,913	Slope:	119/125/123	
	Apr.–Oct. High: July–Aug.			

R	**Grandote Golf and Country Club**	Greens:	$$–$$$	W L
☺☺☺☺	Hwy. 12, La Veta. (719) 742-3122	Carts:	$$	
	18 holes. Par 72/72. Yards: 7,085/5,608	Rating:	72.8/70.7	
	Apr.–Oct. High: July–Sept.	Slope:	133/117	

R	**Great Sand Dunes Country Club**	Greens:	$$$$
☺☺☺	Hwy. 150, Mosca. (719) 378-2357	Carts:	Inquire
	18 holes. Par 72/72. Yards: 7,006/5,327	Rating:	71.2/67.8
	May–Oct. High: July–Sept.	Slope:	126/118

SP	**Hillcrest Golf Club**	Greens:	$	T
☺☺	Rim Dr., Durango. (303) 247-1499	Carts:	$	
	18 holes. Par 71/71. Yards: 6,838/5,252	Rating:	71.3/68.1	
	Mar.–Nov. High: June–Aug.	Slope:	127/111	

R	**Tamarron Resort**	Greens:	$$$$–$$$$$	L R T S J
	Durango. (303) 259-2000	Carts:	Incl.	
☺☺☺☺	*The Cliffs*	Rating:	73.0/71.9	
STATE	18 holes. Par 72/72. Yards: 6,885/5,330	Slope:	144/127	
	May–Nov. High: June–Sept.			

Hawaii

The Hawaiian Islands boast some of the lushest and priciest golf resorts anywhere; they also have more than their share of hidden bargains. Hawaii has two glorious seasons: summer and almost-summer.

Hawaii

The Big Island of Hawaii is larger than all of the other islands in the chain combined, and six times larger than the most populous island of Oahu, but the core of this island is mostly empty. Part of the reason lies in the landscape, which features the active Kilauea Crater, the Mauna Loa volcano, and the Mauna Kea peak. The mountains in the center split the island into two miniclimates. The wet and windy side is to the east, including the major city of Hilo; on the west side the weather is generally better, and it is there that most of the golf resorts are clustered.

The famed **Mauna Kea Beach Golf Course** in Kamuela is sure not to disappoint, with spectacular ocean views and a memorable No. 3 that belongs in any collection of golfing memories—a 200-yard carry over an ocean bay. There are also more than 100 sand traps. The Robert Trent Jones design that sprawls across the lava flows is on the grounds of the spectacular Mauna Kea Beach Hotel, one of the Rockefeller Resorts.

The **Mauna Lani Resort** in Kohala Coast has two first-class challenges that mix black lava flows, ultragreen fairways, and deep blue water. The transcendent South Course is nearly matched by the nearby North holes.

The Kings' Golf Course at the **Waikoloa Beach Resort** in Kamuela is considered by some to be the best on the island. The course is literally carved out of lava flows from the Mauna Kea volcano; it offers links-style challenges where the ocean breezes come into play on most holes.

If your golf game alone is not thrill enough, consider playing a round at the **Volcano Golf and Country Club**, set at the base of the active Mauna Loa volcano.

Things to do—besides golf, that is—include visiting Hawaii Volcanoes National Park on the east side of Mauna Loa.

Kauai

Kauai is perhaps the most unspoiled of the major Hawaiian Islands, although the pace of development has picked up in recent years. There are a double handful or so of first-class golf resorts on the island, all of them about as good as they come. And the pace of life on Kauai is more relaxed than on the bigger and more tourist-bound islands.

The Kiele Course at **Kauai Lagoons Resort** is considered a picturesque, difficult challenge. Another well-thought-of course on the island is the **Poipu Bay Resort Golf Club** in Koloa, where the windy back nine lies along the ocean.

Among the most famous resorts on Kauai is the Princeville Resort, home of the top-rated **Princeville Makai** golf club's three courses. The Ocean and Lakes courses are considered the best here.

Nearby is **The Prince Golf Club**, one of the best resort courses in Hawaii and the nation. Its emphasis is on the varied natural attractions and obstacles of the area, including waterfalls, ravines, and unusual trees and plants. The Prince Course has five tee boxes for most holes, with the back pair restricted to players with handicaps in the single digits. Whichever box you shoot from, unless you are a touring pro or a scratch amateur you can probably expect to enjoy the course more for the challenge and the scenery than for the score on your souvenir card.

One of the signature holes at The Prince is No. 12, the par-4 Eagle's Nest. The tee perches 100 feet above a narrow fairway lined by a dense jungle. The Anini Stream comes into play on all sides of the fern-green backdrop on the second shot.

Sights include the spectacular Waimea Canyon in the western portion, and Kawaikini peak on Mount Waialeale in the center of the island. One of the rainiest places on earth, it receives an average of more than 450 inches of rain each year. By contrast, the southern coast is very dry year-round, and the northern coast, including the Princeville Resort, has a more moderate climate. The lovely Lumahai Beach and Hanalei Bay in the north look little different from when they were used in the filming of *South Pacific* in 1957, or for thousands of years before that, for that matter.

Lanai

Lanai is one of the smallest of the Hawaiian Islands, a privately owned pineapple plantation with just a few thousand residents. Although the island lies just off the northern end of Maui, it is nevertheless a relatively untouched paradise.

A jewel of the isles is **The Challenge at Manele** in Lanai City, with fairways set between lava fields and the ocean.

For an even more impressive setting, there is **The Experience at Koele**, also in Lanai City. The experience begins 500 feet above the elegant lodge, and the front nine is mostly downhill from there into tropical canyons; the back nine is more open, including an island green on the 17th hole.

Maui

The second-largest island was created by two volcanoes, Haleakala on the larger eastern portion and Puu Kukui and the West Maui range at the other end.

A minimall of great golf can be found at the **Kapalua Golf Club**, a resort with no fewer than three top-rated courses. The best of the best is the Plantation Course, a long and wide challenge along the ocean with fairways in the middle of pineapple fields. How long and wide? The famed No. 18 stretches 663 yards, but it runs downhill and usually downwind, making the return home a reasonable par 5 for most players. Next in line is the Village Course with mountain views and uphill shots into the wind; the third jewel is the Bay Course. The beach at Kapalua, by the way, is regularly listed on charts of the world's best strands.

Two more gems can be found at the **Makena Resort Golf Course** in Kihei, where the North and South courses each are on the best-of-state list. The North features views of Haleakala Crater, with most of the natural obstacles of the area (including rock walls, gullies, and lava) left intact. The South Course includes views way out to sea from the 15th and 16th holes.

The Gold Course at **Wailea Golf Club** in Wailea has two kinds of traps: an abundance of sand and some spectacular views including the Mount Haleakala Crater.

Molokai

The rugged island of Molokai features the lovely and relatively uncrowded **Kaluakoi Golf Course** on the western coast. Kaluakoi is a rolling course that takes golfers through the woods and along Kepuhi Beach.

Oahu

Oahu is the center of the Hawaiian tourist scene, including Honolulu and Waikiki Beach; it is also the most populous of the islands, with more than 80 percent of the state's population. It also has nearly half of the 70 or so golf courses in the state. Many of those courses are private or limited to military personnel and their families.

Near the top of any list of courses in Hawaii is the **Koolau Golf Course** in Kaneohea, a very long, very tough public course—in fact it has some of the most difficult ratings in the nation.

A newer rising star, already considered one of the best resorts in the nation, is **Ko Olina** on Oahu's west coast. There is a lot of water on the course, from placid ponds to tumbling waterfalls; the fairways are alive with native plants, and it is all set against the foreboding silhouette of the local volcano range. The resort itself, developed by a Japanese company, has plans for major expansion in coming years for half a dozen luxury hotels, a marina, and more.

Some of the many other appeals of Oahu include the famed Waikiki Beach, Manoa Falls, and the museums and memorials of Pearl Harbor.

As befits a collection of island paradises, golf courses and resorts on Hawaii operate year-round, with little variation in climate except for rainy periods. Variations in rates are more related to the times of year when visitors from distant places crowd the courses and beaches. Expect peak prices in the winter months; some courses also have peak prices in the heart of the summer.

In general, the hottest months of the year are August and September, with temperature readings commonly reaching the 90s; the relatively coolest time is December through February, with lows all the way down to the low 60s. Of more importance for some visitors are the rainy periods, which coincide with the cool period on most of the islands; some places, including Kauai and its famed Princeville Resort, are very rainy all year-round, while the Kohala Coast on the Big Island receives little annual rain.

Econoguide Leader Board: Best Public Courses in Hawaii

Hawaii, the Big Island
- ⊙⊙⊙⊙ Makalei Hawaii Country Club
- ⊙⊙⊙⊙ Mauna Kea Beach Golf Course
- ⊙⊙⊙⊙ Mauna Lani Resort (South)
- ⊙⊙⊙ Waikoloa Beach Resort (Kings)

Kauai
- ⊙⊙⊙⊙ Kauai Lagoons Resort (Kiele)
- ⊙⊙⊙ Poipu Bay Resort Golf Club
- ⊙⊙⊙⊙ The Prince Golf Club
- ⊙⊙⊙⊙ Princeville Makai (Ocean, Lakes, Woods)
- ⊙⊙⊙ Wailua Golf Course

Lanai
- ⊙⊙⊙⊙ The Challenge at Manele
- ⊙⊙⊙ The Experience at Koele

Maui
- ⊙⊙⊙⊙ Kapalua Golf Club (Bay, Plantation, Village)
- ⊙⊙⊙⊙ Makena Resort Golf Course (North, South)
- ⊙⊙⊙ Wailea Golf Club (Blue, Gold)

Molokai
- ⊙⊙⊙ Kaluakoi Golf Course

Oahu

○○○   Ko Olina Golf Club
○○○   Koolau Golf Course

Econoguide Leader Board: Best Deals in Hawaii

$$/○○   Olomana Golf Links (Oahu)
$$/○○○   Pali Municipal Golf Course (Oahu)
$$/○○   Seamountain Golf Course (Hawaii)
$$/○○○   Wailua Golf Course (Kauai)
$/○○○   West Loch Golf Course (Oahu)

Hawaii Golf Guide

Hawaii, the Big Island

R ○○○	**Hapuna Golf Course** Kauna'oa Dr., Kamuela. (808) 880-3000 18 holes. Par 72/72. Yards: 6,875/5,067 Year-round. High: Nov.–Apr.	Greens: Carts: Rating: Slope:	$$$$$ R J Inquire 72.1/63.9 134/117
P ○○○	**Kona Surf Resort and Country Club** Alii Dr., Kailua-Kona. (808) 322-2595 *Mountain Course* 18 holes. Par 72/72. Yards: 6,471/4,906 Year-round. High: Jan.–Mar.	Greens: Carts: Rating: Slope:	$$$$–$$$$$$ T Incl. 71.5/69.2 133/125
○○○	*Ocean Course* 18 holes. Par 72/73. Yards: 6,579/5,499	Rating: Slope:	71.6/71.9 129/127
P ○○○○ STATE	**Makalei Hawaii Country Club** Hawaii Belt Rd., Kailua-Kona. (808) 325-6625 18 holes. Par 72/72. Yards: 7,091/5,242 Year-round. High: Dec.–Mar.	Greens: Carts: Rating: Slope:	$$$$$ R T Incl. 73.5/64.9 143/125
R ○○○○ BEST	**Mauna Kea Beach Golf Course** Manua Kea Beach Dr., Kamuela. (808) 880-3480 18 holes. Par 72/72. Yards: 7,114/5,277 Year-round. High: Nov.–Apr.	Greens: Carts: Rating: Slope:	$$$$$–$$$$$$ R J Incl. 73.6/65.8 135/109
R ○○○○	**Mauna Lani Resort** Kohala Coast. (808) 885-6655 *North Course* 18 holes. Par 72/72. Yards: 6,993/5,474 Year-round. High: Nov.–Apr.	Greens: Carts: Rating: Slope:	$$$$$–$$$$$$ L T Incl. 73.2/71.4 136/124
○○○○ STATE	*South Course* 18 holes. Par 72/72. Yards: 7,029/5,331	Rating: Slope:	73.1/70.3 133/122
R ○○ DEAL	**Seamountain Golf Course** Punaluu. (808) 928-6222 18 holes. Par 72/72. Yards: 6,492/5,663 Year-round. High: Jan.–Feb.	Greens: Carts: Rating: Slope:	$$ R J Incl. 72.5/70.9 135/116
P ○○	**Volcano Golf and Country Club** Volcanoes National Park. (808) 967-7331 18 holes. Par 72/72. Yards: 6,250/5,449 Year-round. High: July–Sept.	Greens: Carts: Rating: Slope:	$$$ Incl. NA 128/117
R ○○○	**Waikoloa Beach Resort** Kamuela. (808) 885-6060 *Beach Golf Course* 18 holes. Par 72/72. Yards: 6,566/5,094 Year-round. High: Dec.–Mar.	Greens: Carts: Rating: Slope:	$$$$$ R T Incl. 71.5/69.4 133/119
○○○ BEST	*Kings Golf Course.* (808) 885-4647 18 holes. Par 72/72. Yards: 7,074/5,459	Rating: Slope:	73.9/69.4 133/121

Hawaii Golf Guide

Hawaii, the Big Island

R ☺☺☺	**Waikoloa Village Golf Club** 68-1792 Melia St., Waikoloa. (808) 883-9621 18 holes. Par 72/72. Yards: 6,791/5,479 Year-round. High: Dec.–Feb.	Greens: $$$–$$$$ T J Carts: Incl. Rating: 71.8/72.1 Slope: 130/119

Kauai

R ☺☺☺☺ BEST	**Kauai Lagoons Resort** Kalapaki Beach, Lihue. (808) 241-6000 *Kiele Course* 18 holes. Par 72/72. Yards: 7,070/5,417 Year-round. High: Jan.–Mar., Aug.	Greens: $$$$$$++ R Carts: Incl. Rating: 73.7/66.5 Slope: 137/123
☺☺☺	*Lagoons Course* 18 holes. Par 72/72. Yards: 6,942/5,607	Greens: $$$$$$ R Carts: Incl. Rating: 72.8/67.0 Slope: 135/116
R ☺☺	**Kiahuna Golf Club** Kiahuna Plantation Dr., Poipu. (808) 742-9595 18 holes. Par 70/70. Yards: 6,353/5,631 Year-round. High: Nov.–Mar.	Greens: $$$ R T Carts: Incl. Rating: 69.7/71.4 Slope: 128/119
R ☺☺☺ STATE	**Poipu Bay Resort Golf Club** Ainako St., Koloa. (808) 742-8711 18 holes. Par 72/72. Yards: 6,959/5,241 Year-round. High: Jan.–May	Greens: $$$$$–$$$$$$+ R T J Carts: Incl. Rating: 73.4/70.9 Slope: 132/121
R ☺☺☺☺ BEST	**The Prince Golf Club** Kuhio Hwy., Princeville. (808) 826-5000 18 holes. Par 72/72. Yards: 7,309/5,338 Year-round. High: Nov.–Mar.	Greens: $$$$$$++ R J Carts: Incl. Rating: 75.6/70.0 Slope: 144/127
R ☺☺☺☺ BEST	**Princeville Makai** Lei O Papa Rd., Princeville. (808) 826-3580 *Ocean/Lakes/Woods* 27 holes. Par 72/72/72. Yards: 6,875/6,886/6,901 Year-round. High: Nov.–Mar.	Greens: $$$$–$$$$$$ L R T J Carts: Incl. Rating: 72.7/72.7/72.3 Slope: 133/134/129
P ☺☺☺ BEST DEAL	**Wailua Golf Course** Kuhio Hwy., Lihue. (808) 245-8092 18 holes. Par 72/72. Yards: 6,981/5,974 Year-round. High: Jan.–Apr.	Greens: $–$$ T S Carts: $ Rating: 73.0/73.1 Slope: 136/122

Lanai

R ☺☺☺☺ STATE	**The Challenge at Manele** Lanai City. (808) 565-2222 18 holes. Par 72/72. Yards: 7,039/5,024 Year-round. High: Nov.–Feb.	Greens: $$$$$$ R Carts: Incl. Rating: NA Slope: NA
R ☺☺☺ STATE	**The Experience at Koele** Lanai Ave., Lanai City. (808) 565-4653 18 holes. Par 72/72. Yards: 7,014/5,425 Year-round. High: Dec.–May	Greens: $$$$$$+++ T J R Carts: Incl. Rating: 73.3/66.0 Slope: 141/123

Maui

R ☺☺☺	**Kaanapali Golf Course** Kaanapali Resort, Lahaina. (808) 661-3691 *South Course* 18 holes. Par 71/71. Yards: 6,555/5,485 Year-round. High: Dec.–Apr.	Greens: $$$$$$ L R T Carts: Incl. Rating: 70.7/69.8 Slope: 127/120
☺☺☺	*North Course* 18 holes. Par 71/72. Yards: 6,994/5,417	Rating: 72.8/71.1 Slope: 134/123
R	**Kapalua Golf Club** Kapalua Dr., Kapalua.	Greens: $$$$$$ R T J Carts: Incl.

Hawaii Golf Guide

Maui

☺☺☺☺ BEST	*The Bay Course.* (808) 669-8820 18 holes. Par 72/72. Yards: 6,600/5,124 Year-round. High: Dec.–Mar.	Rating: Slope:	71.7/69.6 138/121
☺☺☺☺ BEST	*The Plantation Course.* (808) 669-8877 18 holes. Par 72/72. Yards: 7,263/5,627	Rating: Slope:	75.2/73.2 142/129
☺☺☺ BEST	*The Village Course.* (808) 669-8835 18 holes. Par 72/72. Yards: 6,632/5,134	Rating: Slope:	73.3/70.9 139/122

R ☺☺☺☺ STATE	**Makena Resort Golf Course** Makena Alanui, Kihei. (808) 879-3344 *North Course* 18 holes. Par 72/72. Yards: 6,914/5,303 Year-round. High: Dec.–Apr., Aug., Oct.	Greens: Carts: Rating: Slope:	$$$$$$ R T J Incl. 72.1/70.9 139/128
☺☺☺☺ STATE	*South Course* 18 holes. Par 72/72. Yards: 7,017/5,529	Rating: Slope:	72.6/71.1 138/130

P ☺☺	**Pukalani Country Club** Pukalani St., Pukalani. (808) 572-1314 18 holes. Par 72/74. Yards: 6,945/5,574 Year-round. High: Jan.–Mar.	Greens: Carts: Rating: Slope:	$$$–$$$$ L T Incl. 72.8/71.1 121/118
P ☺☺☺	**Sandalwood Golf Course** Honoapiilani Hwy., Wailuku. (808) 572-1314 18 holes. Par 72/72. Yards: 6,469/5,162 Year-round. High: Jan.–Apr.	Greens: Carts: Rating: Slope:	$$$$ R Incl. 71.2/64.8 129/118
P ☺☺	**Silversword Golf Club** Piilani Hwy., Kiehi. (808) 874-0777 18 holes. Par 71/71. Yards: 6,801/5,265 Year-round. High: Jan.–Mar.	Greens: Carts: Rating: Slope:	$$$–$$$$ L T Incl. 72.0/70.0 124/118
P ☺☺	**Waiehu Golf Course** Wailuku. (808) 244-5934 18 holes. Par 72/72. Yards: 6,330/5,511 Year-round. High: Nov.–Mar.	Greens: Carts: Rating: Slope:	$$ $ 69.8/70.6 111/115

R ☺☺☺ BEST	**Wailea Golf Club** Kaukahi St., Wailea. (808) 875-5111 *Blue Course* 18 holes. Par 72/72. Yards: 6,758/5,291 Year-round. High: Dec.–Apr.	Greens: Carts: Rating: Slope:	$$$$$$ R Incl. 71.6/72.0 130/117
☺☺	*Emerald Course* 18 holes. Par 72/72. Yards: 6,825/5,454	Rating: Slope:	NA 134
☺☺☺ STATE	*Gold Course* 18 holes. Par 72/72. Yards: 7,070/5,317	Rating: Slope:	73.0/70.3 139/121

Molokai

R ☺☺☺ STATE	**Kaluakoi Golf Course** Maunaloa. (808) 552-2739 18 holes. Par 72/72. Yards: 6,564/5,461 Year-round. High: Dec.–Mar.	Greens: Carts: Rating: Slope:	$$$–$$$$ L R Incl. 72.3/71.4 129/119

Oahu

SP ☺☺☺	**Ewa Beach International Golf Club** Fort Weaver Rd., Ewa Beach. (808) 565-2222 18 holes. Par 72/72. Yards: 7,039/5,024 Year-round. High: Nov.–Feb.	Greens: Carts: Rating: Slope:	$$$$ S J Incl. 71.7/68.2 126/119
R ☺☺☺	**Ko Olina Golf Club** Aliinui Dr., Kapolei. (808) 676-5300	Greens: Carts:	$$$$$–$$$$$$ R T Incl.

Hawaii Golf Guide

Oahu

BEST		18 holes. Par 72/72. Yards: 6,867/5,392	Rating:	72.8/71.3
		Year-round. High: Dec.–Feb.	Slope:	137/125
P	**Koolau Golf Course**		Greens:	$$$$$–$$$$$$ W L T
☺☺☺	Kionaole, Kaneohe. (808) 236-4653		Carts:	Incl.
BEST	18 holes. Par 72/72. Yards: 7,310/5,119		Rating:	76.5/72.9
	Year-round.		Slope:	155/NA
P	**Makaha Valley Country Club**		Greens:	$$$–$$$$$ W L R
☺☺☺	Makaha Valley Rd., Waianae. (808) 695-7111		Carts:	Incl.
	18 holes. Par 71/71. Yards: 6,369/5,720		Rating:	69.2/72.7
	Year-round. High: Dec.–Mar.		Slope:	133/120
SP	**Olomana Golf Links**		Greens:	$$ W T S
☺☺	Kalanianaole Hwy., Waimanalo. (808) 259-7926		Carts:	Incl.
DEAL	18 holes. Par 72/73. Yards: 6,326/5,456		Rating:	70.3/72.4
	Year-round. High: July–Aug.		Slope:	129/128
P	**Pali Municipal Golf Course**		Greens:	$$ T S J
☺☺☺	Kamehameha Hwy., Kaneohe. (808) 296-7254		Carts:	$
DEAL	18 holes. Par 72/74. Yards: 6,493/6,080		Rating:	78.8/70.4
	Year-round. High: June–Aug.		Slope:	126/127
SP	**Pearl Country Club**		Greens:	$$$$$ T
☺☺☺	Kaonohi St., Aiea. (808) 487-3802		Carts:	Incl.
	18 holes. Par 72/72. Yards: 6,787/5,536		Rating:	72.0/72.1
	Year-round.		Slope:	135/130
R	**Sheraton Makaha Resort and Country Club**		Greens:	$$$$$–$$$$$$ WLRT
☺☺☺	Makaha Valley Rd., Waianae. (808) 695-9544		Carts:	Incl.
	18 holes. Par 72/72. Yards: 7,091/5,880		Rating:	73.2/73.9
	Year-round. High: Jan.–Mar.		Slope:	139/129
R	**Turtle Bay Hilton Golf and Tennis Resort**		Greens:	$$$$–$$$$$$+ R
	Kamehameha Hwy., Kahuku. (808) 293-8574		Carts:	Incl.
☺☺☺	*The Links at Kuilima*		Rating:	75.0/64.3
	18 holes. Par 72/72. Yards: 7,199/4,851		Slope:	141/121
	Year-round. High: Dec.–Mar.			
SP	**Waikele Golf Club**		Greens:	$$$$$ W T
☺☺☺	Paioa Place, Waipahu. (808) 676-9000		Carts:	Incl.
	18 holes. Par 72/72. Yards: 6,663/5,226		Rating:	71.7/65.6
	Year-round. High: Jan.–Feb.		Slope:	126/113
P	**West Loch Golf Course**		Greens:	$ T S J
☺☺☺	Okupe St., Ewa Beach. (808) 671-2292		Carts:	Incl.
DEAL	18 holes. Par 72/72. Yards: 6,479/5,296		Rating:	70.3/68.6
	Year-round. High: Apr.–Sept.		Slope:	123/117

Idaho

The famed **Coeur d'Alene Resort Golf Course** reminds you of one of its most distinct features with its address, 900 Floating Green Drive. The famed 14th hole ends on a green built on a floating pontoon about 75 yards into Lake Coeur d'Alene and reachable only by boat; you've got two tries to land on the green before you must drop a ball on board.

Equally famous around the nation is the **Sun Valley Resort Golf Course** on the grounds of the well-known ski resort.

Most courses in Idaho operate from about March through October or November; expect peak rates to be in effect from spring through the end of summer.

Econoguide Leader Board: Best Public Courses in Idaho

◎◎◎◎ Coeur d'Alene Resort Golf Course
◎◎◎◎ Sun Valley Resort Golf Course

Econoguide Leader Board: Best Deals in Idaho

$$/◎◎◎   Avondale Golf Club
$/◎◎◎   Blackfoot Municipal Golf Course
$$/◎◎◎   The Highlands Golf and Country Club
$/◎◎◎   Pinecrest Municipal Golf Course
$/◎◎◎   Quail Hollow Golf Club

Idaho Golf Guide

Coeur d'Alene Area

SP	**Avondale Golf Club**	Greens:	$$	L T J
◎◎◎	Avondale Loop Rd., Hayden Lake. (208) 772-5963	Carts:	$$	
DEAL	18 holes. Par 72/74. Yards: 6,525/4,719	Rating:	71.1/73.2	
	Mar.–Oct. High: June–Aug.	Slope:	118/123	

R	**Coeur d'Alene Resort Golf Course**	Greens:	$$$$–$$$$$$+	L R
◎◎◎◎	Floating Green Dr., Coeur d'Alene. (208) 667-4653	Carts:	Incl.	
BEST	18 holes. Par 71/71. Yards: 6,309/5,490	Rating:	69.9/70.3	
	Apr.–Oct. High: June–Sept.	Slope:	121/118	

P	**The Highlands Golf and Country Club**	Greens:	$$	W L S J
◎◎◎	Inverness Dr., Post Falls. (208) 773-3673	Carts:	$$	
DEAL	18 holes. Par 72/73. Yards: 6,369/5,115	Rating:	70.7/69.5	
	Mar.–Oct. High: June–Aug.	Slope:	125/121	

R	**Stoneridge Golf Club**	Greens:	$$	R T S J
◎◎	Blanchard Rd., Blanchard. (208) 437-4682	Carts:	$$	
	18 holes. Par 72/72. Yards: 6,522/5,678	Rating:	71.4/72.4	
	Apr.–Oct. High: May–Sept.	Slope:	127/126	

SP	**Twin Lakes Village Golf Course**	Greens:	$–$$	L T S J
◎◎	Rathdrum. (208) 687-1311	Carts:	$$	
	18 holes. Par 71/72. Yards: 6,178/5,370	Rating:	69.7/71.0	
	Apr.–Oct. High: June–Aug.	Slope:	124/121	

P	**University of Idaho Golf Course**	Greens:	$	W T S J
◎◎	Nez Perce, Moscow. (208) 885-6171	Carts:	$$	
	18 holes. Par 72/72. Yards: 6,639/5,770	Rating:	72.0/73.0	
	Mar.–Oct. High: May–Aug.	Slope:	130/130	

Boise Area

P	**Eagle Hills Golf Course**	Greens:	$	W L T S J
◎◎	N. Edgewood Lane, Eagle. (208) 939-0402	Carts:	$	
	18 holes. Par 72/72. Yards: 6,485/5,305	Rating:	70.5/70.2	
	Year-round. High: Mar.–Oct.	Slope:	118/114	

R	**Elkhorn Country Club**	Greens:	$$$$	R
◎◎◎	Elkhorn Rd., Sun Valley. (208) 622-3300	Carts:	Incl.	
	18 holes. Par 72/72. Yards: 7,101/5,424	Rating:	72.4/69.2	
	May–Oct. High: June–Aug.	Slope:	133/120	

P	**Purple Sage Golf Course**	Greens:	$	W
◎◎	Caldwell. (208) 459-2223	Carts:	$	
	18 holes. Par 71/71. Yards: 6,747/5,343	Rating:	70.7/68.9	
	Mar.–Dec. High: May–Aug.	Slope:	117/111	

SP	**Quail Hollow Golf Club**	Greens:	$	W L S J
◎◎◎	N. 36th St., Boise. (208) 344-7807	Carts:	$	
DEAL	18 holes. Par 70/70. Yards: 6,444/4,530	Rating:	70.7/68.0	
	Year-round. High: Mar.–Oct.	Slope:	128/129	

Idaho Golf Guide

Boise Area

P	**Warm Springs Golf Course**	Greens:	$	W T
☺	Warm Springs Ave., Boise. (208) 343-5661	Carts:	$	
	18 holes. Par 72/72. Yards: 6,719/5,660	Rating:	NA	
	Year-round. High: May–Sept.	Slope:	113/113	

Sun Valley

R	**Sun Valley Resort Golf Course**	Greens:	$$$–$$$$$ L R
☺☺☺☺	Sun Valley. (208) 622-2251	Carts:	Incl.
BEST	18 holes. Par 72/73. Yards: 6,565/5,241	Rating:	71.1/70.4
	Apr.–Oct. High: June–Sept.	Slope:	128/125

Pocatello Area

P	**Blackfoot Municipal Golf Course**	Greens:	$	W L
☺☺☺	Teeples Dr., Blackfoot. (208) 785-9960	Carts:	$	
DEAL	18 holes. Par 71/75. Yards: 6,899/6,385	Rating:	71.5/75.0	
	Mar.–Nov. High: May–Oct.	Slope:	123/124	

P	**Highland Golf Course**	Greens:	$	S J
☺☺	Von Elm Rd., Pocatello. (208) 237-9922	Carts:	$	
	18 holes. Par 72/76. Yards: 6,512/6,100	Rating:	67.5/73.0	
	Mar.–Oct. High: May–Sept.	Slope:	114/117	

P	**Pinecrest Municipal Golf Course**	Greens:	$
☺☺☺	E. Elva St., Idaho Falls. (208) 529-1485	Carts:	$
DEAL	18 holes. Par 70/77. Yards: 6,394/6,123	Rating:	69.5/74.0
	Mar.–Nov. High: May–Sept.	Slope:	116/125

P	**Riverside Golf Course**	Greens:	$
☺☺	S. Bannock Hwy., Pocatello. (208) 232-9515	Carts:	$
	18 holes. Par 72/72. Yards: 6,397/5,710	Rating:	69.7/72.2
	Mar.–Oct. High: May–Aug.	Slope:	114/119

P	**Sand Creek Golf Club**	Greens:	$	S J
☺☺	S. 25th E., Idaho Falls. (208) 529-1115	Carts:	$	
	18 holes. Par 72/73. Yards: 6,805/5,770	Rating:	70.5/72.2	
	Mar.–Nov. High: June–Aug.	Slope:	115/116	

Montana

The golfing high points of Montana are the Ridge and Lakes courses of **Eagle Bend** in Bigfork near Kalispell, a long and breathtaking challenge with gorgeous views and abundant wildlife all around.

Not far away in Whitefish are the North and South courses of the **Whitefish Lake Golf Club**, with more mountain scenery and good golfing challenges. Whitefish Lake is also an Econoguide Deal.

The mountain and high-plateau courses of Montana are generally open from about March through November, although snowstorms can eat away at either end of the schedule. Peak rates are usually in effect from April or May through September.

Econoguide Leader Board: Best Public Courses in Montana

| ☺☺☺ | Eagle Bend Golf Club |
| ☺☺☺ | Whitefish Lake Golf Club (North) |

Econoguide Leader Board: Best Deals in Montana

| $$/☺☺☺ | Buffalo Hill Golf Course |
| $/☺☺☺ | Larchmont Golf Course |

$$/○○○   Meadow Lake Golf Resort
$$/○○○   Mission Mountain Country Club
$$/○○○   Polson Country Club
$$/○○○   Whitefish Lake Golf Club (North, South)

Montana Golf Guide

Kalispell Area

P	**Buffalo Hill Golf Course**	Greens:	$$	T
	North Main St., Kalispell. (406) 756-4547	Carts:	$	
○○○	*Championship Course*	Rating:	71.4/70.3	
DEAL	18 holes. Par 72/72. Yards: 6,525/5,258	Slope:	131/125	
	Apr.–Oct. High: May–Sept.			
P	**Eagle Bend Golf Club**	Greens:	$$$	T J
	Bigfork. (406) 837-7302	Carts:	$	
○○○	*Ridge/Lakes Course*	Rating:	71.4/70.0	
STATE	18 holes. Par 72/72. Yards: 6,639/5,382	Slope:	124/119	
	Apr.–Oct. High: June–Aug.			
R	**Meadow Lake Golf Resort**	Greens:	$$	L R T
○○○	St. Andrews Dr., Columbia Falls. (406) 892-2111	Carts:	$	
DEAL	18 holes. Par 72/73. Yards: 6,714/5,344	Rating:	70.9/69.8	
	Apr.–Nov. High: June–Sept.	Slope:	124/121	
P	**Polson Country Club**	Greens:	$$	
○○○	Bayview Dr., Polson. (406) 883-2440	Carts:	$	
DEAL	18 holes. Par 72/72. Yards: 6,756/5,215	Rating:	70.9/68.4	
	Mar.–Nov. High: June–Aug.	Slope:	119/114	
P	**Whitefish Lake Golf Club**	Greens:	$$	R T
	Hwy. 93 N., Whitefish. (406) 862-5960	Carts:	$	
○○○	*North Course*	Rating:	69.8/70.1	
DEAL	18 holes. Par 72/72. Yards: 6,556/5,556	Slope:	118/115	
STATE	Apr.–Oct. High: June–Sept.			
○○○	*South Course*	Rating:	70.5/70.3	
DEAL	18 holes. Par 71/72. Yards: 6,563/5,358	Slope:	122/120	

Missoula Area

P	**Larchmont Golf Course**	Greens:	$	W S J
○○○	Old Fort Rd., Missoula. (406) 721-4416	Carts:	$$	
DEAL	18 holes. Par 72/72. Yards: 7,114/5,936	Rating:	72.7/72.9	
	Mar.–Oct. High: May–Aug.	Slope:	118/118	
SP	**Mission Mountain Country Club**	Greens:	$$	
○○○	Stagecoach Trail, Ronan. (406) 676-4653	Carts:	$$	
DEAL	18 holes. Par 72/73. Yards: 6,478/5,074	Rating:	69.7/67.5	
	Mar.–Oct. High: June–Aug.	Slope:	114/108	

Butte Area

R	**Fairmont Hot Springs Resort**	Greens:	$$	R
○○	Fairmont Rd., Anaconda. (406) 797-3241	Carts:	$$	
	18 holes. Par 72/72. Yards: 6,741/5,921	Rating:	68.5/70.7	
	Mar.–Oct. High: June–Aug.	Slope:	107/109	

Helena

P	**Bill Roberts Municipal Golf Course**	Greens:	$	S J
○○	Cole Ave., Helena. (406) 442-2191	Carts:	$$	
	18 holes. Par 72/72. Yards: 6,782/4,700	Rating:	70.5/65.1	
	Mar.–Nov. High: Apr.–Sept.	Slope:	117/101	

Bozeman Area

P	**Big Sky Ski and Summer Resort**	Greens:	$$	T J
○○	Meadow Village, Big Sky. (406) 995-4706	Carts:	$$	
	18 holes. Par 72/72. Yards:	Rating:	69.0/67.4	
	Year-round. High: June–Aug.	Slope:	111/104	

Billings Area

SP ☺	**Lake Hills Golf Course** Billings. (406) 252-9244 18 holes. Par 72/74. Yards: 6,802/6,105 Year-round. High: May–Sept.	Greens: Carts: Rating: Slope:	$ $ 70.1/72.3 112/109	L S J
P ☺☺	**Peter Yegen Jr. Golf Club** Grand Ave., Billings. (406) 656-8099 18 holes. Par 71/71. Yards: 6,617/4,994 Year-round. High: Apr.–Oct.	Greens: Carts: Rating: Slope:	$ $ 69.7/67.0 112/109	W
R ☺☺	**Red Lodge Mountain Golf Course** Upper Continental Dr., Red Lodge. (406) 446-3344 18 holes. Par 72/72. Yards: 6,779/6,445 May–Oct. High: July–Aug.	Greens: Carts: Rating: Slope:	$$ $ 69.3/70.4 115/115	

Nevada

There are patches of green spread about the great deserts of Nevada—most are in the shadows of the fabulous gambling resorts of the state. (If you're looking to mix a bit of resort travel, you might want to check out another book in the Econoguide series, *Econoguide '97—Las Vegas, Reno, Laughlin, Lake Tahoe* by Corey Sandler.)

Among the best public and resort courses in Nevada is the **Edgewood Tahoe Golf Course** in Stateline at the south end of Lake Tahoe, a mountain course with fabulous views and incomparable facilities; the 17th hole uses a beach on Lake Tahoe as a sand hazard. At the north end of the lake is the Championship Course at the **Incline Village Golf Resort**, a very highly regarded open desert course located 6,400 feet above sea level.

On the other side of the Sierra Nevadas, within easy reach of Reno and Lake Tahoe, is **The Golf Club at Genoa Lakes** in Genoa, a challenging course with

Desert oasis—Las Vegas style
Courtesy of the Sheraton Desert Inn Golf Club, Las Vegas, Nevada.

lots of water . . . and wind. It also is open year-round, even when there is 20 feet of snow on the other side of the range. In nearby Dayton is the **Dayton Valley Country Club**, a superb challenge that is also open year-round.

In Las Vegas, the **Sheraton Desert Inn Golf Club** is worth breaking away from the tables for; although it is right off the Strip, it is so rich with trees, water, and attention to detail you just might be able to forget you are within a wood shot or so of an Egyptian pyramid, a 100-foot-tall lion, and Elvis on Ice. Also worth visiting is the **Las Vegas Hilton Country Club**, the former Sahara Country Club. The **Sun City Las Vegas Golf Club**, a semiprivate facility not affiliated with a casino, has two worthy courses, Highland Falls and Palm Valley.

In Henderson, 10 miles south of Las Vegas, there is **The Legacy Golf Club**, a challenging desert course with a touch of Scotland mixed in.

Courses to the east of the Sierra Nevadas, including those in Las Vegas and Laughlin and some on the plateaus near Reno, are open year-round, with peak-season prices in effect from spring through fall. Some courses reduce their rates in the desert heat of midsummer.

In the high mountain resorts in and around Lake Tahoe, the season runs from May through October, with high-season rates in effect from June through September.

Econoguide Leader Board: Best Public Courses in Nevada

☺☺☺	Dayton Valley Country Club
☺☺☺☺	Edgewood Tahoe Golf Course
☺☺☺☺	The Golf Club at Genoa Lakes
☺☺☺☺	Incline Village Golf Resort
☺☺☺	Las Vegas Hilton Country Club
☺☺☺	The Legacy Golf Club
☺☺☺	Sheraton Desert Inn Golf Club
☺☺☺	Sun City Las Vegas Golf Club (Highland Falls, Palm Valley)

Econoguide Leader Board: Best Deals in Nevada

$$/☺☺☺	Eagle Valley Golf Club (East, West)
$$/☺☺☺	Northgate Golf Course
$$/☺☺☺	Rosewood Lakes Golf Course
$/☺☺☺	Ruby View Golf Course

Nevada Golf Guide

Reno/Carson City Area

SP ☺☺☺ STATE	**Dayton Valley Country Club** Palmer Dr., Dayton. (702) 246-7888 18 holes. Par 72/72. Yards: 7,218/5,161 Year-round. High: May–Oct.	Greens: Carts: Rating: Slope:	$$–$$$$ Incl. 72.9/68.4 136/121	W L T J	
P ☺☺☺ DEAL	**Eagle Valley Golf Club** Centennial Park Dr., Carson City. (702) 887-2380 *East Course* 18 holes. Par 72/72. Yards: 6,658/5,980 Year-round. High: May–Sept.	Greens: Carts: Rating: Slope:	$ $ 68.7/72.8 117/123	T	

Nevada Golf Guide

Reno/Carson City Area

☺☺☺ DEAL	*West Course* 18 holes. Par 72/72. Yards: 6,851/5,293	Greens: Carts: Rating: Slope:	$$ Incl. 73.5/68.8 131/117	T
P ☺☺☺	**Lakeridge Golf Course** Razorback Rd., Reno. (702) 825-2200 18 holes. Par 71/71. Yards: 6,703/5,159 Mar.–Dec. High: Apr.–Oct.	Greens: Carts: Rating: Slope:	$$–$$$ Incl. 70.8/68.5 127/117	L T
R ☺☺☺ DEAL	**Northgate Golf Course** Reno. (702) 747-7577 18 holes. Par 72/72. Yards: 6,966/5,521 Year-round. High: June–Sept.	Greens: Carts: Rating: Slope:	$$ Incl. 72.3/70.2 131/127	W L R T
P ☺☺☺ DEAL	**Rosewood Lakes Golf Course** Pembroke Dr., Reno. (702) 857-2892 18 holes. Par 72/72. Yards: 6,693/5,082 Year-round. High: Apr.–Nov.	Greens: Carts: Rating: Slope:	$–$$ $ 71.1/68.2 127/117	L T S J
P ☺	**Washoe County Golf Club** S. Arlington, Reno. (702) 828-6640 18 holes. Par 72/72. Yards: 6,695/5,863 Year-round. High: Apr.–Oct.	Greens: Carts: Rating: Slope:	$–$$ Inquire 70.0/72.9 119/122	L T S J

Lake Tahoe Area

R ☺☺☺☺ BEST	**Edgewood Tahoe Golf Course** U.S. Hwy. 50, Stateline. (702) 588-3566 18 holes. Par 72/72. Yards: 7,491/5,749 May–Oct. High: July–Sept.	Greens: Carts: Rating: Slope:	$$$$$$+ Incl. 75.1/71.5 136/130	
P ☺☺☺☺ STATE	**The Golf Club at Genoa Lakes** Genoa. (702) 782-4653 18 holes. Par 72/72. Yards: 7,263/5,008 Year-round. High: May–Sept.	Greens: Carts: Rating: Slope:	$$$–$$$$ Incl. 73.5/67.6 134/117	W L
R ☺☺☺☺ BEST	**Incline Village Golf Resort** Incline Village. (702) 832-1144 *Championship Course* 18 holes. Par 72/72. Yards: 6,915/5,350 May–Oct. High: June–Sept.	Greens: Carts: Rating: Slope:	$$$$$$ Incl. 72.6/70.5 129/126	T

Central Nevada

SP ☺☺☺	**Calvada Valley Golf and Country Club** Mt. Charleston Rd., Pahrump. (702) 727-4653 18 holes. Par 71/73. Yards: 7,025/5,948 Year-round. High: Feb.–May, Sept.–Nov.	Greens: Carts: Rating: Slope:	$$$ Incl. 73.2/74.3 124/123	S J
R ☺☺☺	**Oasis Resort Hotel Casino** Hillside Dr., Mesquite. (702) 346-5232 *Palms Golf Course* 18 holes. Par 72/72. Yards: 7,008/6,284 Year-round. High: Jan.–May, Oct.–Nov.	Greens: Carts: Rating: Slope:	$$$$–$$$$$ Incl. 74.9/70.4 137/122	W L R T
P ☺☺☺ DEAL	**Ruby View Golf Course** Elko. (702) 738-6212 18 holes. Par 72/72. Yards: 6,928/5,958 Mar.–Nov. High: June–Aug.	Greens: Carts: Rating: Slope:	$ $ 70.5/72.5 118/123	T

Las Vegas Area

| P

☺☺☺ | **Angel Park Golf Club**
S. Rampart Blvd., Las Vegas. (702) 254-4653
Mountain Course
18 holes. Par 71/72. Yards: 6,722/5,164
Year-round. High: Feb.–June, Sept.–Nov. | Greens:
Carts:
Rating:
Slope: | $$$–$$$$$
Incl.
72.4/69.9
128/119 | L T J |

Nevada Golf Guide

Las Vegas Area

☺☺☺	*Palm Course* 18 holes. Par 70/70. Yards: 6,530/4,570	Rating: Slope:	72.6/67.6 130/110

P ☺☺	**Boulder City Golf Club** Boulder City. (702) 293-9236 18 holes. Par 72/72. Yards: 6,561/5,566 Year-round. High: Spring/Fall	Greens: Carts: Rating: Slope:	$$ Inquire 70.2/70.7 110/113	L T

P ☺☺	**Las Vegas Golf Club** W. Washington, Las Vegas. (702) 646-3003 18 holes. Par 72/72. Yards: 6,631/5,715 Year-round.	Greens: Carts: Rating: Slope:	$$ Inquire 71.8/71.2 117/118	T S J

R ☺☺☺ STATE	**Las Vegas Hilton Country Club** E. Desert Inn Rd., Las Vegas. (702) 796-0013 18 holes. Par 71/71. Yards: 6,815/5,741 Year-round. High: Feb.–May	Greens: Carts: Rating: Slope:	$$$$$$+ Inquire 72.1/72.9 130/127	W L T J

P ☺☺☺ STATE	**The Legacy Golf Club** Henderson. (702) 897-2187 18 holes. Par 72/72. Yards: 7,233/5,340 Year-round. High: Sept.–June	Greens: Carts: Rating: Slope:	$$$$$$ Incl. 74.9/71.0 136/120	T

P ☺☺☺	**Painted Desert Golf Club** Painted Mirage Way, Las Vegas. (702) 645-2568 18 holes. Par 72/72. Yards: 6,840/5,711 Year-round. High: Sept.–June	Greens: Carts: Rating: Slope:	$$$$$ Incl. 73.7/72.7 136/120	L T J

R ☺☺☺ BEST	**Sheraton Desert Inn Golf Club** Las Vegas Blvd. S., Las Vegas. (702) 733-4290 18 holes. Par 72/72. Yards: 7,066/5,791 Year-round. High: Feb.–May	Greens: Carts: Rating: Slope:	$$$$$–$$$$$$ Incl. 73.9/72.7 124/121	L R

SP ☺☺☺ STATE	**Sun City Las Vegas Golf Club** Las Vegas. (702) 254-7010 *Highland Falls Course.* Sun City Blvd. 18 holes. Par 72/72. Yards: 6,512/5,099 Year-round. High: Oct.–May	Greens: Carts: Rating: Slope:	$$–$$$$$ Incl. 71.2/68.8 126/110	W L J

☺☺☺ STATE	*Palm Valley Course.* Del Webb Blvd. 18 holes. Par 72/72. Yards: 6,849/5,502	Rating: Slope:	72.3/71.5 127/124	

R ☺☺	**Wild Horse Golf Club** Showboat Club Dr., Henderson. (702) 434-9009 18 holes. Par 72/72. Yards: 7,053/5,372 Year-round. High: Oct.–May	Greens: Carts: Rating: Slope:	$$$$–$$$$$ Incl. 75.2/71.3 135/125	L T J

Laughlin

P ☺☺	**Emerald River Golf Course** W. Casino Dr., Laughlin. (702) 298-0061 18 holes. Par 72/72. Yards: 6,809/5,205 Year-round. High: Jan.–May, Oct.–Nov.	Greens: Carts: Rating: Slope:	$$–$$$ Incl. NA 144/129	W L R T S J

New Mexico

The best of the public courses in New Mexico is probably the **Piñon Hills Golf Course** in Farmington in the remote northwest corner of the state; it is described as a fair but challenging course in a spectacular setting with views of the La Plata Mountains across the border near Durango, Colorado.

Another winner is the Tamaya and Rio Grande nines at the **Santa Ana Golf Course** in Bernalillo, just north of Albuquerque along the Rio Grande River.

In Albuquerque itself is the long, hilly, and otherwise demanding Championship Course at the **University of New Mexico**.

The **Taos Country Club** is a spectacular desert challenge located just north of Santa Fe. **Cochiti Lake** lies about 35 miles southwest of Santa Fe; it's an excellent challenge with spectacular views.

The **Links at Sierra Blanca** is in Ruidoso, north of Alamogordo; it's a remote high-altitude course. Not far away is the **Inn of the Mountain Gods** in Mescalero. A beautiful place with devilish greens, it is owned by the Mescalero Apache tribe.

Our Econoguide Deals list includes Cochiti Lake, Piñon Hills, Santa Ana, and the Taos Country Club.

In the mountains of New Mexico, courses generally are open from March through November, with peak rates during the summer months of June through September.

Year-round courses elsewhere in the state have peak rates in effect in the summer; some courses offer discounts in the hottest part of the summer.

Econoguide Leader Board: Best Public Courses in New Mexico

☺☺☺	Cochiti Lake Golf Course
☺☺☺☺	Inn of the Mountain Gods Golf Club
☺☺☺	The Links at Sierra Blanca
☺☺☺☺	Pinon Hills Golf Course
☺☺☺	Santa Ana Golf Course (Tamaya, Rio Grande)
☺☺☺☺	Taos Country Club
☺☺☺☺	University of New Mexico Golf Course (Championship)

Econoguide Leader Board: Best Deals in New Mexico

$$/☺☺☺	Cochiti Lake Golf Course
$/☺☺☺	New Mexico State University Golf Course
$/☺☺☺	New Mexico Tech Golf Course
$/☺☺☺☺	Pinon Hills Golf Course
$$/☺☺☺	Santa Ana Golf Course
$$/☺☺☺☺	Taos Country Club

New Mexico Golf Guide

Albuquerque Area

P ☺☺	**Arroyo del Oso Municipal Golf Course** Osuna Rd. N.E., Albuquerque. (505) 884-7505 18 holes. Par 72/73. Yards: 6,892/5,998 Year-round. High: Apr.–Nov.	Greens: $ Carts: $ Rating: 72.3/72.3 Slope: 125/120	T S J
P ☺☺	**Ladera Golf Course** Ladera Dr. N.W., Albuquerque. (505) 836-4449 18 holes. Par 72/72. Yards: 7,107/5,966 Year-round. High: Apr.–Sept.	Greens: $ Carts: Inquire Rating: 73.0/72.8 Slope: 123/116	W L T S J
P ☺☺	**Los Altos Golf Course** Copper St. N.E., Albuquerque. (505) 298-1897 18 holes. Par 72/72. Yards: 6,459/5,895 Year-round. High: May–Aug.	Greens: $ Carts: Inquire Rating: 69.9/71.9 Slope: 110/113	L T S J

New Mexico Golf Guide

Albuquerque Area

P ◎◎◎ DEAL	**New Mexico Tech Golf Course** Canyon Rd., Socorro. (508) 835-5335 18 holes. Par 72/73. Yards: 6,688/5,887 Year-round. High: Apr.–Oct.	Greens: Carts: Rating: Slope:	$ Inquire 71.2/72.8 126/122	W T J
P ◎◎	**Paradise Hills Golf Club** Albuquerque. (505) 898-7001 18 holes. Par 72/74. Yards: 6,801/6,090 Year-round. High: Apr.–Sept.	Greens: Carts: Rating: Slope:	$–$$ $ 71.7/73.5 125/118	L T S
P ◎◎◎◎ DEAL STATE	**Piñon Hills Golf Course** Sunrise Pkwy., Farmington. (505) 326-6066 18 holes. Par 72/72. Yards: 7,249/5,522 Year-round. High: May–Oct.	Greens: Carts: Rating: Slope:	$ $ 73.3/71.1 130/126	W
P ◎◎◎ DEAL STATE	**Santa Ana Golf Course** Prairie Star Rd., Bernalillo. (505) 867-9464 *Tamaya/Rio Grande/Coronado* 27 holes. Par 71/72/71. Yards: 7,108/7,007/7,117 Year-round. High: Mar.–Oct.	Greens: Carts: Rating: Slope:	$–$$ $ 72.7/72.7/72.4 122/123/121	W L T S J
SP ◎◎	**Tierra del Sol Golf Course** Belen. (505) 865-5056 18 holes. Par 72/72. Yards: 6,703/5,512 Year-round. High: Apr.–Oct.	Greens: Carts: Rating: Slope:	$ $ 71.0/71.2 117/114	W T J
P ◎◎◎◎ BEST	**University of New Mexico Golf Course** University Blvd. S.E., Albuquerque. (505) 277-4546 *Championship Course* 18 holes. Par 72/73. Yards: 7,248/6,031 Year-round. High: May–Sept.	Greens: Carts: Rating: Slope:	$–$$$ $$ 74.7/75.1 138/131	W T S J

Santa Fe Area

R ◎◎	**Angel Fire Country Club** Angel Fire. (505) 377-3055 18 holes. Par 72/72. 6,624/5,328 May–Oct. High: June–Sept.	Greens: Carts: Rating: Slope:	$$$ $ NA 128/118	L R
P ◎◎◎ BEST DEAL	**Cochiti Lake Golf Course** Cochiti Hwy., Cochiti Lake. (505) 465-2239 18 holes. Par 72/72. Yards: 6,451/5,292 Year-round. High: Mar.–Oct.	Greens: Carts: Rating: Slope:	$–$$ $ 71.2/70.6 131/121	W
P ◎◎◎ STATE	**The Links at Sierra Blanca** Sierra Blanca Dr., Ruidoso. (505) 258-5330 18 holes. Par 72/72. Yards: 7,003/5,202 Year-round. High: June–Sept.	Greens: Carts: Rating: Slope:	$$–$$$$ $ 72.9/68.9 136/111	W L T S J
P ◎◎	**Los Alamos Golf Club** Diamond Dr., Los Alamos. (505) 662-8139 18 holes. Par 71/74. Yards: 6,440/5,499 Year-round. High: June–Sept.	Greens: Carts: Rating: Slope:	$ $ 69.7/69.8 118/113	W
SP ◎◎◎◎ DEAL STATE	**Taos Country Club** Hwy. 570 W., Rancho de Taos. (505) 758-7300 18 holes. Par 72/72. Yards: 7,302/5,310 Mar.–Nov. High: June–Sept.	Greens: Carts: Rating: Slope:	$$ $$ 73.6/69.0 129/125	W T

Southern New Mexico

R ◎◎◎◎ STATE	**Inn of the Mountain Gods Golf Club** Rte. 4, Mescalero. (505) 257-5141 18 holes. Par 72/72. Yards: 6,834/5,478 Mar.–Dec. High: May–Oct.	Greens: Carts: Rating: Slope:	$$–$$$ $$ 72.1/65.5 132/116	

Southern New Mexico

P	**New Mexico State University Golf Course**	Greens:	$	W T
☺☺☺	Las Cruces. (505) 646-3219	Carts:	$	
DEAL	18 holes. Par 72/72. Yards: 7,040/5,858	Rating:	74.1/70.7	
	Year-round. High: Spring/Fall	Slope:	133/120	

P	**Ocotillo Park Golf Course**	Greens:	$	W T S J
☺☺	N. Lovington Hwy., Hobbs. (505) 397-9297	Carts:	$	
	18 holes. Par 72/72. Yards: 6,716/5,245	Rating:	70.5/69.0	
	Year-round. High: Apr.–Aug.	Slope:	121/108	

Oregon

Portland is Oregon's golfing capital, with four of the state's best in and around the city. The best is probably the Ghost Creek Course at the **Pumpkin Ridge Golf Club** in Cornelius, about 20 miles west of Portland but still inland from the coast. **Eastmoreland** and **Heron Lakes** (its Great Blue Course the best of two there) are in the city itself; both are among the best public courses anywhere.

The best public oceanside course in Oregon—challenging, windy, and full of weather—may be the **Sandpines Golf Resort** in Florence, west of Eugene. Another excellent seaside course is **Salishan Golf Links** in Gleneden Beach, on the coast due west of Salem.

The other direction out of Eugene on the fringes of the Willamette National Forest is the **Tokatee Golf Club** in Blue River, a hidden gem carved out of the mountains, with thousands of green pines framing views of the snow-capped Three Sisters.

On the other side of the mountain range, near Bend, is the superb **Sunriver Lodge and Resort**, where the North Woodlands Course is a difficult woodsy challenge and a lovely resort. Northeast of Bend is the **Black Butte Ranch**, with two winners: the wide-open Big Meadow and the tight mountain track of Glaze Meadow.

Eastmoreland, Heron Lakes, Salishan, and Tokatee are also on both the Econoguide Best and Deals lists.

Many courses in Oregon operate most of the year, generally from about March through November, with peak rates through the summer months. Some courses, including a number around Portland and Salem, are open year-round, with peak rates from about May through October.

Econoguide Leader Board: Best Public Courses in Oregon

☺☺☺	Black Butte Ranch (Big Meadow, Glaze Meadow)
☺☺☺	Eastmoreland Golf Course
☺☺☺	Heron Lakes Golf Course (Great Blue)
☺☺☺☺	Pumpkin Ridge Golf Club (Ghost Creek)
☺☺☺	Salishan Golf Links
☺☺☺☺	Sandpines Golf Resort
☺☺☺☺	Sunriver Lodge and Resort (North Woodlands)
☺☺☺☺	Tokatee Golf Club

Econoguide Leader Board: Best Deals in Oregon

$$/○○○	Eagle Crest Resort (Resort, Ridge)
$/○○○	Eastmoreland Golf Course
$$/○○○	Emerald Valley Golf Club
$$/○○○	Forest Hills Golf Course
$$/○○○	Heron Lakes Golf Course (Great Blue, Greenback)
$$/○○○	Meadow Lakes Golf Course
$/○○○	Quail Valley Golf Course
$$/○○○	River's Edge Golf Course
$$/○○○	Salem Golf Club
$$/○○○	Salishan Golf Links
$$/○○○○	Tokatee Golf Club
$$/○○○	Trysting Tree Golf Club

Oregon Golf Guide

Portland Area

P ○○	**Broadmoor Golf Course** N.E. Columbia Blvd., Portland. (503) 281-1337 18 holes. Par 72/74. Yards: 6,498/5,384 Year-round. High: May–Sept.	Greens: Carts: Rating: Slope:	$–$$ $ 70.3/69.9 118/110	W L
P ○○	**Colwood National Golf Club** N.E. Columbia Blvd., Portland. (503) 254-5515 18 holes. Par 72/77. Yards: 6,400/5,800 Year-round. High: Apr.–Oct.	Greens: Carts: Rating: Slope:	$ $$ 70.2/71.5 113/111	J
P ○○○ BEST DEAL	**Eastmoreland Golf Course** S.E. Bybee Blvd., Portland. (503) 775-2900 18 holes. Par 72/74. Yards: 6,529/5,646 Year-round. High: June–Sept.	Greens: Carts: Rating: Slope:	$ $$ 71.7/71.4 123/117	S J
SP ○○○ DEAL	**Forest Hills Golf Course** S.W. Tongue Lane, Cornelius. (503) 357-3347 18 holes. Par 72/74. Yards: 6,173/5,673 Year-round. High: May–Sept.	Greens: Carts: Rating: Slope:	$$ $$ 69.7/71.7 122/114	J
P ○○	**Glendoveer Golf Course** N.E. Glisan, Portland. (503) 253-7507 *East Course* 18 holes. Par 73/75. Yards: 6,296/5,142 Year-round. High: May–Sept.	Greens: Carts: Rating: Slope:	$ $$ 69.3/73.5 119/120	S J
P ○○○ BEST DEAL	**Heron Lakes Golf Course** N. Victory Blvd., Portland. (503) 289-1818 *Great Blue Course* 18 holes. Par 72/72. Yards: 6,916/5,285 Year-round. High: Mar.–Oct.	Greens: Carts: Rating: Slope:	$$ $–$$ 73.6/69.8 132/120	W S J
○○○ DEAL	*Greenback Course* 18 holes. Par 72/72. Yards: 6,595/5,224	Rating: Slope:	71.4/69.4 124/113	
P ○	**Mountain View Golf Club** S.E. Kelso Rd., Boring. (503) 663-4869 18 holes. Par 71/73. Yards: 6,056/5,294 Year-round. High: Apr.–Oct.	Greens: Carts: Rating: Slope:	$–$$ $$ 69.2/69.2 122/111	W S J
P ○○○○ BEST	**Pumpkin Ridge Golf Club** Old Pumpkin Ridge Rd., Cornelius. (503) 647-9977 *Ghost Creek Course* 18 holes. Par 71/71. Yards: 6,839/5,326 Year-round. High: Apr.–Oct.	Greens: Carts: Rating: Slope:	$$$$ $$ 73.8/71.0 140/121	W L T

Oregon Golf Guide

Portland Area

P	**Quail Valley Golf Course**	Greens:	$$	
☺☺☺	N.W. Aerts Rd., Banks. (503) 324-4444	Carts:	$$	
DEAL	18 holes. Par 72/72. Yards: 6,603/5,519	Rating:	71.6/71.5	
	Year-round. High: June–Sept.	Slope:	122/117	

R	**The Resort at the Mountain**	Greens:	$$	W L R T J
☺☺	Welches. (503) 622-3151	Carts:	$$	
	27 holes. Par 72/70/70. Yards: 6,443/5,776/6,032	Rating:	70.0/68.0/68.0	
	Year-round. High: May–Oct.	Slope:	119/116/116	

P	**Salem Golf Club**	Greens:	$$	L J
☺☺☺	Salem. (503) 363-6652	Carts:	$$	
DEAL	18 holes. Par 72/72. Yards: 6,200/5,163	Rating:	69.6/70.0	
	Year-round. High: July–Sept.	Slope:	118/NA	

R	**Salishan Golf Links**	Greens:	$$	J
☺☺☺	Gleneden Beach. (503) 764-3632	Carts:	$$	
BEST	18 holes. Par 72/72. Yards: 6,439/5,693	Rating:	72.1/73.6	
DEAL	Year-round. High: June–Oct.	Slope:	128/127	

P	**Santiam Golf Club**	Greens:	$$	S J
☺☺	Aumsville. (503) 769-3485	Carts:	$$	
	18 holes. Par 72/72. Yards: 6,392/5,469	Rating:	70.4/72.2	
	Year-round. High: July–Sept.	Slope:	115/122	

P	**Trysting Tree Golf Club**	Greens:	$$	J
☺☺☺	Electric Rd., Corvallis. (503) 752-3332	Carts:	$	
DEAL	18 holes. Par 72/72. Yards: 7,014/5,516	Rating:	73.9/71.3	
	Year-round. High: May–Oct.	Slope:	129/118	

Eugene Area

SP	**Emerald Valley Golf Club**	Greens:	$$	W T S J
☺☺☺	Dale Kuni Rd., Creswell. (503) 895-2174	Carts:	$$	
DEAL	18 holes. Par 72/73. Yards: 6,873/5,371	Rating:	71.7/71.4	
	Year-round. High: June–Sept.	Slope:	123/117	

P	**The Knolls Golf Club**	Greens:	$	T
☺☺	Sutherlin. (503) 459-4422	Carts:	$	
	18 holes. Par 72/73. Yards: 6,346/5,427	Rating:	70.3/71.5	
	Year-round. High: June–Aug.	Slope:	121/122	

P	**Ocean Dunes Golf Links**	Greens:	$$	T S J
☺☺	Munsel Lake Rd., Florence. (503) 997-3232	Carts:	$	
	18 holes. Par 70/72. Yards: 5,670/4,868	Rating:	68.5/69.5	
	Year-round. High: Apr.–Nov.	Slope:	124/124	

P	**Riveredge Golf Course**	Greens:	$–$$	L T S J
☺☺	N. Delta, Eugene. (503) 345-9160	Carts:	$$	
	18 holes. Par 71/71. Yards: 6,256/5,146	Rating:	68.6/67.7	
	Year-round. High: May–Sept.	Slope:	116/112	

P	**Sandpines Golf Resort**	Greens:	$$–$$$	T
☺☺☺☺	35th St., Florence. (503) 997-1940	Carts:	$$	
BEST	18 holes. Par 72/72. Yards: 6,954/5,346	Rating:	74.0/65.8	
	Year-round. High: June–Oct.	Slope:	129/111	

P	**Tokatee Golf Club**	Greens:	$$	J
☺☺☺☺	McKenzie Hwy., Blue River. (503) 822-3220	Carts:	$	
BEST	18 holes. Par 72/72. Yards: 6,842/5,651	Rating:	72.0/71.2	
DEAL	Feb.–Nov. High: June–Sept.	Slope:	126/115	

Bend Area

SP	**Awbrey Glen Golf Club**	Greens:	$$$	L J
☺☺☺	Bend. (503) 388-8526	Carts:	$	

Oregon Golf Guide

Bend Area

	18 holes. Par 72/72. Yards: 7,007/5,459	Rating:	73.7/69.6
	Mar.–Oct. High: May–Sept.	Slope:	135/119

R | **Black Butte Ranch** — Greens: $$–$$$ L
Hwy. 20, Black Butte. (503) 595-6689 — Carts: $$
☺☺☺ *Big Meadow Course* — Rating: 72.0/70.5
STATE 18 holes. Par 72/72. Yards: 6,870/5,716 — Slope: 127/115
Mar.–Nov. High: June–Sept.

☺☺☺ *Glaze Meadow Course* — Rating: 71.5/72.1
STATE 18 holes. Par 72/72. Yards: 6,560/5,616 — Slope: 128/120

R | **Eagle Crest Resort** — Greens: $$ L R J
Cline Falls Rd., Redmond. (503) 923-4653 — Carts: $$
☺☺☺ *Resort Course* — Rating: 71.5/69.8
DEAL 18 holes. Par 72/72. Yards: 6,673/5,395 — Slope: 123/109
Year-round. High: Apr.–Oct.

☺☺☺ *Ridge Course* — Rating: 70.8/NA
DEAL 18 holes. Par 72/72. Yards: 6,477/4,773 — Slope: 123/NA

SP | **Juniper Golf Club** — Greens: $$ W L J
☺ S.E. Sisters Ave., Richmond. (503) 548-3121 — Carts: $$
18 holes. Par 72/72. Yards: 6,525/5,598 — Rating: 71.3/70.9
Year-round. High: May–Oct. — Slope: 124/115

P | **Meadow Lakes Golf Course** — Greens: $$ L
☺☺☺ Prineville. (503) 447-7113 — Carts: $
DEAL 18 holes. Par 72/72. Yards: 6,731/5,155 — Rating: 73.1/69.0
Year-round. High: June–Sept. — Slope: 131/121

P | **River's Edge Golf Course** — Greens: $$ L R T J
☺☺☺ N.W. Mt. Washington Dr., Bend. (503) 389-2828 — Carts: $
DEAL 18 holes. Par 72/73. Yards: 6,647/5,380 — Rating: 72.2/71.8
Year-round. High: May–Sept. — Slope: 139/135

R | **Sunriver Lodge and Resort** — Greens: $$–$$$
Sunriver. (503) 593-1221 — Carts: Incl.
☺☺☺☺ *North Woodlands Course* — Rating: 70.4/72.2
BEST 18 holes. Par 72/72. Yards: 6,880/5,446 — Slope: 115/122
Apr.–Oct. High: June–Aug.

☺☺☺ *South Meadows Course* — Greens: $$–$$$$ L R T J
18 holes. Par 72/72. Yards: 6,960/5,847 — Carts: Incl.
Rating: 72.9/71.7
Slope: 130/116

Medford Area

P | **Cedar Links Golf Course** — Greens: $$
☺☺ Medford. (503) 773-4373 — Carts: $
18 holes. Par 70/71. Yards: 6,142/5,145 — Rating: 68.9/68.7
Year-round. High: May–Sept. — Slope: 114/112

P | **Harbor Links Golf Course** — Greens: $$ W L T S J
☺☺ Harbor Isles Blvd., Klamath Falls. (503) 882-0609 — Carts: $$
18 holes. Par 72/72. Yards: 6,272/5,709 — Rating: 69.3/71.2
Year-round. High: June–Sept. — Slope: 117/119

R | **Kah-Nee-Ta Resort Golf Club** — Greens: $–$$ L S J
☺☺ Warm Springs. (503) 553-1112 — Carts: $$
18 holes. Par 72/73. Yards: 6,352/5,195 — Rating: 73.1/70.0
Year-round. High: Mar.–Oct. — Slope: 123/116

Utah

The **Green Spring Golf Course** in Washington, in the southwest corner of Utah at the Arizona border, is a very difficult canyon course with desert and forest holes. In nearby St. George is the **Sunbrook Golf Club**, a tough mountain course and perhaps the best course in the state.

Park Meadows Golf Club is a spectacular challenge way up in the ski town of Park City, about 30 miles east of Salt Lake City on the back side of the mountains that face the city. **Homestead Golf Club** is another attractive high-mountain course, located in Midway not far from the Alta and Brighton ski areas.

North of Salt Lake City in Layton is **Valley View Golf Course**, an up-and-down long challenge.

And if you've got a few hours to kill before flying away, **Wingpointe** is a tough challenge just outside of downtown Salt Lake City near the airport.

Hobble Creek, in Springville between Salt Lake City and Provo, is a mountain gem and a great deal.

All seven of Utah's Econoguide Best–rated courses are also on the Econoguide Deals list.

High-mountain resorts in Utah are generally open from April to October, with peak rates in effect from June to September. Other courses, including some in the valleys around Salt Lake City, operate year-round, with peak rates in the summer.

Econoguide Leader Board: Best Public Courses in Utah

☺☺☺	Green Spring Golf Course
☺☺☺☺	Hobble Creek Golf Club
☺☺☺	Homestead Golf Club
☺☺☺☺	Park Meadows Golf Club
☺☺☺☺	Sunbrook Golf Club
☺☺☺☺	Valley View Golf Course
☺☺☺	Wingpointe Golf Course

Econoguide Leader Board: Best Deals in Utah

$/☺☺☺	Bonneville Golf Course
$/☺☺☺	Bountiful City Golf Course
$/☺☺☺	Davis Park Golf Course
$/☺☺☺	Eagle Mountain Golf Course
$/☺☺☺	Eaglewood Golf Course
$/☺☺☺	Gladstan Golf Club
$$/☺☺☺	Green Spring Golf Course
$/☺☺☺☺	Hobble Creek Golf Club
$$/☺☺☺	Homestead Golf Club
$/☺☺☺	Logan River Golf Course
$/☺☺☺	Moab Golf Club
$/☺☺☺	Mountain Dell Golf Club (Canyon, Lake)
$$/☺☺☺	Park City Golf Course

$$/○○○○	Park Meadows Golf Club
$/○○○	Spanish Oaks Golf Club
$/○○○○	Sunbrook Golf Club
$/○○○	Tri-City Golf Course
$/○○○○	Valley View Golf Course
$/○○○	West Ridge Golf Course
$/○○○	Wingpointe Golf Course
$$/○○○	Wolf Creek Resort Golf Course

Utah Golf Guide

Salt Lake City Area

P ○○○ DEAL	**Bonneville Golf Course** Connor St., Salt Lake City. (801) 583-9513 18 holes. Par 72/74. Yards: 6,824/5,860 Mar.–Nov. High: Apr.–Sept.	Greens: $ Carts: $ Rating: 71.0/71.6 Slope: 120/119	S J
P ○○○ DEAL	**Bountiful City Golf Course** S. Bountiful Blvd., Bountiful. (801) 298-6040 18 holes. Par 71/72. Yards: 6,630/5,012 Mar.–Nov. High: May–Aug.	Greens: $ Carts: $ Rating: 70.1/68.6 Slope: 117/115	S J
P ○○○ DEAL	**Davis Park Golf Course** E. Nicholls Rd., Fruit Heights. (801) 546-4154 18 holes. Par 71/71. Yards: 6,481/5,295 Mar.–Nov. High: May–Aug.	Greens: $ Carts: $ Rating: 69.3/68.7 Slope: 117/114	S J
P ○○○ DEAL	**Eagle Mountain Golf Course** E. 700 S., Brigham City. (801) 723-3212 18 holes. Par 71/71. Yards: 6,769/4,767 Mar.–Nov. High: Apr.–Sept.	Greens: $ Carts: $ Rating: 71.4/65.4 Slope: 119/101	
P ○○○ DEAL	**Eaglewood Golf Course** E. Eaglewood Dr., N. Salt Lake City. (801) 299-0088 18 holes. Par 71/71. Yards: 6,769/4,767 Mar.–Nov. High: Apr.–Sept.	Greens: $ Carts: $ Rating: 71.1/68.8 Slope: 121/112	W L J
P ○○	**Glendale Golf Course** W. 2100 S., Salt Lake City. (801) 974-2403 18 holes. Par 72/73. Yards: 7,000/5,930 Mar.–Nov. High: May–Aug.	Greens: $ Carts: $ Rating: 70.9/72.5 Slope: 117/120	W S J
P ○○	**Glenmoor Golf and Country Club** S. 4800 W., S. Jordan. (801) 280-1742 18 holes. Par 72/72. Yards: 6,900/5,800 Year-round. High: June–July	Greens: $ Carts: $ Rating: 70.9/72.0 Slope: 117/118	W S
R ○○○ DEAL STATE	**Homestead Golf Club** N. Homestead Dr., Midway. (801) 654-5588 18 holes. Par 72/72. Yards: 6,967/5,131 Apr.–Oct. High: June–Sept.	Greens: $–$$ Carts: $ Rating: 72.8/68.8 Slope: 135/118	W L R T S
P ○○○ DEAL	**Logan River Golf Course** W. 1000 S., Logan. (801) 750-0123 18 holes. Par 71/71. Yards: 6,502/5,048 Mar.–Oct. High: June–Sept.	Greens: $ Carts: $ Rating: 70.5/78.9 Slope: 124/117	S J
P ○	**Meadow Brook Golf Course** S. 1300 W., Taylorsville. (801) 266-0971 18 holes. Par 72/72. Yards: 6,800/5,605 Mar.–Dec. High: May–Oct.	Greens: $ Carts: $ Rating: 70.0/67.9 Slope: 110/104	W S J
P ○○	**Mount Ogden Golf Course** Constitution Way, Ogden. (801) 629-8700 18 holes. Par 71/72. Yards: 6,300/4,980 Mar.–Nov. High: Apr.–Oct.	Greens: $ Carts: $ Rating: 70.5/69.5 Slope: 121/111	

Utah Golf Guide

Salt Lake City Area

P	**Mountain Dell Golf Club**	Greens:	$	W T S J
	Cummings Rd., Salt Lake City. (801) 582-3812	Carts:	$	
☺☺☺	*Canyon Course*	Rating:	71.3/71.1	
DEAL	18 holes. Par 72/73. Yards: 6,787/5,447	Slope:	126/112	
	Apr.–Nov. High: June–Aug.			

☺☺☺	*Lake Course*	Rating:	72.2/67.6	
DEAL	18 holes. Par 71/71. Yards: 6,709/5,066	Slope:	129/109	

P	**Murray Parkway Golf Club**	Greens:	$	J
☺☺	Murray. (801) 262-4653	Carts:	$	
	18 holes. Par 72/72. Yards: 6,800/5,800	Rating:	71.3/71.0	
	Mar.–Nov. High: June–Aug.	Slope:	120/118	

P	**Park City Golf Course**	Greens:	$$	L
☺☺☺	Lower Park Ave., Park City. (801) 649-8701	Carts:	$	
DEAL	18 holes. Par 72/72. Yards: 6,754/5,600	Rating:	71.7/71.4	
	Apr.–Oct. High: May–Sept.	Slope:	127/123	

P	**Park Meadows Golf Club**	Greens:	$$	L T S
☺☺☺☺	Meadows Dr., Park City. (801) 649-2460	Carts:	Incl.	
DEAL	18 holes. Par 72/74. Yards: 7,400/5,816	Rating:	74.4/72.2	
STATE	Apr.–Oct. High: June–Aug.	Slope:	129/125	

P	**Rose Park Golf Club**	Greens:	$	S J
☺☺	N. Redwood Rd., Salt Lake City. (801) 596-5030	Carts:	$	
	18 holes. Par 72/75. Yards: 6,696/5,816	Rating:	69.6/70.8	
	Feb.–Dec. High: May–Sept.	Slope:	109/112	

P	**Schneiter's Riverside Golf Course**	Greens:	$	S J
☺☺	S. Weber Dr., Ogden. (801) 399-4636	Carts:	$	
	18 holes. Par 71/71. Yards: 6,177/5,217	Rating:	68.4/68.5	
	Mar.–Nov. High: May–Aug.	Slope:	114/113	

P	**Stansbury Park Golf Club**	Greens:	$	W L
☺☺	Tooele. (801) 328-1483	Carts:	$	
	18 holes. Par 72/72. Yards: 6,831/5,722	Rating:	71.6/71.5	
	Feb.–Nov. High: June–Aug.	Slope:	125/121	

P	**Tri-City Golf Course**	Greens:	$	S J
☺☺☺	N. 200 E., American Fork. (801) 756-3594	Carts:	$	
DEAL	18 holes. Par 72/75. Yards: 7,077/6,304	Rating:	73.0/75.0	
	Mar.–Oct. High: May–Aug.	Slope:	125/127	

P	**Valley View Golf Course**	Greens:	$	S J
☺☺☺☺	E. Gentile, Layton. (801) 546-1630	Carts:	$	
DEAL	18 holes. Par 72/74. Yards: 6,652/5,755	Rating:	71.2/72.3	
STATE	Mar.–Nov. High: May–Sept.	Slope:	119/120	

P	**West Bountiful City Golf Course**	Greens:	$	S J
☺☺	N. 1100 W., W. Bountiful. (801) 295-1019	Carts:	$	
	18 holes. Par 71/72. Yards: 6,030/4,895	Rating:	67.2/66.5	
	Mar.–Oct. High: June–Aug.	Slope:	113/115	

P	**West Ridge Golf Course**	Greens:	$	W S J
☺☺☺	W. Valley City. (801) 966-4653	Carts:	$	
DEAL	18 holes. Par 71/71. Yards: 6,734/5,027	Rating:	72.2/68.1	
	Mar.–Nov. High: Apr.–Aug.	Slope:	125/118	

P	**Wingpointe Golf Course**	Greens:	$	W L S J
☺☺☺	W. 100 N., Salt Lake City. (801) 575-2345	Carts:	$	
DEAL	18 holes. Par 72/72. Yards: 7,101/5,228	Rating:	73.3/72.0	
STATE	Year-round. High: May–Oct.	Slope:	131/125	

R	**Wolf Creek Resort Golf Course**	Greens:	$$	W L R T
☺☺☺	N. Wolf Creek Dr., Eden. (801) 745-3365	Carts:	$	

Utah Golf Guide

Salt Lake City Area

DEAL	18 holes. Par 72/72. Yards: 6,845/5,332	Rating:	NA
	Mar.–Nov. High: May–Sept.	Slope:	134/127

Provo Area

P	**East Bay Golf Course**	Greens:	$	
☺☺	S. East Bay Blvd., Provo. (801) 379-6612	Carts:	$	
	18 holes. Par 71/72. Yards: 6,932/5,125	Rating:	67.6/66.6	
	Mar.–Nov. High: May–Sept.	Slope:	116/106	

P	**Gladstan Golf Club**	Greens:	$	S J
☺☺☺	Payson. (801) 465-2549	Carts:	$	
DEAL	18 holes. Par 71/71. Yards: 6,509/4,782	Rating:	70.7/67.4	
	Mar.–Nov. High: May–Aug.	Slope:	121/111	

P	**Hobble Creek Golf Club**	Greens:	$	S J
☺☺☺☺	E. Hobble Creek Canyon, Springville. (801) 489-6297	Carts:	$	
DEAL	18 holes. Par 71/73. Yards: 6,315/5,435	Rating:	69.4/69.5	
STATE	Mar.–Nov. High: July–Sept.	Slope:	120/117	

P	**Spanish Oaks Golf Club**	Greens:	$	T S J
☺☺☺	Powerhouse Rd., Spanish Fork. (801) 798-9816	Carts:	$	
DEAL	18 holes. Par 72/73. Yards: 6,358/5,319	Rating:	68.7/68.9	
	Mar.–Oct. High: May–Sept.	Slope:	116/113	

Southern Utah/St. George

P	**Green Spring Golf Course**	Greens:	$–$$	W L T J
☺☺☺	N. Green Spring Dr., Washington. (801) 673-7888	Carts:	$	
DEAL	18 holes. Par 71/71. Yards: 6,717/5,042	Rating:	72.6/69.8	
STATE	Year-round. High: Oct.–May	Slope:	131/119	

P	**Moab Golf Club**	Greens:	$	J
☺☺☺	S.E. Bench Rd., Moab. (801) 259-6488	Carts:	$	
DEAL	18 holes. Par 72/72. Yards: 6,819/4,725	Rating:	72.2/69.6	
	Year-round. High: Spring/Fall	Slope:	125/110	

P	**St. George Golf Club**	Greens:	$$
☺☺	S. 1400 E., St. George. (801) 634-5854	Carts:	Incl.
	18 holes. Par 73/73. Yards: 7,211/5,216	Rating:	73.1/68.9
	Year-round. High: Oct.–May	Slope:	126/114

P	**Southgate Golf Club**	Greens:	$$	L T J
☺☺	S. Tonaquint Dr., St. George. (801) 628-0000	Carts:	$	
	18 holes. Par 70/70. Yards: 6,400/4,463	Rating:	70.2/66.8	
	Year-round. High: Oct.–Apr.	Slope:	120/112	

P	**Sunbrook Golf Club**	Greens:	$–$$	L
☺☺☺☺	St. George. (801) 634-5866	Carts:	$	
DEAL	18 holes. Par 72/72. Yards: 6,800/5,286	Rating:	73.0/71.1	
STATE	Year-round. High: Jan.–May, Oct.–Nov.	Slope:	129/121	

Washington

Way up in the northwest corner of the state on the Canadian border is the **Semiahmoo Golf and Country Club** in Blaine, a spectacular desert course. In Bellingham, the **Shuksan Golf Club** is an exciting newer public course.

The **Classic Country Club** in Spanaway, about 60 miles south of Seattle, is a long, tight challenge with distant views of Mount Rainier. **Kayak Point** in Stanwood, 45 miles south of Seattle, is another narrow, hilly challenge. The **McCormick Woods Golf Course** winds its way through the woods in Port Orchard, about 20 miles northwest of Tacoma. The Tide and Timber nines at the **Port Ludlow Golf Course** in Port Ludlow, about 20 miles northwest of

Seattle, are among the most picturesque and difficult in the state. The Timber Course includes hundreds of stumps of old cedar trees, which were cut down by loggers and left in place as seminatural obstacles.

Indian Canyon is the best of the public courses near Spokane and one of the best in the country, an older course with a challenging heavily wooded track in the hills with views down to the city from the first and tenth holes. The **Meadowwood Golf Course** in Liberty Lake east of Spokane is a hidden gem with some difficult challenges on the back nine.

The **Desert Canyon Golf Resort** in Orondo in the center of the state offers spectacular views of the Columbia River and some excellent desert golf.

Apple Tree in Yakima is set in an apple orchard with an apple-shaped 17th hole.

Indian Canyon, Kayak Point, and Meadowwood are also on the Econoguide Best and Econoguide Deals lists.

Some of Washington's coastal courses are open year-round, with peak rates in effect from May to September. Other courses typically operate from March to October, with peak rates in the summer.

Econoguide Leader Board: Best Public Courses in Washington

☺☺☺☺	Apple Tree Golf Course
☺☺☺	Classic Country Club
☺☺☺☺	Desert Canyon Golf Resort
☺☺☺	Indian Canyon Golf Course
☺☺☺☺	Kayak Point Golf Course
☺☺☺☺	McCormick Woods Golf Course
☺☺☺☺	Meadowwood Golf Course
☺☺☺☺	Port Ludlow Golf Course (Tide, Timber, Trail)
☺☺☺☺	Semiahmoo Golf and Country Club
☺☺☺☺	Shuksan Golf Club

Econoguide Leader Board: Best Deals in Washington

$$/☺☺☺	Avalon Golf Club (North, West, South)
$$/☺☺☺	Canyon Lakes Golf Course
$$/☺☺☺	Capitol City Golf Club
$$/☺☺☺	The Creek at Qualchan Golf Course
$/☺☺☺	Downriver Golf Club
$$/☺☺☺	Dungeness Golf and Country Club
$$/☺☺☺	Gold Mountain Golf Course
$/☺☺☺	Hangman Valley Golf Course
$$/☺☺☺	Indian Canyon Golf Course
$$/☺☺☺☺	Kayak Point Golf Course
$$/☺☺☺	Lake Padden Golf Course
$/☺☺☺	Lake Spanaway Golf Course
$/☺☺☺	Leavenworth Golf Club
$/☺☺☺☺	Meadowwood Golf Course
$$/☺☺☺	Riverside Country Club

$$/⊙⊙⊙	Snohomish Golf Course
$$/⊙⊙⊙	Sudden Valley Golf and Country Club

Washington Golf Guide

Seattle/Tacoma/Bellingham Area

R ⊙⊙	**Alderbrook Golf and Yacht Club** Union. (360) 898-2560 18 holes. Par 72/73. Yards: 6,326/5,500 Year-round. High: Apr.–Oct.	Greens: $$ Carts: $ Rating: 70.9/72.2 Slope: 122/125	W L R S
P ⊙⊙⊙ DEAL	**Avalon Golf Club** Kelleher Rd., Burlington. (206) 757-1900 *North/West/South* 27 holes. Par 72/72/72. Yards: 6,597/6,576/6,771 Year-round. High: May–Sept.	Greens: $$ Carts: $$ Rating: 72.5/72.3/73.3 Slope: 127/129/129	W L T S J
P ⊙	**Battle Creek Golf Course** Meridian Ave. N., Marysville. (206) 659-7931 18 holes. Par 73/73. Yards: 6,575/5,391 Year-round. High: May–Aug.	Greens: $–$$ Carts: $$ Rating: 71.4/70.9 Slope: 125/124	W L S J
P ⊙⊙	**Brookdale Golf Course** Tacoma. (206) 537-4400 18 holes. Par 71/74. Yards: 6,425/5,847 Year-round. High: Apr.–Oct.	Greens: $ Carts: $ Rating: 69.6/72.2 Slope: 112/123	L T S J
P ⊙⊙⊙ DEAL	**Capitol City Golf Club** Yelm Hwy. S.E., Olympia. (206) 491-5111 18 holes. Par 72/72. Yards: 6,536/5,510 Year-round. High: June–Aug.	Greens: $–$$ Carts: $ Rating: 70.9/71.7 Slope: 123/122	W L T S J
P ⊙⊙⊙ STATE	**Classic Country Club** 208th St. E., Spanaway. (206) 847-4440 18 holes. Par 72/72. Yards: 6,793/5,580 Year-round. High: May–Oct.	Greens: $$–$$$ Carts: $$ Rating: 73.6/73.3 Slope: 133/128	W L T S J
SP ⊙⊙⊙ DEAL	**Dungeness Golf and Country Club** Woodcock Rd., Sequim. (206) 683-6344 18 holes. Par 72/72. Yards: 6,372/5,344 Year-round. High: Apr.–Oct.	Greens: $–$$ Carts: $$ Rating: 70.4/70.1 Slope: 121/119	W T J
SP ⊙⊙	**Echo Falls Country Club** 121st Ave. S.E., Snohomish. (206) 668-3030 18 holes. Par 70/71. Yards: 6,123/4,357 Year-round. High: June–Aug.	Greens: $$–$$$ Carts: $ Rating: 68.9/64.6 Slope: 126/115	W L R T S J
P ⊙⊙⊙ DEAL	**Gold Mountain Golf Course** W. Belfair Valley Rd., Bremerton. (206) 674-2363 18 holes. Par 72/75. Yards: 6,749/5,428 Year-round. High: Apr.–Oct.	Greens: $–$$ Carts: Rating: 71.8/70.6 Slope: 120/116	T S J
P ⊙⊙⊙	**Harbour Pointe Golf Club** Mukilteo. (206) 355-6060 18 holes. Par 72/72. Yards: 6,862/4,842 Year-round. High: May–Oct.	Greens: $$–$$$ Carts: $ Rating: 72.8/68.8 Slope: 135/117	W L T S J
P ⊙⊙	**High Cedars Golf Club** 149th St., Orting. (360) 893-3171 18 holes. Par 71/72. Yards: 6,303/5,651 Year-round. High: Apr.–Nov.	Greens: $$ Carts: $$ Rating: 70.2/75.6 Slope: 116/126	W T S J
P ⊙⊙⊙⊙ BEST DEAL	**Kayak Point Golf Course** Marine Dr., Standwood. (360) 652-9676 18 holes. Par 72/72. Yards: 6,719/5,346 Year-round. High: May–Sept.	Greens: $$ Carts: $$ Rating: 72.7/72.8 Slope: 133/129	W S J

Washington Golf Guide

Seattle/Tacoma/Bellingham Area

P ☺☺☺ DEAL	**Lake Padden Golf Course** Samish Way, Bellingham. (206) 738-7400 18 holes. Par 72/72. Yards: 6,675/5,496 Year-round. High: May–Sept.	Greens: Carts: Rating: Slope:	$–$$　　S J $$ 71.3/71.9 122/126
P ☺☺☺ DEAL	**Lake Spanaway Golf Course** Pacific Ave., Tacoma. (206) 531-3660 18 holes. Par 72/74. Yards: 6,810/5,935 Year-round. High: May–Oct.	Greens: Carts: Rating: Slope:	$　　　　W S J $ 71.8/73.4 121/123
SP ☺☺☺ DEAL	**Leavenworth Golf Club** Icicle Rd., Leavenworth. (509) 548-7267 18 holes. Par 71/71. Yards: 5,711/5,343 Apr.–Nov. High: Apr.–Oct.	Greens: Carts: Rating: Slope:	$ $$ 67.0/69.6 116/119
P ☺☺	**Lipoma Firs Golf Course** 110th Ave. E., Puyallup. (206) 841-4396 *Green/Gold/Blue* 27 holes. Par 72/72/72. Yards: 6,722/6,805/6,687 Year-round. High: Apr.–Oct.	Greens: Carts: Rating: Slope:	$–$$　　W L T S J $ 72.2/72.1/72.0 122/122/122
P ☺☺	**Madrona Links Golf Course** 22nd Ave. N.W., Gig Harbor. (206) 851-5193 18 holes. Par 71/73. Yards: 5,602/4,737 Year-round. High: Mar.–Oct.	Greens: Carts: Rating: Slope:	$　　　　T S J $ 65.5/68.1 110/115
P ☺☺☺☺ BEST	**McCormick Woods Golf Course** Port Orchard. (206) 895-0130 18 holes. Par 72/72. Yards: 7,040/5,299 Year-round. High: June–Sept.	Greens: Carts: Rating: Slope:	$$–$$$　W L T S $$ 74.1/71.1 135/122
P ☺☺	**Meadow Park Golf Course** Lakewood Dr. W., Tacoma. (206) 473-3033 18 holes. Par 71/73. Yards: 6,093/5,262 Year-round. High: May–Sept.	Greens: Carts: Rating: Slope:	$　　　　W S J $ 69.0/70.3 114/118
P ☺☺	**Mount Si Golf Course** Snoqualmie. (206) 881-1541 18 holes. Par 72/72. Yards: 6,304/5,439 Year-round. High: Apr.–Sept.	Greens: Carts: Rating: Slope:	$$　　　L S J $ NA 111
P ☺☺	**North Shore Golf and Country Club** N. Shore Blvd. N.E., Tacoma. (206) 927-1375 18 holes. Par 71/73. Yards: 6,305/5,442 Year-round. High: May–Sept.	Greens: Carts: Rating: Slope:	$$　　　W L T J $$ 69.9/70.7 120/119
R ☺☺	**Ocean Shores Golf Course** Canal Dr. N.E., Ocean Shores. (206) 289-3357 18 holes. Par 71/72. Yards: 6,252/5,173 Year-round. High: May–Sept.	Greens: Carts: Rating: Slope:	$–$$　　L S J $$ 70.2/69.6 115/115
R ☺☺☺☺ BEST	**Port Ludlow Golf Course** Highland Dr., Port Ludlow. (206) 437-0272 *Tide/Timber/Trail* 27 holes. Par 72/72/72. Yards: 6,746/6,683/6,787 Year-round. High: May–Sept.	Greens: Carts: Rating: Slope:	$$–$$$　W L R T $ 73.6/73.1/72.7 138/138/131
P ☺☺	**Riverbend Golf Complex** W. Meeker St., Kent. (206) 854-3673 18 holes. Par 72/72. Yards: 6,603/5,485 Year-round. High: Apr.–Sept.	Greens: Carts: Rating: Slope:	$–$$　　W L S J $$ 71.8/70.4 125/124
P ☺☺☺ DEAL	**Riverside Country Club** N.W. Airport Rd., Chehalis. (206) 748-8182 18 holes. Par 71/72. Yards: 6,155/5,456 Year-round. High: Apr.–Sept.	Greens: Carts: Rating: Slope:	$–$$　　L J $$ 68.3/71.0 117/121

Washington Golf Guide

Seattle/Tacoma/Bellingham Area

R	**Semiahmoo Golf and Country Club**	Greens:	$$–$$$$ W L R T
☺☺☺☺	Semiahmoo Pkwy., Blaine. (206) 371-7005	Carts:	$
BEST	18 holes. Par 72/72. Yards: 7,005/5,288	Rating:	74.5/71.6
	Year-round. High: July–Sept.	Slope:	130/126

P	**Shuksan Golf Club**	Greens:	$$ W L T S J
☺☺☺☺	E. Axton Rd., Bellingham. (206) 398-8888	Carts:	Incl.
STATE	18 holes. Par 72/72. Yards: 6,706/5,253	Rating:	70.3/68.5
	Year-round. High: Apr.–Oct.	Slope:	128/118

P	**Snohomish Golf Course**	Greens:	$$ T S J
☺☺☺	147th Ave. S.E., Snohomish. (206) 568-2676	Carts:	$$
DEAL	18 holes. Par 72/74. Yards: 6,858/5,980	Rating:	72.7/74.1
	Year-round. High: May–Sept.	Slope:	126/129

SP	**Sudden Valley Golf and Country Club**	Greens:	$$ W L T J
☺☺☺	Lake Whatcom Blvd., Bellingham. (360) 734-6435	Carts:	$$
DEAL	18 holes. Par 72/72. Yards: 6,553/5,627	Rating:	72.4/72.5
	Year-round. High: July–Sept.	Slope:	129/131

P	**Tumwater Valley Golf Club**	Greens:	$–$$ W L T S J
☺☺	Tumwater Valley Dr., Tumwater. (206) 943-9500	Carts:	$$
	18 holes. Par 72/72. Yards: 7,154/5,504	Rating:	73.1/70.4
	Year-round. High: May–Oct.	Slope:	120/114

P	**West Seattle Golf Course**	Greens:	$ T S J
☺☺	35th Ave. S.W., Seattle. (206) 935-5187	Carts:	$
	18 holes. Par 72/72. Yards: 6,600/5,700	Rating:	70.9/72.6
	Year-round. High: May–Sept.	Slope:	119/123

Southern Washington/Yakima Area

P	**Apple Tree Golf Course**	Greens:	$$–$$$ W L T S J
☺☺☺☺	Occidental Ave., Yakima. (509) 966-5877	Carts:	$
STATE	18 holes. Par 72/72. Yards: 6,892/5,428	Rating:	73.3/72.0
	Year-round. High: Mar.–Oct.	Slope:	129/124

R	**Bridge of the Gods Golf Course**	Greens:	$–$$ L T
☺☺	Skamania Lodge Way, Stevenson. (509) 427-2541	Carts:	$$
	18 holes. Par 70/69. Yards: 5,776/4,362	Rating:	68.9/65.2
	Year-round. High: June–Oct.	Slope:	127/115

P	**Canyon Lakes Golf Course**	Greens:	$–$$ J
☺☺☺	Kennewick. (509) 582-3736	Carts:	$$
DEAL	18 holes. Par 72/72. Yards: 6,973/5,565	Rating:	73.7/71.1
	Year-round. High: Mar.–Nov.	Slope:	135/132

P	**Cedars Golf Club**	Greens:	$ J
☺☺	N.E. 181st St., Brush Prairie. (206) 687-4233	Carts:	$$
	18 holes. Par 72/73. Yards: 6,423/5,216	Rating:	71.2/71.1
	Year-round. High: May–Oct.	Slope:	129/117

SP	**Desert Aire Golf Course**	Greens:	$
☺☺	Desert Aire. (509) 932-4439	Carts:	$
	18 holes. Par 72/73. Yards: 6,501/5,786	Rating:	73.6/73.3
	Year-round. High: June–Oct.	Slope:	133/128

R	**Desert Canyon Golf Resort**	Greens:	$$–$$$ W L T J
☺☺☺☺	Brays Rd., Orondo. (509) 784-1111	Carts:	Incl.
STATE	18 holes. Par 72/72. Yards: 7,293/4,899	Rating:	74.0/67.5
	Mar.–Nov. High: July–Aug.	Slope:	127/104

P	**Quail Ridge Golf Course**	Greens:	$ J
☺☺	Swallows Nest Dr., Clarkston. (509) 758-8501	Carts:	$$
	18 holes. Par 71/71. Yards: 5,861/4,720	Rating:	68.1/66.2
	Year-round. High: Apr.–Sept.	Slope:	114/107

Washington Golf Guide

Southern Washington/Yakima Area

P ◎◎	**Three Rivers Golf Course** S. River Rd., Kelso. (206) 423-4653 18 holes. Par 72/72. Yards: 6,846/5,455 Year-round. High: May–Sept.	Greens: $ Carts: $$ Rating: 72.1/68.5 Slope: 127/120	L T S J
SP ◎◎	**Tri-City Country Club** N. Underwood, Kennewick. (509) 783-6014 18 holes. Par 65/65. Yards: 4,700/4,400 Year-round. High: May–Sept.	Greens: $–$$ Carts: $$ Rating: 62.5/65.2 Slope: 112/115	J

Spokane Area

SP ◎◎	**Chewelah Golf and Country Club** Sand Canyon Rd., Chewelah. (509) 935-6807 18 holes. Par 72/74. Yards: 6,511/5,672 Apr.–Oct. High: May–Sept.	Greens: $ Carts: $$ Rating: 70.9/72.2 Slope: 125/124	S J
P ◎◎◎ DEAL	**Downriver Golf Club** Columbia Circle, Spokane. (509) 327-5269 18 holes. Par 71/73. Yards: 6,130/5,592 Feb.–Nov. High: May–Sept.	Greens: $ Carts: $$ Rating: 68.8/70.9 Slope: 115/114	
P ◎	**Esmeralda Golf Course** E. Courtland, Spokane. (509) 487-6291 18 holes. Par 70/72. Yards: 6,249/5,594 Feb.–Nov. High: May–Aug.	Greens: $ Carts: $$ Rating: 69.2/70.8 Slope: 114/117	T S
P ◎◎◎ DEAL	**Hangman Valley Golf Course** Spokane. (509) 448-1212 18 holes. Par 72/71. Yards: 6,904/5,699 Mar.–Oct. High: May–Sept.	Greens: $ Carts: $$ Rating: 71.9/71.8 Slope: 126/125	S J
P ◎◎◎ BEST DEAL	**Indian Canyon Golf Course** Spokane. (509) 747-5353 18 holes. Par 72/72. Yards: 6,255/5,943 Mar.–Oct. High: May–Sept.	Greens: $$ Carts: $$ Rating: 70.7/65.9 Slope: 126/115	T J
P ◎◎	**Liberty Lake Golf Club** Liberty Lake. (509) 255-6233 18 holes. Par 70/74. Yards: 6,398/5,886 Year-round. High: June–Sept.	Greens: $ Carts: $$ Rating: 69.8/75.7 Slope: 121/134	S J
P ◎◎◎◎ DEAL STATE	**Meadowwood Golf Course** Liberty Lake. (509) 255-9539 18 holes. Par 72/72. Yards: 6,846/5,880 Mar.–Nov. High: May–Aug.	Greens: $ Carts: $$ Rating: 72.4/74.1 Slope: 126/127	S J
P ◎◎◎ DEAL	**The Creek at Qualchan Golf Course** E. Meadowlane Rd., Spokane. (509) 448-9317 18 holes. Par 72/72. Yards: 6,577/5,533 Mar.–Oct. High: May–Sept.	Greens: $–$$ Carts: $$ Rating: 71.1/72.3 Slope: 124/126	J
P ◎◎	**Wandermere Golf Course** Division St., Spokane. (509) 466-8023 18 holes. Par 70/73. Yards: 6,095/5,760 Mar.–Nov. High: June–Sept.	Greens: $ Carts: $$ Rating: 68.6/72.2 Slope: 119/126	S J

Wyoming

The spectacular **Jackson Hole Golf and Tennis Club** is by most accounts the best course in Wyoming and among the best in the nation. Set at the base of Jackson Hole's ski mountain, it offers spectacular views of the Tetons. The Gros Ventre River winds its way through and alongside 12 holes. Nearby in Jackson is the nearly as wonderful, watery **Teton Pines Resort and Country Club**.

Near Sheridan in the north of the state is the well-regarded **Kendrick Golf Course**; in Cody is the **Olive Glenn Golf and Country Club**.

The Kendrick and Olive Glenn clubs share positions on both the Econoguide Best and Econoguide Deals lists.

High mountain courses are generally open from April to October, with peak rates in effect from June to early September. A handful of lower-altitude courses are in operation year-round, again with summer peak rates.

Econoguide Leader Board: Best Public Courses in Wyoming

◎◎◎◎	Jackson Hole Golf and Tennis Club
◎◎◎	Kendrick Golf Course
◎◎◎	Olive Glenn Golf and Country Club
◎◎◎◎	Teton Pines Resort and Country Club

Econoguide Leader Board: Best Deals in Wyoming

$/◎◎◎	Bell Nob Golf Club
$/◎◎◎	Buffalo Golf Club
$/◎◎◎	Kendrick Golf Course
$$/◎◎◎	Olive Glenn Golf and Country Club
$$/◎◎◎	Riverton Country Club

Wyoming Golf Guide

Northern Wyoming

P ◎◎◎ DEAL	**Bell Nob Golf Club** Overdale Dr., Gillette. (307) 686-7069 18 holes. Par 72/72. Yards: 7,024/5,555 Apr.–Oct. High: May–July	Greens: Carts: Rating: Slope:	$ $ 70.8/70.6 119/116
P ◎◎◎ DEAL	**Buffalo Golf Club** Buffalo. (307) 684-5266 18 holes. Par 71/72. Yards: 6,684/5,512 Mar.–Nov. High: May–Sept.	Greens: Carts: Rating: Slope:	$ Inquire 70.9/69.8 116/115
P ◎◎	**Green Hills Municipal Golf Course** J Airport Rd., Worland. (307) 347-8972 18 holes. Par 72/73. Yards: 6,444/5,104 Apr.–Oct. High: June–Aug.	Greens: Carts: Rating: Slope:	$ $ 69.3/68.0 113/113
P ◎◎◎ DEAL STATE	**Kendrick Golf Course** J Big Goose Rd., Sheridan. (307) 674-8148 18 holes. Par 72/73. Yards: 6,800/5,549 Apr.–Oct. High: June–Aug.	Greens: Carts: Rating: Slope:	$ Inquire 71.3/70.8 116/113
SP ◎◎◎ DEAL STATE	**Olive Glenn Golf and Country Club** J Meadow Lane, Cody. (307) 587-5551 18 holes. Par 72/72. Yards: 6,880/5,654 Apr.–Oct. High: June–Aug.	Greens: Carts: Rating: Slope:	$$ $ 71.6/71.2 124/120
R ◎◎◎◎ BEST	**Jackson Hole Golf and Tennis Club** L T Spring Gulch Rd., Jackson. (307) 733-3111 18 holes. Par 72/73. Yards: 7,168/6,036 Apr.–Oct. High: June–Aug.	Greens: Carts: Rating: Slope:	$$$–$$$$ Incl. 72.3/73.2 133/125
R ◎◎◎◎ BEST	**Teton Pines Resort and Country Club** L R J Jackson. (307) 733-1733 18 holes. Par 72/72. Yards: 7,412/5,486 May–Oct. High: June–Sept.	Greens: Carts: Rating: Slope:	$$$$–$$$$$ Incl. 74.2/70.8 137/117

Wyoming Golf Guide

Casper Area

P ⊙⊙	**Casper Municipal Golf Course** Allendale, Casper. (307) 234-2405 18 holes. Par 70/72. Yards: 6,234/5,472 Mar.–Oct. High: May–Aug.	Greens: Carts: Rating: Slope:	$ $ 67.9/69.2 112/112	W
P ⊙⊙	**Douglas Community Club** Douglas. (307) 358-5099 18 holes. Par 71/72. Yards: 6,253/5,323 Apr.–Oct. High: June–Aug.	Greens: Carts: Rating: Slope:	$ $ 68.4/68.5 107/103	W
SP ⊙⊙⊙ DEAL	**Riverton Country Club** Riverton. (307) 856-4779 18 holes. Par 72/72. Yards: 7,064/5,549 Mar.–Oct. High: June–Aug.	Greens: Carts: Rating: Slope:	$$ $ 72.2/71.0 128/119	

Cheyenne Area

P ⊙⊙	**Francis E. Warren AFB Golf Course** Randall Ave., Warren AFB. (307) 775-3556 18 holes. Par 71/75. Yards: 6,585/5,186 Year-round. High: Apr.–Oct.	Greens: Carts: Rating: Slope:	$ $ 68.2/67.0 105/102	T
P ⊙⊙	**Glenn "Red" Jacoby Golf Club** 30th and Willett, Laramie. (307) 745-3111 18 holes. Par 70/72. Yards: 6,540/5,395 Apr.–Oct. High: June–Aug.	Greens: Carts: Rating: Slope:	$ $ 67.3/68.1 108/109	J

FREE

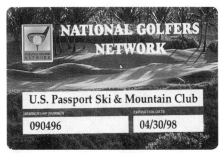

National Discount
Golf Membership
$49.95 Value

- Play over 1,500 golf courses • Up to 50% off green fees
- Discounts on range balls, lessons, and pro shop merchandise

Free membership application on back

Call (800) 754-8326 for a listing of participating courses.

FREE*

Golf Membership

Includes directory listing all courses and discounts

The affordable way to golf!

Order your annual membership card today! Golf memberships make an excellent gift. Order additional memberships for only $9.95.

*Return application with only $5.95 for postage and handling or call (800) 754-8326 to order with credit card.

Your FREE card and directory will ship within 5 days of receipt of this coupon.
*You include only $5.95 for one-time first-class postage and handling to receive your free membership.

Membership valid for approximately 1 year from date ordered.

Please print the information requested below and return coupon to U.S. Passport at 8136 South Grant Way, #C, Littleton, CO 80122, (800) 754-8326.

Name: _____

Address: _____

City: _____ State: _____ Zip: _____

Telephone: _____

Additional memberships ~~$49.95~~ now only $9.95!

Please send me _____ additional membership(s) @ $9.95 each $_____

*Required to receive free membership postage and handling $5.95

( ) Check enclosed made payable to Passport   Total $_____

Please bill ( ) VISA( ) Mastercard

Card #_____ Exp. Date _____

Signature _____

No cash value. No cash refund. One directory per membership card.

This special offer not valid after 12/31/98.

VAIL HOME RENTALS, INC.

15% off from May–August
20% off from September–October

1-bedroom condos to 6-bedroom homes
(Excludes 6/29/97–7/6/97 and 6/28/98–7/6/98)

143 E. Meadow Dr., Vail, CO 81657, (800) 525-9803
E-mail: vail-home-rentals@toski.com
Expires 12/31/98

VAIL HOME RENTALS
143 E. Meadow Drive - Suite 397
Vail, Colorado 81657

GO97-35

VAIL HOME RENTALS, INC.

10% off from 11/10/97–12/12/97
15% off from 4/4/98–4/19/98

1-bedroom condos to 6-bedroom homes

143 E. Meadow Dr., Vail, CO 81657, (800) 525-9803
E-mail: vail-home-rentals@toski.com
Expires 4/19/98

VAIL HOME RENTALS
143 E. Meadow Drive - Suite 397
Vail, Colorado 81657

GO97-36

Crested Butte Accommodations
15% off Lodging on direct bookings only

Just minutes from Skyland Golf Resort, a Robert Trent Jones II-
designed golf course. A wide variety of lodging accommodations and
amenities. Be sure to mention the Econoguide when calling our
friendly, knowledgeable staff. CBA is a full-service travel agency.
Not valid with any other promotions.

CRESTED BUTTE
ACCOMMODATIONS
& TRAVEL AGENCY, ltd.

P.O. Box 5004, Mt. Crested Butte, CO 81225
(800) 821-3718 (970) 349-2448 Fax (970) 349-7621 vrogal@csn.net
Expires 12/31/98.

GO97-30

Play & Save at 400 of the
West's finest courses

Buy One, Get One Free

Proceeds benefit Boys & Girls Clubs of Palm Springs
and Desert Junior Golf

(800) 950-GOLF (4653)
The Golf Passbook
2521 E. 8th St., Tucson, AZ 85711
Expires 12/31/98

the Golf Passbook

Proceeds
benefit Boys &
Girls Clubs of
Palm Springs

GO97-29

Come to Six Flags Magic Mountain and explore ten themed lands of fun, fantasy, and adventure. Discover the most exciting rides and action-packed shows on earth. Six Flags Magic Mountain is open weekends and holidays all year and daily April–October. Park opens at 10 a.m. Call for specific operating days and hours. Schedule subject to change.

26101 Magic Mountain Pky.,Valencia, CA 91355, (805) 255-4129

Introductory Offer

Redeem at any of the following Golf and Country Club locations:

Bonaventure Country Club
200 Bonaventure Blvd., Ft. Lauderdale, (954) 389-2100

Miami Shores Country Club
10000 Biscayne Blvd., Miami Shores, (305) 795-2366

Presidential Country Club
19650 N.E. 18th Ave., North Miami Beach, (305) 933-5266

Pembroke Lakes Golf Course
10500 Taft St., Pembroke Pines, (954) 431-4144

REDEEM AT ANY VF FACTORY OUTLET:

Alabama: Boaz, Foley, Monroeville; **Arizona:** Mesa, Tucson; **California:** Anderson, Cabazon, Gilroy, Lake Elsinore, Vacaville; **Colorado:** Castle Rock; **Delaware:** Rehoboth Beach; **Florida:** Ellenton, Graceville, Sunrise, Orlando; **Georgia:** Calhoun, Commerce; **Illinois:** West Frankfort; **Iowa:** Story City, Williamsburg; **Kentucky:** Carrollton, Hanson; **Louisiana:** Arcadia, Gonzales, Iowa; **Maryland:** Queenstown; **Massachusetts:** North Dartmouth; **Michigan:** Birch Run; **Mississippi:** Tupelo; **Missouri:** Branson, Lebanon; **Nebraska:** Nebraska City; **Nevada:** Las Vegas; **New York:** Bellport, Waterloo; **Pennsylvania:** Grove City; Reading; **Tennessee:** Crossville, Union City; **Texas:** Corsicana, Hempstead, Livingston, Mineral Wells, San Marcos, Sulphur Springs; **Utah:** Draper; **Washington:** Centralia, North Bend

Quick-Find Index to Golf Courses

(See also the detailed Contents)

Airlines 9–18
Balls, golf 5–6, 35–36
Bogey rating 39
Car rentals 20–22
Charter airlines 17–18
Clubs, golf 31–35
Convention fares, airline. 12–13
Discount golf cards 7
Discount hotel companies. 28–29
Econoguide course price ranges 4
Econoguide course ratings 3, 4
Fade. 37
Golf equipment. 4, 6, 31–36
Hooks. 36–37
Hotels. 23–30
Irons 32
Loft. 32
Overbooking, airline. 15–16
Package tours 18–20
Push 37
Shaft, club. 33
Slice 36–37
Standby air travel. 14
Tee-time services 6, 7
Toughest courses in America 39–40
Travel agencies. 18
USGA ratings 37–39
Woods 31–32

THE EAST   **41–94**

Connecticut. 41–45
    Bridgeport area 43
    Danbury area. 44
    Hartford area 44–45
    New Haven area. 43
    New London/Norwich area. 43
    Stamford 43
    Waterbury/Watertown/
      Bristol area. 43
Delaware 45–46
Maine. 46–48
    Augusta area 47
    Bangor area 47
    Central coast 48
    Northern 46–47
    Portland area 47–48
Maryland. 48–51
    Baltimore area 49–50
    DelMarVa Peninsula. 51
    Hagerstown area. 48–49
    Washington, D.C., area. 50–51
    Western. 48
Massachusetts. 51–55

Boston 53–54
Cape Cod/
    Martha's Vineyard. 54–55
    Fall River area 55
    Springfield area 53
    Western. 52
    Worcester area 53
New Hampshire 56–59
    Keene area. 57
    Lebanon area. 57
    Manchester/Concord area 57–58
    Nashua area 58–59
    Northern 56–57
    Portsmouth area 57
New Jersey 59–63
    Atlantic City area. 62
    Cherry Hill/
      Philadelphia suburbs 61–62
    Northern/Newark area 59–61
    Southern 63
    Trenton area 61
New York 63–74
    Adirondack region 68–69
    Albany/capital district. 69–70
    Binghamton/southern tier 70–71
    Buffalo area 65–66
    Catskill region 70
    Long Island 72–74
    New York city/
      northern suburbs. 71–72
    Rochester area 66–67
    Syracuse/central New York 67–68
    Utica-Rome area. 68
Pennsylvania 74–84
    Allentown/Reading/
      Bethlehem area 79–80
    Altoona area 80
    Erie area. 75–76
    Harrisburg/York area. 81–82
    North Central 77
    Philadelphia area 82–84
    Pittsburgh area. 77–79
    Scranton/Wilkes-Barre area 76–77
Rhode Island 84–85
Vermont. 85–88
    Burlington area 87
    Montpelier/Barre area. 87
    Rutland area. 87–88
    Southern 88
    St. Albans 87
Virginia 88–94
    Charlottesville area 91
    Newport/Norfolk/
      Virginia Beach area 93–94

Northern 90–91
Richmond area 91–92
Roanoke. 92
Washington, D.C., area 89–90
Williamsburg area 92–93
Washington, D.C. 94

THE CENTRAL STATES   95–158

Illinois 95–104
Chicago area. 97–102
Dubuque area. 96–97
Kankakee area 102
Peoria area. 103
Quincy 103
Rock Island 97
Springfield/Decatur/
    Champaign area 103
St. Louis area 103–104
Indiana 104–110
Fort Wayne area 106–107
Gary area 105–106
Indianapolis area 107–109
Southeast 109–110
Southwest 109
Iowa 110–113
Cedar Rapids area. 112
Davenport area. 112–113
Des Moines area 111–112
Fort Dodge area 111
Sioux City area. 111
Southeast. 113
Waterloo area. 112
Kansas 113–115
Dodge City 113–114
Garden City. 114
Kansas City area. 115
Topeka area. 114–115
Wichita area 114
Kentucky 115–118
Bowling Green area 116
Covington/Florence area 118
Lexington area 117–118
Louisville area 116–117
Paducah area 116
Michigan 118–125
Detroit/Ann Arbor area 123–125
East-Central 123
Grand Rapids area. 122–123
Northern 120–122
Minnesota 125–131
Central. 127–128
Duluth area 127
Minneapolis/St. Paul area . . . 128–130
Northern 126–127
Rochester area. 130–131
Southern 131
Missouri 131–134
Kansas City area 132–133
Northern 132
Southern 134
Springfield area. 133–134

St. Louis area 133
Nebraska. 134–136
Grand Island area. 135
Lincoln area. 135
McCook and Kearney. 135
Omaha area 135–136
North Dakota 136–138
Eastern 137
Western 137–138
Ohio. 138–148
Akron area 142–143
Cincinnati area. 147–148
Cleveland area. 140–142
Columbus area 145–147
Dayton area 144–145
Northwest 144
Toledo area. 139–140
Youngstown area. 143–144
South Dakota 148–150
Rapid City/Western 149
Sioux City/Eastern 149–150
West Virginia 150–152
Beckley area 151–152
Charleston area 151
Clarksburg area 151
Wheeling. 151
Wisconsin. 152–158
Duluth area/Northern 154
Green Bay area. 154
Madison area 155–156
Milwaukee area. 156–158
Oshkosh area. 155

THE SOUTH   158–235

Alabama 159–162
Birmingham area 160
Huntsville area 160–161
Mobile area. 161–162
Montgomery area. 162
Southern 162
Arkansas. 162–164
Fayetteville area. 163
Fort Smith 163
Little Rock area. 163–164
Northern 164
Florida 164–186
Daytona area 172–173
Fort Lauderdale area 184–185
Fort Myers area. 181–182
Jacksonville area 170–172
Miami area 185–186
Orlando area. 173–177
Palm Beach area 182–184
Pensacola area. 169–170
Tampa area. 177–181
Georgia. 186–194
Atlanta area 188–191
Augusta area. 191–192
Columbus area 192–193
Macon/Warner Robins area. 192
Savannah area 193

Southern. 193–194
Louisiana 194–195
  Baton Rouge area 195
  Lake Charles 194–195
  New Orleans area 195
  Shreveport area 194
Mississippi 195–197
  Columbus area 196
  Gulfport/Biloxi area 196–197
  Hattiesburg area 196
  Northern 196
  Tupelo area 196
North Carolina 197–208
  Asheville area 200-201
  Charlotte area 201–202
  Fayetteville/Pinehurst area . . 203–205
  Greensboro area 202–203
  Raleigh-Durham area 203
  Shore 205–207
  Wilmington area 207–208
  Winston-Salem area 202
Oklahoma. 208–211
  Oklahoma City area 209–210
  Southern 211
  Tulsa area 210–211
  Western 208–209
South Carolina 212–222
  Augusta area 219
  Charlotte area 219–220
  Columbia area 214
  Florence area 215
  Greenville/Anderson area . . . 213–214
  Hilton Head 220–222
  Myrtle Beach region 215–218
Tennessee 222–226
  Chattanooga area 224–225
  Johnson City area 226
  Knoxville area. 225–226
  Memphis area 223
  Nashville area. 223–224
Texas 226–235
  Amarillo area 228
  Austin area 229–230
  Dallas/Fort Worth area 230–233
  El Paso. 228
  Houston area 233–235
  San Antonio area 228–229

**THE WEST, ALASKA,
AND HAWAII   235–300**

Alaska. 235–236
  Anchorage area 236
  Fairbanks. 236
Arizona. 236–243
  Flagstaff area 238
  Lake Havasu City 238
  Phoenix area. 238–243
  Tucson area 243
California. 244–262
  Fresno area 253–254
  Lake Tahoe area 254

Los Angeles area 255–258
Modesto. 252
Monterey area. 252–253
North/North Central 248
Palm Springs area 258–260
Sacramento area 248–249
San Diego area 260–262
San Francisco area. 249–252
Santa Barbara area. 254–255
Colorado. 262–269
  Colorado Springs area 268–269
  Denver area 266–267
  Fort Collins area 267–268
  Grand Junction area. 264
  Rocky Mountain region. 264–266
  Southern 269
Hawaii 269–276
  Hawaii, the Big Island 273–274
  Kauai. 274
  Maui. 274–275
  Molokai 275
  Oahu 275–276
Idaho 276–278
  Boise area 277–278
  Couer d'Alene area. 277
  Pocatello area. 278
  Sun Valley 278
Montana. 278–280
  Billings area. 280
  Bozeman area. 279
  Butte area 279
  Helena. 279
  Kalispell area 279
  Missoula area. 279
Nevada 280–283
  Central 282
  Lake Tahoe area 282
  Las Vegas area. 282–283
  Laughlin 283
  Reno/Carson City area 281–282
New Mexico 283–286
  Albuquerque area 284–285
  Santa Fe area 285
  Southern. 285–286
Oregon. 286–289
  Bend area 288–289
  Eugene area 288
  Medford area 289
  Portland area 287–288
Utah. 290–293
  Provo area 293
  Salt Lake City area 291–293
  Southern/St. George. 293
Washington 293–298
  Seattle/Tacoma/
    Bellingham area. 295–297
  Southern/Yakima area 297–298
  Spokane area 298
Wyoming 298–300
  Casper area 300
  Cheyenne area 300
  Northern 299